PROMOTION AND INTEGRATED MARKETING COMMUNICATIONS

Richard J. Semenik

Professor of Marketing and Dean
College of Business
Montana State University

Board of Directors of
American Advertising Museum

SOUTH-WESTERN
THOMSON LEARNING

Australia · Canada · Mexico · Singapore · Spain · United Kingdom · United States

Promotion and Integrated Marketing Communications
By Richard J. Semenik

Publisher: Dave Shaut
Acquisitions Editor: Pamela Person
Developmental Editor: Mary Draper, Draper Development
Production Editor: Tamborah Moore
Media Development Editor: Sally Nieman
Media Production Editor: Robin Browning
Cover Designer: Michael H. Stratton
Cover Images: Masterfile and Stone
Internal Designer: Michael H. Stratton
Marketing Manager: Marc Callahan
Manufacturing Coordinator: Sandee Milewski
Photo Researcher: James Davis
Production House: The Left Coast Group, Inc.
Printer: Transcontinental Printing, Inc., Beauceville, QC

Photo Credits follow Index

Printed in Canada
1 2 3 4 5 04 03 02 01

For more information contact South-Western, 5101 Madison Road, Cincinnati, Ohio, 45227 or find us on the Internet at http://www.swcollege.com

ISBN: 0-324-06253-2 (core text with InfoTrac)
      0-324-12568-2 (core text only)

For permission to use material from this text or product, contact us by
• **telephone: 1-800-730-2214**
• **fax: 1-800-730-2215**
• **web: http://www.thomsonrights.com**

Library of Congress Cataloging-in-Publication Data
  Semenik, Richard J.
    Promotion and integrated marketing communications/Richard J. Semenik.
      p. cm.
    Includes bibliographical references and index.
    ISBN 0-324-06253-2
    1. Advertising campaigns. 2. Communication in marketing. I. Title.

HF5837 .S45 2001
659.1—dc21   00-068752

ABOUT THE AUTHOR

Richard J. Semenik is the Dean of the College of Business at Montana State University–Bozeman. Professor Semenik spent most of his career at the Eccles School of Business at the University of Utah, where he chaired the Marketing Department on four different occasions, as well as being appointed Associate Dean for Research. Upon leaving the University of Utah, the Eccles School gave him the Distinguished Career Service Award, presented only nine times in the School's history.

Professor Semenik has recently returned from the Ecole Superieure de Commerce in Tours, France, where he was a Visiting Professor of International Business. He was also a Visiting Research Scholar at the Vrije Universiteit in Amsterdam, The Netherlands, and Visiting Scholar at Anahuac Universidad in Mexico City, Mexico. He is frequently asked to speak in Europe and has made presentations in Ireland, Belgium, Portugal, Hungary, the Netherlands, Germany, and France on topics dealing with marketing, advertising and branding strategy. Last year, he delivered the keynote address to the joint conference of the European Association of Advertising Agencies and the International Advertising Association held in Budapest, Hungary.

Professor Semenik received his undergraduate degree from the University of Michigan in 1970, an M.B.A. from Michigan State University in 1971, and his PH.D. from Ohio State University in Marketing in 1976. He has published nearly 60 articles and 10 books on marketing and advertising topics. One of his most recent books, *Advertising,* was released in April 1997 and is now used in 450 universities in the United States, Canada, Australia, and Europe. He serves as a reviewer for major journals in the area of marketing and advertising including *The Journal of Advertising, The International Journal of Advertising, The Journal of Health Care Marketing, The Journal of Consumer Research, Advances in Nonprofit Marketing,* and *The American Academy of Advertising.*

Professor Semenik consults with both small organizations and multinational corporations. He has relationships with IBM, SFX Entertainment, Ethos Marketing Research, The Roundtable Consulting Group, Syntonic Medical Group, FreeChart.com, Premier Resorts (London/Deer Valley), Harris & Love Advertising, the Van Gogh Museum (Amsterdam), and the Breakers Resort. He has been active in local community organizations, having served on the board of the Salt Lake Arts Council and was the first President of the Board of the ArtSpace studio project in downtown Salt Lake City (an urban redevelopment project). In 1999, he was asked to join the National Board of Directors of the American Advertising Museum, and in 2000 he was asked to join the Industry Relations Board of the American Academy of Advertising.

GUIDED TOUR

Promotion and Integrated Marketing Communications

hello...how can I reach you?

by Richard J. Semenik

WELCOME TO THE GUIDED TOUR OF *PROMOTION AND INTEGRATED MARKETING COMMUNICATIONS.*

As you'll see in the illustrated examples that follow, this innovative text offers a broad communications perspective you won't find in any other book on the market. Concise and current, it's just what tomorrow's marketing managers need – a truly integrated marketing communications approach that explores how to use all promotional tools with precision.

Additional information is available at the text's Web site at http://semenik.swcollege.com

A BALANCED APPROACH TO INTEGRATED MARKETING COMMUNICATIONS

- **Promotion and Integrated Marketing Communications** focuses on the full range of promotional tools available in today's business environment. This contemporary perspective is fueled by new database technology, the rise of the Internet as a communication and distribution channel, and more accountability for promotional spending.

- **All promotional tools are covered with the same level of intensity** – reinforcing that effective promotion is a blend of different communication efforts. In Part 3, students are introduced to balanced coverage of every facet of promotion, including advertising, personal selling, sales promotion, sponsorship, direct marketing, e-commerce, point of purchase, public relations and Internet communications.

Part 3: The Tools of Promotion and IMC

Chapter 8: Advertising: Message and Media Strategies

Chapter 9: Internet Advertising

Chapter 10: Direct Marketing and E-Commerce

Chapter 11: Sales Promotion: Consumer, Trade, and Business Market Techniques

Chapter 12: Sponsorship, Point-of-Purchase, and Supportive Communications

Chapter 13: Public Relations and Corporate Advertising

Chapter 14: Personal Selling and Sales Management

- **This comprehensive text offers a solid managerial focus** – reflected by its in-depth coverage of business buyer behavior and measurement of effective promotion across all levels.

GUIDED TOUR

- **Promotion and Integrated Marketing Communications** offers breakthrough coverage of the Internet, e-commerce, and Internet advertising in both business-to-consumer and business-to-business environments. In Chapter 9 (Internet Advertising), students explore the challenges of establishing a Web site and brand in today's "e-community."

- **Chapter 10 (Direct Marketing and E-Commerce)** looks at the explosive growth of direct marketing through e-commerce. Database development and management is covered, along with a model describing the e-commerce process and its importance in the overall marketing strategy.

- **Using the Internet** – These hands-on exercises are designed to get students to use the Internet to examine the nature of promotion, analyze the effectiveness of what they find, and to link chapter concepts to real-life promotions strategies. To make these exercises focused and worthwhile, after their excursion on the Internet, students are required to apply the concepts taught in each chapter by answering application questions provided with each exercise.

hello...how can I reach you?

USING THE INTERNET

Exercise 1

A successful advertising plan should include an integrated marketing communications strategy. The following companies have extensive advertising budgets allocated across multiple media vehicles. Explore the following sites and determine the creative style and type of information available at each site:

Budweiser
http://www.budweiser.com

Guess
http://www.guess.com

Jeep
http://www.jeepunpaved.com

NBA
http://www.nba.com

For each site, answer the following questions:

1. From your experience with past and current promotions for the company or organization, how does the site fit with all these communications? Are there similarities? differences? Does the site reinforce the promotions? Does it offer additional information?

2. In what ways are the differences you have noticed between the site and other media due to the different characteristics of the Internet itself?

3. Create a personal standard for advertising quality by listing several criteria that apply to different media.

Compare the quality of the Web site with that of promotions in other media. In your judgment, did the company or organization allocate too much, too little, or just the right amount of resources on its Web site?

Exercise 2

The Internet's arrival coincided with (and no doubt accelerated) a trend in many industries toward outsourcing those functions not considered "core competencies." And many company sites on the Web are a corporate brand as a thin veneer on top of various off-the-shelf or semi-custom services from myriad providers, from simple site tools to branded e-mail newsletters to even customer service and support. The following companies provide tools or services to backstop other companies' Web presence:

Excite
http://www.excite.com

AskJeeves
http://www.askjeeves.com

TouchScape
http://www.touchscape.com

Where can you find these companies on the Web? In addition to their corporate sites, do you encounter references to them, links, or other signs that they might be behind other companies' Web sites?

- **New Media boxes** in each chapter feature cutting-edge innovations in business-to-consumer and business-to-business promotions.

YOU HAVE E-MAIL (AS A PROMOTION OPTION)

Most of us know e-mail as that useful but sometimes burdensome new technology for professional communications and keeping in touch with relatives in remote places. One firm has emerged that will help marketers use e-mail as another from of promotional communications. The firm, MessageMedia (http://www.messagemedia.com), intends to distinguish itself among e-commerce agencies by offering synchronized marketing communications through e-mail, the Web, and offline media.

The company will handle a firm's in-bound and out-bound e-mail campaigns based on database technology. The applications available from the firm will include customer service and sales messages. But the founder, Larry Jones, is quick to point out the MessageMedia is not a "spamming" organization that sends millions of unsolicited e–mails to unsuspecting and unappreciative Web users. MessageMedia prepares and sends messages only to current customers of his clients – a true relationship-building component of the promotional process.

This is a fast-growing market if you can get the right offer, to the right customer, at the right time, based on the right database. According to Jones, highly targeted e-mail messages draw a 10 percent response rate, while "click-throughs" on Web banner ads are below 1 percent. The key to success for MessageMedia is in the philosophy of the founder, who believes that its not about sending e-mails, it's about understanding the recipient. If MessageMedia's knowledge of the recipients is as good as its advertising suggests (see Exhibit 2.10), this company can't miss.

Source: Dana Blankenhorn, "Message MediaVision Extends Beyond E-mail," *Advertising Age*, August 16, 1999, 44.

- **Web Sightings** in each chapter bring text exhibits online and into real time. Students are encouraged to visit marketers' Web sites, and then evaluate online promotional strategies.

A WORLD OF WEB RESOURCES AT THE WEB SITE

http://semenik.swcollege.com

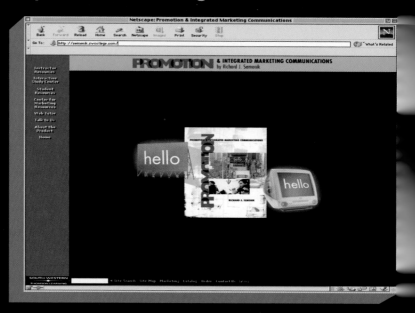

A wealth of Student Resources are available on the te
For example, IMC Web Activities direct students to th
innovative companies – giving them a first-hand look
promotional strategies in progress.

- **Interactive quizzes** strengthen business vocabulary and r
  concepts. In addition, immediate quiz scores and customize
  provide excellent exam preparation.

- **Career Connections** tap into the insights of promotion p
  everywhere. Students benefit from their on-the-job experi
  gleaning tips on how to network for maximum career succ
  up-to-date on the latest promotional strategies, and much

- **Web Sightings** – In keeping with the new media focus of
  will find Web Sightings in each chapter. You can spot these
  by looking for the Web Sightings binoculars found above se
  in each chapter. Students are asked to go to the Web site
  provided to explore the marketer's home page, bringing th
  the book online and into real time. You can think of these
  as in-chapter experiential exercises and real-time cases.
  You can assign these Web Sightings as individual or
  group activities. They are also excellent
  discussion starters.

hello...how can I reach you?

WEB SI

• **IMC LIVE** offers a wealth of promotion industry links –
guiding students to the best networking, education and career
advancement sites.

http://www.tacobell.com

*What drives the sale of a kids meal? Does the food really
matter, or is it the latest cross-promotional G-rated-movie-
tie-in toy that junior needs to collect the complete set? The
tacobell.com site delivers all that and more: contests, trivia
challenges, chat rooms, and more. It's all about brand
building, baby.*

http://www.drpepper.com

*Wouldn't you like to be a Pepper, too? The drpepper.com
site is based upon the latest version of Macromedia flash,
and boasts a number of concurrent promotions and
partnerships including Dr. Pepper Racing, the Collegiate
Golf Challenge, and the Hispanic Heritage Awards. In yet
another cross-promotion, Dr. Pepper-flavored jellybeans
have rocketed to the tops of the Jelly Belly charts.*

• **Crossword Puzzles** (at the student Web site) give students the chance to
have fun solving a puzzle while reinforcing their knowledge of key terms.

• **PowerPoint™ Slides** are available on the Instructor Web site and are also
included on the Instructor's CD-ROM. The slides highlight key concepts and
exhibits from each chapter, along with exhibits of promotions not found in the
textbook. Suggestions for effectively incorporating these PowerPoint slides
into lectures are included in the Instructor's Manual.

• **Career Café** helps students take control of their
professional development – featuring online tips and
resources for resume preparation, salary negotiation,
and networking.

OUTSTANDING PEDAGOGY BRINGS THE REAL WORLD OF MARKETING PROMOTIONS INTO THE CLASSROOM

- **IMC in Practice boxes** highlight a variety of integrated marketing communication strategies and issues — including the compelling *Chainsaw This: 43 Straight Days of Timbersports TV Coverage* from Chapter 4.

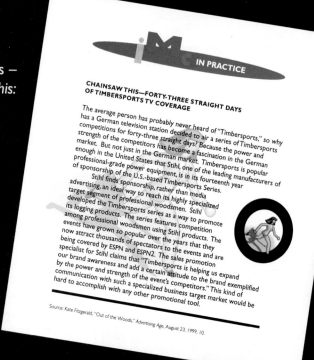

IN PRACTICE

CHAINSAW THIS—FORTY-THREE STRAIGHT DAYS OF TIMBERSPORTS TV COVERAGE

The average person has probably never heard of "Timbersports," so why has a German television station decided to air a series of Timbersports competitions for forty-three straight days? Because the power and strength of the competitors has become a fascination in the German market. But not just in the German market. Timbersports is popular enough in the United States that Stihl, one of the leading manufacturers of professional-grade power equipment, is in its fourteenth year of sponsorship of the U.S.-based Timbersports Series.

Stihl finds sponsorship, rather than media advertising, an ideal way to reach its highly specialized target segment of professional woodsmen. Stihl developed the Timbersports series as a way to promote its logging products. The series features competition among professional woodsmen using Stihl products. The events have grown so popular over the years that they now attract thousands of spectators to the events and are being covered by ESPN and ESPN2. The sales promotion specialist for Stihl claims that "Timbersports is helping us expand our brand awareness and add a certain attitude to the brand exemplified by the power and strength of the event's competitors." This kind of communication with such a specialized business target market would be hard to accomplish with any other promotional tool.

Source: Kate Fitzgerald, "Out of the Woods," *Advertising Age*, August 23, 1999, 10.

- **Chapter-opening vignettes** describe promotional strategies from well-known companies — demonstrating a variety of strategies and providing an excellent launching point for class discussion.

- **Career Profiles** in each chapter investigate the challenges and opportunities surrounding successful promotion professionals. Featured positions include the CEO of a major database marketing firm, a marketing manager for a travel agency, and an account coordinator for a marketing communications agency.

CAREER PROFILE

hello...how can I reach you?

- **Global Issues boxes** provide an insightful real-world look at what companies are doing to compete in the global arena.

 **ISSUES**

IBM COMBS THE GLOBE FOR E-BUSINESS

When is a computer not just a computer? Well, in IBM's way of thinking about things, that would be when a computer is an e-business tool. Faced with potent competitors such as Compaq, Hewlett-Packard, and Dell, IBM needed a way to reposition its laptops and PCs to accelerate its sales. Building on its own much-mimicked e-business concept, it was logical for IBM to pursue a repositioning of these products as e-business tools. The marketing strategy was to launch a revamped product line designed specifically to help companies get on the Internet and other networks to boost their business. A carefully orchestrated ad campaign could help consumers see IBM computers in this new light.

The e-business campaign was launched with extravagant eight-page inserts in various national newspapers. This was followed by giant IBM posters plastered on construction sites, in airports, and in subway stations in major metropolitan markets, along with magazine and TV ads and the ever-present Web site promotion. To add a touch of style and grace to its campaign, IBM employed a photographer who previously specialized in glamour shots for Clinique cosmetics. These stylish black-and-white photos of products such as the IBM ThinkPad were a common element throughout the various media used in this repositioning campaign.

How much to spend on a campaign to promote e-business tools around the world? This yearlong global campaign was funded at the $100-million level. Gee, $100 million here and $100 million there, and all of a sudden you're talking about some real money. IBM spends on the order of $750 million dollars each year on advertising.

Source: Raju Narisetti, "IBM Blitz to Introduce E-Business Tools," *The Wall Street Journal,* April 15, 1998, B4.

- **More than 400 vivid exhibits** reinforce topics throughout the text and spotlight contemporary promotional campaigns.

SOLID SUPPLEMENTS PROVIDE COMPREHENSIVE SUPPORT

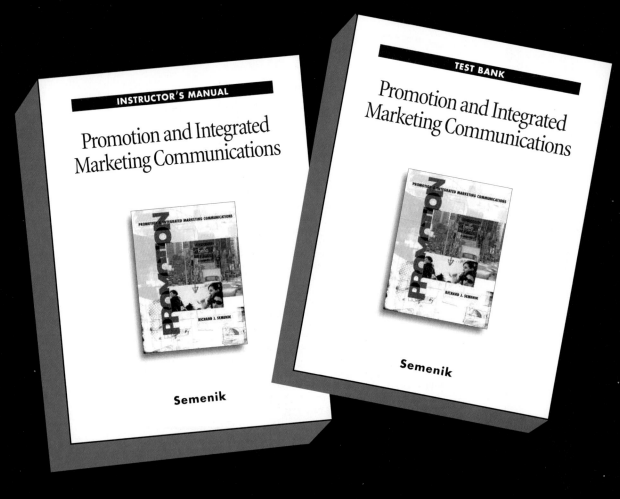

INSTRUCTOR'S MANUAL

Promotion and Integrated Marketing Communications

Semenik

TEST BANK

Promotion and Integrated Marketing Communications

Semenik

The Semenik Supplements Package supports your instruction, providing:

- **Instructor's Manual** with extensive lecture outlines (ISBN: 0-324-06255-9)
- **Test Bank** with a variety of true-false, multiple-choice and essay questions (ISBN: 0-324-06257-5)
- **Computerized Test Bank** (ISBN: 0-324-06258-3)
- **PowerPoint Presentation Slides** (ISBN: 0-324-06256-7)
- **Transparency Acetates** (ISBN: 0-324-06259-1)

- **Awesome Video Package showcasing real companies implementing their marketing strategies** (ISBN: 0-324-06970-7). Designed to support the text, these video cases highlight the experiences of innovative organizations.

- **An Integrated Marketing Communications Exercise** by Bernard C. Jakacki (ISBN: 0-324-01483-X). This supplemental text gives students hands-on experience in creating an IMC program for a hypothetical client – the Tourism Ministry of the Republic of Uruguay.

To my mother, Agustina,
whose strength and
determination are inspiring.

CONTENTS

CONTENTS

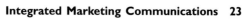

PART 2
Understanding the Market Environment for Promotion and IMC 114

FEELING LUCKY?

PLAY LUCKYSURF.COM
A FREE PLAY A DAY FOR $1 MILLION.

LuckySurf.com

PART 3
The Tools of Promotion and IMC 260

Man has visited the moon
6 times in 30 years.

Sound like your Web site?

Your visitors should do more than explore your site. They should thrive there. Give them the tools they
need to stay connected, share information and to create their own communites—and they'll be back again
and again. Your mission? To increase user loyalty and traffic. Our plan? To seamlessly integrate community
and organizational tools in your branded environment. For a quick, easy way to add customized groupware
to your company's site or intranet, contact us at www.myevents.com/partner. *Mission accomplished.*

Our integrated groupware includes: calendars,
contact managers, photo albums, bulletin boards,
task lists, file sharing, messaging and more.

MyEvents.com

Copyright © 2000 MyEvents.com
As seen in *Business 2.0, Industry Standard* and *Information Week.*

For a healthier sex life you need more iron

THE IRON BED
COMPANY

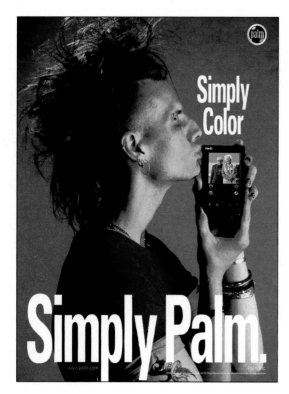

14 Personal Selling and Sales Management   474

PART 4
Evaluation and Measuring the Effectiveness of Promotion and IMC 510

PREFACE

BEYOND ADVERTISING

When a new company is born or a new product is released, the marketing manager responsible for driving awareness and new revenue faces many alternatives and choices. What will be the most effective means to reach the target audience(s)? How can impact be maximized given budget limitations? What mix of promotional and marketing tools will engage and motivate prospects into customers?

This textbook approaches these questions in the same way a marketing professional would—focusing on achieving the desired results through coordinated, integrated use of advertising, personal selling, sales promotion, sponsorship, direct marketing, e-commerce, point-of-purchase (P–O–P), public relations, and Internet communications. Yes, advertising is one tool on the list, but it must be balanced against and coordinated with the others, especially in today's marketplace. Indeed, a new company that might once have been promoted through print and broadcast advertising might now launch itself through an e-mail campaign, the sponsorship of an event, and public relations press releases.

This text stands out from other books that claim to be promotion and integrated marketing communications (IMC) books. These other texts, which are really *advertising* books with some coverage of the other tools of promotion, prepare students for a world that doesn't really exist—one in which advertising is the answer to every marketing challenge. Let's face it, in practice some organizations don't advertise at all, and many others use it only as a lead element of their integrated marketing campaigns.

In contrast, students and instructors will find *Promotion and Integrated Marketing Communications* true to its title. It explores the diverse tools of marketing and promotion individually, as well as how they can best be used together to deliver new customers, new revenue and greater loyalty.

FOCUS ON RESULTS

This book is about getting the job done. The approach is driven entirely by the realities of marketing and promotion—the real world trade-offs, choices and decisions faced by today's marketing professional. *Promotion and Integrated Marketing Communications* differs from other texts in this field in several important ways:

- *A more balanced look at the full range of communications tools.* Advertising, personal selling, sales promotion, sponsorship, direct marketing, e-commerce, point-of-purchase, public relations, and Internet communications are treated with equal emphasis and provided equal stature as options in the communications programs for organizations. No one tool is considered more important than another. As managers will explain, depending on the communications task at hand, a point-of-purchase display effort may be infinitely more effective and appropriate than an advertising effort.

- *A more managerial orientation.* This text looks at marketing problems from the perspective of the manager. Emphasis is on solving problems using all the tools available. For instance, the discussion of measuring effectiveness (Chapter 15) covers *all* the promotional tools, not just advertising and sales promotion. The discussion of message development extends to all forms of promotion, not just the creative aspects of advertising messages. Finally, business buyer behavior is covered in detail (Chapter 5). This is a topic typically ignored in promotion books, but critically important in the world of business-to-business promotion in an e-commerce environment.
- *The Internet and e-commerce as components in promotion.* This is the first book in the field that provides extensive coverage of the Internet, Internet advertising and e-commerce. The Internet is presented not just as a business-to-consumer medium but also as key factor in business-to-business communication and commerce. Further, the Internet and e-commerce are considered as essential integrating forces in the overall promotional effort.

INTEGRATION IS KEY

A book that focuses on the full range of promotional tools rather than predominantly focusing on advertising is completely consistent with the contemporary environment for promotion. This is true for several reasons:

- Database technology allows marketers to use direct marketing, telemarketing, and now e-commerce tools with more precision. These new tools of marketing are implemented with promotional efforts that use multiple promotional programs and rarely rely on advertising alone.
- The rise of the Internet and the role it plays in e-commerce have created a blend of communication/distribution strategies that are properly implemented using a broad communications perspective.
- Trade channel and business-to-business communication rely more on a diverse set of promotional tools.
- Managers manage the communications effort across all promotional tools. The task is managing *promotion,* not managing each tool individually.
- Managers are demanding more specific accountability of the impact of spending on promotion. This results in a greater use of non-advertising communication tools; the effects of which are more easily and more accurately measured.

SPECIFIC ADVANTAGES OF THIS TEXT

Balanced Pedagogy. Most promotions books suffer from trying to be two different or even three different kinds of books: advertising plus promotions plus IMC. This book is a true promotions book that focuses on the integration of promotion tools. This means that advertising is given its due respect as a powerful communications tool but, it is given no more prominence than any other tool in the promotional package.

This feature is demonstrated in the Table of Contents. Note that there is focused attention on planning the promotional effort in Part 1, then the focus moves to researching the environment for promotion in Part 2. Then equal attention is given to each of the tools of promotion in Part 3. The final section, Part 4, fulfills the market trend for greater accountability of the effects of promotion by offering suggestions for measuring effectiveness in each promotional area.

The reason this pedagogy was chosen is because a marketing manager devotes no more administrative time to advertising than event sponsorship or sales promotion or any other promotion device being used. The only time this would not be true is if advertising were being used almost exclusively in the promotional effort, which is extremely uncommon. This book is targeted to those future marketing managers who want and need to know how all the promotional tools work and, more importantly, how to integrate their use for maximum effect.

A Shorter Book. While most promotion books run about 700 pages, this book is shorter at about 550 pages. At least as important, the book is organized into 15 chapters not 20–22 chapters like other books. The reason for the brevity has to do with the fundamental premise of the book: this is a promotions book where discussions of advertising and media don't make up 30–40 percent of the content. Rather, the focus is on the overall promotional planning process and execution of each promotional tool.

Clear, Concise, and Interesting Writing and Presentation. Reviewers and editors have been enlisted to ensure that the writing style is clear, concise, and as interesting as the promotional process itself. In addition, the design principles employed for the presentation offer an interesting and, indeed, integrated look. The medium still can be the message!

Current Coverage, Current Examples. Throughout the text, current, up-to-date examples and issues are presented. As a test, just check any page and see that literature citations are rarely more than a year or two old. And, the fast-paced issues surrounding the Internet, new media, and agency redesign and deployment are all covered, featuring the newest challenges and applications.

ON-TARGET TOPICAL COVERAGE

Part 1: Planning the Promotional Process and Integrated Marketing Communications

In this section, the focus is on planning the promotional effort. This is accomplished by focusing on the process of promotion, the structure of the industry, and a contemporary approach to producing a promotional plan in three chapters.

Chapter 1, Introduction to Promotion and Integrated Marketing Communications, explores how promotion is used by a firm to support the overall marketing program and provide effective communication to target markets. First, there is an evaluation of the relationship between promotion, the promotional mix, and integrated marketing communications. While these terms are common language in all promotion books, there is rarely a clear statement of the relationship between these different processes and activities with an organization. Then, the role of promotion in brand differentiation and positioning is considered. The chapter concludes with a discussion of the nature and prominence of integrated marketing communications as a way to manage the promotional process.

Chapter 2, The Promotion Industry: Marketers, Agencies and Media Organizations, highlights that firms have a wide variety of promotional tools from which to choose in trying to reach and motivate their target markets. And, promotion takes place in a large and complex "communications industry" with many different players and relationships between those players. Our attention turns to understanding how the tools of the promotional mix are managed in a communications industry setting to create brand relationships across all levels of the industry structure. First, we look at the promotion industry as a whole. Then, we consider the different players—particularly advertising and promotion agencies—and the role they play in creating and executing a variety of promotions.

In **Chapter 3, Promotion and IMC Planning and Strategy,** we consider the scope of the promotion and IMC process. First, we look at the full range of elements that make up a promotional plan. Next we consider the way firms choose which tools to emphasize in the promotional mix. This is where a firm decides on how much direct marketing to use relative to event sponsorship, sales promotions, advertising, personal selling and so on. Objective-setting is discussed, differentiating between communications objectives and sales objectives. One of the most difficult and painstaking tasks for managers is setting the promotional budget. We look at several alternatives for promotional budgeting. Finally, a complete model of integrated marketing communications is presented as a tool for planning the IMC effort. This chapter is organized in a way that precisely replicates the planning sequence used by companies and their agencies.

Part 2: Understanding the Market Environment for Promotion and IMC

This section emphasizes that the market environment for promotion needs to be understood completely before commitments and expenditures can be made for particular communications tools. Four chapters in this section explore researching the market environment for promotion.

No decisions are more important to a firm than segmenting the market, targeting high potential segments for different brands, and then positioning the brands for success. The decisions associated with segmenting, targeting, and positioning (STP) are covered in **Chapter 4, Understanding the Marketing Environment: Segmenting, Targeting, and Positioning.** In this chapter, we examine in detail the way organizations decide which consumer and business markets to target and which to ignore as they prepare for promotional campaigns. First, the basics of STP decisions are analyzed. Then we look at segmenting the business-to-business market—a typically overlooked analysis in most situations but critical to the success of both consumer and business products. Finally, we discuss the issue of prioritizing segments and the critical decisions related to brand positioning.

Chapter 5, Understanding Buyer Behavior and Communication Processes, summarizes the concepts and frameworks that are most helpful in understanding two key aspects of buyers. First, the concept of buyer behavior related to both household consumers and business buyers is examined. Because motivations, influences and buying processes differ greatly, it is essential that consumer behavior and business buyer behavior be considered separately. Second, we need to look at the way consumers and business buyers process promotional communications, with our ultimate goal, of course, being to understand which promotional tools will be most effective in communicating to potential buyers—consumers *and* business buyers.

In **Chapter 6, The Regulatory Environment for Promotion and Ethical Issues,** regulation and ethics are covered in concert. The two are examined together because practices that are regulated are often questioned from an ethical standpoint. In some cases, the ethical challenges to promotional practices that lead to regulation are naive and simplistic and fail to take into consideration the complex social, economic, and political environment of contemporary marketing. In other cases, the challenges to promotion are right on. This chapter raises *issues* in the truest sense. It also raises controversies that should make us all think about and debate the very nature of the promotional process.

Chapter 7, The International Market Environment for Promotion and IMC, offers one of the most fascinating topics in all of marketing and promotion. The essential perspective here is that the day has passed when marketers based in industrialized nations can simply "do a foreign version" of their promotions. Today, international marketers must pay detailed attention to local cultures. The essential perspective is clear: the real issue is not nations, but cultures.

This chapter considers the many issues that marketers must understand about the international market environment when promotion needs to cross borders, including cross-cultural research, the challenges of managing marketing efforts across borders, and the use of international promotion agencies. In addition, a key issue in international promotion is the decision to standardize a campaign across all cultures or customize a campaign for every international market. We discuss guidelines for making these decisions. Finally, the issues related to developing and managing a global sales force are presented

Part 3: The Tools of Promotion and IMC

This section examines the role and purpose of each of the major tools in the promotional process. The emphasis throughout these chapters is to first identify the inherent nature of each promotional tool, then examine in detail the communications features of the tool, and finally discuss the value that each tool can add to the IMC effort. Notice that each tool is covered in the same depth, reflecting the core perspective that promotion is truly a blend of many different communications efforts.

Chapter 8, Advertising: Message and Media Strategies, pays proper homage to the advertising process. Advertising is the granddaddy of all the promotional tools. It's the most conspicuous, the most scrutinized and the most controversial. But as prevalent and prominent as advertising is, advertising means different things to different people. It's a business, an art, an institution, and a cultural phenomenon. To the CEO of a multinational corporation, advertising is an essential marketing tool that helps create brand awareness and loyalty and stimulates demand. To a local restaurant owner, advertising is the way to communicate to the neighborhood. To the art director in an advertising agency, advertising is the creative expression of a concept. To a media planner, advertising is the way a marketer uses mass media to communicate to current and potential customers. To scholars and museum curators, advertising is an important cultural artifact, text, and cultural record. Our study of advertising explores the full range of what advertising is and how it can contribute to the promotional process. We begin with a definition of advertising and the key parties involved in its conception. Next we clarify the scope of advertising and the target audiences advertising can reach. The distinguishing feature of advertising among the promotional tools is the creative execution. We look at message strategies that make advertising stand out as a creative effort. Finally, we turn our attention to the media through which advertising is transmitted to the target audiences.

Chapter 9, Internet Advertising, is a key chapter for any contemporary promotions book. Is the Internet a revolution in communication? Well, "revolutions" are more common than they used to be, but we have to be careful about expecting too much. In 1994, executives at Procter & Gamble (P & G) boldly proclaimed that they could envision their promotional programs excluding advertising completely given the power and breadth of new media.[1] The P & G 2000 Annual Report released in September 2000, however, revealed the firm's investment in a B-to-B portal, but makes no mention of the Internet for consumer communications.[2] Still, what *is* truly revolutionary about the Internet is its ability to alter the basic nature

---

1.   Steve Yahn, "Advertising's Grave New World," *Advertising Age,* May 16, 1994, 53.
2.   *P & G 2000 Annual Report,* ©2000, Procter & Gamble, 1–4.

of communication within a commercial channel. Consider that the Internet is being accessed worldwide by about 300 million users.[3] Advertising revenues on the Internet were estimated at about \$4 billion in the year 2000 and are expected to grow to over \$30 billion by the year 2004.[4] This chapter explores the dramatic changes that the Internet is bringing about in the world of advertising. The chapter begins with an overview of cyberspace and some of the basics of the way the Internet works. Then, we consider the different types of advertising that can be used and some of the technical aspects of the process. We look at the issues involved in establishing a Web site and developing a brand in the "e-community." Finally, we explore the IMC challenges of Internet advertising.

New technology has transformed direct marketing as much as any area of marketing and promotion. **Chapter 10, Direct Marketing and E-Commerce,** identifies how firms can manage the direct-marketing opportunities present in the marketplace—both traditional and e-commerce opportunities—in a firm's IMC mix. First, we consider the relationship between direct marketing and e-commerce. Since e-commerce is a phenomenon of the last five or six years, its scope and nature need to be considered in the broader context of the direct-marketing effort. Next, we discuss direct marketing specifically. We look at the popularity of direct marketing, its purposes, and the media used to carry it out. We also explore the development and management of databases. Finally, we examine the new and expanding world of e-commerce. Fueled by consumer and business access to the Internet, e-commerce has become a key issue for both promotion and, quite frankly, overall marketing strategy. A model of e-commerce is proposed which describes how the process works, followed by a discussion of the roles of various participants in the e-commerce process.

Chapter 11, Sales Promotion: Consumer, Trade, and Business Market Techniques, highlights how sales promotions like contests, sweepstakes, sponsorships, and merchandise giveaways can energize the promotional effort, often generating results not possible through traditional advertising. Used properly, sales promotion is capable of almost instant demand stimulation. Sales promotion is also emerging as a global force as firms try to introduce U.S. brands in distant markets. Both consumer *and* trade techniques in sales promotion are covered in this chapter.

Chapter 12, Sponsorship, Point-of-Purchase, and Supportive Communications, meaningfully examines promotional tools that are often given only superficial treatment. Promotional efforts in the areas of point-of-purchase advertising and sponsorship continue to produce impressive results and are receiving more and more funding from many marketers. In addition, two types of supportive communications are being discussed in this chapter: media-based and nonmedia-based. Media-based communications such as billboards and signage have been around for many years, but are enjoying renewed interest from marketers, as are transit and aerial advertising, and directory advertising. In addition, this chapter points out that a marketer must understand and take advantage of the nonmedia supportive communications opportunities inherent in the brand name, logo, and slogan as well as packaging and labeling and word of mouth tactics. A key point made in this chapter is that in *truly* integrated marketing communications, *every* contact with the brand adds to the communication environment for a target customer and these nonmedia factors represent another, potentially powerful communications contact.

Chapter 13, Public Relations and Corporate Advertising, considers in detail the role of these two separate and important areas that must be part of a firm's overall integrated marketing communications effort. Each has the potential to make a distinct and important contribution to the single and unified message and image of an organization, which is the ultimate goal of IMC. Public relations is often a

3.   NUA Internet Surveys, accessed at http://www.nua.net/surveys/ accessed on March 20, 2000.
4.   "Advertising that clicks," *The Economist,* October 9, 1999, 71–72.

"behind the scenes" process. The many tools and objectives of public relations are discussed throughout this chapter. Corporate advertising, on the other hand, uses major media to communicate its unique type of message which is distinct from typical brand advertising a firm might do. While public relations and corporate advertising are rarely the foundation tools of a promotional mix and IMC program, they do represent key tactics under certain conditions. We explore the nature of these two specialized promotional tools and the conditions under which they are ideally suited for the IMC program.

Chapter 14, Personal Selling and Sales Management, provides a complete look at this promotional tool. Many times the role of personal selling effort is given token treatment in discussions of promotion and IMC. That is a mistake. Despite the conspicuousness of advertising, sales promotion, sponsorships and other tools in the promotional mix, personal selling is often the most important force for communication in many corporations. For firms like IBM, Xerox, State Farm Insurance, and a variety of retailing organizations like Dillard's and Nordstrom, the personal selling effort is primarily responsible for customer contact, communication, and culminating sales. This chapter considers the role of personal selling in IMC. We first examine the role of personal selling in the marketing effort and then more specifically with respect to promotional communications. After establishing the role, we identify the types of personal selling a firm can use. Next, the objectives for personal selling are considered. Then, we examine the process of personal selling in great detail including the stages of the personal selling effort. We examine the new, technologically rich environment for personal selling and how these new technologies are changing the way the selling effort is carried out. Finally, we look at sales management in order to understand what steps need to be taken to ensure that this promotional tool is used effectively and efficiently.

Part 4: Evaluation and Measuring the Effectiveness of Promotion and IMC

Chapter 15, Measuring the Effectiveness of Promotion and IMC, highlights the fact that by drawing on research, a marketer can better understand what tools are working in a promotional campaign, and justify the expenditures made to use them. In this chapter, we consider the many issues involved in measuring the effectiveness of the vast array of promotional options. First, we consider issues related to the whole concept of measurement itself. Given the complex nature of communication in a promotional setting, there is a high degree of complexity and more than a little controversy with respect to measurement approaches. Second, we consider measuring the effectiveness of advertising in great detail. Maybe because it is so conspicuous, maybe because of the billions of dollars spent on production, or maybe because it relies so much more on creative execution, advertising has and continues to be the subject of more poking and prodding measurement effort than any other promotional tool. Third, this chapter considers each of the other promotional tools in the order they were presented in the text: Internet advertising, direct mail and e-commerce, sponsorship, P–O–P, supportive media, public relations, corporate advertising, and personal selling. Finally, the chapter concludes with a look at how the effectiveness of the overall IMC program can be measured.

SPECIAL CHAPTER FEATURES

Within each chapter of *Promotion and Integrated Marketing Communications,* you will find dynamic and academically sound features that capture reader attention, clarify important topics, and offer fresh examples of promotions in various business settings.

Chapter Opening Industry Scenarios. Each chapter begins with a vivid story describing promotional strategies from well-known companies. These introductory scenarios demonstrate how chapter concepts are implemented in a variety of businesses and provide an excellent launching point for classroom discussions. For example, Chapter 10 highlights the unfolding story of how The Gap is flourishing after diving into electronic retailing.

IMC in Practice. As already stated, *Promotion and Integrated Marketing Communications* is targeted to future marketing managers who need to know how to integrate all of the promotional tools to achieve synergy and maximum effectiveness. The IMC in Practice boxes highlight interesting and important IMC strategies and issues students will face. Here are some of the titles of IMC boxes in this text:
- *Chainsaw This—Forty-three Straight Days of Timbersports TV Coverage,* Chapter 4
- *Coming Together . . . Over Saturn,* Chapter 5
- *People Who Live In Glass Huts Shouldn't Throw Pizza,* Chapter 6
- *Taking it in the Shorts,* Chapter 8
- *The Mint Wars,* Chapter 12

Global Issues. The Global Issues boxes provide an insightful real-world look at the numerous challenges marketers face internationally. Many international issues are discussed in these timely boxes, including the following:
- *East Meets West for PR Lessons* Chapter 1
- *Good EEEEEEEvening Vietnam!!,* Chapter 7
- *What's So Funny About Iced Coffee?,* Chapter 8
- *Global Promotion? How About Intergalactic?,* Chapter 12
- *Need a High Profile? Go Corporate,* Chapter 13

New Media. New media options add power and impact to promotional mixes. The New Media boxes in each chapter feature innovations in business-to-consumer and business-to-business promotions. Here are some of the titles of New Media boxes in this text:
- *The Internet Is Big—But Will It Ever Be as Big as Seinfeld?,* Chapter 1
- *Brand Loyalty is Tough for Dot-Coms,* Chapter 5
- *Third in Sales but First in E-Commerce,* Chapter 7
- *Ten Web Design Goofs That Can Be Fatal to a Web Site,* Chapter 9
- *Television Advertising Is Direct-Response Advertising,* Chapter 10

Web Sightings. In keeping with the new media distinctiveness of this book, you will find "Web Sightings" in each chapter, marked by the man with binoculars found above selected exhibits. These internet addresses take students to the marketer's home page, bringing the textbook exhibit into real time. Questions are provided to prompt students to explore, explain, describe, compare, contrast, summarize or analyze the content or features of the marketer's home page.

Career Profiles. The field of promotions offers a rich variety of job opportunities, each contributing to the overall success of the promotional campaign. Each chapter in this text includes a Career Profile that investigates the challenges and opportunities of successful promotions professionals. Some examples of the positions featured include an account coordinator for a marketing communications agency, a marketing manager for a travel agency, a group account director for one of the largest interactive advertising agencies in the United States, and president and CEO of a major database marketing firm.

Key Terms with Page Citations. Each chapter ends with a listing of key terms found in the chapter along with page citations for easy reference. Key terms also appear in boldface in the text. Students can prepare for exams by scanning these lists to be sure they can define or explain each term. Students can also have fun with key terms at the text Web site where they can work online crossword puzzles that use key terms from the text.

Experiential Exercises. At the end of each chapter, Experiential Exercises require students to apply the material they have just read by researching topics, writing short papers, preparing brief presentations, or interacting with professionals from the promotions industry. They require students to go beyond the classroom to seek information not provided in the text. A number of these exercises are especially designed for teamwork. Additional Experiential Exercises can be found in the *Instructor's Manual.*

Using the Internet. Every chapter includes Using the Internet Exercises that take students online to explore promotional strategies for a variety of organizations. A series of questions guide students as they study how organizations are using World Wide Web technology to implement their promotional campaigns.

SUPERLATIVE SUPPORT PACKAGE

InfoTrac® College Edition. With InfoTrac® College Edition, students get complete, 24 hour-a-day access to full-text articles from hundreds of scholarly journals and popular periodicals such as *Newsweek, Time,* and *USA Today.* InfoTrac® College Edition is perfect for all students, from dorm-dwellers to commuters and distance learners.

***Instructor's Manual* with Extensive Lecture Outlines.** The author-written Instructor's Manual provides comprehensive lecture outlines for each of the text's 15 chapters. The outlines offer a complete and structured approach for presenting class lectures. The *Instructor's Manual* also contains additional video cases and suggested answers for all end-of-chapter activities. [ISBN: 0-324-06255-9]

Test Bank. The test bank provides a vast resource of test questions that test understanding of major concepts and terminology. Each chapter includes true-false, multiple choice, and essay questions. [ISBN: 0-324-06257-5]

Computerized Test Bank. All items from the printed *Test Bank* are available on *ExamView* Testing Software, an automated testing program that allows instructors to create exams by selecting questions, modifying questions, and adding new questions. The software is available in Windows and is provided free to instructors at educational institutions that adopt this text. Custom exams also available by calling 1-800-423-0563 (Thomson Learning Academic Resources). [ISBN: 0-324-06258-3]

PowerPoint Slides with Example Advertisements. All images prepared as transparency masters in the *Instructor's Manual* are also available on PowerPoint software. The PowerPoint images can also be downloaded from the Web site at http://semenik.swcollege.com. [ISBN: 0-324-06256-7]

WebTutor™. This content-rich, Web-based teaching and learning aid reinforces and clarifies complex concepts. For each chapter, WebTutor™ includes a summary of key topics, a variety of quizzes to determine where a student needs additional study, flashcards, quizzes, additional Web links, threaded discussion, and more. [ISBN: WebTutor for WebCT 0-324-12362-0; WebTutor for Blackboard 0-324-130589].

Web Site at http://semenik.swcollege.com. Timely, innovative, and comprehensive, the Web site for this textbook is a valuable source of industry news, career advice, and the latest promotional campaigns from well-known companies. An interactive study center provides a Pretest and Posttest for each chapter and e-lectures that review key topics. In addition, a comprehensive set of Internet Exercises guide students through the analysis of IMC campaigns.

Instructor's Resource CD-ROM. The instructor's resource disk includes the *Exam View Testing Software, Test Bank,* the *Instructor's Manual,* and PowerPoint slides. [ISBN: 0-324-06254-0]

Color Transparency Package. Also available to instructors is a high-quality selection of full-color overhead transparencies. These transparencies include both ads and exhibits from the textbook and an abundant number of additional ads not found in the text. Suggestions for incorporating these ads into lectures are included in the *Instructor's Manual* lecture outlines. [ISBN: 0-324-06259-1]

Video Package. Written and designed by a team of academics to enrich and support chapter concepts, the videos highlight promotional strategies used by a variety of service and manufacturing organizations. The video cases, included in the Instructor's Manual and written by the text author, challenge students to develop solutions to business problems. [ISBN: 0-324-06970-7]

IMC: An Integrated Marketing Communications Exercise. This comprehensive supplementary package by Bernard C. Jakacki puts students in the role of client services manager at a major full-service integrated marketing communications agency. The client, the Tourism Ministry of the Republic of Uruguay, wants the agency to create and manage a total promotions program for a new resort in Uruguay called *Punta del Este.* [ISBN: 0-324-01483-X]

ACKNOWLEDGMENTS

A large number of reviewers participated in the development of this text, and I would like to recognize their contributions:

Avery Abernethy
Auburn University

Soumava Bandyopadhyay
Lamar University

Kenneth Bartkus
Utah State University

Ronald J. Bauerly
Western Illinois University

Paul N. Bloom
University of North Carolina

Jennifer Chang
Penn State University

Lauren DeGeorge
University of Central Florida

James Haefner
University of Illinois at Urbana–Champaign

Michael A. McCollough
University of Idaho

Darrel D. Muehling
Washington State University

Betty Parker
Western Michigan University

Denise Schoenbachler
Northern Illinois University

Sanjaya Shunglu
Penn State University

James Swartz
Cal State Poly University–Pomona

Charles M. Wood
University of Tulsa

Rajiv Vaidyanathan
University of Minnesota–Duluth

Sincere appreciation is extended to Michael McCollough, University of Idaho, for developing a comprehensive test bank and Martin Meyer, University of Wisconsin–Stephens Point, for writing the interactive quizzes for the Web site and quiz questions for WebTutor under a tight deadline. Nick Bean channeled his creative energies into developing innovate Web content, and his involvement with this project is appreciated. Robert Cannell, Roosevelt University, developed Appendix A, and I appreciate his role in describing a captivating IMC success story. In addition, special thanks are extended to Carolyn Lawrence who wrote the superior Career Profiles.

I want to thank James Davis for his tenacious effort in gaining permission for the use of the hundreds of advertisements, illustrations and tables used in this book. James simply does not take no for an answer and almost always prevails. Mary Draper was an author's dream come-true as a developmental editor. She accepted my ideas and helped me make them work. I want to thank my good friends and colleagues Chris Allen and Tom O'Guinn who gave me their blessing in venturing off on this project.

There are several people as South-Western/Thomson Learning who have supported me for a number of years. At the top of the list are Dave Shaut and Steve Momper. Dave signed my first book—and has been trying to recover ever since. Seriously, we have worked through all sorts of good times and hard times. Thanks Dave for all your support. Steve Momper has been with me since my first book as well. Despite the fact that he has believed in every idea I have ever had, he has risen through the ranks to upper management. I thank you for that unwavering faith. Pamela Person inherited me and this project as her first project. I hope it wasn't too weird for you Pamela. You did a great job. Special thanks goes to Marc Callahan for managing the marketing and sales efforts; Michael Stratton for exceptional internal, cover, and Web designs; and Tamborah Moore for carefully managing the production effort.

Richard J. Semenik

PROMOTION AND INTEGRATED
MARKETING COMMUNICATIONS

PART 1

PLANNING THE PROMOTIONAL PROCESS AND INTEGRATED MARKETING COMMUNICATIONS

This opening section of the book reveals the breadth, complexity, and power of the promotional process. Modern-day promotion is an exciting combination of communication and technology. We will explore how companies are relying on the different tools of promotion to communicate through both traditional and new technology methods. In addition, the concept of managing the promotional process in an integrated and coordinated manner is introduced. This approach to managing the promotional effort has become known as integrated marketing communication, or IMC. IMC is a way of managing diverse promotional efforts from advertising through event sponsorship to personal selling so that a cohesive communication program is the result. An IMC approach allows firms to more effectively and efficiently use the tools of promotion. A final goal for this section is to learn how to plan the overall promotional effort. The overall promotional plan is considered as an introduction to the content area of Part 2 of the text.

1

Introduction to Promotion and Integrated Marketing Communications explores how promotions is used by a firm to support the overall marketing program and provide effective communication to target markets. First, we evaluate the relationship among promotion, the promotional mix, and integrated marketing communications (IMC). Then we look at the role of promotion in marketing strategy. The chapter also describes how IMC provides a new perspective on the way in which communication options are exercised to compete effectively, develop customer loyalty, and generate profits.

2

The Promotion Industry: Marketers, Agencies, and Media Organizations looks at the basic structure of the promotion industry and how it is changing due to advances in technology. Advertising agencies, research firms, special production facilitators, media companies, and Web site developers are just some of the organizations that form the structure of the industry. Each plays a different role, and billions of dollars are spent every year for the services of various participants.

3

Promotion and IMC Strategy and Planning explains how promotional plans are developed. The chapter begins with a detailed look at each element of the promotion plan and goes on to explore how firms set objectives for the promotional effort. A key issue here is the difference between communications objectives and sales objectives. We will look at several alternatives for promotional budgeting and conclude with a complete model of integrated marketing communications. The Appendix to Chapter 3 demonstrates an integrated marketing communications success story.

After reading this chapter, you will be able to:

1 Define promotion, the promotional mix, and integrated marketing communications.

2 Explain the relationship between promotion, the promotional mix and integrated marketing communications.

3 Identify and describe the tools of the promotional mix.

4 Identify the role of promotion in marketing strategy.

5 Discuss the rise in prominence of integrated marketing communications (IMC) as a way of managing the promotional process

It really was the "Ultimate Driving Experience" for the 49,886 prospective BMW customers (including nearly 5,000 teenagers) who got to drive a new BMW M3 around a test track for up to four hours. The company has been developing a variety of special events and promotions—including the driving-school event—in order to reach customers in new and different ways. Because of their success, BMW has increased spending on them at a rate of 20 percent per year. The events are aimed at getting drivers behind the wheel of its latest models with a specific emphasis on future customers, including teenagers. The events will complement BMW's extensive advertising campaigns, dealer showroom programs, and growing Internet presence.

Initially launched in thirteen major U.S. cities, this was much more than just a driving event. The adults and teens who took part in the first yearlong run of the " Ultimate Driving Experience" couldn't have had a greater thrill. With the help of a professional driver, prospective customers spent more than two hours behind the wheel of a 3-Series BMW sedan learning high-performance driving techniques, accident avoidance skills, and traction tricks. Teens got a special four-hour session emphasizing basic driving skills and safe driving techniques and could test their skills against their peers. The first year of the event

was so successful that BMW upped its investment significantly by building its own facility for the test.

While this was the "Ultimate Driving Experience" for participants, it really was close to the ultimate promotional event for the firm. For all the fun the drivers were having, this was a carefully planned and broad-based promotional event. Aside from introducing prospective customers to the thrill of driving a new BMW, the firm used the event as an opportunity to showcase a gallery of its latest models, let participants shop in a BMW "lifestyle shop" featuring logo wear and accessories, and then treated them to lunch in the mobile M Café where free Internet access was provided to the company's Web site, http://www.bmw.com.

This event is just one component of an elaborate promotional mix used by the company to inform and persuade customers about the values and superiority of its brand. Advertising, of course, is a cornerstone of BMW's promotional mix, with about $140 million invested in television, magazines, and newspaper ads (see Exhibit 1.1). The firm is beefing up its Web site to build and solidify relationships with existing customers. The "Owners Circle" Web area allows customers to register at the site and maintain an ongoing dialogue with product specialists from the firm. The company is in the process of

EXHIBIT 1.1

Advertising in mass media, like this magazine ad, is a key component of the promotional mix for BMW cars. But the firm also uses special events, brand placement in films, a comprehensive Web site, and a large sales force to communicate with target audiences.

completing the BMW Performance Center, where owners and prospective owners can pay between $495 and $865 for instruction by professional drivers in programs ranging from a New Drivers School to the M5 school, which offers advanced skill training in an M5 sedan (0–60 mph, 4.8 seconds). In addition, if you were lucky, you might have been one of a few dozen BMW owners who participated in the screening of the then-newest James Bond film, *The World Is Not Enough,* which featured the new $100,000+, Z8 BMW. The firm negotiated a $20 million agreement with Metro-Goldwyn-Mayer for sponsorship of the Bond films in return for featuring BMW products in the films. All these promotion and advertising activities are anchored in a carefully planned and monitored dealer network where the sales staff gets annual training on features of new BMW models.

The goal of the promotional program for BMW, in the words of Jim McDowell, VP of Marketing for BMW of North America, is "to reinforce the choice people make with BMW and give them a variety of ways to discover the cars' features in ways that are not apparent through mere description or advertising." Overall, for anyone interested in a BMW, these events seem to offer not only the "Ultimate Driving Experience" but also the "Ultimate Promotional Experience."[1]

INTRODUCTION

The many promotional tactics used by BMW mean that the company's strategists are putting together a complex promotional program to communicate with target customers about the values of BMW. Like most firms, BMW's promotional program includes a variety of tools, all designed to complement each other and support the firm's strategic marketing objectives. This chapter explores how promotion is used by a firm to support the overall marketing program and provide effective communication to target markets. First, we will evaluate the relationship between promotion, the promotional mix, and integrated marketing communications. Then, we will look at the role of promotion in marketing strategy. Finally, we will discuss the nature and prominence of integrated marketing communications as a way to manage the promotional process.

The Relationship Between Promotion, the Promotional Mix, and Integrated Marketing Communications ❶ ❷

We need to be clear about one thing at the outset: the communications process called promotion is not just about advertising—not by a long shot. And we need to understand some basic vocabulary and relationships in the area of promotion—specifically, the definitions of and relationships among promotion, the promotional mix, and integrated marketing communications.

Promotion is the communications process in marketing that is used to create a favorable predisposition toward a brand of product or service, an idea, or even a person. Promotion for a brand of product or service is the most common kind of promotion. Chevrolet promotes Chevy trucks. E*Trade promotes its online brokerage service, and Altoids promotes its "curiously strong" mints (see Exhibit 1.2). An example of the promotion of an idea is a public service advertising campaign for gun safety (like the one in Exhibit 1.3) or when a firm sponsors a special event like a 10K run to raise money for a local hospital. Promotion of a person is most common in politics and entertainment. When a politician holds a fund-raiser, meets with the press, and uses newspaper and television advertising to try to get elected, then a person is being promoted. When Bruce Willis shows up on the *Tonight Show with Jay Leno,* Bruce (and his agent) is doing person promotion.

---

1.   Information taken from Kate Fitzgerald, "It's the Wheel Thing," *Advertising Age,* November 15, 1999, 30, 32.

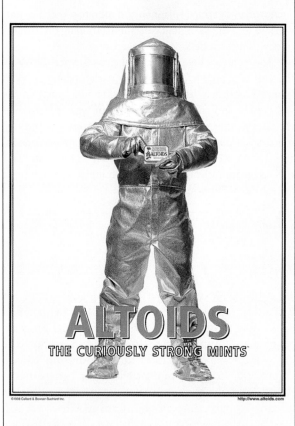

EXHIBIT 1.2

Promotion is about attracting attention to brands and creating a favorable impression. The "Curiously Strong Mint" campaign for Altoids mints has been highly successful at doing both.

EXHIBIT 1.3

This public service advertising campaign is promoting an idea: gun safety.

The **promotional mix** is a blend of communications tools used by a firm to carry out the promotion process and to communicate directly with target markets (or audiences in the language of communications). These communications tools include advertising, the Internet, direct marketing and e-commerce, sales promotion, event sponsorships, point-of-purchase displays, support communications (like directories, brand placement in films, and specialty items), public relations, and personal selling. As we saw in the introductory scenario, BMW used mass-media advertising, special events, brand placement in films, a Web site, and salespeople in a large dealer network in the promotional mix. Each of these tools is capable of communicating in a different way to achieve a different kind of impact on people. We will be taking a closer look at each of these communications tools later in the chapter and in great detail in Chapters 8 to 14.

Finally, **integrated marketing communications (IMC)** is the process of using promotional tools in a unified way so that a synergistic communications effect is created. That is, every form of communication being used—from the company's business cards and stationery through the most elaborate full-production television ad—is evaluated to be sure that a clear, consistent, and compelling message is being communicated to the intended audiences. Notice that the word "audiences" is used. That's because corporate communications these days have to be aimed at not just

EXHIBIT 1.4

The relationship between promotion, the promotional mix, and IMC

household consumers, but also business and trade customers like wholesalers, retailers, and suppliers. If a brand isn't properly promoted to the business and trade market, it will never reach the consumer market. And some companies only sell to business and trade customers.

In summary, promotion is the communications *process* itself. The promotional mix represents the *tools and activities* of promotion. IMC is *a way of managing the process and activities* so that they are coordinated and a synergistic effect is achieved. Exhibit 1.4 graphically illustrates this relationship. At this point, we want to take a closer look at the different communications options in the promotional mix.

THE PROMOTIONAL MIX ❸

Now that we have the basic parts of promotion and IMC defined, let's look at the tools in the promotional mix more closely. Just as a firm develops an overall marketing mix based on a blend of product design, pricing, distribution, and promotional decisions, the promotional area itself is a blend of activities. The promotional mix can include some combination of many approaches, as mentioned in the previous section, or just one or two promotional tools. Exhibit 1.5 lists the approximate amount invested in the different tools of promotion in 1999. Notice that while advertising is clearly the largest, at over $200 billion annually, the other factors in the promotional mix also attract huge dollar amounts. (If you add various forms of sales promotion together, then sales promotion is actually larger than advertising.) The New Media box discusses the current level of investment in the Internet and highlights this new medium as a communications option as well. With this as a perspective, we can consider a brief overview of each of the promotional mix factors.

THE INTERNET IS BIG—BUT WILL IT EVER BE AS BIG AS *SEINFELD*?

You know those annoying little boxes that slow down the loading of the Internet page you want to be on and then flash incessantly while you're browsing? They are called banner ads, and big companies like Xerox and small companies like Boo.com (an online sportswear retailer) are currently investing about $3.3 billion dollars to reach Web surfers with banner ads. But how well do they work? One survey has determined that less than 1 percent of Web users ever click on a banner ad. Not very impressive, but that doesn't mean the ad didn't communicate some information while the surfer was moving around a Web page.

At this point, the investment in Web advertising is only about 1.5 percent of the investment companies are making in traditional media like television, radio, newspapers, and magazines. And in its heyday a 30-second spot on *Seinfeld* cost about $500,000. Will the Internet ever get that big? Probably not.

Source: "Advertising That Clicks," *The Economist*, October 9, 1999, 71–72.

Advertising

Advertising tends to be the most glamorous and elaborate of all the promotional tools. Around the world, nearly $500 billion is spent annually on advertising—and that is just for media time and space! If you add in all the costs of producing ads and the salaries of people working in the industry, the amount invested in advertising is well over $1 trillion dollars a year. **Advertising** is defined

Promotional Mix Tool	Annual Expenditures
Advertising	$201.00
Premium Incentives	25.30
Point-of-Purchase	13.70
Specialty Items	13.20
Sponsorships	6.80
Couponing	6.45
Interactive	1.02
Sampling	1.01

Sources: Data for advertising expenditures obtained from "Leading National Advertisers," *Advertising Age,* September 27, 1999. Data for Internet Advertising obtained from "Advertising That Clicks," *The Economist,* October 9, 1999, 71. All other data obtained from The 1999 Annual Report of the Promotion Industry, *Promo,* July 1999, S5.

as a paid, mass-mediated attempt to persuade.[2] To appreciate the nature of advertising, a good starting point is to recognize the importance and scope of the process in the United States. One measure of the importance of advertising is the growth in advertising expenditures in the United States as the economy has grown. Since the early 1900s, advertising media expenditures have grown from about $200 million to today's level of $200 billion.[3]

Another perspective on advertising is the amount firms spend on advertising relative to total sales. Across all industries, U.S. firms spend about 7 percent of gross sales on advertising. This exceeds the average amount, across all industries, spent by firms on research and development. Exhibit 1.6 gives some examples of advertising-to-sales ratios in several industries and the spending by some of the firms in those industries. Notice that in personal care and food products—where consumers perceive homogeneity between brands—the advertising-to-sales ratio is a relatively high 10 to 12 percent, compared to higher-priced items like automobiles and computers where about 2.5 percent of sales is spent on advertising.

But advertising is about much more than spending big dollars. The advertising process is a complex system of strategic planning and creative genius. It requires careful planning and precision execution. Advertising is, therefore, actually carried out in a structured fashion, which we will examine in Chapter 8.

Internet Advertising

Internet advertising is a form of advertising in which the message is carried over the Internet rather than traditional mass media. A global collection of computer networks linking both public and private computer systems, the **Internet** represents a process and a medium that is unique and warrants special attention. The scope of the Internet is truly impressive given that it is a communications medium that is less than a decade old. Currently, 106 million people in the United States, or about 40 percent of the population, are online. About 200 million people worldwide, or 4.7 percent of the population, are online.[4] In 1999, $3.3 billion was spent on

---

2.   Thomas C. O'Guinn, Chris T. Allen, and Richard J. Semenik, *Advertising* (Cincinnati, OH: South-Western College Publishing, 2000), 6.

3.   Ibid, 42.

4.   Data obtained from NUA Internet Surveys data at http://www.nua.net/surveys, accessed November 20, 1999.

EXHIBIT 1.6

Advertising-to-sales ratios in selected industries

Source: Industry averages were obtained from "1998 Advertising to Sales Ratios for the 200 Largest Ad Spending Industries," *Advertising Age,* June 29, 1998, 22. Advertising spending for individual firms was obtained from "100 Leading National Advertisers," *Advertising Age,* September 28, 1998, 547. Reprinted with permission from the June 29, 1998 and September 28, 1998 issues of *Advertising Age,* Crain Communications, Inc., 1998.

Industry	Advertiser	U.S. Ad Spending	U.S. Sales	Advertising Spending as % of Sales
Apparel				**5.30**
	Levi Strauss	$ 244.6	$ 4,600.0	5.30
	Nike	501.7	5,055.0	9.10
Automobiles				**2.70**
	General Motors	3,087.4	127,128.0	2.42
	Ford	1,281.8	120,474.0	1.06
	Volkswagen	204.9	6,791.0	3.00
	Honda	578.1	21,190.7	2.72
Computers				**2.30**
	IBM	924.9	32,663.0	2.82
	Intel	630.5	11,053.0	5.69
	Microsoft	407.4	4,356.0	9.35
Food				**10.5**
	Nestlé SA	460.9	15,353.0	2.99
	Kellogg	558.2	3,961.8	14.08
	Campbell Soup	342.5	4,850.0	7.05
Personal care				**12.0**
	Procter & Gamble	2,743.2	18,460.0	14.8
	Gillette	578.4	3,682.8	15.6
	Estée Lauder	519.2	2,200.0	23.5
Retail				**3.30**
	JCPenney	906.2	30,546.0	2.96
	Circuit City Stores	450.2	8,870.8	5.07
	Wal-Mart	290.2	112,005.0	0.25

Internet advertising, and that amount is expected to grow to over $30 billion by the year 2004.[5]

Nearly everything about the way the Internet works as a communications medium is different from the way traditional advertising works. The key similarity is that both represent important ways to reach a target audience. There are four main components of the Internet through which communication can occur:

- *Electronic mail (e-mail):* Allows people (or advertisers) to send messages directly to individuals' computers. In 1999, over 1 trillion e-mails were sent from within the United States alone.
- *Internet Relay Chat (IRC):* Allows people to "talk" over the Internet in real time despite their geographic separation. RCA Records used this form of Internet communication to "chat up" a new album by Christina Aguilera before turning to more traditional promotional communications.[6]

5.   "Advertising That Clicks," *The Economist,* October 9, 1999, 71–72.
6.   Erin White, " 'Chatting' a Singer Up the Pop Charts," *The Wall Street Journal,* November 5, 1999, B1, B4.

- *Usenet:* A link of individuals with common interests that provides a forum for sharing knowledge that is separate from the e-mail system; an electronic bulletin board.
- *World Wide Web (WWW):* Most of us think the WWW is the Internet. Actually, it is that part of the Internet where people and organizations can access an immense database of information through programs called Web browsers (such as Internet Explorer and Netscape). Access to the Web is provided by connection to the network. Access for most household users is gained by signing up with a commercial service like AT&T WorldNet or AOL (see Exhibit 1.7), but access is also available through a local Internet provider or an educational institution.

The Internet's role as an advertising vehicle is still being defined. So far, most companies are struggling to integrate their Internet communications with their overall promotional communications.[7] We will look at Internet advertising in depth in Chapter 9 and the way marketing transactions (e-commerce) occur through the Internet in Chapter 10.

http://www.att.net/wns/maxim

EXHIBIT 1.7

Distill AT&T's offer and what have you got? Just one of many, many providers of a nearly commodity service—literally, just a service to move bits on a wire (albeit the one over which a lot of interesting things might pass) to your house. The message, though, speaks to being both hip and conservatively secure. Traditional telecommunications providers like AT&T have myriad competitors, from cable TV services to wireless providers, in offering access to the Net to consumers.

Sales Promotion

Sales promotion is the use of incentives to generate a specific and short-term response in a household consumer, trade buyer (a retailer like Nordstrom's), or business buyer (like Xerox). Free samples, coupons, premiums, sweepstakes and contests, rebates, and price discounts are some of the primary methods of sales promotion in the consumer market. The business market relies more on trade shows, demonstrations, premiums, price or merchandise allowances, and sales force or dealer contests as sales promotion techniques. Sales promotion is designed to stimulate short-term purchasing in a target market and enhance dealer effectiveness in promoting a firm's brand. This promotional option is valuable to marketers because it provides a way to get a consumer who is using a competitor's brand to switch to the marketer's brand. It is also a way to move stagnant inventory and create needed cash flow.

---

7.   Gene DeRose and Michele Slack, "Online in the Media Mix," *Critical Mass,* Fall 1999, 108.

Firms have to be careful when they use sales promotion techniques, though. The frequent use of sales promotion can make it difficult to attract customers without it. But, used judiciously and with careful timing, sales promotion provides an incentive to consumers like no other promotional tool.

Direct Marketing and E-Commerce

Direct marketing is an interactive system of marketing that uses one or more advertising media to effect a measurable response and/or transaction at any location.[8] This definition distinguishes direct marketing from other primary promotional tools in three ways:

- *Direct marketing uses a combination of media.* Any medium can be used in a direct marketing program, and a combination of media is often used to increase effectiveness.
- *Direct marketing is often designed to elicit a direct response.* An example of this would be getting the message receiver to phone or mail in an order. Other forms of promotion like traditional advertising, public relations, or event sponsorship are not designed to elicit immediate action.
- *Direct marketing transactions can occur anywhere.* This includes the buyer's home, by mail, or literally any place the consumer can communicate with the marketer.

EXHIBIT 1.8

Direct marketing is another way to reach consumers with a message about a brand. But it also offers the consumer the chance to place an order—like the toll-free number listed here to order a subscription to National Geographic.

Today, the primary methods of direct marketing are direct mail; telemarketing using the telephone sales solicitation; and direct-response advertising in magazines, newspapers, and on television and radio (see Exhibit 1.8). The widespread use of direct-marketing techniques and their sophisticated use by firms like L. L. Bean and Time Warner is an indication of the importance and potency of direct marketing as a promotional mix tool.

Online ordering via the Internet is another form of direct marketing and has come to be known as "e-commerce" because of the totally electronic communication between buyers and sellers. **E-commerce** is business conducted between buyers and sellers using electronic exchange media. E-commerce is quickly emerging as a significant form of direct marketing. In 1998, about $7.8 billion in merchandise was purchased by consumers online from firms like The Gap and Amazon.com.[9] More significantly, business-to-business online e-commerce currently totals about $50 billion annually, with firms like Dell Computer, General Electric, and General Motors insisting that vendors and suppliers move most of their ordering and order servicing to the Internet.[10] In addition, trade markets are emerging where buyers in specific industries are creating e-marketplaces to enhance the efficiency of the exchange process.[11]

8. Bob Stone, *Successful Direct Marketing Methods* (Lincolnwood, IL: NTC Business Books, 1994), 5.
9. Mohanbir Sawhney and Steven Kaplan, "Let's Get Vertical," *Business 2.0,* September 1999, 85.
10. Ibid.
11. Jeffrey Davis, "How It Works," *Business 2.0,* February 2000, 2112–114.

Sponsorship, Point-of-Purchase, and Supportive Communications

Sponsorship involves funding an event (like a motocross competition) or a charitable cause (such as a public television fund-raiser), or creating an event in order to highlight a firm's brand to a specific target audience. When a firm sponsors or cosponsors an event such as a golf tournament, museum exhibit, or rock concert, the brand featured in the event gains widespread visibility and credibility with the event audience. That audience already has a positive attitude toward and affinity for the situation they are in because they chose to attend or participate. When this audience encounters a brand in such a favorable environment, the brand experiences a positive, "halo" effect—the audience likes the event and will be more positive toward the brand. Exhibit 1.9 shows an ad announcing that Mountain Dew will be sponsoring a large-scale snowboarding festival. Sponsorship has become the fifth most popular form of promotion used by U.S. firms, with about $7 billion allocated annually to event sponsorships.[12]

http://www.mountaindew.com

EXHIBIT 1.9

Event sponsorship is a popular promotional mix tool because it allows marketers to reach a highly targeted market in a very favorable setting. Here, Mountain Dew is one of the sponsors of a high-profile snowboarding event. Web site addresses (universal resource locators, "URLs") are also well suited to being plastered on the side of a NASCAR racer, or on the barrier behind home plate. How much does Mountain Dew's Web presence match the "Gen X" feel of this event?

Point-of-purchase (P–O–P) promotion refers to materials used in the retail setting to attract shoppers' attention to a company's brand. P–O–P materials typically convey a specific brand feature or highlight special short-term price discounts. In-store displays, banners, end-of-aisle displays, wall units, and floor stands are ways to attract a little extra attention to a brand. The "Tylenol Store" display unit in Exhibit 1.10, for example, was created for Wal-Mart.

Supportive communications include a variety of ways a marketer communicates to target audiences outside of mainstream media or electronic communications. The most widely used supportive communications are directories, specialty advertising items, and brochures. Directories, most prominently the Yellow Page directories, are the most important form of supportive communications. Yellow Page directory listing is a crucial communications tool for many types of retail organizations with predominantly local markets—restaurant, entertainment, and repair service retailers in particular.

Specialty items carry a marketer's logo and are typically given away free to customers. Items like pens, calendars, key chains, mouse pads, and baseball caps are typical of the specialty items used by advertisers. Even the new dot-com Internet firms have discovered the value of specialty items. The leading Internet auction site, eBay, launched a road tour with a 34-foot motorhome pulling a trailer emblazoned with the eBay brand name. The tour was dubbed "From our homepage to your hometown." The tour hit state fairs, flea markets, and antique shows and gave away free hats, T-shirts, and pens.[13]

12. "1999 Annual Report of the Promotion Industry," *Promo* magazine, July 1999, S5.
13. "eBay Site Organizes Road Trip to Gather Its Users Together," Events & Promotions, *Advertising Age*, September 9, 1999, 10.

Brochures are prepared by the marketer and made available to members of the trade—retailers and wholesalers—and the company's sales force as a way to ensure that accurate and complete information is available to target audiences about the company's brand. You will often hear brochures referred to as "collateral" materials. A key to the IMC strategy in Cincinnati Bell's introduction of AT&T Wireless Services to the Cincinnati, Ohio, metropolitan area was the extensive use of collateral materials at the retail level as shown in Exhibit 1.11.

Another form of supportive communication includes the package, logo, slogans, and even mascots or spokespersons—like the Pillsbury doughboy, Snoopy (Met Life), the Jolly Green Giant, or Ronald McDonald—that are associated with a brand. These factors all carry information and communicate a message for a brand. The package represents the last chance to communicate with a consumer just before a purchase is made. Spokespersons or mascots can be a very powerful reminder of a brand. A whopping 96 percent of all American kids recognize Ronald McDonald, and a company spokesperson said the red-haired clown is "inseparable from the McDonald's brand."[14]

Public Relations

As part of being a good corporate and community citizen, a firm will use public relations as a way to establish a good image and reputation. **Public relations (PR)** focuses on communication that can foster goodwill between a firm and its many constituent groups. These constituent groups include customers, stockholders, suppliers, employees, government entities, citizen action groups, and the general public.

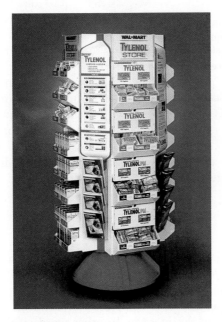

EXHIBIT 1.10

Point-of-purchase displays help marketers promote their brands with trade. This "Tylenol Store" aisle display was created for one of Tylenol's biggest trade customers, Wal-Mart.

EXHIBIT 1.11

Brochures, or collateral material, represent the chance to communicate about a brand in the retail setting. These are the brochures Cincinnati Bell Wireless created for retail stores during the launch of AT&T Wireless Services in Cincinnati.

14.   Louise Kramer, "McDonald's Execs Explore Makeover for Ronald Icon," *Advertising Age,* August 16, 1999, 14.

Public relations is used to highlight positive events in an organization, such as quarterly sales and profits or noteworthy community service programs carried out by the firm. Conversely, public relations is used strategically for "damage control" when adversity strikes an organization. Public relations uses techniques like press releases, newsletters, and community events as ways to reach target audiences.

In one of the most successful public relations efforts of all time, Johnson & Johnson relied heavily on public relations in 1982 when its Extra-Strength Tylenol product had been tampered with and caused several people to die. Johnson & Johnson's public relations people handled literally hundreds of inquiries from the public, distributors, the press, and police. Then the firm quickly and carefully issued coordinated statements to the general public, the press, and government authorities to provide clarification wherever possible. The result was that through conscientious and competent PR activities, Johnson & Johnson came through this disaster viewed as a credible and trustworthy organization and recouped sales levels of Tylenol in less than a year from the incident.

Public relations is emerging as a more prominent tool in the promotional mix of many firms. As mass media become more cluttered with ads and as consumers retain a healthy skepticism of advertising, public relations communications are being viewed as an important addition to the mix. Its use is also becoming more favored on a worldwide basis, as the Global Issues box demonstrates.

GLOBAL ISSUES

EAST MEETS WEST FOR PR LESSONS

Public relations has been a decidedly Western marketing practice and the sole province of economies dedicated to capitalism and free enterprise. But in a world where Western marketing techniques are being relied on to help ailing economies, public relations has suddenly been discovered in other cultures.

One such culture with an economy in transition is China. Until recently, public relations in China was nothing more than an exercise in government protocol. But now, PR is described in China as being "as varied and sprawling as the largest and most populated country in the world." For example, the China Global Public Relations Company is owned by a news agency and employs nearly 100 PR specialists. China Global has many Western clients, including General Motors, Lockheed, and Chrysler, who need help understanding the culture.

At this point, marketing and communications in China are a matter of fundamentals. Before marketing communications can get too elaborate or creative, the more rudimentary elements of customer relations must be considered. Basic public relations is an excellent starting point.

Source: David Ritchey, "Mastering the Fundamentals of PR in China," *Tactics*, September 1997, 16.

Personal Selling

Personal selling is the presentation of information about a firm's products or services by one person to another person or to a small group of people. Personal selling is distinguished from all other forms of promotion in that it is the only one-on-one communication that can deliver a completely customized message based on feedback from the receiver of the message. In other words, if you are in an electronics shop considering the purchase of a DVD player, the salesperson can tell you about different brands and focus the message content on features of each brand based on the questions you ask or information you request. No other form of promotion—not even the Internet—can customize a message in this way.

Personal selling is the dominant variable in the promotional mix of many corporate marketers. Complex products and services, high purchase prices, and negotiated contracts warrant the customized communication of personal selling. When GE Capital Services negotiates financing with a major construction company, a team of highly trained salespeople will negotiate financing levels and terms. In business-to-business markets, there are many instances where advertising, sales promotion, and other promotional mix variables simply do not achieve the needed communications effect. But this is not always the case in business-to-business sales. While personal selling is the major strategy in the promotional mix for Andersen Consulting, for example, the firm also annually sponsors a high-profile, international professional golf tournament that gets widespread television coverage.

IN PRACTICE

WHAT? YOU HAVE ONLY *ONE* $12,000 WATCH?

In a sudden revelation, the watch industry has awakened to the power of branding. In a product category where a $20 Timex performs in precisely the same way as a $20,000 Rolex, creating value for a brand in consumers' minds with various communication efforts is a must.

But the watch industry has only recently concluded that a marketing strategy that builds brand images is key to success. A Gallup survey found that just 51 percent of U.S. consumers owned two or more watches. This meant, of course, that nearly half of the U.S. public has only one, or perhaps, no timepiece at all. The Movado Group has been the most aggressive in the use of multiple promotional techniques for this area. The firm held a "premier" party in Los Angeles for its ESQ line of watches. The upscale party was part of a tie-in with the brand's placement on the Fox TV show *Time of Your Life*. Retailer in-store events (featuring the TV characters) and contests were quickly followed by television commercials. The capstone effort was a six-page special advertising section in *Vogue* timed with the holiday buying season.

Other watchmakers like Fendi, Tag Heuer, Ebel, and Gucci have all upped their investment in promotion as well to develop and position brands. So, how many $12,000 Rados do you have?

Source: Mercedes Cardona, "Watchmakers Find Time Ripe for Building Brands," *Advertising Age*, October 18, 1999, 20.

The Role of Promotion in Marketing Strategy 4

To truly understand promotion and IMC, we have to understand the role promotion plays in a firm's overall marketing strategy. Every organization must make marketing strategy decisions about its brands. For the sake of clarity, **branding** is establishing a name, term, symbol, or design that identifies for consumers that a product is being offered by a particular seller and clearly distinguishes the product of that seller from those offered by competitors. Nike is a brand. Sketchers is a brand. Sony is a brand. Each of these firms develops elaborate marketing strategies to try to ensure the success of all the items that carry the brand name. The IMC in Practice box tells the story of how the watch industry has suddenly discovered the value of the branding process (also see Exhibit 1.12).

The marketing strategy decisions related to branding include managing existing and new brands, pricing, promoting, and distributing brands for target audiences. The role of promotion in marketing strategy affects three key aspects of decision making with respect to brands: creating the marketing mix; achieving effective market segmentation, product differentiation, and positioning; and enhancing revenues and profits.

The Role of Promotion in the Marketing Mix

Marketing assumes a wide range of responsibilities related to the conception, pricing, promotion, and distribution brands referred to as the **marketing mix.** Many of you know from your introductory marketing course that the word "mix" is used to describe these responsibilities because decision makers plan the proper strategic emphasis between the product features, pricing strategy, promotional activities, and distribution when a brand is marketed to consumers. This blend, or mix, then results in the overall marketing mix for a brand.

Promotion plays a key role in the marketing mix because it is essential to the successful implementation of the three other mix factors. Let's consider each area of the mix and see how promotion has a positive and supportive impact.

Product (Brand). Perhaps the most obvious effect of promotion is on product management in the marketing mix. When we talk about the "product" area of the marketing mix, we are really talking about brand management in an individual firm. A brand would be at a significant competitive disadvantage without effective communication provided by promotion. Specifically, promotion affects the product area of the marketing mix in four important ways, as follows.

1. *Information and persuasion.* This is the fundamental role played by promotion in the marketing mix, and it relates most directly to managing the brand. Target audiences learn about a brand's features and benefits through the communications transmitted by various promotional mix tools. Advertising, personal selling, events, and the other promotional mix tools all inform or persuade target audiences about the values a brand has to offer. No other variable in the marketing mix is designed to accomplish this communication. Recall that this communication occurs to both consumers and trade target audiences.

EXHIBIT 1.12

Watchmakers have discovered that the promotional process is essential to creating a brand preference among consumers. From everyday watches like Timex, through high-end competitors like Patek Phillipe, watch marketers are using promotional events, brand placements in movies and TV shows, and ads like this for Fendi to make their brands distinctive in the minds of consumers.

2. *Introduction of new brand or brand extensions.* Promotion is essential when firms introduce a new brand or extensions of existing brands. A **brand extension** is an adaptation of an existing brand to a new product area. For example, the Snickers Ice Cream bar is a brand extension of the original Snickers candy bar, and Ivory shampoo is a brand extension of Ivory dishwashing liquid. When new brands or extensions are brought to market, the promotional process is largely responsible for attracting attention to the new market offering. This is often accomplished with sales promotions and P–O–P displays. It is also the role of promotion to communicate to a target audience the values of a new brand or the features a brand extension has to offer, typically through advertising.

   Again, trade buyers are key to the success of new brands or brand extensions. Marketers have little hope of successfully introducing a brand if there is no cooperation in the trade channel among wholesalers and retailers. Direct support to the trade in terms of displays, contests, and other incentives helps insure the success of a brand. And the trade responds readily to news that a brand will have hefty promotional support in terms of consumer promotion like advertising and sponsorships.

3. *Building and maintaining brand loyalty among consumers.* Loyalty to a brand is one of the most important assets a firm can have. **Brand loyalty** occurs when a consumer repeatedly purchases the same brand to the exclusion of competitors' brands. While the product itself is the most important influence on building and maintaining brand loyalty, promotion plays a key role in the

process as well. Advertising reminds consumers of the values—tangible and intangible—of the brand. Promotions often provide an extra incentive to consumers to remain brand loyal. Direct marketing can tailor communications to existing customers. Other promotional tools can also offer similarly valuable communications that will help build and strengthen lasting and positive associations with a brand. When a firm creates and maintains positive associations with the brand in the mind of consumers, the firm has developed **brand equity.**[15]

4. *Building and maintaining brand loyalty within the trade.* It might not seem like wholesalers and retailers can be brand loyal, but they will favor one brand over others given the proper support from the manufacturer. Promotion is an area where support can be given. Marketers can provide the trade with sales training programs, collateral materials, displays, and traffic-building special events. All these devices contribute to brand loyalty in the trade.

Price. Consumers look beyond the product and its features in making their choices. They balance the price of brands against those features. The promotional mix affects two aspects of price—one at the consumer level and one related to the trade.

1. *Pricing effects in the consumer market.* Because consumers are always balancing brand values against cost, a well-conceived promotional mix provides a balanced communication consistent with the target audience's needs: advertising can offer an image; personal selling can provide performance information; sales promotions can offer a price concession or an incentive to buy a brand. Coupons reduce the price in an obvious way, and rebates give consumers a choice on how to use an extra "bonus" in the pricing system. But incentives like premiums (for example, 2-for-1 offers) or a sweepstakes give consumers another reason to buy the featured brand because of extra value in the pricing scheme. Direct price concessions like coupons reduce consumer risk, while incentives offer an extra value in the mind of consumers.

2. *Pricing effects in the trade market.* Pricing effects in the trade means very simply that a marketer construct a price arrangement that wholesalers and retailers find attractive. It means setting a price margin on brand so that the trade realizes an attractive profit. But promotional tactics can also contribute. Special promotions like case-lot discounts, co-op advertising (where the marketer pays some or all of local advertising costs), and incentive contests all affect the end price at the trade level and can affect the wholesalers' and retailers' preference for one brand over others.

Distribution. The effect of promotion on the distribution variable of the marketing mix has mainly to do with securing distribution at the trade level. But promotional tactics can affect consumer access to a brand in retail outlets as well.

1. *Consumer access to brands.* Related to the pricing effects in the trade market discussed above, consumer access to brands is facilitated by promotions. When special P–O–P or brochure materials are used at the retail level, consumer access to a brand is increased. Also, if co-op advertising is used, consumers are informed of the location of outlets where brands are carried. Overall, promotions that excite the trade will increase the breadth of distribution of a brand, thus positively affecting consumer access.

2. *Securing trade distribution.* Co-op advertising, slotting fees, vendor support programs, and incentive programs (discussed in great detail in Chapter 11) are

15. Kevin L. Keller, *Strategic Brand Management: Building, Measuring, and Managing Brand Equity* (Upper Saddle River, NJ: Prentice-Hall, 1998), 2.

promotional techniques that convince wholesalers to carry a brand. In addition, large-scale promotional efforts aimed at consumers, like advertising and event sponsorships, convince trade sellers that a brand will be a success and help secure trade distribution.

As you can see, the tools of the promotional mix can affect all the other variables in the marketing mix in a positive and substantive way. But promotion has positive effects on other elements of marketing strategy as well.

The Role of Promotion in Effective Market Segmentation, Differentiation, and Positioning

The second important marketing strategy that is affected by promotional activities has to do with some of the most basic brand strategies for cultivating customers: market segmentation, product differentiation, and positioning. Promotion plays an important role in helping a firm effectively execute these marketing strategies.

Market segmentation is the breaking down of a large, widely varied (heterogeneous) market into submarkets or segments that are more similar (homogeneous) than dissimilar in terms of what values customers are looking for. Underlying the strategy of market segmentation are the facts that consumers differ in their wants and that the wants of one person can differ under various circumstances. Promotion's role in the market segmentation process is to develop communications and use the different tools of promotion to appeal to the wants and desires of different segments. The segment for minivans may be highly interested in brand features (personal selling) and a manufacturer's rebate (sales promotion). Conversely, members of the target audience for the new $100,000 BMW Z8 are more concerned with image (advertising) and symbolic value of the brand (recall that BMW has a negotiated brand placement, a sales promotion technique, in James Bond films).[16]

Product differentiation is the process of creating a perceived difference, in the mind of the consumer, between an organization's brand and the competition's. Notice that this definition emphasizes that product differentiation is based on *consumer perception*. The perceived differences can be tangible, or they may be based on intangible image or style factors. The critical issue is that consumers *perceive* a difference between brands. If consumers do not perceive a difference, then whether "real" differences exist or not does not matter. Product differentiation is one of the most critical of all marketing strategies. If a firm's brand is not perceived as distinctive and attractive by consumers, consumers will have no reason to choose the brand over one from the competition or to pay higher prices for the "better" brand.

Promotion is key to creating a difference, in the mind of the consumer, between an organization's brand and its competitors' brands. An advertisement may highlight a brand feature that is distinctive like the Honda del Sol ad in Exhibit 1.13, or it may create the difference with imagery and deep meaning for a brand. The message for Schiff vitamins in Exhibit 1.14 creates meaning for the product that goes far beyond any nutritional value that vitamins provide.

EXHIBIT 1.13

Advertising can be used help differentiate a brand from competition by highlighting a distinctive brand feature, like the removable roof on a Honda del Sol.

16. Dave Guilford and Hillary Chura, "BMW Loads Up Bond Push to Precede Film Premier," *Advertising Age,* November 1, 1999, 12.

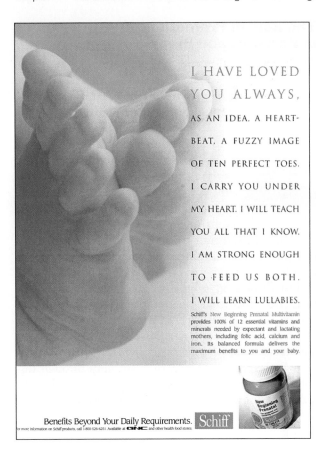

I HAVE LOVED

YOU ALWAYS,

AS AN IDEA. A HEART-

BEAT. A FUZZY IMAGE

OF TEN PERFECT TOES.

I CARRY YOU UNDER

MY HEART. I WILL TEACH

YOU ALL THAT I KNOW.

I AM STRONG ENOUGH

TO FEED US BOTH.

I WILL LEARN LULLABIES.

Schiff's New Beginning Prenatal Multivitamin provides 100% of 12 essential vitamins and minerals needed by expectant and lactating mothers, including folic acid, calcium and iron. Its balanced formula delivers the maximum benefits to you and your baby.

Benefits Beyond Your Daily Requirements. **Schiff**
For more information on Schiff products, call 1-800-526-6251. Available at **GNC** and other health food stores.

EXHIBIT 1.14

What is the "deep meaning" in this message for Schiff vitamins that helps differentiate this brand from its competitors?

In yet another way, sales promotion can create a difference in the mind of a consumer by offering a discount to the suggested retail price. The reduced price (and therefore risk) makes the brand different from nondiscounted brands. Or a special event can situate the brand socially in a way that is more appealing to consumers than the competitors' brands and create a difference in perception. The essential task for promotion is to use the right tools at the right time so that the firm's brand is perceived as distinctive.

Positioning is the process of designing a brand so that it can occupy a distinct and valued place in the target consumer's mind relative to other brands, and then communicating this distinctiveness through promotion. Notice that positioning, like product differentiation, is dependent on a perception. The importance of positioning can be understood by recognizing that consumers will create a *perceptual space* in their minds for all the brands they might consider. A perceptual space is how one brand is seen on any number of dimensions—such as quality, taste, price, or social display value—in relation to those same dimensions in other brands.

The positioning decision is really comprised of two different decisions. A firm must decide on the **external position** for a brand—that is, the niche the brand will pursue relative to all the competitive brands on the market. Additionally, an **internal position** must be achieved with regard to the other similar brands a firm markets.

With regard to the external-positioning decision, a firm must achieve a distinctive competitive position based on design features, pricing, distribution, or promotional strategy. Some brands, like a Donna Karan sweater at $150, are positioned at the top of their product category. Other brands, like a sweater from The Gap at $35, seek a position at a more moderate level in the market.

Effective internal positioning is accomplished by either developing vastly different products within a product line or creating advertising messages that appeal to different consumer needs and desires. Procter & Gamble successfully avoids cannibalization in its laundry detergent line by internally positioning very similar brands using a combination of product design and effective advertising. While some of these brands assume different positions in the line due to substantive differences (a liquid versus a powder soap, for example), others with minor differences achieve distinctive positioning through advertising. One P&G brand is advertised as being effective on kids' dirty clothes, while another is portrayed as effective for preventing colors from running (see Exhibit 1.15). In this way, advertising helps create a distinctive position, both internally and externally, and minimizes cannibalization among similar brands.

The methods and strategic options available to an organization with respect to market segmentation, product differentiation, and positioning will be fully discussed in Chapter 4. For now, recognize that promotion plays an important role in assisting an organization in putting these essential market strategies into action.

MOST LEADING DETERGENTS DON'T HAVE WHAT IT TAKES TO KEEP COLORS FROM RUNNING WILD IN THE WASH. AND THAT CAN MEAN REAL TROUBLE. CHEER WITH ADVANCED COLOR GUARD, ON THE OTHER HAND, IS SPECIALLY FORMULATED TO CLEAN YOUR CLOTHES, PROTECT YOUR COLORS AND KEEP YOU OUT OF TROUBLE. IN FACT, WASH AFTER WASH, THERE'S NO BETTER GUARD AGAINST COLORS THAT RUN. THAT OUGHTA TAKE A LOAD OR TWO OFF YOUR MIND, RIGHT?

Run out of Cheer and you could run into trouble.

http://www.cheer.com

http://www.tide.com

http://www.clothesline.com

EXHIBIT 1.15

When a firm has multiple brands in a product category, it must be careful to position those brands distinctively to avoid cannibalization of one brand's sales by another. Here, Procter & Gamble successfully achieves both a competitive external position and a distinctive internal position for Cheer laundry detergent by promoting the brand as the leader in preventing colors from running. Contrast Cheer with Tide, another P&G brand, and the Tide ClothesLine site.

The Role of Promotion in Revenues and Profits

The fundamental purpose of marketing can be stated simply: to generate revenue. No other part of an organization has this primary purpose. In the words of highly regarded management consultant and scholar Peter Drucker, "Marketing and innovation produce results: all the rest are 'costs.'"[17] The results Drucker is referring to are revenues. The marketing process is designed to generate sales and therefore revenues for the firm.

The contribution to creating sales as part of the revenue-generating process is where promotion plays another important role in marketing strategy. Recall in our discussion of the role of promotion in the marketing mix that various promotional tools can communicate descriptive and persuasive information and help implement strategies in the marketing mix. The techniques of promotion, which can help highlight brand features, price, or availability through distribution, attract customers. When a brand has the *right* features, the *right* price, the *right* distribution, and the *right* communication, sales will likely occur, and the firm generates revenue. In this way, promotion makes a direct contribution to the marketing goal of revenue generation. Notice that promotion *contributes* to the process of creating sales and revenue—it cannot be viewed as solely responsible for creating sales and revenue. Some organizations will mistakenly see promotion as a panacea, the salvation for a marketing mix that is deficient in some way. Promotion cannot be held solely responsible for sales. Sales occur when a brand has a well-conceived, complete marketing mix—including good promotion.

The effect of promotion on profits is a bit more involved, but may be the most important role that promotion plays in marketing strategy overall. This effect comes about when promotion can help give a firm greater flexibility in the price it charges for the brand. Promotion can help create pricing flexibility by (1) contributing to economies of scale, and (2) creating brand loyalty.

When a firm creates large-scale demand for its product, the quantity of product produced is increased. As production reaches higher and higher levels, fixed costs (such as rent and equipment costs) are spread over a greater number of units produced. The result of this large-scale production is that the cost to produce each item is reduced. Lowering the cost of each item because of high-volume production is known as **economies of scale.**

When Colgate manufactures hundreds of thousands of tubes of its new Colgate Total toothpaste and ships them in large quantities to warehouses, the fixed costs of

17. Peter F. Drucker, *People and Performance: The Best of Peter Drucker* (New York: HarperCollins, 1977), 90.

production and shipping per unit are greatly reduced. With lower fixed costs per unit, Colgate can realize greater profits on each tube of toothpaste sold. Promotion contributes to demand stimulation in both consumer and trade markets. By communicating features and availability of a brand with advertising, direct marketing, event sponsorship, or Internet strategies, promotion helps stimulate demand in consumer markets. By using personal selling, P–O–P displays, and incentives, the promotional process helps secure widespread and preferred distribution within the trade market. This demand stimulation, in turn, contributes to large quantity production, leading to economies of scale, which ultimately translates into higher profits per unit.

Recall that promotion contributes to brand loyalty and that brand loyalty occurs when a consumer repeatedly buys the same brand. This loyalty can result from pure habit, brand images and brand names that are prominent in the consumer's memory, barely conscious associations with a brand's image, or some fairly deep meanings consumers have attached to the brands they buy. Consumers who are brand loyal, through whatever set of these influences and meanings are generally less sensitive to price increases for the brand. In economic terms, this is known as **inelasticity of demand.** When consumers are less price sensitive, firms have the flexibility to raise prices and increase profit margins. Research has demonstrated that when promotion contributes to differentiation and brand loyalty, the brand is less subject to price challenges by competitors.[18] That is, inelasticity of demand is achieved, and you can charge more for your product.

INTEGRATED MARKETING COMMUNICATIONS

Earlier in the chapter, we introduced the concept of integrated marketing communications (IMC). The rise in prominence of IMC makes it essential that this evolving perspective on communication be understood in relation to the promotional process. On the client side, sophisticated marketers such as Starbucks, Citibank, and Ford Motor Company are taking an IMC approach and using promotional tools such as advertising direct marketing, event sponsorship, sales promotions, and public relations to build their brands.[19] On the agency side, a recent search for "integrated marketing communication agencies" on the Internet turned up over 200 agencies that were described as IMC service providers. Article after article in the trade press maintains that IMC has once and for all moved beyond the stage of a fad or buzzword to a lasting philosophical shift in the way marketers communicate with their customers.[20]

What Is IMC?

We offered a definition of IMC early in the chapter and have referred to it many times throughout. But we need to go into more depth at this point. Let's see how three industry experts define IMC.

[A] concept of marketing communications planning that recognizes the added value of a comprehensive plan that evaluates the strategic role of a variety of communications disciplines—for example, general advertising, direct response, sales promotion, and public relations—and

---

18. William Boulding, Eunkyu Lee, and Richard Staelin, "Mastering the Mix: Do Advertising, Promotion, and Sales Force Activities Lead to Differentiation," *Journal of Marketing Research,* vol. 31, May 1994, 159–171.
19. For a discussion of how marketers are turning to an IMC approach to managing the promotional process, see Laura Petrecca, "Ikea Homes In on Office," *Advertising Age,* August 10, 1998, 16; and Betsy Spethmann, "Is Advertising Dead?," *Promo,* September 1998, 32–36.
20. Kate Fitzgerald, "Beyond Advertising," *Advertising Age,* August 3, 1998, 1, 14.

CAREERPROFILE

Name:	Don Halcombe
Title:	Public Relations Manager
Company:	Discovery.com, Bethesda, Maryland
	http://www.discovery.com
Education:	B.A., Mass Communications

Don Halcombe was fresh out of college when he was offered a temporary job in the publicity department of Discovery Communications, the parent company of the Discovery Channel and Discovery.com. Although some might shy away from taking a temporary job, Don saw it as an opportunity. "Temping seemed like a good way to get acclimated to the work world and I thought it might let me make connections," he says.

The gamble paid off. Within a few months, Don moved into a permanent, full-time job as the publicity coordinator for the company's CD-ROM/Multimedia unit. Although his initial job was sending out press kits about Discovery's products, he soon took on additional responsibilities. "If I knew a press release needed to be written, I would ask 'Do you mind if I take a first crack?'," says Don. "No one's going to turn down help, especially in a fast-paced work environment." Eventually, Don's job grew to include organizing media tours, budget tracking, and giving input into marketing decisions.

Several years later, Don was offered an exciting opportunity as marketing manager for Discovery Communications' new Your Choice TV subsidiary. "My first job was to put together a brand identity for the subsidiary that would tie all of our promotional activities together," says Don. "The concept we decided on was that this was 'smart and friendly TV' that let you do things you couldn't do before."

Don then had to work closely with Your Choice TV's advertising agency to develop a company logo, direct mailings explaining the concept to consumers, and advertisements. "It was a challenge to make sure the agency people understood what our message should be," says Don.

Don is now Public Relations Manager for Discovery.com. He works closely with Discovery.com's marketing group. "We meet and discuss what type of promotion and advertising they are planning and then I develop public relations programs that complement that," says Don. "Since the Internet is still relatively new to many people, there's still a lot of publicity opportunities to tell stories about what Discovery.com does."

To learn more about careers in promotion, marketing, and public relations, visit these Web sites:

American Marketing Association Career Center
http://www.ama.org/jobs

Wall Street Journal Career Journal
http://www.careerjournal.com/careers/resources/document/cwc-sales.htm

combines these disciplines to provide clarity, consistency, and maximum communications impact.[21]

What is integrated marketing communications? It's a new way of looking at the whole, where once we only saw parts such as advertising, public relations, sales promotion, purchasing, employee communications, and so forth. It's realigning communications to look at it the way the customer sees it—as a flow of information from indistinguishable sources.[22]

IMC is the strategic coordination of multiple communication voices. Its aim is to optimize the impact of persuasive communication on both the consumer and nonconsumer (e.g., retailers, sales personnel, opinion leaders) audiences by coordinating such elements of the marketing mix as advertising, public relations, promotions, direct marketing, and package design.[23]

Notice that each of these definitions is compatible with the one we offered early in the chapter: IMC is the process of managing the promotional tools in such a way that a synergistic communications effect is created.

Factors Contributing to IMC's Rising Prominence

Why has IMC become so popular over the past decade? Several significant and pervasive changes in the marketing and communications environment have contributed to its growing prominence.

- *Fragmentation of media.* Media options available to marketers have proliferated at an astounding rate. Broadcast media now offer "narrow-casting" so specific that advertisers can reach consumers at precise locations, such as airports and supermarket checkout counters. The print media have proliferated dramatically as well. Currently, over 1,000 different magazine titles are published in the United States! The proliferation and fragmentation of media have resulted in less reliance on mass media and more emphasis on other promotional options, such as direct mail and event sponsorship.

21. This is the definition used by the American Association of Advertising Agencies. It appeared in Don E. Schultz, "Integrated Marketing Communications: Maybe Definition Is in the Point of View," *Marketing News,* January 18, 1993, 17.

22. Don E. Schultz, Stanley I. Tannenbaum, and Robert F. Lauterborn, *Integrated Marketing Communications* (Lincolnwood, IL: NTC Business Books, 1993), xvii.

23. Esther Thorson and Jeri Moore, *Integrated Communications: Synergy of Persuasive Voices* (Mahwah, NJ: Erlbaum Press, 1996), 1.

- *Better audience assessment through database technology.* The ability of firms to generate, collate, and manage databases has created diverse communications opportunities beyond mass media. Databases can be used to create customer and noncustomer profiles. With this information, it is possible to more accurately identify and target specific market segments such as Asian-Americans, teenagers, Hispanics, and dual-income households with no kids (DINKs). This leads the marketer away from mass media to promotional tools that reach only the segment that has been targeted.
- *Consumer empowerment.* Consumers today are more powerful and sophisticated than their predecessors. Fostering this greater power are more single-person households, smaller families, higher education levels, and more experienced consumers. Empowered consumers are more skeptical of commercial messages and demand information tailored to their needs.
- *Increased advertising clutter.* Not only are consumers becoming more sophisticated, they are becoming more jaded as well. The proliferation of advertising stimuli has diluted the effectiveness of any single message. In one recent evaluation of network television breaks it was found that not only were the breaks lasting up to five full minutes, but in one break there were nineteen separate messages![24] There is no end in sight to this "message" proliferation.
- *Shifting channel power.* In some product and market categories, there has been a shift in power away from big manufacturers toward big retailers. The new "power retailers," such as Wal-Mart, The Gap, Toys "R" Us, and Home Depot, are able to demand promotional fees and allowances from manufacturers, which diverts funds away from advertising and into special events, in-store displays, or other promotions.
- *Desire for greater accountability.* In an attempt to achieve greater accountability for promotional spending, firms have reallocated marketing resources from advertising to more short-term and more easily measurable methods, such as direct marketing and sales promotion.

All these factors have contributed to an increase in the diversity and complexity of the communications tools used by firms to inform and persuade target audiences. Mass media advertising still plays an important role in the communications programs of most firms, whether they are IMC oriented or not. But the opportunity to use other communication tools makes coordination and integration much more challenging than in the past. Both clients and advertising agencies, however, see the payoff as great:

Integrated marketing communications is emerging as one of the most valuable "magic bullets" a firm can use to gain competitive advantage.

—James C. Reilly, IBM

Integrated marketing communications identifies the dynamics of today's marketplace and teaches us how easy it is to prosper under the new rules of communication.

—Richard Fizdale, Leo Burnett[25]

The Participants in IMC

Earlier in the chapter, we learned that integrated marketing communications is a philosophy about how to manage promotional communications and tools. But who actually gets involved in this management process? Exhibit 1.16 presents a hierarchy

---

24. Chuck Ross, "Now Many Words from Our Sponsors," *Advertising Age,* September 27, 1999, 3, 87.
25. These quotes were taken from Schultz, Tannenbaum, and Lauterborn, *Integrated Marketing Communications,* ix, xi, xii.

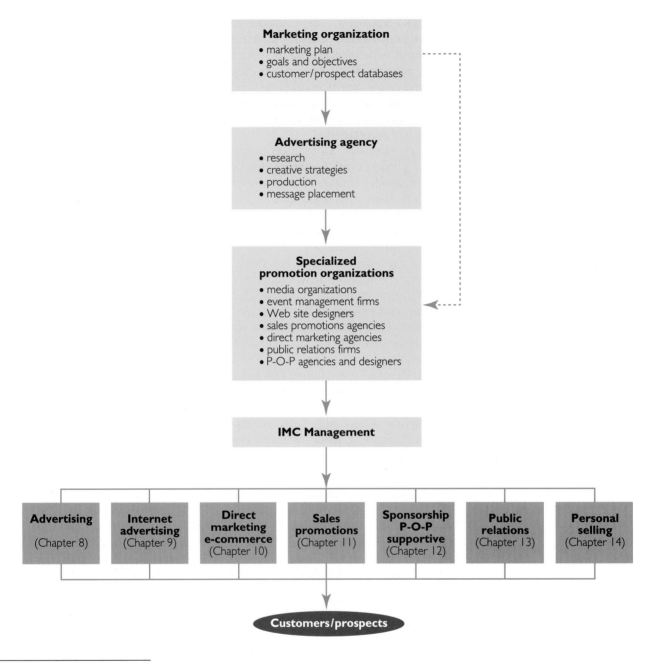

EXHIBIT 1.16

The Participants in IMC Management

of participants in the IMC management process that helps illustrate the challenges marketers will encounter when they try to manage multiple promotional activities.

Notice that the marketer typically brings to the process a marketing plan, goals and objectives, and perhaps a database that will identify current and prospective customers. These databases are developed from customer contacts or are purchased from specialty research firms. Typically, a marketer will be working with an advertising agency that will help research the market, suggest creative strategies, and produce IMC materials. In addition, agencies can assist in placing materials in outlets that range from conventional mass media to event sponsorship to Internet advertising.

Exhibit 1.16 also shows the number of specialized marketing communication organizations that may need to be hired in conjunction with or in place of the firm's ad agency to execute an IMC campaign. This is where the process starts to get messy.

The fact is that many ad agencies simply do not have all the internal expertise necessary to develop and manage every promotional mix tool. First and foremost, the ad agency is the expert in the development and placement of mass-media advertising. This is especially the case for large advertising agencies. Most successful ad agencies are successful because of their prowess in mass-media advertising. Because they have a lot invested in this area of expertise, they are routinely criticized for the tendency to push mass media as the best communication solution for any client.[26] So, when marketers want communication options other than traditional advertising in mass media, they often must turn to external facilitators to get the expertise they are looking for. For example, companies like Avon and Ford's Lincoln Mercury division retain Wunderman Cato Johnson–Chicago just to help them with event management. Pepsi and Philip Morris retain Cyrk-Simon Worldwide to design and run their Pepsi Stuff and Marlboro Miles branded-merchandise reward programs.[27] The dashed line on the right side of Exhibit 1.16 is meant to show that in many instances marketing organizations must literally bypass their traditional advertising agency to get the expertise they require for building their brands.

Coordination and integration of a promotional mix becomes much more complex as various external facilitators are brought into the picture. These diverse specialists often will view one another as competitors for the client's marketing dollars, and will most likely champion their particular specialty, whether event sponsorship, sales promotions, the Internet, direct marketing, or whatever. This is just human nature in a free-enterprise system. But instead of ending up with coordination and integration, we now have conflict and disintegration. Of course, conflict and disintegration are *not* what the marketer wants for a brand.

Advertising agencies of all sizes are well aware of these challenges, and many are attempting to redesign themselves to add more internal expertise that can foster the goals of IMC. Sometimes this redesign comes in the form of new cross-functional work units launched within the traditional agency under nifty names like J. Walter Thompson USA's 35-person Total Solutions Group; or DDB Needham Worldwide's 140-person Beyond DDB.[28] Other times, expertise is added when big companies buy out smaller specialist firms to supplement their range of services.[29] As you can see, this whole business of IMC is about bringing together the right combination of expertise to serve a particular client's marketing needs. This is always a complex undertaking with no easy answers.

The IMC process as depicted in Exhibit 1.16 shows the participants and the tools of IMC. Notice that where each of the promotional tools is listed, there is also a chapter listing. The tools of the promotional mix are discussed in these chapters in Part 3 of this book.

At this point, we have the basics of promotion and integrated marketing communication defined and discussed. In Chapter 2, we turn our attention to how the promotion industry is structured to handle the communication effort.

26. For example, see Jim Osterman, "This Changes Everything," *Adweek,* May 15, 1995, 44–45 and Betsy Spethmann, "Is Advertising Dead?" *Promo,* September 1998, 32–36, 159–162.
27. Spethmann, "Is Advertising Dead?", 32–36, 159–162.
28. Kate Fitzgerald, "Beyond Advertising," *Advertising Age,* August 3, 1998, 1, 14.
29. Spethmann, "Is Advertising Dead?", 32–36, 159–162.

SUMMARY

1 Define promotion, the promotional mix, and integrated marketing communications.

Promotion is the communications process in marketing that is used to create a favorable predisposition toward a brand of product or service, an idea, or even a person. Product and service promotion for a brand of a product or service is the most common kind of promotion. Idea promotion includes the promotion of causes like gun safety and safe sex. Person promotion is most common in politics and entertainment.

The promotional mix is a blend of communications tools used by a firm to carry out the promotion process and communicate directly with a target market (or audience, in the language of communications).

Finally, integrated marketing communications (IMC) is the process of managing promotional tools in such a way that a synergistic communications effect is created.

2 Explain the relationship between promotion, the promotional mix, and integrated marketing communications.

The relationship between promotion, the promotional mix and integrated marketing communications is as follows: promotion is the communications *process* itself. Promotional mix represents the *tools and activities* of promotion. IMC is *a way of managing the process and the tools* so that they are coordinated and a synergistic effect is achieved.

3 Identify and describe the tools of the promotional mix.

The tools of the promotional mix include all the options available to marketers for communicating with target audiences—both consumer and business audiences. These tools are:

a. Advertising is a mass-mediated attempt to persuade. Advertising is the most conspicuous form of promotion and uses mass media like television, magazines, newspapers, and radio to communicate with target audiences.

b. Internet advertising is a form of advertising in which the message is carried over the Internet rather than through traditional mass media.

c. Sales promotion is the use of incentives techniques to generate a specific and short-term response from a household consumer, trade buyer (a retailer like Nordstrom's), or business buyer (like Xerox).

d. Direct marketing is an interactive system of marketing that uses one or more advertising media to effect a measurable response and/or transaction at any location. E-commerce is business conducted between buyers and sellers using electronic exchange media—primarily the Internet.

e. Sponsorship involves providing funding for an event or a charitable cause or creating an event in order to highlight a firm's brand to a specific target audience. Point-of-purchase (P–O–P) promotion refers to materials used in the retail setting to attract shoppers' attention to a company's brand. Supportive communications include a variety of ways a marketer communicates to target audiences outside of mainstream media or electronic communications. The most widely used supportive communications are directories, specialty advertising items, and brochures.

f. Public relations is a form of communication that can foster goodwill between a firm and its many constituent groups.

g. Personal selling is the presentation of information about a firm's products or services by one person to another person or to a small group of people. Personal selling is distinguished from all other forms of promotion in that it is the only one-on-one communication that can deliver a completely customized message based on feedback from the receiver of the message.

4 Identify the role of promotion in marketing strategy.

Promotion plays a role in marketing strategy by contributing to the implementation of marketing strategy in three areas:

a. *Promotion affects the implementation of the marketing mix.* The product, price, and distribution tactics of the marketing mix can be positively affected by promotion. Promotion enhances the branding effort, helps create flexibility in the pricing area, and helps secure and enhance the distribution of the brand.

b. *Promotion increases the effectiveness of market segmentation, product differentiation, and positioning.* Through the process of attracting attention of target audiences and creating a unique and positive perception of a brand within target audiences, promotion aids in both the implementation and management of market segmentation, product differentiation, and positioning.

c. *Promotion enhances revenue generation and profit margins.* Promotion plays a key role in demand stimulation, which contributes to revenue generation. In addition, demand stimulation can create economies of scale and brand loyalty, which contributes positively to profit margins.

5   Discuss the rise in prominence of integrated marketing communications as a way of managing the promotional process.

The rise in the prominence of IMC has been fostered by six changes in the marketing and communications environment.

a. *Fragmentation of media.* Traditional media options available to marketers have proliferated so as to fragment media coverage. Such fragmentation has led to greater reliance on more broad-based promotional programs that require greater coordination.

b. *Better audience assessment through database technology.* The ability of firms to generate, collate, and manage databases has created diverse communications opportunities beyond mass media. Databases can be used to create customer and noncustomer profiles. With this information, highly targeted communications programs can be implemented.

c. *Consumer empowerment.* Today's consumers are more educated, more affluent, and more independent than their predecessors. This translates into a sense of power. Empowered consumers are more skeptical of commercial messages and are demanding information tailored to their precise information desires.

d. *Increased advertising clutter.* More and more advertisers are using mass media to achieve a wide reach for their messages. Record spending on traditional media has created a cluttered communication environment.

e. *Shift in channel power.* In some product and market categories, there has been a shift in power away from big manufacturers and toward big retailers. The new "power retailers," like Wal-Mart, The Gap, Toys "R" Us, and Home Depot, are able to demand promotional fees and allowances from manufacturers, which diverts funds away from advertising and into activities like allowances, events, and in-store promotions.

f. *Desire for more accountability.* In an attempt to achieve greater accountability for promotional spending, firms have begun to allocate more promotional dollars in the short term and more easily measurable methods like direct response and sales promotion techniques.

KEY TERMS

promotion, 7
promotional mix, 8
integrated marketing
   communications (IMC), 8
advertising, 9
Internet advertising, 10
Internet, 10
sales promotion, 12
direct marketing, 13

e-commerce, 13
sponsorship, 14
point-of-purchase (P–O–P), 14
supportive communications, 14
public relations (PR), 15
personal selling, 16
branding, 17
marketing mix, 17
brand extension, 18

brand loyalty, 18
brand equity, 19
market segmentation, 20
product differentiation, 20
positioning, 21
external position, 21
internal position, 21
economies of scale, 22
inelasticity of demand, 23

QUESTIONS FOR REVIEW AND CRITICAL THINKING

1. Distinguish promotion from integrated marketing communications. How are they different? How are they related?

2. Which variable in the promotional mix attracts the most money annually? Why?

3. How is personal selling different from every other promotional tool a marketer might use?

4. Explain how promotion helps a firm in its market segmentation strategy.

5. Why is brand loyalty important to a company? How does the promotional process help create brand-loyal consumers?

6. What is the difference between sales promotion for the consumer market and sales promotion for the trade market? Which one is more important?

7. If spending on promotion is an expense for a firm, how is it that promotion can contribute to greater profitability in a firm?

8. Of the many reasons why IMC has become a more prominent method of managing the promotional process, which one do you think is most important? Defend your decision.

EXPERIENTIAL EXERCISES

1. **In-class exercise:** The IMC in Practice Box discussed the fact that major watch marketers around the world are using all forms of promotion to increase demand. The discussion also mentioned that a recent Gallup poll discovered that 49 percent of Americans own one or no watches. Let's do an in class survey that has three parts.

   a. First, let's find out how many watches people own: 0, 1, 2, 3, 4, etc. (As a sidelight to this first question, how many people in the class are not wearing a watch today!) The person who owns the most watches will get a prize to be determined by your instructor (no, it will not be another watch).

   b. Second, let's get a brand share ranking by finding out which brands are owned by class members

   (Seiko, Timex, Wenger, Swatch, etc.) and rank-order them on the board.

   c. Third, let's find out how many people plan on getting another watch and which brands they are considering and rank-order them.

2. **Out-of-class exercise:** Pick a brand of a product that you either own or are interested in. For the next week, try to find as many forms of promotion as you can for that brand. Keep your eye out for TV, magazine, newspaper, and other major media ads; try to find a Web site; see if the brand is included in event sponsorship, and so forth. Record your findings and decide how well the firm has integrated the various promotional tools.

USING THE INTERNET

Exercise 1

For many users of the Internet, the first stop is always a search engine site. Try queries on each of the following search engines:

AltaVista
http://www.altavista.com

HotBot
http://www.hotbot.com

Excite
http://www.excite.com

Google
http://www.google.com

Each site has its particular features, angling to provide an interesting tool to encourage bookmarking and return visits. Google has a "cache" feature, where a copy of the page that was indexed is saved—if you follow the main link, you see a copy of the page as it is now (if it's still *there* now). AltaVista was the first search engine site to provide for multilingual translation.

1. Which sites features do you find most useful?

2. In searching, there's often a balance between precision and recall: does the search return *only* what you're looking for, and does it return *all* the pages you're looking for? Look for things you know the search engine should find (such as your favorite sports team or a favorite book). Does it find everything you'd expect it to, and how much "chaff" does it dredge up along with the "wheat"?

Mamma.com and Dogpile are "meta search engines": that is, they take the user's query, execute it on several other search engines (such as HotBot, AltaVista, or Excite), and then arrange and present the combined results.

Mamma.com
http://www.mamma.com

Dogpile
http://www.dogpile.com

3. What advantages do meta search engines offer?

Exercise 2

The HotBot search engine site permits queries on "links to" particular Web sites. While many site visitors might come via a hierarchical site like Yahoo!, or via a search engine, querying on keywords, many visitors come because of these links-referrals from other sites. Go to the HotBot site and choose the query option of "links to this URL," and see how many and what sorts of sites link to sites you're familiar with. Try this same query on:

http://www.yahoo.com
http://www.ibm.com
http://www.mtv.com
http://www.thex-files.com

1. There are more than half a million links to the Yahoo! Web site, on pages across the Web. Why do you think this is?

2. Why might a Web site developer include a link to IBM's corporate Web site?

3. One major problem with Web links is their brittleness: a link to a subpage on one of these sites could become broken if the site is reshuffled. What are the trade-offs between links to specific pages, and general links to the top level of a Web site?

4. How does *The X-Files* television program site benefit from its community of fans?

After reading this chapter, you will be able to:

1 Discuss six important trends transforming the promotion industry.

2 Describe the participants in the promotional communications process.

3 Discuss the role played by advertising and promotion agencies, the services provided by these agencies, and how they are compensated.

4 Identify key external facilitators who assist in planning and executing promotional campaigns for marketers.

5 Discuss the role played by media organizations and trade partners in executing effective promotional programs.

CHAPTER 2

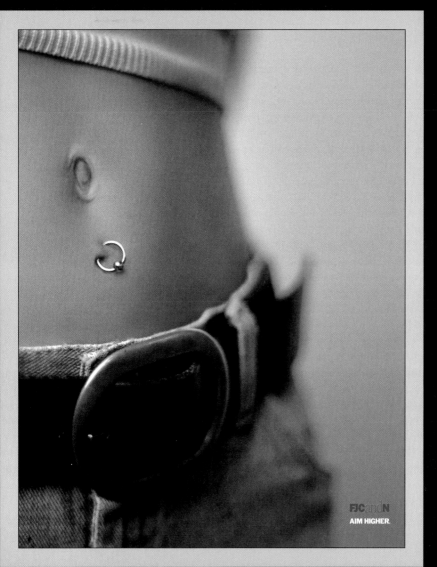

To say that the promotion industry is in an era of dynamic change is a colossal understatement. Consider this situation at Leo Burnett Co., one of the largest U.S. advertising agency. The company has spent decades developing effective and award-winning advertising for United Airlines, McDonald's, Miller Brewing, Kraft International, and Reebok International, a group of clients that any advertising agencies would be proud to list in its account stable. But what about an advertising agency that loses the business of these prestigious clients over a 24-month period? That is exactly what happened to Leo Burnett Co., and the agency had to cope with this massive loss immediately.

The exodus of such high-profile clients was devastating. Leo Burnett was supposed to be the Rock of Gibraltar of advertising—conservative, confident, and very stable. Most of the defections were explained by the clients' feeling that Burnett's processes were too tradition bound and bureaucratic, with too much emphasis on advertising and not enough creative promotion using other techniques.[1] The Miller Lite account went to Fallon McElligott, where "ads by Dick" were created (no bargain there). United Airlines went to friendlier skies. Adding insult to injury, McDonald's took a large part of its business a few blocks away to DDB Needham, where Burnett got the account from in the first place way back in the late 1970s. The Reebok business was lost because the client said it wanted to look "outside the mainstream to tap new ideas."[2] This was *not* supposed to happen at Leo Burnett, but it did.

While this type of account jumping is becoming common among clients looking for more "impact" and flashier promotions, the really interesting part of the story is how Burnett responded. First, the agency quickly recouped revenue losses by adding $575 million in new media-buying assignments from Procter & Gamble and, surprisingly, Miller Brewing and by adding more than $713 million in other new business including a prestigious $100 million brand strategy assignment from Delta Airlines.[3] And the agency maintained a long and impressive list of clients, including Pillsbury, Procter & Gamble, Oldsmobile, Motorola (see Exhibit 2.1), Philip Morris, and others.

Next, agency management took the question of its creative abilities and responsiveness to clients' broad-based promotional needs seriously and initiated massive changes. The main thrust was to consider ways to make

EXHIBIT 2.1

Despite massive client defections, Leo Burnett (http://www. leoburnett.com) maintained a long list of marquee clients including newly rejuvenated Motorola.

it more nimble, more interactive, more broad based in its promotional services, and ultimately to improve the creative environment. In response, Burnett added some "edginess" by acquiring 49 percent of the hot British creative shop Bartle Bogle Hegarty. Next, a big boost in interactive creativity came by employing Red Spider, another edgy British creative/management group specializing in brand strategy development. Then the agency established Vigilante, a New York "urban culture" unit that combs the streets of urban America looking for leading-edge trends.[4] But the acquisitions and changes didn't stop there. Through 1999, Burnett had formed the following agencies and alliances through "The Leo Group": Lapiz (Hispanic marketing), LB NorthStar (direct/

1. Mercedes M. Cardona, "Burnett Splitting Agency into Seven Mini-Shops," *Advertising Age,* November 17, 1997, 6.
2. Jeff Jensen and Chuck Ross, "Burnett USA Resigns $100 Mil Reebok Biz," *Advertising Age,* May 5, 1997, 68.
3. David Goetzl, "Delta's new $100 Mil Push Signals Shift in Branding," *Advertising Age,* March 13, 2000, 8.
4. Dirk Johnson, "Not So Jolly Now, A Giant Agency Retools," *The New York Times,* March 22, 1998, accessed at http://archives.nytimes.com/archives on December 23, 1999.

database/promotion marketing), The Lab/Unexpected Solutions (strategic consultancy), Giant Step (interactive), TFA/Leo Burnett Technology Group (business-to-business), Capps Digital (production), Williams-Labadie (medical), and Moroch & Associates (retail marketing).

Finally, the biggest maneuver of all—a merger. The Leo Group and The MacManus Group announced they would merge, creating a new top-tier global advertising and diversified marketing services company headquartered in Chicago with more than $1.7 billion in annual revenues, 500 operating units in 90 countries and 16,000 employees. Revenues of the new holding company, called B Com3 Group, will be split evenly between U.S. and overseas markets and between general advertising and diversified marketing services. To make the deal truly global, Tokyo-based Dentsu Inc., the world's largest

single brand agency, will make a significant investment in the combined entity. Dentsu's ownership stake is expected to be approximately 20 percent, making it the largest shareholder in B Com3 Group, which will be Dentsu's major partner in serving clients outside Asia.[5]

So, in the end, Leo Burnett overcame the problem of being "too traditional" and reinvented itself into an interactive, multimethod advertising agency serving a wide range of promotional communication needs for global clients. But it was more than overcoming a problem. At the end of this long and challenging series of changes, The Leo Group was named "Global Agency Network of the Year" by *Advertising Age*.[6] Now, that's a response to change! Let's focus our attention now on how promotion is really a communications industry, and big agencies like Leo Burnett and small agencies all over the world serve the promotion needs of their clients.

INTRODUCTION

As we saw in Chapter 1, firms have a wide variety of promotional tools from which to choose in trying to reach and motivate their target markets. But no matter what tools are being used, we need to always remember that promotion is first and foremost "communication." And promotion takes place in a large and complex industry structure with all sorts of players and relationships between those players.

In order to fully understand promotion, we need to understand that it is a "communications industry." This is where we will turn our attention now, to exploring how the tools of the promotional mix are managed in a communications industry setting to create brand relationships across all levels of the structure. First, we will look at the promotion industry as a fairly well-structured communications industry. Then we will consider the different players—particularly advertising and promotion agencies—and the role they play in creating and executing promotion. In this way, we will better comprehend how the promotional tools work when consumers encounter a promotional message.

THE PROMOTION INDUSTRY IN TRANSITION

The loss of clients, and ultimately the reorganization of a large and respected U.S. advertising agency such as Leo Burnett Co., signals the nature and magnitude of change that is occurring in the promotion industry. We will examine these changes in more detail shortly. But first we need to realize that the fundamental process of promotion, and the role it plays in organizations, remains steadfastly rooted in the process of persuasive communications designed to stimulate demand in target audiences. That has not—and cannot be—changed.

5.   Laura Petrecca and Hillary Chura, "Merged Leo-MacManus Could Be Valued at $5 bil," *Advertising Age,* November 8, 1999, 3.
6.   Hillary Chura, "Leo Group Posts Stunning Turnaround," *Advertising Age,* January 31, 2000, S6, S22.

What has changed over the past ten years and what Leo Burnett has reacted to is that the structure of the promotion industry is (again) in transition. How has the industry changed, and how is it continuing to change? Interactive media options, agency structure, client demands for immediate results, and creative techniques are just a few of the aspects of the industry undergoing significant and fundamental change.

The central issues in the Leo Burnett story highlight two key aspects of change that have taken place in the structure of the promotion industry. First, marketers believe that to maintain brand leadership in highly competitive markets characterized by impatient consumers, new and different creative promotions are essential. Second, traditional factory-like advertising agencies are being replaced with new, more adaptable, and responsive multimethod promotional agencies. Similarly, many marketers are branching out from their traditional ad agencies and using smaller "boutique" promotion agencies and consultants as a way to revitalize creative promotion.[7]

The acquisitions and diversification of advertising agencies is just one symptom of the important changes in the promotions industry. The structure of the promotion industry today is being altered by six important trends, as follows:

1. *Information in the marketplace has become an interactive system between marketers and consumers.* Historically, marketers have controlled information and the flow of information—it was a one-way communication. Now, consumers are in greater control of information about products and services and do not just receive information, but give information to the firm. This has created a brand relationship situation between marketers and advertisers where

GLOBAL IMC ONE PERSON AT A TIME

While many firms are anxious to communicate with consumers in the seamless, multimethod style of IMC, few have embraced the concept as aggressively and effectively as Nestlé, a Swiss-based firm with operations on every continent. The president, Peter Brabeck-Letmathe, takes the IMC philosophy of communication very seriously, stressing direct communication with Nestlé's consumers in as many ways as possible.

Brabeck believes in building one-to-one relationships with customers in ways that advertising alone cannot accomplish. His interest is fostered by what he sees as fragmented consumer segments and splintered media markets. Also, Nestlé is feeling the pressure from growth in retailers' power relative to manufacturers. To cope with diverse consumer segments and media options, Nestlé has relied more on a wide range of communications/promotional alternatives:

Dialogue Clubs. These clubs encourage consumers to communicate with the company via phone, letter, or e-mail and participate in new product development. Clubs are set up in Europe and North America and were formed from databases Nestlé was originally developing for its direct-marketing program.

Direct Marketing. Following through on the initial database concept, Nestlé has a direct selling program through the clubs. Club members are mailed a special catalog that allows them to purchase Nestlé products through the mail.

TV Shopping Networks. Nestlé joined a TV shopping test and set up "Easy Shop," a proprietary shopping program in two Swiss villages.

Internet. Nestlé maintains a corporate Web site as well as individual sites for every brand it markets.

Nestlé Loyalty Cards. Swipe cards provide Nestlé buyers with discounts and contribute to the now highly sophisticated database. Each time a shopper buys a Nestlé product, the retailer can "swipe" the card and contribute to the customer's Nestlé points. These points can be exchanged for discounts or free products.

Joint Promotions. The firm has partnered with an Italian airline and a food catalog retailer to copromote both brands' loyalty programs.

Ultimately, Brabeck wants "to know what my consumer is feeling, how he is changing, and what he is desiring."

Source: Suzanne Bidlake, "Nestlé CEO Strives for Dialogue That Individualizes Consumers," *Ad Age International,* January 1998, 33.

7.   Comments made by Martin Sorrell as represented in "Agencies Face New Battlegrounds: Sorrell," *Advertising Age,* April 13, 1998, 22.

promotional communication needs to be sensitive to the interactive nature of the communication environment.[8]

2. *The proliferation of cable television and direct-marketing technology, and alternative new media, has caused media fragmentation.* Media fragmentation has spawned new specialized agencies to sell and manage the media options.

3. *A growing investment in advertising from television ads to billboards to banner ads on the Internet, has resulted in so much clutter that the probability of any one ad breaking through and making a real difference continues to diminish.* With a lack of faith in advertising alone, promotion options like online communication, brand placement in film and television, point-of-purchase (P–O–P) displays, and sponsorships are more attractive to marketers.

4. *New communication/distribution channels, including catalogs, TV shopping networks, online shopping, and price clubs are growing in influence.* Consumers do not just want a communications experience, they want a "commerce experience."[9]

5. *Fragmentation of marketing budgets within companies has occurred, with a greater proportion of these budgets going to trade and consumer sales promotions.*

6. *Improved information systems are allowing retailers and distributors to exercise more control over many kinds of marketing and promotional decisions.*

As a result of these changes, marketers are rethinking the way they try to communicate with consumers. Fundamentally, there is a greater focus on integrated marketing communications (IMC) programs as a way to address the changes. More than ever, marketers are looking to the full complement of promotional opportunities in sales promotions, event sponsorships, new media options, and public relations as means to support and enhance the primary advertising effort. And IMC is a global phenomenon, as the Global Issues box highlights.

For years to come, these fundamental changes will affect the way marketers think about promotional communications. In response, advertising and promotion agencies will think about the way they serve their clients, and the way marketing communications are delivered to audiences. Big spenders like Procter & Gamble, Nestlé, and General Motors are already demanding new and innovative programs to enhance the impact of their promotional dollars. While the goal of persuasive communication remains intact—attract attention and develop preference for a brand— the changing marketplace and the changes it is causing in the structure of the promotion industry is the central topic of this chapter.

THE STRUCTURE OF THE PROMOTION INDUSTRY ❷

To fully appreciate the structure of the promotion industry, let's first consider its size. Remember from Chapter 1 that the promotion industry is huge—about $300 billion spent in the United States alone on various categories of advertising and promotion. But that figure does not even consider the revenues earned by agencies in the promotion business. Exhibits 2.2 and 2.3 show, respectively, the ten largest advertising agencies and the ten largest promotional agencies in the United States. (Note: At this point, the industry still distinguishes between *advertising* agencies and *promotion* agencies even though many advertising agencies, as we saw with Leo Burnett, do provide services in direct marketing, interactive media, and event sponsorship. So for now, we still need two lists of agencies.)

8.   Tom Duncan and Sandra Moriarty, "Brand Relationships Key to the Agency of the Future," *Advertising Age,* October 18, 1999, 44.
9.   Lauren Barack, "Chiat's New Day," *Business 2.0,* December 1999, 130–132.

Rank				U.S. Gross Income		
1999	1998	Agency	Headquarters	1999	1998	Percentage of Change
1	1	Grey Advertising	New York	$535.8	$477.5	12.2
2	2	J. Walter Thompson Co.	New York	496.2	415.3	19.5
3	4	McCann-Erickson Worldwide	New York	466.9	393.5	18.7
4	3	FCB Worldwide*	New York	452.8	403.7	12.2
5	5	Leo Burnett USA	Chicago	396.8	371.7	6.7
6	9	Euro RSCG Worldwide	New York	378.4	313.8	20.6
7	6	Y&R Advertising	New York	365.1	339.2	7.6
8	7	BBDO Worldwide	New York	361.1	336.6	7.3
9	8	DDB Worldwide Communications	New York	342.8	316.6	8.3
10	10	Ogilvy & Mather Worldwide	New York	327.7	289.9	13.0

Source: 56th Annual Agency Report, *Advertising Age*, April 24, 2000, 52.

EXHIBIT 2.2

The ten largest advertising agencies (although they handle promotion for clients as well) in the United States ranked by gross income in U.S. millions of dollars.

Rank Agency ($15 Million and Up)	1998 Net Revenues	Percentage of Growth
DraftWorldwide	$176	216 %
Wunderman Cato Johnson	140	13 %
Cyrk-Simon Worldwide	137	59 %
Alcone Marketing	123	8 %
Gage Marketing Group	99	-18 %
Frankel & Company	85	28 %
TLP, Inc.	63	53 %
The Integer Group	59	102 %
Flair Communications Agency	52	81 %
Aspen Marketing Group	46	187 %

EXHIBIT 2.3

The ten largest promotion agencies in the United States ranked by net revenues in U.S. millions of dollars

The main reason we need to understand the structure of the promotion industry is so we can know who does what in what order during the promotional process. The industry is actually a collection of a wide range of talented people, all of whom have specialized expertise and perform key tasks in planning, preparing, and executing promotion campaigns. Exhibit 2.4 shows the structure of the promotion industry by outlining the different participants in the process.

Exhibit 2.4 demonstrates that marketers (like Kellogg's and Visa Card) can employ the services of advertising and promotion agencies (like Leo Burnett for advertising, Gage Marketing Group for promotions, Hill & Knowlton for public relations, and Insignia POPS for point-of-purchase materials) that may (or may not) contract for specialized services with various external facilitators (like Simmons Market Research). Together, these agencies create promotions that are transmitted with the help of various media organizations (like Nickelodeon cable

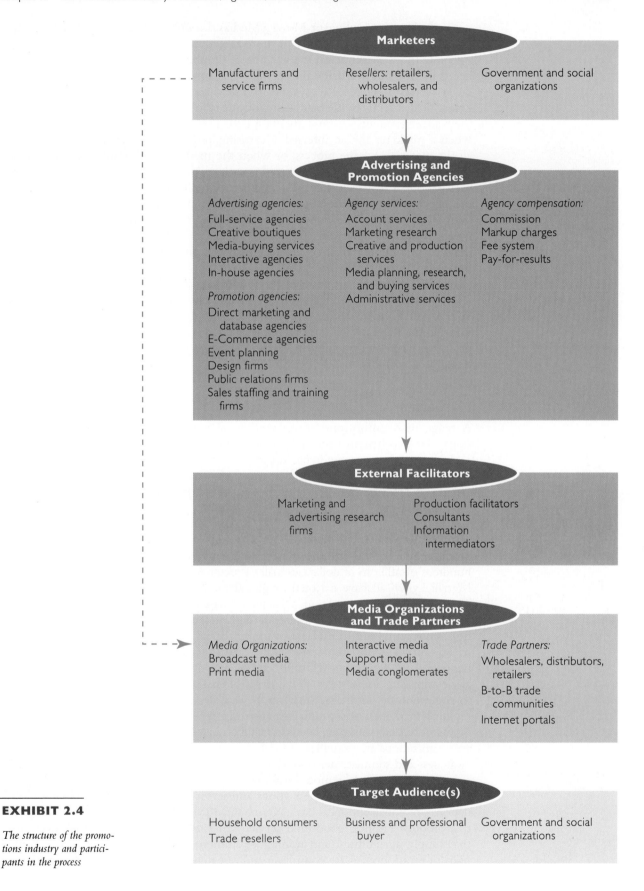

EXHIBIT 2.4

The structure of the promotions industry and participants in the process

network, America Online, or MessageMedia) through trade partners (like Wal-Mart, Dillard's, or VerticalNet) to one or more target audiences.

Note the dashed line on the left side of Exhibit 2.4. This line indicates that marketers do not always employ the services of advertising and promotion agencies. Nor do marketers or agencies always seek the services of external facilitators. Some marketers deal directly with media organizations or trade partners for placement of their advertisements or implementation of their promotions. This happens either when a marketer has an internal advertising/promotions department that prepares all the materials for the process, or when the media organizations (especially radio, television, and newspapers) and trade partners provide technical assistance in the preparation of materials. The new interactive media formats also provide marketers the opportunity to work directly with entertainment programming firms, such as Walt Disney and Sony, to provide integrated programming that features brand placements in films or television programs. And, as you will see, many of the new media agencies provide the creative and technical assistance marketers need to implement campaigns through new media.

Each level in the structure of the industry is complex. Let's take a look at each level, with particular emphasis on the nature and activities of promotion agencies. When you need to devise a promotion, no source of information will be more valuable than the advertising or promotion agency you work with. Advertising and promotion agencies provide the essential creative firepower to the process and represent a critical link in the structure.

Marketers

A range of organizations—from your local pet store to multinational corporations—seek to benefit from the effects of promotion. Different types of marketers each use promotion somewhat differently, depending on the type of product or service they sell or the position in the trade channel they occupy. The following categories describe the different types of marketers and the role promotion plays for them.

Manufacturers and Service Firms. Large national manufacturers of consumer products and services are the most prominent users of promotion, often spending hundreds of millions of dollars annually. Procter & Gamble, General Foods, MCI, and Merrill Lynch all have national or global markets for their products and services. These firms' use of promotion, particularly mass-media advertising and trade promotions, is essential to creating awareness and preference for their brands. But promotion is not useful just to national or multinational firms; regional and local producers of household goods and services also rely heavily on promotion. For example, regional dairy companies sell milk, cheese, and other dairy products in regions usually comprising a few states. These firms often use couponing and sampling as ways to communicate with target markets. Several breweries and wineries also serve only regional markets. Local producers of products are relatively rare, but local service organizations are common. Medical facilities, hair salons, restaurants, auto dealers, and art organizations are examples of local service providers that use promotion to create awareness and stimulate demand. What car dealer in America has not used a "holiday event" promotion or a remote local radio broadcast to attract attention!

Firms that produce business goods and services also use promotion on a global, national, regional, and local basis. Xerox and IBM are examples of global companies that produce business goods and services. At the national and regional level, firms that supply agricultural and mining equipment and repair services are common users of promotion, as are consulting and research firms. At the local level, firms that supply janitorial, linen, and bookkeeping services use promotion.

SEE WHAT THE BUZZ IS ALL ABOUT

WHAT'S THAT NOISE? AN ENTIRE INDUSTRY BEING REBUILT. THE $627 BILLION U.S. CONSTRUCTION INDUSTRY. BUZZSAW.COM MOBILIZES THE POWER OF THE WEB TO DELIVER THE MOST COMPLETE BUSINESS-TO-BUSINESS E-COMMERCE AND COLLABORATION SERVICES FOR EVERYONE IN DESIGN AND CONSTRUCTION. WHAT'S THE ATTRACTION? A FASTER, MORE FLEXIBLE, AND ULTIMATELY MORE PROFITABLE WAY TO WORK. A COMPLETELY NEW WAY TO BUILD. THAT'S THE BUZZ.

buzzsaw.com™
an Autodesk® venture

EXHIBIT 2.5

Business-to-business "vertical trade communities" like Buzzsaw (http://www.buzzsaw.com), which specializes in the construction industry, have emerged as a way for manufacturing and service firms to promote their goods and services to each other over the Internet.

Trade Resellers. The term **trade reseller** is simply a general description for all organizations in the marketing channel of distribution that buy products to resell to customers. As Exhibit 2.4 shows, resellers can be retailers, wholesalers, or distributors. These resellers deal with both household consumers and business buyers at all geographic market levels.

Retailers that sell in national or global markets are the most visible reseller advertisers. Sears, The Limited, and McDonald's are examples of national and global retail companies that use various forms of promotion to communicate with customers. Regional retail chains, typically grocery chains such as Albertson's or department stores such as The May Company, serve multistate markets and use promotions suited for their regional customers. At the local level, small retail shops of all sorts rely on newspaper, radio, television, and billboard advertising and special promotional events to reach a relatively small geographic area.

Wholesalers and distributors, such as American Lock & Supply (which supplies contractors with door locks and hardware), are a completely different breed of reseller. Technically, these two groups deal with business customers only, since their position in the distribution channel dictates that they sell products either to producers (who buy goods to produce other goods) or to retailers (who resell goods to household consumers). Occasionally, an organization will call itself a wholesaler and sell to the public. Such an organization is actually operating as a retail outlet.

Wholesalers and distributors have little need for the mass-media communication such as media like television and radio. Rather, they use trade publications, directory advertising such as the Yellow Pages and trade directories, and direct mail as their main advertising media. In this new era of Internet communications, these firms also participate in business-to-business "vertical trade communities" like VerticalNet and Buzzsaw (see Exhibit 2.5). These vertical trade communities act as comprehensive sources of information, interaction, and electronic commerce: the buying and selling of goods and services over the Internet.

Federal, State, and Local Governments. At first, you might think it is odd to include governments as promotion users, but government bodies invest millions of dollars in advertising annually. In fact, in 1998 the U.S. government was the twenty-fifth largest spender on advertising in the United States with expenditures exceeding $790 million in 1998.[10] And that was just on advertising. If you add in the expense of collateral, recruiting fairs, and the personal selling expense of recruiting offices, the cost is well over $2 billion annually. The federal government's spending on promotion is concentrated in two areas: armed forces recruiting and social issues. As an example, the U.S. government once used a television ad campaign with a budget of $55 million for U.S. Army recruiting. The government purchased time on

10. AdAge DataPlace, "100 Leading National Advertisers 1998," accessed at http://www.adage.com on December 27, 1999.

The Nature Conservancy.

Saving the Last Great Places

THE MISSION OF
The Nature Conservancy
is to preserve plants,
animals and natural
communities that
represent the diversity of
life on Earth by protecting
the lands and waters
they need to survive.

Share Our Conservation Vision

KATHARINE
ORDWAY
ASSOCIATES

Leave a Lasting Legacy.

Join a special group of visionary conservationists
in protecting Earth's precious natural habitats.
Katharine Ordway Associates are members of The Nature Conservancy
whose annual gifts of $1,000 or more help support our mission of Saving
the Last Great Places. Your tax-deductible gift will help secure critical land
protection opportunities. Demonstrate your commitment by joining the
Katharine Ordway Associates today.

For more information on the
Katharine Ordway Associates,
please visit our Web site at
www.tnc.org/koa
or call
1-888-2JoinTNC

For information on
making a gift of appreciated
stock, please contact
Anne Hubbard at
ahubbard@tnc.org
or
(703) 841-4859

The Nature Conservancy
International Headquarters
4245 North Fairfax Drive
Suite 100
Arlington, VA
22203-1606

www.tnc.org/koa

EXHIBIT 2.6

*Social organizations like The Nature Conservancy use advertising as a
way to promote donations to the organization* (http://www.tnc.org).

MTV and during NCAA basketball games to reach its target audience.[11] The other big promotion expense for government is in direct marketing. Each year, dozens of government publications are mailed to millions of businesses and individuals, particularly small businesses, to alert them to government programs or regulations and tax law changes. State and local government agencies, especially health care and welfare organizations, attempt to shape behaviors (reduce child abuse, for example) or communicate with citizens who can use their services, such as potential Social Security and Medicare recipients. State governments also invest millions of dollars in promoting state lotteries and tourism.

Social Organizations. Promotion by social organizations at the national, state, and local levels is common. The Nature Conservancy and the United Way promote their programs, seek donations, and attempt to shape behavior (for example, to deter drug use or encourage breast self-examination procedures). National organizations such as these use both the mass media and direct mail (see Exhibit 2.6) to promote their causes and services. Every state has its own unique statewide organizations, such as Citizens Against Hunger, a state arts council, a tourism office, or a historical society. Social organizations in local communities represent a variety of special interests, from computer clubs to neighborhood child care organizations. The promotions used by social organizations have the same fundamental purposes as those carried out by major multinational corporations: to stimulate demand and disseminate information. While big multinationals might use global advertising, local organizations rely on promotions like bike-swaps or bake sales.

Few of the marketers just discussed have the in-house expertise or resources to strategically plan and then prepare effective promotion. This is where advertising and promotion agencies play such an important role in the structure of the advertising industry.

Agencies ❸

Marketers are fortunate to have a full complement of agencies that specialize in literally every detail of every promotional tool. Let's take a closer look at the types of agencies marketers rely on to help create their promotional communications.

Advertising Agencies. Most marketers choose to enlist the services of an advertising agency. An **advertising agency** is an organization of professionals who provide creative and business services to clients in planning, preparing, and placing advertisements. The reason so many firms rely on advertising agencies is that those agencies can offer professionals with very specialized talent, experience, and expertise that simply cannot be matched by in-house employees.

---

11.   Kevin Goldman, "Army Launches New TV Ad Campaign," *The Wall Street Journal,* March 7, 1995, B10.

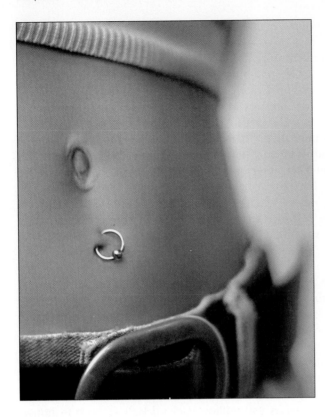

EXHIBIT 2.7

Full-service advertising agencies, from large global agencies to smaller regional shops, provide a wide range of services for clients. Their greatest contribution to the process, though, is their creative prowess. Here, FJCandN, a regional agency, is imploring marketers to "aim higher." A nice bit of creative to tout the agency's creative talents.

Advertising agencies can be found in most big cities and small towns in the United States, but they are often global businesses as well. The top 500 advertising agencies had worldwide income of more than $25 billion on gross billings of nearly $200 billion in 1998.[12] This 15.0 percent increase over 1997 shows the strength of investment in advertising globally.

The types of agency professionals who can help marketers in the planning, preparation, and placement of both advertising and other promotional activities include:

- Account planners
- Account supervisors
- Art directors
- Creative directors
- Copywriters
- Radio and television producers
- Researchers
- Artists
- Technical staff—printing, film editing, and soforth
- Marketing specialists
- Media buyers
- Public relations specialists
- Sales promotion and event planners
- Direct-marketing specialists
- Web developers
- Interactive media planners

As this list suggests, and as we saw with the story of Leo Burnett's evolution, some advertising agencies can provide marketers with a host of services, from campaign planning through creative concepts to e-strategies to measuring effectiveness. Several different types of agencies are available to the marketer. A short description of the major types of agencies follows.

Full-Service Agency. A **full-service agency** typically includes an array of advertising professionals to meet all the promotional needs of clients. Often, such an agency will also offer a client global contacts. Young & Rubicam and McCann-Erickson Worldwide are examples. Full-service agencies are not necessarily large organizations employing hundreds or even thousands of people. Small local shops can be full service with just a dozen or so employees (see Exhibit 2.7). And big accounts can often go to smaller agencies. When American Honda Motor Co. put its Acura account up for review recently, it wanted "outstanding creative talent" no matter what size agency did the work. The account went to midsize agency Suissa Miller in Santa Monica, California.[13]

Creative Boutique. A **creative boutique** typically emphasizes creative concept development, copywriting, and artistic services to clients. A marketer can employ this alternative for the strict purpose of infusing greater creativity into the message

12. AdAge, DataPlace, "Agency Report," accessed at http://www.adage.com/dataplace/archives on December 27, 1999.
13. Advertising Age Viewpoint editorial, "Why Midsize Shops Survive," *Advertising Age,* October 28, 1998, 26.

theme or individual advertisement. As one advertising expert put it, "If all clients want is ideas—lots of them, from which they can pick and mix to their hearts' delight—they won't want conventional, full-service agencies. They'll want fast, flashy fee-based idea factories."[14] Creative boutiques are these "idea factories." Some large global agencies such as McCann-Erickson Worldwide are setting up "creative-only" project shops that mimic the services provided by creative boutiques.[15]

Interactive Agency. The era of new media has created a new form of agency—the **interactive agency.** This kind of agency helps marketers prepare communications for new media such as the Internet, interactive kiosks, CD–ROMs, and interactive television. Interactive agencies have so far been focused on banner ads and Web site development. Other "cyberagencies," which we will talk about shortly, specialize in online promotions. One of the best interactive agencies is Red Sky Interactive. They have prepared corporate Web sites for Nike, Levi Strauss, Absolut, and Lands' End. Check out their work at http://www.redsky.com.

In-House Agency. An **in-house agency,** often referred to as the advertising department in a firm, takes responsibility for the planning and preparation of advertising materials. This option has the advantage of greater coordination and control in all phases of the advertising and promotion process. The marketer's own personnel have control over and knowledge of marketing activities, such as product development and distribution tactics. Another advantage is that the firm can essentially keep all the profits from commissions an external agency would have earned. As the senior VP for advertising and corporate communications at NEC explained about the firm's prospects for moving much of its $40 million Packard Bell account in-house, "We're certainly looking at taking some of the work in-house because it's more efficient."[16] While the advantages of doing advertising work in-house are attractive, there are two severe limitations. First, there may be a lack of objectivity, thereby constraining the execution of all phases of the advertising process. Second, it is highly unlikely that an in-house agency could match the breadth and depth of expertise available in an external agency.

Media-Buying Service. While not technically an agency, a **media-buying service** is an independent organization that specializes in buying media time and space, particularly on radio and television, as a service to advertising agencies and marketers. The task of buying media space has become more complex because of the proliferation of media options. An agency or marketer will do the strategy planning for media placement and then turn to a media-buying service to do the actual buying of time and space. One additional advantage of using a media-buying service is that since it buys media in large quantities, it often acquires media time at a much lower cost than an agency or advertiser could. Also, media-buying services often acquire time and space in "inventory" and offer last-minute placement to advertisers.

Promotion Agencies. While marketers often rely on an advertising agency as a steering organization for their promotional efforts, many specialized agencies called **promotion agencies** often enter the process. This is because advertising agencies, even full-service ones, will concentrate on the advertising process and only provide ancillary services for other promotional efforts. This is particularly true in the current era where new media are offering so many different ways to communicate to

14. Sorrell, "Agencies Face New Battle Grounds," 22.
15. Melanie Wells, "McCann Eyes Boutique," *Advertising Age,* June 27, 1994, 4.
16. Bradley Johnson, "NEC May Move $40 Mil In-House," *Advertising Age,* April, 6, 1998, 48.

target markets. As an indication of the proliferation and diversification of promotion agencies, look at the sample listing from *Promo* in Exhibit 2.8 of the promotion agencies available. Notice these agencies can handle everything from sampling to event promotions to in-school promotional tie-ins. A list of the types of agencies and their services follows (although in reality many agencies are hybrids and offer multiple promotion services as you can see in Exhibit 2.8).

Direct-Marketing and Database Agencies. **Direct-marketing** and **database agencies** (sometimes called **direct-response agencies**) provide a variety of direct-marketing services. These firms maintain and manage large databases of mailing lists as one of their services. They can design direct-marketing campaigns through either mail, tele-marketing, or direct-response campaigns using all forms of media. These agencies help marketers construct databases of target customers, merge databases, develop pro-motional materials, and then execute the campaign. In many cases, these agencies maintain **fulfillment centers,** which ensure that customers receive the product ordered through direct mail. Direct Media (http://www.directmedia.com) is the world's largest list management and list brokerage firm, providing clients with services in both the consumer and busi-ness-to-business markets across the country and around the world.

Many of these agencies are set up to provide cre-ative and production services to clients. These firms will design and help execute direct-response cam-paigns using traditional media like radio, televi-sion, magazines, and newspapers. Also, they can prepare **infomercials**—a 5- to 60-minute "information" program that promotes a brand and offers direct purchase to view-ers—for their clients. Firms that provide infomercial services maintain directors and producers on staff. Exhibit 2.9 shows the largest direct-market-ing agencies in the United States.

E-Commerce Agencies. There are so many new and dif-ferent kinds of e-commerce agencies that it is hard to categorize them all. The **e-commerce agency** han-dles a variety of planning and execution activities related to promotions using electronic commerce. Note that these agencies are different from the inter-active agencies discussed above. They do not create Web sites or banner ads but rather help firms conduct all forms of promotion through electronic media, particularly the Internet. They can run sweepstakes, issue coupons, help in sampling, and do direct-response campaigns.[17] A firm like e-Centives (http://www.ecentives.com)offers marketers the option of providing consumers with online coupons and sales offers. Blockbuster, Hickory Farms, Orvis, and Mrs. Fields cookies are a few of the firms that have signed on with e-Centives. Another specialized firm

http://www.promomagazine.com

EXHIBIT 2.8

A wide range of agencies is available to marketers for their promotional needs. A multipage listing like this appears in every issue of Promo *to help marketers find the right agency. Of course, with the Web, companies have a good many more means to be found by those who need them. How is* Promo *making use of the Web, and what pressures do you think it, as a print magazine, might face from the Web? How might an industry-specific publication make best use of the Web?*

---

17. Al Urbanski, "Off-the-Rack Web Programs," *Promo* magazine, December 1999, i.4.

EXHIBIT 2.9

Direct-marketing agencies prepare direct-marketing and direct-response promotions for marketers. These are the top direct-marketing agencies in the United States.

http://www.messagemedia.com

EXHIBIT 2.10

New e-commerce agencies are popping up faster than pop-up screens. This agency, MessageMedia, helps marketers use the Internet to send e-mail messages to highly targeted audiences. MessageMedia helps firms develop the databases as well. Like many new frontiers, the Internet is seeing many new entrants who may not last, though others have rapidly become the "gorillas" in their niches—for example, in e-mail promotions, or managing special-event Webcasts. How will all these new entrants relate to older, established agencies, which served "old commerce" so well?

is MessageMedia (http://www.messagemedia.com) Message Media (featured in the New Media box and in Exhibit 2.10) provides clients with e-mail messaging services and database management to direct those messages to highly targeted audiences. Another new media e-commerce organization is DoubleClick (http://www.doubleclick.com), which provides services related to Internet advertising, the targeting technology, complete ad management software solutions, direct-response Internet advertising, and Internet advertising developed for regional and local businesses. There is even an organization that will handle all your online public relations news releases: PR Newswire (http://www.prnewswire.com). The best way to view these new ecommerce agencies is to understand that they can provide all forms of promotion using new media technology usually specializing in Internet solutions.

Sales Promotion Agencies. These specialists design and then operate contests, sweepstakes, special displays, or coupon campaigns for advertisers. It is important to recognize that these agencies can specialize in **consumer sales promotions** and will focus on price-off deals, coupons, sampling, rebates, and premiums. Other firms will specialize in

trade sales promotions designed to help marketers use promotions aimed at wholesalers, retailers, and vendors. These agencies are expert in incentive programs, trade shows, sales force contests, and in-store merchandising and P–O–P materials.

These agencies often work closely with the direct-marketing agencies in the preparation of materials to ensure coordination and timing of promotions. These agencies also help firms develop catalogs and assist in fulfillment like the direct-marketing agencies.

YOU HAVE E-MAIL (AS A PROMOTION OPTION)

Most of us know e-mail as that useful but sometimes burdensome new technology for professional communications and keeping in touch with relatives in remote places. One firm has emerged that will help marketers use e-mail as another from of promotional communications. The firm, MessageMedia (http://www.messagemedia.com), intends to distinguish itself among e-commerce agencies by offering synchronized marketing communications through e-mail, the Web, and offline media.

The company will handle a firm's in-bound and out-bound e-mail campaigns based on database technology. The applications available from the firm will include customer service and sales messages. But the founder, Larry Jones, is quick to point out the MessageMedia is not a "spamming" organization that sends millions of unsolicited e-mails to unsuspecting and unappreciative Web users. MessageMedia prepares and sends messages only to current customers of his clients—a true relationship-building component of the promotional process.

This is a fast-growing market if you can get the right offer, to the right customer, at the right time, based on the right database. According to Jones, highly targeted e-mail messages draw a 10 percent response rate, while "click-throughs" on Web banner ads are below 1 percent. The key to success for MessageMedia is in the philosophy of the founder, who believes that its not about sending e-mails, it's about understanding the recipient. If MessageMedia's knowledge of the recipients is as good as its advertising suggests (see Exhibit 2.10), this company can't miss.

Source: Dana Blankenhorn, "MessageMedia Vision Extends Beyond E-Mail," *Advertising Age*, August 16, 1999, 44.

Event-Planning Agencies. Event sponsorship can also be targeted to household consumers or the trade market. **Event-planning agencies** and organizers are experts in finding locations, securing dates, and putting together a team of people to create a promotional event—audiovisual people, caterers, security experts, entertainers, participants, or whoever is necessary to make the event come about. The event-planning organization will also often take over the task of advertising the event and making sure the press provides coverage (publicity) of it. When a marketer sponsors an entire event, like a PGA golf tournament, managers will work closely with the event-planning agencies. If a marketer is just one of several sponsors of an event, like a NASCAR race, it has less control over planning.

Design Firms. Designers and graphics specialists do not get nearly enough credit in the promotional process. If you take a job in promotions, your designer will be one of your most important partners. While designers rarely are involved in promotional strategy, they are intimately involved in the execution of the promotional effort. In the most basic sense, **designers** help a firm create a **logo,** the graphic mark that identifies company and other visual representations that promote a firm's identity. This mark will appear on everything from advertising to packaging to the company stationery, business cards, and signage. But beyond the logo, graphic designers will design everything used in promotions including coupons, phone cards, in-store displays, brochures, outdoor banners for events, newsletters, and direct-mail pieces. They are key, if somewhat anonymous, participants in the process.

Public Relations Firms. The **public relations firm** manages an organization's relationships with the media, the local community, competitors, industry associations,

CAREERPROFILE

Name:	Jieun Lee
Title:	Account Coordinator
Company:	Frankfurt Balkind, New York, New York
	http://www.frankfurtbalkind.com
Education:	B.A., English with Advertising minor

"This job allows me to explore many different options and get a feel for the industry, as well as produce something that's great and tangibly inspired," says recent college graduate Jieun Lee of her job as an account coordinator at Frankfurt Balkind. The 130-person marketing communications agency helps clients as diverse as Schering-Plough, Pitney Bowes, and the Guggenheim Museum strategically position their products and brands through advertising, Web site development, and other communications programs.

As an account coordinator, she interacts with various departments, both within the agency and at client offices, to ensure that projects proceed smoothly. "Essentially, I push work through the agency at different levels, ensuring that each department does what they have to do to reach deadlines according to client and agency expectations," explains Jieun.

Jieun's job is never dull. She meets at least daily with the agency's account executives to discuss the day's priorities and upcoming deadlines. Next, she may touch base with one of the agency's copywriters or artists to discuss how specific marketing strategies should be incorporated into an advertisement they're developing. Later, she may call the production department for an estimate on the cost and schedule of printing a brochure for a different client. Or she'll switch to coordinating the details of a photography shoot for the filming of a television commercial.

Jieun's advice to others considering this career path? Simple: Work hard. "It won't go unrecognized. You're expected to do a certain amount, but that won't always be enough for you to grow from," she says. "Also, be smart about who manages you. Even though you may only be starting out, you have the right to ask for good people to manage you and to make sure you learn how to do your job."

To learn more about advertising and marketing communications agencies, visit these Web sites:

Advertising Agencies.com
http://www.americanadagencies.com

American Advertising Federation
http://www.aaf.org

American Association of Advertising Agencies
http://www.aaaa.org

and government organizations. As we saw in Chapter 1, the tools of public relations include press releases, feature stories, lobbying, spokespersons, and company newsletters. Some public relations firms can conduct research to develop and test the impact of public relations efforts. Most marketers do not like to handle their own public relations tasks for two reasons. First, public relations takes highly specialized skill and talent not normally found in the firm. Second, managers are too close to public relations problems and may not be capable of handling a situation—particularly a negative one—with measured public responses. For these reasons, marketers, and even advertising agencies, turn to outside public relations firms.

Sales Staffing, Training, and Assessment Firms. There are a wide variety of firms available to marketers for staffing, developing, training, and evaluating the sales force. Whether the sales force is at the retail level or is a corporate sales force selling to business buyers and the trade, a large number of highly specialized tasks need to be handled. Often, firms turn to outside agencies to handle these tasks. For example, Sales Staffers International Inc. (http://www.salesstaffers.com) is a sales force outsourcing firm that can provide temporary staff, sales training, and evaluation. Vital Learning (http://vital-learning.com) provides sales force training programs and helps firms equip their salespeople with the latest automation productivity tools. Marketers can find agencies to help with all stages of the personal selling and sales force management process.

Agency Services

Advertising and promotion agencies offer a wide range of services. The marketer may need a large, global, full-service advertising agency to plan, prepare, and execute its promotion strategy. On the other hand, a creative boutique may offer the right combination of services. Similarly, a large promotions firm might be needed to manage events and promotions, while a design firm is enlisted for design work but nothing else. The most important issue, however, is for the marketer and the agency to negotiate and reach agreement on the services being provided before any agency is hired. The types of services commonly offered by advertising and promotion agencies include the following.

Account Services. **Account services** include managers who, with titles such as account executive, account supervisor, or account manager, work with clients to determine how the brand can benefit most from promotion. Account services entail identifying the benefits a brand offers, its target audiences and the best competitive positioning, and then developing a complete promotion plan. In some cases, account services in an agency can provide basic marketing and consumer behavior research, but the client should really bring this information to the table. Knowing the target segment, the brand's values, and positioning strategy are really the responsibility of the marketer (more on this in Chapters 4 and 5).

Account services managers also work with the client in translating cultural and consumer values into advertising and promotional messages through the creative services in the agency. Finally, they work with media services to develop an effective media strategy for determining the best vehicles for reaching the targeted audiences. One of the primary tasks in account services is to keep the various agency teams—creative, production, media—on schedule and within budget (more about this in Chapter 3).

Marketing Research Services. Research conducted by an agency for a client usually consists of the agency locating studies (conducted by commercial research organizations) that have bearing on a client's market or promotional objectives. The research group will help the client interpret the research and communicate these interpretations to the creative and media people. If existing studies are not sufficient, research may actually be conducted by the agency. As mentioned in the account services discussion, some agencies can assemble consumers from the target audience to evaluate different versions of proposed advertising and determine whether messages are being communicated effectively. The ad agency BBDO has several proprietary research methods it employs for clients designed to understand both broad consumer trends and very specific aspects of consumer behavior in well-defined target audiences.

Many agencies have established the position of account planner to coordinate the research effort. An **account planner** is an individual assigned to clients on an equal level with an account executive and will ensure that research input is included at each stage of development of promotional materials. Some agency leaders, like Jay Chiat of Chiat/Day think that account planning is "the best new business tool ever invented."[18] Others are more measured in their assessment. Jon Steel, Director of Account Planning at Goodby, Silverstein, and Partners, described account planning this way: "Planning, when used properly, is the best business tool ever invented."[19] Either way, agencies are understanding that research, signaled by the appointment of an account planner, is key to successful promotional campaigns.

Creative and Production Services. **Creative services** comes up with the concepts that express the value of a company's brand in interesting and memorable ways. In simple terms, the creative group develops the promotional message that will be delivered though advertising, sales promotion, direct-marketing, or public relations. The creative group in an agency will typically include a creative director, art director, illustrators or designers, and copywriters. In specialized promotion agencies, event planners, contest experts, and interactive media specialists will join the core group.

Production services includes producers (and sometimes directors) who take creative ideas and turn them into advertisements, direct-mail pieces, or events. Producers generally manage and oversee the endless details of production of the

18. John Steel, *Truth, Lies & Advertising: The Art of Account Planning* (New York: John Wiley & Sons, 1998), 42.
19. Ibid, 43.

finished advertisement or other promotion activity. Advertising agencies maintain the largest and most sophisticated creative and production staffs.

Media-Planning and -Buying Services. **Media-planning and -buying services** handle the placement task in the promotional effort. The central challenge is to determine how a client's message can most effectively and efficiently reach the target audience. Media planners and buyers examine an enormous number of options to put together an effective media plan within the client's budget. But media planning and buying is much more than simply buying ad space, timing a coupon distribution, or scheduling an event. A wide range of media strategies can be implemented to enhance the impact of the message. Agencies are helping clients sort through the blizzard of new media options such as CD–ROM, videocassettes, interactive media, and the Internet. Years ago, most large agencies, such as Chiat/Day and Fallon McElligott, set up their own interactive media groups in response to client demands that the Internet media option be made available to them.[20] And new specialized media planning organizations have emerged to serve marketers' needs for Internet placement. The three positions typically found in the media area are media planner, media buyer, and media researcher. This is where the client's money is spent and is thus very important.

Administrative Services. Like other businesses, agencies have to manage their business affairs. Agencies have personnel departments, accounting and billing departments, and sales staffs that go out and sell the agency to clients. Most important to clients is the traffic department, which has the responsibility of monitoring projects to be sure that deadlines are met. Traffic managers make sure the creative group and media services are coordinated so that deadlines for getting promotional materials to printers and media organizations are met. The job requires tremendous organizational skills and is critical to delivering the other services to clients.

Agency Compensation

The way agencies get paid is somewhat different from the way other professional organizations are compensated. While accountants, doctors, lawyers, and consultants often work on a fee basis, agencies frequently base compensation on a commission or markup system. Promotion agencies occasionally work on a commission basis, but more often on a fee or contract basis. We will examine the four most prevalent agency compensation methods: commissions, markup charges, fee systems, and newer pay-for-results plans.

Commissions. The traditional method of agency compensation is the **commission system,** which is based on the amount of money the marketer spends on media. Under this method, 15 percent of the total amount billed by a media organization is retained by the advertising or promotion agency as compensation for all costs in creating advertising/promotion for the marketer. The only variation is that the rate typically changes to 16⅔ percent for outdoor media.

Over the past ten years, the wisdom of the commission system has been questioned by both advertisers and agencies themselves. As the chairman of a large full-service agency put it, "It's incenting us to do the wrong thing, to recommend network TV and national magazines and radio when other forms of communication like direct marketing or public relations might do the job better."[21] About half of all

20. Kevin Goldman, "Ad Agencies Slowly Set Up Shop at New Addresses on the Internet," *The Wall Street Journal,* December 29, 1994, B5.
21. Patricia Sellers, "Do You Need Your Ad Agency?" *Fortune,* November 15, 1993, 148.

advertisers compensate their agencies using a commission system based on media cost. But only about 14 percent of marketers responding to a recent survey still use the traditional 15 percent commission. More marketers are using other percentage levels of commission—often negotiated levels—as the basis for agency compensation. Unilever, the Dutch consumer products company with extensive U.S. revenues, has some agencies on rates as low as 10.75 percent, depending on the agreement negotiated.[22]

Markup Charges. Another method of agency compensation is to add a percentage **markup charge** to a variety of services the agency purchases from outside suppliers. In many cases, an agency will turn to outside contractors for art, illustration, photography, printing, research, and production. The agency then, in agreement with the client, adds a markup charge to these services. The reason markup charges became prevalent in the industry is that many promotion agencies were providing services that did not use traditional media. Since the traditional commission method was based on media charges, there was no way for these agencies to receive payment for their work. This being the case, the markup system was developed. A typical markup on outside services is 17.65 to 20 percent.

Fee Systems. A **fee system** is much like that used by consultants or attorneys, whereby the marketer and the agency agree on an hourly rate for different services provided. The hourly rate can be based on average salaries within departments or on some agreed-upon hourly rate across all services. This is the most common method for promotion agencies to get compensated. GM, the largest U.S. advertiser, agreed to a fee system in which compensation will be based on agency work and its thinking.[23] Recently, agencies that have been inundated with requests from dot-com companies to prepare campaigns have initiated a fee system that requires an "upfront" payment for anticipated expenses plus a "fair profit margin."[24] Some agencies feel that some dot.coms won't be around long enough to make a commission system work.

Another version of the fee system is a fixed fee, or contract, set for a project between the client and the agency. It is imperative that the agency and the marketer agree on precisely what services will be provided, by what departments in the agency, over what specified period of time. In addition, the parties must agree on which supplies, materials, travel costs, and other expenses will be compensated beyond the fixed fee. Fixed-fee systems have the potential for causing serious rifts in the client-agency relationship because out-of-scope work can easily spiral out of control when so many variables are at play.

Pay-for-Results. Recently, many marketers and agencies alike have been working on compensation programs called **pay-for-results,** which base the agency's fee on the achievement of agreed-upon results.[25] Historically, agencies have not agreed to be evaluated on "results" because "results" have often been narrowly defined as sales. The key effect on a sales result is based on factors outside the agency's control such as product features, pricing strategy, and distribution programs (that is, the overall marketing mix, not just promotions). These newer pay-for-results compensation plans tie the advertising or promotion agency compensation to a pre–agreed upon achievement of specified objectives. An agency may agree to be compensated based on achievement of sales levels, but more often (and more appropriately)

22.   Pat Sloan and Laura Petrecca, "Unilever Panel to Propose Hike in Fees for Agencies," *Advertising Age,* November 3, 1997, 2.
23.   Jean Halliday, "GM to Scrap Agency Commissions," *Advertising Age,* November 16, 1998, 1, 57.
24.   Alice Z. Cuneo, "Dot-Compensation: Ad Agencies Feel the Net-Effect," *Advertising Age,* February 7, 2000, 1.
25.   Laura Petrecca, "Pay-for-Results Plans Can Boost Agencies: Execs," *Advertising Age,* September 8, 1997, 18, 20.

communications objectives such as awareness, brand identification, or brand feature knowledge among target audiences will serve as the results criteria. A recent mandate by Procter & Gamble has all 200 of its brands and the agencies that handle them on a brand sales model that began on July 1, 2000.[26]

One of the most difficult tasks in the compensation system is coordinating all the agencies and how they get paid. As you have seen, more marketers are using more different forms of promotion and enlisting the help of multiple agencies. A key to IMC here is integrated agency communication. When all of a marketer's agencies are working together and coordinating their efforts, not only integrated marketing communication, but better relations between agencies, is achieved.[27] However, not all clients see it that way, as the IMC in Practice box suggests.

As if this long list of agencies and intricate compensation schemes wasn't complicated enough, let's complicate things a bit more and consider a fairly long list of external facilitators that marketers and their agencies rely on to create and execute promotional campaigns.

External Facilitators ④

While agencies offer clients many services and are adding more, marketers often need to rely on specialized external facilitators in planning, preparing, and executing promotional campaigns. **External facilitators** are organizations or individuals that provide specialized services to marketers and agencies. The most important of these are discussed in the following sections.

Marketing and Advertising Research Firms. Many firms rely on outside assistance during the planning phase of advertising. Research firms such as Burke International and Simmons can perform original research for advertisers, using focus groups, surveys, or experiments to assist in understanding the potential market or consumer perceptions of a product or services. Other research firms, such as SRI International, routinely collect data (from grocery store scanners, for example) and have these data available for a fee.

Marketers and their agencies also seek measures of promotional program effectiveness after a campaign has run. After an advertisement or promotion has been running for some reasonable amount of time, firms such as Starch INRA Hooper will run recognition tests on print advertisements. Other firms such as Burke offer day-after recall tests of broadcast advertisements. Some firms specialize in message testing to determine whether consumers find advertising messages appealing and understandable. The exact nature and full range of research that can be conducted to measure effectiveness are covered in Chapter 15.

Consultants. A variety of **consultants** specialize in areas related to the promotional process. Marketers can seek out marketing consultants for assistance in the planning stage. Creative and communications consultants provide insight on issues related to message strategy and message themes. Consultants in event planning and sponsorships offer their expertise to both marketers and agencies. Public relations consultants often work with top management. Media experts can help an advertiser determine the proper media mix and efficient media placement.

Two new types of consultants have emerged in recent years. One is a database consultant, who works with both marketers and agencies. Organizations such as Shepard Associates help firms identify and then manage databases that allow for the

---

26. Betsy Spethmann, "Pay Day," *Promo* magazine, November 1999, 47–50; and Kathryn Kranhold, "P&G Expands Its Program to Tie Agency Pay to Brand Performance," *The Wall Street Journal,* September 16, 1999, B12.
27. Allen Winneker, "Avoiding Bonus Envy," *Promo* magazine, November 1999, 35–37.

development of integrated marketing communications programs. Diverse databases from research sources discussed earlier can be merged or cross-referenced in developing effective communications programs. The other new type of consultant specializes in Web site development and management. These consultants typically have the creative skills to develop Web sites and corporate home pages and the technical skills to advise marketers on managing the technical aspects of the user interface.

IN PRACTICE

I WANT MY IMC–SORT OF

As much lip service as marketers give to pursuing the "one voice" and "seamless communication" that a well-designed IMC program can provide, there seems to be one major roadblock to implementation: the marketers themselves! This is the opinion of one industry expert who has studied the IMC process for many years.

John McLaughlin, a marketing consultant, believes that major IMC efforts actually started with major advertising agencies about 25 years ago, when agencies began designing their organizations to provide all sorts of communications capabilities to their clients in addition to traditional advertising, as a way to ensure keeping all of their clients' business. These agencies added sales promotion, public relations, and direct-mail departments, but the vast majority of clients didn't respond. The reasons:

- Clients didn't see a clear-cut cost advantage in dealing exclusively with a primary agency rather than several suppliers.
- Clients didn't have confidence in the ability of advertising agencies to deliver specialized services.
- Clients had strategic concerns about putting all their eggs in one creative/executional basket. If a client decided to replace an agency, a house of cards would come tumbling down around the firm's entire communication/promotional program.

Because of these concerns, marketers not only hesitated to use their agencies' newly developed multiple capabilities, but also delayed implementing IMC altogether. The task of developing multiple relationships with multiple agencies proved to be dysfunctional and expensive—but the original concerns about dealing with a sole agency remained. Creative constipation set in.

In the meantime, since agencies were not realizing widespread new business from newly formed divisions, many of them were disbanded or sold off. While some agencies still maintain broad-based staffs from multiple communications needs of clients, others choose to partner with outside agencies.

So, if IMC has not spread as quickly as everyone thinks it should have, McLaughlin says simply, "Blame it on the clients."

Source: John P. McLaughlin, "Why Is IMC Taking So Long? Blame It on the Clients," *Marketing News,* September 15, 1997, 27.

Production Facilitators. External **production facilitators** offer essential services both during and after the production process. Production is the area where marketers and their agencies rely most heavily on external facilitators. All forms of media advertising require special expertise that even the largest full-service agency, much less a marketer, typically does not retain on staff. In broadcast production, directors, production managers, songwriters, camera operators, audio and lighting technicians, and performers are all essential to preparing a professional, high-quality radio or television ad. Production houses can provide the physical facilities, including sets, stages, equipment, and crews, needed for broadcast production. Similarly, in preparing print advertising, brochures, and direct-mail pieces, the agency or firm may hire outside graphic artists, photographers, models, directors, and producers to provide the specialized skills and facilities needed. In-store promotions is another area where designing and producing materials requires the skills of a specialty organization.

The specific activities performed by external facilitators and the techniques employed by the personnel in these firms will be covered in greater detail in Part 3 of the text. For now, it is sufficient to recognize the role these firms play in the promotion industry.

Information Intermediators. This form of external facilitator has emerged as a result of new technology and the desire on the part of marketers to target audiences more precisely. **Information intermediators** collect customer purchase transaction histories, aggregate them across many firms that have sold merchandise to these

EXHIBIT 2.11

Information intermediators like AllAdvantage play an important role in providing marketers with media access, in this case the Internet, to highly targeted audiences.

customers, and then sell the customer names and addresses back to the firms that originally sold to these customers. Firms such as American Express, AT&T, and regional telephone companies are uniquely situated in the information management process to accumulate and organize such data, and they will likely emerge as information intermediators. These firms will gather and organize information on consumer transaction histories across a variety of different companies selling goods and services. Once this information is organized by an intermediator, it allows an advertiser to merge information about important target segments—what they buy, when they buy, and how they buy. With this information, both message themes and media placement can be more effectively and efficiently developed.

A variety of firms have emerged as specialty information intermediators for the Internet. The way the Internet works is uniquely suited to track the Web surfing behavior and also the purchase behavior of users (a point we will discuss as an ethical issue in Chapter 6). Exhibit 2.11 features one of the new breed of Internet infomediary firms, AllAdvantage.com (http://www.alladvantage.com), which uses a brand mascot called "Infomediary Man." AllAdvantage has a unique system for attracting and then tracking consumers for marketers. This company "pays" Web surfers to join their system (there is an hourly and referral rate for surfing) for the right to post advertising and promotional messages on members' computer screens as they surf. The company describes its service to marketers in this way:

Once consumers download our free Viewbar software, they are continuously exposed to the ads we deliver while they surf the Web. In a sense, we're renting digital billboards on millions of computer screens around the world. But the Viewbar is much more than just a billboard. It allows us to track actual surfing behavior. That means we can target and deliver advertising and other content more precisely, more efficiently than ever before. We can deliver messages to consumers who are already interested in buying online, who we know to be interested in your product, at the time when they are most receptive, regardless of where they are on the Internet—every search and every site. Our international community of over 3 [now 4] million Internet users consent to this responsible use of their information because we reward them for doing something they enjoy—surfing the Web. And we bring them ads, offers, and information about things that actually interest them. Members also know that AllAdvantage's privacy policy protects them from unwanted reuse of their data. And they can turn off the Viewbar anytime they want to—so they're in control.[28]

This issue of consumers "controlling information" is an important one that discussed in Chapter 3. The communications environment is much more an interactive system where consumers are controlling the information flow than ever before.[29]

Media Organizations and Trade Partners ⑤

The next level in the industry structure, shown in Exhibit 2.12, comprises the media available to marketers and the role of trade partners. The media available for placing advertising, such as broadcast and print media, are well known to most of us simply because we're exposed to them daily. In addition, the Internet has created media organizations through which marketers can direct and distribute their advertising and promotional messages. One such media organization, Real Media (http://www.realmedia.com), has a global network of over 1,000 Web sites for placement of marketers' advertising and promotional materials (see Exhibit 2.13). But with other forms of promotion, like event sponsorship, in-store displays, sampling, and retail sale people, the marketer must rely on various trade partners. Examining Exhibit 2.12 again shows that these trade partners are also a "media" link in delivering promotion to consumers.

Media Organizations. Marketers and their agencies turn to **media organizations** that own and manage the media access to consumers. In traditional media, major television networks such as NBC or Fox, as well as national magazines such as *U.S. News & World Report* or *People,* provide advertisers with time and space—at considerable expense—for their messages.

Other media options are more useful for reaching narrowly defined target audiences. Specialty programming on cable television tightly focused direct-mail pieces, and a well-designed Internet campaign may be better ways to reach a specific audience. Note the inclusion of "Media Conglomerates" in this list. This category is included because organizations such as Time Warner and Viacom own and operate companies in broadcast, print, and interactive media. Most recently, Disney has vastly expanded its media presence with the purchase of the ABC television network and partial ownership in multiple Web sites, including ESPN SportsZone, NBA.com, NFL.com, and ABCnews.com.[30]

The support media organizations shown in Exhibit 2.12 include all those places that marketers want to put their messages but are not mainstream, traditional media.

28. Quote taken from "Advertisers" page of the AllAdvantage Web site accessed at http://www.alladvantage.com on December 29, 1999.
29. Don Schultz and Beth Barnes make very strong statements about the interactive nature of information in the twenty-first century marketplace. For their basic premise, see Don E. Schultz and Beth E. Barnes, *Strategic Brand Communications Campaigns* (Lincolnwood, IL: NTC Business Books, 1999), 12.
30. Chuck Ross, "Disney Eyes Stake in Excite as Part of Bold Web Strategy," *Advertising Age,* June 1, 1998, 1, 52.

Broadcast

Television
Major network
Independent station
Cable

Radio
Network
Local

Print

Magazines
By geographic coverage
By content

Direct Mail
Brochures
Catalogs
Videos

Newspapers
National
Statewide
Local

Specialty
Handbills
Programs

Interactive Media

Online Computer Services

Home-Shopping Broadcasts

**Interactive Broadcast
Entertainment Programming**

Kiosks

CD-ROM

Internet

Support Media

Outdoor
Billboards
Transit
Posters

Directories
Yellow pages
Electronic directories

Premiums
Keychains
Calendars
Logo clothing
Pens

Point-of-Purchase Displays

**Film and Program Brand
Placement**

Event Sponsorship

Media Conglomerates

Multiple Media Combinations
Time Warner
Viacom
TCI
Turner Broadcasting
Comcast
AT&T

Trade Partners

Wholesalers
Distributors
Retailers
Internet Portals
B-to-B Trade Communities

EXHIBIT 2.12

One key agency service is media buying and placement for marketers' promotional materials, particularly advertising messages. New media organizations like Real Media have emerged to direct promotions to targeted audiences on the Internet.

EXHIBIT 2.13

Internet media organizations like Real Media provide marketers with access to audiences through a vast worldwide network of branded Web sites and portals. The range of these properties enables Real Media to customize advertising and promotions to a marketer's specific needs.

Often referred to as "out-of-home" media, these support media organizations include transit companies (bus and taxi boards), billboard organizations, directory companies, and sports and performance arenas for sponsorships, display materials, and premium items.

Trade Partners. Trade partners constitute an interesting link in the structure of the promotion industry these days. The traditional **trade partners** include wholesalers, distributors, and retailers who help carry out the promotion for a brand through personal selling and in-store promotions like sampling, shelf coupons, and in-store displays. But we cannot ignore the impact of new media trade partners that include business-to-business trade communities, like VerticalNet (and Buzzsaw, featured earlier in the chapter). In addition, the big consumer Internet portals like Yahoo! and Go2Net are clearly media through which marketers can reach a targeted audience with a persuasive promotion—the essence of the promotional process. These new media "partners" must be considered for all the opportunities they present. Will they replace major media? Probably not. Do they constitute a viable vehicle for reaching target customers with promotional messages? Absolutely.

Audiences

The structure of the promotion industry (check Exhibit 2.4 again) and the flow of communication would obviously be incomplete without an audience—no audience, no communication. One interesting thing about the audiences for promotional communications—with the exception of household consumers—is that they are also the marketers who use promotional communications. We are all familiar with the type of advertising directed at us in our role as consumers—toothpaste, window cleaner, sport utility vehicles, soft drinks, insurance, and on and on.

http://www.instinet.com

http://www.govcon.com, http://www.verticalnet.com

EXHIBIT 2.14

While we tend to think of promotions as being directed to consumer audiences, business and government organizations are audiences for promotion as well. Here, Instinet, the world's largest agency brokerage firm, targets a professional business audience. Because the Net can be used to slice and dice the online population into any sort of vertical or horizontal subset, there are myriad "portal" sites attracting specialized audiences for pinpoint targeting. GovCon, for example, is aimed at government contractors; it was bought by VerticalNet, an online community aggregator.

But the business and trade audiences and government are key to the success of a large number of firms who sell only to business and government buyers. While many of these firms rely heavily on personal selling (Chapter 14) in their promotional mix, many also use a variety of promotional tools. Andersen Consulting uses high-profile television and magazine advertising and sponsors a major PGA golf tournament. Many business and trade sellers regularly have need for public relations, and most use direct mail to communicate with potential customers as a prelude to a personal selling call. Throughout the chapter, we have discussed the use of corporate Web sites as a way to communicate detailed information about a firm's offering in the business-to-business and business-to-government markets. Exhibit 2.14 is an example of a business organization, Instinet (http://www.instinet.com), communicating with securities brokers by using magazine advertising.

SUMMARY

① Discuss six important trends transforming the promotion industry.

Recent years have proven to be a period of dramatic change for the promotion industry. Many factors have propelled this change. Consumers' access to and greater control over information has made the communications process much more interactive between marketers and consumers. Cable television has increased its reach, and the growing popularity of direct-marketing programs and home shopping has diluted the impact of advertising delivered via mass media. Internet aggregators of radio and TV broadcasts and streaming video offer new hybrid media options for advertisers to consider. In addition to the growth and diversity of media, marketers have altered their budget allocations, with more funding going to sales promotion and event sponsorship and less to conventional advertising. These changes have contributed to the emphasis on integrated marketing communications.

② Describe the participants in the promotional communications process.

Many different types of organizations make up the promotion industry. To truly appreciate what promotion is all about, one must understand who does what and in what order in the creation and delivery of a promotional campaign. The process begins with an organization that has a message it wishes to communicate to a target audience. This is the marketer. Next, advertising and promotion agencies are typically hired to launch a campaign, but other external facilitators are often brought in to perform specialized functions, such as assisting in the production of materials or managing databases for efficient direct-marketing campaigns. These external facilitators also include consultants who work with marketers and their agencies in making promotional strategy decisions. All promotional campaigns must use some type of media and trade partners to reach target markets. Marketers and their agencies must therefore also work with companies that have media time or space to sell and establish partnerships with wholesalers, retailers, and Internet portal organizations.

③ Discuss the role played by advertising and promotion agencies, the services provided by these agencies, and how they are compensated.

Advertising and promotion agencies come in many varieties and offer diverse services to clients with respect to planning, preparing, and executing promotion campaigns. These services include market research and marketing planning, the actual creation and production of ad materials, the buying of media time or space for placement of the ads, and traffic management—keeping production on schedule. Some advertising agencies appeal to clients by offering a full array of services under one roof; others—such as creative boutiques—develop a particular expertise and win clients with their specialized skills. Promotion agencies specialize in one or more of the other forms of promotion beyond advertising. New media agencies are proliferating to serve the Internet needs of marketers. The four most prevalent ways to compensate an agency for services rendered are commission systems, markup charges, fee systems, and the new pay-for-results programs.

④ Identify key external facilitators who assist in planning and executing promotional campaigns for marketers.

Marketing and advertising research firms assist marketers and their agencies in understanding the market environment. Consultants of all sorts from marketing strategy through event planning and retail display are another form of external facilitator. Perhaps the most widely used facilitators are in the area of production of promotional materials. In advertising, a wide range of outside facilitators are used in the production of both broadcast and print advertising. In promotions, designers, and planners are called on to assist in creation and execution of promotional mix tools. Information intermediators fill a new role in the structure of the industry. These firms help manage the vast information on consumer preferences and purchasing behavior, particularly with respect to the Internet.

⑤ Discuss the role played by media organizations and trade partners in executing effective promotional programs.

Media organizations and trade partners are the essential link in delivering promotional communications to target audiences. There are traditional media organizations like television, radio, newspapers, and magazines. Interactive media options include not just the Internet but CD–ROM communications, electronic kiosks, and various other creative new media. Media conglomerates like AT&T and Viacom control several different aspects of the communications system from cable broadcast to Internet connections.

With respect to trade partners, the traditional channel partners, which include distributors, wholesalers, and retailers, are essential to carrying through on promotions that require in-store execution. These include coupons, premiums, price deals, sampling, and in-store displays. Nontraditional trade partners like business-to-business trade communities and large search engine portals are essential to reaching target audiences over the Internet.

KEY TERMS

trade reseller, 41
advertising agency, 42
full-service agency, 43
creative boutique, 43
interactive agency, 44
in-house agency, 44
media-buying service, 44
promotion agencies, 44
direct-marketing agency, 45
database agency, 45
direct-response agency, 45
fulfillment centers, 45

infomercial, 45
e-commerce agencies, 45
consumer sales promotions, 46
trade sales promotions, 47
event-planning agency, 47
designers, 47
logo, 47
public relations firm, 47
account services, 49
account planner, 49
creative services, 49
production services, 49

media-planning and -buying
   services, 50
commission system, 50
markup charge, 51
fee system, 51
pay-for-results, 51
external facilitators, 52
consultants, 52
production facilitators, 53
information intermediaries, 53
media organizations, 55
trade partners, 57

QUESTIONS FOR REVIEW AND CRITICAL THINKING

1. Describe why Leo Burnett lost several major clients and how the agency reinvented itself in response to changes in the promotional industry.

2. As cable-TV channels continue to proliferate and Web TV becomes a reality, how would you expect the promotion industry to be affected?

3. The U.S. Army spends millions of dollars each year trying to recruit young men and women. What forms of promotional communication would be best suited to this recruiting effort?

4. Huge marketers such as Procter & Gamble spend billions of dollars on advertising every year, yet they still rely on advertising agencies to prepare most of their ads. Why doesn't a big company like this just do all its own advertising in-house?

5. As marketers become more enamored with the idea of integrated marketing communications, why would it make sense for an advertising agency to develop a reputation as a full-service provider?

6. Explain the viewpoint that a commission-based compensation system may actually give ad agencies an incentive to do the wrong things for their clients.

7. Why would advertisers and their agencies be likely to call on external facilitators for expertise and assistance in producing promotional materials?

8. Give an example of how the skills of a public relations firm might be employed to reinforce the message that a sponsor is trying to communicate through other forms of promotion.

EXPERIENTIAL EXERCISES

1. **In-class exercise.** During a two-day period, observe and list all the media you come in contact with that carry promotional messages and offers. Which media are most suitable for local advertisers? Which medium do you think is most effective in reaching you? Which do you think is least effective? If you were planning to open a pizza restaurant, which promotional tools would you use and which media choices do you think would be best? Present your findings to the class and explain your reasoning.

2. **Out-of-class exercise.** Make an appointment with an account executive at an advertising or promotion agency in your city. Ask this person what he or she believes are the biggest challenges facing the promotion industry from his or her perspective. How does that perspective match the issues raised at the beginning of this chapter?

USING THE INTERNET

Exercise 1

Visit the following five sites:

Ogilvy & Mather
http://www.ogilvy.com

Modem Media. Poppe Tyson
http://www.poppe.com

Magnet Interactive
http://www.magnetinteractive.com

J. Walter Thompson
http://www.jwtworld.com

Proxicom
http://www.proxicom.com

For each site, answer these questions:

1. Is this a full-service advertising agency or a boutique that specializes in Internet advertising services?

2. What specific services does the firm offer? What is its client base?

3. Based on the Web site, what is the creative style of each firm?

4. If you were a company selling mountain bikes, which firm would you choose? Justify your choice based on your answers to the preceding questions.

Exercise 2

As with any other business, part of an advertising firm's Web strategy is to use its presence to attract customers (clients).

1. How do you think the agencies in the previous exercise attract "eyeballs" to their Web sites?

2. Are the agencies listed in all the places they should be, for example, in the correct categories on the Yahoo! site?

Use one or more of the search engines described in Chapter 1's Using the Internet section to search on one of the companies by name.

3. What sort of pages does your query find? How often are they official or authoritative content from the agency or its clients, for example, press releases—how often are they "mainstream" news, and what other sources did you encounter?

Use the "links to this URL" query described in Chapter 1's Using the Internet section to find the links to one of these agencies' sites.

4. Do agency clients often, seldom, or never mention the agency on their own Web sites?

After reading this chapter, you will be able to:

1 Describe the basic elements of a promotional plan.

2 Explain the way an organization makes the strategic decisions regarding which promotional tools to emphasize in a promotional campaign.

3 Discuss the difference between communications and sales objectives in promotional planning.

4 Explain the different methods for setting a budget for promotional spending.

5 Describe a model used for planning integrated marketing communications and understand the components of an IMC plan (appendix).

www.apple.com

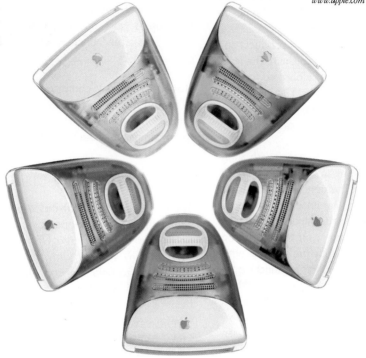

Collect all five.

Think different.™

The battle cry in all the advertising and promotion for Apple Computer as the new millennium approached was "Think Different." But it seemed that no one was listening. The once high-flying computer manufacturer was floundering in a PC/Windows onslaught. In June 1998, Apple's U.S. retail market share had fallen to a mere 2 percent.[1] The company that once had rocked the computer business with its innovative Macintosh computer and its provocative and landmark "1984" TV commercial was approaching virtual extinction.

The severity of the company's problems went well beyond the need for a fresh promotional campaign and a catchy slogan like "Think Different." Could Apple be saved? To rebound, it would need inspired leadership and, most important, a series of innovative new products and effective promotion to draw attention to them. The leadership would have to come from its celebrated founder and on-again/off-again CEO—Steve Jobs. The new product designed to salvage the company was the iMac personal computer. The promotional campaign was outstanding.

Steve Jobs decided to revive the company with an innovative new product launched by an integrated, comprehensive promotional campaign. The new product was designed under Jobs's supervision. The iMac was to be the first in a new generation of Internet appliances. As described by Jobs, "iMac lets anyone get on to the Internet quickly and easily." Regarding the introductory promotional campaign, Jobs went on to say, "We're launching this campaign because we want the world to know that iMac is the computer for the tens of millions of consumers who want to get to the Internet easily, quickly, and affordably."[2] Jobs was not just grasping at straws. The promotional planning process at Apple provided market research that showed one of consumers' primary motives for buying a personal computer was to hook up to the Internet.

As the new iMac was going on sale, Apple executives also announced the start of the largest promotional campaign in the history of the company. Paid media advertising costs alone were expected to run more than $100 million between August 15 and December 31, 1998. What follows are the key elements of the campaign:[3]

ADVERTISING

Television. National TV ads began August 16 on *The Wonderful World of Disney* and continued on programs such as *News Radio* and *The Drew Carey Show,* and on cable shows such as *South Park* and *Larry King Live.* Spot TV ads were also placed in the top ten metro markets in the U.S. Television ads began airing in Europe and Asia in September 1998.

Outdoor Billboards also went up in the top ten metro markets. As shown in Exhibit 3.1, they featured a photo of the iMac and one of the following copy lines: "Chic. Not geek"; "Sorry, no beige"; "Mental floss"; and "I think, therefore iMac."

Magazine An informative twelve-page iMac insert was distributed through leading magazines such as *Time, People, Sports Illustrated,* and *Rolling Stone.* Over 15 million copies were put in consumers' hands in the first few weeks after launch. Four pages from this insert are displayed in Exhibit 3.2.

Radio A five-day countdown to the iMac launch was executed through a network of twenty nationwide radio companies. Apple's was the most comprehensive radio campaign in the United States the week of August 10, 1998.

PROMOTIONS

Trade Partners Alliances Apple joined forces with its local retailers in cooperative advertising and promotional efforts around the United States. For example, the company worked with the New York dealer Data Visions Inc. to help sponsor iMac ads on movie screens in all 600 of Long Island's theaters. Other dealers participated in software and T-shirt giveaways, and CompUSA launched newspaper ads that for the first time promoted Apple products exclusively.

Web Site Features Of course, everything the world could ever want to know about the iMac and the iMac product launch was available at http://www.apple.com.

Sales Promotion In conjunction with the radio coverage, iMac giveaways were announced each day of the week preceding Midnight Madness opening of Apple retail shops on August 14.

PUBLIC RELATIONS

While the iMac went on sale August 14, 1998, its launch campaign was actually initiated three months before with extensive public relations activities:

1. Bradley Johnson, "Jobs Orchestrates Ad Blitz for Apple's New iMac PC," *Advertising Age,* August 10, 1998, 6.
2. "Apple Launches Its Largest Marketing Campaign Ever for iMac," accessed at http://www.apple.com/pr/library/ on January 20, 2000.
3. Ibid.

- Steve Jobs made a surprise unveiling of the machine before an audience of media types in the same auditorium where Macintosh was introduced. The iMac prototype was kept behind a veil on stage until he was ready to spring it on his unsuspecting audience. He stated at the time: "We figured we'd have a surprise and then let people feed on it before they could get it."[4]
- In the weeks leading up to August 14, Jobs's sneak preview had the desired effect of creating an iMac publicity buzz across Web sites frequently visited by loyal Mac users.
- Working with loyal retailers, Apple's PR people created 20-foot-high inflatable iMac balloons to fly above retail stores at the Midnight Madness event on August 14, 1998 (iMacs went on sale at 12:01 A.M.). A Cupertino, California, retailer added giant searchlights and delivered part of its midnight iMac inventory using four Volkswagen New Beetles on loan from a local dealer.
- Television crews from every station in the San Francisco Bay Area were there to cover the sale of the first iMacs in the United States, reporting it all to the world the next day. Summarizing the state of affairs at ground zero, one salesperson at a CompUSA Superstore in San Francisco said: "I don't think even Apple expected it to be this crazy; We're having trouble keeping iMacs on the shelves."[5]

Early reports suggested that the iMac promotional campaign had the kind of effect that Steve Jobs wanted. Without a doubt, the extensive use of promotional tools, managed in true IMC fashion, created renewed consumer interest in the Apple brand. Market research showed that iMac was winning over previous Windows users as well as households buying their first personal computer.[6] The weekend following the launch, Apple's retail channel was reporting massive demand and completely empty shelves.[7] By the end of 1998, Apple's share of the U.S. PC market had climbed from 3.4 percent to 4.5 percent.[8] And, by the end of 1999, its market share had reached about 6 percent of all U.S. PC shipments. Still only good enough for seventh place in the United States, but a far cry from the 2 percent market share of June 1998. And, in a true test of marketing strategy and promotion, profits at the firm had nearly doubled from the prior year to over $600 million. Now the company is holding secret meetings to plot its next era in the Internet appliance world.[9] No doubt another leap forward is in the offing.

EXHIBIT 3.1

The launch of the Apple iMac used a wide range of promotional tools to draw attention to the brand (again) and to announce this new product. Here, billboards were used as part of the advertising campaign.

4.   Jim Carlton, "From Apple, a New Marketing Blitz," *The Wall Street Journal,* August 14, 1998, B1.
5.   "iMac Makes a Midnight Debut," accessed at http://www.macweek.com on August 15, 1998.
6.   Jim Carlton, "Apple Reports Tripling in Profit: Sales Jump Is First in Three Years," *The Wall Street Journal,* January 14, 1999, B6.
7.   "Retailers Experience Record Consumer Demand for iMac," company press release, August 19, 1998.
8.   Brooke Crothers, "Surveys: World PC Shipments Rebound," CNET News.com, January 29, 1999, accessed at http://www.cnet.com/news on January 4. 2000.
9.   Brent Schlender, "Steve Jobs' Apple Gets Way Cooler," *Fortune,* January 24, 2000, 66–71.

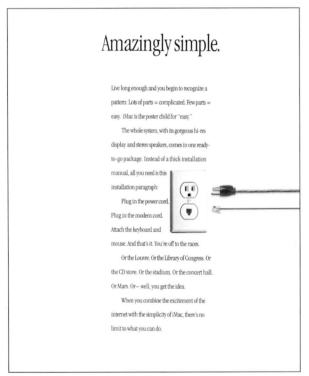

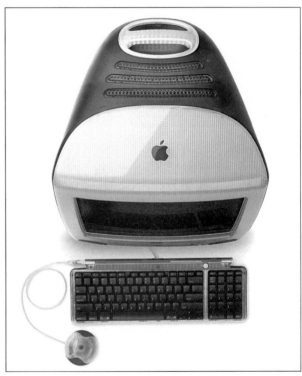

EXHIBIT 3.2

A key to the introduction of the iMac was to show its distinctive colors. Magazine advertising was well suited to this task and Apple used this multipage insert to get the message across.

INTRODUCTION

The launch of the iMac gives you some sense of the complexity—and importance—of executing a comprehensive promotional campaign designed and planned as an IMC effort. And it should be clear that you don't go out and spend over $100 million promoting a new product that is vital to the success of a firm without giving the entire endeavor considerable forethought.

In this chapter, we will consider the scope of the promotion and IMC process. First, we will look at the full range of elements that make up a promotional plan. Next, we will consider how firms decide which tools to emphasize in the promotional mix. This is where a company determines how much advertising to use relative to event sponsorship, sales promotions, personal selling, and so on. At this point, we will consider the way firms set objectives for the promotional effort. A key issue here is the difference between communications objectives and sales objectives. One of the most difficult and painstaking tasks for managers is setting the promotional budget. We will look at several alternatives for promotional budgeting. Finally, a complete model of integrated marketing communications will be presented as a tool for planning the IMC effort.

The first two chapters described the areas of promotion and IMC. In this chapter, we take on the challenge of planning the effort. The chapter is organized in a way that precisely replicates the planning sequence used by companies and their advertising and promotion agencies.

THE PROMOTION PLAN ❶

The promotion plan should be a direct extension of a firm's marketing plan. As the discussion in Chapter 1 stated explicitly, promotion is about building a brand and building the perception of a brand's value within the market. A statement of what the brand is supposed to stand for in the eyes of the target segment derives from the firm's marketing strategy, and will guide all promotional planning activities.

A **promotion plan** specifies the analysis, strategy, and tasks needed to conceive and implement an effective promotional effort. The iMac campaign illustrates the wide array of options that can be deployed in creating interest and communicating the value of a brand. Jobs and his agencies choreographed public relations activities; promotions and giveaways; cooperative, broadcast, and billboard advertising; Web site buzz; and blimps as part of the iMac launch. A promotion planner should review all the options before selecting an integrated set of promotional tools to communicate with the target market.

Exhibit 3.3 shows the components of a promotional plan. It should be noted that there is a great deal of variation in promotional plans from marketer to marketer. A manufacturing firm in the packaged goods business will likely have a promotional plan that is vastly different from a services marketer in the banking industry. But all the marketers discussed in Chapter 2 (review Exhibit 2.4) will need to produce a plan for using promotional tools and managing the tools. Our discussion will focus on the six major elements of a promotion plan:

- Executive summary and overview
- Situation analysis
- Objectives
- Budgeting
- Strategy
- Evaluation

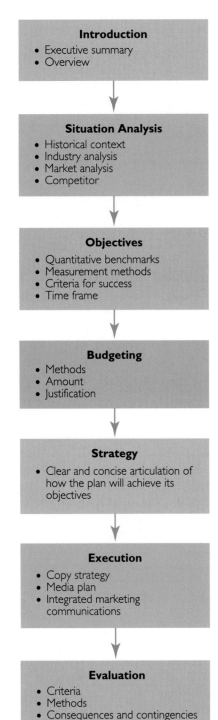

EXHIBIT 3.3

The stages of the promotion plan

Executive Summary and Overview

The introduction of a promotion plan consists of an executive summary and an overview. An **executive summary,** typically two paragraphs to two pages long, is offered to state the most important aspects of the plan. This is the take-away—that is, what the reader should remember from the plan. It is the essence of the plan.

As with many documents, an overview is also customary. An **overview** ranges in length from a paragraph to a few pages, sets out what is to be covered, and structures the context. All plans are different, and some require more of a setup than others. Don't underestimate the benefit of a good introduction. It's where you can make or lose a lot of points with your boss or client.

Situation Analysis ❷

A promotional plan **situation analysis** is where the marketer and agencies lay out the most important factors that define the situation facing the firm and then explain the importance of each factor.

An infinite list of potential factors internal and external to the firm define a situation analysis. But the key is to choose those few important factors that *really* describe the situation, and then explain how the factors relate to the promotion task at hand.

Let's say you represent American Express. How would you define the firm's current promotion situation? Think about how credit card marketing is influenced by the economic conditions of the day and the cultural beliefs about the proper way to display status. In the early eighties, it was acceptable for marketers to tout the self-indulgent side of plastic (for example, MasterCard's slogan "MasterCard, I'm bored"). Today, charge and credit card ads often point out just how prudent it is to use your card for the right reasons. Now, instead of just suggesting you use your plastic to hop off to the islands when you feel the first sign of boredom, credit card companies are far more likely to detail a few of the functional benefits of their cards, like the Citibank message in Exhibit 3.4 for its Visa and MasterCard. Notice that the card can rack up points for the purchase of a new car or frequent flier miles on several different airlines. The factors most commonly described in a situation analysis are considered in the following sections.

Demographic Trends. Basic demographic trends may be the single most important situational factor in promotion plans. Whether it's baby boomers or Generation X, Y, or Z, where the numbers are is usually where the sales are. As the population distribution varies with time, new markets are created and destroyed. The baby-boom generation of post–World War II disproportionately dictates consumer offerings and demand simply because of its size. As the boomers age, companies that offer the goods and services needed by tens of millions of aging boomers will have to devise new appeals. And what of the X'ers? Are the needs of the current twentysomethings fundamentally different from those of boomers? And what about Generations X, Y, and Z? How do we communicate to new consumers with different values and attitudes (see Exhibit 3.5). And, as discussed in the IMC in Practice box, the next great challenge for marketers will be finding effective ways to reach a new generation who are skeptical of media advertising.

http://www.citibank.com/us/cards/

EXHIBIT 3.4

A decade ago, credit card issuers would compete either on rates or on the solidity of their banks' good names. Today, cards are bundled with a variety of offers, and spun to fit any of a number of lifestyles or interests. Visit Citibank's site to see what they mean when they say, "A card for every purchase": The bank offers cards for cash back toward a new car, along with those granting frequent flyer miles, points toward Sony products, or monthly golf tips. Any wonder why American consumers have run up high personal debt? Too much going on to notice that they send bills as well!

EXHIBIT 3.5

Generation Y (today's teens) and Generation Z (today's preteens) are a massive market force with $27 billion of their own money to spend. But marketers have to reach them with not only the right message, but also the right attitude—like this one.

Historical Context. No situation is entirely new, but all situations are unique. Just how a firm arrived at the current situation is very important. Before trying to design Apple's iMac campaign, an agency should certainly know the history of all the principal players, the industry, the brand, the corporate culture, critical moments in the company's past, its big mistakes and big successes. All new decisions are situated in a firm's history, and the firm should be diligent in studying that history. For example, would a firm consider a promotional campaign for Green Giant without knowing something of the brand's history and the rationale behind using the Green Giant as an icon for the brand? The history of the Green Giant dates back decades. No matter what promotional decisions are made in the present, the past has a significant impact.

Industry Analysis. An **industry analysis** focuses on developments and trends within an industry. An industry analysis should describe factors that might affect the character and growth in an industry like technology, regulations, economic

GEN X WAS EASY COMPARED TO REACHING GENERATIONS Y AND Z

During the 1990s, everybody was pretty excited about Generation X. But consider Generation Y (today's teens) and Generation Z (today's preteens). First, Generations Y and Z have $27 billion of their own money to spend, and their disposable income is growing at a rate of 20 percent per year. Second, Y and Z, with both parents working or in single-parent families, are taking on more household responsibilities. Many times this includes doing the shopping for the family. Marketers know that brand familiarity established at a young age can turn into brand loyalty as that consumer ages. If you wait until they reach twentysomething, it may already be too late to start. And, third, there is the little matter of market size: Generation Y is projected to top out at 35 million consumers by 2010, making them a larger cohort than the aging baby boomers!

But here's the basic problem with respect to promotion and cultivating these new demographic target segments: these kids are very skeptical of traditional broadcast advertising, maybe because they are bombarded with so many marketing messages. Researchers estimate that Generation Z is exposed to 3,000 to 5,000 messages a week, compared to about 1,000 per week for Generation X at a similar life stage. Relying on the traditional broadcast media simply can't be enough with youthful and media-savvy consumers. But the future appears bright for the marketer who has learned how to capitalize on the interactive properties of the World Wide Web, especially for engaging Generation Z. While most marketers are still learning on this front, today's most popular Web sites with Generation Z—such as http://www.disney.com, http://www.zapme.com, and http://www.nick.com—provide some clues about what works.

Principle 1: You have to give young consumers more than text and pretty pictures; they want to be involved and build something or solve something or win something. *Principle 2:* Kids want to connect and be recognized. Herein lies the beauty of the Web as a promotional tool: Its infinite capacity for interactivity lets inventive marketers create games and contests that allow winners to be recognized and contestants to interact with one another. This is the power of the Web to engage your new consumer. And this may the promotional tool with the power to win over skeptical young consumers.

Source: David Vaczek, "Problem Children," *Promo*, July 1998, 37–46.

conditions, or social trends. For example, if you were designing promotion for Blockbuster Video, you might be concerned that movie rentals have been significantly lower industrywide. Are consumers watching fewer movies? The answer is actually no, they are not watching fewer movies. Rather, the industry and the channels through which consumers are acquiring movies is changing. Film distributors are discovering that they can make more money by selling films directly to the public at deeply discounted prices. Also, satellite distribution of movies is cutting directly into sales at video rental chains. There is also the problem of changing home technologies. What if the new DVD completely wipes out the inferior videocassette?

Or what if new cable rules allow distribution of films through the Internet? (More on this in Chapter 6.)

Certainly these issues have an impact on the long-term future of companies like Blockbuster, but even in the short term they have meaning. If you're Blockbuster, you want someone to come up with a promotional plan that slows or reduces this trend. You want your agencies to figure out what is unique about going to a video store. Maybe it means more integrated promotion efforts, such as tie-ins with fast-food restaurants and toy stores, appearances by celebrities, or a chance to win tickets to a sporting event. One thing is clear—you can't ignore the trends in an industry, no matter what industry you are in.

Market Characteristics. Characteristics of the market within which communication will take place is an important influencing factor on decision making. The effect of the external environment is unavoidable in all areas of marketing. With respect to promotional mix strategy decisions, three influences from the market will have a primary effect on promotional planning: type of consumer, geographic considerations, and competition.

Type of Customer. Depending on which of the three basic customer groups—household consumers, business buyers, or the trade—a firm needs to communicate with, there will be a different emphasis among the promotional mix tools. Typically, the business buyer and members of the distribution channel are more knowledgeable and more price and service oriented. The individualized communication provided by personal selling best addresses the needs of these types of customers.

The household consumer, on the other hand, often needs to be reached through a much broader combination of promotional tools. The large number of potential buyers spread across a wide geographic area make advertising a logical choice. Consumer tendencies to comparison shop in some product categories call personal selling and the Web into play. The growing demand for convenience in the consumer market, increased access to cable television, and a continued willingness to accumulate credit card debt makes direct marketing a legitimate choice.

Trade buyers are a critical link in the marketing and promotion process. Unless we can convince the buyers at Wal-Mart or Costco or whichever trade partner we desire that our brand is worth selling, the consumer will never have access. Trade buyers need personal selling and Web access to brand ordering. Personal selling can take place either with a site visit, trade show displays, or telemarketing.

Many firms deal with more than one of the customer types for every product they sell. Colgate-Palmolive, for example, has a broad line of consumer products. It spends nearly $450 million annually on media advertising to communicate with household consumers. Colgate must also stimulate demand within the distribution trade. It directs a considerable amount of money and effort in its promotional mix at wholesalers and retailers through personal selling and sales promotions.

Geographic Considerations. Emphasis in the promotional mix can vary greatly depending on the local, regional, national, or international scope of the firm's market. As the scope of the market broadens, more emphasis will be placed on advertising just to reach target markets. As regional variations enter the marketing plan, promotions can be implemented that are uniquely tailored to regional differences. Local retailers will rely heavily on advertising in local media and promotions that have limited geographic reach. Of course, the Internet allows marketers to reach any market, even a global market, with relative ease.

Competition. Competitors' strategies cannot be ignored as the promotional mix is being devised. This is not to say that firms copy each other's promotional strategies. But in many industries, firms tend to come to the same conclusions with regard to the use of promotional mix options. Each competitor often recognizes the same influences. However, a strategic maneuver by one competitor may force all the others to follow suit. For example, one competitor may suddenly increase advertising in a business target market with heavy geographic concentration—a condition that would normally dictate heavy reliance on personal selling. To meet such a competitive thrust, the other firms in the industry are likely to follow suit.

Product Characteristics.

The product or service a firm is promoting is an overriding consideration in promotional mix decision making. The effect here comes from fundamental characteristics of the product rather than from specific differences between brands. These fundamental characteristics are the product category and stage in the product life cycle.

Product category. One of the most informative considerations for determining the weight of each variable in the promotional mix is the product category of the item. Convenience goods, shopping goods, specialty goods, and services in the consumer market require a different blend of variables in the promotional mix.

Convenience goods, which are frequently purchased and simple items characterized by brand switching, have broad demographic and geographic market

CAREERPROFILE

Name:	*Tara Zanecki*
Title:	*Director of Marketing*
Company:	*Massive Media Group, Santa Monica, California*
	http://www.massivemediagroup.com
Education:	*B.A., Mass Communications*

Tara Zanecki loves the challenge of helping new high-tech firms launch successful marketing programs. "In a traditional company, it can take ages to get marketing decisions made, but in a start-up they have to be made right away," she says.

Massive Media Group's goal is to develop new ways for entertainment firms to protect their copyrights on content sold over the Internet. "It's a new business model," says Tara. "A huge part of my job is crafting the messages we'll use both externally and internally."

She began by interviewing the firm's founders about their vision for Massive Media. "I spent about 45 minutes with each person trying to get a sense of how they thought we should portray the company and what we do," says Tara. "Our goal is to be the 'thought leader' in the minds of entertainment and advertising executives looking to protect their content on the Internet. We want to be the first name they think of," she says.

Like most start-ups, Massive Media's initial promotion budget is tight. "We'll only be doing limited advertising. Most of our promotion will be public relations based," says Tara. "Cost-wise, it's a much cheaper method than advertising. Exposure-wise, it will also give us the most benefits at this stage."

The Internet will also be a promotional tool. "You really have to plan out what you want your Web site to convey and how it will fit with your other promotional efforts. We want our image and our message to be reflected in our site," she says. To accomplish this, Tara is planning to put value-added information like research, statistics, and news on the firm's site.

Massive Media is the third start-up Tara has worked for, and she doubts it will be the last. Her advice to students hoping to land a job like hers? "Get as much real-world experience from internships and part-time jobs as you can before you graduate."

To learn more about developing promotional plans for start-up firms, visit these Web sites:

Silicon Valley Small Business Development Center
http://www.siliconvalley-sbdc.org

Bplans.com
http://www.bplans.com/marketing.htm

Guerilla Marketing
http://www.gmarketing.com

Entrepreneur Magazine
http://www.entrepreneurmag.com

segments. All the packaged goods in your grocery store—like toothpaste, shampoo, or dog food—are convenience goods. Promotion for convenience goods relies on advertising and sales promotion because consumers are unable to make an extensive judgment of these products at the point of purchase (the store managers hate it when you tear open a bag of cookies and sample them!). In contrast, **shopping goods,** which are higher priced and full of features—like automobiles, televisions, and clothes—would require a different mix of promotional tools. Shopping goods need advertising to create brand awareness, but there is a greater emphasis on personal selling because of higher price, complexity, and the fact that consumers comparison shop and judge the product at the point of purchase. **Specialty goods** are high-priced luxury goods where consumers seek out brand names. Designer clothes and expensive watches are examples of specialty goods. The emphasis on brand name in the specialty goods category reduces the usefulness of sales promotion in this category. However, because of the exclusive nature of distribution, advertising is often needed to identify for consumers' outlets where the product can be obtained.

Services often require the combined use of advertising and personal selling. Advertising is used to inform consumers of the availability of the service. Personal selling is used because most services are tailored to each consumer's specific needs. Sales promotions are often used because of the intense competition in service products, and discounts often allow customers to try a new service provider at reduced risk. Often you will see ads for service organizations, such as carpet cleaning services, where advertising is used to reach customers, a free estimate is offered (personal selling), and the ad also contains a coupon for a discount (sales promotion).

The promotional mix for business goods relies more heavily on personal selling for several reasons already mentioned. Higher unit cost, larger order size, fewer and more educated customers, customization, and support services all warrant a greater reliance on personal selling. Sales promotions are also widely used. Trade show demonstrations, premiums, and dealer contests help attract the attention of business buyers.

Stage in the Product Life Cycle. As you recall from your introductory marketing class, every product passes through several stages of market development. During each stage, promotional requirements change. In the introductory state, the need for personal selling is acute as the firm tries to gain acceptance for the product in the trade channel. Also, at this stage, advertising may be used to stimulate **primary demand** (demand for the entire product category, not just the brand). Advertising will continue to be dominant through the growth stage as selective demand stimulation for a brand begins. The middle stages of the life cycle will see a decline in emphasis on personal selling as the members of the trade have already been cultivated. The middle stages will also see periodic heavy emphasis on sales promotion. In these stages, firms make minor alterations in differentiation and positioning strategy, and coupons and contests may be used to attract attention to the brand. During the maturity stage and especially during the decline stage, sales promotions become prominent and advertising is usually minimized. The goal here is to clear out inventories and reduce promotional costs.

Characteristics of the Firm. The nature of the promotional mix is also influenced by a variety of factors internal to the firm. In many cases, firms will be using promotional mix strategies that seem totally inappropriate given the nature of the external environment and characteristics of the product. The explanation for these somewhat unusual promotional mix decisions usually lies with influences unique to the characteristics of the firm itself.

Push (vs.) pull strategy. Reliance on the tools in the promotional mix varies greatly depending on whether a firm decides to use a push or pull promotional strategy. The most common is a **push strategy,** where a manufacturer promotes the product to wholesalers and distributors, who then promote the product to retailers, who in turn use promotional tools to communicate with consumers. When promotion is used within the channel of distribution in this fashion, it is said to be "pushed" through the channel to the consumer. Manufacturers and wholesalers/distributors primarily use personal selling and sales promotion, whereas retailers use the full range of promotional tools. In a **pull strategy,** a marketer uses advertising to stimulate demand among consumers, who then demand the product from retailers, who in turn demand it from wholesalers, who then order it from the manufacturer. In this situation, consumers "pull" the product through the channel. Exhibit 3.6 graphically depicts the difference between a push and a pull strategy. In a push strategy, personal selling and trade sales promotions dominate the promotional mix. A pull strategy most often relies on advertising to directly communicate with consumers. In recent years, pharmaceutical firms have advertised prescription drugs directly to consumers (referred to in the industry as DTC) in an effort to pull the drugs through the distribution channel. By 1999, big drug companies were spending $2 billion a year on advertising to encourage consumers to "ask your doctor" about various prescription drugs.[10]

Funds Available. A lack of funds available for promotion can dictate a heavy reliance on personal selling, trade shows, and a Web site. When a firm is strapped for funds, it is more feasible to maintain a sales force that works on commission, pay a small fee for a trade show booth, or maintain a Web site for a few thousand dollars than to undertake expensive advertising campaigns. With limited funds, a firm can deploy a sales staff and try to cultivate wholesaler and retailer support. Also, the sales staff can be used to set up and service dealer displays and attend trade shows. Web sites can, of course, be accessed by potential customers from anywhere at any time. Web

10. Kathryn Kranhold, "Drug Makers Prescribed Direct Mail Pitch," *The Wall Street Journal,* December 16, 1999, B16.

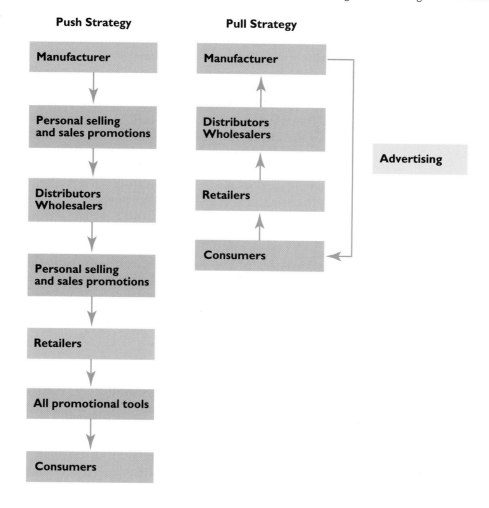

Push Strategy

Pull Strategy

Manufacturer

Personal selling
and sales promotions

Distributors
Wholesalers

Personal selling
and sales promotions

Retailers

All promotional tools

Consumers

Manufacturer

Distributors
Wholesalers

Retailers

Consumers

Advertising

EXHIBIT 3.6

Manufacturers will use a different promotional mix for a "push" versus a "pull" strategy. This graphic shows that various promotional tools are used when a brand is pushed through the distribution system to the end user. Conversely, when a brand is pulled through the distribution system, advertising is a dominant force in the promotional mix.

sites also do not need an extensive staff to maintain them, although timely updates are critical.

Size of the Sales Staff. When an organization has a relatively small sales staff, it may rely on other forms of promotion or on members of the trade for promotional support. A small sales staff severely constrains a firm's ability to effectively reach all customers. One common solution is to deploy a small sales staff to trade shows rather than calling on individual customers. Another is to use direct response advertising to generate sales leads. Sales promotion and direct marketing are used to bolster the weakness in the sales staff. The same is true when a firm has a competitively inferior sales staff. Certainly, no organization wants to carry on for very long knowing its sales staff is inadequate. However, the talent available in some industries can be so limited that firms often have to accept the fact that areas other than personal selling will be emphasized until the sales force can be bolstered in either size or capability.

Extent of the Firm's Product Line. When a firm has a broad and deep product line, the nature of the promotional mix changes in several ways. Extensive product lines lighten the personal selling task at the wholesale and retail levels because the efficiency of the firm's sales staff is greatly increased when each staff member has several items to sell. Also, depending on the branding strategy, advertising efficiency can be greatly enhanced. Using any of several "family" branding strategies, where every product in the line carries the same brand name, means that communication about each brand in the line will automatically promote all the other brands in the line. Finally, joint brand efforts in couponing and in-store displays are feasible with an extensive product line.

Characteristics of the Distribution System.
Marketing mix strategies related to the distribution system have direct bearing on the promotional mix. Three types of distribution decisions will affect the promotional mix configuration: the intensity of distribution, length of the trade channel, and types of trade partners.

Intensity of Distribution. The total number of trade distributors and retailers that carry a product affects promotional strategy; this is referred to as the **intensity of distribution. Intensive distribution** places the brand in as many different types of outlets as possible. Convenience goods are intensively distributed. The more intensely (extensively) a product is distributed, the more advertising can be used to presell the product before a consumer contacts the distribution outlet. Recall our earlier discussion of convenience goods that are intensively distributed. The wider the distribution and the less complicated a product is, the more advertising is a necessary tool in the promotional mix.

When a more **selective distribution** strategy is used, retailers have a vested interest in generating store traffic for an item, and cooperative efforts, like sales promotions, with the manufacturing firm are more common. Also, retailers will use personal selling at the point of purchase for selectively distributed products like washing machines and stereo products. Products that are distributed on a highly restrictive basis (**exclusive distribution**) need advertising to inform consumers where they can be purchased. This type of distribution is typically reserved for the specialty goods described earlier.

Length of the Trade Channel. "Length" in trade channel terminology is not measured in physical distance. Rather, **channel length** refers to the number of levels of distribution a product passes through before it reaches the end user. As more levels are used in the distribution strategy, channel length increases. A channel that includes sales agents, distributors, and retailers is a "long" channel. A channel where a consumer accesses a Web site, orders with a credit card, and gets FedEx delivery is a short channel. One common effect of channel length on the promotional mix is an increased need for personal selling as there are more levels in a channel. Each level of the channel will need promotion to "push" the brand to the next level. Firms need to try to gain tighter control over distributors, wholesalers, and retailers and will deploy salespeople to help manage a long channel.

The shortest channel strategy, which distributes the brand directly to the end user, will rely on either personal selling or direct-marketing techniques. Advertising is often employed in short channels as a supportive effort to create a favorable predisposition. Avon, Century 21 Real Estate, and Charles Schwab Discount Brokerage are examples of firms that use short channels and support the personal selling effort with mass media advertising. Every dot-com company has a short channel, and we have seen the extensive use of mass media to support their marketing efforts.

Types of Trade Partners. The types of distributors, wholesalers, and retailers used in the channel change the promotional plan and strategy. Wholesalers with large sales staffs and complete delivery and installation services relieve the marketer of the

©1997 Mercedes-Benz of North America, Inc., Montvale, N.J., Member of the Daimler-Benz Group.

Love

EXHIBIT 3.7

A key objective for promotion is creating and maintaining the image of a brand. Mercedes-Benz has masterfully developed and maintained an image of quality and luxury over many years and in very creative ways.

responsibility for stimulating demand at the retail level. If a firm chooses lower-cost wholesalers who do not provide promotion and service, the firm itself will have to design a promotional mix to cultivate retail support.

At the retail level, the type of retail outlet carrying the product has a pervasive effect on promotional strategy. In some cases, the retailer will be the dominant force in the promotional program. This is especially true in product categories where retailers are typically better known than the manufacturers, such as in the furniture and plumbing fixtures product categories. Another important consideration at the retail level is the amount of in-store personal selling that retailers provide. Many self-service retailers, like Costco, carry the same items as full-service department stores. Products like home entertainment items and hardware items are examples. The more a retailer is self-service oriented, the more the manufacturer must presell items to consumers through advertising. As the retail outlet provides more communication at the point of purchase through personal selling, the marketer can rely on this communication to consumers and adjust the promotional mix strategy accordingly.

Objectives

Promotional objectives lay the framework for the subsequent executions in a promotional campaign and take many different forms. Objectives identify the goals of a marketer in concrete, measurable terms. The marketer, more often than not, has more than one objective for a campaign. Common promotional objectives include the following:

1. To create and maintain an image for a brand.
2. To increase consumer awareness of and curiosity about a brand.
3. To change consumers' beliefs or attitudes about a brand.
4. To influence the purchase intention for a brand.
5. To stimulate trial use of a brand.
6. To convert one-time product users into repeat purchasers.
7. To switch consumers from a competing brand.
8. To encourage brand loyalty.
9. To stimulate more frequent use.
10. To increase sales.

We'll discuss each of these objectives briefly in the following paragraphs. Realize that a marketer may have more than one objective for a single promotional campaign. For example, a swimwear company may state its promotional objectives as follows: to maintain the company's brand image as the market leader in adult female swimwear and to increase trial use by males of a new product line.

Creating an image for a brand is perhaps the most sustainable and important long-term objective set by marketers. Recall from Chapter 1 the important role played by promotion in successfully establishing the brand in the mind of consumers. **Brand image** is the perception of a brand held by consumers. Of course, all marketers strive for a positive brand image. A positive and clear brand image is one of the most valuable assets a marketer can have. Because images are based mainly on emotional appeals, it is very difficult for competitors to knock a competitor out of an image position. The competitors typically must take up a different position based on a different set of perceptions by consumers. Advertising is the main staple of image development in promotion. Mercedes-Benz has been outstanding at developing an image of quality and luxury and maintaining that brand image with advertising (see Exhibit 3.7).

IBM COMBS THE GLOBE FOR E-BUSINESS

When is a computer not just a computer? Well, in IBM's way of thinking about things, that would be when a computer is an e-business tool. Faced with potent competitors such as Compaq, Hewlett-Packard, and Dell, IBM needed a way to reposition its laptops and PCs to accelerate its sales. Building on its own much-mimicked e-business concept, it was logical for IBM to pursue a repositioning of these products as e-business tools. The marketing strategy was to launch a revamped product line designed specifically to help companies get on the Internet and other networks to boost their business. A carefully orchestrated ad campaign could help consumers see IBM computers in this new light.

The e-business campaign was launched with extravagant eight-page inserts in various national newspapers. This was followed by giant IBM posters plastered on construction sites, in airports, and in subway stations in major metropolitan markets, along with magazine and TV ads and the ever-present Web site promotion. To add a touch of style and grace to its campaign, IBM employed a photographer who previously specialized in glamour shots for Clinique cosmetics. These stylish black-and-white photos of products such as the IBM ThinkPad were a common element throughout the various media used in this repositioning campaign.

How much to spend on a campaign to promote e-business tools around the world? This yearlong global campaign was funded at the $100-million level. Gee, $100 million here and $100 million there, and all of a sudden you're talking about some real money. IBM spends on the order of $750 million dollars each year on advertising.

Source: Raju Narisetti, "IBM Blitz to Introduce E-Business Tools," *The Wall Street Journal*, April 15, 1998, B4.

Creating or maintaining brand awareness and interest is a popular promotional objective. **Brand awareness** is an indicator of consumer knowledge about the existence of the brand and how easily that knowledge can be retrieved from memory. Advertising, with its broad reach through mass media and superior creative execution using color, action, and sound, is ideally suited for creating and maintaining brand awareness and interest. For example, a marketer might ask a consumer to name five brands of fast food. **Top-of-the-mind awareness** is represented by the brand recalled first. Ease of retrieval from memory is important because for many goods or services, it is predictive of market share. Awareness was important to IBM as the Global Issues box describes.

Beliefs are the knowledge and feelings people accumulate about an object (brand) or issue. For example, you may believe that FedEx is the most reliable next-day delivery service or that Saturn has a no-pressure sales environment. You may believe that gingivitis is the scourge of the Western world, and no one is safe from it. These are all important beliefs for marketers to understand in their respective product categories. In the case of Crest or any other toothpaste that promises to prevent gingivitis, the idea that this disease is prevalent is important when setting promotional objectives.

Creating or changing attitudes is another popular promotional objective. An **attitude** is defined as an overall evaluation of an object (brand), person, or issue. Attitudes vary along a continuum from positive to negative or favorable to unfavorable. One way to go about changing people's attitudes is to give them new information designed to alter their beliefs. Alternatively, attitude change may be pursued by consistently associating one's brand with other likable objects or settings to effect a direct change in liking. Information-dense ads are designed to change attitudes by first altering beliefs, whereas entertaining ads are designed to influence attitudes through direct affect transfer. And even for an information-intensive service such as a mutual fund, there are times when the most prudent advertising goal is to build brand awareness and make your fund more likable by using entertaining or humorous advertising. In 1998 there were 8,900 different mutual funds being marketed to U.S. consumers.[11] Similarly, the world of e-trading in stocks and bonds has produced dozens of competitors. If your advertising and promotion can attract attention and make your brand likeable, your chances of success greatly increase (see Exhibit 3.8). We will discuss both beliefs and attitudes as a basis for promotional objectives in Chapter 6.

Purchase intent is another popular criterion in setting objectives. **Purchase intent** is determined by asking consumers whether they intend to buy a product or

Trying to make money is only half the fun.
No...that's pretty much it.

Everyone likes money, that's why you invest. And that's why E·TRADE® gives you the tools you need to make better investing decisions. From market insights directly off the street to Smart Alerts that keep tabs on your investments. And at E·TRADE, you never have to spend your precious money on high commissions. Trades start as low as $4.95† with active investor rebate. For more information, visit etrade.com or call us at 1-800-ETRADE-

It's time for
E✳TRADE

http://www.etrade.com http://www.ameritrade.com

http://www.datek.com

WEB SIGHTING

EXHIBIT 3.8

If an advertisement can create good feelings, it may affect attitude toward the brand positively. That would seem to be the whole idea behind this ad for E✳Trade. Online stock brokerages like E✳Trade, Ameritrade, and Datek Online are all scrambling to sign up millions of new traders, and using imagery such as this—putting Joe Consumer into the adrenaline rush of the Wall Street trading floor—is a powerful hook. But how much do these services differ in what they offer?

11.   Vanessa O'Connell, "Alliance Capital Tries to Spice Up Funds with Offbeat TV Spots," *The Wall Street Journal,* March 25, 1998, B8.

service in the near future. The appeal of influencing purchase intent is that intent is closer to actual behavior, and thus closer to the desired sale, than are attitudes. While this makes sense, it does presuppose that consumers can express their intentions with a reasonably high degree of reliability. Sometimes they can, sometimes they cannot. Purchase intent, however, is fairly reliable as an indicator of relative intention to buy, and it is, therefore, a worthwhile promotional objective.

Trial usage reflects actual behavior and is commonly used as a promotional objective. Many times, the best that we can ask of promotion is to encourage the consumer to try our brand once. At that point, the brand must live up to the expectations of the consumer for providing satisfaction. In the case of new products, stimulating trial usage is critically important. Coupons, trial offers, sampling, and premium packs all stimulate trial use.

The **repeat purchase** objective is aimed at the percentage of consumers who try a new product and then purchase it a second time. A second purchase is reason for great rejoicing. The odds of long-term product success go way up when this percentage is high. In-package coupons are the best way marketers have discovered to increase the probability of repeat purchase. Of course, the greatest impact on repeat purchase comes from the performance of the brand in the hands of the consumer.

Brand switching as a promotional objective focuses on encouraging users of competitive brands to switch to the marketer's brand. In some brand categories like toothpaste and potato chips, switching is commonplace, even the norm. In others it is rare. When setting a brand-switching promotional objective, the marketer must neither expect too much nor rejoice too much over a temporary gain. Persuading consumers to switch brands can be a long and arduous task. To encourage immediate brand switching, marketers typically will use low-price sales, contests and sweepstakes, coupons, and giveaways.

Encouraging brand loyalty is at the other end of the continuum from brand switching. A **brand loyalty** objective is designed to retain current users as regular buyers of the marketer's brand. It is really too much to ask that a consumer never switch brands. Brand loyalty is considered extremely high if a marketer can retain a buyer three or four times out of five purchases. Images developed by advertising, frequency programs, event sponsorships, and multipacks are ways of encouraging brand loyalty.

Similar to the brand loyalty objective is increasing the frequency of use. **Increasing the frequency of use** encourages consumers to use a brand they already use more often. The Sun-Kist orange juice campaign with the slogan "Orange Juice Isn't Just for Breakfast Anymore" encouraged orange juice drinkers to drink the juice as a snack drink instead of soda. In an innovative campaign that combines brand switching, brand loyalty, and frequency of use, American Express is offering to give away free Friday nights at several participating hotels when you use your American Express card to pay for five nights (see Exhibit 3.9).

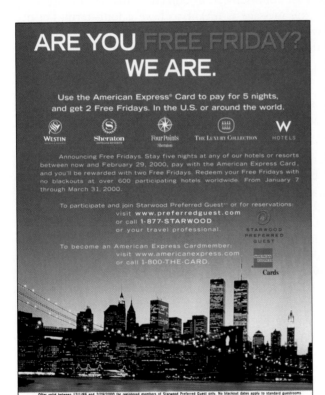

EXHIBIT 3.9

Increasing the frequency of use of a brand is a common promotional objective. Here, American Express is using a giveaway of free Friday night stays if you use your American Express Card to pay for five other nights. A classic example of trying to increase the frequency of use of a brand.

Communications Versus Sales Objectives. ③ Note that the tenth common objective listed is "to increase sales." Some analysts argue that as a single variable in a firm's overall marketing mix, it is not reasonable to set sales expectations for promotion when other variables in the mix might undermine the promotional effort. That is, good promotion cannot overcome a bad product, bad pricing, or bad distribution that might be preventing sales from happening. While this is true, some promotional tools are better designed for communication and others move consumers very close to—and are actually related to—closing a sale.

It is worth discussing when communications is the proper emphasis for promotional objectives and when sales can be used. In a well-articulated statement, Don Schultz and Beth Barnes see it this way [brackets added]:

[T]he marketing organization is trying to either deliver a message [communications] or deliver an incentive [sales] to the customer or prospect. From the consumer's view, this idea is quite simple: either the marketer wants the consumer to understand and store away something about its product or service, which would constitute a message, or the marketer wants the consumer to do something with regard to the product or service, generally within a specific time frame, which would be an incentive.[12]

When we say that firms will set communication objectives that are not focusing on sales, we mean simply that the message is meant to have a long-term, positive developmental effect on receivers and will focus on communications goals. A few examples of how communications objectives would be stated are:

- Increase the awareness of the brand name to 40 percent of all consumers in the western United States.
- Create trial use by 15 percent of all teenagers aged thirteen to fifteen.
- Communicate superior brand performance features to the target audience with a series of advertisements over the next six months.

From the standpoint of communications objectives, advertising, public relations, and event sponsorship would be best suited to the task. These tools in the promotional mix create awareness of a brand, communicate brand features or availability, or develop a favorable attitude that can lead to consumer preference for a brand. Conversely, sales promotions, direct marketing, point-of-purchase (P–O–P), and personal selling are all out to create an incentive for the consumer to buy—a sales objective.

The main problem that keeps cropping up with the communications versus sales issue is that marketers keep wanting to state advertising objectives in sales terms rather than communications terms. The desire by organizations to tie their advertising effort to sales is certainly understandable. After all, the average person assumes a fairly direct relationship between advertising and sales. With more and more emphasis on accountability in spending, firms are scrutinizing budgets and the performance of all aspects of the marketing program, including advertising.

Despite all the compelling arguments to maintain a heavy emphasis on communications, firms still have a keen eye trained on sales. And this is where the other variables in the promotional mix should come into play. Direct marketing (especially direct response), e-commerce strategies, coupons, and P–O–P displays are very close to the sales decision. Granted, a bad price, poor distribution, and a poor product will all still override the effect of a promotion. But the essence of these other promotional techniques is much closer to sales than advertising is. Finally, the personal selling effort in the promotional mix is, indeed, directly related to sales. Unless a firm has designated the sales force program as a missionary (nonselling) effort, then sales objectives should, by all means, be set for sales force performance.

12.   Don E. Schultz and Beth E. Barnes, *Strategic Brand Communication Campaigns* (Lincolnwood, IL: NTC Business Books, 1999), 70–71.

As you can see, while there is a natural tension between those who advocate sales objectives and those who push communications objectives, nothing precludes a marketer from using both categories when developing and managing a promotional effort. Indeed, combining sales objectives such as market share and household penetration with communication objectives such as awareness and attitude change can be an excellent means of motivating and evaluating a promotional campaign.[13] When Mead Johnson pharmaceuticals turned to RTCdirect to help with the promotion for Enfamil infant formula, the agency came up with a program that had both communications and sales objectives. RTCdirect created a campaign where new mothers received literature and coupons via direct mail, were offered a 24-hour hotline, and a Web site was developed to help them with their new role as mom.[14] This campaign had both measurable communications (the hotline and Web site) and sales (coupons) objectives.

Characteristics of Workable Promotional Objectives. Objectives that allow a firm to make intelligent decisions about resource allocation must be stated in terms that make sense. Articulating such well-stated objectives is easier when promotion planners do the following:

- *Establish a quantitative benchmark.* Objectives for promotion are measurable only in the context of quantifiable variables. Promotion planners should begin with quantified measures of the current status of market share, awareness, attitude, repeat purchase, or any other factor that promotion is expected to influence. The measurement of effectiveness in quantitative terms requires a knowledge of the level of variables of interest *before* a promotional effort, and then afterward. For example, a statement of objectives might be "Increase the market share of heavy users of the product category using our brand from 22 to 25 percent." In this case, a quantifiable and measurable market share objective is specified.
- *Specify measurement methods and criteria for success.* It is important that the factors being measured are directly related to the objectives being pursued. It is of little use to try to increase the awareness of a brand with advertising and then judge the effects based on changes in sales. If changes in sales are expected, then measure sales. If increased awareness is the goal, a change in consumer awareness is the only legitimate measure of success. This may seem obvious, but in a classic study of advertising objectives, it was found that claims of success for advertising were unrelated to the original statements of objective in 69 percent of the cases studied.[15] A recent complication for measurement comes from the Web and other interactive media. The interactive media have presented a substantial challenge with respect to establishing success criteria.[16] Fortunately, these measurement factors are being worked out and are covered in detail in Chapter 15.
- *Specify a time frame.* Objectives for promotion should include a statement of the period of time allowed for the desired results to occur. In some cases, as with direct-response advertising, the time frame may be immediate or perhaps a 24-hour period. For communications-based objectives, the measurement of results may not even be possible until the end of an entire multiweek campaign. The point is that the time period for accomplishing an objective and the measurement period must be stated in advance in the promotion plan.

---

13. John Philip Jones, "Advertising's Crisis of Confidence," *Marketing Management,* vol. 2, no. 1 (1993), 15–24.
14. Rebecca Gardyn, "Relationships Rule at D.C. Direct Shop," *Advertising Age,* October 11, 1999, 46.
15. Stewart Henderson Britt, "Are So-Called Successful Advertising Campaigns Really Successful?" *Journal of Advertising Research,* vol. 9 (1969), 5.
16. Sally Beatty, "P&G, Rivals and Agencies Begin Attempt to Set On-Line Standards," *The Wall Street Journal,* August 24, 1998, B6.

These criteria for setting objectives help ensure that the planning process is organized and well directed. As in all things, however, moderation is a good thing. A single-minded obsession with watching the numbers can be dangerous in that it minimizes or entirely misses the importance of qualitative and intuitive factors.

Budgeting ④

One of the most agonizing tasks is budgeting the funds for a promotional effort. Firms like IBM and Nokia routinely spend hundreds of millions of dollars on promotion. Within a firm, budget recommendations typically come up through the ranks, from a brand manager to a category manager and ultimately to the executive in charge of marketing. The sequence then reverses itself for the allocation and spending of funds. In a small firm, such as an independent retailer, the sequence just described may include only one individual who plays all the roles. Each of the major promotional mix areas has somewhat different ways in which budgets can be determined. First, we'll look at the basic methods for budgeting; then we'll consider the unique budgeting issues for each promotional mix tool.

Budgeting Methods. To appreciate the benefits (and failings) of each method, we will consider them separately. Each of these budgeting methods can be applied to all the promotional mix tools. We cover the tools separately so you can see the items typically charged against each area:

Percentage of Sales. A **percentage-of-sales approach** to budgeting calculates a budget based on a percentage of the prior year's sales or the projected year's sales. This technique is easy to understand and operationalize. The budget decision makers merely specify that a particular percentage of either last year's sales or the current year's estimated sales will be allocated to the promotion process. It is common to spend between 2 and 12 percent of sales on promotion.

While simplicity is certainly an advantage in decision making, the percentage-of-sales approach is fraught with problems. First, when a firm's sales are decreasing, the promotion budget will automatically decline. Periods of decreasing sales may be precisely the time when a firm needs to increase spending on promotion; if a percentage-of-sales budgeting method is being used, this won't happen. Second, this budgeting method can easily result in overspending on promotion. Once funds have been earmarked, the tendency is to find ways to spend them. Third, the most serious drawback from a strategic standpoint is that the percentage-of-sales approach does not relate promotion dollars to overall promotional objectives. Basing spending on past or future sales just doesn't make sense. It implicitly presumes a direct cause-and-effect relationship between promotion and sales in all instances, which we know is not true, particularly for promotional efforts with long-term image objectives.

Unit of Sales. A variation on the percentage-of-sales approach that firms may use is the **unit-of-sales approach,** which simply allocates a specified dollar amount of promotion to each unit of a brand sold (or expected to be sold). This is merely a translation of the percentage-of-sales method into dollars spent per unit. The unit-of-sales approach has the same advantages and disadvantages as the percentage-of-sales approach.

Share of Market/Share of Voice. With **share of market/share of voice,** a firm monitors the amount spent by various significant competitors on promotion and allocates an equal amount or an amount proportional to (or slightly greater than) the firm's market share relative to the competition.[17]

With this method (also referred to as **competitive parity**), a marketer will achieve a share of voice, or a promotional presence in the market, equal to or greater than a designated competitor's share of voice. This method is often used for budget allocations in new-brand introductions. Conventional wisdom suggests that some multiple, often 2.5 to 4 times the desired first-year market share, should be spent in terms of share-of-voice promotional expenditures. For example, if a marketer wants a 2 percent first-year share, it would need to spend up to 8 percent of the total dollar amount spent in the industry (for an 8 percent share of voice). The logic is that a new brand will need a significant share of voice to gain notice among a group of existing, well-established brands.[18] To achieve significant share of voice for its new toothpaste with baking soda and peroxide, Colgate-Palmolive spent $40 million in the first six months on advertising alone.[19]

Although this technique is sound in the sense that it shows a heightened awareness of competitors' activities, there is some question as to whether it can or should be used. First, there is really no good way to get timely information on competitors' spending. Second, there is no reason to believe that competitors have a clue on how to spend their money. Third, a key flaw in logic in this method is the presumption that every promotional effort is of the same quality and will have the same effect on consumers. Nothing could be farther from the truth. Multimillion-dollar campaigns have been miserable failures, while limited-budget campaigns have been big successes.

Funds Available. The **funds-available method** is also referred to as the "all you can afford" approach to budgeting. In some situations, an organization is so concerned with accountability that the promotional budget is the result of leftovers. Only after all direct costs for manufacturing, administration, legal, taxes, and marketing have been accounted for, plus a profit allocation, does the decision maker identify funds for advertising and promotion. The typical result is that insufficient funds are made available. Granted, there are times when firms are in a crisis situation regarding cash flow and financial liquidity. Notwithstanding these pressures, budgeting for promotion on this basis is simply inappropriate. It fails to draw on information relevant to the objectives for promotion or the nature of the environment within which promotion will be carried out.

Objective and Task. The methods for setting a budget just discussed all suffer from the same fundamental deficiency: a lack of specification of how expenditures are related to promotional objectives. The only method of budget setting that focuses on the relationship between spending and objectives is the **objective-and-task approach.** This method begins with the stated objectives for a promotional effort. The budget is then formulated by identifying the specific tasks necessary to achieve different objectives.

There is a lot to recommend this procedure for budgeting. A firm identifies any and all tasks it believes are related to achieving its objectives. Should the total dollar figure for the necessary tasks be beyond the firm's financial capability, a reconciliation must take place. But even if a reconciliation and a subsequent reduction of the budget occurs, the firm has at least identified what *should* have been budgeted to pursue its promotional objectives.

17.   The classic treatment of this method was first offered by James O. Peckham, "Can We Relate Advertising Dollars to Market-Share Objectives?" in *How Much to Spend for Advertising,* Malcolm A. McGiven, Ed., (New York: Association of National Advertisers, 1969), 24.

18.   James C. Shroer, "Ad Spending: Growing Market Share," *Harvard Business Review* (January–February 1990), 44.

19.   Pat Sloan, "Colgate Packs $40M Behind New Toothpaste," *Advertising Age,* December 12, 1994, 36.

EXHIBIT 3.10

Advertising budgets are typically the largest in the promotional mix. Big-time TV productions like this one for American Express featuring Seinfeld can cost up to $2 million for a 30-second ad.

The objective-and-task approach is the most logical and defensible method for calculating and then allocating a budget. It is the only budgeting method that specifically relates promotional spending to the promotional objectives being pursued. It is widely used among major marketers.

Budgeting for Advertising. Typically, advertising budgets are the largest in the promotional mix. While a shifting of funds to other promotional tools has happened in recent years, spending on mass media advertising has been setting records. The reason advertising commands such a large budget has to do with the items that are charged to advertising. They include:

- Market research
- Message research
- Production costs—production companies, talent, site costs
- Media costs
- Agency commissions/fees
- Account personnel travel and expenses

While the list for advertising may be a bit shorter than the list for other promotional tools, the categories can generate some whopping costs. Production costs for a fully produced, 30-second television ad shot in film (the highest quality) average about $700,000, with $2 million production not uncommon (see Exhibit 3.10). As you know, big advertisers like GM and P&G spend billions of dollars on media. And when billions of dollars are spent on media, then hundreds of millions are spent on agency commissions and fees.

Budgeting for advertising relies on all of the budgeting techniques discussed at the outset of this section, depending on the individual firm. In one of the few surveys dealing with the budgeting issue, about 50 percent of all firms surveyed used the objective-and-task approach to allocate funds to advertising.[20]

Budgeting for Sales Promotion. As mentioned at the end of Chapter 1, more managers are investing in sales promotions because of a perception that these techniques are more "accountable" for the funds spent. In other words, the effect of coupons, cents-off, and premium techniques seems easier to trace than advertising. Budgets for sales promotion will typically include charges for the following items:

- Coupon values and dealer handling charges
- Contest and sweepstakes materials and charges
- Brochures and collateral material
- Trade shows and exhibits
- Trade channel partner meetings and entertainment
- Premiums
- Point-of-purchase materials
- Trade allowances

---

20. Survey results cited in James E. Lynch and Graham J. Hooley, "Increasing Sophistication in Advertising Budget Setting," *Journal of Advertising Research* (February–March 1990), 67.

- Trade incentives
- Trade training programs
- Refunds/rebates

Perhaps because of the long-standing reliance on sales promotion techniques, methods of budgeting are the same as for advertising. The percentage of sales, unit-of-sales, share of market/share of voice, and objective-and-task approach are all ways to determine a budget for sales promotion. While the objective-and-task approach is still the preferred method, using a unit-of-sales approach makes more sense for sales promotion than it does for advertising. Cents-off coupons are the most obvious example of budgeting on a per-unit basis. Planners can know before a campaign is run exactly the value of a coupon, the number of coupons distributed, and the historic coupon redemption rate, and then add in the dealer handling charges. A similar "build-up" analysis can be used for premiums, contests, sweepstakes, refunds, and rebates. The other factors charged to sales promotion, like dealer programs and trade shows, are better handled using an objective-and-task approach. Again, the percentage-of-sales approach rarely produces a budget that makes logical sense.

Budgeting for Direct Marketing. Of all the promotional mix tools, direct marketing is in many ways the easiest to budget. The cost of a direct-mail marketing program can be accurately estimated using simple cost-based estimates. Marketers will get exact bids from external facilitators regarding printing, sorting, bundling, mailing, and fulfillment (servicing and shipping to customers). These bids will come to the marketer on either a project basis or a cost-per-thousand bid. Marketers will be able to obtain similar cost estimates for telemarketing campaigns, infomercials, and catalog selling. These direct-marketing and direct-response techniques all include activities that can be priced out in advance with little chance of dramatic cost changes.

The two areas of direct marketing where there is some difficulty in using a cost-based budgeting approach are Web site sales and direct-response ads in major media. With regard to the Web, it is difficult to charge the entire cost of Web development and maintenance if the Web site serves information, content, and selling purposes. In terms of direct-response campaigns using radio, television, newspaper, or magazine media, the question becomes whether to budget media expenses as advertising or direct marketing.

Budgeting for Web Sites and Banner Ads. Web site development and maintenance is a key issue in this new era of reaching consumers and businesses via the Web. Pure-play e-commerce sites and traditional corporations that have built and maintain a Web presence spent a combined $10 billion worldwide in 1999.[21] To give you some feeling for the cost of developing and maintaining a site, consider these numbers:[22]

Average cost to build a Web site:	$37,000
Cost to build a Web site in Europe:	$77,000
Cost to build a Web site in the United States:	$34,000
Cost to build a portal or media site:	$78,000
Cost to build a business-to-consumer site	$68,000
Cost to build a business-to-business site	$30,000
Cost to maintain a site by profitable firms	$26,000
Cost to maintain a site by firms yet to make a profit:	$30,000

21. "Europeans Pay More for Web Development," accessed at http://www.nua.net/surveys on January 12, 2000.
22. "Real Numbers Behind Net Profits 1999," *Activmedia,* accessed at http://www.activemedia.com on January 13, 2000.

The numbers above are worldwide averages. You can probably get your brother-in-law or neighbor to set up a Web page for nothing—and even pay nothing to have it maintained if you comply with certain provider requests (e-messages to you and banners on your site). Or you may be able to find a small firm in town that will build a site for $5,000 to $10,000. In the fierce world of e-commerce competition, a fast and appealing Web site is a must (see Exhibit 3.11). If you want to see what a really good site looks like and how a good site performs, go to http://www.zapme.com.

There are two other issues with Web site development: maintenance and management. First, somebody in the firm or in the support agencies is going to have to manage and evaluate the site. Second, if a firm plans on selling directly from the site, then fulfillment (getting stuff to buyers) is another cost that must be factored into the budget.

The price for placing banner ads has been falling over the last few years. As more banner ads are being placed on the Internet, the cost per thousand (CPM) has been falling dramatically. In 1998, the average cost for banner ads was about $30 CPM. By 2000, big-banner advertisers like eBay were paying only about $10.50 CPM. Remember that if you are reaching 1 million people at a site, even $10 CPM will cost you some big money.[23]

Budgeting for Public Relations. It's hard to say that you actually "budget" for public relations. Did Exxon have a public relations "budget" to deal with the Valdez disaster? Did Coke have a public relations budget to deal with its products being removed from nearly all shops in Europe in 1999? Probably not. For the ongoing routine public relations (PR) efforts that include press releases, press conferences, and sponsoring events, a budget is fairly easy to calculate. A simple objective-and-task budget can be put together following standard procedure. For the bad news disasters that may dominate managerial time for weeks, there is simply no way to estimate or anticipate a cost of the damage control needed from the PR effort.

In the case of disasters, there is really no good way to have a budget ready. If a firm faces a PR crisis, a "funds available" approach makes the most sense: spend the money you need to take care of the problem. This will likely mean spending on press conferences, media releases, and extra staff meetings and travel. During the aftermath of a PR crisis, firms will often initiate a corporate image advertising campaign (see Chapter 13) as a way to reestablish the brand's (and the firm's) stature in the market.

Budgeting for Personal Selling. Setting a budget for the personal selling effort is a big job. Normally, the factors charged to personal selling include:

- Recruiting costs
- Training costs
- Travel expenses
- Promotional materials—samples, catalogs, product brochures
- Salaries and benefits
- Incentive programs—bonuses, awards

Recruiting, training, travel, salary, and benefit expenses are cost factors that are self-explanatory. Promotional materials are those materials provided to salespeople to support their selling effort, such as samples or demonstration kits. In selling college textbooks, literally thousands of samples of a new text will be mailed to prospective adopters at colleges and universities. College professors need a sample textbook in order to make an informed decision. The cost of sending samples to professors can be tens of thousands of dollars.

---

23. "Banner Ads Drop in Price," *Wired,* November 4, 1998, accessed at http://www.wired.com on January 14, 2000; "Portals Get Majority of Ad Impressions," October 26, 1999, accessed at http://www.adrelevance.com on January 14, 2000.

http://www.fashionmall.com

http://www.kmart.com

http://www.bluelight.com

EXHIBIT 3.11

While the ad is deceptively spare, a business-to-consumer (B2C) Web site like Fashionmall.com can be both complex, and expensive. And technical costs can be dwarfed by those of creating and promoting a new brand for the venture. By early 2000, some B2C plays, such as European retailer Boo.com, had gone bankrupt after spending tens of millions of dollars. "Bricks and clicks" (traditional "real world" retailers with a complementary Web presence), such as Kmart may have an easier time building a consumer base by leveraging an established brand.

The methods used to set a budget for personal selling are standard. A percentage-of-sales approach can be used, but it suffers from a lack of recognition of unique challenges facing the sales force, such as introducing a new product or expanding into a new geographic territory. A competitive parity approach can be used particularly with salary, benefit, and bonus programs relative to what other firms in the industry are doing. Again, this technique is inappropriate because the objectives of competitors and therefore the activities of their salespeople might be quite different. The competitive parity approach can easily result in over- or under-paying salespeople.

Once again the objective-and-task method for budget determination is the most effective. Management assesses the objectives that are established for the overall selling effort. Based on those objectives, tasks for the salesforce are specified, as are compensation and incentive programs. All costs associated with the tasks are determined, and the budget is then projected.

EXHIBIT 3.12

This ad for Danskin is an excellent example of a firm using promotion to strategically reposition a brand. The slogan says it all: "Danskin—Not Just for Dancing."

Strategy

Strategy is the mechanism by which something is to be done. It is an expression of the means to an end. All of the activities in a firm are supposed to support an overall strategy. Strategy is what you do given the situation and objectives. The basis for promotional strategy will be drawn from the situation analysis conducted at the outset of the promotional plan. Depending on the nature of the market and product, competition, the distribution system, and the characteristics of the firm, a strategic mix of promotional tools will be decided on.

There are an infinite number of possible promotional strategies. For example, if you are trying to get more top-of-the-mind awareness for your brand of chewing gum, a simple strategy would be to employ a high-frequency, name-repetition campaign. Exhibit 3.12 presents an ad from Danskin's campaign designed to broaden the appeal of its products beyond dance accessories to the much larger fitness-wear market. This would be an attempt to introduce new products with the Danskin name. Promotion for the unique "fitness" features of the brand were emphasized using celebrities as implicit endorsers.

Strategy formulation is a creative endeavor. It is best learned through the study of what others have done in similar situations and through a thorough analysis of the target consumer. To assist in strategy, a growing number of agencies have created a position called the **account planner.** This person's job is to synthesize all relevant consumer research and draw inferences from it that will help define a coherent advertising and promotion strategy. As with so many things, experience counts in this crucial role.

Evaluation

Last but not least in a promotion plan is the evaluation stage. This is where a marketer determines how the promotional program has performed—factor by factor. For now, we need to realize that the main basis for evaluation will be the communications and sales objectives set for the program. Chapter 15 will cover in detail all the methods that can be used for measurement.

INTEGRATED MARKETING COMMUNICATIONS MANAGEMENT AND PLANNING

Chapter 1 highlighted that once the promotional tools are decided on and execution begins, managing the promotional mix becomes an IMC task. One could argue that Rhino Records is the undisputed champion of creative IMC management.

Rhino Records began as a used-album record store in West Los Angeles. Records were displayed in fruit crates on sawhorses. Rhino management would do just about anything to get attention. First, they ran ads and put up posters offering customers a nickel if they would take home a copy of a Danny Bonaduce album and promise to actually listen to it.[24] Then they pressed records in the shapes of animals. Perhaps their greatest feat was recording and selling a kazoo-orchestra recording of Led Zeppelin's "Whole Lotta Love." It sold 15,000 copies. Then Rhino asked a well-known street person in Los Angeles, Wild Man Fischer, to record a tune called "Go to Rhino Records." At first the recording was given out as a promotional bonus to customers, but then it found its way to the BBC in London and actually made the pop charts in the United Kingdom.[25]

It is highly unlikely that management at Rhino had a clear and highly structured IMC plan back in the 1970s. But an evaluation of their promotions shows that everything the company did had a synergy and integration to it. And Rhino is still at it today. If you visit the company's Web site at http://www.rhino.com, you'll find not only information on CDs and videos, but contests and special promotions—all folded into the same brand image and customer loyalty emphasis of those early Rhino promotions.

The lesson from Rhino Records is that no matter how you get there, understanding customers and crafting a broad-based set of brand communications is key to growing a reputation and brand loyalty in the market. Today, things are bit more complicated than in the early days of Rhino. Firms need a more structured approach to managing the many pieces of a promotional program. There is nothing new about planning promotional efforts around a mix of different promotional tools. Depending on a firm's marketing and promotional objectives, different tools and different combinations of tools are used for different purposes, as we have already discussed. But managing in an IMC fashion goes beyond merely using the right tool under the right conditions.

---

24. Stephen Fried, "Loony Tunes: Rhino Records' Utterly Gonzo Sensibility Is Turning Out to Be Good Business," *GQ,* April 1992, 76.
25. B-Rated Rock and Roll," *Newsweek,* October 7, 1985, 90.

Strategic planning of IMC is distinguished from the traditional use of multiple promotional tools in four important ways:[26]

- *An outside-in approach is used for planning.* In some organizations, communications are planned from the inside out; that is, firms begin the planning process by setting communications objectives that match what the *managers* believe to be brand information needs for differentiation/positioning objectives. In planning IMC, a firm starts with the customer and works backward, identifying what the customer deems to be important information. What is key about this approach is that it also helps verify the *way* in which consumers want information about a brand, from sales promotion to event sponsorship through the Internet and media advertising.

CEO, CFO, CWO(?)

We all know that the CEO is the Chief Executive Officer and the CFO is the Chief Financial Officer, but what is a CWO? Well, it had to happen, this is the Chief Web Officer and it is a reality at Colgate-Palmolive, the packaged-goods conglomerate. Colgate has just created the CWO position to oversee the company's Internet strategy. The CWO will be responsible for both Web marketing and e-commerce and develop a global strategy to coordinate all of the company's Internet activities. Is Colgate serious about this? Absolutely. The company issued this statement after announcing the position: "The Web officer is going to be second in importance only to the chief marketing officer" of the company.

Part of the Colgate move is to counter actions by major competitors Procter & Gamble and Unilever. In 1996, P&G made a big deal out of committing the firm to more interactive media, particularly the Web. Unilever has gained attention lately for its interactive marketing efforts by cutting deals with AOL and Microsoft estimated to be worth about $100 million.

Colgate's interactive efforts have been a bit sparse to date compared to the competition. The appointment of the CWO is meant to change all that. The CWO's first assignment? Establish Colgate-owned Hill's Science Diet brand pet foods as a leader in Web-based pet products marketing. While this may seem odd, consider the situation (remember the "situation analysis" from the promotional plan). The global premium pet food market is a multibillion dollar industry that Colgate leads with about $1 billion in annual sales. With the proliferation of pet product Web sites like http://www.Petopia.com and http://www.pets.com, Web sales of premium pet foods could explode. Having a CWO on hand to guide expansion in this area alone makes sense for Colgate.

Source: Jack Neff, "Colgate Leaps by Rivals with 1st Chief Web Officer," *Advertising Age*, September 6, 1999, 28.

- *IMC management planning requires comprehensive and detailed knowledge about customers and prospects.* An IMC planning approach is much more database driven than traditional promotional programs. This feature is highlighted by American Express. With its huge database of cardholders and travelers, AmEx has detailed information on tens of millions of people—so detailed, in fact, that it can send out special promotions in monthly bills to as few as 20 people.[27]

- *An IMC management plan is built around brand communications.* Brand communications are *all* the ways in which customers or prospective customers come in contact with the company's brand: packaging, employee contacts, in-store displays, sales literature, media exposure, and so on. This issue was raised in Chapter 1 as a key dimension of the brand-building process using the promotional mix. Now, in managing the promotional mix, each communication must be evaluated for clarity and consistency within the overall promotional program.

- *Control of IMC management and planning should be centralized.* The effectiveness of an IMC program is greatly increased by appointing a single person or a group to control and evaluate all communications with customers and prospects and to manage the overall plan. Firms

---

26. Don E. Schultz, "Maybe We Should Start All Over with an IMC Organization," *Advertising Age*, October 25, 1993, 8.

27. Jonathan Berry, "Database Marketing," *Business Week*, September 5, 1994, 56.

are now starting to appoint IMC or marketing communications managers to handle this management task. Colgate has one of the most comprehensive IMC management structures to the extent that the firm has appointed a Web officer to oversee its global online strategy, as the New Media box highlights.[28]

A Model of IMC Management and Planning

Integrated marketing communications takes a truly systems-oriented approach to the planning: All communications are designed to maximize overall impact, not the impact of an individual component. IMC implementation shares database information with the marketing program. This database foundation is considered critical to the success of IMC programs by nine out of ten marketing and agency people questioned.[29]

A general planning model for IMC is shown in Exhibit 3.13. This gives you the lay of the land in terms of the scope and sequence of managing the promotional effort. We will specifically address different aspects of the process throughout the rest of the text.

Notice that the management process must begin with an awareness of and allegiance to overall corporate and marketing plans. It does an organization no good whatsoever if the promotional effort goes off in a direction that contradicts corporate and marketing planning. Notice that customer/prospect databases relating to demographics, psychographics (lifestyles), geodemographics, and product use are the foundation of the planning. These databases help profile current and potential customers. Specialized research agencies can provide marketers with databases to identify and understand target markets. North Castle Partners agency developed a database on teen shopping behaviors that helped develop promotions for Phisoderm that were highly successful in profiling teens' interests and behaviors.[30] You will learn all about generating and using these types of databases in Chapter 4 and Chapter 10.

From these databases, various market segments and target markets can be identified. The model shows four basic markets: brand-loyal users, competitors' brand-loyal users, brand switchers, and nonusers of the product category. The nature of the first two target markets is obvious. The brand switchers are those consumers who are highly "deal prone" and exhibit little loyalty to any one brand—yet. The nonusers of the product category constitute two types of potential target markets. For new product areas, promotion can have a solid impact on informing and persuading nonusers to try the product. For mature products, like milk, potato chips, chewing gum, or any other product that has been around a long time, promotion cannot affect people who choose, for whatever reason, not to use the product category. Attempting to turn nonusers into users in mature product categories is a futile effort. That's why there is no continuing planning effort on that side of the model. You'll learn more about this issue (called primary demand) later in the text.

As we continue down Exhibit 3.13, we see that different marketing objectives will be set for these segments. Depending on the segment, maintaining loyalty or inducing trial and building loyalty are the main goals. These objectives in turn affect the marketing mix, which then affects promotional objectives. As we saw earlier in the chapter, both communications and sales objectives can be appropriate, depending on the marketing objectives set and the promotional tools available.

Finally, notice at the bottom of the model that a firm must decide which promotional tools to use to cultivate each target market. Remember that each segment will likely require a different "blend" in the promotional mix. Trial use will likely

28. Jack Neff, "Colgate Leaps by Rivals with 1st Chief Web Officer," *Advertising Age,* September 6, 1999, 28.
29. Adrienne Ward Fawcett, "Integrated Marketing Door Open for Experts," *Advertising Age,* November 8, 1993, S2.
30. Denis Lavoie, "Agency Aims to Get Inside Teenagers' Minds," *Marketing News,* September 27, 1999, 8.

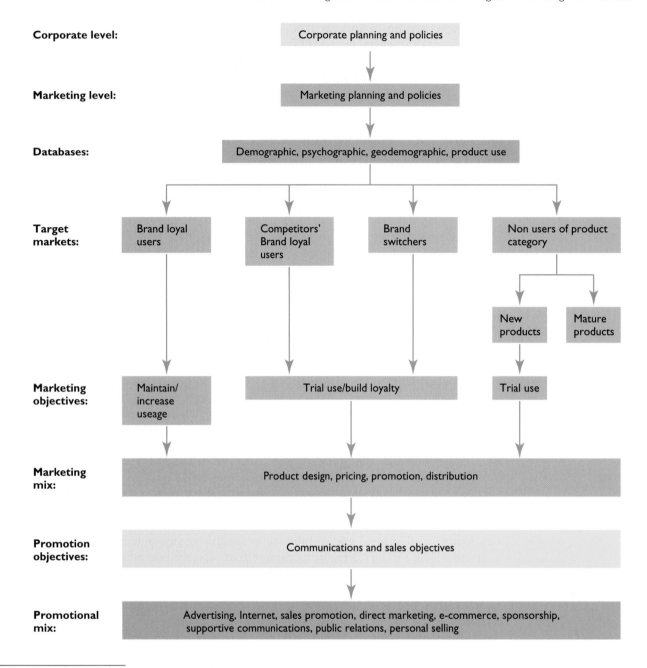

EXHIBIT 3.13

IMC Management and Planning Model

depend heavily on sales promotions, and maintaining brand loyalty will be more dependent on advertising. The strategic application of promotional mix tools will be discussed in great detail in Part 3.

While the tools of IMC can be clearly identified, it is less clear how these various ways of communicating with segments can be truly integrated. Recent industry studies of IMC show that firms believe an IMC approach will be valuable because the process helps focus messages on key target audiences and reduces wasted circulation. But these same firms express concern that ego conflicts and turf battles within the firm and among the many specialty communications agencies that serve the firm could undermine the process.[31] And there is disagreement about who is responsible for the integration and coordination. Some firms feel it is their own responsibility, whereas others believe the outside agencies should make it their business to integrate their individual communications efforts.

This chapter introduced you to the full scope of the promotional effort. The promotional plan lays out all the areas of planning and preparation that need to be undertaken before the promotional effort can begin. In addition, the way in which IMC management and planning fits with promotional planning was also presented. The appendix to this chapter illustrates a complete IMC plan, including a marketing mix, media plans, and creative samples for the consumer and trade market. The chapters from this point forward will provide you with the knowledge you need to develop the detailed promotion and IMC plans introduced here.

31. Thomas R. Duncan and Stephen E. Everett, "Client Perceptions of Integrated Marketing Communications," *Journal of Advertising Research* (May–June 1993), 30–39.

SUMMARY

1 Describe the basic elements of a promotion plan.

A **promotion plan** is motivated by the marketing planning process and provides the direction that ensures proper implementation of the promotion effort begins with an **executive summary** and **overview.** A promotion plan incorporates information from the firm's situation analysis, including an assessment of the market and competition, and objectives for the process. The plan should also specify the dollars budgeted for the campaign and the strategy for achieving objectives. The final part of the plan is a commitment to evaluation and a specification of criteria to be used for measurement.

2 Explain the way an organization makes the strategic decisions regarding which promotional tools to emphasize in a promotional campaign.

A firm determines which tools to emphasize in the promotional mix during the situation analysis of a promotional plan. There are a broad range of factors that influence the choice of and emphasis on different promotional tools. In the situation analysis of a promotional plan, strategists will consider the historical context for the brand and all the promotional campaigns that have preceded the one being planned, characteristics of the market, the product, the firm, and the distribution system when considering the mix of promotional factors. Differences across brands and situations will result in more or less reliance on the tools of promotion in any given situation.

3 Discuss the difference between communications and sales objectives in promotional planning.

Setting appropriate objectives is a crucial step in developing any promotion plan. These objectives are typically stated in terms of communications or sales goals. Both types of goals have their proponents, and the appropriate types of objectives to emphasize will vary with the situation. Communications objectives feature goals such as building **brand awareness** or reinforcing consumers' beliefs about a brand's key benefits. Sales objectives are just that: They hold promotion directly responsible for increasing sales of a brand. Communications goals typically relate to advertising, sponsorship, and efforts, while sales objec-

tives are better suited to those promotional tools that affect the consumer at the point of purchase like direct marketing, the Internet, or coupons.

4 Explain the different methods for setting a budget for promotional spending.

Perhaps the most challenging aspect of any campaign is arriving at a proper budget allocation. Companies and their agencies work with several different methods to arrive at a budget. A **percentage-of-sales approach** is a simple but naive way to deal with this issue. A variation on that approach is the **unit-of-sales approach** that allocates funds on a per-unit basis rather than percentage-of-sales basis. In the **share-of-market/share-of-voice approach,** the activities of key competitors are factored into the budget-setting process. A **funds available** (or all-you-can-afford) method is used when firms are strapped for cash and need to cover costs and preserve profitability. The **objective-and-task approach** is difficult to implement, but will yield the best value for a firm's promotional investment.

Each of the promotional mix tools has unique considerations in the budgeting process. Costs that need to be charged against the promotional budget vary greatly from one promotional tool to another. The proper budget approach will depend on the target segment and the communications and sales objectives set for overall promotion and the unique mix of tools used to pursue those objectives.

5 Describe a model used for planning integrated marketing communications and understand the components of an IMC plan (see the Appendix, pages 97–113).

IMC management and planning considers the complete process of using promotion to communicate to target markets and effectively deploy promotional tools. At the outset, corporate and marketing plans and objectives must be understood and adopted as fundamental premises of the management process. Next, databases will help identify and profile target markets. From the target markets will emerge marketing objectives and the marketing mix configuration to pursue those objectives. Finally, promotional objectives relating to communications and sales will dictate what mix of promotional tools will be appropriate to pursue each different target market.

KEY TERMS

promotion plan, 67
executive summary, 68
overview, 68
situation analysis, 68
industry analysis, 69
convenience goods, 71
shopping goods, 72
specialty goods, 72
primary demand, 73
push strategy, 73
pull strategy, 73
intensity of distribution, 75

intensive distribution, 75
selective distribution, 75
exclusive distribution, 75
channel length, 75
brand image, 77
brand awareness, 77
top-of-the-mind awareness, 77
beliefs, 77
attitude, 77
purchase intent, 78
trial usage, 79
repeat purchase, 79

brand switching, 79
brand loyalty, 79
increasing the frequency of use, 79
percentage-of-sales approach, 82
unit-of-sales approach, 82
share of market/share of voice, 82
competitive parity, 83
funds-available method, 83
objective-and-task approach, 83
strategy, 88
account planner, 89

QUESTIONS FOR REVIEW AND CRITICAL THINKING

1. Review the materials presented in this chapter (and anything else you may be able to find) about Apple's launch of the iMac. Based on the promotion techniques used, which ones fulfilled communications objectives and which fulfilled sales objectives?

2. Find an example of cooperative advertising in your local newspaper where a retailer features a manufacturer's brand in the ad. Why would computer manufacturers such as Apple, IBM, or Compaq want to participate in cooperative advertising programs with their retailers?

3. Explain the differences between marketing strategies and promotional plans. How do target markets enter into this relationship?

4. Describe five key elements in a situation analysis, and provide an example of how each of these elements may ultimately influence the final form of a promotional campaign.

5. How would it ever be possible to justify anything other than sales growth as a proper objective for advertising? Is it possible that advertising could be effective yet not yield growth in sales?

6. What types of objectives would you expect to find in a promotional plan that featured direct-response advertising?

7. Write an example of a workable promotional objective that would be appropriate for a product like Crest Tartar Control toothpaste. Identify the promotional tools you have chosen and how they affect your objective.

8. In what situations would share of voice be an important consideration in setting an advertising budget? What are the drawbacks of trying to incorporate share of voice in budgeting decisions?

9. What is it about the objective-and-task method that makes it the preferred approach for the sophisticated marketer? Describe how build-up analysis is used in implementing the objective-and-task method.

10. Choose what you believe is the key element in the IMC management model. Why do you believe it is important with respect to managing the promotional process?

EXPERIENTIAL EXERCISES

1. **In-class exercise.** In this chapter you read about the role of industry analysis in promotion planning. Divide into teams and select one product category, such as soft drinks, fast foods, vitamin supplements, health foods, or athletic footwear. Identify the external variables that tend to influence that industry. Assign the variables to group members. Describe how each variable should be monitored by industry marketers.

2. **Out-of-class exercise.** Pick a product that you use regularly—your watch or even your favorite bookstore. Based on your personal knowledge, identify what you think would be an effective promotional advertising objective for this brand. Next, describe a promotional mix based on all the brand contacts you have with the brand.

USING THE INTERNET

Exercise 1

A successful advertising plan should include an integrated marketing communications strategy. The following companies have extensive advertising budgets allocated across multiple media vehicles. Explore the following sites and determine the creative style and type of information available at each site:

Budweiser
http://www.budweiser.com

Guess
http://www.guess.com

Jeep
http://www.jeepunpaved.com

NBA
http://www.nba.com

For each site, answer the following questions:

1. From your experience with past and current promotions for the company or organization, how does the site fit with all these communications? Are there similarities? differences? Does the site reinforce the promotions? Does it offer additional information?

2. In what ways are the differences you have noticed between the site and other media due to the different characteristics of the Internet itself?

3. Create a personal standard for advertising quality by listing several criteria that apply to different media.

Compare the quality of the Web site with that of promotions in other media. In your judgment, did the company or organization allocate too much, too little, or just the right amount of resources on its Web site?

Exercise 2

The Internet's arrival coincided with (and no doubt accelerated) a trend in many industries toward outsourcing those functions not considered "core competencies." And many company sites on the Web are a corporate brand as a thin veneer on top of various off-the-shelf or semi-custom services from myriad providers, from simple site tools to branded e-mail newsletters to even customer service and support. The following companies provide tools or services to backstop other companies' Web presence:

Excite
http://www.excite.com

AskJeeves
http://www.askjeeves.com

TouchScape
http://www.touchscape.com

Where can you find these companies on the Web? In addition to their corporate sites, do you encounter references to them, links, or other signs that they might be behind other companies' Web sites?

APPENDIX A

THE LAUNCH OF CINCINNATI BELL WIRELESS: AN INTEGRATED MARKETING COMMUNICATIONS SUCCESS STORY

INTRODUCTION: PLANNING THE IMC CAMPAIGN ⑤

What is needed to plan and execute a successful IMC campaign?

1. A planning model
2. IMC Resources
3. A Budget
4. Team Leadership

The **planning model** presented in Chapter 3 is commonly used throughout the marketing communications industry, sometimes with minor variations. It is a basic and time-tested outline for organizing the details of a comprehensive plan.

IMC resources, of course, include a wide array of marketing, promotional, creative, and production services. Marketing research is needed to identify prospects and their information needs. Marketing professionals write the strategies and objectives, decide on tactics to be used, determine budgets, and coordinate the planning. Specialists in advertising, public relations, direct marketing, and sales promotion each bring their knowledge to the process. Writers and graphic artists craft the creative messages. Production experts in photography, computer graphics, Internet, printing, television, and radio each contribute importantly to the overall effort.

The **budget,** including each tactical element of a plan, is critical because it is the final yardstick of evaluation. In the end, management will ask: Did the plan yield the results expected for the budget invested? Every planned element carries a price tag, and the IMC manager plays a key role in consolidating all of the elements into one cohesive budget. As described in Chapter 3, there are several budgeting methods commonly used, and determining the overall budget for a sizeable IMC effort calls for smart judgment and careful attention to detail.

If you're getting the idea that building an IMC plan is slightly more complicated than tic-tac-toe, you're absolutely right. Tension, stress, creativity, deadlines, collaboration, synergy, conflict, misunderstandings, expertise, complexity, details, details, details—these are all things that characterize the process of preparing to launch an IMC campaign.

This appendix was written by Robert J. Cannell, Associate Professor, Integrated Marketing Communications, Roosevelt University. In addition to teaching IMC, Mr. Cannell operates his own marketing and creative services practice in Chicago.

How is it possible for people to survive and work through the array of challenges? How is it possible for order to emerge from the chaos?

Team leadership turns chaos into order, ideas into reality. To use a familiar metaphor, executing an IMC campaign is very much like the performance of a symphony orchestra. It only sounds right if the maestro brings it all together at the critical moment. This raises the question: Who is the IMC "maestro"?

Clearly, there will be many team leaders involved in a comprehensive IMC plan. But who sits at the top of the hill? Who has final authority and responsibility? Some marketers give a great deal of the responsibility to their advertising agencies, public relations firms, and others, but it is the client who hires these experts and ultimately pays the bills.

Many agencies today position themselves as being in the IMC business, that is, having all of the tools necessary to orchestrate the total IMC plan. Full service in the IMC sense includes advertising, public relations, sales promotion, events management, and direct marketing. Some marketers hire such agencies and rely on them to lead the entire process, even though as clients, they still have ultimate authority because they pay the bills.

When the marketer chooses to hire a variety of specialized resources, rather than an IMC agency, it stands to reason that more of the "orchestration" rests with the marketing director or brand manager of that organization. In other words, the principal IMC leadership role in this case is with the marketer.

CINCINNATI BELL, INC.: ESTABLISHED COMPANY WITH A NEW PRODUCT

This is an IMC case example in which a marketer and its IMC agency launch a new wireless phone service. The client is Cincinnati Bell, Inc.; the product, Cincinnati Bell Wireless (CBW); the agency, Northlich Stolley LaWarre (NSL). The story will help you understand and appreciate the challenges and benefits of sophisticated IMC campaigns.[1]

The case covers the period May to December, 1998. During that short period of time, CBW launched its new digital wireless PCS (personal communication services) and won over 16,800 new wireless customers. Just two years later, they have over 200,000 customers and their wireless service introduction has been described as one of the most successful in the country. John F. (Jack) Cassidy, then president of CBW, has since been named president of Cincinnati Bell, Inc.[2]

AN IMC AGENCY

Northlich Stolley LaWarre, based in Cincinnati, Ohio, is ranked by *Adweek* magazine among the top fifty Midwest ad agencies (1998) with reported net revenue of $15.9 million from billings of over $100 million. NSL serves a diverse list of clients including ChoiceCare/Humana Managed Healthcare, Fidelity Institutional Retirement Services, and a number of Procter & Gamble assignments. It became the agency of record for Cincinnati Bell, Inc. in 1996.

---

1.   The Cincinnati Bell Wireless case study is abridged from Thomas C. O'Guinn, Chris T. Allen, and Richard J. Semenik, *Advertising,* 2nd Edition, Cincinnati, OH: South-Western College Publishing, 2000), 124, 131, 292–301, 429–433, 640–647.

2.   Mike Boyer, "Cincy Bell Names New President," http://enquirer.com, accessed at *The Cincinnati Enquirer,* on May 23, 2000.

While the folks at NSL usually refer to their company as an advertising agency, it is probably more accurate to think of it as an IMC agency. In the mid-1990s, the agency underwent restructuring to become more of an integrated services provider, a significant change from its earlier position as a conventional mass media-oriented ad agency. Among the 150 staffers at NSL are people skilled in marketing research, strategic marketing planning, direct marketing, public relations, advertising, collateral, packaging, point-of-purchase, and other IMC materials. The key to their new direction is to provide their clients with multidisciplinary teams to plan and execute programs.

At NSL, IMC means using whatever marketing tools are appropriate for the marketing problem at hand. That might mean that direct marketing used in conjunction with image-oriented advertising could be a recommended solution, or PR used with sales promotion, or any number of other IMC combinations. To truly leverage the power of a brand name and motivate consumers, it takes an intimate understanding of all IMC tools, and of how to orchestrate a multidisciplinary approach using different media and messages. The overriding goal is always to build the strength of the client's brand. This is what NSL did in launching Cincinnati Bell Wireless.

CINCINNATI BELL, INC.: IN PURSUIT OF IMC

Cincinnati Bell, Inc. is a diversified and innovative communications company employing about 30,000 people in 1997. The company consists of three major business domains: information services, teleservices, and communication services.

In communication services, its units include Cincinnati Bell Telephone Company (CBT), Cincinnati Bell Long Distance, and Cincinnati Bell Supply Company, providing local and long-distance phone service, Yellow Pages and directory service, and telecommunications equipment in the Greater Cincinnati metropolitan market. CBT is explicitly dedicated to a strategy of being more than just "the phone company." Their commitment is to superior service, quality, innovation, and value.

In 1997, Cincinnati Bell, Inc. signed a landmark agreement with AT&T Wireless Services that marked the birth of Cincinnati Bell Wireless. The stage was set for CBW and its IMC agency to prepare to launch—in just six months—advanced personal communication services: voice, paging, and e-mail messaging, with other features and associated products.

CINCINNATI BELL WIRELESS: SITUATION ANALYSIS

Brand Historical Context

1998 was the year of the CBW launch. However, this particular launch was just one in a continuing series of new products and services involving the Cincinnati Bell brand name. All this fit into a broad strategic campaign titled "Celebrating 125 Years of Innovation." Some important milestones in the history of the company are listed in Exhibit A-1.

In addition, a common theme across ads for its various products and services was the slogan "People you know you can rely on." See Exhibit A-2 for examples from the various campaigns. Given this context, the launch of CBW should not be viewed as an isolated event. Clearly, the Cincinnati Bell name, widely known in the local market, carried with it brand value that provided a sound foundation for the CBW launch. This was a tremendous asset.

A Corporate Timeline . . .
1873—City & Suburban Telegraph Association (now Cincinnati Bell) founded
1876—Alexander Graham Bell invents the telephone
1877—First telephone installed in Cincinnati
1907—First Yellow Pages directory published
1975—911 emergency service activated
1984—First fiber optic cable installed
1990—Cincinnati Reds sweep Oakland in the World Series
1992—Cincinnati Bell pioneered the self-healing fiber optic network
1996—First telecommunication company to offer Internet access: Fuse
1997—1,000,000th access line installed
1997—Ranked one of the nation's top two providers of trouble-free local phone service
1998—First to offer Internet Call Manager
1998—Ranked highest independent telecommunications company for Web technology
1998—Cincinnati Bell: Celebrating 125 years of innovation

EXHIBIT A.1

Cincinnati Bell: Celebrating 125 years of innovation

Industry Analysis and Competition

Telecommunications is a dynamic, technical, and complex business. It is important to understand some key industry issues at that time.

The phone marketplace in Cincinnati, and, for that matter, nationwide, was on the brink of bedlam. Cincinnati Bell management realized that in a marketplace typified by chaos, the rewards would go to companies that offered consumers simple solutions and good value. Out of chaos often comes a wonderful business opportunity.

Critical to understanding this opportunity is the distinction between analog cellular and digital PCS wireless phones. CBW would launch a new digital PCS offering to the Greater Cincinnati marketplace. Its primary competition at launch would be analog cellular providers. Analog cellular was established technology that introduced most of us to the concept of a wireless phone.

Across the United States, analog service providers all relied on the same transmission methods and thus handled calls for each other's customers, for a heavy "roaming fee." Travelers could make an analog cellular call almost anywhere in the United States. A wide variety of phone models was also available.

For more information on the industry, the following Web sites will be helpful: http://www.wow-com.com; http://www.ksg.harvard.edu/project6/; http://www.gsm-pcs.org/; http://www.cincinnati.com/technology/.

Product Advantages

Digital PCS, the new kid on the block, offered important advantages over analog:

1. The sound quality of digital is better than analog.
2. Digital PCS could be marketed at lower prices than analog because digital technology allows providers to expand capacity to handle calls much more easily.
3. Digital technology also opens the door for add-on services such as e-mail and Internet access.
4. Digital service always relies on a computer-mediated stream of ones and zeros, meaning messages can be more easily encrypted, thus eliminating many forms of "cellular fraud" that plague analog systems.

EXHIBIT A.2

Cincinnati Bell sample ads prior to the wireless launch

In addition, the agreement between Cincinnati Bell, Inc. and AT&T Wireless Services made CBW part of a nationwide system that would allow customers to use their phones in 400 cities across the United States. CBW realized that it needed to get its value proposition in front of consumers before the competition.

Another built-in advantage for CBW was distribution potential through company stores known as Stores@Cincinnati Bell. The complete distribution system, however, included other CBW-authorized outlets.

Local Competition

In 1998, only one other PCS provider existed in the Cincinnati market under the brand name GTE Wireless. However, GTE Wireless had not been aggressive in convincing Cincinnatians of the benefits of digital PCS, and was further hampered by a very limited calling area. More established competition came from analog cellular providers, and two of these—Ameritech Cellular and AirTouch Cellular—had strong brand identity in the local market.

A Key Decision

CBW and NSL had to resolve a fundamental dilemma created by the local competition. That is, should they concentrate the launch campaign on signing up first-time wireless phone users, or should they seek to steal customers away from the entrenched analog competition? The answer would come from a thorough segmentation analysis.

Market Trends

Demand for both digital PCS and analog cellular was surging. Nationwide, the market had more than doubled from 1995 to 1998, to over 60 million subscribers. Market growth rates approaching 30 percent annually had several companies scrambling to take advantage of the opportunity (for example, Sprint would introduce its PCS service to the Cincinnati market in November 1998), so CBW executives pressed for their launch as soon as was humanly possible.

The Federal Communications Commission estimates the Cincinnati market to be about 1.9 million people. Given a national penetration rate of 25 percent, this translates into a potential market of 475,000 wireless phone subscribers in Greater Cincinnati. Who among these should be targeted in the CBW launch? How many of these could CBW hope to sign on to its service in the first 90 days after launch? These questions would be hotly debated by NSL and CBW personnel leading up to their May 11 blastoff.

Target Segment Analysis

Both quantitative and qualitative research tools uncovered important consumer insights such as:

1. The number-one motivation for sign-up among new users was concern for safety of a family member.
2. Many consumers felt confused and overwhelmed by the growing number of wireless phone deals and options.
3. Consumers rated corporate identity and credibility as increasingly important in the decision about which wireless service to choose.

Further, an in-depth analysis led to the segmentation model show in Exhibit A-3. As you study this, remember that compelling advertising begins with descriptions

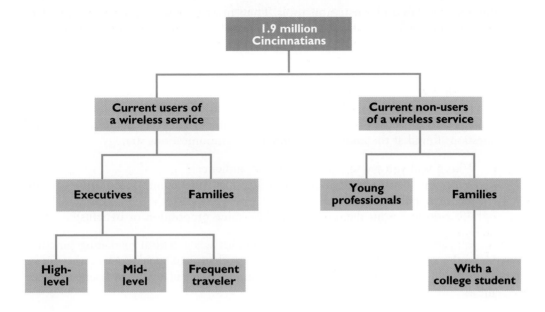

EXHIBIT A.3

The CBW/NSL segementation framework: Spring 1998

and insights about one's target segments that are both personal and precise. Consider these two selected segments, one a business audience and the other general consumers, for example:

Midlevel Executives—Profile and Motivations

- Current users of another wireless service
- Primarily college-educated males
- Early adopters who embrace advancing technology
- Internet users
- See wireless phone as productivity tool for work
- Receptive to new features that improve productivity
- Would switch for better price
- Concerned about poor customer service, erratic sound quality, restrictive calling zones

Families with a Child in College—Profile and Motivations

- Current nonusers
- Motivated by safety and security
- Phone service purchased by parent, used by student
- See wireless as quicker, more reliable communication
- Concerned about children misusing phone, cost control
- Unsure about options such as contracts, pricing, coverage zones, add-on features
- Reassured by familiar brand names

Once again, these profiles raise the question of targeting alternatives—on the one hand, getting present users to switch; on the other hand, getting new customers to take the plunge and sign on for a new technological advancement.

It should be clear that CBW cannot have it both ways. That is, the fast-track business executive and the concerned parent of a college student would require very different appeals and persuasion tools. They must choose one target segment or risk having a diluted message that would leave all segments confused about their value proposition.

Marketing Strategy and Objectives

Having analyzed the marketing situation, it was time for CBW and NSL to set their strategy and objectives for the new product launch. They faced the three critical questions found at the core of all marketing communications strategy:

- Whom will you try to reach (the target audience)?
- What are their current beliefs and attitudes (the communications problems and/or opportunities)?
- What do you want them to believe (the value proposition or benefits)?

As you can see, CBW had choices to make. This was a critical marketing juncture. Make the best choices, and you have the best chance of success. Make the wrong choices and your IMC campaign could flounder and fail while competitors move ahead.

The Target Market Decision

Here is a case where the decision was based more on the quality of prospects than on their quantity—not on the greatest number of people who might buy wireless service, but on those people who would be the "heavy users" of it. CBW and NSL selected mid- and high-level executives who currently were using another wireless service as the primary target. Rationale: This demographic segment of business

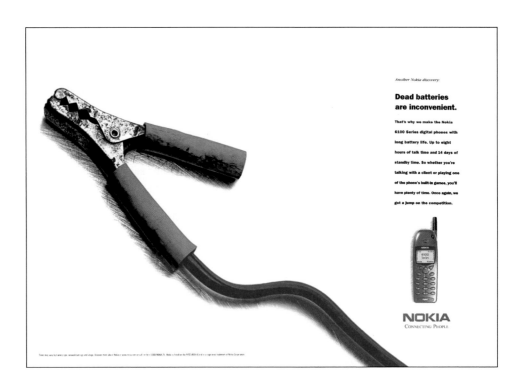

EXHIBIT A.4

Another asset in the CBW launch: The Nokia 6100 Series Digital Phone

users—managers, owners, professionals, and entrepreneurs (MOPEs)—makes much heavier use of the wireless service in terms of minutes called per month than household users who want to keep the wireless phone handy in case they need it. MOPEs represent a much greater revenue opportunity for Cincinnati Bell.

Product Benefits and the Value Proposition

Using various media and IMC methods, the value proposition to be featured in the IMC campaign would cover these key benefits of this new service:

- *Simple pricing, better value.* No contracts to sign; subscribers choose a simple pricing plan, like 500 minutes for $49/month or 1,600 minutes for $99/month.
- *Access in over 400 cities at one "hometown rate."* As a member of AT&T's nationwide network, CBW offered a strong incentive to business travelers.
- *Worry-free security.* Digital PCS allows secure business transactions that may be compromised over analog cellular.
- *Latest technology and style, a feature-packed phone.* CBW launched its service with the Nokia 6160 wireless phone, describing it as "the coolest phone on the planet," and the kind of phone you want people to see you using.

In addition to these important benefit claims, CBW had a tremendous advantage from the standpoint of the combined brand equities of the strategic partners. Nokia's strength had been established by brand-building ads, plus event sponsorship such as the Nokia Sugar Bowl. See Exhibit A-4 for an example of Nokia's brand-building national advertising. In combination, the Cincinnati Bell, AT&T, and Nokia brand names were an imposing triad that would establish instant credibility for CBW.

LAUNCHING THE CINCINNATI BELL WIRELESS PROMOTION

Marketing and Marketing Communications Objectives

When creating objectives, it is important to differentiate what is meant by a marketing objective versus a marketing communications objective.
Marketing objectives typically address:

- *Sales volume*—in dollars, product units, or number of customers
- *Share of market*—a percentage of the available business
- *Distribution goals*—channels to be established to sell the product

Marketing communications objectives typically address:

- *Awareness goals*—a percentage of targeted prospects you want to remember the brand name
- *Association goals*—a percentage of targeted prospects you want to associate the brand with key benefits
- *Action goals*—the specific actions you want the prospects to take as a result of receiving the message (for example, call a phone number, visit a store, etc.)

Jack Cassidy, CBW's president, stated the initial marketing objective for the launch simply and forcefully: "Get me activations!" Although activating a customer does not necessarily create a satisfied or profitable customer, everything starts with this. NSL's work would be judged initially on the basis of the number of new customers who signed on. Specifically, CBW set these measurable marketing objectives:

- Against an estimated target audience of 475,000 potential wireless users, gain 3.5% penetration in calendar year 1998 (from a May launch date).
- Activate over 16,000 new user accounts.

IMC Category	Tools/Techniques	Strengths/Reasons to Use
Public Relations	News releases, media interviews, press kits and conferences, feature articles	Your news delivered through journalists, editors, media broadcasters. Publicity for your brand or company. Enhanced by the high credibility of the news media.
	Newsletters	Economical news delivery-vehicle to employees, trade channels, customers.
	Annual reports, company magazines	Image-building pieces with high-production values. Reach financial stakeholders, employees, customers.
	Executive speeches to industry groups; conferences and seminars	Build reputation as voice of authority. Gain media coverage and credibility for organization and its brands.
Media Advertising	Television commercials	High visibility, rapid awareness building, potential for broad exposure through "talked about" creativity. National, regional or local market flexibility through broadcast and cable outlets.
	TV Infomercials	Direct marketing tool to sell products direct to consumer.
	Radio commercials	High message repetition at reasonable cost. Local market targeting by programming: for example, music format, news, talk, sports.
	Magazine ads: national and regional	Reach special interest audience segments. Attractive, colorful showcase for good creative work, product information and image.
	Magazine ads: business-to-business	Reach highly specialized and segmented business markets by Standard Industry Classification (SIC).
	Newspaper ads: local	Deliver where-to-buy retail message to shoppers in communities, towns, large metro areas.
	Newspaper ads: national	High image-building potential from association with respected media; puts your message in "good company" with well-known leading advertisers and brand names.
	Out-of-home media: transit posters, billboards	Reinforce and extend the impact of broadcast and print campaigns. Add high-visibility impact for launching new products. Direct traffic to a nearby sales outlet.
	Internet advertising and e-commerce	Highly targeted vehicle for reaching market segments of computer users; selling directly on the Internet. Fastest growing medium.
Collateral— Sales Support	Brochures, flyers, spec sheets, bill inserts	Deliver detailed product data, consumer information, promotional announcements, and reminders.
	Specialty advertising premiums	Brand name builders, reminders: messages on buttons, T-shirts, caps, pens, mugs, key chains, etc.
	Multipiece packages, self-mailers, postcards, sales letters, e-mail	Many targeting options, rental lists available. Flexibility from simple, inexpensive postcard or letter to sophisticated and costly high-impact pieces. Internet e-mailings growing rapidly.
	Direct marketing catalogs	Selling broad product offerings: apparel, housewares, gift.

continued

EXHIBIT A.5

IMC tools and their strengths

IMC Category	Tools/Techniques	Strengths/Reasons to Use
Direct Mail	Trade incentives: stocking allowances, coop advertising, tie-in promotions	Create marketing "push." Build distribution channels, move product into reseller inventories. Motivate retailers to promote your product.
Sales Promotion	Coupons, sampling, bonus packs	Stimulate trial. Build store traffic.
	Contests, sweepstakes	Create brand excitement. Build store traffic. Collect names for prospect database.
	Point-of-purchase displays	Reinforce media advertising. Create interaction and impulse buying. Motivate retailers.
	Trade shows, events, sponsorships	Create opportunity for face-to-face contact with trade and consumer prospects. Introduce new products. Collect names for databases. Build brand image through association.
Telemarketing	Selling by phone	Direct marketing tool using outbound or inbound phone programs.

EXHIBIT A.5, *continued*

IMC tools and their strengths

Also key to the marketing effort was a plan to expand geographically to include the Dayton, Ohio, market ninety days into the launch. This increased the overall scope of the market from 1.9 million to 3.2 million people.

Marketing communications objectives were stated generally as:

- Create brand awareness for Cincinnati Bell Wireless.
- Generate interest in the brand's value proposition (benefits to the target audience).
- Bring prospects into retail outlets offering the Nokia 6160 phone at a special introductory price of $99.

Budget Allocation

From a start date in May, the eight-month budget (for the balance of the calendar year), was set at $3 million. This was a very significant budget level for a Cincinnati-Dayton market campaign. By comparison, to launch at this level in the top fifty metro areas of the United States would translate into a $225 million national effort—on a par with what Apple Computer spent in launching the iMac in the second half of 1998.

The IMC Promotional Mix

How do IMC professionals determine which tools to use? Considering the wide variety of options, it is important to have a general understanding of the opportunities presented by each communications technique. See Exhibit A-5, which lists typical IMC communications tools and their strengths.

For the CBW launch, Northlich Stolley LaWarre used a multilayered campaign with different elements called on to contribute the best of what each has to offer.

Public Relations

Public relations efforts often are initiated in advance of conventional advertising, giving the media a chance to scoop the news before it breaks in ads. As early as February 1998, press releases announced newsworthy developments such as the signing of the partnership agreement between Cincinnati Bell and AT&T. An employee newsletter previewed the CBW launch with news of the advertising campaign to come (see Exhibit A-6).

Other internal, corporate communications included a special invitation to attend an employees-only sneak preview on May 5, 1998. Hundreds of employees

EXHIBIT A.6

CBW internal newsletter: launch preview

turned out to watch the official countdown and blastoff. But in addition to employees, the press was there, making it an informative media event for reporters as well.

Advertising

Television. May 11 began the television campaign, using three different commercials. One is shown here in Exhibit A-7. As you've learned, good advertising is based on an understanding of the consumers' beliefs, attitudes, and concerns, and that is what comes through in the CBW television commercials. Consumer research told NSL that consumers were frustrated by the complexity of the wireless category. The commercials emphasized the simplicity of CBW's proposition—simple pricing plans and no contracts.

Print, Radio, and Outdoor. NSL made heavy use of both print and radio ads to complement the television campaign. Because television is usually the most expensive medium, the less expensive print and radio elements build repetition into the program cost-effectively. In addition, print ads typically help the audience absorb more information than broadcast messages. Actual spending levels for TV, radio, print, and outdoor are detailed in Exhibit A-8.

Print ads in newspapers and regional magazines kept the offer visible on almost a daily basis. Ads like the one in Exhibit A-9 hammered away at the point that CBW is simply a better deal and that the world's most advanced digital phone was part of the package. Additionally, the actor shown in the print ads also appears in the TV spots, reinforcing the integrated message and visual look of the campaign.

Again, in radio, the same actor delivered the message. Using radio for high repetition, the NSL commercials reinforced messages of best geographic coverage, a great phone, no contracts, and much better prices than cellular. See the sample radio copy in Exhibit A-10.

Outdoor advertising was not a major element, but instead played its traditional role as a support medium (see Exhibit A-11). Billboard and transit ads bolstered the basic proposition that CBW is clearer, smarter, and better than cellular.

Promotions and Events

The schedule of launch events and promotions shown in Exhibit A-12 served a variety of purposes. Citywide spring outdoor events provided exposure and lead generation at virtually no cost. Audiences at these events also allowed CBW to gauge the appeal of their service with a broader base of potential users, without diluting the focus of the primary advertising campaign.

Price promotions geared to gift-giving occasions such as Mother's Day and Father's Day used special radio, print, and direct mail. Telephone bill inserts were another cost-effective way to announce promotions.

EXHIBIT A.7

Cincinnati Bell Wireless storyboard: "Classroom"

Finally, CBW's participating sponsorship of professional baseball and the women's professional golf tour boosted awareness. "Businessmen's special" promotions at Cincinnati Reds games hit the primary target segment—MOPEs.

Direct Marketing

To build on the broad awareness being created by the PR, advertising, events, and promotions, NSL's direct-marketing specialists prepared a coordinated and extensive direct-mail campaign. The goal was to create action in one of several ways:

- Sign up for wireless service by calling an 800 number.
- Get more details at the CBW Web site.
- Sign up by visiting any Store@Cincinnati Bell, or another CBW-authorized dealer.

In the mailing, MOPEs received a letter from the marketing director detailing benefits of the wireless service to business users. Also included was a $10 coupon redeemable with purchase. The objective was to sway hesitant MOPEs to close the deal (see Exhibit A-13).

Description	January	February	March	April	May	June	July
TV					$142,982	$95,887	$0
Radio					49,904	22,844	27,536
Print					153,977	65,265	63,374
Outdoor					8,339	8,339	6,589
Production Totals	$19,179	$50,053	$281,165	$344,835	246,118	202,306	169,507
Media Totals	0	0	0	0	355,202	192,335	97,499
Total Spending	19,179	50,053	281,165	344,835	601,320	394,641	267,006

EXHIBIT A.8

CBW launch: Media billing summary for the first half of 1998

EXHIBIT A.9

Sample print ad from the CPW launch

A list broker that specialized in geo-demographic segmentation identified nearly 100,000 MOPE households. The campaign was designed with a built-in experiment to yield information that would benefit future mailings. Four groups were created:

1. 46,000 MOPE households received the complete mailing package plus outbound telemarketing follow-up and extra offer of a free leather case for their Nokia 6160 phone.
2. 46,000 more MOPE households received the complete mailing package plus outbound telemarketing follow-up, but no offer for the free leather case.
3. 5,000 MOPE households received the complete mailing package with follow-up by a second direct-mail contact in place of telemarketing.
4. 1,500 MOPE households received outbound telemarketing only.

Results: Direct mail followed by outbound telemarketing was the most effective tactical combination, as expected. In addition, they learned that the incremental responses generated by the leather case offer were not enough to justify the extra costs associated with that offer.

Sales Support, Collateral, Point-of-Purchase Advertising

An IMC campaign is characterized by brand contacts—the many ways in which prospects come in contact with the organization. In addition to the mass media communications—advertising, media publicity, sponsored events, direct-mail campaigns—there are many smaller, but also important, ways of making

EXHIBIT A.10

Radio copy: Roadside America *(:60)*

(Sound effects: outdoor, nature sounds.)

Scott: This truly is a modern way to travel, Roy.

Roy: Yeah, the largest mobile home ever made. Theater-style seating. Sleeps 52. So big, it beeps when I back up . . . and when I'm going forward.

Scott: Wow! Now where have you been, what have you seen?

Roy: The world's largest talking cow in Georgia. A bicycle-eating tree in Washington. And pretty much everything in between.

Scott: Oh, that's great . . . now, you know, if you had a Cincinnati Bell Wireless phone, you could talk to virtually anyone, anywhere you went.

Roy: Oh yeah, is that right, even at the sand sculpture of the last supper?

Scott: Oh, the sand sculpture of the last supper . . .

Roy: All right, how about the lickable house of salt?

Scott: Oh . . . yeah, wherever that is. You know . . . plus home-rate roaming in AT&T cities across the U.S.

Roy: Well, what are we waiting for?!

(Sound effects: engine starts, then the familiar beeping sound a truck makes when it's backing up, continues under Scott.)

Scott: Get the nationwide coverage and simple more affordable rates than cellular: 100 minutes for 25 bucks or 500 minutes for $50. Stop by the Store@Cincinnati Bell or call 565-1CBW for details.

Note: This ad was voted *Best of Show* by the 1998–99 Addy Awards, Cincinnati Advertising Club.

contact. Person-to-person contacts through salespeople, packaging, sales literature, in-store displays—each is a point of contact that must be evaluated for consistency of message and brand image.

At Stores@Cincinnati Bell, prospective customers were reminded of the larger IMC campaign in many ways. Brochures, package sleeve designs, store design elements—all tied in visually to the campaign's graphic look. See brochure examples in Exhibit A-14. In-store salespeople were well versed in the messages and details of the larger IMC campaign. The multiple benefits of CBW's wireless service—the value proposition—were written as a top ten list, featured on in-store placards and window posters.

In all of these ways, the CBW launch integrated promotional elements. This is the payoff of integrated marketing communications. And how did it work for Cincinnati Bell Wireless?

EXHIBIT A.11

CBW launch billboard facing

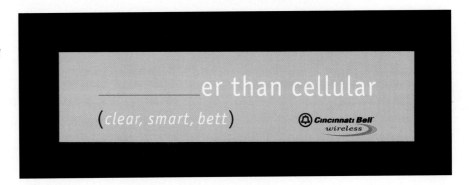

Evaluating Results

Were the objectives achieved? Did the client consider the campaign a success? Think back to the objectives. The campaign's goal was to activate over 16,000 new subscriber accounts in calendar year 1998. They soon realized that this number was too conservative when, after one week into the campaign, they had 10,500 activations.

By year's end they had over 60,000 activations, over three-and-half times the original goal. And the profile of these subscribers told another story. Almost exactly half of these activations came from MOPEs who were converting to CBW from another mobile phone service. The other 30,000 came from young professionals who hadn't previously subscribed to a mobile phone service.

EXHIBIT A.12

CPW launch: promotion and events schedule

May	June
Taste of Cincinnati Target: Adults 25–54 Objective: Introduce CBW and build awareness; generate leads (database) Vehicles: Event only Promo: Booth at event; free trial (phone calls); contest entry	**Day in Eden** Target: Adults 25–54 Objective: Introduce CBW and build awareness; generate leads (database) Vehicles: Event only Promo: Booth at event; free trial (phone calls); contest entry
Mother's Day Target: Users and nonusers Objective: Drive response; store traffic Message: Safety; multiple phones per household Vehicles: Radio and print; bill inserts Promo: Special price package; radio contest (best mother; mother in most need of wireless)	**Kid Fest** Target: Users and nonusers Objective: build awareness; drive response Message: Safety Vehicles: Event only Promo: Booth at event giving away safety-related item (windshield distress sign; emergency flag) logo'd CBW; special offer to sign up for service and receive family pass to local amusements
Graduate Program (high school and college) Target: Nonusers (soon to be young professionals); users (families) Objectives: Drive response Message: Safety and productivity benefits Vehicles: Radio and print; bill inserts Promo: Special price package	**Father's Day** Target: Users and nonusers Objective: Drive response; traffic in stores Message: Productivity benefits Vehicles: Radio and print; bill inserts Promo: Special price package; radio contest (best father; father in most need of wireless)
Baseball Target: Businessmen (Businessmen's Special) Objective: Build awareness; drive response Message: Productivity benefits Vehicles: Event only Promo: Coupon on back of ticket for discount; raffle free phone/service	**LPGA** Target: Nonusers and Users Objective: Drive response Message: Safety and convenience Vehicles: Event only Promo: Coupon on back of ticket for discount; raffle free phone/service

EXHIBIT A.13

CBW launch: direct mail piece

EXHIBIT A.14

CBW launch: P-O-P brochures

The *no hassles, great pricing,* and *cool phone* elements of the value proposition had broader appeal than imagined. Further indications of marketing success included:

1. *Customer loyalty.* Compared to an industry churn rate (customers lost per month) of 4 percent per month, CBW ran at 1 percent.
2. *High revenues.* MOPEs were targeted because they are heavy users of wireless services. While analog cellular companies average $29 revenue per month per customer, and other digital service provider average $45, CBW's average hit $60.
3. *IMC budget doubled.* Recognizing the strength of their early results, CBW spent $6 million in the first calendar year, rather than the original $3 million budgeted.

No wonder investment analysts, AT&T executives, business journalists and CBW president Jack Cassidy drew the same conclusions about this campaign: By any measure, this was the most successful PCS digital launch ever in North America.

UNDERSTANDING THE MARKET ENVIRONMENT FOR PROMOTION AND IMC

Good communication is based on broad knowledge of the market and consumers in the market. In this section of the book, we'll learn how to understand the environment within which a promotional effort will take place. Gathering this essential market knowledge starts with basic marketing strategies: segmenting, targeting, and positioning. These are the strategies upon which a firm has built its overall marketing effort and, in turn, form the foundation for the promotional effort. From these basic strategies, the well-informed promotional planner will then turn to researching and understanding consumer behavior. The influences on consumer decision making will create a desire for information on the part of consumers. Different tools in the promotional process can provide different types of information in different forms, so understanding consumer behavior is an essential task.

Another perspective in this section is that every promotional effort is a communication effort. How consumers process information is essential to preparing and delivering messages through promotion. Next, there is a critical need to understand the regulatory and ethical environment for promotion. While regulations are pretty clear, the ethical issues in promotion are anything but clear. Careful consideration by the promotional planner in these areas is fundamental to understanding the market environment. Finally, having an international perspective on the market is a must. Every organization must be aware of the influence of culture on the communication effort. Even if a firm thinks it will never need to promote its brand outside the United States, the potential for international business and the communication it requires is ever present.

4

Understanding the Marketing Environment: Segmenting, Targeting, and Positioning explains that a firm's most important decisions include segmenting the marketing, targeting high potential segments for different brands, and then positioning the brands for success. This chapter addresses how to segment both the consumer market and business-to-business market—a typically overlooked analysis in most situations but critical to the success of both consumer and business products. Finally, we will discuss the issue of prioritizing segments and the critical decisions related to brand positioning.

5

Understanding Buyer Behavior and Communication Processes summarizes the concept of buyer behavior of household consumers and business buyers and how each processes promotional communications. Our ultimate goal, of course, is to understand which promotional tools are most effective in communicating to both types of potential buyers. Underlying the success of any promotions effort is a good understanding of the communication process, so this chapter concludes with an explanation of this process.

6

The Regulatory Environment for Promotion and Ethical Issues considers both the regulation of promotion and the ethical debates that accompany the practices of promotion. The chapter identifies the main regulatory issues related to the promotional process and evaluates the effectiveness of self-regulation. Finally, the chapter explores the debates surrounding various ethical issues such as truth in advertising, consumer privacy, and deception in sales-promotion offers.

7

The International Market Environment for Promotion and IMC introduces issues related to planning promotional efforts aimed to international audiences. Global forces are creating markets that are more affluent, accessible, and predictable. In the midst of these trends toward international trade, marketers are redefining the nature and scope of the markets for goods and services while adjusting to the creative, media, and regulatory challenges of competing across national borders.

After reading this chapter, you will be able to:

1 Explain the process of segmenting and targeting markets and then positioning brands within those markets.

2 Describe the different techniques marketers use to identify target segments in the consumer market.

3 Identify the ways marketers segment the business-to-business market.

4 Discuss the criteria used by marketers to decide which segments to target.

5 Discuss the key elements of an effective brand positioning strategy.

CHAPTER 4

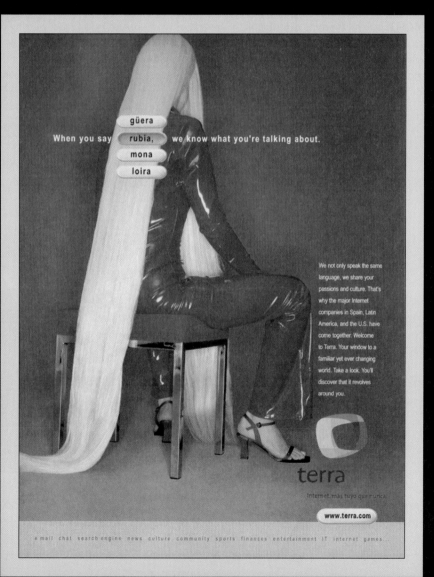

It would be fair to say that executives at The Gillette Company in Boston, Massachusetts, have become prisoners of their own success. King C. Gillette invented the safety razor in 1903, and since then male grooming habits and the "wet shave" have been the company's obsession. Few companies have experienced the growth and global success that Gillette has achieved in the twentieth century. This firm is able to make the extraordinary claim that roughly two-thirds of all wet shaves around the world involve one of its razors.[1] Its advertising slogan—"Gillette: The Best a Man Can Get"—and products like its SensorExcel and MACH3 shaving systems are ubiquitous. Thus, the challenge for Gillette executives is how to maintain the company's success at growing sales and profits around the world. They can try to keep introducing more expensive (and more profitable) shaving systems like the MACH3, and try to reach every last wet-shaving male on the face of the planet, but at some point they literally will run out of new faces.

To find sources for new growth, Gillette, like a lot of companies, needed to identify someone other than wet-shaving males to target with its new products and promotional campaigns. To make a long story short, Gillette decided to target wet-shaving females. The quintessential male-focused company will finally devote some of its considerable resources to addressing the unique shaving needs of women. And not by just putting pink handles on men's razors (like the Daisy disposable razor, a failed Gillette product in the mid-1970s), but a complete line of products developed by women for women. When the

EXHIBIT 4.1

This is one of the ads from the promotional campaign used by Gillette to launch the firm's wet-shaving product line for women. Notice the ad features a summer scene—the season when the company spends most of its budget to reach this target segment.

EXHIBIT 4.2

Another in the series of advertisements from the promotional campaign targeting women with wet-shaving products. This ad highlights an emotional appeal as the basis for the benefits of using the Gillette brand.

1. Mark Maremont, "Gillette Finally Reveals Its Vision of the Future, and It Has 3 Blades," *The Wall Street Journal,* April 14, 1998, A1, A10.

strategy was announced, one competitor quipped, "What's your headline—Gillette discovers women?"[2] Actually, that wasn't far from being right.

Gillette has identified 15-to-24-year-old women as a new target segment. The thinking is that winning over youthful, wet-shaving young females will create customers for life. Gillette had the global marketplace in mind when it launched its "Gillette for Women: Are You Ready?" campaign. While women around the world are less likely to remove body hair than their counterparts in the United States (for example, Gillette estimates that 84 percent remove body hair in the United States vs. 18 percent in Germany), younger women worldwide are more receptive to the idea. Gillette has set out to tap the growth potential represented by the target segment of 15-to-24-year-old females around the world.

The program Gillette has launched is multifaceted. It started with the Sensor shaving system for women, created by a female industrial designer, that featured a flat, wafer-shaped handle to give women better control while shaving. Other products have followed, such as a high-end disposable razor named Agility and a line of shaving creams and after-shave products marketed under the brand name Satin Care. More money was allocated for global promotional campaigns featuring ads like those shown in Exhibits 4.1 and 4.2. This "Gillette for Women: Are You Ready?," advertising was based on market research that showed most women perceive shaving as a nuisance or chore. Hence, they treat razors as a commodity item and are satisfied with inexpensive disposables. Gillette's advertising was designed to make this routine grooming chore more important and more glamorous, and, in the words of Gillette's VP of female shaving, "elevate the role of shaving beyond the practical to a more emotional realm."[3] In this "emotional realm," Gillette's hopes are that more women will be willing to pay a bit extra for products like Sensor and Satin Care.

By targeting wet-shaving young women, Gillette executives have found a way to keep the company's sales and profits growing. Annual growth rates for women's products are around 20 percent, outperforming the men's division. Gillette's sales gains have been followed with increases in its promotion budgets in an effort to reach a goal of $1 billion in revenues from women's products worldwide by the year 2001.[4] No matter how you cut it, that's a whole lot of wet shaves.

INTRODUCTION

No decisions are more important to a firm than segmenting the market, targeting high potential segments for different brands, and then positioning the brands for success. The decisions associated with segmenting, targeting, and positioning (STP) are complex and depend on precise information. The information gathered is then used to understand the market environment well enough to take strategic action.

Virtually every organization must compete for the attention and business of some customer groups while de-emphasizing or ignoring others. In this chapter, we examine in detail the way organizations decide which consumer and business markets to target and which markets to ignore in laying the foundation for their marketing programs and promotional campaigns. We first consider the basics of STP decisions with respect to how markets are analyzed. Then we look at segmenting the business-to-business market—a typically overlooked analysis in most situations but critical to the success of both consumer and business products. Finally, we will discuss the issue of prioritizing segments and the critical decisions related to brand positioning.

STP MARKETING AND THE EVOLUTION OF MARKETING STRATEGIES ❶

The Gillette example illustrates that marketers decide who to market to and what sort of promotion will be needed to communicate to the market. Gillette executives started with the diverse market of all women, and they broke the market down by

---

2.   Mark Maremont, "Gillette's New Strategy Is to Sharpen Pitch to Women," *The Wall Street Journal*, May 11, 1998, B1, B16.
3.   Ibid.
4.   Ibid.

age segments. Recall from Chapter 1 that this is the process called **market segmentation,** where a firm takes a diverse, heterogeneous market and breaks it into submarkets or segments that are more homogeneous. Once a basic segmentation analysis was done, Gillette selected 15-to-24-year-old females as their target segment. A **target segment** is a subgroup (of the larger segment) chosen as the focal point for a marketing program and promotional campaign.

While markets are segmented, products are positioned. To pursue the target segment, a firm organizes its marketing and promotional efforts around a coherent positioning strategy. **Positioning** is the act of designing and representing a brand so that it will occupy a distinct and valued place in the consumer's mind relative to other brands. **Positioning strategy** involves the selection of key themes or concepts that the organization will feature when communicating this distinctiveness to the target segment. In Gillette's case, its executives first designed a line of products for the youthful female wet-shaver target market. They then came up with the positioning theme "Gillette for Women: Are You Ready?" to clearly distinguish this new line from their traditional male-oriented shaving systems and from competitors' shaving products. Finally, through skillful promotions, they communicated distinctive functional and emotional benefits to the target segment.

Notice the specific sequence, illustrated in Exhibit 4.3, that is used to segment, and target markets, and then position brands for those target markets. This is the sequence played out in the Gillette example: The marketing strategy evolved as a result of segmenting, targeting, and positioning. This sequence of strategic marketing planning activities has come to be known as **STP marketing,** and it represents a sound basis for generating effective promotion. While there are no formulas that guarantee success, the STP approach is strongly recommended for markets characterized by diversity in consumers' needs and preferences. In markets with any significant degree of diversity, it is impossible to design one product that will appeal to everyone, or one promotional campaign that will communicate with everyone. Organizations that lose sight of this simple premise often run into trouble.

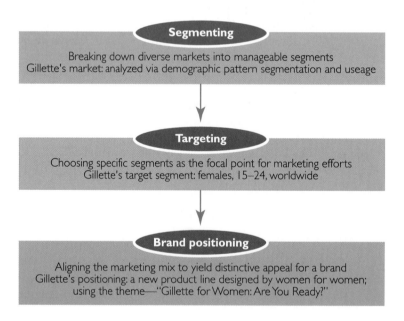

EXHIBIT 4.3

Segmenting and targeting the market and positioning the brand—referred to as STP marketing—lay the foundation for effective promotional campaigns.

Indeed, in most product categories one finds that different consumers are looking for different things, and the only way for a company to take advantage of the sales potential represented by different customer segments is to develop and market a different brand for each segment. No company has done this better than cosmetics juggernaut Estée Lauder. Lauder has over a dozen cosmetic brands, each developed for a different target segment of women.[5] For example, there is the original Estée Lauder brand, for women with conservative values and upscale tastes. Then there is Clinique, a no-nonsense brand that represents functional grooming for Middle America. Bobbi Brown Essentials are for the working mom who skillfully manages a career and her family and manages to look good in the process. M.A.C. is a brand for those who want to make a bolder statement: its spokespeople have been RuPaul, a 6-foot 7-inch drag queen, and k. d. lang, the talented lesbian vocalist. Prescriptives is marketed to a hip, urban, multiethnic target segment, and Origins, with its earthy packaging and natural ingredients, is for consumers who are concerned about the environment. These are just some of the cosmetics brands offered by Estée Lauder to appeal to diverse target segments.

We offer the Estée Lauder example to make two key points before we move on. First, the Gillette example may have made things seem too simple: STP marketing is a lot more complicated than just deciding to target women or men. Gender and age alone are rarely specific enough to serve as a sufficient basis for determining a target segment. Second, the cosmetics example shows that many factors beyond just age and gender can come into play when trying to identify valid target segments. For these diverse cosmetics brands, we see that considerations such as attitudes, lifestyles, and basic values all may play a role in identifying and describing customer segments.

To illustrate this point, consider the two ads in Exhibits 4.4 and 4.5. Both these ads ran in *Seventeen* magazine in the same issue, so it is safe to surmise that the marketers were trying to reach adolescent females. But as you compare these ads, it should be pretty obvious that the marketers were really trying to reach out to very different segments of that market. To put it bluntly, it would be hard to imagine a marine captain wearing Hard Candy lip gloss when preparing for a combat exercise. Again, even though both of these ads are targeted to the same demographic segment of adolescent females, they are clearly designed to reach different segments of that market.

The Value of STP Marketing

The value of a carefully orchestrated STP marketing effort is that it enhances performance across all phases of the marketing and promotional campaign. There are often dramatic effects on both the efficiency and effectiveness of activities. From human resource needs to the speed of implementing promotion, a firm is able to more astutely make decisions when segmentation, targeting, and positioning have been done properly. Specifically, STP marketing analysis enhances a firm's efforts related to:

- The precise specification of marketing objectives.
- A better understanding of the needs, desires, and motives of consumers.
- A better understanding of why customers purchase and noncustomers do not.
- More efficient allocation of human and financial resources.
- The ability to assess competitive strengths and weaknesses of the firm's marketing and promotional activities.
- The ability to identify more precisely the messages to use across promotional mix tools.

5. Nina Munk, "Why Women Find Lauder Mesmerizing," *Fortune,* May 25, 1998, 96–106.

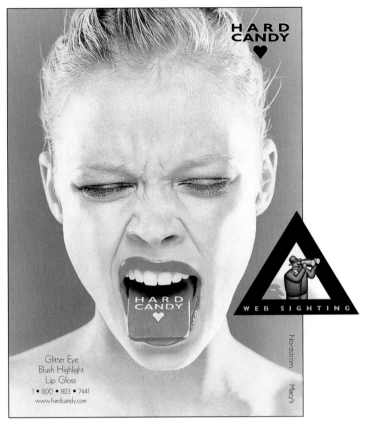

http://www.hardcandy.com; http://www.urbandecay.com;
http://www.lancome.com

EXHIBIT 4.4

The U.S. Armed Forces, including the Marines, are very aggressive and sophisticated advertisers. Here the Marines direct a message to basically the same target segment (from an age and gender standpoint) that was the focal point in Gillette's "Are You Ready?" campaign.
http://www.usmc.mil/

EXHIBIT 4.5

Hard Candy comes by its hip style, perhaps in large part, because of its uninhibitedly energetic founding by Gen X twentysomething Dinch Mohajer, who was unhappy with the choices traditional cosmetics firms offered her and her market demograph. There must be something in that California air. Internet technology company Cisco co-founder Sandy Lerner created Urban Decay—another alternative for the fashion-mad—out of a similar dissatisfaction with the offerings of companies like Lancôme.

- The ability to better provide IMC management of the promotional effort.
- The ability to respond more quickly to changes in the external environment.

The reason a firm will realize these benefits is that STP marketing analysis forces an organization to focus its efforts within well-defined parameters. This makes decision makers more knowledgeable and more sensitized to factors that affect a firm's marketing and promotional efforts. The effect is really one of specialization versus generalization. As the decision makers in an organization become "specialists" on a particular group of consumers—the target segment—then the ability to understand the brand's value and the means to deliver it are greatly increased.

Beyond STP Marketing

If an organization uses STP marketing as a framework for strategy development, at some point it will find the right strategy, develop the right promotion, make a lot of money, and live happily ever after. Right? As you might expect, it's not quite that simple. Even when STP marketing yields profitable outcomes, one must presume that success will not last indefinitely. Indeed, an important feature of marketing and promotion—a feature that can make these professions both terribly interesting and terribly frustrating—is their dynamic nature. To paraphrase a popular saying, "shifts happen," and consumer preferences and markets change. Competitors improve their marketing strategies, or technology changes and makes popular product obsolete. Successful marketing strategies need to be modified or may even need to be reinvented as shifts occur in the organization's competitive environment. As a matter of fact, Gillette is now in a period where it needs to reassess and reassert itself. While the move into women's wet shaves was well conceived and is still a good idea, sales and profits in the entire blade and razor category have slowed considerably, dropping from about a 20 percent growth rate to about 5 percent annually.[6] Will Gillette abandon STP marketing as a way to cultivate markets? Absolutely not! Quite to the contrary, the firm will rededicate itself to the process as a way to discover new and profitable products and brands for different segments.

To maintain the vitality and profitability of its brands, an organization has two options. The first is to reassess the segmentation strategy. This may come about through a detailed examination of the current target segment and developing new and better ways to meet its needs, or it may be necessary to adopt new targets and position new products to them, as was the case with "Gillette for Women."

The second option is to pursue a product differentiation strategy. As we defined in Chapter 1, **product differentiation** focuses the firm's efforts on emphasizing or even creating differences for its brands to distinguish them from the offerings of established competitors. Recall that promotion plays a critical role as part of the product differentiation strategy because often the consumer will have to be convinced that the difference being portrayed is meaningful. Product differentiation strategies try to make a brand appear different from competing brands, but it is consumers' perceptions of the difference that will determine the success of the strategy. As one highly respected marketing consultant, Jack Trout, put it, "In this global killer economy, marketers have to find a way to differentiate themselves or they better have a very, very low price."[7]

For example, when Church & Dwight Company introduced its Arm & Hammer Dental Care baking soda toothpaste, major toothpaste marketers such as Procter & Gamble and Colgate-Palmolive were not impressed. This new brand had a distinctive difference from traditional brands like Crest and Colgate, but would consumers find this difference meaningful? The answer turned out to be yes—the slightly salty taste and gritty texture of the Arm & Hammer brand proved popular with consumers; in no time, sales of baking soda toothpastes approached $300 million annually.[8]

The basic message is that marketing strategies and the promotion that supports them are never really final. Successes realized through proper application of STP marketing can be short-lived in highly competitive markets where any successful innovation is almost sure to be copied by competitors. Thus, the brand identity process for marketers is continuous; STP marketing must be pursued over and over again and may be supplemented with product differentiation strategies.

6.   Richard McCaffery (TMF Gibson), "Gillette Closes Out Grim 1999," accessed at http://www.fool.com/news on January 28, 2000.
7.   Jack Trout, "Being Different Is Where It's At," *Advertising Age,* November 22, 1999, 27.
8.   Kathleen Deveny, "Anatomy of a Fad: How Clear Products Were Hot and Then Suddenly Were Not," *The Wall Street Journal,* March 15, 1994, B1.

IDENTIFYING TARGET SEGMENTS ❷

The first step in STP marketing involves breaking down large, diverse markets into more manageable submarkets or customer segments through the market segmentation process. This can be accomplished in many ways, but keep in mind that marketers need to identify a segment with common characteristics that will lead consumers in that segment to respond distinctively to a marketing program. Additionally, for a segment to be really useful, marketers must be able to reach that segment with communications about the brand. Typically, this means that the segment must be reachable with at least some but preferably many forms of promotion. For example, teenage males can be reached efficiently through media such as MTV; selected rap, contemporary rock-and-roll, or alternative radio stations; promotional gear like T-shirts and ball caps; and the Internet. As described in the New Media box, one of the particularly appealing aspects of the Internet for marketers is the way it allows them to reach valued and specific target segments.

In this section, we will review several ways that consumer markets are commonly segmented. Markets can be segmented on the basis of demographic and geographic characteristics, usage patterns and commitment levels, psychographics and lifestyles, or benefits sought. Many times, segmentation schemes evolve in such a way that multiple variables are used to identify and describe the target segment. Such an outcome is desirable because more knowledge about the target will usually translate into better promotional programs.

TRUTH IS, GEN X IS STILL OUT THERE, IF YOU KNOW WHERE AND HOW TO LOOK

The twentysomething consumer, referred to loosely as Generation X, remains a high priority in the segmentation strategies of many companies. One simple fact helps explain why: Their projected aggregate income by the year 2001 will be in the neighborhood of $1.8 trillion. Of course, like any other age cohort, there is too much diversity within this group to treat them as a single entity. There are, at the very least, four submarkets of Gen X'ers to consider—college and graduate students, up-and-coming professionals, and married couples with and without children. To reach the Gen X segment, you really must know who it is you're targeting within that segment. Then you can pick an advertising medium that will help you get your message to them.

Increasingly, the medium that marketers rely on is the Internet. Again, a simple fact helps explain why. The twentysomething cohort spends an average of 9.3 hours a week surfing the Net, compared to an average of 8.4 hours a week for the population in general, and 6.3 hours for people over age 50. Volkswagen of America is often cited as an example of a company that has been successful in communicating with Gen X'ers, and its Web site is a critical part of that dialogue. But it's not enough just to build a Web site and then expect Gen X to show up. The Web site works only as part of an integrated campaign where traditional broadcast advertising does its part by generating some curiosity and getting the consumer to use the Web. Easier said than done, because Gen X'ers have been raised on sophisticated advertising campaigns and can be very cynical about advertisers' motives.

Source: "Want to Catch Gen X? Try Looking on the Web," *Marketing News,* June 8, 1998, 20.

Demographic Segmentation

The starting point for many segmentation efforts is demographic segmentation. **Demographic segmentation** breaks a market down by basic physical descriptors of individuals such as age, gender, ethnic background, marital status, income, education, and occupation. Demographic information has special value in the market segmentation process because if a marketer knows the demographic characteristics of the target segment, choosing advertising media and promotional channels to efficiently reach that segment is much easier.

Demographic information has two specific applications. First, demographics are commonly used to describe or profile segments that have been identified with some other variable. If an organization had first segmented its market in terms of product usage rates (to be discussed shortly), the next step would be to describe or profile its heavy users in terms of demographic characteristics such as age or income. In fact, one of the most common approaches for identifying target segments is to combine information about usage patterns with demographics.

Mobil Oil Corporation used such an approach in segmenting the market for gasoline buyers and identified five basic segments: Road Warriors, True Blues, Generation F3, Homebodies, and Price Shoppers.[9] Extensive research on more than 2,000 motorists revealed considerable insight about these five segments. At the one extreme, Road Warriors spend at least $1,200 per year at gas stations; they buy premium gasoline and snacks and beverages and sometimes opt for a car wash. Road Warriors are generally more affluent, middle-aged males who drive 25,000 to 50,000 miles per year. (Note how Mobil combined information about usage patterns with demographics to provide a detailed picture of the segment.) In contrast, Price Shoppers spend no more than $700 annually at gas stations, are generally less affluent, rarely buy premium, and show no loyalty to particular brands or stations. In terms of relative segment sizes, there are about 25 percent more Price Shoppers on the highways than Road Warriors. If you were the marketing vice president at Mobil Oil Corporation, which of these two segments would you target? Think about it for a few pages—we'll get back to you.

Second, as stated earlier, demographic categories are frequently used as the starting point in market segmentation. This was the case in the Gillette example, where teenage females turned out to be the segment of interest. It was also the method used by filmmakers such as Konica USA, Kodak, and Fuji who have attempted to tap into diverse demographic segments with products such as high-speed "baby film" for new parents, complete photo-hobby kits for preteens, and hassle-free cardboard cameras for older people who want last-minute photos of the grandchildren.[10]

One demographic group that will receive increasing attention from marketers in the years to come is the "woopies," or well-off older people. In the United States, consumers over 50 have more discretionary income than all other age segments combined. By the year 2025, the number of people over 50 will grow by 80 percent to become a third of the U.S. population. This growth in the woopie segment will be even more dramatic in other countries, such as Japan and the nations of Western Europe.[11] What's more, this group will bring to their latter years unprecedented wealth. Beginning in the year 2005, the first woopies will be able to draw on their 401(k) retirement plans in the United Sates without any tax penalties.[12] Still, like any other age segment, older consumers are a diverse group, and the temptation to stereotype must be resisted. Some marketers advocate partitioning older consumers into groups aged 50–64, 65–74, 75–84, and 85 or older as a means of reflecting important differences in needs.

Another key factor for demographic segmentation is ethnic background. Ethnic groups are growing much more rapidly in the United States than the nonethnic population. The population of Hispanic-origin consumers is growing at about 4.5 percent per year in the. United States compared with a 1.2 percent growth rate for the overall population, and now represent over 32 million U.S. consumers.[13]

9. Allanna Sullivan, "Mobil Bets Drivers Pick Cappuccino over Low Prices," *The Wall Street Journal,* January 30, 1995, B1.
10. Joan E. Rigdon, "Photography Companies Focus on Niches," *The Wall Street Journal,* March 12, 1993, 1.
11. "The Rich Autumn of a Consumer's Life," *The Economist,* September 5, 1992, 67–68.
12. Peter G. Peterson, "Bracing for the Age Wave," *Bloomberg Personal Finance,* July/August 1999, 38.
13. Christine Galea and Sara Lorge, "The Power of the Survey," *Sales & Marketing Management, 1999 Survey of Buying Power,* 6.

The Asian population in the United States is experiencing a similar heightened growth rate and now numbers about 11 million. Marketers track demographic changes and trends with publications like *Marketing & Sales Management* magazine's Annual Survey of Buying Power and by keeping close tabs on government publications that provide demographic data. These government publications include the Census of Population, Census of Housing, Census of Retail Trade, and Survey of Current Business.

Marketers are finding that communicating with ethnic populations requires using a broad range of promotional tools. Certainly there are media targeted to ethnic populations, but that only covers the advertising effort. Promoting events in ethnic regions of the country has proved effective in targeting ethnic populations; it also bolsters and instills a strong sense of community. The Ethnic Marketing Manager for Lincoln Mercury Co. believes that the main challenge of marketing to ethnic populations is "about reaching the market and then taking the vehicles to the market via events." Lincoln Mercury sponsors the Latin Business Expo in California and the National Black MBA Luncheon in Los Angeles.[14]

Geographic Segmentation

Geographic segmentation needs little explanation other than to discuss how useful geography is as a segmentation method. **Geographic segmentation** may be conducted within a country by region (for example, the Pacific Northwest versus New England), by state or province, by city, or even by neighborhood. Climate and topographical features yield dramatic differences in consumption by region for products such as snow tires and surfboards, but geography can also correlate with other differences that are not so obvious. Food preferences and preparation habits, entertainment preferences, recreational activities, and other aspects of lifestyle have been shown to vary along geographic lines. Exhibits 4.6 and 4.7 show U.S. consumption

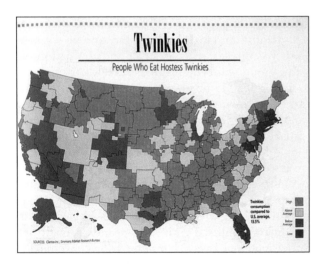
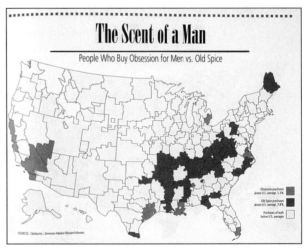

EXHIBITS 4.6 AND 4.7

Where people live wouldn't seem to matter with respect to what products they use. But if you look at these geodemographic maps of Hostess Twinkies and Old Spice versus Obsession cologne, it appears where people live does have something to do with consumption patterns.

14.   Cara Beardi, "Community Events Key for Automakers," *Advertising Age,* November 15, 1999, 41.

GLOBAL GEODEMOGRAPHICS

Given the success of the PRIZM geodemographic segmentation process being used in the United States, it was logical to expect the same methods and technology to be applied on an international scale. Experian, based in Nottingham, England, and Orange, California, is doing just that. Experian (http://www.experian.com) is a global information solutions company that specializes in helping organizations make informed strategic segmentation decisions. The company is one of the world's leading suppliers of information on consumers, businesses, motor vehicles, and property. By combining its databases with advanced technology and consultancy services, Experian assists its clients in targeting and acquiring new customers, building successful customer relationships and managing financial risk.

Experian has developed a geodemographic segmentation system for eighteen countries (accounting for about 800 million consumers), including most of Western Europe, Australia and New Zealand, Japan, South Africa, and the United States. Such a system can prove very powerful for marketers with global aspirations, because it can tell them whether the segment they are pursuing in one country also exists in others. When a common customer segment exists in many countries (for example, middle-income, urban office workers), a single marketing and advertising campaign can sometimes be used to appeal to both segments in different countries. Expect these systems to grow in popularity as the tools and technology spread around the world.

Sources: Susan Mitchell, "Parallel Universes," *Marketing Tools*, November/December 1997, 14–17; Bruno Rost and Julie Springer, "Experian Selected to Support Morgan Stanley Dean Witter in Launch of New Credit Card," accessed at http://www.experian.com on February 10, 2000.

patterns for Twinkies, and for Obsession versus Old Spice cologne. While you wouldn't think so, geographic location does seem to affect the consumption of these product types and consumer preferences.

In recent years, skillful marketers have merged information on where people live with the U.S. Census Bureau's demographic data to produce a form of market segmentation known as geodemographic segmentation. **Geodemographic segmentation** identifies neighborhoods (by zip codes) around the country that share common demographic characteristics. One such system, known as PRIZM (potential rating index by zip marketing), identifies 62 market segments that encompass all the zip codes in the United States.[15] Each of these segments indicates similar lifestyle characteristics and can be found throughout the country.

The "American Dreams" segment, for example, is found in many metropolitan neighborhoods and comprises upwardly mobile ethnic minorities, many of whom were foreign-born. This segment's product preferences are different from those of people belonging to the "Rural Industrial" segment, who are young families with one or both parents working at low-wage jobs in small-town America. Systems such as PRIZM are very popular because of the depth of segment descriptions they provide, along with their ability to precisely identify where the segment can be found. The process of geodemographic segmentation can be so useful in preparing promotional efforts that it has gone global, as the Global Issues box discusses.

Usage Patterns and Commitment Levels

One of the most common ways to segment markets is by consumers' usage patterns or commitment levels. In this sense, marketers don't care who you are or where you live—they just zoom in on what you buy and how you use it. One of the key aspects of usage patterns is the realization that for most products and services, a small percentage of the users use a large percentage of the products. These are called the heavy user segments. It is common to find that **heavy users** in a product category—like soft drinks or salty snacks—often account for the majority of a product's sales and thus become the preferred or primary target segment. For example, Campbell Soup Company has discovered what it refers to as its extra-enthusiastic core

15.   Christina Del Valle, "They Know Where You Live—and How You Buy," *Business Week,* February 7, 1994, 89.

users: folks who buy nearly 320 cans of soup per year.[16] That's enough soup to serve Campbell's at least six days a week every week! To maintain this level of devotion to the product, marketing wisdom holds that it is in Campbell's best interest to know about these heavy users in great detail and make them a focal point of the company's marketing strategy.

While being the standard wisdom, the heavy-user focus has some potential downside risk. For one, devoted users may need no encouragement at all to keep consuming. This means that spending money on promotion, particularly couponing or cents-off promotions, may be a complete waste of money. In addition, a heavy-user focus takes attention and resources away from those who do need encouragement to purchase the marketer's brand. Perhaps most important, various heavy users may be significantly different in terms of their motivations to consume, their approach to the product, or their image of the product. This makes a single promotional campaign for the heavy-user segment difficult to develop.

Another segmentation option combines prior usage patterns with commitment levels to a product category or a brand within a product category. This combination of usage and commitment yields four fundamental segment types: nonusers, brand-loyal customers, switchers (or variety seekers), and emergent consumers.[17] Each segment represents a unique opportunity for a marketer.

Nonusers, those consumers who do not use the product category, offer the lowest level of opportunity relative to the other three groups. It is very difficult to convince someone who is not a chewing gum user, or beer drinker, or football fan to develop an affinity for a product category that they have, for whatever reason, rejected for years. Promotional efforts aimed at nonusers will be unsuccessful in mature product categories like chewing gum or beer or football. In new product categories, like DVD players or electronic organizers, nonusers are a segment with potential. **Brand-loyal users,** consumers who repeatedly buy the same brand, are a tremendous asset if they are the marketer's customers, but they are difficult to convert if they are loyal to a competitor. **Switchers, or variety seekers,** often buy what is on sale or choose brands that offer discount coupons or other price incentives. Whether they are pursued through price promotions, high-profile advertising campaigns, or both, switchers turn out to be an expensive segment to try to win. Much can be spent in getting their business merely to have it disappear just as quickly as it was won. But as we saw in Chapter 3, for short-term promotional objectives that focus on sales, switchers can represent good potential for spiking demand for a brand.

Emergent consumers offer the organization an important business opportunity. In most product categories, there is a gradual but constant influx of first-time buyers. The reasons for this influx vary by product category and include purchase triggers such as puberty, college graduation, marriage, birth of a child, divorce, job promotions, and retirement. Immigration can also be a source of numerous new customers for many product categories. The segment of emergent consumers called the "new rich" is certainly attracting the attention of marketers. Households in the United States with a net worth over $1 million have grown from about 1.3 million in 1990 to nearly 7 million by 1999, and the percentage of millionaires who are under 55 has nearly doubled during that time. These kinds of statistics are attracting marketers like online trading companies and life insurance companies, who are targeting the new rich with all forms of promotions.[18]

16. Rebecca Piirto, *Beyond Mind Games: The Marketing Power of Psychographics* (Ithaca, NY: American Demographics Books, 1991), 230.

17. Further discussion of this four-way scheme is provided by David W. Stewart, "Advertising in Slow-Growth Economies," *American Demographics* (September 1994), 40–46.

18. Mercedes M. Cardona, "Phoenix Home Life Targets Ad Effort at Newly Wealthy," *Advertising Age,* January 10, 2000, 16.

Emergent consumers are motivated by many different factors, but they share one important characteristic: Their brand preferences are still under development. Targeting emergents with promotional communications that fit their age or social circumstances may produce modest effects in the short run, but it eventually may yield a brand loyalty that pays handsome rewards for the discerning organization. This was the thinking behind the promotional campaign for Rogaine run by Pharmacia & Upjohn.[19] The company started a promotional campaign urging young men who have a full head of hair, but who still see strands going down the drain, to start using Rogaine as a preventive measure. As another example, credit card marketers actively recruit college students who have limited financial resources in the short term, but excellent potential as long-term customers. Exhibit 4.8 shows an American Express direct-marketing campaign run in a college catalog that was designed to tap this emergent segment.

http://www.americanexpress.com

http://www.jostens.com

EXHIBIT 4.8

Emergent consumers represent an important source of future revenue for marketers. This direct-marketing promotion by American Express targets new college graduates. What other product categories have a significant "emergent" market? College is the perfect window of opportunity for Amex: Students won't have had a credit card before coming to school (they were too young), and will have significant independence for the first time and a host of purchase opportunities. How might Jostens, the class ring people, see that same market? Where might you find either of these two companies advertising on the Web?

19.   Kathryn Kranhold, "Rogaine Urges the Nonbald to Use Ounces of Prevention," *The Wall Street Journal*, September 20, 1999, B1.

Psychographics and Lifestyle Segmentation

Psychographics is a term that marketers created in the mid-1960s to refer to a form of research that emphasizes the understanding of consumers' activities, interests, and opinions (AIOs).[20] Back in the 1960s, many advertising and promotion agencies were using demographic variables for segmentation purposes, but they wanted insights into consumers' motivations, which demographics alone could not provide. Psychographics were created as a tool to supplement the use of demographic data. Because a focus on consumers' activities, interests, and opinions often produces insights into differences in the lifestyles of various segments, this approach has come to also be known as lifestyle segmentation. Knowing details about the lifestyle of a target segment can be valuable for creating advertising messages and promotional programs that ring true to the consumer.

Lifestyle segmentation (or psychographic segmentation) can be customized with a focus on the issues germane to a single product category, or it may be pursued so that the resulting segments have general applicability to many different product or service categories. An example of the former is research conducted for Pillsbury to segment the eating habits of American households.[21] This "What's Cookin' " study involved consumer interviews with more than 3,000 people and identified five segments of the population, based on their shared eating styles:

- *Chase & Grabbits,* at 26 percent of the population, are heavy users of all forms of fast food. These are people who can make a meal out of microwave popcorn; as long as the popcorn keeps hunger at bay and is convenient, this segment is happy with its meal.
- *Functional Feeders,* at 18 percent of the population, are a bit older than the Chase & Grabbits but no less convenience oriented. Since they are more likely to have families, their preference for convenience foods involves frozen products that are quickly prepared at home. They constantly seek faster ways to prepare the traditional foods they grew up with.
- *Down-Home Stokers,* at 21 percent of the population, involve blue-collar households with modest incomes. They are very loyal to their regional diets, such as meat and potatoes in the Midwest versus clam chowder in New England. Fried chicken, biscuits and gravy, and bacon and eggs make this segment the champion of cholesterol.
- *Careful Cooks,* at 20 percent of the population, are more prevalent on the West Coast. They have replaced most of the red meat in their diet with pastas, fish, skinless chicken, and mounds of fresh fruit and vegetables. They believe they are knowledgeable about nutritional issues and are willing to experiment with foods that offer healthful options.
- *Happy Cookers* are the remaining 15 percent of the population but are a shrinking segment. These cooks are family oriented and take substantial satisfaction from preparing a complete homemade meal for the family. Young mothers in this segment are aware of nutritional issues but will bend the rules with homemade meat dishes, casseroles, pies, cakes, and cookies.

Even these abbreviated descriptions of Pillsbury's five psychographic segments should make it clear that very different marketing and promotional programs are called for to appeal to each group.

As noted, lifestyle segmentation studies can also be pursued with no particular product category as a focus, and the resulting segments will prove to be useful for

---

20. Piirto, *Beyond Mind Games,* 21–23.
21. Ibid., 222–23.

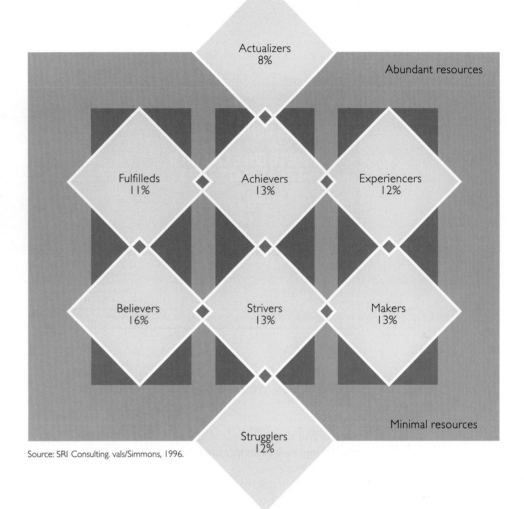

Source: SRI Consulting. vals/Simmons, 1996.

EXHIBIT 4.9

SRI International, a research firm, has produced the VALS 2 system as a way to segment the U.S. consumer market into eight distinct segments.

many different marketers. A notable example of this approach is the VALS (values and lifestyles) system developed by SRI International and marketed by SRI Consulting of Menlo Park, California.[22] The VALS framework was first introduced in 1978 with nine potential segments, but in recent years it has been revised as VALS 2 with eight market segments.

As shown in Exhibit 4.9, these segments are organized in terms of personal descriptions (which include more than age, income, and education) and personal orientation. For instance, the Experiencer is relatively affluent and action oriented. This enthusiastic and risk-taking group has yet to establish predictable behavioral patterns. Its members look to sports, recreation, exercise, and social activities as

22. Ibid.; see Chapters 3, 5, and 8 for an extensive discussion of the VALS system.

EXHIBIT 4.10

For years, Volvo has used a benefit segmentation strategy that features safety as a benefit of owning a Volvo.

outlets for their abundant energy. SRI Consulting sells detailed information and marketing recommendations about the eight segments to a variety of marketing organizations.

It is important to note that a marketer need not turn to a syndicated research service like SRI to get lifestyle data. The firm itself can research the target segment and develop a profile of activities, interests, and opinions. This may, indeed, take some original research using the help of one of the firm's advertising or promotional agencies. The research might be expensive, but the payoff in terms of knowing what kinds of messages to develop and which promotional tools to deploy can make a huge difference in the effectiveness of the overall IMC effort.

Benefit Segmentation

Another segmentation approach developed by researchers and used extensively over the past 30 years is benefit segmentation. In **benefit segmentation,** target segments are identified by the various benefit packages that different consumers want from the same product category. For instance, different people want different benefits from their automobiles. Some consumers just want economical and reliable transportation; others want speed and excitement; still others want luxury, comfort, and prestige. One product could not possibly serve such diverse benefit segments. For years, Volvo has staked a claim on the safety benefit segment of the auto market, as Exhibit 4.10 shows.

This notion of attempting to understand consumers' priorities and assess how different brands might perform based on criteria deemed important by various segments needs to be understood through a thorough consumer behavior analysis. We will take up this task in the next chapter. In particular, we will learn how multiattribute attitude models (MAAMs) allow marketers to identify various factors that motivate choice—including benefits sought. The importance weights collected from individual consumers in MAAMs research often provide the raw material needed for identifying benefit segments.

SEGMENTING BUSINESS-TO-BUSINESS MARKETS ❸

Thus far, our discussion of segmentation has focused on ways to segment consumer markets. **Consumer markets** are the markets for products and services purchased by individuals or households to satisfy their consumption needs. Consumer marketing is often compared and contrasted with business-to-business marketing. **Business markets** are comprised of institutional and government buyers who purchase items to be used in the production of other products and services or to be resold to other businesses or households. Although advertising is much more prevalent in consumer markets, products and services such as fax machines, cellular phones, and tax consulting are commonly promoted to business customers. When Microsoft launched Windows 2000, a large portion of the $200 million multimedia advertising campaign was aimed at the business market with the theme "The Business Internet."[23]

The goal of segmentation analysis in business-to-business markets is the same as in consumer markets: to take the heterogeneous business market and break it into segments that are more homogeneous and manageable. Motorola is a firm that takes the process of segmentation seriously. This highly successful global semiconductor and communications firm identifies six distinct segments in its annual report: the Semiconductor Products Segment (semiconductors), General Systems Segment (cellular telephones), Communications Segment (wireless paging and data transmission), Government and Systems Technology Segment (global personal communications), Information Systems Segment (data compression and networking), and the Automotive and Industrial Electronics Group (lighting and energy products). Firms like Motorola recognize the value of focusing their resources on well-defined product/customer segments in the business market.

There are six basic approaches to segmenting the business market for goods and services: type of organization, standard industrial classification (SIC), size of organization, geographic location, end-use segmentation, and horizontal versus vertical market segmentation.

Type of Organization Segmentation

The broadest means of segmenting the business market is to recognize the types of organizations that constitute potential customers. In the most general sense, the market can be described as consisting of five basic organizational types:

1. *Users.* These are organizations that purchase finished products for use in their businesses. The goods are not changed or incorporated in the manufacturing of other products. Machine tools, computers, vehicles, and office supplies are examples. Recently, Gateway has started to target the business PC user. Historically a consumer products brand, Gateway has initiated a broad-based promotional campaign using advertising, direct marketing, Internet, and sales promotion techniques and created the Gateway@Work division to target business users.[24]
2. *Manufacturers, processors, assemblers.* This class of customer purchases products to use in the production process or buys component parts of the finished product

---

23. Tobi Elkin, "Microsoft Ads Tout Windows 2000 as Open for Business," Advertising Age, January 21, 2000, 3.
24. Beth Snyder, "Gateway Pursues Business PC Users," *Advertising Age,* January 3, 2000, 1.

CAREERPROFILE

Name:	Tara Regan
Title:	Director of Marketing and Business Development
Company:	Perdue Office Interiors, Jacksonville, Florida
	http://www.perdueoffice.com
Education:	B.A., Interior Design

A degree in interior design might seem like an odd background for a marketing job, but Tara Regan says it's a huge asset in her position at Perdue Office Interiors, a dealer of Steelcase office furnishings. It gives her insight into how clients buy and use furniture. "In order to be successful in marketing, you have to really understand your products and how various customers use them," she says. "It's very hard to position your products and company correctly if you don't have that insight."

Consumers looking for furniture for their home offices or small businesses, for example, are concerned with price, appearance, and functionality. They can preview furniture options on Perdue's Web site, but before they buy they often prefer to see the furniture in person. "We try to have examples of what we sell on our Web site on our showroom floor," says Tara. "That way, they can come in and touch and feel the furniture before they buy."

"Our large corporate accounts are handled totally differently," says Tara. "We're usually dealing with facility managers who may be furnishing offices for thousands of employees in many different locations." Price isn't always the priority with these clients. "They want to buy from a company that is knowledgeable about space planning and the array of applications in which office systems affect employee productivity," says Tara. Architects and design professionals form another target segment. "With this group, our job is to keep them in the loop about the products and services we provide," explains Tara. "We're positioning ourselves as being a source to help them serve their clients better."

In developing marketing programs for these various market segments, Tara must keep Perdue's overall corporate marketing strategy in mind. "Although we're selling to different segments, we have to make sure that all of our marketing strategies blend together cohesively," she says.

To learn more about positioning, targeting and segmentation, visit these Web sites:

American Demographics
http://www.demographics.com

University of Texas Advertising Department Targeting and Segmentation Resources Page
http://advertising.utexas.edu/world/Target.htm#Top

Abbot Wool's Market Segment Resource
http://www.awool.com/awool

they sell. Raw materials, drive belts, and computer chips are examples of products sold to these buyers.

3. *Resellers.* These are wholesalers, distributors, and retailers who buy finished products and resell them in the same form to business buyers or household consumers.

4. *Corporate service organizations.* It is important to distinguish this class of customer as organizations that provide an intangible product to their customers. Service organizations typically purchase finished items, like carpeting and office furniture and operating supplies like stationery. These organizations are also high-potential customers for other services such as computer consulting. Examples would be Young & Rubicam advertising agency and Arthur Andersen corporate tax consulting (see Exhibit 4.11).

5. *Institutional service organizations.* These are not-for-profit organizations that by virtue of their unique status represent an entirely different customer class. All forms of government, educational institutions, research and teaching hospitals, and foundations are included here. In total, this group represents enormous purchasing power.

Standard Industrial Classification Segmentation

The SIC prepared by the U.S. Census Bureau, Bureau of the Budget, serves as an ideal tool for business segmentation. The SIC codes are assigned in nine major groups with forty-eight total categories. The SIC provides uniformity in definitions and identifies the number of establishments engaged in each type of business. Category segmentation by SIC is one of the most common approaches to identifying business target markets.

The SIC data can provide very specific information. A firm is able to identify types of organizations, the number of establishments, and the number of employees in the relatively specific area of a single county within a state. While this type of information is somewhat superficial, it indicates the market potential of a specific area. For example, if NCR wanted to determine the market for its inventory tracking systems in Cuyahoga County, Ohio, the firm could immediately identify that there are 8,773 retail operations in the area. This information would give NCR a general description of the business segment.

EXHIBIT 4.11

Business-to-business marketers use segmenting, targeting, and brand positioning in the same way as consumer products marketers. Here, Arthur Andersen is using advertising as part of a promotional campaign targeting corporations that need tax consulting services.

Size of Organization Segmentation

Size of organization segmentation can be based on total sales volume of a potential customer or number of employees—both of which can be obtained from SIC code data. With these data, a firm can identify prospects based on size relative to the number of employees and the total payroll expenditures of the firms. One well-known firm has operationalized this type of segmentation in the insurance industry. The leading property and casualty insurer USF&G has launched a program to provide increased building and general liability coverage to small businesses that competitors have ignored. The firm expects to increase its small business premiums from $240 million to over $1 billion.

Another basis for size segmentation relates to large users or small users of the product category. This is much like the "usage pattern" analysis used in consumer market segmentation. A new competitor often finds a marketing opportunity among low volume users who are ignored by the large, established suppliers. This is precisely the strategy employed by Geneva Steel. This firm sells to steel-service centers that buy, process, and then sell steel to midsize and small users. Geneva avoids big, demanding buyers like the automakers with this segmentation scheme.

Geographic Location Segmentation

Geographic location is a frequent basis for segmentation in the business market because of the tendency for some industries to be geographically concentrated. Some business markets are regional in character due to the basic nature of the industry. Coal mining and other natural resource industries are examples. Some industries have become concentrated in certain areas of the country due to the emergence of one or more key competitors that ultimately attracted other competitors and suppliers. Textiles, automobile manufacturing, furniture, computer software, and pharmaceuticals are all examples of industries where firms have gravitated to the same region(s) of the country. Firms that serve industries based on a geographic segmentation scheme will often locate in or near the same geographic area in order to provide prompt and individualized service.

When industries are concentrated geographically, a firm can take advantage of this market feature and use a sales force effectively in the promotional mix. Similarly, sponsoring local or regional events will also reach a concentrated market where advertising might result in a lot of wasted circulation of the communication.

End-Use Segmentation

End-use segmentation refers to segmenting the market based on the final use or application of a product. If an electronic component is to be used in an inexpensive car stereo, the care exercised in the product development and manufacturing process and the scrutiny of the item by the buyer will be considerably different from that

http://www.interconti.com; http://www.russiantearoom.com

EXHIBIT 4.12

Marshal McLuhan's quote about the "global village" referred to communications media remaking the world as a much smaller place; Inter-Continental's message is that, if you're in their target demographic, the same quality of service and accommodation experience will be everywhere you might find yourself, from Dallas to Dubai. How would strategies differ, trying to sell a quality hotel experience to any business traveler in the developed world, versus a quality meal in one particular business destination, such as New York City's Russian Tea Room?

given to a similar component that is to be used in the control system of a passenger airplane. The use characteristics of different buyers can, therefore, form a basis for segmenting the business market. For example, there are chain saws and there are chain saws. Stihl makes a line of heavy-duty industrial chain saws for professional lumberjacks that the average weekend do-it-yourselfer could hardly lift.[25] The firm targets the professional lumberjack and uses a variety of promotional events to promote to this segment, as the IMC in Practice box discusses.

Another aspect of end use as a basis for segmentation relates to original equipment manufacturers (OEM) versus aftermarket buyers. OEM customers buy products that are incorporated in the final product they manufacture. Aftermarket customers are buying items to resell to their customers. An example is the automobile battery market. Ford Motor Company is an OEM that buys batteries to install in vehicles as they are assembled on the production line. Conversely, NAPA Auto Parts stocks batteries to sell in the retail aftermarket. These two types of business firms represent very different segments and would require different promotional mixes. Ford Motor Company would be communicated to almost exclusively with personal selling. But NAPA Auto Parts would need incentive programs at the retail level to motivate individual stores to feature a particular brand of battery. In-store displays and sales incentives would be used as motivators at the retail level.

Horizontal and Vertical Market Segmentation

Horizontal market segmentation is the process of identifying potential customers across industries. **Vertical market segmentation** is the process of segmenting the market based on identifying potential customers *within* a single organizational type or industry. A company like Goodyear sells horizontally across several

25.   Kate Fitzgerald, "Out of the Woods," *Advertising Age,* August 23, 1999, 10.

IN PRACTICE

CHAINSAW THIS—FORTY-THREE STRAIGHT DAYS OF TIMBERSPORTS TV COVERAGE

The average person has probably never heard of "Timbersports," so why has a German television station decided to air a series of Timbersports competitions for forty-three straight days? Because the power and strength of the competitors has become a fascination in the German market. But not just in the German market. Timbersports is popular enough in the United States that Stihl, one of the leading manufacturers of professional-grade power equipment, is in its fourteenth year of sponsorship of the U.S.-based Timbersports Series.

Stihl finds sponsorship, rather than media advertising, an ideal way to reach its highly specialized target segment of professional woodsmen. Stihl developed the Timbersports series as a way to promote its logging products. The series features competition among professional woodsmen using Stihl products. The events have grown so popular over the years that they now attract thousands of spectators to the events and are being covered by ESPN and ESPN2. The sales promotion specialist for Stihl claims that "Timbersports is helping us expand our brand awareness and add a certain attitude to the brand exemplified by the power and strength of the event's competitors." This kind of communication with such a specialized business target market would be hard to accomplish with any other promotional tool.

Source: Kate Fitzgerald, "Out of the Woods," *Advertising Age,* August 23, 1999, 10.

industries: automobiles, large commercial trucks, farm equipment, recreational vehicles. A company like Intel is predominantly (for now) a microprocessor firm and sells vertically to OEM PC and file server makers. As you have probably guessed, the promotional mix for firms using vertical market segmentation is much more complex than in horizontal market segmentation. Vertical markets will likely need a different message for each market. In horizontal markets, the values of buyers across markets are similar enough so that a fairly standardized message can be used.

Inter-Continental Hotels and Resorts is a classic case of an organization that needs to use horizontal market segmentation in serving business customers. Business travelers from all kinds of businesses from all over the world are potential customers for the hotel properties (see Exhibit 4.12). But the needs of a traveler from the banking industry are pretty much the same as the needs of traveler from the medical industry.

Overall, business-to-business market segmentation is more direct than consumer market segmentation. The more narrowly defined nature of the business market makes segmentation and the promotional process somewhat more manageable.

PRIORITIZING TARGET SEGMENTS ❹

Whether it is done through usage patterns or demographic characteristics or geographic location or benefit packages or any combination of options, segmenting markets typically yields a mix of segments that vary in their attractiveness to the marketer. In pursuing STP marketing, the marketer must get beyond this potentially confusing mixture of segments to a selected subset that will become the target for its marketing and promotional programs. Recall the example of Mobil Oil Corporation and the segments of gasoline buyers it identified via usage patterns and demographic descriptors. What criteria should Mobil use to help decide between Road Warriors and Price Shoppers as possible targets? There are several criteria that can be used to prioritize segments: capabilities of the organization, size and growth potential of the segment, and competitive field.

Capabilities of the Organization. Perhaps the most fundamental criteria in segment selection revolve around what the members of the segment want versus the organization's ability to provide it. Every organization has distinctive strengths and weaknesses (often referred to as "core competencies") that must be acknowledged when choosing its target segments. The organization may be particularly strong in some aspect of manufacturing, like Gillette, which has expertise in mass production of intricate plastic and metal products. Or perhaps its strength lies in well-trained and loyal service personnel, like those at Nordstrom who can effectively implement outstanding communications at the point of purchase. To effectively serve a target segment, an organization may have to commit substantial resources to acquire or develop the capabilities needed to provide what that segment wants. If the price tag for these new capabilities is too high, the organization must find another segment.

Size and Growth Potential of the Segment. Another major consideration in segment selection entails the size and growth potential of the segment. Segment size is a function of the number of people, households, or institutions in the segment, plus their willingness to spend in the product category. When assessing size, advertisers must keep in mind that the number of people in a segment of heavy users may be relatively small, but the extraordinary usage rates of these consumers can more than make up for that. In addition, it is not enough to simply assess a segment's size as of today. Segments are dynamic, and it is common to find marketers most interested in devoting resources to segments projected for dramatic growth. As we have already seen, the purchasing power and growth projections for people age 50 and older have made this a segment that many companies are targeting.

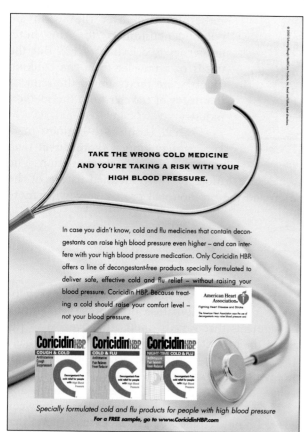

EXHIBIT 4.13

A market niche is a relatively small group of consumers targeted by a firm. Here, a line of cold and flu remedies is being marketed to a pretty small niche—people with high blood pressure.

Competitive Field. So does bigger always mean better when choosing target segments? The answer is a function of the third major criterion for segment selection. In choosing a target segment, a marketer must also look at the **competitive field** of companies pursuing the segment's business—and then decide whether it has a particular expertise, or perhaps just a bigger budget, that would allow it to serve the segment more effectively.

When a marketer factors in the competitive field, it often turns out that smaller *is* better when selecting target segments. Almost by definition, large segments are usually established segments that many companies have identified and targeted previously. Trying to enter the competitive field in a mature segment isn't easy because established competitors can be expected to respond aggressively with advertising campaigns or price promotions in an effort to repel any newcomer. This happens every time a new toothpaste or snack food is introduced to the market.

Alternatively, large segments may simply be poorly defined segments; that is, a large segment may need to be broken down into smaller categories before a company can understand consumers' needs well enough to serve them effectively. Again, the segment of older consumers—age 50 and older—is huge, but in most instances it would simply be too big to be valuable as a target. Too much diversity exists in the needs and preferences of this age group, so further segmentation based on other demographic variables, or perhaps via psychographics, is called for before an appropriate target can be located.

The smaller-is-better principle has become so popular in choosing target segments that it is now referred to as niche marketing. A **market niche** is a relatively small group of consumers who have a unique set of needs and who typically are willing to pay a premium price to the firm that specializes in meeting those needs. The small size of a market niche often means it would not be profitable for more than one organization to serve it. Thus, when a firm identifies and develops products for market niches, the threat of competitors developing imitative products to attack the niche is reduced. Exhibit 4.13 is an example of an ad directed toward a very small niche—people with high blood pressure who need cold and flu products.

Niche marketing will continue to grow in popularity as the mass media splinter into a more and more complex and narrowly defined array of specialized vehicles. Specialized programming—such as the Health & Fitness Channel, the Cooking Channel, or the 24-hour Golf Channel—attracts small and very distinctive groups of consumers, providing advertisers with an efficient way to communicate with market niche.[26]

But now let's return to the question faced by Mobil Oil Corporation. Whom should it target—Road Warriors or Price Shoppers? Hopefully, you will see this as a straightforward decision. Road Warriors are a more attractive segment in terms of both segment size and growth potential. Although there are more Price Shoppers in terms of sheer numbers, Road Warriors spend more at the gas station, making them the larger segment from the standpoint of revenue generation. Road Warriors are much more prone to buy those little extras, such as a sandwich and a car wash, that could be extremely profitable sources of new business. Mobil also came to the conclusion that too many of its competitors were already targeting Price Shoppers. Mobil thus selected Road Warriors as its target segment and developed a positioning strategy it referred to as "Friendly Serve." Gas prices went up at Mobil stations, but Mobil also committed new resources to improving all aspects of the gas-purchasing experience.[27] Cleaner restrooms and better lighting alone yielded sales gains between 2 percent and 5 percent. Next, more attendants were hired to run between the pump and the snack bar to get Road Warriors in and out quickly—complete with their sandwich and beverage. Early results indicated that helpful attendants boosted station sales by another 15 to 20 percent. The Mobil case is a good example of how the application of STP marketing can rejuvenate sales, even in a mundane product category such as gasoline.

FORMULATING A POSITIONING STRATEGY FOR A BRAND ⑤

Now that we have discussed the ways markets are segmented and the criteria used for selecting specific target segments, let's turn our attention to positioning strategy for a brand. If a firm has been careful in segmenting the market and selecting its targets, then a positioning strategy—such as Mobil's "Friendly Serve" or Gillette's "The Best a Man Can Get"—should occur naturally. In addition, as an aspect of positioning strategy, we begin to entertain ideas about how a firm can best communicate to the target segment what it has to offer. This is where promotional tools play their vital role. A positioning strategy will include particular ideas or themes that must be communicated effectively if the marketing program is to be successful.

Essentials of Effective Brand Positioning Strategies

Any sound positioning strategy includes several essential elements. Effective positioning strategies are based on meaningful commitments of organizational resources

26.   Patricia Sellers, "The Best Way to Reach Your Buyers," *Fortune,* Autumn/Winter 1993, 14–17.
27.   Chad Rubel, "Quality Makes a Comeback," *Marketing News,* September 23, 1996, 10.

to produce substantive value for the target segment. They also are consistent internally and over time, and they feature simple and distinctive themes. Each of these essential elements is described and illustrated in this section.

Substantive Value. Let's begin with the issue of substance. For a brand positioning strategy to be effective and remain effective over time, the organization must be committed to creating substantive value for the customer. Take the example of Mobil Oil Corporation and its target segment, the Road Warriors. Road Warriors are willing to pay a little more for gas if it comes with extras such as prompt service or fresh coffee. So Mobil must create a promotional campaign that depicts its employees as the brightest, friendliest, most helpful people you'd ever want to meet. The company asks its ad agency to come up with a catchy jingle that will remind people about the great services they can expect at a Mobil station. It spends millions of dollars running these ads over and over and wins the enduring loyalty of the Road Warriors. Right? Well, maybe, and maybe not. Certainly, a new promotional campaign will have to be created to make Road Warriors aware of what the company has to offer, but it all falls apart if they drive in with great expectations and the company's people do not live up to them.

Effective brand positioning begins with delivering substantive value, in a real sense not just a promotional promises sense, to consumers. In the case of Mobil's "Friendly Serve" strategy, this means keeping restrooms attractive and clean, adding better lighting to all areas of the station, and upgrading the quality of the snacks and beverages available in each station's convenience store. It also means hiring more attendants, outfitting them in blue pants, blue shirts, ties, and black Reeboks, and then training and motivating them to anticipate and fulfill the needs of the harried Road Warrior.[28] Effecting meaningful change in service levels at its 8,000 stations nationwide is an expensive and time-consuming process for Mobil, but without some substantive change, there can be no hope of retaining the Road Warrior segment's lucrative business.

Consistency. A brand positioning strategy also must be consistent internally and consistent over time. Regarding internal consistency, everything must work in combination to reinforce a distinct perception in the consumer's mind about what a brand stands for. If we have chosen to position our airline as the one that will be known for on-time reliability, then we certainly would invest in things like extensive preventive maintenance and state-of-the-art baggage-handling facilities. There would be no need for exclusive airport lounges as part of this strategy, nor would any special emphasis need to be placed on in-flight food and beverage services. If our target segment wants reliable transportation, then this and only this should be the obsession in running our airline. This particular obsession has made Southwest Airlines a very formidable competitor, even against much larger airlines, as it has expanded its routes to different regions of the United States.[29]

A strategy also needs consistency over time. Breaking through the clutter of the hundreds of promotional messages that bombard consumers and establishing what a brand stands for is a tremendous challenge for any marketer, but it is a challenge made easier by consistent positioning. If year in and year out a marketer communicates the same basic theme to the target segment, then the message may get through and shape the way consumers perceive the brand. An example of a consistent approach is the long-running "Good Neighbor" ads of State Farm Insurance. While

---

28. Ibid.
29. Scott McCartney, "Southwest Airlines Lands Plenty of Florida Passengers," *The Wall Street Journal,* November 11, 1997, B4.

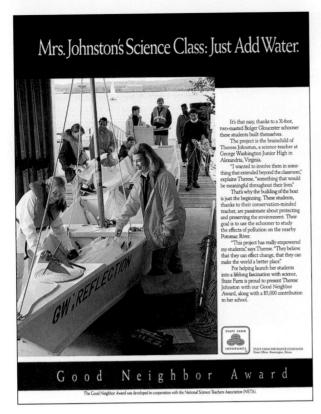

Mrs. Johnston's Science Class: Just Add Water.

It's that easy, thanks to a 31-foot, two-masted Bolger Gloucester schooner these students built themselves.

The project is the brainchild of Therese Johnston, a science teacher at George Washington Junior High in Alexandria, Virginia.

"I wanted to involve them in something that extended beyond the classroom," explains Therese, "something that would be meaningful throughout their lives."

That's why the building of the boat is just the beginning. These students, thanks to their conservation-minded teacher, are passionate about protecting and preserving the environment. Their goal is to use the schooner to study the effects of pollution on the nearby Potomac River.

"This project has really empowered my students," says Therese. "They believe that they can effect change, that they can make the world a better place."

For helping launch her students into a lifelong fascination with science, State Farm is proud to present Therese Johnston with our Good Neighbor Award, along with a $5,000 contribution to her school.

STATE FARM INSURANCE COMPANIES
Home Office, Bloomington, Illinois

Good Neighbor Award

The Good Neighbor Award was developed in cooperation with the National Science Teachers Association (NSTA).

EXHIBIT 4.14

Consistency is a foundation of good positioning strategy. The "Good Neighbor" campaign by State Farm Insurance is a model of consistency.

the specific copy changes, the thematic core of the campaign does not. Exhibit 4.14 shows a contemporary ad from this long-running campaign.

Simplicity and Distinctiveness. Finally, there is the matter of simplicity and distinctiveness. Simplicity and distinctiveness are essential to the promotional task—and the essence of an IMC approach to promotion as well. No matter how much substance has been built into a brand, it will fail in the marketplace if the consumer doesn't accurately perceive what the brand can do. Keep in mind, in a world of harried consumers who can be expected to interrupt, ignore, or completely forget most of the promotional messages they are exposed to, complicated, imitative messages simply have no chance of getting through. The basic premise of a brand positioning strategy must be simple and distinctive if it is to be communicated effectively to a target segment.

The value of simplicity and distinctiveness in positioning strategy is nicely illustrated by the success of GM's Pontiac division in the mid-1980s. This was a period when Japanese automakers were taking market share from their U.S. counterparts, and no American car company was being hit harder than General Motors. Pontiac, however, grew its market share in this period with a brand positioning strategy that involved a return to Pontiac's heritage from the 1960s as a performance car.[30] Pontiac's positioning strategy, which was communicated with a relentless barrage of advertisements, was "We Build Excitement."

This was certainly a distinctive claim relative to GM's other, stodgier divisions of that era, and its beauty was its simplicity. Pontiac's Grand Am featured distinctive styling and mechanics that furnished the substance to support the communication, and it became a best-seller for Pontiac. Indeed, in this Pontiac positioning strategy we see substance, consistency, simplicity, and distinctiveness—all the essential elements for an effective brand positioning strategy.

Fundamental Brand Positioning Themes

Brand positioning themes that are simple and distinctive help an organization make internal decisions that yield substantive value for customers, and they assist in the development of focused campaigns to break through the clutter of competitors' promotions. Thus, choosing a viable brand positioning theme is one of the most important decisions faced by marketers and advertisers. In many ways, the raison d'être for STP marketing is to generate a viable brand positioning theme.

Themes can take many forms, and like any other aspect of marketing and promotion, they can benefit from creative breakthroughs. Yet while novelty and creativity are valued in developing positioning themes, there are basic principles that should be considered when selecting a theme. Whenever possible, it is helpful if the organization can settle on a single premise—such as "Good Neighbor" or "We

30. Paul Ingrassia, "Pontiac Revives 'Sporty' Image, Setting a Marketing Example for Other GM Units," *The Wall Street Journal,* August 15, 1986, 13.

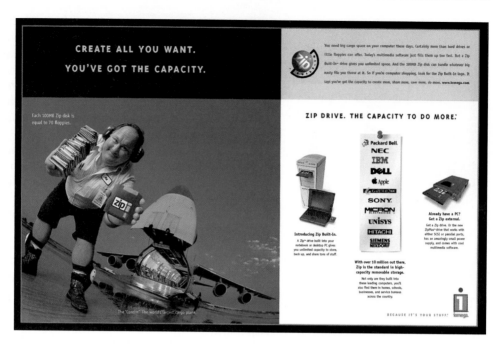

EXHIBIT 4.15

One positioning theme is benefit position. Iomega promises the benefit
of all the capacity you need to do what you need to do.

Build Excitement" or "Friendly Serve" or "Gillette for Women: Are You Ready?"—
to reflect its positioning strategy.[31] In addition, three fundamental options should
always be considered in selecting a positioning theme. These options are benefit
positioning, user positioning, and competitive positioning.[32]

Benefit Positioning. "We Build Excitement" and "Friendly Serve" are examples
of benefit positioning. **Benefit positioning** offers the consumer a positive result
from use and ownership of a brand and can feature either functional or emotional
benefits. Notice in these premises that a distinctive customer benefit is featured.
This single-benefit focus is the first option that should be considered when formulating a brand positioning strategy. While it might seem that more compelling brand
positioning themes would result from promising consumers a wide array of benefits, keep in mind that multiple-benefit strategies are hard to implement. Not only
will they send mixed signals within an organization about what a brand stands for,
but they will also place a great burden on coordinating the promotional effort.
Exhibit 4.15 shows an ad that executes benefit positioning. In this ad for Iomega
Zip drives (and disks), the benefit promised is that you have all the capacity you
need to create documents and data files.

Benefit positioning either can rely on functional product features, like the
Iomega appeal, or it can be built on the emotional benefits of brand ownership
and use. Functional benefits are the place to start in selecting a positioning theme,
but in many mature product categories, the functional benefits of brands in the

31. A more elaborate case for the importance of a single, consistent positioning premise is provided in Al Ries and
Jack Trout, *Positioning: The Battle for Your Mind* (New York: Warner Books, 1982).
32. Other basic options are discussed in David A. Aaker and J. Gary Shansby, "Positioning Your Product," *Business
Horizons,* May/June 1982, 56–62.

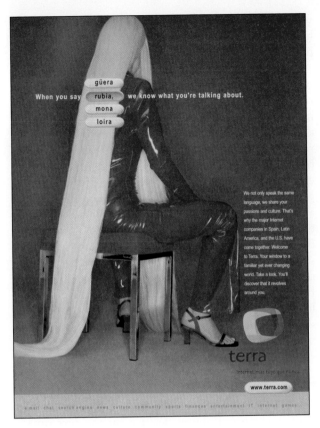

EXHIBIT 4.16

Positioning a brand based on the profile of a target user group is a user positioning strategy. Terra is a Web portal for Hispanic consumers and a good example of user positioning.

competitive field are essentially the same. In these instances, the organization may turn to emotion in an effort to distinguish its brand. Emotional benefit positioning may involve a promise of exhilaration, like Pontiac's "We Build Excitement," or may feature a way to avoid negative feelings—such as embarrassment in social settings from bad breath, dandruff, or perspiration odor.

User Positioning. Besides benefit positioning, another fundamental option is user positioning. Instead of featuring a benefit or attribute of the brand, **user positioning** takes a specific profile of the target user as the focal point of the brand positioning strategy.

User-oriented positioning themes are common when demographic and psychographic variables have been combined to reveal a target segment's distinctive lifestyle. The task then becomes the positioning of products or services to fit that lifestyle. This positioning technique is shown in Exhibit 4.16 where ethnic users form the basis for user positioning. Terra (http://www.terra.com) is an Internet portal company started in Spain that has cultivated partnerships in South America, Central America and the United States to provide Spanish language content for Hispanic Internet users. Notice the appeal Terra uses in its position advertising. The firm focuses not just on language as a distinctive feature but also on the culture and lifestyle of its Hispanic target segment. Any usage pattern factor can be used as the basis for implementing a user-focused positioning strategy.

Competitive Positioning. The third option for a positioning theme is competitive positioning. In some ways, every position effort is a competitive effort, but **competitive positioning** focuses on the relative merits of a firm's brand relative to the competitors' brands. With new products, competitive positioning is often used as a way to distinguish the new brand as unique. When Pepsi introduced its Fruit Works brand into the flavored fruit drinks market, it positioned the brand as lighter and less sweet than competitor Fruitopia and simpler than the herb-fortified brands marketed by SoBe.[33] To bring home the point, Pepsi relied on sampling and event sponsorships to provide a personal connection to the teen and young adult target segment.

The competitive positioning option is also useful in well-established product categories with a crowded competitive field. Here, the goal is to use an explicit reference to an existing competitor to help define precisely what your brand can do. Many times this approach is used by smaller brands to carve out a position relative to the market share leader in their category. For instance, in the analgesics category, many competitors have used market leader Tylenol as an explicit point of reference in their positioning strategies. Excedrin, for one, has attempted to position itself as the best option to treat a simple headache, granting that Tylenol might be the better choice to treat the various symptoms of a cold or the flu. As shown in Exhibit 4.17, Excedrin's strategy must have been effective, because Tylenol came back

33. Stephanie Thompson, "Pepsi Favors Sampling Over Ads for Fruit Drink," *Advertising Age,* January 24, 2000, 8.

Do you want caffeine...

Check the label...a single dose of some pain relievers has more caffeine than a cup of coffee.

Of course, there's no caffeine in Tylenol. Only the proven, powerful pain reliever doctors recommend most for headaches.

So if you're thinking about cutting back on caffeine, the way many people are these days, make sure you're not getting it in an unexpected place. Your pain reliever.

or decaf with that headache?

EXTRA STRENGTH TYLENOL
Geltabs

The Pain Reliever Hospitals Use Most

McNEIL
©McN-PPC Inc. 1997. Use only as directed.

EXHIBIT 4.17

Competitive positioning is a commonly used technique in mature product categories where the performance of brands does not change much over time. Here Tylenol is using a competitive comparison to Excedrin as a way to implement competitive positioning.

with a very pointed reply. In fact, Exhibit 4.17 highlights one of the risks of competitive positioning—a potent response from a tough competitor.

Now that you've seen the three fundamental options for creating a brand positioning strategy, we need to make matters a bit more messy. There is nothing that would prevent a person from combining these options to create a hybrid involving two or more of them working together. The combinations of benefit and user, and benefit and competitive, are quite common in creating brand positioning strategies. For example, the two Gillette ads you examined at the beginning of the chapter are hybrids involving the benefit/user combination. Do keep in mind that the key elements of brand positioning strategy—substance, consistency, and simplicity and distinctiveness—are primary to the strategy ultimately chosen. But the last thing we'd want to do is give you guidelines that would shackle your creativity. So don't be shy about looking for creative combinations of positioning strategies.

Repositioning Brands

Since STP marketing is far from a precise science, marketers do not always get it right the first time.[34] Furthermore, markets are dynamic. Things change. Even when marketers do get it right, competitors can react, or consumers' preferences may shift for any number of reasons, and what once was a viable positioning strategy must be altered if the brand is to survive. One of the best ways to revive an ailing brand or to fix the lackluster performance of a new market entry is to redeploy the STP process to arrive at a revised brand positioning strategy. This type of effort is commonly referred to as **repositioning.**

While repositioning efforts are a fact of life for marketers, they present a tremendous challenge. When brands that have been around for some time are forced to reposition, perceptions of the brand that have evolved over the years must be changed through product redesign and promotion. When Oldsmobile promised that "This Is Not Your Father's Oldsmobile," but did not change the vehicle design, the new younger, upscale market that was targeted with the promotion responded simply by saying, "Yes it is." This problem is common for brands that become popular with one generation but fade from the scene as that generation ages and emergent consumers come to view the brand as passé.[35]

Faced with fierce competition and plummeting market share, Nabisco set out to reposition its "new and improved" line of SnackWell's cookies and crackers in the summer of 1998.[36] In fact, this was the second attempt to reposition the failing SnackWell's line in less than a year, a sure sign that the brand had lost its luster. And

34. Michael Gershman, *Getting It Right the Second Time* (Reading, MA: Addison-Wesley, 1990).
35. Robert L. Simison and Rebecca Blumenstein, "Cadillac and Lincoln Try to Regain Their Cachet," *The Wall Street Journal,* July 3, 1997, B1, B8.
36. Vanessa O'Connell, "Nabisco Ads Push Cookies for Self-Esteem," *The Wall Street Journal,* July 10, 1998, B5.

rather than feature the good taste or the low-fat content of its snacks, Nabisco attempted emotional benefit brand positioning. Their target segment was baby-boomer women with a high sense of self-worth. Their research had revealed that for this segment, "wellness" is not about looking good in a bathing suit, but about celebrating competencies and accomplishments. To feed into this celebration of self, one commercial opined: "At SnackWell's, we like to think that snacking shouldn't be just about feeding yourself, but, in some small way, about feeding your self-esteem."[37] The message here may be that failing brands in cluttered product categories can get pretty desperate for something compelling to say to the customer.

A highly successful repositioning executed in the 1990s was that of Mountain Dew, which was taken from relative obscurity to the official brand of Generation X. Advertising and promotion from Mountain Dew's popular "Thrill" campaign features mountain biking, skateboarding, rollerblading, and other extreme sports. Repositioning may also be pursued by prosperous brands in an effort to renew and amplify that prosperity.

The STP process is essential to preparing effective promotional campaigns. Drawing on the basic marketing strategies of segmenting, targeting, and brand positioning allows promotional strategists to develop effective messages and deploy the proper mix of promotional tools more effectively. But segmenting, targeting, and brand positioning are not enough—in isolation. A complete examination of consumer behavior tendencies and motivations is also needed. We will turn our attention to the topic of consumer behavior in the next chapter.

SUMMARY

❶ Explain the process of segmenting and targeting markets and then positioning brands within those markets.

The term STP marketing refers to the process of segmenting, targeting, and brand positioning. Marketers pursue this set of activities in formulating marketing and promotional strategies. STP marketing should always be considered when consumers in a category have heterogeneous wants and needs. It allows marketers to identify target segments that are more homogeneous and devise a promotional mix that effectively and efficiently cultivates the target segment(s).

❷ Describe the different techniques marketers use to identify target segments in the consumer market.

In market segmentation, the goal is to break down a heterogeneous market into more manageable subgroups or segments. Many different bases can be used for this purpose. Markets can be segmented on the basis of usage patterns and commitment levels, demographics, geography, psychographics, lifestyles, or benefits sought. Multiple bases are typically applied for segmenting consumer markets.

❸ Identify the ways marketers segment the business-to-business market.

There are six basic approaches to segmenting the business-to-business market for goods and services: type of organization, standard industrial classification (SIC), size of organization, geographic location, end-use segmentation, and horizontal versus vertical market segmentation. The values of market segmentation that apply in the consumer market also apply to the business-to-business market. Business-to-business marketers benefit from the increased knowledge of the target segment and the efficiency in reaching targeted segments that come from segmentation.

37. Ibid.

4 Discuss the criteria used by marketers to decide which segment to target.

In pursuing STP marketing, an organization must get beyond the stage of segment identification and settle on one or more segments as a target for its marketing and advertising efforts. Several criteria are useful in establishing the organization's target segment. First, the organization must decide whether it has the proper skills to serve the segment in question. The size of the segment and its growth potential must also be taken into consideration. Another key criterion involves the intensity of the competition the firm is likely to face in the segment. Often, small segments known as market niches can be quite attractive because they will not be hotly contested by numerous competitors

5 Discuss the key elements of an effective brand positioning strategy.

The P in STP marketing refers to the brand positioning strategy that must be developed as a guide for all marketing and promotion activities that will be undertaken in pursuit of the target segment. As exemplified by Pontiac's "We Build Excitement" campaign, effective positioning strategies are rooted in the substantive benefits offered by the brand. They are also consistent internally and over time, and they feature simple and distinctive themes. Benefit positioning, user positioning, and competitive positioning are options that should be considered when formulating a positioning strategy.

KEY TERMS

market segmentation, 120
target segment, 120
positioning, 120
positioning strategy, 120
STP marketing, 120
product differentiation, 123
demographic segmentation, 124
geographic segmentation, 126
geodemographic segmentation, 127
heavy users, 127

nonusers, 128
brand-loyal users, 128
switchers, or variety seekers, 128
emergent consumers, 128
psychographics, 130
lifestyle segmentation, 130
benefit segmentation, 132
consumer markets, 133
business markets, 133
end-use segmentation, 135

horizontal market segmentation, 136
vertical market segmentation, 136
competitive field, 138
market niche, 139
benefit positioning, 142
user positioning, 143
competitive positioning, 143
repositioning, 144

QUESTIONS FOR REVIEW AND CRITICAL THINKING

1. While STP marketing often produces successful outcomes, there is no guarantee that these successes will last. What factors can erode the successes produced by STP marketing, forcing a firm to reformulate its marketing strategy?

2. Why does the persuasion required with a product differentiation strategy present more of a challenge than the persuasion required with a market segmentation strategy?

3. Explain the appeal of emergent consumers as a target segment. Identify a current promotional campaign targeting an emergent-consumer segment.

4. It is often said that psychographics were invented to overcome the weaknesses of demographic information for describing target segments. What unique information can psychographics provide that would be of special value to advertisers?

5. What criteria did Mobil Oil Corporation weigh most heavily in its selection of Road Warriors as a target segment? What do you think will be the biggest source of frustration for Mobil in trying to make this strategy work?

6. Explain why smaller can be better when selecting segments to target in marketing strategies.

7. What essential elements of a positioning strategy can help overcome the consumer's natural tendency to ignore, distort, or forget most of the advertisements he or she is exposed to?

8. Identify examples of current promotional campaigns that feature benefit positioning, user positioning, and competitive positioning.

9. Carefully examine the Gillette ads displayed in Exhibits 4.1 and 4.2. What brand positioning theme

(benefit, user, or competitive) is the basis for these ads? If you say benefit positioning, what form of benefit promise (functional, emotional, or self-expressive) is being made in these ads? Write a statement of the value proposition that you believe is reflected by these two ads.

10. Look around your room or apartment and find a product that you consider one of your favorite brands. Consider what it is about this brand that makes it a personal favorite for you. Is it functional or emotional, or some combination of these different types of benefits that you particularly value about this brand?

EXPERIENTIAL EXERCISES

1. **In-class exercise.** Bring to class three ads that you think target different segments. Speculate as to what segments are being targeted. Be prepared to defend your position in front of the class.

2. **Out-of-class exercise.** General Motors is attempting to reposition the Oldsmobile in the minds of consumers. Ask three adults to discuss with you their current impression of, beliefs about, and attitudes toward Oldsmobile. Would they purchase an Oldsmobile today? Why or why not? Briefly describe what each adult said and indicate the extent to which you think the brand needs to be repositioned. Now ask three people your age about their impression of, beliefs about and attitudes toward Oldsmobile. How do the responses match up?

USING THE INTERNET

Exercise 1

The same products can be advertised to different market segments through different media outlets, with differing appeals—for example, emphasizing a car's safety rating in a family-oriented publication, and its power and agility in a magazine targeting single men. Many companies using the Internet, however, have a single Web page for a given product, and most likely a single, corporate Web site.

Some companies have been energetic in securing Internet domain names, beyond the one for their corporate Web site. Procter & Gamble (http://www.pg.com), for instance, has created Web sites for many of its brands (such as Head & Shoulders), and for many generic words associated with their products, or with conditions that might recommend their products (for example, diarrhea.com, which they've reserved, but haven't yet used for a Web site, which might be a good thing!). Visit:

Procter & Gamble
http://www.pg.com
http://www.vsassoon.com
http://www.headandshoulders.com

1. How does the Internet pose a challenge to segmenting markets?

2. How might a company ensure that its messages best match its audiences on the Web?

Exercise 2

While the Internet originated in and has seen its greatest growth in the United States, it's making tremendous inroads in foreign markets and with foreign audiences. While the Net does much to render distance irrelevant, language and culture provide opportunities for segmentation and specialization. Visit:

Zona Financiera
http://www.zonafinanciera.com

Zona Financiera is attempting to become the leading "portal" for Latin American financial information and opportunities.

1. How does the Zona Financiera site further subdivide the rather large market it has chosen to address?

2. What language issues need to be addressed?

After reading this chapter, you will be able to:

1 Describe the four stages of consumer decision making.

2 Explain how consumers adapt their decision-making processes as a function of involvement and experience.

3 Explain consumer decision making in a sociocultural consumption context.

4 Describe the business buyer behavior process.

5 Describe both the mass and personal communication processes that show how consumers and business buyers receive and interpret promotional communications.

THE **FASHION GODS CAN**
GET DOWN ON THEIR KNEES
AND PRAY TO ME.

Dr AirWair
Martens

Legendary anthropologist Margaret Mead was famous for studying the indigenous people of Samoa. Claude Lévi-Strauss slogged through the Amazon rain forest in a last-ditch effort to observe and understand disappearing native traditions. Mary Isherwood poked around people's kitchens to grasp the "meaning of goods." So what do modern-day anthropologists do? They study a new tribe called consumers. Really. Since consumer behavior is about human behavior in the context of consumption, anthropologists, psychologists, sociologists, and consumer behavior researchers all study consumers doing what they do best—consuming.

This new breed of highly trained social scientists finds consumers every bit as interesting as tribes. This is because commercially viable subcultures exist everywhere. The Internet has spawned subcultures in chat rooms. Starbucks has (re)created the "café" subculture in the United States, and shopping malls have become the new field for hunting and gathering.

Because of the huge payoffs that come from a clear understanding of consumer behavior, these consumer behavior researchers are analyzing consumer activities and preferences at the request of a wide range of marketers. But instead of being armed with notepads and bug

spray, these researchers arm themselves with video cameras, tape recorders, and pagers. They track the behavior and rituals of consumers and help marketing and promotional strategists craft products and communications that resonate positively within target markets.

One of these new-era researchers is Rick Robinson, founder of a consumer research firm called E-Lab (the "E" stands for experience). He does consumer behavior research and analysis for firms like Pepsi, Netscape, Frito-Lay, Nokia, and JanSport. To help a client design a new cold remedy, Robinson studied how people get sick and what they do while they are sick. He hung around sporting goods stores long enough to help JanSport design a completely new way of displaying its backpacks at the point of purchase. His take on consumer behavior is, "Every consumer behavior has a particular framework and a theory that it is based upon. Ideas, beliefs, and attitudes all come from somewhere. Our job is a matter of finding the meaningful patterns that exist. We don't ask customers what they want, we watch what they do."[1]

The Pleasant Company (a division of Mattel) takes its consumer behavior analysis very seriously. The firm's American Girl brand, which began with history books and pricey dolls, has expanded into lifestyle books, apparel, furniture, fashion shows, and a newsletter to parents. Strategists at The Pleasant Company are meticulous in their research on the seven- to twelve-year-old market. How do they know the audience so well? From letters, mostly. The *American Girl* gets 12,000 letters after each issue. The girls write about their interests, give advice to fellow readers, and offer ideas for activities and crafts.[2] In addition, operators at customer service lines handle comments as well as orders. Based on the research, Pleasant introduces new products that have both educational merit and entertainment value and appeal to both the kids and their parents (see Exhibit 5.1).

Whether it's highly trained consumer behavior researchers doing observational research or marketers like The Pleasant Company paying very close attention to their customers' behavior, it's all about understanding what consumers want, what they feel, and what they do. In a nutshell, that's the study of consumer behavior.

EXHIBIT 5.1

Marketers like The Pleasant Company go to great lengths to understand the behavior of their customers—both off- and online. Marketers need good information on consumer behavior so they can plan and execute promotional campaigns using the right tools with the right messages. The Pleasant Company IMC campaign uses direct-mail catalogs, a newsletter, the Web site pictured here, and fashion show events.

1. Gene Koprowski, "The Science of Shopping," *Business 2.0,* June 1999, 140.
2. "Living the American Girl Dream," *Promo,* December 1999, 23.

INTRODUCTION

This chapter summarizes the concepts and frameworks that are most helpful in trying to understand two key aspects of buyers. First, the concepts of buyer behavior related to both household consumers and business buyers will be examined. Household consumer behavior (referred to from hereon as "consumer behavior") and business buyer behavior need to be discussed separately. The motivations and influences on these two types of buyers and the processes they use in making buying decisions are vastly different and need separate examination. Years of developmental research have produced good frameworks for how the consumer and business buyer behavior processes work. We will examine each in detail. Second, we need to look at the way consumers and business buyers process promotional communications. Our ultimate goal, of course, is to understand which promotional tools to use and which will be the most effective in communicating to potential buyers—consumers *and* business buyers. To achieve this goal, we need to know how communication itself works. These communication processes are fairly complex, but this chapter provides a straightforward framework that illustrates how the process takes place in concert with promotion.

CONSUMER BEHAVIOR

Consumer behavior is defined as the complex process by which individuals acquire, use, and dispose of products or services to satisfy their needs and desires. Notice that this definition of behavior includes not just the buying act itself, but also the using and disposing of products. We will describe consumer behavior and explain its diversity from two different perspectives. The first portrays consumers as reasonably systematic decision makers who seek to maximize the benefits they derive from their purchases. The second views consumers as active interpreters of the social context in which they live, as beings whose membership in various cultures, societies, and communities significantly affects their interpretation and response to marketing and promotional activities. These two perspectives are different ways of looking at the exact same people and the exact same behaviors. Although different in essential assumptions, both perspectives are valuable in actually getting the work of promotion done.

PERSPECTIVE ONE: THE CONSUMER AS DECISION MAKER

One way to view consumer behavior is as a logical, sequential process culminating with the individual reaping a set of benefits from a product or service that satisfies that person's perceived needs. In this basic view, we can think of individuals as purposeful decision makers who take matters one step at a time. All consumption episodes can then be conceived as a sequence of four stages:

1. Need recognition
2. Information search and alternative evaluation
3. Purchase
4. Postpurchase use and evaluation

The Consumer Decision-Making Process

A brief discussion of what typically happens at each stage will give us a foundation for understanding consumers, as well as illuminate opportunities for developing powerful advertising.

EXHIBIT 5.2

When consumers look to the performance and price of a brand, they are evaluating the functional benefits. This Geo Metro ad is a direct appeal to this kind of consumer evaluation.

Need Recognition. The consumption process begins when people perceive a need. A **need state** arises when our desired state of affairs differs from our actual state of affairs. Need states are accompanied by a mental discomfort or anxiety that motivates action; the severity of this discomfort can be widely variable depending on the genesis of the need. For example, the need state that arises from running out of toothpaste would involve very mild discomfort for most people, whereas the need state that accompanies the breakdown of one's automobile on a dark and deserted highway in Minnesota in mid-February can approach true desperation.

One way promotion works is to point to and thereby activate needs that will motivate consumers to buy a product or service. For instance, nearly every fall, marketers from product categories as diverse as autos, snowblowers, and footwear roll out predictions for another severe winter and encourage consumers to prepare themselves before it's too late. Such an appeal is very productive when the previous winter was especially severe and the advertiser does a good job of capturing the sights and sounds of last year's terrible storms.

Following an especially severe winter in the Northeast, Jeep dealers in New York State warned, "Last year's winter produced 17 winter storms. . . . This year, the *Old Farmer's Almanac* is predicting another winter with above-average snowfall." As a result of this campaign, Jeep dealers in the New York region sold every vehicle they could get their hands on.[3] Consumers in New York obviously responded to the advertiser's effort to activate a need state. Many factors can influence the need states of consumers. The central point is that a variety of needs can be fulfilled through consumption, and it is reasonable to suggest that consumers are looking to satisfy needs when they buy products or services.

Products and services should provide benefits that fulfill consumers' needs; hence, one of promotion's primary jobs is to make the connection between the two

---

3.   Fara Warner, "Relishing and Embellishing Forecasts for Frigid Winter," *The Wall Street Journal,* December 1, 1994, B1.

for the consumer. Benefits come in many forms. Some are more **functional benefits**—that is, they derive from the more objective performance characteristics of a product or service. Convenience, reliability, nutrition, durability, and economy are descriptors that refer to functional benefits. The Geo Metro ad in Exhibit 5.2 is a clear example of appealing to functional needs.

Consumers may also choose products that provide emotional benefits; these are not typically found in some tangible feature or objective characteristic of a product. **Emotional benefits** are more subjective and may be perceived differently from one consumer to the next. They may include needs like love and belonging, esteem, prestige, security, or pleasure. These are powerful consumption motives that advertisers often try to activate. What sort of emotional benefits are promised in Exhibit 5.3?

Information Search and Alternative Evaluation. Once the consumer has recognized a need, it is often not obvious what the best way to satisfy that need would be. Need recognition simply sets in motion a process that may involve an extensive information search and careful evaluation of alternatives prior to purchase.

Information for the decision is acquired through an internal or external search. The consumer's first option for information is an **internal information search** drawing on personal past experience and prior knowledge. An internal search can also tap into information that has accumulated in one's memory as a result of repeated exposure to promotional communications. Affecting people's beliefs about a brand before their actual use of it, or merely establishing the existence of the brand in the consumer's consciousness, is a critical function of promotions. This internal search for information may be all that is required. When a consumer has considerable prior experience with the products in question, attitudes about the alternatives may be well established and drive the choice.

If an internal search does not turn up enough information to yield a decision, the consumer can proceed with an external search. An **external information search** involves visiting retail stores to examine the alternatives, seeking input from friends and relatives about their experiences with the products in question, or perusing professional product evaluations furnished in various publications such as *Consumer Reports* or *Stereo Review*. Online evaluations of brands provided by Web sites like CNET or Cameras.com offer consumers a new and extensive source of external information. At the CNET site (http://www.cnet.com), for example, you will find the "CNET Buying Adviser" for different product categories (see Exhibit 5.4). Consumers who are in an active information-gathering mode may be receptive to considering detailed, informative promotional messages delivered through any of the print media; encountering a brand at a sponsored event; or posting a product inquiry on a corporate Web site.

After an information search, which will vary in intensity from consumer to consumer, alternatives will be considered. Alternative evaluation will be structured by the consumer's consideration set and evaluative criteria. The **consideration set** is the

SOME DAY SOON, HE'LL HAVE A SUPERHERO LUNCHBOX, A SEAT ON THE BUS, AND A NEW BEST FRIEND.

NOW, WHILE YOU CAN, JOHNSON'S BABY HIM.

Johnson's Baby Bath: still the mildest baby bath you can buy. And now the number one choice of hospitals. Today, teach him the meaning of gentle, with Johnson's Baby Bath. The mildest you can buy, it's clinically proven as gentle to his eyes as pure water—yet cleans far better than water ever could. It's hypoallergenic and carefully pH-balanced, too. No wonder it's the number one choice of hospitals. He'll grow up soon enough. For now, just Johnson's Baby him.

PROTECT THEM.
SHELTER THEM.
JOHNSON'S BABY THEM.

EXHIBIT 5.3

Every parent worries about doing the right thing. This ad communicates the emotional benefits of using Johnson's Baby Bath—"Protect them. Shelter them. Johnson's Baby them."

http://www.cnet.com; http://www.consumerreports.com

EXHIBIT 5.4

When consumers go into information search, they now have a whole new set of resources on the Web. Sites like CNET provide consumers with evaluations of many brands within a product category. Consumer electronics is, in fact, one of the more heavily covered categories— it lends itself particularly well to Web-based shopping. In addition to commercially oriented sites, one finds more neutral reviewers, such as Consumer Reports. *Just how do these sites make money, and who pays whom for what?*

subset of brands from a particular product category that become the focal point of a consumer's evaluation. Most product categories contain too many brands for all to be considered, so a consumer finds some way to focus the search and evaluation. For example, for autos, consumers may consider only cars priced less than $10,000, or only cars that have antilock brakes, or only foreign-made cars, or only cars sold at dealerships within a five-mile radius of their work or home. A critical function of promotion is to make consumers aware of the brand and keep them aware, so that the brand has a chance to be part of the consideration set. Virtually all advertising tries to do this.

As the search-and-evaluation process proceeds, consumers form evaluations based on the characteristics or attributes that brands in their consideration set have in common. These product attributes or performance characteristics are referred to as **evaluative criteria.** Evaluative criteria differ from one product category to the next and can include many factors, such as price, texture, warranty terms, color, scent, or fat content.

It is critical for marketers to have as complete an understanding as possible of the evaluative criteria that consumers use to make their buying decisions. By knowing these criteria, a promotional mix can be devised that emphasizes them. Advertising themes can highlight whatever attributes consumers value most. Similarly, sales promotions can feature price discounts, in-store displays can focus on premiums, or events can nurture the proper image affiliation. Understanding consumers' evaluative criteria furnishes a powerful starting point for any promotional campaign and is examined in more depth later in the chapter.

Purchase. At this third stage, purchase occurs. The consumer has made a decision, and a sale is made. Great, right? Well, to a point. As nice as it is to make a sale, things are far from over. In fact, it would be a mistake to view purchase as the culmination of the decision-making process. No matter what the product category, the consumer is likely to buy from it again in the future. So, what happens after the sale is very important to advertisers.

Postpurchase Use and Evaluation. The goal for marketers must not be simply to generate a sale; it must be to create satisfied and, ultimately, loyal customers. The data to support this position are quite astounding. Research shows that about 65 percent of the average company's business comes from its present, satisfied customers, and that 91 percent of dissatisfied customers will never buy again from the company that disappointed them.[4] Thus, consumers' evaluations of products in use become a major determinant of which brands will be in the consideration set the next time around.

Customer satisfaction obviously results from a favorable *postpurchase* experience. Consumers rarely derive their satisfaction from a brand during the search process itself—they obviously have to own and use a brand to gain satisfaction. This satisfaction may develop after a single use, but more likely it will require sustained use. Promotion can play an important role in inducing customer satisfaction by creating appropriate expectations for a brand's performance before a purchase and by helping the consumer who has already bought the advertised brand to feel good about doing so.

Cognitive dissonance is the anxiety or regret that lingers after a difficult decision. Promotion plays an important role in alleviating the cognitive dissonance that can occur after a purchase. If the goal is to generate satisfied customers, this dissonance must be resolved in a way that leads consumers to conclude that they did make the right decision after all. Purchasing high-cost items or choosing from categories that include many desirable and comparable brands can yield high levels of cognitive dissonance. When dissonance is expected, it makes good sense for the marketer to reassure buyers with detailed information about its brands. Postpurchase reinforcement programs might involve a variety of promotional communications like direct mail, e-mail, or other types of personalized contacts with the customer such as phone contact from a salesperson. This postpurchase period represents a great opportunity for the marketer to have the undivided attention of the consumer and to provide information and advice about brand use that will increase customer satisfaction.[5] These postpurchase communications can also help a marketer get consumers to think about their new purchase in an idealized way. For an example, see the ad for Isuzu shown in Exhibit 5.5.

EXHIBIT 5.5

Consumers often need positive reinforcement after an important purchase. The message in this Isuzu Trooper ad reassures consumers by suggesting that the vehicle is not only a great hauler, but also stylish enough to make friends and family envious.

4.   Terry G. Vavra, *Aftermarketing: How to Keep Customers for Life Through Relationship Marketing* (Homewood, IL: Business One Irwin, 1992), 13.
5.   Ibid.

Four Modes of Consumer Decision Making ❷

You may be thinking that consumers aren't always deliberate and systematic; sometimes they are hasty, impulsive, or even irrational. The search time that people put into their purchases can vary dramatically for different types of products. Would you give the purchase of a toothbrush the same amount of effort as the purchase of a new stereo system? Why is that T-shirt you bought at a concert more important to you than the brand of orange juice you had for breakfast this morning? Does buying a Valentine's gift from Victoria's Secret create different feelings from buying new furniture for your office?

Some purchase decisions are just more engaging than others. In the following sections, we will elaborate on the view of consumer as decision maker by explaining four decision-making modes that help marketers appreciate the richness and complexity of consumer behavior. These four modes are determined by a consumer's involvement and prior experiences with the product or service in question.

Sources of Involvement. To fully understand the complexity of consumer behavior, those who study the issues typically talk about the "involvement level" of any particular decision. **Involvement** is the degree of perceived relevance and personal importance accompanying the choice of a certain product or service within a particular context. Many factors contribute to an individual's level of involvement with any given decision. People can develop interests and avocations in many different areas, such as cooking, photography, pet ownership, or exercise and fitness.

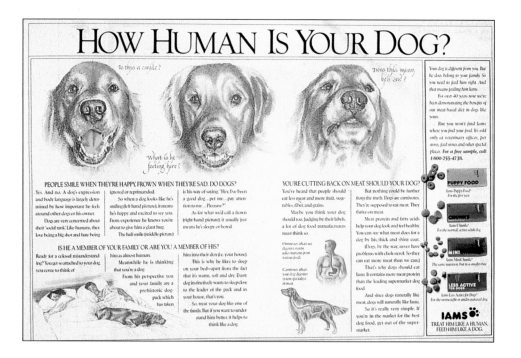

EXHIBIT 5.6

Many people take decisions about their pet's health very seriously. This creates a high-involvement type of consumer decision making situation. Marketers, like IAMS, provide extensive information to satisfy the consumer's sense of involvement.

6.   Gilles Laurent and Jean-Noel Kapferer, "Measuring Consumer Involvement Profiles," *Journal of Marketing Research,* February 1985, 41–53.

EXHIBIT 5.7

Four modes of consumer decision making based on involvement and past experience.

	High Involvement	Low Involvement
Low Experience	Extended problem solving	Limited problem solving
High Experience	Brand loyalty	Habit or variety seeking

Such ongoing personal interests can enhance involvement levels in a variety of product categories. Also, any time a great deal of risk is associated with a purchase—perhaps as a result of the high price of the item, or because the consumer will have to live with the decision for a long time—one should expect elevated involvement.

Consumers can also derive important symbolic meaning from products and brands.[6] Ownership or use of some products can help people reinforce some aspect of their self-image or make a statement to other people who are important to them. Think about the symbolic meaning and commitment of buying a wedding ring. The combination of high price, long-term commitment, and huge symbolic meaning creates a highly involving event for most people.

Involvement levels vary not only among product categories for any given individual, but also among individuals for any given product category. For example, some pet owners will feed their pets only the expensive canned products that look and smell like people food. The company IAMS, whose ad is featured in Exhibit 5.6, understands this and made a special premium dog food for consumers who think of their pets as humans. Many other pet owners, however, are perfectly happy with 50-pound economy packages.

Prior Experience. Prior experience is the extent to which a consumer has either direct or indirect experience with purchasing and using products in a product category. With many frequently purchased household items, like laundry detergent or paper towels, we all accumulate family experiences growing up. Even some high-priced items such as automobiles or stereo equipment can be ingrained in our consumption sociology. But changes in life (moving away from home) and changes in lifestyle (getting married or having kids) may challenge us with purchases where we have little prior experience. Purchases of life insurance, kids' clothes, home appliances, and the like may be unsettling, new-purchase decisions that present a challenge.

Now we will use the ideas of involvement and prior experience to describe four different types of consumer decision making. These four modes are shown in Exhibit 5.7. Any specific consumption decision is based on a high or low level of prior experience with the product or service in question, and a high or low level of involvement. This yields the four modes of decision making: (1) extended problem solving, (2) limited problem solving, (3) habit or variety seeking, and (4) brand loyalty. Each is described in the following sections.

Extended Problem Solving. When consumers are inexperienced in a particular consumption setting yet find the setting highly involving, they are likely to engage in **extended problem solving.** In this mode, consumers go through a deliberate decision-making process that begins with explicit need recognition, proceeds with careful internal and external information search, continues through alternative evaluation and purchase, and ends with a lengthy postpurchase evaluation. Examples of extended problem solving are choosing a home or a diamond ring, as shown in Exhibit 5.8. These products are expensive, are publicly evaluated, and can carry a considerable amount of risk in terms of making an uneducated choice.

A MAN'S GUIDE *to buying* DIAMONDS

She's expecting DIAMONDS.
Don't PANIC. We can help.

The way to a man's heart is through his stomach, but the way to a woman's usually involves a jeweler. Just think of golf clubs, or season tickets wrapped in a little black velvet box. That's how women feel about diamonds.

To know diamonds is to know her. Find out what she has her heart set on. Is it a pendant, anniversary band, or ear studs? You can find out by browsing with her, window shopping, watching her reaction to other women's jewelry. Go by body language, or just by what she says. Then, once you know her style, you can concentrate on the diamond itself.

Like people, no two diamonds are alike. Formed in the earth millions of years ago, found in the most remote corners of the earth, rough diamonds are sorted by DeBeers into over 5,000 grades before they're cut and polished. So be aware of what you're getting. Two diamonds of the same size can differ in quality. And if a price looks too good to be true, it probably is.

Maybe a jeweler is a man's best friend. You want a diamond you can be proud of. So don't be attracted to a jeweler because of "bargain prices." Find someone you can trust. Ask questions. Ask friends who've gone through it. Ask the jeweler you choose why two diamonds that look the same are priced differently. You want someone who will help you determine quality and value using four characteristics called *The 4Cs.* They are: *Cut*, not the same as shape, but refers to the way the facets or flat surfaces are angled. A better cut offers more brilliance; *Color*, actually, close to no color is rarest; *Clarity*, the fewer natural marks or "inclusions" the better; *Carat weight*, the larger the diamond, usually the more rare. Remember, the more you know, the more confident you can be in buying a diamond you'll always be proud of.

Learn more. For the booklet *"How to buy diamonds you'll be proud to give,"* call the **American Gem Society**, representing fine jewelers upholding gemological standards across the U.S., at **800-340-3028**.

Compromise now? Where's your heart? Go for diamonds beyond her wildest dreams. Go for something that reflects how you really feel. You want nothing less than a diamond as unique as your love. Not to mention as beautiful as that totally perplexing creature who will wear it.

Diamond Information Center
Sponsored by De Beers Consolidated Mines, Ltd., Est. 1888.
A diamond is forever. DeBeers

http://www.adiamondisforever.com; http://www.bluenile.com

EXHIBIT 5.8

A high-involvement and low-experience decision usually means the consumer will seek out a lot of information. Here, DeBeers offers help at the Diamond Information Center. Contrast this site with the Blue Nile site. What differences do you note? Who's selling what to whom?

Limited Problem Solving. In **limited problem solving**, experience and involvement are both low. A consumer is less systematic in his or her decision making. The consumer has a new problem to solve, but it is not a problem that is interesting or engaging, so the information search is often limited to simply trying the first brand encountered. For example, let's say a young couple has a baby, and suddenly they perceive a *very* real need for disposable diapers. The hospital gave them trial packs of several products, including Pampers disposables. They try the Pampers and find them an acceptable solution to their messy new problem. They take the discount coupon that came with the sample to their local grocery and buy several packages. Smart marketers realize that promotions that feature trial offers can be a very effective method for new shoppers to collect information about brands, and they facilitate a trial of their brands through free samples, inexpensive "trial sizes," or discount coupons.

Habit or Variety Seeking. Habit and variety seeking occur under conditions of low involvement but high experience. In terms of sheer numbers of decisions, habitual purchases are probably the most common. Consumers find a brand of laundry detergent that suits their needs, they run out of the product, and they buy the same brand again. The cycle repeats itself dozens of times a year in an almost mindless fashion. Getting in the habit of buying just one brand can be a way to simplify life and minimize the time invested in "nuisance" purchases. When a consumer perceives little difference between competitive brands, it is easier to buy the same brand repeatedly.

In some product categories where a buying habit would be expected, an interesting phenomenon called variety seeking may be observed instead. Remember, **habit** refers to buying a single brand repeatedly as a solution to a simple consumption problem. This can be very tedious, and some consumers fight the boredom through variety seeking. **Variety seeking** refers to the tendency of consumers to switch their selection among various brands in a given category in a seemingly random pattern. This is not to say that a consumer will buy just any brand; he or she probably has two to five brands that all provide similar levels of satisfaction. However, from one purchase to the next, the individual will switch brands from within this set, just for the sake of variety. Variety seeking is most likely to occur in frequently purchased categories where sensory experience, such as taste or smell, accompanies product use. Product categories such as soft drinks and alcoholic beverages, snack foods, breakfast cereals, and fast food are prone to variety seeking.

Brand Loyalty. The final decision-making mode is typified by high involvement and rich prior experience. In this mode, brand loyalty becomes a major consideration in the purchase decision. Consumers demonstrate **brand loyalty** when they repeatedly purchase a single brand. In one sense, brand-loyal purchasers may look as if they have developed a simple buying habit; however, it is important to distinguish brand loyalty from simple habit. Brand loyalty is based on highly favorable attitudes toward a brand and a conscious commitment to find this brand each time the consumer purchases from this category. Conversely, habits are merely consumption simplifiers for consumers that are not based on deeply held convictions. Habits can be disrupted with a skillful combination of advertising and sales promotions. That is what Yahoo! has tried to do with its advertising that ties the Yahoo! experience not just to Web surfing but to shopping opportunities accessed *through* Yahoo![7] On the other hand, depending on advertising dollars to persuade truly brand-loyal consumers to try an alternative brand can be a great waste of resources.

BRAND LOYALTY IS TOUGH FOR DOT-COMS

In an environment where technology is ubiquitous and one Web site operates, from a technology standpoint, about the same as another, getting consumers to be brand loyal is pretty tough. From big sites like http://www.Yahoo.com and http://www.Pets.com to smaller sites likes http://www.Stamps.com and http://www.Computers.com, the new dot-coms have been turning to advertising and promotion to try to ingrain some brand loyalty in surfers. Yahoo! has launched a TV advertising campaign that now touts the shopping opportunities at Yahoo! as a way to try to attract repeat business and provide an anchor for brand loyalty. Yahoo's original advertising focused on first the search engine then the portal nature of the site.

The similarity of technology across sites is not the only deterrent to site loyalty. Much of the advertising run by dot.coms tells you what they offer, but gives no compelling differentiated reason to come to the site. Some branding executives believe that the problem starts with the name. Names like Pets.com and Drugstore.com project a commodity image that is hard to overcome. One site relies heavily on contests as a promotional tool to differentiate the site and attract repeat users: http://www.iWon.com. Here, $10,000 is given away every week and $10 million on tax day as a way to attract attention and keep surfers coming back to the portal. Sounds like it might work, but how long can they keep it up? And, is a contest a good enough foundation for brand loyalty?

Sources: Alice Z. Cuneo, "Yahoo! TV Ads Connect the brand with Shopping," *Advertising Age,* November 1, 1999, 62; Laurie Freeman, "Who Are You?" *Marketing News,* February 14, 2000, 1, 8.

Brands such as Sony, Levi's, Harley-Davidson, FedEx, and the Grateful Dead inspire loyal consumers. Brand loyalty is something that every marketer aspires to have, but in a world filled with savvy consumers and endless brand proliferation, it is becoming harder and harder to attain. Brand loyalty may emerge because the consumer perceives that one brand simply outperforms all others in providing some critical functional benefit. For example, the harried business executive may have grown loyal to FedEx's overnight delivery service as a result of repeated satisfactory experiences with FedEx.

Perhaps more importantly, brand loyalty can be due to the emotional benefits that accompany certain brands. Strong emotional benefits might be expected from consumption decisions that we classify as highly involving, and they are major determinants of brand loyalty. Indeed, with so many brands in the marketplace, it is becoming harder and harder to create loyalty for one's brand through functional benefits alone. To break free from this brand-parity problem and provide consumers with lasting reasons to stay loyal, marketers are investing more and more effort in communicating the emotional benefits that might be derived from brands in categories as diverse as soup (Campbell's—"Good for the Soul") and cellular service (AirTouch—"Empowerment . . . Boundless . . . It can change your life"). In addition, as suggested by the New Media box, dot-com brands are struggling to attract new visitors, but they are also trying to instill brand loyalty in Web surfers—not an easy task in an environment where one site seems about as good as another to the average consumer.

7.   Alice Z. Cuneo, "Yahoo! TV Ads Connect the Brand with Shopping," *Advertising Age,* November 1, 1999, 62.

Key Psychological Processes

To complete our consideration of the consumer as a thoughtful decision maker, one key issue remains: the psychological influences on the process. What does promotion leave in the minds of consumers that ultimately may influence their behavior? This is an important question in deciding which tools to use in a promotional mix. Several ideas borrowed from psychology and social psychology are usually the center of attention when discussing the psychological aspects of promotion. These include attitudes and beliefs, multiattribute attitude models, perception, and experiential-hedonic influences.

Attitudes and Beliefs.   **Attitude** is an overall evaluation of any object, person, or issue that varies along a continuum, such as favorable to unfavorable or positive to negative. Attitudes are learned, and if they are based on substantial experience with the object or issue in question, they can be held with great conviction. Attitudes make our lives easier because they simplify decision making; that is, when faced with a choice among several alternatives, we do not need to process new information or analyze the merits of the alternatives. We merely select the alternative we think is the most favorable. For promotional purposes, marketers are most interested in one particular class of attitudes—brand attitudes.

Brand attitudes are summary evaluations that reflect preferences for various brands of products and services. The next time you are waiting in a checkout line at the grocery, look at the items in your cart. Those items are a direct reflection of your brand attitudes. Where do brand attitudes come from? Here we need a second idea from social psychology. To understand why people hold certain attitudes, we need to assess their specific beliefs. **Beliefs** represent the knowledge and feelings a person has accumulated about an object or issue. They can be logical and factual in nature, or biased and self-serving. A person might believe that Cadillacs are large and unstylish, garlic consumption promotes weight loss, and pet owners are lonely people. For that person, all these beliefs are valid and can serve as a basis for attitudes toward Cadillacs, garlic, and pets.

People have many beliefs about various features and attributes and brands. Some beliefs are more important than others in determining a person's final evaluation of a brand. Typically, a small number of beliefs—on the order of five to nine—underlie brand attitudes.[8] These beliefs are the critical determinants of an attitude and are referred to as **salient beliefs.** Clearly, we would expect the number of salient beliefs to vary between product categories. The loyal Harley owner who proudly displays a tattoo will have many more salient beliefs about his or her bike than about a brand of salsa.

Multiattribute Attitude Models.   Since belief shaping and reinforcement are principal goals of various tools of promotion, it should come as no surprise that marketers make belief assessment a focal point in their attempt to understand consumer behavior. **Multiattribute attitude models (MAAMs)** provide a framework and set of procedures for collecting information from consumers to assess their salient beliefs and attitudes about competitive brands.

Any MAAMs analysis will feature four fundamental components:

- **Evaluative criteria** are the attributes or performance characteristics that consumers use in comparing competitive brands. In pursuing a MAAMs analysis, a marketer must identify all evaluative criteria relevant to its product category.

8.   Icek Ajzen and Martin Fishbein, *Understanding Attitudes and Predicting Social Behavior* (Englewood Cliffs, NJ: Prentice-Hall, 1980), 63.

- **Importance weights** reflect the priority that a particular evaluative criterion receives in the consumer's decision-making process. Importance weights can vary dramatically from one consumer to the next; for instance, some people will merely want good taste from their bowl of cereal, while others will be more concerned about fat and fiber content.

- The **consideration set** is that group of brands that represents the real focal point for the consumer's decision. For example, the potential buyer of a luxury sedan might be focusing on Acuras, BMWs, and Saabs. These and comparable brands would be featured in a MAAMs analysis. Cadillac could have a model, like its Seville, that aspired to be part of this consideration set, leading General Motors to conduct a MAAMs analysis featuring the Seville and its foreign competitors. Conversely, it would be silly for GM to include the Geo Metro in a MAAMs analysis with this set of imports.

- **Beliefs** represent the knowledge and feelings that a consumer has about various brands. In a MAAMs analysis, beliefs about each brand's performance on all relevant evaluative criteria are assessed. Beliefs can be matters of fact—Raisin Nut Bran has five grams of fat per serving, the same as the six-inch Subway Club— or highly subjective—the Acura Integra sports coupe is the sleekest, sexiest car on the road. It is common for beliefs to vary widely among consumers.

In conducting a MAAMs analysis, we must specify the relevant evaluative criteria for our product category, as well as our direct competitors. We then go to consumers and let them tell us what's important and how our brand fares against the competition on the various evaluative criteria. The information generated from this research will give us a better appreciation for the salient beliefs that underlie brand attitudes, and it may suggest important opportunities for changing our promotional mix to yield more favorable brand attitudes. To see how this might work, consider these three situations where the findings from MAAMs would affect the promotional campaign.

First, a MAAMs analysis may reveal that consumers do not have an accurate perception of the relative performance of our brand on an important evaluative criterion. For example, consumers may perceive that Crest is far and away the best brand of toothpaste for fighting cavities, when in fact all brands with a fluoride additive perform equally well on cavity prevention. Correcting this misperception could become our focal point if we compete with Crest.

Second, a MAAMs analysis could uncover that our brand is perceived as the best performer on an evaluative criterion that most consumers do not view as very important. The task for promotion in this instance would be to persuade consumers that what our brand offers (say, our mouthwash prevents gingivitis) is more important than they had thought previously.

Third, the MAAMs framework may lead to the conclusion that the only way to improve attitudes toward our brand would be through the introduction of a new attribute to be featured in our promotion. For example, the advertisement in Exhibit 5.9 makes the case that a platinum sensor in the thermostat is something you should be looking for the next time you purchase an oven.

When marketers use the MAAMs approach, good things can result in terms of more favorable brand attitudes and improved market share. When marketers carefully isolate key evaluative criteria, bring products to the marketplace that perform well on the focal criteria, and develop promotions that effectively shape salient beliefs about the brand, the results can be dramatic.

Perception. **Perception** is the manner in which an individual interprets stimuli from his or her environment. Each of us uses perception to create our own "reality." Because the human mind has limits on the amount of stimulation it can handle, we

http://www.thermador.com

http://www.intel.com

EXHIBIT 5.9

Thermador wants you to get inside their product (not literally, of course), but also to add to your evaluative criteria a new factor you've not thought about before. Intel has raised this to a high art: Its "Intel Inside" campaign for the Pentium microprocessor is an integrated marketing communications masterpiece—how many other chips do you know by name, and what other products would you recall by a simple, short audio "stinger"?

screen information from the environment in a way that is consistent with what each of us believes to be important and relevant. Perception creates an orientation to the world that is the result of past experiences, attitudes, cultural norms, and learned behavior. Perceptions are actually the combined influence of many of the psychological influences discussed so far.

The implication of perceptual processes is that consumers will ignore stimuli they deem irrelevant and interpret all stimuli in a way that is consistent with their personal version of "reality." As such, information about products, their use, and benefits must be consistent with the *consumer's* definition of what is relevant. For example, health issues have created a heightened awareness among consumers of the fat and cholesterol content of foods. Firms have altered products to reduce fat and cholesterol and prominently display these reductions in advertising, on product packages, and in other promotional communications.

Experiential-Hedonic Influences. An important and typically underemphasized set of influences on consumption behavior has to do with the experiential and pleasure (hedonic) aspects of consuming products.[9] The influences discussed so far in this chapter suggest the human mind is working overtime to separate, evaluate, and direct consumption decisions. Experiential and hedonic motives emphasize the pleasure and personal enhancement that result from consumption. That is, consumers buy and consume things because it feels good—period. There would appear to be a trend beginning in the United States toward greater pleasure seeking. A few years ago, Americans began exercising less, eating more pork, and not trying nearly as hard to avoid cholesterol.

The effects of psychological influences on the consumer behavior process must be considered in the context of several environmental factors that also affect the consumer. We now turn our attention to these environmental factors and try to understand the consumer as a social being.

PERSPECTIVE TWO: THE CONSUMER IN A SOCIOCULTURAL CONSUMPTION CONTEXT ③

The view of the consumer as a decision maker is a popular one. It is not, however, without its limitations or its critics. Certainly, it tells only part of the story. In its effort to isolate psychological mechanisms, this approach often takes consumer behavior out of its natural social context, making consumers appear oddly utilitarian and overly rational.

9.   Elizabeth C. Hirschman and Morris B. Holbrook, "Hedonic Consumption: Emerging Concepts, Methods, and Propositions," *Journal of Marketing*, vol. 46, no. 2 (September 1982), 92–101.

This section presents a second perspective on consumer behavior, a perspective concerned with social and cultural processes. It draws on basic ideas from anthropology, sociology, and communications, and it should be considered another part of the larger story of how promotion works. But remember, this is just another perspective. We are still talking about the same consumers discussed in the preceding section; we are just viewing their behavior from a different vantage point: consumers consume in a sociocultural context. To examine consumption and the promotional process as a purely individual act leaves a wealth of information undiscovered. The major components of this sociocultural context for consumer decision making are culture, values, rituals, society, social class, family, reference groups, race and ethnicity, gender, and community.

Culture

Culture is what a people do, or "the total life ways of a people, the social legacy the individual acquires from his (her) group."[10] It is the way we eat, groom ourselves, celebrate, and mark our space and position. It is the way things are done. Cultures are often thought of as large and national, but in reality they are usually smaller and not necessarily geographic, such as urban hipster culture, teen tech-nerd culture, Junior League culture, and so on. No company is better at understanding the culture of its customers than American Girl—the division of Mattel that sells pricey dolls and has expanded into history books, apparel, and furniture. The company gets 12,000 letters from its pre-teen customers and potential customers after an issue of *American Girl* is released. Mattel pores over the comments and are in a constant dialogue with their customers.[11]

It's usually easier to see and note culture when it's more distant and unfamiliar. For most people, this is when they travel to another place. If you were to point this out to one of the locals, say to a Parisian, and say something like, "Boy, you guys sure do things funny over here in France," you would no doubt be struck (perhaps literally) with the locals' belief that it is not they, but you, who behave oddly. This is a manifestation of culture and points out that members of a culture find the ways they do things to be perfectly natural. Culture is thus said to be invisible to those who are immersed in it. Everyone around us behaves in a similar fashion, so we do not think about the existence of some large and powerful force acting on us all. But it's there; this constant background force is culture. Make no mistake, culture is real, and it affects every aspect of human behavior, including consumer behavior and consumers' responses to promotion.

When marketers consider why consumers consume certain goods or services, or why they consume them in a certain way, they are considering culture itself. Culture informs consumers' views about food, the body, gifts, possessions, a sense of self versus others, mating, courtship, death, religion, family, jobs, art, holidays, leisure, satisfaction, work . . . just about everything. For example, if you are Ocean Spray, you want to understand how the cultural ritual of Thanksgiving works so that you can sell more cranberries. What is Thanksgiving? Why do Americans value it? Why do they perform the particular rituals performed on that day? Or who makes up the rules of gift giving? If you are Tiffany, Barnes & Noble, or Hallmark, you have a very good reason to understand why people do things a certain way (for example, buy things for some holidays but not others). The list is endless. When you're in the promotion business, you're in the culture business.

---

10. Gordon Marshall, ed., *The Concise Oxford Dictionary of Sociology* (New York: Oxford University Press, 1994), 104–105.
11. "Living the American Dream Girl," *Promo*, December 1999, 23.

THE FASHION GODS CAN
GET DOWN ON THEIR KNEES
AND PRAY TO ME.

EXHIBIT 5.10

Americans prize their individuality. This Dr. Martens ad beautifully expresses that cultural value.

Values. **Values** are the defining expressions of culture. They express in words and deeds what is important to a culture. For example, some cultures value individual freedom, while others value duty to society as a whole. Some value propriety and restrained behavior, while others value open expression. Values are cultural bedrock. Values are enduring. They cannot be changed quickly or easily. In this way, they are very different from attitudes, which marketers believe can be changed through a single promotional campaign.

Typically, marketers try to either associate their product with a cultural value or criticize a competitor for being out of step with one. For example, in America, to say that a product "merely hides or masks odors" would be damning criticism indeed, because it suggests that anyone who would use such a product doesn't really value cleanliness and thus is out of step with a closely held cultural value.

Promotional communications must be consistent with the values of a people. If they are not, they will likely be rejected. Many argue that the most effective communications are those that best express and affirm core cultural values. For example, one core American value is said to be individualism. This value has been part of American culture since at least the Boston Tea Party. A communication that is consistent with or even celebrates this value will strike a responsive chord. The Dr. Martens ad in Exhibit 5.10 shows an advertisement that leans heavily on this value.

Rituals. **Rituals** are "often-repeated formalized behaviors involving symbols."[12] Cultures affirm, express, and maintain their values through rituals. For example, ritual-laden holidays such as Thanksgiving, Christmas, and the Fourth of July help perpetuate aspects of American culture through their repeated reenactment. Because they include consumption (for example, feasts and gift giving), they help intertwine national culture and consumption practices (see Exhibit 5.11). For example, Jell-O may have attained the prominence of a national food because of its regular usage as part of the Thanksgiving dinner ritual.[13] In the American South, it is common to eat black-eyed peas on New Year's Day to ensure good luck.

But rituals don't have to be the biggest events of the year. There are also everyday rituals, such as the way we eat, groom, and work. Think about all the habitual things you do from the time you get up in the morning until you crawl into bed at night. These things are done in a certain way; they are not random. Members of a common culture tend to do them one way, and members of other cultures do them other ways. Again, if you've ever visited another country, you have no doubt noticed significant differences. An American dining in Paris might be surprised to have sorbet to begin the meal and a salad to end it.

---

12. Ibid, 452.
13. Melanie Wallendorf and Eric J. Arnould, "We Gather Together: Consumption Rituals of Thanksgiving Day," *Journal of Consumer Research,* vol. 18, no. 1 (June 1991): 13–31.

we make it *Simple*
so you can make it a *Holiday*

The Holiday Flavors of Kraft.

CoolWhip JELL-O PHILADELPHIA CREAM CHEESE Stove Top Velveeta   KRAFT

EXHIBIT 5.11

Rituals are often accompanied by consumption. Holiday rituals in the United States are no exception.

Society

While culture is essentially what a people do, **society** is "a group of people who share a common culture, occupy a particular territorial area, and feel themselves to constitute a unified and a distinct entity."[14] Examples are American society, Southern society, and Eastern society. Within a society, many social forces and social institutions operate. Consumer behavior and promotion depend on the actions of these social institutions, agents, and forces. Social factors such as class, family, reference groups, race and ethnicity, gender, and community all have a significant impact on consumer behavior and the way consumers respond to promotion.

Social Class. **Social class** refers to a person's relative standing in a social hierarchy resulting from systematic inequalities in the social system. (These systematic inequalities are also known as *social stratification.*) Wealth, power, prestige, and status are not distributed equally within any society. People are rich or poor, are powerful or powerless, possess low status or high status, and so on. Thus, a cross section of American society would reveal many different levels (or strata) of the population along these different dimensions.

Social class has historically been a slippery concept. For example, some individuals possess higher social class than their income indicates, and vice versa. Successful plumbers often have higher incomes than college professors, but their occupation is (perhaps) less prestigious. Education also has something to do with social class, but a person with a little college experience and a lot of inherited wealth will probably rank higher than an insurance agent with an MBA. Thus income, education, and occupation are three important variables for indicating social class, but are still individually, or even collectively, inadequate at capturing its full meaning. Clearly, "complex combinations of social rewards and social opportunities compose social class."[15] Others have argued that the emergence of the New Class, a class of technologically skilled and highly educated individuals with great access to information and information technology, will change the way we define social class: "Knowledge of, and access to, information may begin to challenge property as a determinant of social class."[16]

Here, we use the term social class in a very inclusive sense. To us, social class includes not only economic criteria (such as income and property), but prestige, status, mobility, and a felt sense of similarity or communal belonging. Members of a social class tend to live in a similar way; have similar views and philosophies; and, most critically, tend to consume in similar ways. Markers of social class include what one wears, where one lives, and how one talks. In a consumer society, consumption marks

14. Marshall, *Concise Oxford Dictionary of Sociology,* 498.

15. James R. Kluegel and Eliot R. Smith, *Beliefs About Inequality: Americans' View of What Is and What Ought to Be,* (New York: Aldine de Gruyter, 1986).

16. Alvin W. Gouldner, "The Future of Intellectuals and the Rise of the New Class," in *Social Stratification in Sociological Perspective: Class, Race, and Gender,* ed. David B. Grusky (San Francisco: Westview Press, 1994), 711–729.

or indicates social class in a myriad of ways. In fact, some believe that social class is the single biggest predictor of consumer behavior and consumer response to promotions.

One reason for this is the power of social class in determining consumption tastes and preferences, including media habits, and thus exposure to various promotional vehicles—for example, the magazines *RV Life* versus *Wine Spectator.* We think of tennis more than bowling, chess more than checkers, and Brie more than Velveeta as belonging to the upper classes. Ordering wine instead of beer has social significance, as does wearing Tommy Hilfiger rather than Wrangler jeans. Social class and consumption are undeniably intertwined. In fact, cultural theorist Pierre Bourdieu argues that social class is such a powerful force that it "structures the whole experience of subjects," particularly when it comes to consumption.[17]

Family. The consumer behavior of families is also of great interest to marketers. Marketers want not only to discern the needs of different kinds of families, but also to discover how decisions are made within families. The first is possible; the latter is much more difficult. For a while, consumer researchers tried to determine who in the traditional nuclear family (that is, Mom, Dad, and the kids) made various purchasing decisions. This was largely an exercise in futility. Due to errors in reporting and conflicting perceptions between husbands and wives, it became clear that the family purchasing process is anything but clear. While some types of purchases are handled by one family member, many decisions are actually diffuse nondecisions, arrived at through what consumer researcher C. W. Park aptly calls a "muddling through" process.[18] These "decisions" just get made, and no one is really sure who made them, or even when. For a marketer to influence such a diffuse and vague process is indeed a challenge. The consumer behavior of the family is a complex and often subtle type of social negotiation. One person handles this, one takes care of that. Sometimes specific purchases fall along gender lines, but sometimes they don't.[19] While they may not be the buyer in many instances, children can play important roles as initiators, influencers, and users in many categories, such as cereals, clothing, vacation destinations, fast-food restaurants, and even computers.

We also know that families have a lasting influence on the consumer preferences of family members. One of the best predictors of the brands adults use is the ones their parents used. This is true for cars, toothpaste, household cleansers, and many more products. Say you go off to college. You eventually have to do laundry, so you go to the store and buy Tide. Why Tide? Well, you're not sure, but you saw it around your house when you lived with your parents, and things seemed to have worked out okay for them, so you buy it for yourself. The habit sticks, and you keep buying it. This is called an **intergenerational effect.**

Marketers often focus on the major or gross differences in types of families, because different families have different needs, buy different things, and are reached by different media. There are a lot of single parents and second and third marriages. Family is a very open concept. In addition to the "traditional" nuclear family and the single-parent household, there is the extended family (nuclear family plus grandparents, cousins, and others), the blended family (resulting from second and third marriages), and the so-called alternative family (single and never-married mothers, and gay and lesbian households with and without children, for example).

17.   Pierre Bourdieu, "Distinction: A Social Critique of the Judgement of Taste," in *Social Stratification in Sociological Perspective: Class, Race, and Gender,* ed. David B. Grusky (San Francisco: Westview Press, 1994), 404–429.
18.   C. Whan Park, "Joint Decisions in Home Purchasing: A Muddling-Through Process," *Journal of Consumer Research,* vol. 9 (September 1982): 151–162.
19.   For an excellent article on this topic, see Craig J. Thompson, William B. Locander, and Howard R. Pollio, "The Lived Meaning of Free Choice: An Existential-Phenomenological Description of Everyday Consumer Experiences of Contemporary Married Women," *Journal of Consumer Research,* vol. 17 (December 1990): 346–361.

Reference Groups. Other people and their priorities can have a dramatic impact on consumer consumption priorities. A **reference group** is any configuration of other people that a particular individual uses as a point of reference in making his or her own consumption decisions.

Reference groups can be small and intimate (you and the people sharing your neighborhood) or large and distant (you and all other people taking a promotion course). Reference groups can also vary in their degree of formal structure. They can exist as part of some larger organization—such as an employer—with formal rules for who must be part of the group and what is expected of the group in terms of each day's performance. Or they may be informal in their composition and agenda, such as a group of casual friends who all live in the same apartment complex.

Another way of categorizing reference groups involves the distinction between membership groups and aspirational groups.[20] **Membership groups** are those that we interact with in person on some regular basis; we have personal contact with the group and its other members like our work group or church group. **Aspirational groups** are made up of people we admire or use as role models but are unlikely to interact with in any meaningful way. However, because we aspire to be like the members of this group, they can set standards for our own behavior. Professional athletes, movie stars, rock-and-rollers, and successful business executives become role models whether they like it or not. Of course, marketers are keenly aware of the potential influence of aspirational groups, and they commonly employ celebrities, from Grant Hill to Hanson, as endorsers for their products in advertising or in-store promotions, or as participants in special events.

Reference groups affect our consumption in a variety of ways. At the simplest level, they can furnish information that helps us evaluate products and brands, and if we will actually consume a particular product (for example, tonight's dinner) with the group, the group's references may become hard to distinguish from our own. Additionally, reference groups play an important role in legitimizing the symbolic value of some forms of consumption—that is, individuals choose some brands because they perceive that using these products will enhance their image with a reference group or signal to others that they belong to a particular reference group. In this way, brands end up offering consumers important self-expressive benefits.

And how do brands get their symbolic meaning that makes them valuable as props for reference group communications? Just how did Nike become a symbol of devotion to performance? Such symbolism is shaped and reaffirmed by years of consistent (IMC) communications—in the proper sociocultural context. Even great promotions cannot succeed against social and cultural trends. And remember, much of what a brand means is determined by consumers, not just handed down by marketers and their promotional themes.

Race and Ethnicity. Race and ethnicity provide other ways to think about important social groups. Answering the question of how race figures into consumer behavior is difficult. Our discomfort stems from on the one hand having the desire to say, "Race doesn't matter, we're all the same," and on the other hand not wanting (or not being able) to deny the significance of ethnic culture as an influence on a wide variety of behaviors, including consumer behavior. Obviously, a person's pigmentation in itself has almost nothing to do with preferences for one type of product over another. But because race has mattered in culture, it matters in consumer behavior. Race clearly affects cultural and social phenomena. The United States is becoming an increasingly diverse culture (Exhibit 5.12). But how do we (and should we) deal with this reality?

---

20. For additional explanation of this distinction, see Michael R. Solomon, *Consumer Behavior* (Upper Saddle River, NJ: Prentice-Hall, 1996), 342–344.

Year	White	Black	Hispanic	Asian	American Indian
1996	194.4 (73.3%)	32.0 (12.1%)	27.8 (10.5%)	9.1 (3.4%)	2.0 (0.7%)
2000	197.1 (71.8%)	33.6 (12.2%)	31.4 (11.4%)	10.6 (3.9%)	2.1 (0.7%)
2010	202.4 (68.0%)	37.5 (12.6%)	41.1 (13.8%)	14.4 (4.8%)	2.3 (0.8%)
2020	207.4 (64.3%)	41.5 (12.9%)	52.7 (16.3%)	18.6 (5.7%)	2.6 (0.8%)
2030	210.0 (60.5%)	45.4 (13.1%)	65.6 (18.9%)	23.0 (6.6%)	2.9 (0.8%)
2040	209.6 (56.7%)	49.4 (13.3%)	80.2 (21.7%)	27.6 (7.5%)	3.2 (0.9%)
2050	207.9 (52.8%)	53.6 (13.6%)	96.5 (24.5%)	32.4 (8.2%)	3.5 (0.9%)

Source: U.S. Census Bureau.

EXHIBIT 5.12

Ethnic diversity in the United States: projected U.S. population by race in millions of people (and percent of total population)

Race does provide social identity to varying degrees. African-Americans, Hispanics, Asian-Americans, and other ethnic groups have culturally related consumption preferences based on history, tradition, and culturally situated holidays. It is not enough, however, for marketers to say one group is different from another group. If they really want a good, long-term relationship with their customers, marketers must acquire, through good consumer research, a deeper understanding of who their customers are and how this identity from race and ethnicity is informed by culture. In short, they must ask why (or if) groups of consumers are different, and not settle for an easy answer. It wasn't until the mid- to late 1980s that most American corporations made a concerted effort to court the African-American consumer. Efforts to serve the Hispanic consumer have been intermittent and inconsistent. But now the size, growth, and economic power of these groups, along with Asian-Americans, have made all of them highly prized consumers for a wide range of marketers. As an example, with over 40 million Spanish-language consumers now online, specialized Web sites like latino.com (http://www.latino.com) and Terra.com (http://www.terra.com) are providing Web content in Spanish (including regional variations) and also cultural content of interest to Hispanic audiences.[21] In addition, big marketers like GM are developing communications and promotions directed at ethnic markets for mainstream products like SUVs.[22] Sample ads directed at diverse audiences based on race and ethnicity are shown in Exhibits 5.13 and 5.14.

Gender. **Gender** is the social expression of sexual biology, sexual choice, or both. Obviously, gender matters in consumption. But are men and women really that different in any meaningful way in their consumption behavior, beyond the obvious? Again, to the extent that gender informs a "culture of gender," the answer is yes. As long as men and women are the products of differential socialization, they will continue to be different in some significant ways. Is there any question that gender socialization plays a role in the way the ad in Exhibit 5.15 tries to communicate based on gender? There is, however, no definitive list of gender differences in consumption, because the expression of gender, just like anything else social, depends on the situation and the social circumstances. In the late 1970s, marketers discovered working

21.   Evantheia Schibsted, "Americas Online," *Business 2.0,* January 2000, 70–74.
22.   Jean Halliday, "GMC Revises Ad Tactics for 2000," *Advertising Age,* January 31, 2000, 10.

EXHIBITS 5.13 AND 5.14

Because of the growth and economic power of ethnic groups in the United States, marketers are developing specialized promotional communications for these target segments.

women, and over time the portrayal of women in more diverse roles has worked its way into promotional communications. Changes in gender roles that result in changes in household duties create different social realities for men and women.

These social realities need to be part of the promotional plan when male versus female target segments are identified for promotional programs. Recent research findings verify that 48 percent of married women bring in at least half of the household income, while 25 percent out-earn their husbands. Women make 80 percent of the purchase decisions, including 66 percent of the decisions regarding computer equipment for the home. This behavior has carried over to the Internet, where 56 percent of all new Web users are women and women are expected to be spending nearly $20 billion on online purchases by the year 2002.[23] From a promotional standpoint, any firm with a female target audience that is not at least considering a strong Web presence may be heading for a communications disadvantage.

Community. Community is a powerful and traditional sociological variable, considered by some to be the fundamental concept in sociology. **Community** is defined as a "wide-ranging relationship of solidarity over a rather undefined area of life and interests."[24] This means that people come together and affiliate based on

23. Ellen Pack, "She's Gotta Have It," *Business. 2.0*, June 1999, 145.
24. Marshall, *Concise Oxford Dictionary of Sociology*, 72–73.

EXHIBIT 5.15

Is there any doubt that this communication is based on gender evaluation in consumer behavior analysis?

shared experiences and interest areas. Its meaning extends well beyond the idea of a specific geographic place, however. Communities can be imagined and, in today's world of Internet communication, even virtual. As people find others like themselves in chat rooms or even "virtual nightclubs" (where participants share live audio feeds from nightclubs), a sense of community emerges on the Internet.[25]

Marketers are becoming increasingly aware of its power. Community is important in at least two major ways. First, when products have social meanings, community is the social domain for that meaning to be interpreted. Communities may be the fundamental reference group, and they exhibit a great deal of power. A community may be your neighborhood, or it may be people like you with whom you feel a kinship, such as members of social clubs, other consumers who collect the same things you do, or people who have the same interests you do. In a consumer society, goods and services figure prominently in the symbolic fabric of communities. Communities may exist through a common consumer bond like a product or a brand. For example, skateboarders form a community and so do owners of Range Rovers.

Second, the extent to which brands can derive power is determined in part by brand community. **Brand communities** are groups of consumers who feel a commonality and a shared purpose grounded or attached to a consumer good or service.[26] When owners of Dr. Martens, Bang & Olufsens, Harley Davidsons, or Saturns experience a sense of connectedness by virtue of their common ownership or usage, a brand community exists. When two perfect strangers stand in a parking lot and act like old friends simply because they both own Saturns, a type of community is revealed. Indeed, Saturn's Spring Hill Homecoming, described in the IMC in Practice box, is considered a great marketing success story in the area of cultivating brand community.

BUSINESS BUYER BEHAVIOR ❹

We have seen that consumer behavior is an elaborate and complex interaction of psychological process and sociocultural contexts. Business buyer behavior is not quite so complex, but it still requires careful analysis and examination. Just as in consumer buying behavior, the buying process in business markets takes place in a series of stages. These stages are actually quite similar to the consumer buying behavior process:

1. Need recognition
2. Product and scheduling specifications
3. Evaluation of products
4. Evaluation of suppliers and services
5. Product and supplier choice
6. Product and supplier evaluation

25. Khanh T. L. Tran, "On the Internet, Lifting the Velvet Rope, *The Wall Street Journal,* August 30, 1999, B1.
26. Albert Muniz Jr. and Thomas O'Guinn, "Brand Community" (Berkeley, CA: unpublished manuscript).

IN PRACTICE

COMING TOGETHER . . . OVER SATURN

It sounded like a goofy idea: Invite every Saturn owner (about 600,000) to a "homecoming" at the Spring Hill, Tennessee, plant where their cars were "born." After all, who in their right mind would plan their vacation around a remote manufacturing facility? About 44,000 Saturn owners, that's who. Owners came from as far away as Alaska and Taipei; one couple ended up getting married by a United Auto Workers chaplain, with the Saturn president there to give away the bride. Another 100,000 Saturn owners participated in related, dealer-sponsored programs all over the United States. Add in the national publicity provided from the news media and ensuing Saturn ads depicting the event, and the idea isn't so goofy any more. It's a masterly integrated marketing communications campaign that used about five different promotional tools to help build allegiance to the Saturn brand. The strength of the Saturn brand community is the envy of the automotive industry.

The genius of the Spring Hill Homecoming is that Saturn's primary marketing strategy revolves around strong customer relations and service. The four-day event at the Tennessee plant rewarded customers for their purchase behavior and provided reassurance for new-car shoppers seeking the trust and relationships that allay service-related fears and the general mystery of new-car buying. Saturn's innovative approach is also integral to the overall strategy of its parent company, General Motors: The overwhelming majority of Saturn sales come from previous import owners, and not at the expense of other GM divisions. A key issue in the introduction of Saturn was to take sales from the popular Japanese cars and not cannibalize other GM nameplates. Actually, Saturn's retention programs just may be the greatest tangible benefit to arise from GM's earthshaking $5 billion initial investment in the Saturn project.

An essential factor in the overall strategy is the promotional execution. In order to maintain and nurture the community of Saturn owners, a wide range of promotional tools has been and needs to be used. Direct communication through mail and telephone contact, events like the Spring Hill gathering, public relations, and traditional advertising have all played an important role.

Sources: "Savvy Companies Hold Customers," *Sales & Marketing Management*, December 1994, 15; Kevin L. Keller, *Strategic Brand Management* (Upper Saddle River, NJ: Prentice-Hall, 1998), 244–245; for an in-depth analysis of Saturn's brand building programs, see David Aaker, *Building Strong Brands* (New York: Free Press, 1996), Chapter 2.

While there are similarities to consumer decision making, these stages reflect both similarities and differences between the consumer buying process and the business buying process. Like their consumer counterparts, business buyers initiate a decision based on need recognition, but this need recognition is much more narrowly defined. First, due to production schedule demands and the nature of business products, the business buyer typically enters the decision process based on out-of-stock or functional need states. By virtue of the "diffused" buying responsibilities of multiple participants in the buying process (discussed in the next section), the business buyer is often influenced or directed by other members of the organization (such as engineers or end users of the product) in seeking out products to purchase.

Next, product evaluation is predominantly based on functional and benefits-of-use criteria rather than on emotional criteria. This is not to say that business buyers are not subject to emotion in the decision-making process. Just because they don a role in an organization does not turn them into "decision-making" robots. But emotions tend to give way to the more rational bases for decision making in this highly structured and professional decision-making context. Finding the supplier who carries the product that meets the designated product and service specifications becomes an overriding consideration.

A notable distinction between consumer and business buyers is this emphasis placed on choosing the supplier and scheduling the ordering of products. The source of supply is more important to the business buyer since a variety of benefits result from choosing the right business suppliers as partners. In the world of supply chain management, these benefits that result from partnerships are referred to as **relationship marketing**: the trust and interdependence that develops between suppliers and business buyers.[27] Similarly, the pressures of keeping an organization running

27. An early piece that established the importance of relationships in the business marketing process is Jonathan R. Copulsky and Michael J. Wolf, "Relationship Marketing: Positioning for the Future," *Journal of Business Strategy*, July/August 1990, 16–20.

Is success on the Internet a matter of chance?

Is success on the Internet a matter of will?

Is success on the Internet a matter of survival?

On the Internet, success can be elusive. And one thing you can't afford is an Internet service that tries to be everything to everyone. Enter UUNET. With products engineered exclusively with business in mind, we provide the award-winning service and support you need to not just survive. But to prevail. Call us at 1-877-862-6554. Code: Focus. Or visit www.info.uu.net.

The Business Side Of The Internet.

UUNET
A WorldCom Company

Canada: 1 888 242 0653 ©2000 UUNET Technologies, Inc., a subsidiary of WorldCom, Inc. All rights reserved. The UUNET logo is a trademark.

EXHIBIT 5.16

While business buyers put a premium on rational, functional evaluations, there is still an element of emotion in the decision-making process—particularly with respect to developing sound relationships with suppliers. What language in this communication suggests UUNET wants to establish a relationship with its customers?

smoothly with the needed production supplies and equipment place greater emphasis on the scheduling of purchases. As consumers, we can do with that new camcorder for a day or two. But what would happen to Dell Computer's mass customization assembly line process if Xilinx doesn't deliver parts on time? The ad in Exhibit 5.16 highlights the benefits of supplier partnerships and relationship marketing—very emotional criteria in the choice process.

In the business market, product and supplier evaluation are much more formalized *after* a purchase than in the consumer market. While we often evaluate our decisions in the postpurchase stage and try to deal with the anxiety of a particularly tough decision, business buyers have a more formalized—even institutionalized—procedure for rating product and supplier performance. This feature of business buying behavior has heightened the awareness of "relationship" marketing, as we have discussed before. Buying and selling organizations now understand that nurturing, long-term partnerships reap tremendous rewards for both organizations. This feature of business buyer behavior is somewhat threatened in the new context of vertical trade communities on the Internet. When a bid or auction system is used to seek the best price or when multiple trade partners assemble at a trade portal, long-standing relationships may be threatened by the price emphasis that such trade systems promote. This is discussed in more detail in Chapter 10.

The Nature of Decision Making in the Business Market

Psychological and sociological factors mediate consumer decision making. In business decision making, the nature of the process is affected by three factors: the decision styles used by business buyers, the type of decision that is being made, and the buying center concept.

Decision Styles. **Decision styles** refers to the fact that business buyers typically use one of two very different styles in going about the decision-making process. The **rational decision style** is characterized by an effort on the part of the buyer to maximize the value of the purchase. The buyer will scrutinize price, product features, and delivery schedule, and in general be very deliberate in progressing through the stages of decision making. Conversely, the buyer using a **conservative decision style** will place primary emphasis not on the monetary or economic aspects of the purchase but on reducing risk. The conservative-style decision maker will rely on past experience with vendors and relationships as primary factors in decision making. Some estimates suggest that as many as 70 percent of all business decision makers are using this conservative decision-making style, thus placing risk aversion above economic considerations in the purchase process. But again, in the context of Internet access to a wide range of information and potential suppliers, the tendency to build relationships may be on the way out.

Rational and conservative decision makers will place different value on factors in the marketing mix of the firms with which they are doing business. Rational decision makers will emphasize the product and pricing variables, while conservative decision makers will be more sensitive to distribution (that is, availability and delivery of stock) and other aspects of the relationship between buyer and seller. Each, therefore, will respond to different types of promotional appeals. The rational buyer will see information-intensive promotion provided by direct mail, manuals, or personal selling. The conservative buyer will also value personal selling, but training and posttransaction service may be more highly valued. Properly appealing to rational and conservative decision makers will require completely different promotional mixes.

Type of Decision. The type of decision factor includes three possibilities: straight rebuy, modified rebuy, or new task buying decision.

- The **straight rebuy** is a common situation where a buyer is purchasing an item on a routine basis and engages in little information search. Vendors are usually chosen from a preapproved list. This type of decision is typical for operating supplies and small component parts and not unlike the consumer's habitual decision-making effort.
- The **modified rebuy** is also a recurring purchase, but product and vendor specifications can change over time, requiring that information search be initiated.
- The **new task buying decision** is characterized by extensive information search. It is a new purchase decision and is typical for infrequently purchased business goods like installations and accessory equipment. It can also occur when major changes in sources of supply are considered for raw materials and operating supplies. Recently, new technologies have resulted in more new task decision making. This includes not just hardware but a wide range of services needed to cope with developing online activities.

Buyer Center. The typical business purchase order is signed by a purchasing agent, but that person is likely *not* the person who made the decision about what to buy. Unfortunately, it is often quite difficult to figure out who *is* actually responsible for the decision to buy. Production workers, research and development staff, design engineers, techies, or top-level executives may be the ones who determine the specifications for products. But while one group may make the specifications, it is common for several different people to be involved in a single decision. This is known as the **buying center** concept, because several people are involved in the process. Specifically, it is possible that as many as six different types of decision makers may be involved in any particular business purchase decision. These are described in Exhibit 5.17.

The importance of the buying center concept is obvious. Depending on who is actually making the decision, different messages and different promotional mix tools will need to be used. If a CEO or CFO is typically making the decision for your product category, you will never get a salesperson or a piece of direct mail through. But advertising on *Meet the Press* or in *Fortune,* or sponsoring a golf tournament, just might get the attention (and name recognition) you need to communicate with the head honcho.

Different members of an organization have different values and objectives in the decision process. This means different promotional messages and different promotional tools. The buyer may want a selling team assembled to make a formal presentation. Or a trade show may be the only way to reach all the different participants in the decision. And it is absolutely necessary to understand the communications environment. An example of this is a clerical staffperson who is the gatekeeper for all product and service information that flows to the ultimate decision makers. If the marketer does not properly understand this individual's role and influence, the brand will never even make it to the consideration stage.

Participant	Role in the Decision-Making Process
1. Initiator	This person who first suggests that a purchase needs to be made. This person may be directly involved in operations or may be from a different part of the organization entirely, such as the home office. Also, an initiator may actually be from outside the organization. Often, outside consultants recommend the purchase of equipment or services to enhance a firm's operations.
2. User	This, of course, is the individual within the organization who ultimately uses the product. A scientist in the research and development laboratory may require a specially designed microscope or an engineer may need a high-powered computer work station. The user often establishes product specifications and submits an evaluation of product performance.
3. Decision Maker	The ultimate decision maker in an organization can literally be anyone. The user is many times the decision maker. The purchasing agent can be the decision maker. In some organizations, the president or chief executive officer may become involved as the ultimate decision maker.
4. Influencer	An influences in an diffused buying process is someone in the organization who, because of experience or specialized expertise, exerts an influence on other members of the organization involved in the decision.
5. Buyer	This person simply places the order for the item. In most organizations, this will be a purchasing agent or the equivalent position.
6. Gatekeeper	This individual is critical to the process. Gatekeepers control the flow of information into an organization. Information about products from literature or directly from salespeople is controlled by the gatekeeper. Gatekeepers can be purchasing agents or even clerical staff in an organization.

EXHIBIT 5.17

The potential participants in a buying center

Business Buyer Behavior on the Internet. Because of the business buyer's knowledge about product categories and drive to evaluate products thoroughly, marketers need to recognize that the Internet provides an ideal venue for business buyers. Internet buying offers business buyers a highly efficient way to search for product alternatives, evaluate prices, and even negotiate a deal. As proof of the power and value of the Internet as a business-to-business marketplace, business-to-business e-commerce is expected to reach nearly $3 trillion in the United States by the year 2004. Worldwide, transactions will likely total over $5 trillion.[28] At sites like VertiNet, ProPurchase, and Chemdex, specialized vertical trade communities allow business buyers to seek product and pricing information from literally dozens of different suppliers at the same time. At Chemdex, a business buyer can search through information from 120 suppliers of approximately 250,000 life-science chemicals.[29] Sites like MetalSite, PlasticsNet, and PaperExchange offer the same sort of broad information environment. These used to be highly fractionated markets. Now this sort of buying environment provides business buyers much greater efficiency than seeing dozens of salespeople or wading through dozens of direct-mail catalogs. Mainstream business marketers like Intel and Dell have turned to the 'Net to serve their customers as well. By the beginning of the year 2000, both Intel and Dell were seeing about 50 percent of their transactions taking place over the Internet.[30]

28. Forrester Research, "B2B to Be Marked by New eMarketplaces," February 10, 2000, accessed at http://www.nua.net/surveys on February 20, 2000.
29. Bob Donath, "Value Eliminates Marketing Distractions," *Marketing News,* December 6, 1999, 13.
30. "Intel Sells Half of All Its Computer Chips over the Internet," Associated Press, October 7, 1999, accessed via the Internet on October 7, 1999.

Evaluation Criteria Used in Business Decision Making

In analyzing consumer behavior, we found that both psychological and sociological factors influenced consumer decisions. Business buyers are subject to a variety of influences, both economic and emotional, as we discussed in the decision-styles section. These influences on the business buyer translate directly into evaluation criteria used in the decision-making process. The following are criteria used by business buyers to evaluate products, services, and the vendors who supply them.

Efficiency of Product Supplied. This can be based on such qualities as speed of performance, wear and repair qualities of an item, and ease of use or installation. For example, a product might have features that make it possible to use low-cost, semi-skilled workers. This is often the case when antiquated production processes are enhanced with robotics. Or, in the case of PCs and Web sites, clerical productivity can be increased to such a degree that fewer staff may be needed to achieve the same level of output. One of the most powerful appeals a seller can make to a business buyer is that the product will enhance the efficiency of the buyer's operations.

Certainty of Supply. A supplier may entice the buyer with low prices, but without the ability to guarantee dependable, long-term supply, business buyers will balk at establishing a relationship. No matter how attractive a price is, if the buyer fears that a supplier can't deliver, that buyer will likely shy away from the relationship.

Dependability in Meeting Schedules. Business customers must meet their own schedules in production and sales and must assure themselves of supplies in the specified quantities and on the dates promised. Consider the disastrous circumstance of an automobile production line being held up because a 59-cent, molded-plastic piece for the dashboard did not arrive on schedule!

Technical Assistance. This includes information on qualities and use of products or processes as well as advice on maximizing the customer's efficiency. Solving problems of installing and incorporating equipment into existing production methods is also important to the customer in this area. Lanier, the supplier of office equipment, offers service contracts to buyers where the firm will respond within two hours to a request for technical assistance or repair.

Product Features and Supplier Patronage Motives. Business buyers base their purchase decisions on criteria related to both the product and the supplier of the product. To get an idea of the range of evaluation criteria used in these two areas, the following list will be helpful. Some typical product features emphasized by business buyers are:

- Efficiency
- Economy
- Quality, strength, durability
- Speed
- Protection from loss (warranty or guarantee)
- Dependability or reliability
- Accuracy
- Uniformity and stability
- Low maintenance cost
- Simplicity

Note that this list includes items that relate to all area of product evaluation: function, emotion (risk aversion), and benefits. Each item on the list suggests appeals that the business buyer might find relevant in promotional communications.

CAREERPROFILE

Name: Lisa Rubin
Title: Marketing Manager
Company: Anderson Travel & Cruises, San Diego, California
               http://www.andersontravel.com
Education: B.S., Advertising and Marketing

When she graduated from college, Lisa Rubin knew several things about the type of job she wanted. "I wanted to work in an industry where people are happy," she says. "I also wanted to work in a people-oriented job. And, I love to travel."

After a stint working for a special events planning firm, Lisa found a job that seems like a perfect fit. As Marketing Manager for Anderson Travel & Cruises, a nine-office travel agency in Southern California, she develops advertising and communications programs promoting vacations in exotic destinations.

A large portion of Lisa's workday is spent coordinating the agency's weekly newspaper advertisements. The ads are designed to attract the attention of consumers who are ready for a vacation. "Our ads paint a picture that makes customers say 'I want to be on that beach. I've worked hard and I deserve a vacation,'" explains Lisa.

For each ad, Lisa also develops a package of information for the firm's travel agents. "The idea is to give them every possible piece of information about the programs we're advertising so that when customers call, they are ready to answer questions," says Lisa. "We do all of the research for them so they can do their primary job, which is informing and persuading clients."

That knowledge is vital, says Lisa, because when consumers are shopping for a vacation, they want to be reassured that they're making the right choice. "When the customer comes in, they're sold on the emotional rewards of taking a trip, but they can't really touch and see before they buy a vacation. It's very important that our agents be able to explain to customers exactly what they're buying." Price is also part of the decision-making process. "Even people who can afford expensive vacations want to feel they're spending their money wisely," says Lisa.

Anderson's Web site is rich with information about options and pricing. "Our Web site is a tool that gives customers the option to do some research on their own and to get a feel for prices prior to purchasing," says Lisa. "Some customers feel comfortable buying online, but there are also those customers that want that person-to-person transaction. They still want to be able to sit across a table from someone when they're buying a vacation and say 'this is going to be good, right?' Because of that, I think 'brick and mortar' travel agencies are never going to go away entirely."

To learn more about travel and tourism marketing, visit these Web sites:

The Travel and Tourism Research Association
http://www.ttra.com

The Association of Travel Marketing Executives
http://www.atme.org

To learn more about consumer behavior, visit these Web sites:

American Demographics
http://www.marketingtools.com

The Society for Consumer Psychology
http://www.consumerpsych.org

The trigger factor that determines choice in the business market can also be the buyer's image of the selling institution. This is especially important when the decision relates to goods that are so nearly alike that it is difficult to see clear differences between competitive brands. Products such as operating supplies and raw materials fall into this category, as do services where buyers might find it difficult to come up with hard criteria on which to base a judgment. When the product itself is hard to judge, the supplier evaluation criteria carry the greatest weight in the choice process. Typical of the criteria used to evaluate suppliers are:

- Completeness of line and inventory
- Offer of free service
- Reputation in trade
- Reciprocal patronage
- Price and discount policies
- Monopoly position
- Financial or managerial connection
- Relationships
- Past services
- Research and pioneering

Analyzing buyer behavior is a critical component in developing a promotional mix. As you have seen, an understanding of how consumers and business buyers make decisions gives insights into what is important in their decision-making processes. But if we come up with the information or the incentive (such as promotional deals or premiums) that has a good chance of working, how do we communicate with consumers and business buyers? The next sections present the basics of communication and raise some issues about information processing.

THE COMMUNICATION PROCESS **⑤**

The fundamental process underlying each element in the promotional mix is communication. Communicating with current and potential customers is a firm's chance to tell them what it has to offer and why the offer has value. Each element in the promotional mix can be better understood when we have a basic understanding of the communication process.

Communication is the process of sending a message to a receiver. The traditional and widely accepted definition is the process of establishing a commonness or oneness of thought between a sender and a receiver.[31] Exhibit 5.18 is a model of communication that represents how the process takes place in promotion. Each component in the model warrants some discussion to truly appreciate how this communication process works.

Intentions

A mass communication effort in marketing begins with intentions for message content and the behavioral effect the communication is expected to have on those who receive the message. **Intended message content** identifies the informational, persuasive, and visual content in a promotional communication. As we have seen, household and business buyers will seek out information during the decision-making process. Intentions for message content will emphasize providing "relevant" information. What information is "relevant" to buyers? Relevance depends on consumers' perceiving that a brand meets their psychological or sociocultural needs. In the case of business buyers, the criteria for evaluating products and suppliers will be the basis for relevance.

The **intended behavioral effect**—how receivers respond to a communication—is rarely immediate. One class of communications is designed to create a favorable predisposition toward a firm's product, and a delayed response is to be expected. In most cases this means a favorable image or attitude toward a brand. Then, at some future point in time, the goal is to have receivers recall the communication and judge the brand as one that can satisfy their current needs. Another class of communication messages implores consumers to take immediate action. Advertisements, infomercials, Internet, and direct-marketing communications that

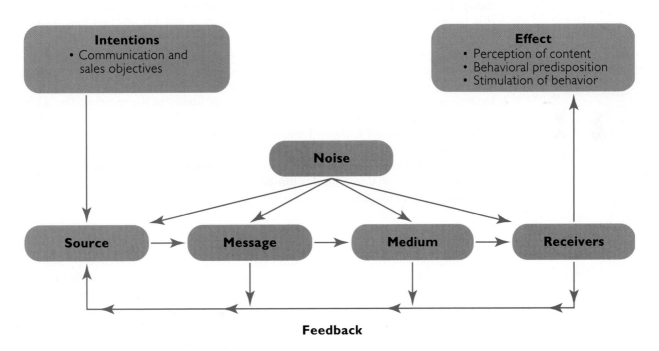

EXHIBIT 5.18

The communication process in promotion

---

31. Wilbur Schram, *The Process and Effects of Communication* (Urbana, IL: University of Illinois Press, 1955), Chapter 1.

urge consumers to call to place an order are designed to elicit an immediate response. This would be an actual behavior—purchase behavior. Review the discussion of communications versus sales objectives for promotion in Chapter 3. When a marketer uses personal selling as a promotional tool, the sales force is also able to close a sale. Again, this would make the behavior effect of sales a legitimate intention for the communication process.

Source

The **source** of a communication is the marketer of the brand and, in personal selling, the salesperson who represents the marketer. Both consumers and business buyers can have preconceived notions and attitudes about marketers that affect their response to communications. Source credibility is a key issue here. **Source credibility** is the receiver's perception that the source of the message is knowledgeable, believable, trustworthy, and unbiased and has the knowledge to offer relevant information. If a communicator is perceived to be knowledgeable, then receivers believe the communicator has the expertise to provide persuasive information in a communication. If a source is perceived to be trustworthy, consumers also believe it to be honest and ethical. In communications research, sources that are perceived to be expert and trustworthy are more credible and persuasive than sources that are perceived to be less expert or trustworthy.[32]

Source credibility is a big reason why many marketers use spokespersons in their advertising and promotion to try to increase the credibility of the communication. Celebrities are often used to increase source credibility. If Tiger Woods says a golf ball is great, the message gains some persuasive power because he would know such things. If auto racer Jeff Burton wears a Chevy hat and drives a Chevy, Chevrolets may be perceived as more durable and well engineered. What if Michael Jordan touts a battery or a long-distance service? Is this message more believable and persuasive?

Aside from celebrity spokespersons, people perceived as experts are often used to increase the credibility of a communication. Promotional communications that feature the endorsement of experts such as doctors or engineers provide a basis for believability and trustworthiness that boosts the credibility of the message. The ad in Exhibit 5.19 uses an expert source, a dental hygienist, as a way to increase the credibility of the claims for Colgate Total. Another credible source is the average person who should have practical knowledge about the way a brand performs. When an average person champions a brand, this is called a **testimonial** and can increase the persuasive impact of a communication because we tend to believe and trust people we perceive to be similar to ourselves.

Message

The **message** contains the information designed to inform or persuade consumers and business buyers that a marketer's brand provides superior satisfaction. When the mass media are used for promotional communications, one difficulty is constructing a message that is suitable for a large number of receivers. The message must be a generalized representation of many different judgment criteria that might be used by a diverse set of consumers—even within the same segment. If the situation analysis and target marketing plans are done well, the message can contain reasonably specific information relating to the target's judgment criteria. Remember, those criteria can relate to functional features or perceived emotional benefits.

32. William McGuire, "The Nature of Attitudes and Attitude Change," in *Handbook of Social Psychology,* 2nd ed., G. Lindsey and E. Aronson, Eds. (Cambridge, MA: Addison-Wesley Publishing Co., 1969), 135–199.

EXHIBIT 5.19

Credible sources make a message more believable. Using the testimonial of a dental hygienist increases the believability of this communication.

A great advantage of personal selling in communication is the opportunity for the salesperson to tailor the message for each receiver. The values of the product can be portrayed differently according to each receiver's unique perspective, needs, and judgment criteria. Further, the salesperson can respond to inquiries or objections raised by the receiver. The mass communication message must remain general in order to be relevant to as many receivers as possible. In personal communication, a different message can be constructed during each contact. The tools in the promotional mix that allow personal communication include personal selling, telemarketing, some forms of direct marketing, and customized e-mail.

The overriding consideration for message content is, again, that it is deemed *relevant* by consumers. If consumers perceive a message to be irrelevant or contradictory to their attitudes and beliefs, it will be ignored. We'll spend quite a bit of time on message development issues in Part 3 of the book when we get to applying the tools of promotion and IMC.

Medium

The **medium** is the vehicle through which a message is transmitted to receivers. Newspapers, radio, television, magazines, billboards, the Internet (which includes Web sites, e-mail, and banner ads), and direct mail constitute standard media for transmitting mass communications messages. Each of these media has the capability of reaching a large number of receivers at a low cost per contact and frequent intervals.

The medium chosen has much to do with effective communication. The broadcast media of radio and television have the advantage of audio and/or audiovisual presentation messages. The print media can provide more detailed information, but a brand is left pretty lifeless on a printed page. The Internet allows consumers to pursue information at whatever level of depth and intensity they choose. Marketers often use a combination of media to achieve overall communications goals. The makers of Titleist golf equipment can use advertisements in *Golf Digest* to communicate functional features of its golf balls, and then use television ads during a major golf tournament that feature a celebrity to send an emotional appeal to receivers.

In personal selling, the salesperson is both the source and the medium for the message, which puts a lot of pressure on the individual or team that carries out the communication. In other forms of personal communication like telemarketing, highly customized direct marketing, or individualized e-mails, there is still a medium involved.

Receivers

The **receivers** of a message are the consumers or business buyers targeted by a firm in its STP strategy. Reaching these consumers is accomplished by carefully choosing promotional tools and the mass media needed to send the message. The media organizations we discussed in Chapter 2 provide access to target segments and have up-to-date information on their readers, viewers, listeners, or surfers. In this phase of the mass communication process, the most important information is a firm's strategy regarding segmentation and positioning. The target segment constitutes the audience to whom the message is directed. The positioning strategy affects message content.

Effects

The **effects** in a mass communication process are determined by identifying receivers' perception of message content, behavioral predisposition toward the product, and the amount and type of behavior actually stimulated by the communication. Identifying what was *actually perceived* relative to the intentions can be a lengthy and costly process. Only through evaluation can such information be obtained. There are a wide range of techniques that can be used to measure and evaluate the effect of each tool in the promotional mix. This is a topic we take up in great detail in Chapter 15.

The critical issue about content perception is the degree to which intentions for the content match the perception of content. Behavioral predisposition as an effect of mass communication is measured by identifying the overall image of or attitude toward brand created by the communication. Another dimension of behavioral predisposition is receivers' intention to buy after exposure to a message.

The amount and type of behavior stimulated is an important measure of communication effect. Unfortunately, it is the most difficult to measure. Because consumers and business buyers may not draw on information obtained from a communication for a long time, being able to attribute behavior to a particular message is nearly impossible, as we discussed in Chapter 3. For direct-response messages in advertising, infomercials, or through e-commerce, the task is a bit easier. It would simply entail monitoring calls received or orders received after a message was sent.

Noise and Feedback

In a mass communication effort, **noise** is any disturbance that inhibits message transmission to the intended receiver. As Exhibit 5.18 shows, noise is pervasive in the system. Noise affecting intentions comes in the form of inaccurate or incomplete information in the situation analysis that results in a poor understanding of receivers. Noise emanating from the source of the message occurs when a brand's features do not match what receivers deem to be relevant to their search for satisfaction. Another form of noise at the source level is an episode of bad publicity that may change receivers' attitudes toward a brand or a company. The unexplained spontaneous acceleration of the Audi 5000 or the allegations that Nike was using child labor affected attitudes toward those firms and their brands among some potential customers. The message itself contributes to noise if the language used or visualizations are confusing to receivers. Clutter in a medium produces noise as competing messages interfere with one another. Finally, noise is present at the receiver level if distractions occur during message reception. Overall, noise reduces the impact of a mass communication, or it can result in total lack of reception.

Feedback in mass communication typically tries to measure one or more of the following:

- Who were the actual receivers of the message?
- What was the perceived content of the message?
- What behavioral predisposition toward the product resulted from receipt of the message?
- What type of behavior was stimulated by exposure to the message?

Once this valuable information is obtained, changes throughout the system can be made: message content can be changed, media placement can be adjusted, or new receivers can be targeted. The feedback process provides the opportunity to enhance future mass communications efforts.

ISSUES IN COMMUNICATION AND INFORMATION PROCESSING

A model of communication provides a useful framework for understanding the overall process and dimensions of communication. But while models offer a broad perspective, there are issues that need to be considered with regard to how the information is managed by consumers and business buyers. The key issues are information processing and perceptual defenses, and persuasion via a peripheral route.

Information Processing and Perceptual Defense

At this point, you may have the impression that creating effective promotion is a pretty straightforward exercise. We carefully analyze consumers' beliefs and attitudes, construct communications to address any problems that might be identified, and choose various promotional tools to get the word out to our target market. Yes, it would be easy if consumers and business buyers would just pay attention to and believe everything we tell them, and if our competition would kindly stop all of its promotion so that ours would be the only message that the target market had to worry about. Of course, these things aren't going to happen.

Why would we expect to encounter resistance from our target market as we attempt to influence their beliefs, attitudes, and understanding about our brand? One way to think about this problem is to portray the receiver as an information processor who must advance through a series of stages before our message can have its intended effect. If we are skillful in selecting appropriate promotional tools to reach our target, then receivers must (1) pay attention to the message, (2) comprehend it correctly, (3) accept the message exactly as we intended, and (4) retain the message until it is needed for a purchase decision. Unfortunately, problems can occur at any or all of these four stages, completely negating the effect of our campaign.

There are two major obstacles that we must overcome if our message is to have its intended effect. The first—the cognitive consistency impetus—stems from the way individuals deal with information. Remember, a person develops and holds beliefs and attitudes for a reason: They help him or her make efficient decisions that yield pleasing outcomes. **Cognitive consistency impetus** is a mental state where a consumer is satisfied with an attitude and belief structure and the outcomes they produce. New information that challenges existing beliefs can be ignored or disparaged to prevent modification of the present cognitive system. Cognitive consistency is a comfortable and pleasing state, and individuals do whatever they can to maintain it. The individual's desire—consumer or business buyer—to maintain cognitive consistency can be a major roadblock for a marketer that wants to change beliefs and attitudes.

The second obstacle—**information overload**—comes from the context in which messages are processed. Even if a person wanted to, it would be impossible to process and integrate every promotional message that he or she is exposed to each day. Pick up today's newspaper and start reviewing every ad you come across. Will you have time today to read them all? The overload problem is further magnified by competitive brands making very similar performance claims. Now, was it Advil, Anacin, Aleve, Avia, Motrin, Nuprin, or Tylenol Gelcaps that promised you twelve hours of relief from your headache? (Can you select the brand from this list that isn't even a headache remedy?) The fact is that each of us is exposed to hundreds of promotions each day, and no one has the time or inclination to sort through them all.

Because of information overload, consumers employ perceptual defenses to simplify and control their own information processing. Perception is the way in which people select, organize, and interpret information. It is important here to see that the consumer is in control, and the marketer must find some way to engage the consumer if a message is to have any impact. Of course, the best way to engage consumers is to offer them information about a brand that addresses an active need state. Simply stated, it is difficult to get people to process a message about your headache remedy when they don't have a headache. The consumer is able to enlist a whole series of screening mechanisms through the perception process to deal with information overload.

- **Selective exposure** is the ability to allow stimuli into the field of awareness. When consumers change the television or radio station or throw out direct-mail pieces without even opening them, that is selective exposure. If a business buyer refuses to accept an appointment with a salesperson or passes by a company's booth at a trade show, that is also selective exposure.
- **Selective attention** is the mind's capacity to screen out information that is deemed irrelevant. This is certainly the marketer's greatest challenge, creating a tremendous waste of promotional dollars. Most promotional communications are given a quick assessment and then simply ignored by consumers.
- **Selective comprehension** occurs when a receiver interprets a message in a way that is consistent with his or her existing attitude and belief structure. Any information that contradicts or challenges this structure will be rejected as biased or untruthful. If a salesperson tells you that Nokia phones are inferior and you really like your Nokia, you will reject the information as erroneous.
- **Selective retention** is the process of choosing to store only some of the information that is attended to and comprehended. This is the ultimate result of information overload—we just don't have enough room in our brainpans for all the information we encounter. This is the fundamental way in which consumers and business buyers deal with too much information—only the most relevant and important (and interesting) information gets remembered.

Marketers employ a variety of tactics to break through the information overload that activates perceptual defenses. Popular music, celebrity spokespersons, sexy models, rapid scene changes, wild demonstrations, and anything that is novel are devices for combating the selective perception defenses. While marketers will try almost anything to break down these defenses, some consumers around the world seem to be actually seeking out more information—not less. The Global Issues box tells an interesting story on this subject about Japanese consumers.

Let's assume that a communication gets attention and the receiver comprehends its claims correctly. Will acceptance follow and create the enduring change in brand attitude that is desired, or will there be further resistance? If the message is trying to alter beliefs about the brand, expect more resistance. When the receiver is involved and attentive and comprehends a claim that challenges current beliefs, the cognitive consistency impetus kicks in, and cognitive responses can be expected. Cognitive responses are the thoughts that occur to individuals at that exact moment in time when their beliefs and attitudes are being challenged by some form of persuasive communication. When these thoughts are negative in any way, the advertiser's goals are not served.[33]

GLOBAL ISSUES

INFORMATION, INFORMATION EVERYWHERE

While marketers always worry that consumers will screen out their promotional messages because of information overload, a new breed of Japanese consumers seems to be looking for information everywhere they go. The reason: a wireless Web connection that's just about free. Young Japanese consumers can get cellular phone service with Web access for a few dollars a month. This compares to a 24-hour on-line connection over a leased fixed line at about $360 a month.

Web-smart phones in Japan will exceed 20 million units by the year 2002. That compares with only 17 million computer users who went online between 1995 and 2000. One young Japanese consumer users her "featherweight" 90-gram net phone constantly. She checks her e-mail several times a day, scours real estate Web sites for a new apartment, and orders books online through the small screen text. And this might just be the beginning. Before too long, a "third-generation" wireless Web service will be launched in Japan. Known as wideband CDMA, it will allow lightning-fast data transmission and high-quality video communication. Looks like marketers will be able to reach consumers with advertising over their cell phones before too long. One wonders if this will become cell phone information overload.

Source: Irene M. Kunni, "I'm Online All the Time," *Business Week,* October 18, 1999, 24.

Shaping Attitudes via a Peripheral Route

For low-involvement products, such as batteries or tortilla chips, cognitive responses to promotional claims are really not expected.[34] In such situations, attitude formation will often follow a more peripheral route, and peripheral cues become the focal point for judging the message impact. **Peripheral cues** refer to features of the message other than the actual arguments about the brand's performance. They include an attractive or comical spokesperson, novel imagery, a catchy jingle, an eye-popping display, or a compelling demonstration. Any feature of a promotion that prompts a pleasant emotional response can be thought of as a peripheral cue.

In the peripheral route, the receiver can still learn from a promotional message, but the learning is passive and typically must be achieved by frequent association of the peripheral cue (for example, the Eveready Energizer Bunny) with the brand in question. It has even been suggested that classical conditioning principles might be

33. For an expanded discussion of these issues, see Richard E. Petty, John T. Cacioppo, Alan J. Strathman, and Joseph R. Priester, "To Think or Not to Think: Exploring Two Routes to Persuasion," in *Persuasion: Psychological Insights and Perspectives,* Sharon Shavitt and Timothy C. Brock, Eds. (Boston: Allyn and Bacon, 1994), 113–147.
34. Ibid.

employed by marketers in their communications to facilitate and accelerate this associative, peripheral learning process.[35] As consumers and business buyers learn to associate pleasant feelings and attractive images with a brand, their attitude toward the brand should become more positive.

What do LeAnn Rimes, Jerry Seinfeld, Junji Takada, the Pillsbury Doughboy, Shaq, the Budweiser amphibians, and the pleasant tones that accompany the "Intel Inside" reminder have in common? They—and many other stars, icons, and techniques like them—have all been used as peripheral cues in promotional campaigns. When all brands in a category offer similar benefits, the most fruitful avenue for promotion is likely to be the peripheral route, where the marketer merely tries to maintain positive or pleasant associations with the brand by constantly presenting it with appealing peripheral cues. Event sponsorship and highly likeable ads, especially ads that use humor, are key techniques in peripheral route persuasion.

This strategy can be especially important for mature brands in low-involvement categories where the challenge is to keep the customer from getting bored. But it is expensive because any gains made along the peripheral route are short-lived.[36] Expensive TV airtime, lots of repetition, and a never-ending search for the freshest, most popular peripheral cues demand huge promotional budgets. When you think of the peripheral route, think of the promotional campaigns for high-profile, mature brands such as Coke, Pepsi, Miller Lite, McDonald's, and Doritos. They entertain in an effort to keep you interested.

---

35. For additional discussion of this issue, see Frances K. McSweeney and Calvin Bierley, "Recent Developments in Classical Conditioning," *Journal of Consumer Research,* vol. 11 (September 1984): 619–631.
36. The rationale for cultivating brand interest for mature brands is discussed more fully in Karen A. Machleit, Chris T. Allen, and Thomas J. Madden, "The Mature Brand and Brand Interest: An Alternative Consequence of Ad-Evoked Affect," *Journal of Marketing,* vol. 57 (October 1993), 72–82.

SUMMARY

❶ Describe the four stages of consumer decision making.

Advertisers need a keen understanding of their consumers as a basis for developing effective promotion. This understanding begins with a view of consumers as systematic decision makers who follow a predictable process in making their choices among products and brands. The process begins when consumers perceive a need, and it proceeds with a search for information that will help in making an informed choice. The search-and-evaluation stage is followed by purchase. Postpurchase use and evaluation then become critical as the stage in which customer satisfaction is ultimately determined.

❷ Explain how consumers adapt their decision-making processes as a function of involvement and experience.

Some purchases are more important to people than others, and this fact adds complexity to any analysis of consumer behavior. To accommodate this complexity, advertisers often think about the level of involvement that attends any given purchase. Involvement and prior experience with a product or service category can lead to four diverse modes of consumer decision making. These modes are extended problem solving, limited problem solving, habit or variety seeking, and brand loyalty.

❸ Explain consumer decision making in a sociocultural consumption context.

Culture and society provide the context in which promotional communications will be interpreted. Marketers who overlook the influence of the sociocultural consumption context are bound to struggle in their attempt to communicate with the target audience. Several key concepts relate to managing the impact of the sociocultural environment. These include culture, values, rituals, society, social class, family, reference groups, race, ethnicity, gender, and community.

❹ Describe the business buyer behavior process.

Business buyers go through a decision process that is similar to consumers. These stages of the business buying behavior process are:

a. Need recognition
b. Product and scheduling specifications
c. Evaluation of products
d. Evaluation of suppliers and services
e. Product and supplier choice
f. Product and supplier evaluation

Business buyers do put more emphasis on scheduling their purchases and on the product and supplier choice and evaluation effort. It is also necessary to recognize that business buyers will typically use one of two types of decision styles: rational or conservative. The rational style emphasizes information search and evaluation. The conservative style emphasizes relationships with established suppliers.

❺ Describe both the mass and personal communication processes that show how consumers and business buyers receive and interpret promotional communications.

The communication process that helps us understand how consumers and business buyers receive and manage promotional communications has several components. The process begins with intentions for the communication on the part of the source of the message. These intentions have to do with message content, behavior effects, and overall communication and sales objectives. The next element of the model is the source which represents the marketer sending the message. In personal selling, the salesperson becomes the source (as well as the medium) for the message. The source then constructs a message for the targeted market (receivers).

The content of the messages is based on an understanding of the target market's evaluative criteria for judging brands in the product category. Consumers and business buyers have different criteria in the way they judge brands. The medium for communication are the mass media and in the case of personal selling, the salesperson.

Noise is pervasive through the communication process. Noise is any disruption or interference within the process, and it affects each element. When the message reaches receivers, there are effects. These effects relate to perceptions, behavioral intentions, and actual behaviors on the part of receivers. Finally, the source receives and solicits feedback from receivers and uses feedback to alter the communication effort in the future.

KEY TERMS

consumer behavior, 151
need state, 152
functional benefits, 153
emotional benefits, 153
internal information search, 153
external information search, 153
consideration set, 153
evaluative criteria, 154
customer satisfaction, 155
cognitive dissonance, 155
involvement, 156
prior experience, 157
extended problem solving, 157
limited problem solving, 158
habit, 158
variety seeking, 158
brand loyalty, 158
attitude, 160
brand attitudes, 160
beliefs, 160
salient beliefs, 160
multiattribute attitude models
　(MAAMs), 160

evaluative criteria, 160
importance weights, 161
perception, 161
culture, 163
values, 164
rituals, 164
society, 165
social class, 165
intergenerational effect, 166
reference group, 167
membership groups, 167
aspirational groups, 167
gender, 168
community, 169
brand communities, 170
relationship marketing, 171
decision styles, 172
rational decision style, 172
conservative decision style, 172
straight rebuy, 173
modified rebuy, 173
new task buying decision, 173
buying center, 173

communication, 176
intended message content, 177
intended behavioral effect, 177
source, 178
source credibility, 178
testimonial, 178
message, 178
medium, 179
receivers, 180
effects, 180
noise, 180
feedback, 181
cognitive consistency impetus, 182
information overload, 182
selective exposure, 182
selective attention, 182
selective comprehension, 182
selective retention, 182
peripheral cues, 183

QUESTIONS FOR REVIEW AND CRITICAL THINKING

1. When consumers have a well-defined consideration set and a list of evaluative criteria for assessing the brands in that set, they in effect possess a matrix of information about that category. Drawing on your experiences as a consumer, set up and fill in such a matrix for the category of fast-food restaurants.

2. Is cognitive dissonance a good thing or a bad thing from a marketer's point of view? Explain how and why marketers should try to deal with cognitive dissonance their consumers may experience.

3. Most people quickly relate to the notion that some purchasing decisions are more involving than others. What kinds of products or services do you consider highly involving? What makes these products more involving from your point of view?

4. Explain the difference between brand-loyal and habitual purchasing. When a brand-loyal customer arrives at a store and finds her favorite brand is out of stock, what would you expect to happen next?

5. Describe three attitude-change strategies that could be suggested by the results of a study of consumer behavior using multiattribute attitude models. Provide examples of different advertising campaigns that have employed each of these strategies.

6. Watch an hour of prime-time television, and for each commercial you see, make a note of the tactic the advertiser employed to capture and hold the audience's attention. How can the use of attention-attracting tactics backfire on an advertiser?

7. How do consumers and business buyers differ in their decision-making processes? Is it true that business buyers completely eliminate emotion from their decisions?

8. Give three examples of highly visible cultural rituals practiced annually in the United States. For each ritual you identify, assess the importance of buying and consuming for effective practice of the ritual.

9. Are you a believer in the intergenerational effect? Make a list of the brands in your cupboards, refrigerator, and medicine cabinet. Which of these brands would you also expect to find in your parents' cupboards, refrigerator, and medicine cabinet?

10. It's one thing to understand consumer and business buyer decision making, another to understand the communication process. What more do we learn about consumers and business buyers by studying communication and information process issues associated with communication?

EXPERIENTIAL EXERCISES

1. **In-class exercise.** In this chapter, you learned about MAAMs. Divide into teams. Discuss your personal brand preferences for toothpaste, cereal, and shampoo. Create a list of attributes consumers would use in evaluating brands in each product category. Which attributes are especially important to team members when buying a brand in this product category? Which attributes do team members find irrelevant?

2. **Out-of-class exercise.** Watch people watch advertising, in a real situation. Take notes while observing. Record the conversation topics, the responses to the ads, the background noise, and all the other stuff going on. Then write a paragraph or two explaining what happens when people watch ads on TV. How could a marketer use what you've learned in this chapter to make a better promotional message in an advertisement?

USING THE INTERNET

Exercise 1

Consumers often follow a predictable decision-making process when purchasing products. Web sites can be configured to influence a specific stage or several stages of the decision-making process. Visit the following sites:

Edmund's Automobile Buyer's Guides
http://www.edmund.com

Isuzu
http://www.isuzu.com

1. What stage or stages of the consumer decision-making process does each site address?

2. How do the sites differ in addressing the process of buying a car?

3. How do the sites differ in addressing functional and emotional benefits?

   Now, compare the Amazon.com and Reebok sites:

Amazon.com
http://www.amazon.com

Reebok
http://www.reebok.com

4. What stage or stages of the consumer decision-making process does each site address?

5. How do the sites differ in developing brand loyalty?

6. How do the sites differ in producing customer satisfaction?

Exercise 2

One of the most powerful aspects of the Internet is that, being digital, all transactions can easily be monitored and measured if you're in the right place. (This can also be, from a privacy standpoint, one of its most threatening aspects.) Some companies are "surveilling" consumers to better understand consumer behavior and to advise corporate clients as to how best to meet their needs. Visit the following sites:

e-Satisfy
http://www.e-satisfy.com

comScore
http://www.comscore.com

1. Some of the information collection on consumer behavior can be done passively—for example, by analyzing Web site logs—while other data are collected via such tools as pop-up surveys. What drawbacks and benefits do the various means to gauge consumer interests present?

2. What can be done on the Web that can't be done in a "bricks-and-mortar" store, in terms of measuring consumer shopping behavior?

3. Are there areas in which a bricks and mortar store might have an advantage in understanding its customers?

After reading this chapter, you will be able to:

1 Assess the benefits and problems of promotion in a free-enterprise, capitalistic society.

2 Identify the role of government agencies in the regulation of promotion.

3 Explain the meaning and importance of self-regulation of promotion.

4 Discuss the regulatory issues related to the promotional process.

5 Debate the ethical issues that arise from the use of promotional tools.

FEELING LUCKY?

PLAY LUCKYSURF.COM
A FREE PLAY A DAY FOR $1 MILLION.

LuckySurf.com

http://www.donnelleymarketing.com

http://www.epic.org

EXHIBIT 6.1

Database America (now a subsidiary of Donnelley Marketing) is in the business of collecting, compiling, and cashing in on information about consumers. On the one hand, such data can be used to precisely target advertising, or for a charitable appeal; on the other hand, companies in the private sector are amassing information on individuals so effectively as to make the government surveillance in Orwell's 1984 seem amateurish.

Anne Marie is a consumer just like you and me. When she saw the Eddie Bauer edition of the Ford Explorer as a sweepstakes giveaway, she dreamed about winning her dream car. But, in the end, she decided that entering the sweepstakes created a nightmare. "Every Jeep dealer in the Galaxy was calling me after that, she said. "There was a span of about two weeks that a different car dealer called or mailed something about me coming in to test-drive a car. I was furious."[1]

Does this sound familiar? What happened to Anne Marie happens to millions of Americans every day. Marketers call it "database marketing." Contests, sweepstakes, supermarket discount cards, and product warranty cards are common methods used by retailers and direct-marketing companies to gather information about customers and create a database to be used for promotional strategies. Big data "warehouse" companies like Metromail, Acxiom, and R L. Polk specialize in collecting massive amounts of consumer information. Exhibit 6.1 shows an ad for an Internet-based data company that provides "profiling" of consumers' online behavior and then delivers personalized online coupons. They then sell the data—including names, addresses, and phone numbers—to companies that use direct marketing such as catalog publishers, Internet companies, charities, book clubs, and music clubs. With the data, these firms can put together highly targeted promotions using direct mail, telemarketing, banner ads on Web pages, or even magazine ads.

While marketers call this process database marketing, consumer advocates are calling it an invasion of privacy. The leader of Junkbusters, a consumer advocacy group that opposes invasions of consumer privacy, calls the practice of database development "Orwellian" because "George Orwell's *1984* described a world where each home had a television-like device that actually watched what individuals were doing."[2]

But marketers defend the practice as good marketing research that leads to greater efficiency and more value for customers. The information gathered about consumers is stored (or warehoused) in a giant database and then "mined" or scrutinized for meaning. Once it is mined, consumers can be targeted with products or discount offers that match their previous buying patterns. As one direct marketer put it, "The more effective direct marketers get, the more they know about you, the better they can serve you."[3] For example, grocers argue that

1.   Teena Massingill, "Buyer Beware: Retailers Sharing Data," Knight Ridder News Service, September 17, 1999.
2.   Bradley Johnson, "Gov't Agencies Eye Online Profiling," *Advertising Age,* November 8, 1999, 102.
3.   Erika Rasmusson, "What Price Knowledge?" *Sales and Marketing Management,* December 1998, 56.

with the databases, they can target coupon and other special offers to the people most likely to use them, instead of wasting money on coupons and mailings that are never used. Consumer advocates are arguing for "permission marketing," where marketers can only direct promotions to people who give them express permission to do so. Groups like the Privacy Rights Clearinghouse are taking up the fight for consumers, and the issue is currently being debated in Federal Trade Commission hearings. So far, nothing about database development is illegal. We will need to wait and see if any restrictions are placed on the database process by either government mandate or consumer pressure. Or we could all do what some people do. They rarely shop on the Internet, junk mail and surveys go directly into the trash, and they have unlisted phone numbers.

INTRODUCTION

The story of Anne Marie and her encounter with database marketing raises issues about both the regulation of promotion and the ethics of gathering personal information about consumers—the two main topics of this chapter. The reason regulation of promotion is discussed in the same breath with the ethics of promotion is that the two often go hand in hand. Practices that are regulated are often questioned from an ethical standpoint.

In some cases, the ethical challenges to promotional practices that lead to regulation are naive and simplistic and fail to take into consideration the complex social, economic, and political environment of contemporary marketing. In other cases, the challenges to promotion are right on. This chapter raises *issues* in the truest sense. It also raises controversies that should make you think about and debate the very nature of the promotional process. These issues and controversies are critical to your understanding of promotion because promotion affects individuals' lives and has an impact on society as a whole. In this chapter, we consider both the regulation of promotion and the ethical debates that accompany the practices of promotion. But first we need to consider the contemporary context within which these debates take place.

REGULATION, ETHICS, AND A FREE ENTERPRISE ECONOMY

At the outset of a discussion of regulatory and ethical issues relating to promotion, it is important to understand the context for these discussions. Recall that promotion was not the brainstorm of gray-flanneled, Madison Avenue schemers. Marketing processes, including promotion, will naturally emerge in highly industrialized, high-consumption societies from a need to efficiently and effectively move all the "stuff" people buy. The fundamental basis for the existence of the promotional process is both economic and social. From an economic standpoint, products that are centrally located and produced in large quantities typically cost less and are more easily obtained. But those products need to be promoted so that the economies of large-scale production and distribution can be maintained. If all the stuff people buy sits in warehouses and retail shops, companies fail and the economy suffers. In a **free-enterprise economy,** where competition between organizations is fostered and encouraged, a process such as promotion is implicitly required—people need to know about all the stuff they can buy and where to get it. The competitive structure of a free enterprise system motivates firms to strive for competitive advantage. The route to competitive advantage demands strategies that lead to superior product design, efficiency that keeps prices low, attractive distribution, and compelling promotion.

3.   Erika Rasmusson, "What Price Knowledge?" *Sales and Marketing Management,* December 1998, 56.

Government Agency	Regulatory Focus
Federal Trade Commission (FTC)	Most widely empowered agency. Controls methods of unfair competition regarding advertising. Also regulates credit claims, labeling, and packaging.
Federal Communications Commission (FCC)	Prohibits obscenity, fraud, and lotteries on radio and television. Ultimate power lies in the ability to revoke broadcast licenses.
Food and Drug Administration (FDA)	Regulates the advertising of food, drug, cosmetic, and medical products. Recent focus on direct-to-consumer (DTC) prescription drug advertising. Can require special labeling for hazardous products.
Securities and Exchange Commission (SEC)	Regulates the advertising of securities and the disclosure of information in annual reports.
U.S. Postal Service	Responsible for regulating direct-mail advertising and prohibiting lotteries and gaming using the mail system. Can impose fines for obscene materials sent through the mail.
Bureau of Alcohol, Tobacco, and Firearms	Regulation of alcohol advertising. This was the agency responsible for putting warning labels on alcoholic beverages and for banning active athletes from beer ads. It has the power to determine what is misleading advertising in these product areas.
U.S. Department of Transportation	Can regulate and give approval for claims appearing in airline advertising.
U.S. Department of Agriculture	Regulates the advertising of seed products, insecticides, and advertising for meat products.
Consumer Products Safety Commission	Can require remedies from advertisers of defective consumer products.

EXHIBIT 6.2

Federal government agencies with the power to affect promotional activities

However, we have to realize that the economy of the United States and most other high-consumption societies functions only partially on the principles of free markets. The complex nature of an industrial state has brought about regulations and government intervention. The result is that a **mixed economy** has evolved where restrictions and guidelines have been imposed on fundamental economic processes including promotion. Most economies now function as somewhat free, partly socialistic, and heavily regulated.

So, as we consider the performance of promotion on regulatory and ethical grounds, keep in mind that the overall process of any individual firm in using promotional techniques is affected by the broader context: a free enterprise economic system regulated by government intervention.

THE REGULATION OF PROMOTION: GOVERNMENT, INDUSTRY, AND CONSUMERS ❷

The term "regulation" immediately brings to mind government scrutiny and control of the promotional process. There are, indeed, various government bodies that regulate advertising, but that's not the only way promotion gets regulated. Consumers themselves and several different industry organizations exert as much regulatory power over promotion as government agencies do. Three primary groups—government bodies, industry organizations, and consumers—regulate promotion in the truest sense; together they shape and restrict the process. The government relies on legal restrictions, whereas consumers and industry groups use less formal controls. Like the topic of ethics, the regulation of promotion can be controversial, and opinions about what does and doesn't need to be regulated can be highly variable. Moreover, the topic of regulation could easily be an entire course of study in its own right, so here we present just an overview of major issues and major players.

First, we consider the groups that regulate promotion. Then we'll consider the legal issues associated with each major area of the promotional mix.

Federal Government Regulation

The federal government has a powerful tool available for regulating promotion: the threat of legal action. In the United States, several different federal agencies have been given the power and responsibility to regulate the promotional process. Exhibit 6.2 identifies nine federal government agencies that have the most legal mandates concerning promotion and their areas of regulatory responsibility. Several other agencies have minor powers in this area; they include the Civil Aeronautics Board (advertising by air carriers), the Patent Office (trademark infringement), and the Library of Congress (copyright protection). Also, Exhibit 6.3 shows the major laws enacted by the federal government that affect promotional practices.

THE 'NETS VERSUS THE NET'S

As the Internet companies expand at an exponential rate and twenty new retailers emerge on the Web every day, these bastions of new technological commerce have run into a virtual brick wall: the U.S. Congress. Congress was putting the final touches on a bill that would force TV networks to license programs to satellite broadcasters. At the last minute, two influential lawmakers, Orrin Hatch of Utah and Howard Coble of North Carolina, were persuaded by owners of copyrighted TV material to amend the satellite bill with one tiny little phrase that would "exclude online digital communications." The result is that Internet companies would not have the same access to programs as satellite companies. The 'Net would not be able to broadcast programs that were being broadcast over the Net'.

But the television networks are not alone in battling the Internet providers. Also lined up against them are Major League Baseball, the National Basketball Association, and associations of Hollywood producers, music companies, and composers. These groups claim that once a broadcast of a show or an event gets on the Internet, perfect copies can be sent around the globe almost instantly—depriving studios, team owners, or producers of distribution rights. And don't overlook this one small point of concern to network TV broadcasters: When a program goes out over the Internet, advertising revenues go out the window (or monitor, as it were).

As one lobbyist explained it, "The battleground of the future will be between technology companies with global reach and older companies looking to protect existing markets." This round of legislation in Congress appears to be just the beginning.

Source: Paula Dwyer, "On Capitol Hill, The Internet Wars Are Just Beginning," *Business Week*, December 6, 1999.

The agencies listed in Exhibit 6.2 are the most directly involved in promotional regulation. The Food and Drug Administration (FDA) focuses on food and drug products and is the federal agency responsible for monitoring information packages and labels. But the FDA has recently been involved in advertising issues. As more pharmaceutical firms practice "direct to consumer" (DTC) advertising for prescription drugs (see Exhibit 6.4), the FDA has issued federal guidelines regarding such advertising.[4] The Federal Communications Commission (FCC) deals mostly with broadcast licensing issues, but those issues can have a direct effect on the advertising process.[5] As the FCC monitors cable-television ownership arrangements, the ability of cable operators to attract advertisers will be affected. Also, the FCC prohibits lotteries on radio and television, which may affect similar gaming practices on the Internet.

The Securities and Exchange Commission (SEC) is charged with making sure that advertising in the securities industry is truthful and offers full disclosure. While traditional advertisers have dealt with the SEC for years, the new dot-com Internet brokers have had to learn the rules and regulations. The U.S.

4.   David Goetzl and Laura Petrecca, "Acquisitions Latest DTC Side Effect," *Advertising Age,* November 15, 1999, 16.

5.   Kathy Chen, "New FCC Cable Rules Could Hurt AT&T," *The Wall Street Journal,* September 9, 1999, B9.

Federal Act	Area of Regulation
Sherman Antitrust Act (1890)	Prohibits contracts, combinations, or conspiracies which retrain interstate trade. Makes it illegal to monopolize or attempt to monopolize any part of interstate trade or commerce. (Regulates the use of promotional allowances and co-op advertising.)
Federal Trade Commission Act (1914)	Prohibits unfair methods of competition and (by the addition of the Wheeler-Lea Amendment of 1938) unfair or deceptive acts or practices deemed to be harmful to consumers. (Regulates truthfulness and competitive fairness in advertising)
Clayton Act (1914)	Supplemented the Sherman Antitrust Act and defined more precisely certain prohibited practices regarding price discrimination, tying clauses, exclusive dealer agreements and stock ownership in directly competing companies where the effect may be to substantially lessen competition. (Regulates promotional allowances, personal selling, and advertising.)
Robinson-Patman Act (1936)	Amendment to the Clayton Act that makes it illegal to discriminate between buyers in price or terms of sale for commodities of like quality and quantity. Prohibits brokerage fees except to independent brokers. Forbids promotional allowances or provisions of services except on "proportionately equal" terms. This regulation was brought on by differential practices by manufacturers trying to win the business of large chain store operations. (Regulates use of allowances to distributors and retailers. Also regulates price negotiations in the personal selling process.)
Lanham Trademark Act (1947)	This regulation was originally designed to allow registration of and protection of trademarks as a dimension of fair competition. The act has recently been invoked in disputes regarding comparative advertising. (Regulates use of trademarks, tradenames, and comparative advertising practices.)
Fair Packaging and Labeling Act (1967)	Requires accurate and fair labels and containers. Requires manufacturers to include on the label contents of the package, identity of the manufacturer, and amount contained in the package. (Regulates label and packaging practices.)
Consumer Credit Protection Act (1968)	(encompassing Truth in Lending Act) Requires full disclosure of the cost of credit and loans. (Regulates language in credit promotions though advertising, direct marketing, and brochures.)
Magnuson-Moss Warranty Act (1975)	Sets forth requirements for full and limited express warranties. (Regulates language in advertising, packaging, direct marketing, and brochures.)
Foreign Corrupt Practices Act (1977)	Makes it illegal for U.S. firms to use bribery of company or government officials or political parties as a condition of doing business in foreign markets. (Regulates the activities of personal selling.)
Alcoholic Beverage Labeling Act (1988)	Mandates that all containers of alcoholic beverages contain the following warning: "Government Warning: (1) According to the Surgeon General, women should not drink alcoholic beverages during pregnancy due to the risk of birth defects. (2) Consumption of alcoholic beverages impairs your ability to drive a car or operate machinery and may cause health problems."
Nutrition Labeling and Education Act (1990)	Requires uniformity in nutrition labeling of food products and establishes strict rules for health claims and nutritional attributes of food products. (Regulates advertising and packaging language.)
Children's Television Act (1990)	Limits the minutes of advertising allowable during television programs for children. Limits are 10.5 minutes per hour on weekends and 12 minutes per hour on weekdays. (Regulates advertising.)

EXHIBIT 6.3

Major federal laws affecting promotional activities

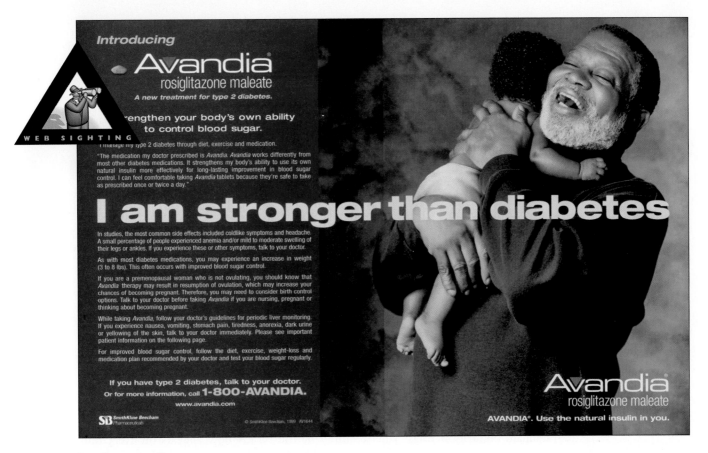

http://www.avandia.com

EXHIBIT 6.4

More pharmaceutical firms are advertising prescription drugs directly to consumers (known as DTC advertising). Because of DTC advertising's growing popularity, the U.S. Food and Drug Administration has issued regulatory guidelines on the use of ads like this one—you've likely noticed ads that take great pains not to make specific claims, or, if they do, include a page or more of medical detail and disclaimers to qualify them. This ad further suggests you "talk to your doctor" as an extra spoonful of legal liability preventive. How useful is the internet in promoting pharmaceuticals?

Postal Service has the most control of direct marketing carried out through the mail and can impose fines and restrictions for fraud or misrepresentation. Finally, the Bureau of Alcohol, Tobacco, and Firearms only occasionally gets involved in regulating and prosecuting promotional activities, but if it does, the impact can be far-reaching. This is the agency that was responsible for the warnings that appear on alcoholic beverages and for banning active athletes from acting as spokespeople in beer commercials. While these federal agencies get involved in issues relating to promotion, not all issues are settled by them. The New Media box demonstrates that when revenues from promotion are at stake, the controversies can reach the U.S. Congress.

However, by far the most active among the federal government agencies is the Federal Trade Commission (FTC), which has the greatest power and is most directly involved in controlling the promotional process. The FTC has been granted legal power through legislative mandates and also has developed programs for regulating advertising, labeling, and trade promotion practices.

The FTC's Legal Powers. The Federal Trade Commission was created by the FTC Act in 1914. The original purpose of the agency was to prohibit unfair methods of competition. In 1916, the FTC concluded that false advertising was one way a firm could take unfair advantage of another, and advertising was established as a primary concern of the agency.

It was not until 1938 that the effects of deceptive advertising on consumers became a key issue for the FTC. Until the passage of the Wheeler-Lea Amendment (1938), the commission was primarily concerned with the direct effect of advertising on competition. The amendment broadened the FTC's powers to include regulation of advertising that was misleading to the public (regardless of the effect on competition). Through this amendment, the agency could apply a cease-and-desist order, which required a firm to stop its deceptive practices. It also granted the agency specific jurisdiction over drug, medical device, cosmetic, and food advertising.

Several other acts provide the FTC with legal powers over advertising. The Robinson-Patman Act (1936) prohibits firms from granting phantom cooperative advertising allowances as a way to court important dealers. The Wool Products Labeling Act (1939), the Fur Products Labeling Act (1951), and the Textile Fiber Products Identification Act (1958) provided the commission with regulatory power over labeling and advertising for specific products. Consumer protection legislation, which seeks to increase the ability of consumers to make more informed product comparisons, includes the Lanham Act (1947), which prohibits false advertising; the Fair Packaging and Labeling Act (1966); the Truth in Lending Act (1969); and the Fair Credit Reporting Act (1970). The FTC Improvement Act (1975) expanded the authority of the commission by giving it the power to issue trade regulation rules. Recent legislation has expanded the FTC's role in monitoring and regulating product labeling and advertising. For example, the 1990 Nutrition Labeling and Education Act (NLEA) requires uniformity in the nutrition labeling of food products and establishes strict rules for claims about the nutritional attributes of food products. The standard "Nutrition Facts" label required by the NLEA now appears on everything from breakfast cereals to barbecue sauce. The NLEA is a unique piece of legislation from the standpoint that two government agencies—the FTC and the FDA—play key roles in its enforcement.

The law also provides the FTC and other agencies with various means of recourse when advertising practices are judged to be deceptive or misleading. The spirit of all these acts relates to the maintenance of an equitable competitive environment and the protection of consumers from misleading information. It is interesting to note, however, that direct involvement of the FTC in advertising practices more often comes about from its regulatory programs and remedies than from the application of legal mandates.

The FTC's Regulatory Programs and Remedies. The application of legislation has evolved as the FTC exercises its powers and expands its role as a regulatory agency. This evolution of the FTC has spawned several regulatory programs and remedies to help enforce legislative mandates in specific situations.

The **advertising substantiation program** of the FTC was initiated in 1971 with the intention of ensuring that advertisers make available to consumers supporting evidence for claims made. The program was strengthened in 1972 when the commission forwarded the notion of "reasonable basis" for the substantiation of advertising. This extension suggests not only that advertisers should substantiate their claims, but also that the substantiation should provide a reasonable basis for believing the claims are true.[6] Simply put, before a company runs an ad, it must

6.   For a discussion of the FTC advertising substantiation program and its extension to provide a require a reasonable basis for advertising claims, see Debra L. Scammon and Richard J. Semenik, "The FTC's 'Reasonable Basis' for Substantiation of Advertising: Expanded Standards and Implications," *Journal of Advertising,* vol. 12, no. 1 (1983), 4–11.

have documented evidence that supports the claim it wants to make in that ad. The kind of evidence required depends on the kind of claim being made. For example, health and safety claims will require competent and reliable scientific evidence that has been examined and validated by experts in the field (go to http://www.ftc.gov/ for additional guidance).

The consent order and the cease-and-desist order are the most basic remedies used by the FTC in dealing with deceptive or unfair advertising. In a **consent order,** an advertiser accused of running deceptive or unfair advertising agrees to stop running the advertisements in question, without admitting guilt. For advertisers who do not comply voluntarily, the FTC can issue a **cease-and-desist order,** which generally requires that the advertising in question be stopped within thirty days so a hearing can be held to determine whether the advertising is deceptive or unfair. For products that have a direct effect on consumers' health or safety (for example, foods), the FTC can issue an immediate cease-and-desist order.

Affirmative disclosure is another remedy available to the FTC. An advertisement that fails to disclose important material facts about a product can be deemed deceptive, and the FTC may require **affirmative disclosure,** whereby the important material absent from prior ads must be included in subsequent advertisements. The absence of important material information may cause consumers to make false assumptions about products in comparison to the competition. Such was the case with Geritol; the FTC ordered the makers of the product to disclose that "iron-poor blood" was not the universal cause of tiredness.

The most extreme remedy for advertising determined to be misleading is **corrective advertising.** In cases where evidence suggests that consumers have developed incorrect beliefs about a brand based on deceptive or unfair advertising, the firm may be required to run corrective ads in an attempt to dispel those faulty beliefs. The commission has specified not only the message content for corrective ads, but also the budgetary allocation, the duration of transmission, and the placement of the advertising. The goal of corrective advertising is to rectify erroneous beliefs created by deceptive advertising, without imposing undue harm to the reputation of a brand or the manufacturer of the brand.[7]

Another area of FTC regulation and remedy involves **celebrity endorsements.** The FTC has specific rules for advertisements that use an expert or celebrity as a spokesperson for a product. In the case of experts (those whose experience or training allows a superior judgment of products), the endorser's actual qualifications must justify his or her status as an expert. In the case of celebrities (such as Michael Jordan as a spokesperson for McDonald's), FTC guidelines indicate that the celebrity must be an actual user of the product, or the ad is considered deceptive.

These regulatory programs and remedies provide the FTC a great deal of control over the advertising process. Numerous ads have been interpreted as questionable under the guidelines of these programs, and advertisements have been altered. It is likely also that advertisers and their agencies, who are keenly aware of the ramifications of violating FTC precepts, have developed ads with these constraints in mind.

It is certainly fair to conclude that advertising regulation is a dynamic endeavor that will challenge regulators far into the future. Of course, the most notable new challenge that regulators around the world must learn to cope with is advertising on the Internet. For instance, while U.S. government agencies such as the FTC and FDA intend to extend their jurisdiction to the Internet, they clearly have a tiger by the tail.

7.   For a summary of the original intent of the corrective advertising remedy and evidence of its effectiveness, see Debra L. Scammon and Richard J. Semenik, "Corrective Advertising: Evolution of the Legal Theory and Application of the Remedy," *Journal of Advertising,* vol. 11, no. 1 (1982), 10–20; and William L. Wilkie, Dennis L. McNeill, and Michael B. Mazis, "Marketing's Scarlet Letter: The Theory and Practice of Corrective Advertising," *Journal of Marketing,* vol. 48 (Spring 1984), 11–18.

State Government Regulation

State governments do not have extensive policing powers over the promotional activities of firms. Since the vast majority of companies are involved in interstate marketing of goods and services, any violation of fair practice or existing regulation is a federal government issue.

There is typically one state government organization, the attorney general's (AG) office, which is responsible for investigating questionable promotional practices. It was the AG offices in Texas and New York that launched an investigation of claims made by Kraft that its Cheez Whiz spread used real cheese.[8] Similarly, it was the state AG in Texas that claimed a demonstration used by Volvo was misleading. In the ad, a monster truck with oversized tires was shown rolling over the roofs of a row of cars, crushing all of them except a Volvo. The problem was, the Volvo in the test had its roof reinforced while the other cars' roof supports had been weakened.[9]

Since the 1980s, the National Association of Attorneys General (NAAG), represented by the attorneys general from all fifty states, has been active as a group in monitoring advertising and sharing their findings. In 1988, attorneys general from twenty-two states challenged the safety of Honda's three-wheeled ATV, claiming that the vehicle posed an unreasonable risk of injury. Part of the challenge was that Honda advertising encouraged dangerous riding behavior.[10] Overall, states will rely on the vigilance of the federal agencies discussed earlier to monitor promotional practices and then act against firms with questionable activities.

Finally, in 1995, thirteen states passed prize notification laws regarding sweepstakes and contests. The new laws require marketers to make full disclosure of rules, odds, and retail value of prizes. The states were responding to what they felt was widespread fraud and deception. Some states have aggressively prosecuted the sweepstakes companies in court.

Industry Self-Regulation ❸

The promotion industry has come far in terms of self-control and restraint. Some of this improvement is due to tougher government regulation, and some to industry self-regulation. **Self-regulation** is the promotion industry's attempt to police itself. Supporters say it is a shining example of how unnecessary government intervention is, while critics point to it as a joke, an elaborate shell game. According to the critics, meaningful self-regulation occurs only when the threat of government action is imminent. How you see this controversy is largely dependent on your own personal experience and level of cynicism.

Several industry and trade associations and public service organizations have voluntarily established guidelines for promotion within their industries. The reasoning is that self-regulation is good for the promotion community as a whole and creates credibility, and therefore enhances the effectiveness, of promotion itself. Exhibit 6.5 lists some organizations that have taken on the task of regulating and monitoring promotional activities, and the year when each established a code of standards.

The purpose of self-regulation by these organizations is to evaluate the content and quality of promotion specific to their industries. The effectiveness of such organizations depends on the cooperation of members and the policing mechanisms used. Each organization exerts an influence on the nature of promotion in its industry. Some are particularly noteworthy in their activities and warrant further

---

8. "Deceptive Ads: The FTC's Laissez-Faire Approach Is Backfiring," *Business Week,* December 2, 1985, 130.
9. Steven W. Colford and Raymond Serafin, "Scali Pays for Volvo Ad: FTC," *Advertising Age,* August 26, 1991, 4.
10. Paul Harris, "Will the FTC Finally Wake Up?" *Sales and Marketing Management,* January 1988, 57.

EXHIBIT 6.5

Selected business organizations and industry associations with self-regulation programs

Organization	Code Established
Advertising Associations	
American Advertising Federation	1965
American Association of Advertising Agencies	1924
Association of National Advertisers	1972
Business/Professional Advertising Association	1975
Public Relations Society of America	1988
Point-of-Purchase Advertising Institute	1990
Special Industry Groups	
Council of Better Business Bureaus	1912
Household furniture	1978
Automobiles and trucks	1978
Carpet and rugs	1978
Home improvement	1975
Charitable solicitations	1974
Children's Advertising Review Unit	1974
National Advertising Division/National Advertising Review Board	1971
Media Associations	
American Business Press	1910
Direct Mail Marketing Association	1960
Direct Selling Association	1970
National Association of Broadcasters	
Radio	1937
Television	1952
Outdoor Advertising Association of America	1950
Selected Trade Associations	
American Wine Association	1949
Wine Institute	1949
Distilled Spirits Association	1934
United States Brewers Association	1955
Pharmaceutical Manufacturers Association	1958
Proprietary Association	1934
Bank Marketing Association	1976
Motion Picture Association of America	1930
National Swimming Pool Institute	1970
Toy Manufacturers Association	1962

discussion. Beyond the U.S organizations discussed here, there are some global movement as well (see the Global Issues box).

The National Advertising Review Board. One important self-regulation organization is the Council of Better Business Bureaus' National Advertising Review Board (NARB). The NARB is the operations arm of the National Advertising Division (NAD) of the Council of Better Business Bureaus. Complaints received from consumers, competitors, or local branches of the Better Business Bureau are forwarded to the NAD. Most such complaints come from competitors. After a full review of the complaint, the issue may be forwarded to the NARB and evaluated by a panel. The complete procedure for dealing with complaints is detailed in Exhibit 6.6.

The NAD maintains a permanent professional staff that works to resolve complaints with the advertiser and its agency before the issue gets to the NARB. If no resolution is achieved, the complaint is appealed to the NARB, which appoints a panel made up of three advertiser representatives, one agency representative, and one public representative. This panel then holds hearings regarding the advertising in question. The advertiser is allowed to present the firm's case. If no agreement can be reached by the panel either to dismiss the case or to persuade the advertiser to change the advertising, the NARB initiates two actions. First, it publicly identifies the advertiser, the complaint against the advertiser, and the panel's findings. Second, it forwards the case to an appropriate government regulatory agency (usually the FTC).

The NAD and the NARB are not empowered to impose penalties on advertisers, but the threat of going before the board acts as a deterrent to deceptive and questionable advertising practices. Further, the regulatory process of the NAD and the NARB is probably less costly and time-consuming for all parties involved than if every complaint were handled by a government agency.

State and Local Better Business Bureaus. Aside from the national Better Business Bureau (BBB), there are more than 140 separate local

GLOBAL ISSUES

SELF REGULATION—WITH FULL GOVERNMENT APPROVAL

As the opening scenario to this chapter highlighted, consumers, marketers, and advocacy groups have been struggling with the issue of privacy when it comes to harvesting information about consumers' personal lives and shopping behavior. The controversy swirls around what data marketers could, should, or might obtain, and how they might use it once they have it.

The controversy over privacy in direct-marketing programs is raging in the United States and Europe, but Australians seem to have come up with a solution that, for the time being, seems to be satisfying everyone. Termed "enhanced self-regulation" by Rob Edwards, CEO of the Australian Direct Marketing Association (ADMA) (one of the plan's architects), a code of behavior has been proposed for direct marketers that focuses on five aspects of the direct-marketing process. An industry body called the Code Administration Authority will review consumer complaints related to these aspects:

- Compulsory use of the Do Not Mail/Do Not Call service, which gives consumers the right to limit the number of direct-marketing solicitations they receive. Consumers request the service by calling a toll-free number.
- A seven-day cooling off period during which the consumer can cancel a direct-marketing contract.
- Compulsory adoption of the National Privacy Principles as set down by the Federal Privacy Commissioner. The principles include an "opting out" clause so consumers can avoid getting any more direct-marketing offers.
- An independent Code Authority made up of consumers and industry representatives. A negative ruling by this body could result in the expulsion of a member from ADMA.
- A set of international "best practices" for e-commerce. The list would be distributed to the more than 400 members of ADMA.

So while most of the world debates and consternates over privacy issues, the Australians have taken bold and specific steps to improve the industry and reassure consumers of direct marketers' professionalism.

Source: Don E. Schultz, "Australian's 'It' When It Comes to Privacy," *Marketing News*, November 8, 1999, 18.

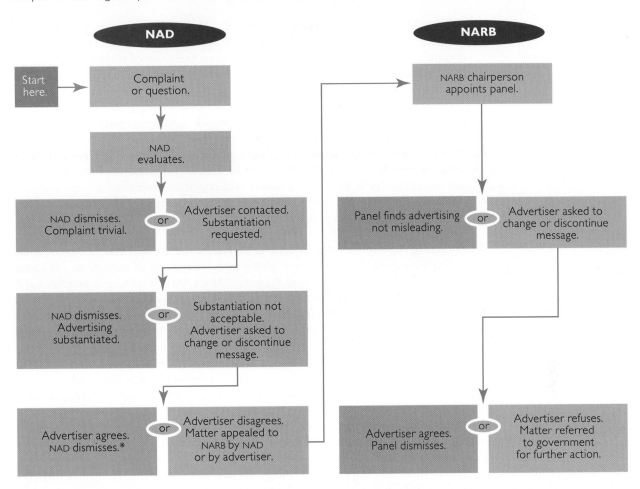

*If the complaint originated outside the system, the outside complainant can appeal at this point to the NARB chairperson for a panel adjudication. Granting of such an appeal is at the chairperson's discretion.

EXHIBIT 6.6

Flow diagram of NAD and NARB regulatory process

bureaus. Each local organization is supported by membership dues paid by area businesses. The three divisions of a local BBB—merchandise, financial, and solicitations—investigate the advertising, telemarketing, and personal selling practices of firms in their areas. A local BBB has the power to forward a complaint to the NAD for evaluation.

Beyond its regulatory activities, the Better Business Bureau tries to avert problems associated with promotions by counseling new businesses and providing information to marketers and agencies regarding legislation, potential problem areas, and industry standards.

Better Business Bureau Code of Online Business Practices. Most recently, the Better Business Bureau has established BBB *OnLine* and is developing a Code of Online Business Practices (http://www.bbbonline.org/business/code). The code was developed based on an evaluation of more than 5,000 commercial Web sites and draws on the bureau's eight decades of setting business standards. Five basic principles drive the detailed recommendations of the code:

- *Disclose, Disclose, Disclose.* Online businesses shall disclose to their customers and prospective customers, clearly, conspicuously and in easy-to-understand language, accurate information about the business, any goods or services offered through an online transaction and, if applicable, the transaction itself.

- *Tell the Whole Truth and Nothing but the Truth.* Online businesses shall not engage in deceptive or misleading trade practices with regard to any aspect of electronic commerce, including advertising, marketing, or their use of technology.
- *Have Respectful Information Practices.* Online businesses shall adopt information practices that respect the consumer's concerns and treat the information with care. They shall post and adhere to a privacy policy based on fair information principles, take appropriate measures to provide adequate security, and respect consumer preferences regarding unsolicited email.
- *Aim to Please.* Online businesses should make online shopping a positive consumer experience and shall seek to resolve disputes that are raised by their customers, clients, or licensees in a timely and responsive manner.
- *Take Special Care with Children.* If online businesses target children under the age of 13, they shall take special care to protect them.[11]

Advertising Agencies and Promotion Trade Associations. It makes sense that advertising agencies and their industry associations would engage in self-regulation. An individual agency is legally responsible for the advertising it produces and is subject to reprisal for deceptive claims. The agency is in a difficult position in that it must monitor not only the activities of its own people, but also the information that clients provide to it. Should a client direct an agency to use a product appeal that turns out to be untruthful, the agency is still responsible.

The American Association of Advertising Agencies (4As, http://www.aaaa.org) has no legal or binding power over its agency members, but it can apply pressure when its board feels industry standards are not being upheld. The 4As also publishes guidelines for its members regarding various aspects of advertising messages. One of the most widely recognized industry standards is the 4As' Creative Code. The code outlines the responsibilities and social impact advertising can have and promotes high ethical standards of honesty and decency.

Direct mail may have a poor image among many consumers, but its industry association, the Direct Marketing Association (DMA, http://www.the-dma.org), is active in promoting ethical behavior and standards among its members. It has published guidelines for ethical business practices. In 1971, the association established the Direct-Mail Preference Service, which enables consumers who wish to have their names removed from most direct mail lists.

The Point of Purchase Advertising Institute (POPAI, http://www.popai.org) in Washington, DC, and the Promotional Products Association (PPA, http://www.promotion-clinic.ppa.org) in Dallas have extensive programs for members to maintain the quality and professionalism of their industries. Seminars, trade shows, association publications, and member Web sites are techniques used to promote the industry and maintain high standards.

Media Organizations. Individual media organizations evaluate the advertising they receive for broadcast and publication. The National Association of Broadcasters has a policing arm known as the Code Authority, which implements and interprets separate radio and television codes. These codes deal with truth, fairness, and good taste in broadcast advertising. Newspapers have historically been rigorous in their screening of advertising. Many newspapers have internal departments to screen and censor ads believed to be in violation of the newspaper's advertising standards. While the magazine industry does not have a formal code, many individual publications have very high standards.

---

11. "Better Business Bureau System Posts Draft of New Code of Online Business Practices and Solicits Public Comment," Better Bureau Press Release, November 22, 1999, accessed at http://www.bbb.org on December 5, 1999.

Internet Self-Regulation. Because there are few federal guidelines established for advertising and promotion on the Internet, the industry itself has been the governing body. So far, no industrywide trade association has emerged to offer guidelines or standards. You will see later in the chapter that several special-interest groups are questioning the ethics of some Internet promotional practices. And there are those who are skeptical that the industry can regulate itself.

A new group, the Global Business Dialog on Electronic Commerce (GBDe), is trying to establish itself as a trade association for the online industry. But while it counts some big companies among its 200 members—for instance, Time Warner, DaimlerChrysler, Toshiba—not one of the Internet heavyweights like Amazon.com or Yahoo! has joined the ranks. The GBDe has drawn up a proposal for dealing with harmful content (pornography), protecting personal information, enforcing copyrights, and handling disputes in e-commerce. But the organization's efforts have not created great enthusiasm. Lester Thurow, the prominent public policy professor from MIT, said that "Self-regulation can play a role if you have real regulation that will come piling in if you don't do it."[12]

A review of all aspects of industry self-regulation suggests not only that a variety of programs and organizations are designed to monitor promotion, but also that many of these programs are effective. Those whose livelihoods depend on promotion are just as interested as consumers and legislators are in maintaining high standards. If promotion deteriorates into an unethical and untrustworthy business activity, the economic vitality of many organizations will be compromised. Self-regulation can help prevent such a circumstance and is in the best interest of all the organizations discussed here.

Consumers as Regulatory Agents

Consumers themselves are motivated to act as regulatory agents based on a variety of interests, including product safety, reasonable choice, and the right to information. Promotion tends to be a focus of consumer regulatory activities because of its conspicuousness. Consumerism and consumer organizations have provided the primary vehicles for consumer regulatory efforts.

Consumerism, the actions of individual consumers or groups of consumers designed to exert power in the marketplace, is by no means a recent phenomenon. The earliest consumerism efforts can be traced to seventeenth-century England. In the United States, there have been recurring consumer movements throughout the twentieth century.

In general, these movements have focused on the same issue: Consumers want a greater voice in the whole process of product development, distribution, and information dissemination. Consumers commonly try to create pressures on firms by withholding patronage through boycotts. Some boycotts have been effective. Firms as powerful as Procter & Gamble, Kimberly-Clark, and General Mills all have responded to threats of boycotts by pulling advertising from programs consumers found offensive.[13] Recently, a coalition of large firms—Procter & Gamble, General Motors, IBM, Johnson & Johnson, and Sears—have started paying the Warner Brothers Network to develop prime-time programming that is more family friendly.[14] These advertisers are growing weary of shows featuring sex and violence, and given the history of boycotts, they believe more wholesome shows are a safer bet.

12. Neal Boudette, "Internet Self-Regulation Seen Lacking Punch," Reuters News Services, September 14, 1999, accessed at http://biz.yahoo.com/ on September 14, 1999.

13. Alix M. Freedman, "Never Have So Few Scared So Many Television Sponsors," *The Wall Street Journal,* March 29, 1989, B4.

14. "Anything for a Ratings Boost," *Marketing News,* September 13, 1999, 3.

CAREERPROFILE

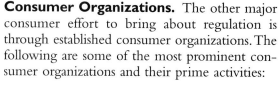

Name:	Jackie Bueres
Title:	Assistant Product Manager
Company:	Noven Pharmaceuticals, Miami, Florida
	http://www.noven.com
Education:	B.S., Communications; M.B.A., Marketing

"I couldn't market something if I didn't believe in the product or the ethics of the corporation," says Jackie Bueres. As an assistant product manager at Noven Pharmaceuticals, she has no qualms about either. Bueres manages promotional and marketing activities for Noven's Vivelle-Dot™ Estrogen Replacement Patch, a small, self-adhesive patch that dispenses estrogen through the skin. "I really believe we have the best product of its type on the market," says Bueres.

A large part of Bueres's job is staying on top of the ethical issues and legal regulations required for marketing drug products. "There's quite a bit of information to know about Federal Drug Administration rules," says Bueres. "You have to make sure all of your messages are FDA-approved." The process begins with the marketing plan. "It highlights how our products will be marketed, taking FDA regulations into account," says Bueres. "The whole marketing team sticks to it."

One of Bueres's primary tasks is managing an ongoing direct-mail program. She prepares five direct-mail packages a year. They are sent to physicians to explain Vivelle-Dot™ uses and benefits. Before each mailing can go out, however, it goes through an approval process that includes a review by Noven's internal medical affairs and legal regulatory offices. It usually takes about a week to get all approvals. "It's good to have an extra set of eyes evaluate what's going out," she says. "The last thing we want is a complaint going to the FDA."

Her job also includes alerting salespeople to FDA and company guidelines. "We focus a lot on ethical and legal regulations during sales force meetings," she says. "We have to make sure our sales representatives understand what they can and cannot say when they call on doctors."

Does Bueres feel that all of these rules and regulations get in the way of creative marketing? Not at all. "All of our competitors are playing in the same field. They have to follow the same rules so it really doesn't inhibit us at all."

To learn more about marketing ethics and regulations, visit these Web sites:

The Arent Fox Advertising Law Research Center
http://www.arentfox.com/
quickGuide/businesslines/advert/
advertisingLaw/advertisinglaw.html

The University of Texas Advertising Law & Ethics page
http://www.advertising.utexas.edu/
research/law

Consumer Organizations. The other major consumer effort to bring about regulation is through established consumer organizations. The following are some of the most prominent consumer organizations and their prime activities:

- *Consumer Federation of America (CFA).* This organization, founded in 1968, now includes over 200 national, state, and local consumer groups and labor unions as affiliate members. The goals of the CFA are to encourage the creation of consumer organizations, provide services to consumer groups, and act as a clearinghouse for information exchange between consumer groups.

- *Consumers Union.* This nonprofit consumer organization is best known for its publication *Consumer Reports.* Established in 1936, Consumers Union has as its stated purpose to provide consumers with information and advice on goods, services, health, and personal finance; and to initiate and cooperate with individual and group efforts to maintain and enhance the quality of life for consumers. This organization supports itself through the sale of publications and accepts no funding, including advertising revenues, from any commercial organization.

- *Action for Children's Television (ACT).* This group has been active in conjunction with the national Parent-Teacher Association in initiating boycotts against the products of advertisers who sponsor programs that are violent in nature. On its own, ACT has lobbied government bodies to enact legislation restricting the use of premiums in advertising to children and the use of popular cartoon characters in promoting products.

These three organizations are the most active and potent of the consumer groups, but there are literally hundreds of such groups organized by geographic location or product category. Consumers have proven that faced with an organized effort, corporations can and will change their practices. In one of the most publicized events in recent times, consumers applied pressure to Coca-Cola and, in part, were responsible for forcing the firm to remarket the original formula of Coca-Cola (as Coca-Cola Classic). If consumers are able to exert such a powerful and nearly immediate influence on a firm like Coca-Cola, one wonders what other changes they could effect in the market.

ISSUES IN THE REGULATION OF PROMOTION

The last section describes the regulatory agents—government bodies, industry organizations, and consumers themselves—that can affect the promotional practices of marketers. At this point, we will turn our attention to the promotional mix areas and consider the regulatory issues that relate to each.

Issues in the Regulation of Advertising ❹

There are three basic issues with respect to the regulation of advertising: the content of advertising, competitive issues, and advertising to children. Each area is a focal point for regulation. Probably the majority of complaints against advertisers and their advertising efforts has to do with the content of advertising. In general, critics and those who desire greater regulation of the advertising process feel that advertising does not provide enough information for consumers to make informed decisions. There are two main issues in the regulation of content: deception and unfairness.

Deception and Unfairness. Nobody likes to be lied to, and there is widespread agreement that deception in advertising is unacceptable. The problem, of course, is that it is difficult to determine what is deceptive both from a regulatory and from an ethical standpoint. The FTC's policy statement on deception was worked out several years ago. It remains the authoritative source when it comes to defining deceptive advertising. Below are the three factors the FTC believes are essential in declaring an ad deceptive:[15]

- There must be a representation, omission, or practice that is likely to mislead the consumer.
- This representation, omission, or practice must be judged from the perspective of a consumer acting reasonably in the circumstance.
- The basic question is whether the act or the practice is likely to affect the consumer's conduct or decision with regard to the product or service. If so, the practice is material, and consumer injury is likely because consumers are likely to have chosen differently if not for the deception.

If this definition of deception sounds like carefully worded legal jargon, that's because it is. It is also a definition that can lead to diverse interpretations when it is actually applied to advertisements in real life. Fortunately, as represented in Exhibit 6.7, the FTC now provides highly practical advice for anticipating what can make an ad deceptive (go to http://www.ftc.gov/bcp/guides/guides.htm under the section "Frequently Asked Advertising Questions"). One critical point about the FTC's approach to deception is that both implied claims and information that is missing from an ad can be bases for deeming an ad deceptive. Obviously, the FTC expects any explicit claim made in an ad to be truthful, but they also are on the lookout for ads that deceive through allusion

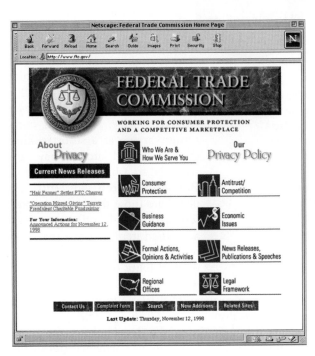

EXHIBIT 6.7

The Federal Trade Commission exerts the most regulatory power over advertising. In an effort to clarify the commission's policies and procedures, an extensive Web site has been created. The site provides information on all FTC programs and policies, including programs related to the Internet. http://www.ftc.org

---

15. For additional discussion of the FTC's definition of deception, see Gary T. Ford and John E. Calfee, "Recent Developments in FTC Policy on Deception," *Journal of Marketing*, vol. 50 (July 1986), 82–103.

IN PRACTICE

PEOPLE WHO LIVE IN GLASS HUTS SHOULDN'T THROW PIZZA

Pizza Hut won a major battle with archrival Papa John's International over advertising claims. Papa John's, the number-four pizza chain in the United States had been using "Better Ingredients. Better Pizza." as its advertising tag line. The phrase alone is fairly harmless and borders on advertising "puffery," a perfectly legal form of commercial braggadocio. But when Papa John's brash founder John Schnatter was featured in one of the spots and claimed that consumers preferred his chain's sauce over Pizza Hut's "remanufactured paste," Pizza Hut, the market leader, took exception to the claim and sued Papa John's in federal court. After three weeks of testimony that included dough experts and sauce demonstrations, a jury sided with Pizza Hut in its allegation that Papa John's was misleading consumers.

The settlement resulted in Papa John's losing the rights to the slogan and paying damages of $468,000—far less than the $12.5 million sought by Pizza Hut. But with about $300 million invested in the advertising, the four-year campaign had built up market recognition. The "Better Ingredients. Better Pizza." slogan appeared on everything from pizza boxes and napkins to the company's Web page. But market analyst F. Fitzhugh Taylor III doesn't believe dropping the slogan/tag line will result in long-term damage to Papa John's. "Some restaurant chains change their slogans annually, so I don't think this is a big deal," said Taylor. By the way, Pizza Hut didn't exactly come out of all this unscathed. Aside from the time, effort, and money involved in bringing and arguing this case, the jury also found that Pizza Hut also misled consumers with its own campaign counterattack on Papa John's. Pizza Hut said Papa John's used old dough to make its pizza—the jury didn't buy that either.

Sources: Louise Kramer, "Jury Finds Papa John's Ads Misled," *Advertising Age,* November 22, 1999, 46; Marcus Kabel, "Judge to Set Damages in Pizza Hut, Papa John's Fight," Reuters News Services, November 29, 1999, accessed on the Internet on December 3, 1999; Marcus Kabel, "Papa John's Ordered to Drop Slogan in Pizza Ads," Reuters News Services, January 3, 2000, accessed on the Internet on January 5, 2000.

and innuendo, or ads that deceive by not telling the whole story. The IMC in Practice box tells the story of how Papa John's Pizza and Pizza Hut got into a legal battle over claims alleged to be deceptive and misleading.

Many instances of deceptive advertising have resulted in formal government programs designed to regulate such practices. The most common occurrences of deceptive advertising occur with respect to:

- *False testimonials.* When an advocacy position is taken by a spokesperson in an advertisement, this is known as a **testimonial.** Testimonials can be delivered by an "average person," a celebrity, or an expert. Since consumers perceive spokespersons to be offering an opinion based on knowledge and experience, there is the potential for deception if the spokesperson is neither an expert nor experienced with the product or service.

- *Bait-and-switch advertising.* Bait-and-switch advertising is an offer to sell an advertised product at an attractive price, but when consumers arrive at a store seeking the advertised item, they are switched to a higher-priced item. **Bait-and-switch** ads that are illegal are those that do not represent a bone fide offer to sell an advertised item, or those that misrepresent the actual price, quality, or availability of a product.[16]

- *Misleading demonstrations.* Advertising intended to mislead consumers is deemed deceptive. Under certain conditions, it is permitted that additives be used in food products to make them appear realistic in the filming of television commercials (marketers had previously been prosecuted for deception for this practice). But physically altering a product to enhance its performance (recall the Volvo example earlier) is deemed deceptive and misleading.

- *"Free Offers."* Some special product promotions are advertised as offering a "free" product. If obtaining the product for "free" is contingent on purchasing another product, or if the buyer incurs unreasonable additional costs, like exorbitant shipping charges, then the FTC has determined that these are deceptive offers.

16.　Ray Werner, "Legal Developments in Marketing," *Journal of Marketing,* vol. 55 (July 1991), 66.

- *Puffery.* There can be complications in regulating puffery, however. **Puffery** is the use of absolute superlatives in advertising like "best" and "greatest." Conventional wisdom has argued that consumers don't actually believe extreme claims and realize that advertisers are just trying to attract attention. There are those, however, who disagree with this view of puffery and feel that it actually represents "soft-core" deception, because some consumers believe these exaggerated claims.[17] Recent court challenges may make puffery claims more difficult to use.[18]

While the FTC and the courts have been reasonably specific about what constitutes deception, the definition of unfairness in advertising has been left relatively vague until recently. In 1994, Congress ended a long-running dispute in the courts and in the advertising industry by approving legislation that defines unfair advertising as "acts or practices that cause or are likely to cause substantial injury to consumers, which is not reasonably avoidable by consumers themselves, and not outweighed by the countervailing benefits to consumers or competition."[19] This definition obligates the FTC to assess both the benefits and costs of advertising, and rules out reckless acts on the part of consumers, before a judgment can be rendered that an advertiser has been unfair.

Competitive Issues. Because the large dollar amounts spent on advertising may foster inequities that literally can destroy competition, several advertising practices relating to competition can result in regulation. Among them are cooperative advertising, comparison advertising, and using monopoly power.

Vertical cooperative advertising is an advertising technique whereby a manufacturer and dealer (either a wholesaler or retailer) share the expense of advertising. This technique is commonly used in regional or local markets where a manufacturer wants a brand to benefit from a special promotion run by local dealers. There is nothing illegal per se about the technique, and it is used regularly. The competitive threat inherent in the process, however, is that dealers (especially since the advent of the new power retailers like Wal-Mart, Home Depot, and Costco) can be given bogus cooperative advertising allowances. These allowances require no effort or expenditure on the part of the dealer and thus represent hidden price concessions. As such, they are a form of unfair competition and are deemed illegal. If an advertising allowance is granted to a dealer, that dealer must demonstrate that the funds are applied specifically to advertising.

The potential exists for firms to engage in unfair competition if they use comparison ads inappropriately. **Comparison advertisements** are those in which an advertiser makes a comparison between the firm's brand and competitors' brands. The comparison may or may not explicitly identify the competition. Again, comparison ads are completely legal and are used frequently by all sorts of organizations. Exhibit 6.8 is an example of a straightforward comparison ad that follows all the rules and is fair in its comparison.

But the frequency of use of comparison ads has resulted in a large increase in complaints to the National Advertising Division of the BBB from marketers who dispute the competitive comparative claims.[20] If a comparative advertisement is carried out in such a way that the comparison is not fair, then there is an unjust competitive effect. The American Association of Advertising Agencies has issued a set of

17.   Ivan Preston, *The Great American Blowup* (Madison, WI: University of Wisconsin Press, 1975), 4.
18.   James Heckman, "'Puffery Claims No Longer So Easy to Make," *Marketing News,* February 14, 2000, 6.
19.   Christy Fisher, "How Congress Broke Unfair Ad Impasse," *Advertising Age,* August 22, 1994, 34. For additional discussion of the FTC's definition of unfairness see Ivan Preston, "Unfairness Developments in FTC Advertising Cases," *Journal of Public Policy and Marketing,* vol. 14, no. 2 (1995), 318–332.
20.   Jack Neff, "Household Brands Counter Punch," *Advertising Age,* November 1, 1999, 26.

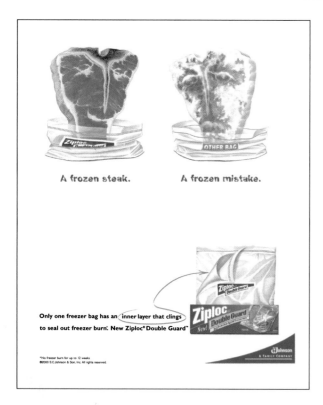

A frozen steak.   A frozen mistake.

Only one freezer bag has an inner layer that clings
to seal out freezer burn: New Ziploc® Double Guard™

*No freezer burn for up to 12 weeks
©2000 S.C.Johnson & Son, Inc. All rights reserved.

EXHIBIT 6.8

*Comparison advertising is regulated by a variety of government laws
and industry self-regulation guidelines. This ad for Ziploc bags is
an example of a fair and fact-based comparison that fits everybody's
guidelines.*

guidelines, shown in Exhibit 6.9, regarding the use of comparison ads. Further, the Federal Trade Commission may also get involved in a disputed comparative advertising situation. A firm using a comparison may be required to substantiate claims made in an advertisement under the FTC's advertising substantiation program discussed earlier. In addition, the Lanham Act prohibits false advertising, and comparative claims that are false or have the tendency to deceive may be prosecuted under the Lanham Act guidelines.[21]

Finally, some firms are so powerful in their use of advertising that **monopoly power** by virtue of large-scale spending on advertising can become a problem. This issue normally arises in the context of mergers and acquisitions. As an example, the U.S. Supreme Court blocked the acquisition of Clorox by Procter & Gamble because the advertising power of the two firms combined would (in the opinion of the Court) make it nearly impossible for another firm to compete.

This issue may become more prevalent than it has been in many years in the context of the Internet. Since technological capability on the Internet is homogeneous and ubiquitous, the success of one dot-com versus another may come down to brand management and brand strategy. Which in turn, may come down to which dot.com has the most money to spend on advertising to develop brand awareness and recognition. Those without the capability to spend big on advertising may not be able to compete on that basis alone.

Advertising Aimed at Children. Critics argue that continually bombarding children with persuasive stimuli can alter their motivation and behavior. While government organizations such as the FTC have been active in trying to regulate advertising directed at children, industry and consumer groups have been more successful in securing restrictions. The consumer group Action for Children's Television was actively involved in getting Congress to approve the Children's Television Act (1990). This act limits the amount of commercial airtime during children's programs to ten minutes on weekdays and twelve minutes on weekends. The Council of Better Business Bureaus established a Children's Advertising Review Unit and has issued a set of guidelines for advertising directed at children. These guidelines emphasize that advertisers should be sensitive to the level of knowledge and sophistication of children as decision makers. The guidelines also urge advertisers to make a constructive contribution to the social development of children by emphasizing positive social standards in advertising, such as friendship, kindness, honesty, and generosity. Similarly, the major television networks have set their own guidelines for advertising aimed at children. The guidelines restrict the use of celebrities, prohibit exhortive language (such as "Go ask Dad"), and restrict the use of animation to one-third of the total time of the commercial.

---

21. Maxine Lans Retsky, "Lanham Have It: Law and Comparative Ads," *Marketing News,* November 8, 1999, 16.

The Board of Directors of the American Association of Advertising Agencies recognizes that when used truthfully and fairly, comparative advertising provides the consumer with needed and useful information. However, extreme caution should be exercised. The use of comparative advertising, by its very nature, can distort facts and, by implication, convey to the consumer information that misrepresents the truth. Therefore, the Board believes that comparative advertising should follow certain guidelines:

1. The intent and connotation of the ad should be to inform and never to discredit or unfairly attack competitors.
2. When a competitive product is named, it should be one that exists in the marketplace as significant competition.
3. The competition should be fairly and properly identified, but never in a manner or tone of voice that degrades the competitive product or service.
4. The advertising should compare related or similar properties or ingredients of the product, dimension to dimension, feature to feature.
5. The identification should be for honest comparison purposes and not simply to upgrade by association.
6. If a competitive test is conducted, it should be done by an objective testing source, preferably an independent one, so that there will be no doubt as to the veracity of the test.
7. In all cases, the test should be supportive of all claims made in the advertising based on the test.
8. The advertising should never use partial results or stress insignificant differences to cause the consumer to draw an improper conclusion.
9. The property being compared should be significant in terms of value or usefulness of the product to the consumer.
10. Comparatives delivered through the use of testimonials should not imply that the testimonial is more than one individual's thought unless that individual represents a sample of the majority viewpoint.

Source: American Association of Advertising Agencies

EXHIBIT 6.9

The American Association of Advertising Agencies has issued guidelines for using comparative ads. Unfair comparisons between brands harms competition.

Issues in the Regulation of Direct Marketing and E-Commerce

The most pressing regulatory issue facing direct marketing and e-commerce was discussed at the outset of the chapter—database development and the privacy debate that accompanies the practice. But that earlier discussion just scratched the surface of the debate. The real privacy concerns have to do with the developing ability of firms to merge offline databases with online Web search and shopping behavior of consumers.

Privacy. The online e-commerce privacy issue focuses on the "cookies" (online tracking devices) that advertisers place on a Web surfer's hard drive to track that person's online behavior. This alone is annoying and feels like an invasion of privacy. But it is nothing compared to the emerging possibilities. You see, cookies do not reveal a person's name or address. What is looming as a real possibility is that offline databases with the consumer's name, address, phone number, credit cards, medical records, credit records, and social security number can be merged with the online tracking data.[22] With this combination of data, the following could easily happen: You are browsing a Web page on mutual funds and seconds later, you get a phone

22. Marcia Stepanek, "Protecting E-Privacy: Washington Must Step In," *Business Week E.Biz,* July 26, 1999, EB30; Michael Krauss, "Get a Handle on the Privacy Wild Card," *Marketing News,* February 28, 2000, 12.

http://www.luckysurf.com; http://www.havenco.com

EXHIBIT 6.10

Luckysurf. com is an Internet provider of sweepstakes games (although they never quite call it that) where $1 million can be won. Some states have enacted bans on Internet gambling, and the U.S. Congress has considered nationwide restrictions. But the nature of the Internet makes any legal jurisdiction on the globe just a click away, and some countries would happily provide havens for "virtual casinos" to give your money a place to play. And in 2000, an Internet start-up, HavenCo., set up shop on Sealand, an abandoned World War II era artificial island off the coast of England that claims sovereignty; HavenCo. hopes to become a magnet for online gaming companies and others with a need for discrete data repositories. If you were a state legislator, what would you think of Net gambling?

call from a telemarketer trying to sell you financial services! Sure feels like an invasion of privacy. This situation is serious enough that Congress and the FTC are carefully scrutinizing mergers of firms that would create such comprehensive online and offline databases.[23]

Contests and Sweepstakes. While privacy is a huge direct-marketing and e-commerce issue, it is not the only one. The next biggest legal issue has to do with sweepstakes and contests. Because of the success and widespread use of sweepstakes in direct marketing (like Publishers Clearinghouse sweepstakes), Congress has proposed limits on such promotions. The limits on direct-mail sweepstakes include the requirement that the phrases "No purchase necessary to win" and "A purchase will not improve an individual's chance of winning" must be repeated three times in letters to consumers and again on the entry form. In addition, penalties can be

23.   Jennifer Gilbert and Ira Teinowitz, "Privacy Debate Continues to Rage," *Advertising Age,* February 7, 2000, 44.

imposed on marketers who do not promptly remove consumers' names from mailing lists at the consumer's request.[24]

The online version of sweepstakes and contests has also had the attention of the U.S. Congress. "Games" like the one promoted by Luckysurf.com in Exhibit 6.10 don't call themselves sweepstakes, lotteries, games, or contests—but they play a lot like them. At the Luckysurf site, you merely need to register (providing name, address, e-mail address, and password), pick seven numbers, and then click on one of four banner ads to activate your entry in a $1 million-a-day drawing—guaranteed by Lloyd's of London. So far, these online games have avoided both lawsuits and regulation, but they have attracted the attention of policy makers.[25]

Telemarketing. Another legal issue in direct marketing has to do with telemarketing practices. The Telephone Consumer Fraud and Abuse Prevention Act of 1994 (later strengthened by the FTC in 1995) requires telemarketers to state their name, the purpose of the call, and the company they work for. The guidelines in the act prohibit telemarketers from calling before 8 A.M. and after 9 P.M. and from calling the same customer more than once every three months. In addition, telemarkers may not use automatic dialing machines that contain prerecorded messages and must keep a list of consumers who do not want to be called.[26]

Issues in the Regulation of Sales Promotion

Regulatory issues in sales promotion focus on three areas: premium offers, trade allowances, and sweepstakes and contests.

Premium Offers. With respect to **premiums** (an item offered for "free" or at a greatly reduced price with the purchase of another item), the main area of regulation has do with requiring marketers to state the fair retail value of the item offered as a premium.

Trade Allowances. In the area of trade allowances, marketers need to be familiar with the guidelines set forth in the Robinson-Patman Act of 1936. Even though this is an old piece of legislation, it still applies to contemporary trade promotion practices. The guidelines of the Robinson-Patman Act require marketers to offer similar customers similar prices on similar merchandise. This means that a marketer cannot use special allowances as a way to discount the price to highly attractive customers. This issue was raised earlier in the context of vertical cooperative advertising.

Contests and Sweepstakes. In the area of sweepstakes and contests, the issues discussed under direct marketing and e-commerce apply, but there are other issues as well. The FTC has specified that there are four violations of regulations that marketers must avoid in carrying out sweepstakes and contests:

- Misrepresentations about the value (that is, stating an inflated retail price) of the prizes being offered.
- Failure to provide complete disclosure about the conditions necessary to win—are there behaviors required on the part of the contestant?
- Failure to disclose the conditions necessary to obtain a prize—are there behaviors required of the contestant after the contestant is designated a "winner"?

24. Ira Teinowitz, "Congress Nears Accord on Sweepstakes Limits," *Advertising Age,* August 9, 1999, 33.
25. James Heckman, "Online, but Not on Trial, Though Privacy Looms Large," *Marketing News,* December 6, 1999, 8.
26. Ford and Calfee, "Recent Developments in FTC Policy on Deception," op. cit.

- Failure to ensure that a contest or sweepstakes is not classified as a lottery, which is considered gambling. A contest or sweepstakes is a lottery if a prize is offered based on chance and the contestant has to give up something of value in order to play.

Issues in the Regulation of Public Relations

Public relations is not bound by the same sorts of laws as other elements of the promotional mix. Because PR activities deal with public press and public figures, much of the regulation relates to these issues. The PR activities of a firm may place it on either side of legal issues with respect to rights of privacy, copyright infringement, or defamation through slander and libel.

Rights of Privacy. The rights-of-privacy problems facing a public relations firm center on the issue of appropriation. **Appropriation** is the use of pictures or images owned by someone else without permission. If a firm uses a model's photo or a photographer's work in an advertisement or company brochure without permission, then the work has been "appropriated" without the owner's permission. The same is true of PR materials prepared for release to the press or as part of a company's PR kit.

Copyright Infringement. Copyright infringement can occur when a public relations effort uses written, recorded, or photographic material. As with appropriation, written permission must be obtained to use such works.

Defamation. When a communication occurs that damages the reputation of an individual because the information in the communication was untrue, this is called **defamation** (you many have heard it referred to as "defamation of character"). Defamation can occur through either slander or libel. **Slander** is oral defamation, which in the context of promotion would occur during television or radio broadcast of an event involving a company and its employees. **Libel** is defamation that occurs in print and would be related to magazine, newspaper, direct mail, or Internet reports.

The public relations practitioner's job is to protect clients from slanderous or libelous reports about a company's activities. The inflammatory TV "investigative" news programs are often sued for slander and libel because they are challenged to prove the allegations they make about a company and its personnel. The issues revolve around whether negative comments can be fully substantiated.[27] Erroneous reports in major magazines and newspapers about a firm can result in a defamation lawsuit as well. Less frequently, PR experts need to defend a client from having made defamatory remarks (unless, of course, the client is a media organization).

Issues in the Regulation of Personal Selling

Several legal issues relate to the personal selling process. The most formal regulatory mandate affecting personal selling is specified in the Clayton (1914) and Robinson-Patman (1936) Acts and focuses on discriminatory pricing practices and bribery.

Price Discrimination. Firms are prohibited from **price discrimination** in the channel of distribution that occurs when different prices are charged to different

---

27. One of the most widely publicized lawsuits of this time involved Philip Morris's $10 billion libel suit against ABC's news program DayOne. For a summary of this suit see Steve Weinberg, "ABC, Philip Morris, and the Infamous Apology," *Columbia Journalism Review,* November/December 1995, accessed at http://www.cjr.org on December 7, 1999.

trade buyers who are buying similar quantities of goods. An exception is allowed if different service levels are provided to the different buyers. Since it is the sales force that negotiates the selling price with the trade in many instances, salespeople need to be aware of the guidelines set down in these regulations.

A related pricing issue is **price fixing,** which is the act of setting prices in concert with competitors. It is illegal under the mandates of the Clayton Act (1914). **Tying agreements,** also illegal under the Clayton Act, attempt to bind a buyer to the purchase of additional products as a condition of buying a desired product. Since salespeople are often the key price negotiators in the trade channel, these legal issues apply most directly to them.

Bribery. Bribery, the act of providing financial or other incentives in return for favorable treatment, is illegal in the United States and strictly prohibited in the personal selling process. The Foreign Corrupt Practices Act (1977) prohibits U.S. firms from using bribery in foreign markets as well, even though the practice may be prevalent and even accepted in those markets. The dividing line between bribery and "courting" a client is a fine one. Taking a client to dinner, treating a client's employees to a golf tournament, or "hosting" a sales incentive cruise to the Caribbean, are all legal if they are related to sales or service goals in an incentive promotional program. But direct gifts of money or other goods of value without these gifts being tied to sales or service performance criteria could be construed as bribery.

ETHICAL ISSUES IN PROMOTION ⑤

At the outset of the chapter, the proposition was offered that much of what gets regulated in promotion is also an ethical controversy. **Ethics** are moral standards and principles against which behavior is judged. Honesty, integrity, fairness, and sensitivity can be included in the broad definition of ethical behavior. We have to remember, though, that corporations are not unethical; people are unethical. As we discuss each promotional mix variable, think about two things. First, what is ethical will always come down to an individual, personal judgment. Second, as long as people make decisions about promotion, there are going to be some ethical lapses.

Ethical Issues in Advertising

Maybe because advertising is so conspicuous, or maybe because so much money is spent on advertising, the fact is that there are more ethical questions regarding advertising practices than about all other forms of promotion combined. Ethical issues in advertising would affect not only individuals, but broad social groups as well. Some of the common criticisms of advertising follow.

Advertising Is Superficial. Critics argue that advertising does not provide good product information. The basic criticism of advertising here is that it frequently carries little, if any, actual product information. What it does carry is said to be hollow adspeak. Ads are rhetorical; there is no pure "information." All information in an ad is biased, limited, and inherently deceptive. Critics claim that ads should contain information on functional features and performance results. Critics of advertising would prefer that all advertising be like the ad in Exhibit 6.11.

Advertisers argue in response that, in many instances, consumers are interested in more than a physical, tangible good with performance features and purely functional value. The functional features of a product may be secondary in importance to consumers in both the information search and the choice process. Advertising's critics misunderstand the totality of product benefits, including the hedonic

EXHIBIT 6.11

Critics of advertising would prefer that all advertising focus on the functional features of a brand much like this ad does for the Nissan Pathfinder.

(pleasure-seeking) aspects. The relevant information for a buyer may relate to the criteria being used to judge the satisfaction potential of the product, and that satisfaction is quite often nonutilitarian. Advertisers would offer the ad in Exhibit 6.12 as an example of their position.

Advertising Wastes Resources.   One of the traditional criticisms of advertising is that it represents an inefficient, wasteful process that channels monetary and human resources of a society to the "shuffling of existing total demand," rather than to the expansion of total demand.[28] Critics say that a society is no better off with advertising because it does not stimulate demand—it only shifts demand from one brand to another. Similarly, critics argue that brand differences are trivial and the proliferation of brands does not offer a greater variety of choice, but rather a meaningless waste of resources, with confusion and frustration for the consumer.

Advertisers counter with the argument that advertising's role in demand stimulation for a brand can result in much lower prices as economies of scale are achieved (recall the discussion from Chapter 1). When this happens, resources are being used efficiently to serve demand, and there is the related effect of delivering a higher standard of living at lower cost to consumers.

28. Richard Caves, *American Industry: Structure, Conduct, Performance* (Englewood Cliffs, NJ: Prentice-Hall, 1964), 102.

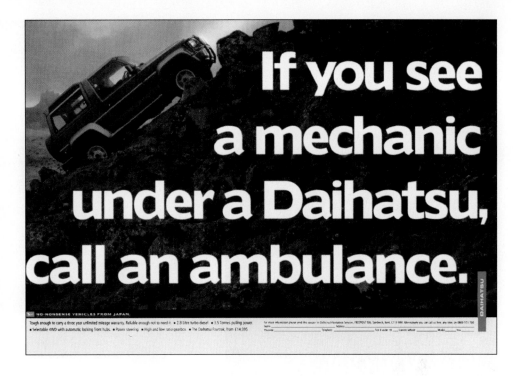

EXHIBIT 6.12

Advertisers believe that consumers use a wide range of criteria in evaluating and choosing a brand, and not all of these criteria relate to functional features.

Advertising Creates Needs. A common cry among critics is that advertising creates needs and makes people buy things they don't really need or even want. The argument is that consumers are relatively easy to seduce into wanting the next shiny bauble offered by marketers. For example, a quick examination of any issue of the magazine *Seventeen* reveals a medium intent on teaching the young women of the world to covet slim bodies and a glamorous complexion (see Exhibit 6.13).

Advertisers counter such a claim by arguing that human beings come fully equipped with a set of life needs—the need to be loved, esteem needs, and the need for security. Advertisers merely place their brands in the social context of these need states. Advertising is not nearly powerful enough to create needs. Advertisers point out that if ads were as powerful as critics believe, no product would ever fail.

Advertising Promotes Materialism. It is also claimed that an individual's wants and aspirations may be distorted by advertising. The long-standing argument is that in societies characterized by heavy advertising, there is a tendency for conformity and status-seeking behavior, both of which are considered materialistic and superficial.[29] Material goods are placed ahead of spiritual and intellectual pursuits. It creates wants and aspirations that are artificial and self-centered. This results in an overemphasis on the production of private goods, to the detriment of public goods (such as highways, parks, schools, and infrastructure).

Although advertising is undeniably in the business of promoting the good life, defenders of advertising argue that it did not create the American emphasis on materialism. For example, in the United States, major holidays such as Christmas (gifts), Thanksgiving (food), and Easter (candy and clothing) have become festivals of

29.   Vance Packard, *The Status Seekers* (New York: David McKay, 1959).

EXHIBIT 6.13

Critics of advertising argue that ads like these create needs in young women. What do you think?

EXHIBIT 6.14

Advertisers are recognizing the diversity reality of consumers' lives. This ad for Dove is a beautiful example of representing that diversity.

consumption. While we clearly live in the age of consumption, goods and possessions have been used by all cultures to mark special events, to play significant roles in rituals, and to serve as vessels of special meaning, long before there was modern advertising. Still, have we taken it too far? Is excess what we do best in consumer cultures?

Advertising Perpetuates Stereotypes. Advertisers often portray their target customer in advertisements, with the hope that individuals will relate to the ad and attend to its message. Critics charge that this practice yields a very negative effect— it perpetuates stereotypes. The portrayal of women, the elderly, and ethnic minorities is of particular concern. It is argued that women are still predominantly cast as homemakers, or as objects of desire, despite the fact that women now hold top management positions and head households. The elderly are often shown as helpless or ill, even though many active seniors enjoy a rich lifestyle. Critics contend that advertisers' propensity to feature African-American or Latin athletes in ads is simply a more contemporary form of stereotyping.

Advertisers counter with the fact that few ads typecast women or minorities anymore and would offer the ad in Exhibit 6.14 as an example. Advertising is in the business of reflecting the world as a way to be relevant to that world. Unrealistic portrayals of women or minorities is not in the best interest of the group or the advertiser.

Advertising Is Often Offensive and in Poor Taste. A pervasive and longstanding criticism of advertising is that it is often offensive and the appeals are typically in poor taste. Moreover, some would say that the trend in American advertising is to be rude, crude, and sometimes lewd, as advertisers struggle to grab the attention of consumers who have learned to tune out the avalanche of advertising messages they are confronted with each day.[30] Of course, taste is just that, a personal and inherently subjective evaluation. What is offensive to one person is merely satiric to another. A television ad depicting Adolf Hitler as a reformed spokesperson for a brand of potato chips, complete with the Nazi swastika morphing into the brand's logo, caused a predictable outcry in Thailand. Leo Burnett, the agency that prepared this ad for the Thai market, quickly withdrew it after protests from the Israeli embassy in Bangkok, and maintained the ad "was never intended to cause ill feelings.[31] Benetton regularly gets itself in trouble with the media and regulators with its extreme advertising. Most recently, Benetton ads, featuring death-row inmates were too much for several state attorneys general, who called for a ban on the campaign.[32]

But not all advertising deemed offensive has to be as extreme as these examples. Many times, advertisers get caught in a firestorm of controversy because certain, and sometimes relatively small, segments of the population are offended. The AIDS prevention campaign run by the Centers for Disease Control and Prevention(CDC) has been criticized for being too explicit. A spokesperson for the Family Research Council said about the ads, "They're very offensive—I thought I was watching *NYPD Blue.*" A highly popular ad seen as controversial by some was the "People Taking Diet Coke Break" ad. In this television spot, a group of female office workers is shown eyeing a construction worker as he takes off his T-shirt and enjoys a Diet Coke. Coca-Cola was criticized for using reverse sexism in this ad.[33] While Coca-Cola and the CDC may have ventured into delicate areas, consider these advertisers, who were caught completely by surprise in finding that their ads were deemed offensive:

- In a public service spot developed by Aetna Life & Casualty insurance for measles vaccine, a wicked witch with green skin and a wart resulted in a challenge to the firm's ad from a witches' rights group.
- A Nynex spot was criticized by animal-rights activists because it showed a rabbit colored with blue dye.
- A commercial for Black Flag bug spray had to be altered after a war veterans' group objected to the playing of taps over dead bugs.

It should be emphasized that most consumers probably did not find these ads particularly offensive. Perhaps it is the spirit of political correctness that causes such scrutiny, or maybe it is that consumers are so overwhelmed with ads that they have simply lost their tolerance. Or maybe some people just have too much time on their hands. And sometimes they correctly point to insensitivity on the part of advertisers. Whatever the explanation, marketers today are well advised to take care in broadly considering the tastefulness of their ads.

Advertisers Deceive with Subliminal Stimulation. There is much controversy, and almost a complete lack of understanding, regarding the issue of **subliminal** (below the threshold of consciousness) communication and advertising. Since there is much confusion surrounding the issue of subliminal advertising, perhaps this is the most appropriate point to provide some clarification: No one ever sold anything by putting images of breasts in ice cubes or the word "sex" in the background of an ad. Furthermore, no one at an advertising agency, except the very bored or the very eager to retire, has time to sit around dreaming up such things. We realize it makes for a great story, but hiding pictures in other pictures doesn't work to get anyone to buy anything. Although it is true that there is some

30. Stuart Elliot, "A New Pitch for U.S. Ads: Lewd, Crude, and Rude," *International Herald Tribune,* June 20, 1998, 1, 4.
31. Pichayaporn Utumporn, "Ad with Hitler Causes a Furor in Thailand," *The Wall Street Journal,* July 5, 1998, B8.
32. Michael McCarthy, "Shock Advertising Receives Jolts of Criticism," *USA Today,* February 22, 2000, B1.
33. Kevin Goldman, "From Witches to Anorexics, Critical Eyes Scrutinize Ads for Political Correctness," *The Wall Street Journal,* May 19, 1998, B1, B10.

evidence for some types of unconscious ad processing, these are effects generally related to ease of recall from memory, not the ability of a subliminal message to create behaviors. If the rumors are true that advertisers are actually using subliminal messages in their ads (and they aren't), the conclusion should be that they're wasting their money.[34]

Advertising Affects Programming on Mass Media. Critics argue that advertisers who place ads in media have an unhealthy effect on shaping the content of information contained in the media. For example, if a magazine that reviews and evaluates stereo equipment tests the equipment of one of its large advertisers, the contention is that the publication will hesitate to criticize the advertiser's equipment.

Another charge leveled at advertisers is that they purchase airtime only on programs that draw large audiences. Critics argue that these mass-market programs lower the quality of television because cultural and educational programs, which draw smaller and more selective markets, are dropped in favor of mass-market programs.[35] Additionally, television programmers have a difficult time attracting advertisers to shows that may be valuable yet controversial. Programs that deal with abortion, sexual abuse, or AIDS may have trouble drawing advertisers who fear the consequences of any association with controversial issues.

Marketers argue that they are delivering what audiences desire. If *World Wrestling Federation, Cops,* and *America's Dumbest Criminals* are preferred programming, then consumers have a right to choose. This controversy probably goes well beyond advertising's role in programming and relates to the deeper issue of the intellectual atmosphere and value system of the citizenry.

Advertising Causes People to Use Alcohol and Tobacco Products. No advertising issue in the last two decades of the twentieth century is as volatile as this one. From 1980 forward, the press regularly has carried stories about the tobacco industry's courtroom trials. Few products have motivated as much press or as much passionate debate. Many medical journals have published survey research claiming that advertising "caused" cigarette and alcohol consumption—particularly among teenagers.[36] The main controversy in the tobacco debates swirled around the use of characters like "Joe Camel."

Interestingly, these studies contradicted the research since the 1950s carried out by marketing, communications, psychology, and economics researchers—including assessments of all the available research by the FTC.[37] These early studies (as well as several Gallup Polls during the 1990s) found that family, friends, and peers—not advertising—are the primary influence on the use of tobacco and alcohol products. And while children at a very early age can recognize tobacco advertising characters like Joe Camel, they also recognize the Energizer Bunny, the Jolly Green Giant, and Snoopy—all characters associated with adult products. Kids are also aware that

---

34. Timothy Moore, "Subliminal Advertising: What You See Is What You Get," *Journal of Marketing,* vol. 46 (Spring 1982), 38–47.

35. Chuck Ross, "Marketers to Blame for Lack of Diversity on TV: JWT report," *Advertising Age,* August 16, 1999, 4.

36. See, for example, Joseph R. DiFranza, et al., "RJR Nabisco's Cartoon Camel Promotes Camel Cigarettes to Children," *Journal of the American Medical Association,* 266(22), 3168–3153.

37. For a summary of over sixty articles that address the issue of alcohol and cigarette advertising and the lack of relationship between advertising and cigarette and alcohol industry demand, see Mark Frankena, et al., "Alcohol, Consumption, and Abuse," Bureau of Economics, Federal Trade Commission, March 5, 1985. A similar listing of research articles and the same conclusions were drawn during Congressional Hearings on the topic, see "Advertising of Tobacco Products," Hearings before the Subcommittee on Health and the Environment, Committee on Energy and Commerce, House of Representatives, Ninety-ninth Congress, July 18 and August 1, 1986, Serial No. 99-167.

cigarettes cause disease and know that they are intended as an adult product.[38] It is also true that the Surgeon General of the United States reported in 1994 that "Tobacco use begins primarily through the dynamic interplay of sociodemographic, environmental, behavioral, and personal factors" and that "To date, however, no longitudinal study of the direct relationship of cigarette advertising to smoking initiation has been reported in the literature".[39] Research in Europe offers the same conclusions in that "Every study on the subject [of advertising effects on the use of tobacco and alcohol] finds that children are more influenced by parents and playmates than by the mass media."[40]

Why doesn't advertising cause people to smoke and drink? The simple answer is that advertising just isn't that powerful. Eight out of ten new products fail, and if advertising were so powerful, no new products would fail. The more detailed answer is that advertising cannot create primary demand in mature product categories. **Primary demand** is creating demand for an entire product category. With mature products, advertising isn't powerful enough to have that effect. Research across several decades has demonstrated repeatedly that advertising does not create primary demand for tobacco or alcohol.[41]

No one has ever said that smoking or drinking is good for you (except for maybe that glass of wine with dinner). That's not what we are saying here, either. The point is that these behaviors emerge in a complex social context, and the vast weight of research evidence suggests that advertising is not a causal influence on initiation behavior, but rather plays its fundamental role in helping people make brand choices after they choose to begin a behavior.

Ethical Issues in Sales Promotion, Direct Marketing, and E-Commerce

The main ethical issues in direct marketing and e-commerce center on the question of privacy, which has been thoroughly discussed in the context of legal issues. Within the trade channel, ethical issues in sales promotion have to do with the recently acquired power retailers like Wal-Mart and Costco have developed. With this power, retailers can pressure manufacturers into unethical behavior such as providing allowances not available to buyers in general. There are those who would say that **slotting fees,** a charge paid by a marketer to a retailer on a per store basis to carry the marketer's brand (discussed in detail in Chapter 11) is really just a form of bribery. Similarly, it is also considered unethical for salespeople to spend lavishly on dinners, shows, or other entertainment as means of acquiring the business of a trade channel member.

There is also the ethical issue of promoters not following through the promised rewards of a promotion. Failing to send a rebate or adding conditions to winning a prize are forms of unethical behavior. Also, placing conditions on winning a sweepstakes or contest without informing contestants is unethical. You might get notified that you just won a trip to the Caribbean, but a condition of winning is that you first must attend a sales presentation in your hometown on "condo opportunities" in the Caribbean!

38.   See, for example, Lucy L. Henke, "Young Children's Perceptions of Cigarette Brand Advertising: Awareness, Affect and Target Market Identification," *Journal of Advertising,* vol. 24, no. 4 (Winter 1995), 13–27; and Richard Mizerski, "The Relationship Between Cartoon Trade Character Recognition and Attitude Toward the Product Category," *Journal of Marketing,* vol. 59 (October 1995), 58–70.

39.   Surgeon General's Report 1994, "Preventing Tobacco Use Among Young People," 123, 188.

40.   Jeffrey Goldstein, "Children and Advertising—the Research," *Commercial Communications,* July 1998, 4–8.

41.   For research on this topic across several decades, see Richard Schmalensee, *The Economics of Advertising* (Amsterdam-London: North-Holland Publishing Company, 1972); Mark S. Albion and Paul W. Farris, *The Advertising Controversy,* (Boston,: Auburn House Publishing Co., 1981); and Michael J. Waterson, "Advertising and Tobacco Consumption: An Analysis of the Two Major Aspects of the Debate," *International Journal of Advertising,* 9, 1990, 59–72.

Ethical Issues in Public Relations

You will hear people argue that public relations per se is unethical. That's because many of the tools of public relations don't look or sound like promotion. A news conference, a press release, or a speaker at a civic event are sometimes not identified as "speaking for" a corporation. It is this "publicity" issue that is often questioned ethically. It is the job of the PR specialist to be the "standard bearers of corporate ethical initiatives."[42] In addition, PR consultants must take the responsibility to counsel their clients to deal ethically with a problem and not hide the truth about a situation.

The Public Relations Society of America (http://www.prsa.org) has a Code of Profession Standards that highlights the honesty and integrity aspects of the process in the first eight standards of the code. Notice that these standards deal with serving both the client and the media.

1. A member shall conduct his or her professional life in accord with the public interest.
2. A member shall exemplify high standards of honesty and integrity while carrying out dual obligations to a client or employer and to the democratic process.
3. A member shall deal fairly with the public, with past or present clients or employers, and with fellow practitioners, giving due respect to the ideal of free inquiry and to the opinions of others.
4. A member shall adhere to the highest standards of accuracy and truth, avoiding extravagant claims or unfair comparisons and giving credit for ideas and words borrowed from others.
5. A member shall not knowingly disseminate false or misleading information and shall act promptly to correct erroneous communications for which he or she is responsible.
6. A member shall not engage in any practice which has the purpose of corrupting the integrity of channels of communications or the processes of government.
7. A member shall be prepared to identify publicly the name of the client or employer on whose behalf any public communication is made.
8. A member shall not use any individual or organization professing to serve or represent an announced cause, or professing to be independent or unbiased, but actually serving another or undisclosed interest.

Ethical Issues in Personal Selling

The ethics of personal selling were touched on earlier in the discussion of trade sales promotion. It almost goes without saying that high-pressure selling tactics that attempt to embarrass or even threaten a customer into making a decision are clearly unethical. In the past, selling programs for vacation resort time-shares was plagued by high-pressure sales tactics. Typically, the elderly or the uneducated are targeted by unethical salespeople because they are more vulnerable to high-pressure tactics.

Aside from high-pressure selling techniques, a salesperson can also be tempted to make unsubstantiated claims during a sales pitch. Since personal selling often takes place on a one-on-one basis in the privacy of an office, the opportunity to make such claims "confidentially" is ever present. Consumers often acquiesce to a salesperson's recommendations thinking that the seller has their best interest in mind.

Finally, we need to revisit the issue of ethics and bribery. While bribery is illegal in the United States (and for U.S. nationals selling in foreign markets), the policing of bribery is a very personal process. No one will know if a bribe has been offered or carried out except for the parties involved. The moral and ethical standards of the people involved in sales negotiations is the only way bribery can be avoided or exposed.

---

42. Fraser P. Seitel, *The Practice of Public Relations* (Upper Saddle River, NJ: Prentice-Hall, 1998), 89.

SUMMARY

1 Assess the benefits and problems of promotion in a free-enterprise, capitalistic society.

Marketing processes, including promotion, will naturally emerge in industrialized, high mass consumption societies where people want their "stuff" moved around in a highly efficient and effective way. In a free-enterprise economy, where competition between organizations is fostered and encouraged, a process such as promotion is implicitly required. The competitive structure of a free enterprise system motivates firms to strive for competitive advantage. The route to competitive advantage demands strategies that lead to superior product design, efficiency that keeps prices low, distribution that gets people their stuff quickly, *and* compelling promotion.

But the complex nature of high mass consumption societies like the United States has brought about regulations and government intervention. The result is that a mixed economy has evolved where restrictions and guidelines have been imposed on fundamental economic exchange processes. Marketing, and the promotional process, has progressed and evolved simultaneously with the economy. It now functions as part of a somewhat free, partly socialistic, and heavily regulated economy.

2 Identify the role of government agencies in the regulation of promotion.

Both federal government and state agencies regulate promotional activities. By far, federal agencies exert an influence on using promotional tools. This is true for two reasons. First, the federal government and its key regulatory agencies—the FTC, FDA, and FCC—have the regulatory power by virtue of legal mandate. Second, most promotional violations involve interstate commerce, which makes the violation a federal offense. States have developed some regulatory power and authority through the state attorneys general offices.

Overall, federal and state agencies are interested in maintaining fair competition by restricting unfair business practices. In addition, keeping consumers informed and protecting them from deceptive practices is a primary role of government regulation. More than a dozen major pieces of legislation (review Exhibit 3.3) have been enacted to protect fair competition and shield consumers from deceptive promotional practices.

3 Explain the meaning and importance of self-regulation of promotion.

Self-regulation is the promotion industry's attempt to police itself. Supporters say it is a shining example of how unnecessary government intervention is, while critics point to it as a joke, an elaborate shell game. According to the critics, meaningful self-regulation occurs only when the threat of government action is imminent.

Several industry and trade associations and public service organizations have voluntarily established guidelines for promotion within their industries. The importance of self-regulation relates to the fact that a well-run, ethical industry is good for the promotion community as a whole and creates credibility for, and therefore enhances the effectiveness of, promotion itself. Exhibit 3.5 lists some organizations that have taken on the task of regulating and monitoring promotional activities, and the year when each established a code of standards.

4 Discuss the regulatory issues related to the promotional process.

The main regulatory issues related to the promotional process are:

Advertising
a.   Deception and unfairness
b.   Competitive issues
c.   Advertising aimed at children

Direct Marketing and E-Commerce
a.   Privacy
b.   Sweepstakes and contests
c.   Telemarketing

Sales Promotion
a.   Premium offers
b.   Trade allowances
c.   Contests and sweepstakes

Public Relations
a.   Rights of privacy
b.   Copyright infringement
c.   Defamation

Personal Selling
a.   Price discrimination
b.   Bribery

5 Debate the ethical issues that arise from the use of promotional tools.

It is somewhat redundant to ask you to debate the ethical issues in promotion, because ethical issues, by definition, are debatable. Since ethics entail developing personal standards that will determine your behavior, each of us will impose a different standard on each area of the promotional mix.

Far and away advertising has the most ethical issues to debate—nearly a dozen, ranging from the superficiality and materialism that advertising promotes to wasting resources, creating needs, and causing people to smoke and drink. The other areas of the promotional mix have issues related to privacy (direct marketing), slotting fees and deception in offers (sales promotion), the public interest (sales promotion), and coercive behavior (personal selling). Each of these issues is debatable on both sides—they are issues in the truest sense.

KEY TERMS

free-enterprise economy, 191
mixed economy, 192
advertising substantiation program, 196
consent order, 197
cease-and-desist order, 197
affirmative disclosure, 197
corrective advertising, 197
celebrity endorsements, 197
self-regulation, 198

consumerism, 203
testimonial, 206
bait-and-switch, 206
puffery, 207
vertical cooperative advertising, 207
comparison advertisements, 207
monopoly power, 208
premiums, 211
appropriation, 212
defamation, 212

slander, 212
libel, 212
price discrimination, 212
price fixing, 213
tying agreements, 213
bribery, 213
ethics, 213
subliminal, 217
primary demand, 219
slotting fees, 219

QUESTIONS FOR REVIEW AND CRITICAL THINKING

1. How does the fact that the United States is a "mixed economy" affect the way promotional activities are carried out by firms?

2. Which of the federal government agencies has the most authority and power over promotional activities? What is the nature of that power?

3. What is the difference between the advertising substantiation program and corrective advertising? How are these two legislative remedies related to each other?

4. Identify two ways in which the Better Business Bureau is involved in the regulation of promotion.

5. Identify two promotion industry trade associations and explain their activities with respect to regulating the promotional activities of firms.

6. What areas of direct marketing and e-commerce are most heavily regulated?

7. How is personal selling regulated? Which two laws are most directly related to personal selling activities?

8. Debate two ethical issues regarding advertising. Offer arguments that both criticize advertising in this regard and defend the practice of advertising.

EXPERIENTIAL EXERCISES

1. **In-class exercise.** Divide the class in half. You have twenty minutes to come up with arguments and examples on the ethical issue "Advertising creates needs." Half of the class will argue that it does, while the other half of the class will take the opposite position. Defend your argument on conceptual grounds and provide examples.

2. **Out-of-class exercise.** Search a popular press business magazine or newspaper and locate an article on either a legal or an ethical issue stemming from a promotional practice (lawsuits are easy to find). Read the article and write a one-page discussion of how you feel about the issue raised in the article.

USING THE INTERNET

Exercise 1

Protection of children has been used as the basis for a number of legislative and regulatory proposals regarding the Internet. In addition to the problem of their exposure to inappropriate content, children might also be targeted by marketers in order to collect information that a more savvy, informed adult might regard as private. The Center for Media Education is one of the nonprofit groups concerned with children's exposure to advertising in the new media. TRUSTe is a nonprofit consortium thath has established "trust marks" to indicate how a Web site handles information collected on site visitors; it has a Children's Privacy Seal Program to address the special concerns for young children's privacy, for example, regarding parental consent.

Center for Media Education
http://www.cme.org

TRUSTe
http://www.truste.org

1. How does the Internet compare with traditional media in terms of segregating audiences, for example, to limiting children's exposure to advertising?

2. If you were a Web site manager, how might you try to filter your audience, whether to bar children (or, for that matter, adults) or to separate audiences by age group?

3. Why might children require additional privacy protections?

Exercise 2

Given the global nature of the Internet, disagreements between *national* regulatory regimes can quickly blow up into *international* policy disputes. The issue of individual privacy is at the core of a major disagreement between the United States and Europe regarding commerce on the World Wide Web—most European countries have strong national policies regarding protection of citizen privacy, and the European Union (EU) is promoting a uniform policy that would drastically curtail what sort of information a company could collect and maintain on an individual. The EU further insists that this policy should apply to any foreign (for example, the U.S.) company receiving information from an EU country—think of, say, a U.S. airline with offices in Frankfurt or Paris, and booking flights to Europeans. In the U.S., the Federal Trade Commission has suggested the need for regulation, while industry is promoting self-regulation.

The European Union in the United States
http://www.eurunion.org

The U.S. Federal Trade Commission
http://www.ftc.gov

1. What companies should be the most concerned with these international-scale regulatory differences?

2. How could companies accommodate the differences through their structures or operations?

After reading this chapter, you will be able to:

1 Understand that international communications is about cultures, not nations.

2 Explain the different types of cross-cultural research that can provide key information to the process of effective communication in international markets.

3 Identify three distinctive challenges that complicate the execution of advertising as a promotional tool in international settings.

4 Discuss the advantages and disadvantages of standardized versus customized promotional campaigns.

5 Discuss the development and management of an international sales force.

If you are famous, extremely wealthy, and can buy anything you want, then you are likely to get an entire wardrobe for free—from Tommy Hilfiger. The Tommy Hilfiger brand has become a worldwide success, and dressing celebrities stylishly in casual red, white, and blue clothes is just one of the many promotional strategies used by the founder, Tommy Hilfiger himself. The overall success of the company has been stunning. In a recent financial reporting year, sales increased to $2 billion and profits are well over $200 million. The brand is now the most successful designer label in America, outselling both Ralph Lauren and Calvin Klein.

While the overall success of the brand is impressive, the promotional strategy used to product launch the brand in Europe was remarkable. In 1996, the Tommy Hilfiger brand was virtually unknown in Europe. Now, recognition is nearly 100 percent. The key to this phenomenal rise in success and awareness is the venturesome way Tommy Hilfiger used a vast array of promotional tools—and his personal fascination with celebrities to launch the brand.

The assault on Europe actually started well before the brand was even distributed on the Continent. Hilfiger figured it this way: If you want to create a buzz, you have to start from the top. So, from the top, he spent $5 million a year sending out free clothes to the likes of President Clinton, British Princes Harry and William, and pop musician Snoop Doggy Dogg. In addition to U.S., British, and rap royalty, a long list of celebrities was more than happy to fly the red, white, and blue Hilfiger flag. The princes even wrote to Hilfiger and asked for more clothes.

Once the celebrities were fully outfitted, Hilfiger put his promotional machinery to work and created one of the most intense one-week promotional campaigns in history. First, there was a Pan-European public relations effort that achieved its purpose of getting every newspaper and glossy magazines across the U.K. and the Continent talking about Hilfiger. Simultaneously, there was an advertising blitz for the new Tommy fragrance; the announcement that Hilfiger would open a shop in London's prestigious New Bond Street at London's highest-ever retail rent of $1.7 million annually; and bookings of Claudia Schiffer, Naomi Campbell, Kate Moss, and Stella Tennant at $25,000 a day each to launch the clothes down the catwalk at London's Fashion Week. And this was all in one week! By the end of the week, celebrities were fighting to get invited to Hilfiger's party at Oxo Tower on the banks of London's river Thames.[1]

What a promotional campaign—advertising, event sponsorship, public relations, and sampling. But as you know, Hilfiger has not let up. The brand is still prominent among the best fashion magazines in the world. Hilfiger maintains his fascination with celebrities and still sponsors several rock and pop tours annually (see Exhibit 7.1). In the end, widespread use of promotion brought the Hilfiger brand from anonymity to rock star status.

Aside from the stunning success of the overall Hilfiger brand, what is important about Hilfiger's promotional strategy is that it was successful in an international setting. Many U.S. firms are adept at competing in the domestic market, but when it comes to reaching beyond the borders, well, things don't always go as well as Hilfiger's European launch:

- The name Coca-Cola in China was first rendered as "Ke-kou-ke-la." Unfortunately, Coke did not discover until after thousands of signs had been printed that the

EXHIBIT 7.1

Tommy Hilfiger has built a global brand by using all forms of promotion. Here, the sponsorship of a Lenny Kravitz concert is advertised in GQ magazine.

1. Information for this scenario was drawn from Dan Keeler, "How Does He Do It?" *EuroBusiness,* November 1999, 82–92.

phrase means "bite the wax tadpole" or "female horse stuffed with wax," depending on the dialect. Coke then researched 40,000 Chinese characters and found a close phonetic equivalent, "ko-kou-ko-le," which can be loosely translated as "Happiness in the mouth."

- In Taiwan, the translation of the Pepsi slogan "Come alive with the Pepsi Generation" came out as "Pepsi will bring your ancestors back from the dead."

- Scandinavian vacuum manufacturer Electrolux used the following in an American ad campaign: "Nothing sucks like an Electrolux."

- When Parker Pen marketed a ballpoint pen in Mexico, its ads were supposed to say, "It won't leak in your pocket and embarrass you." Instead the ads said, "It won't leak in your pocket and make you pregnant."[2]

INTRODUCTION

Humorous or not, such episodes remind us that communicating with consumers around the world is a complex and important challenge. **International promotion** is promotion that reaches across national and cultural boundaries. Unfortunately, a great deal of international advertising and promotion in the past was nothing more than translations of domestic advertising and promotion. Often, these translations were at best ineffective, at worst offensive like the ones above. The day has passed, however—if there ever was such a day—when marketers based in industrialized nations can simply "do a foreign translation" of their messages. Today, international marketers must pay greater attention to local cultures. The essential perspective is clear: The real issue is not nations, but cultures.

This chapter considers the many issues that marketers must understand about the international market environment when promotion needs to cross borders. We begin with an examination of the complex notion of culture and communication. Cross-cultural research, the next topic, gives us a way to learn about cultures so that effective promotion can be prepared. We look at the international challenges in preparing advertising, sales promotion, direct marketing, e-commerce, and public relations. Promotion agencies can be critical to overcoming the challenges of international promotion, and we look at the options available to marketers.

A key issue in international promotion is the decision to standardize a campaign across all cultures or customize a campaign for every international market. Guidelines that can be used in making this decision, are identified near the end of the chapter. Finally, the issues related to developing and managing a global sales force are presented. In many cases, successfully entering international markets is highly dependent on cultivating customers with the personal contact of a sales force rather than other forms of promotion.

CULTURE AND COMMUNICATIONS ❶

Culture is the total life ways of a people, the social legacy the individual acquires from his or her group.[3] Culture is typically invisible to those who are immersed within it, which makes communicating across cultures difficult. It is, in fact, one of the most difficult of all communication tasks, largely because there is no such thing as "culture-free" communication. Promotion, and particularly advertising, is a cultural

---

2. These examples are posted (along with others) on the University of Texas at Austin Advertising Department Web site (http://www.advertising.utexas.edu) accessed December 10, 1999.
3. Gordon Marshall, ed., *The Concise Oxford Dictionary of Sociology* (New York: Oxford University Press, 1994), 104.

product; it means nothing outside of the culture within which it is created. Culture surrounds promotion, informs it, gives it meaning. To transport a promotion across cultural borders, one must respect, and hopefully understand, the power of culture.

The Importance of International Communication

Promotion depends on effective communication, and effective international communication depends on creating shared meaning between cultures. The degree of shared meaning is significantly affected by cultural membership. When an advertiser in culture A wants to communicate with consumers in culture B, it is culture B that will surround the created message, form its cultural context, and significantly affect how it will be interpreted. Exhibit 7.2 graphically illustrates the "shared meaning" basis for effective communications.

Some products and brands may belong to a global consumer culture more than to any one national culture, which makes creating a shared meaning relatively easy. Such brands travel well, as do their advertising and promotions, because there is already common cultural ground on which to build effective communication. The Libertel phone and McDonald's ads in Exhibits 7.3 and 7.4 provide examples of products and brands with wide, if not "global," meaning. Wireless phones have emerged as a global product seemingly overnight, providing functionality that is easy to appreciate so that many consumers share the same meaning for the value of a cellular phone. McDonald's, although clearly an American icon, has become a part of the global landscape, thus facilitating something of a global image. Such examples, however, are few and far between, and as global as they may be, they are still affected by the local culture as to their use and, ultimately, their meaning.

As communications technology has progressed in the latter half of the twentieth century, international communications, and particularly commercial communications, has become extremely important. As one international communications scholar put it:

No activity, national or international, is exempt from the corporate sponsor—not even, apparently, the world wide programs of the United Nations. Corporate sponsorships could be magnificently expanded from the Grand Prix and Olympic events to the United Nations itself.[4]

While this comment is decidedly cynical, it makes the point that promotion is a global phenomenon with far-reaching effects. Other international scholars point out that the importance and complexity of international communications can be under-

EXHIBIT 7.2

Communication in international markets requires creating "shared meaning" between cultures.

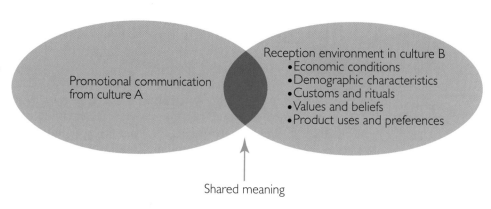

Promotional communication from culture A

Reception environment in culture B
- Economic conditions
- Demographic characteristics
- Customs and rituals
- Values and beliefs
- Product uses and preferences

Shared meaning

4.   Elli Lester, "International Advertising and Theory," in Basil G. Englis (editor), *Global and International Advertising* (Hillsdale, NJ: Lawrence Erlbaum Associates), 1994, 5.

stood by assessing the complex social, economic, and political changes that affect the international communications environment. Specifically, international developments that are particularly relevant to commercial communications are:

- The development of the triad trading blocs in Europe, Asia, and North America, perhaps as a prelude to a rise in nationalism.
- The loosening of political and economic constraints on ethnic groups in Central and Eastern Europe and the former Soviet Union.
- The liberalization of the flow of labor and the increase of movements by people across European borders (and other parts of the world), leading to increased ethnic tensions.
- The growing size of ethnic groups by virtue of their elevated birthrate relative to "dominant" populations in various countries.
- The rise of cultural borders and barriers within the European Union even as the economic borders begin to fall.[5]

EXHIBIT 7.3

In some product categories, creating shared meaning across cultures is quite easy. This Dutch ad for cellular phones says, "I got my eyes from my mother, I got my sense of humor from my mother. And I got my mobile phone from my father." Sound familiar? http://www.libertel.com

EXHIBIT 7.4

McDonald's is the quintessential global brand, succeeding in literally dozens of international markets around the world. It would appear that a "Big Mac" creates shared meaning across cultures.

5.   Janeen Arnold Costa and Gary J. Bamossy, *Marketing in a Multicultural World* (Thousand Oaks, CA: Sage Publications, 1995), viii.

All this complexity is emerging at a point in time when marketers worldwide are seeking new outlets for their brands and new sources of revenue—just like Tommy Hilfiger's move into the British and European markets. The Internet alone would be enough of a catalyst for the increase in international promotion and commerce. But the drive into foreign markets began way before the Internet was ever an issue, and marketers have been working hard to understand how to successfully market and promote on foreign soil.

OVERCOMING CULTURAL BARRIERS IN INTERNATIONAL PROMOTION

Global trade initiatives such as the General Agreement on Tariffs and Trade (GATT) and the North American Free Trade Agreement (NAFTA) are designed to encourage trade and economic development across national borders. These initiatives signal the emergence of international markets that are larger, more accessible, and perhaps more homogeneous in some ways and more nationalistic in others. In the midst of this trend toward more and more international trade, marketers are redefining the nature and scope of the markets for their goods and services, which, in turn, redefines the nature and scope of the promotional effort. This means that firms must be more sensitive to the social and economic differences of various international markets.

All the firms listed in Exhibit 7.5 compete in either consumer products or the automotive markets. These are international corporate titans such as Procter & Gamble (P&G), Nestlé, Toyota, and Coke. Today, however, most companies consider their markets to extend beyond national boundaries and across cultures. This international orientation means that marketers must come to terms with how they are going to effectively overcome cultural barriers in trying to communicate with consumers around the world.

Barriers to Creating Successful International Promotions

Adopting an international perspective is often difficult for marketers. The reason is that experiences gained over a career and a lifetime create a cultural "comfort zone"—that is, one's own cultural values, experiences, and knowledge serve as a subconscious guide for decision making and behavior. International promotions are particularly beset with this problem because we are "comfortable" with our natural way of communicating and it is hard to step back and consciously block a natural tendency.

Because of this subconscious tendency to communicate within our comfort zone, promotional strategists must overcome two related biases to be successful in international markets. **Ethnocentrism** is the tendency to view and value things from the perspective of one's own culture. **Self-reference criterion (SRC)** refers to the unconscious reference to one's own cultural values, experiences, and knowledge as a basis for decisions. These two closely related biases are primary obstacles to success when conducting marketing and promotion planning that demands a cross-cultural perspective.

A decision maker's SRC and ethnocentrism can inhibit his or her ability to sense important cultural distinctions between markets. This in turn can blind marketers to their own culture's "fingerprints" on the promotions they've created. Sometimes these are offensive or, at a minimum, markers of "outsider" influence. Outsiders aren't always welcome; other times, they just appear ignorant.

For example, AT&T's "Reach Out and Touch Someone" advertising campaign was viewed as much too sentimental for most European audiences even though it was a huge success in the United States. Similarly, AT&T's "Call USA" campaign,

Marketer	Headquarters	1998 Ad Spending Outside the U.S.
Procter & Gamble	Cincinnati	$3,018.2
Unilever	Rotterdam/London	2,737.3
Nestlé	Vevy, Switzerland	1,559.3
Volkswagen	Wolfsburg, Germany	1,070.4
Ford Motor Co.	Dearborn, Michigan	1,049.5
General Motors	Detroit	1,039.3
Toyota Motors	Toyota City, Japan	1,034.9
Coca-Cola	Atlanta	1,011.5
Peugeot Citroën	Paris	854.9
L'Oréal	Paris	840.9

Source: Advertising Age, AdAge Dataplace accessed at http://www.advantage.com on December 10, 1999

EXHIBIT 7.5

Top ten global marketers ranked by advertising spending outside the United States. Figures are in millions of U.S. dollars.

aimed at Americans doing business in Europe, was negatively perceived by many Europeans. The ad featured a harried American businessman whose language skills were so poor that he could barely ask for assistance to find a telephone in a busy French hotel. European businesspeople are typically fluent in two or three languages and have more than enough language competence to ask for a telephone. This ad, with its portrayal of Americans as culturally inept and helpless, created a negative association for AT&T among European businesspeople. Granted, the target market was Americans in foreign assignments, but the perspective of the ad was still decidedly ethnocentric and offensive to Europeans and violated a core concept of IMC—speak in a clear and appealing voice to all constituents at all times.

The only way you can have any hope of counteracting the negative influences that ethnocentrism and SRC have on international promotionals is to be constantly sensitive to their existence and to the virtual certainty of important differences between cultures that will somehow affect your best effort. The way to get sensitive about cultures is to do cross-cultural audience research.

Cross-Cultural Audience Research

Analyzing audiences in international markets can be a humbling task. If firms have worldwide product distribution networks—as do Nestlé, Ford, Unilever, and Philip Morris—then international audience analysis may require dozens of separate analyses. There really is no way to avoid the task of specific audience analysis. This typically involves research in each different country, generally from a local research supplier. There are, however, good secondary resources that may provide broad-based information to advertisers about international markets. The U.S. Department of Commerce has an International Trade Administration (ITA) division that helps companies based in the United States develop foreign market opportunities for their products and services. The ITA (http://www.ita.doc.gov) publishes specialized reports that cover most of the major markets in the world and provide economic and regulatory information. The United Nations' *Statistical Yearbook* is another source of general economic and population data (http://www.un.org). The yearbook, published annually, provides information for more than 200 countries. This type of source provides some helpful information for the international marketer.

An international audience analysis will also involve evaluation of economic conditions, demographic characteristics, values, custom and ritual, and product use and preferences. To begin an analysis like this, a good source of information is the World Bank's *World Tables,* which summarizes valuable data on living patterns for 124 countries, including such indicators as radio, television, telephone, and auto ownership per thousand households. Another publication from the World Bank is *The World Bank Atlas,* which is published annually. The atlas has information on population size, population growth trends, life expectancy, infant mortality, education levels, and gross national product (GNP). Other World Bank (http://www.worldbank.org) publications include information on productivity, level of industrialization, trade, energy use, and government spending on social and military programs.

A good international market analysis will rely on such **secondary data**—data gathered by someone else for some other purpose—but the need to understand very specific aspects of a foreign market may require specific data collection unique to a promotional situation, called **primary data** collection. Some combination of secondary and primary data collection will be required in four areas: economic conditions; demographic characteristics; values, customs, and rituals; and product use and preferences.

EXHIBIT 7.6

In newly industrialized countries, marketers are using all forms of promotion. This contest run by Tropicana, which features a wide array of consumer products as prizes, is an example.

Economic Conditions. One way to think about the economic conditions of a potential international audience is to break the world's markets into three broad classes of economic development: less developed countries, newly industrialized countries, and highly industrialized countries. These categories provide a basic understanding of the economic capability of the average consumer in a market and thus help place consumption in the context of economic realities.

Less developed countries represent nearly 75 percent of the world's population, many of which are plagued by drought, civil war, and economies that lack almost all the resources necessary for development such as capital, infrastructure, political stability, and trained workers. Many of the products sold in these less developed economies are typically not consumer products, but rather business products used for building infrastructure (such as heavy construction equipment) or agricultural equipment.

Newly industrialized countries have economies defined by change; they are places where traditional ways of life that have endured for centuries are changing and modern consumer cultures have emerged in a few short years. This creates a unique set of problems for the outside advertiser trying to hit a moving target or a culture in rapid flux.

Rapid economic growth in countries such as Singapore, Malaysia, and Taiwan has created a new middle class of consumers with radically different expectations than their counterparts of a mere decade ago. Asian consumers are relatively heavy users of media-based information. The latest global trends in fashion, music, and travel have shorter and shorter lag times in reaching this part of the world. Many U.S. firms already have a strong presence in these markets with both their products and their promotions, like the contest being run by Tropicana brand shown in Exhibit 7.6.

The **highly industrialized countries** of the world are the countries with both a high gross domestic product (GDP) and a high per capita income. These countries have also invested heavily over many years in infrastructure—roads, hospitals, airports, power-generating plants, and educational institutions. Within this broad grouping, an audience assessment will focus on more detailed analyses of the market, including the nature and extent of competition, marketing trade channels, lifestyle trends, and market potential. Firms pursuing opportunities in highly industrialized countries proceed with market analysis in much the same way it would be conducted in the United States. While the advertising in these countries will often vary based on unique cultural and lifestyle factors, consumers in these markets are accustomed to seeing a full range of creative appeals and promotions for goods and services. The IMC in Practice box highlights how marketers in foreign countries are accustomed to using a full range of promotional tools when they come to the United States and try to cultivate target markets.

Demographic Characteristics. Information on the demographic characteristics of nations is generally available. Both the U.S. Department of Commerce and the United Nations publish annual studies of population for hundreds of countries. Marketers using promotion must be sensitive to the demographic similarities and differences in international markets. The demographics of a population, including size, age and income distribution, education levels, occupations, literacy rates, and household size, can dramatically affect the type of promotion prepared for a market. For example, those thinking of entering international markets should keep in mind that roughly 20 percent of the world's population, generally residing in the highly industrialized countries, controls 75 percent of the world's wealth and accounts for 75 percent of all consumption.[6]

6.   "The World in 1999," *The Economist,* Winter 1999, 2.

While much has been written about the graying of the U.S. population, other parts of the world do not follow this pattern. In the Middle East, Africa, and Latin America, roughly 40 percent of the population is currently under the age of 25.[7] Increases and decreases in the proportion of the population in specific age groups are closely related to the demand for particular products and services. As populations continue to increase in developing countries, new market opportunities emerge for products and services for young families and teens. The most effective promotional mix for a young population may be very different than the promotional mix that will click with an older population.

IN PRACTICE

BRINGING DISCO BACK HOME

Usually, we think of "international marketing" as U.S. firms trying to sell in foreign markets. But don't forget that U.S. consumers are the most voracious consumers in the world, and every marketer everywhere *in* the world would love to market and promote to American consumers. This is certainly the case for Fiorucci, a Milan-based sportswear company that specializes in disco-style designs.

The company's (re)introduction into the U.S. market was spearheaded by avant-garde retail stores and a multifaceted promotional campaign. The New York store, for example, features a café, tattoo parlor, and special events to keep young shoppers coming in. Media spending on advertising is budgeted at "a couple of million dollars." The true strength of the promotional program, though, is in supportive tactics like wild posters, bus boards, taxi tops, and posters in bus shelters.

Fiorucci hopes that this new approach to the market sticks for good this time. You see, in the early 1980s, Fiorucci was *the* hippest clothing company. When the firm celebrated its fifteenth anniversary at Studio 54 in 1983, Madonna jumped out of the birthday cake. By the early 1990s, management had to be replaced and most U.S. distribution had been cut off. But this time, the brand is steering clear of celebrities and is, instead, developing a Web presence (http://www.fioruccisafetyjeans.com), adding a catalog, and introducing a new line, Elio Fiorucci Collection targeted at women over twenty-five. Now that's a nice set of IMC plans.

Source: Mercedes M. Cardona, "Fiorucci Boogies Back onto Scene," *Advertising Age,* May 31, 1999, 20.

One of the most interesting demographic evolutions is taking place in India. Currently, 47 percent of India's 1 billion population is under twenty years old—160 million of them are teenagers. Not only is this population young, but they are embracing the concepts of capitalism. They find advertising on fifty cable and satellite channels and are technically very savvy. This young group of consumers is open to all forms of promotion from advertising to events and contests.[8] A similarly young population resides throughout Asia and will also be in tune with western-style promotional practices.

Values. **Cultural values** are enduring beliefs about what is important to the members of a culture. They are the defining bedrock of a culture. They are an outgrowth of the culture's history and its collective experience. Even though there are many cultures within any given nation, many believe that there are still enough shared values to constitute a meaningful "national culture,"
like "American culture." Again, India's billion residents are a case in point. The older population idealizes Gandhi-style poverty and socialist theory and grew up amid famines. The younger population—which, recall, is nearly 500 million people under twenty years old—admires capitalism, wants to get rich, and grew up with MTV and food surpluses.[9]

Discovering predominant and evolving cultural values must be considered both within and between cultures. Oriental cultures are very collectivist in their orientation to the world (although they don't particularly like that word). For example, in

7.   Ibid, 17.
8.   Manjeet Kripalani, "India's Youth," *Business Week,* October 11, 1999, 74-78.
9.   Ibid, 78.

Taiwanese, there is no word for "individualism," a concept that is very difficult for Americans to appreciate and understand. More important, the cultural values must be discovered and understood well enough so that advertising messages and promotional tactics are consistent with and respectful of foreign market value systems.

Custom and Ritual. Among other things, **rituals** are acts that perpetuate a culture's connections to its core values. They seem perfectly natural to members of a culture, and they can often be performed without much thought (in some cases, hardly any) regarding their deeper meaning, whereas to consumers outside a culture the acts may seem odd and unexplainable. Many consumer behaviors involve rituals, such as grooming, gift giving, or preparing food. To do a good job in cross-cultural promotion, the rituals of other cultures must be not only appreciated, but also understood. This requires in-depth and extended research efforts. Quick marketing surveys rarely do anything in this context except invite disaster. Often, **ethnographic research,** which employs depth interviewing and extended interaction with consumers in natural settings, is needed to truly understand customs and rituals in a culture. For example, in 1991, General Mills and Nestlé teamed up to introduce General Mills cereals in Europe. It seemed a sure-fire combination: Nestlé had the European name recognition and distribution, General Mills had the cereal production expertise, and the cereal market in Europe was growing at 30 percent per year. The result—nearly a complete flop. Did anyone mention that Europeans don't prefer cold cereals? The breakfast custom and ritual in some parts of Europe features a fairly large breakfast with meat, eggs, various breads, and perhaps some cereal, but it will either be hot or a granola-type cereal often purchased in bulk. Ethnographic research would have caught the distinction where broad survey research did not.

One of the most devastating mistakes a marketer can make is to presume that consumers in one culture have the same rituals as those in another. Religion is an obvious expression of values in a culture. In countries adhering to the precepts of Islam, which includes most Arab countries, traditional religious beliefs restrict several products from being advertised at all, such as alcohol and pork. Other restrictions related to religious and cultural values include not allowing women to appear in advertising and restricting the manner in which children can be portrayed in advertisements. Each market must be evaluated for the extent to which prevalent customs or values translate into product choice and other consumer behaviors. When Taco Bell entered the market in Singapore, they did so in the trendiest nightclub with hip-hop dancers and an MTV-style DJ—but without Giget, the Taco Bell Chihuahua. You see, Singapore has a large Muslim population that does not revere dogs as we do in the United States. To even touch a dog is considered taboo to Muslims.[10]

Understanding values and rituals can represent a special challenge (or opportunity) when economic development in a country or region creates tensions between the old and the new. The classic example is the dilemma that marketers face as more wives leave the home for outside employment, creating tensions in the home about who should do the housework. Most recently, this tension over traditional gender assignments in household chores has been particularly acute in Asia, and marketers there have tried to respond by featuring husbands as homemakers in promotional materials. For example, an ad for vacuum cleaners made by Korea's LG Electronics showed a woman lying on the floor exercising and giving herself a facial with slices of cucumbers, while her husband cleaned around her. The ad received mixed reviews from women in Hong Kong and South Korea, with younger women approving but their mothers disapproving.[11] (Sound familiar?) The advertiser's

10.   Normandy Madden and Andrew Hornery, "As Taco Bell Enters Singapore, Gidget Avoids the Ad Limelight," *Ad Age International,* January 11, 1999, 13.
11.   Louise Lee, "Depicting Men Doing Housework Can Be Risky for Marketers in Asia," *The Wall Street Journal,* August 14, 1998, B6.

CESARE CATINI®

Обувь от Cesare Catini. Эксклюзивный дистрибьютор в Украине «Solo Moda»
Магазин в Киеве: ул. Горького, 10 тел.: +(044) 220-61-67, факс: +(044) 227-51-48

http://www.cesarecatini.com;
http://www.cosmo.women.com/cos/;
http://www.cosmopolitan.ru;
http://www.cosmohispano.com

EXHIBIT 7.7

A decade after the Cold War's thaw, the former Soviet Bloc is now fertile ground for high-fashion sales, as indicated by this Cesare Catini in the Russian-language edition of Cosmopolitan. Cosmo *seems to have gotten to wherever high fashion might be worn and the highly fashionable might be talked about, with several regionally targeted variations: How well do you think such advertising might fare in the land of vodka and potatoes?*

dilemma in situations like these is how to make ads that reflect real changes in a culture, without alienating important segments of consumers by appearing to push the changes. Not an easy task!

Product Use and Preferences. Information about product use and preferences is available for many markets. The major markets of North America, Europe, and the Pacific Rim typically are relatively heavily researched. In recent years, ACNielsen has developed an international database on consumer product use in twenty-six countries. Also, Roper Starch Worldwide has conducted global studies on product preferences, brand loyalty, and price sensitivity in forty different countries. The Roper Starch study revealed that consumers in India were the most brand loyal (34 percent of those surveyed), and that German and Japanese consumers showed the greatest tendency for price sensitivity (over 40 percent of survey consumers in each market).[12] Obviously the Germans and the Japanese are prime targets for sales promotions, whereas Indian consumers may not need an extra incentive to stay loyal to a brand.

Studies by firms such as Nielsen and Roper Starch do not dispute that consumers around the world display vastly different product use characteristics and preferences. One area of great variation is personal-care products. There is no market in the world like the United States, where consumers are preoccupied with the use of personal-care products such as toothpaste, shampoo, deodorant, and mouthwash. Procter & Gamble, maker of brands such as Crest, Pert, Secret, and Scope, among others, learned the hard way in Russia with its Wash & Go shampoo. Wash & Go (comparable to Pert in the United States) was a shampoo and conditioner designed for the consumer who prefers the ease, convenience, and speed of one-step washing and conditioning. Russian consumers, accustomed to washing their hair with bar soap, didn't understand the concept of a hair conditioner, and didn't perceive a need to make shampooing any more convenient. After that misstep, P&G spent over a year researching and testing the introduction of Secret brand deodorant into the German market. The main concern? While stick-type deodorants are the best selling in the United States with 49 percent of the market, only 10.1 percent of Germans use rollons. Rather Germans prefer spray deodorants that can be used by the whole family.[13]

Other examples of unique and culture-specific product uses and preferences come from Brazil and France. In Brazil, many women still wash clothes by hand in

12. Leah Rickard, "Ex-Soviet States Lead the World in Ad Cynicism," *Advertising Age,* May 5, 1995, 3.
13. Dagmar Mussey, "Europe Gets U.S. Secret," *Advertising Age International,* November 1999, 13.

metal tubs, using cold water. Because of this behavior, Unilever must specially formulate its Umo laundry powder and tout its effectiveness under these washing conditions.

Marketers must be astute with respect to the evolving nature of product use and preference. While Russian consumers are still somewhat skeptical of western marketing and promotion, some segments of society have embraced greater style and less function in the products they use. The ad in Exhibit 7.7 appeared in the Russian edition of *Cosmopolitan*. For Russian consumers, this is quite a departure from the days of standing in long lines to get a pair of government-issue modified combat boots.

CHALLENGES IN INTERNATIONAL ADVERTISING

Cross-cultural audience research on basic economic, social, and cultural conditions is an essential starting point for planning international advertising. But even with excellent audience analysis, three formidable and unique challenges face the marketer in using promotional materials: the creative challenge, the media challenge, and the regulatory challenge.

The Creative Challenge in Advertising

Written or spoken language is a basic barrier to cross-cultural communication. The area of promotion most affected by this challenge is advertising. Advertising materials prepared in German are typically difficult for those who speak only Arabic—this much is obvious. We've all heard stories of how some literal translation of an ad said something very different from what was intended. Much like the stories earlier in the chapter, when Sunbeam introduced the Mist-Stick mixer into the German market, the firm ran into a fairly severe language problem. The word "Mist" spelled and pronounced precisely the same way in German means "manure." The word "Stick" translates roughly as "wand." Sunbeam was attempting to introduce a "manure wand" for use in German food preparation.[14]

What is less obvious, however, is the role of picturing in cross-cultural communication. **Picturing** involves communication with visual images rather than words. There is a widely held belief that pictures are less culturally bound than are words, and that pictures can speak to many cultures at once. International advertisers are increasingly using ads that feature few words and rely on pictures to communicate. This is, as you might expect, a bit more complicated than it sounds.

First, picturing is culturally bound. Different cultures use different conventions or rules to create representations (or pictures) of things. Pictures, just like words, must be "read" or interpreted, and the "rules of reading" pictures vary from culture to culture. People living in Western cultures assume that everyone knows what a certain picture means. This is not true and is another example of ethnocentrism. Photographic two-dimensional representations are not even recognizable as pictures to those who have not learned to interpret such representations. Symbolic representations that seem so absolute, common, and harmless in one culture can have varied, unusual, and even threatening meaning in another. A picture may be worth a thousand words, but those words may not mean something appropriate—or they may be entirely unintelligible or tasteless—to those in another culture. Think about the pictures used in the three ads in Exhibit 7.8. Which of these ads seems culture bound? Which would seem to easily cross cultural borders? Why?

---

14. David Ricks, *Big Business Blunders: Mistakes in Multi-National Marketing* (Homewood, IL: Dow Jones-Irwin, 1983), 46.

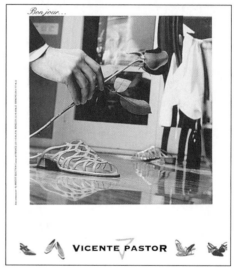

EXHIBIT 7.8

How much are the pictures used in these ads dependent on cultural context for their meaning?

All these ads depend on knowing the way to correctly interpret the picture in the ad, but some require more cultural knowledge than others. For example, if the audience doesn't know the story of the dish that ran away with the spoon, then the Oneida ad in Exhibit 7.8 is probably not as engaging as it otherwise might be. What does giving a rose mean in other cultures? Is a big bare belly going to reflect the same level of status in Germany, India, and Argentina?

A few human expressions, such as a smile, are widely accepted to mean a positive feeling. Such expressions and their representations, even though culturally connected, have widespread commonality. But cultureless picture meanings do not exist. A much larger contributor to cross-cultural commonalities are those representations that are a part of a far-flung culture of commerce and have thus taken on similar meanings in many different nations. With sports playing an ever-larger role in international commerce, the sports hero is often used to symbolize common meaning across cultural boundaries. What do you think? Is Michael Jordan Michael Jordan, no matter what he is selling, or where he is selling it?[15]

15. Roger O. Crockett, "Yikes! Mike Takes a Hike," *Business Week,* January 25, 1999, 74.

Other creative challenges relate to the specific sort of appeal used in a particular market. Humorous ads are highly popular in the United States and the United Kingdom, but German consumers don't respond particularly well to them. Nudity in advertising (Exhibit 7.9) is readily accepted in France, the Netherlands, Italy, and Brazil, but many other societies, including the United States, tend to find the use of nudity in poor taste. The choice of the right creative technique is highly dependent on local market knowledge. A local agency, discussed later in the chapter, can help a marketer with these advertising message strategy decisions.

The Media Challenge in Advertising

Of all the challenges faced by advertisers in international markets, the media challenge may be the greatest. Exhibit 7.10 gives examples of some of the media options for reaching consumers around the world.

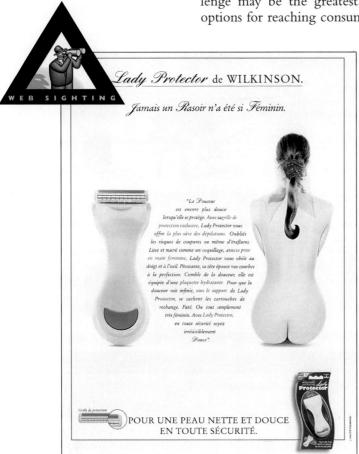

WEB SIGHTING

Lady Protector de WILKINSON.

Jamais un Rasoir n'a été si Féminin.

POUR UNE PEAU NETTE ET DOUCE
EN TOUTE SÉCURITÉ.

http://www.wilkinson-sword.com

EXHIBIT 7.9

It's been said that "all politics is local," but so too is personal hygiene. The U.K.'s Wilkinson might encounter difficulties in selling its Lady Protector, specifically designed for shaving women's leg and underarms, in France, a country where that has generally not been the custom. The company's Web site is admirably multilingual, though, appealing to British, French, and Germans. Might Wilkinson have done better with an "Americanized" Web site as well?

Media Availability and Coverage. Some international markets simply have too few media options, others have too many. In addition, even if diverse media are available in a particular international market, there may be severe restrictions on the type of advertising that can be done or the way in which advertising is organized in a certain medium.

Many countries have dozens of subcultures and language dialects within their borders, each with its own newspapers and radio stations. This complicates the problem of deciding which combination of newspapers or radio stations will achieve the desired coverage of the market. The presence of a particular medium in a country does not necessarily make it useful for advertisers if there are restrictions on accepting advertising. The most prominent example is the BBC networks in the United Kingdom, where advertising is still not accepted. While the United Kingdom does have commercial networks in both radio and television, the BBC stations are still widely popular and viewers of these stations are unreachable with advertising. Or consider the situation with regard to television advertising in Germany and the Netherlands. On the German government-owned stations, television advertising is banned on Sundays and holidays and restricted to four 5-minute blocks on other days. In the Netherlands, television advertising cannot constitute more than 5 percent of total programming time, and most time slots must be purchased nearly a year in advance. Similar circumstances exist in many markets around the world.

Newspapers are actually the most localized medium worldwide, and they require the greatest amount of local market knowledge to be correctly used as an advertising option. In Mexico, for example, advertising space is sold in the form of news columns, without any notice or indication that the "story" is a paid advertisement. This situation influences both the placement and layout of ads. Turkey

Media	Ownership	Circulation or Number of Households
PRINT		
Business Week	The McGraw-Hill Cos.	1.08 million
Computerworld/InfoWorld	IDG	1.9 million
The Economist	The Economist Group	684,416
Elle	Hachette Filipacchi	5.1 million
Elle Deco	Hachette Filipacchi	1.5 million
Financial Times	Pearson PLC	363,525
Forbes Global Business & Finance	Forbes	860,000**
Fortune	Time Warner	915,000
Harvard Business Review	Harvard Business School Publishing	220,000
International Herald Tribune	The New York Times/ The Washington Post Co.	222,930
National Geographic	National Geographic Society	8.8 million
Newsweek Worldwide	The Washington Post Co.	4.2 million
PC World	IDG	3.6 million
Reader's Digest	Reader's Digest Association	26 million
Scientific American	Yerlagsgruppe Hoitzbrinck	562,150
TIME	Time Warner	5.6 million
USA Today International	Gennett Co.	2.2 million† (Mon.–Thurs.) 2.6 million (Friday edition)
The Wall Street Journal	Dow Jones & Co.	4.3 million
TV		
Animal Planet	Discovery Communications/BBC	4.9 million*
BBC World	BBC Worldwide	60 million
Cartoon Network	Time Warner	125.5 million
CNBC	NBC/Dow Jones & Co. (only 100% NBC-owned in U.S.)	136 million**
CNN International	Time Warner	221 million
Discovery Networks International	Discovery Communications	144 million
ESPN	Walt Disney Co./Hearst Corp.	242 million
MTV Networks	Viacom	285 million
TNT	Time Warner	104.2 million

*Includes 45 million homes in the United States
**Excludes Latin America
†For international edition only

Source: *Advertising Age International*, February 8, 1999, 23.

EXHIBIT 7.11

International marketers are finding more media available to reach foreign markets. CNBC offers complete coverage of the European market.

EXHIBIT 7.12

Direct broadcast by satellite allows households around the world to receive television transmission via a small, low-cost dish. This is an ad promoting satellite TV provided by SkyPort to the Asian market.

has more than 350 daily national newspapers; the Netherlands has only three. And, many newspapers (particularly regional papers) are positioned in the market based on a particular political philosophy. Advertisers must be aware of this, making certain that their brand's position with the target audience does not conflict with the politics of the medium.

The best news for advertisers from the standpoint of media availability and coverage is the emergence of several global television networks made possible by satellite technology (see Exhibit 7.11). Viacom bills its combined MTV Networks (MTVN) as the largest TV network in the world, with a capability to reach over 300 million households worldwide.[16] The company not only can provide media access, but also offers expertise in developing special promotions to Generations X, Y, and Z around the world. It has facilitated international campaigns for global brands such as Pepsi, Swatch, Sega, and BMX bikes.[17] The worldwide news network, CNN can be seen in 100 countries and specifically offers newly acquired access to the vast Indian market.[18]

Another development affecting Europe and Asia is direct broadcast by satellite (DBS). Transmissions by DBS are received by households through a small, low-cost receiving dish. Satellite Televisions Asian Region (STAR TV) currently sends BBC and U.S. programming to 17 million Asian households and hotels. Revenues for these pan-regional cable and satellite channels are increasing at over 20 percent per

16. "On-Air Opportunities," *Television Business International,* vol. 49, January 1998, 1.
17. Ibid.
18. Todd Pruzan, "India Will Allow CNN Broadcasts," *Ad Age International,* July 12, 1995, 9.

year.[19] Ultimately, STAR TV could reach 3 billion people, making it the most widely viewed medium in the world. An ad for one of STAR TV's partners in the Asian market is shown in Exhibit 7.12. Additionally, global expansion of the Internet may one day offer marketers economical access to huge new markets. But that day has yet to arrive. It would be inappropriate to presume that the Internet is equally accessible or equally important to consumers in various parts of the world (see Chapter 9).

Media Costs and Pricing. Confounding the media challenge is the issue of media costs and pricing. As discussed earlier, some markets have literally hundreds of media options (recall the 350 Turkish newspapers). Whenever a different medium is chosen, separate payment and placement must be made. Additionally, in many markets, media prices are subject to negotiation—no matter what the official rate cards say. The time needed to negotiate these rates is a tremendous cost in itself.

Global coverage is an expensive proposition. For example, a four-color ad in *Reader's Digest* costs over half a million dollars. If an advertiser wants to have full impact with *Reader's Digest,* then the ad should be prepared in all 20 of the different languages for the international editions—again, generating substantial expense.

Exhibit 7.13 provides a nice summary of advertising expenditures in different media around the world, and documents that ad spending is on the rise just about everywhere. Both ad rates and the demand for ad space are on the increase. In some markets, advertising time and space are in such short supply that, regardless of the published rate, a bidding system is used to escalate the prices. With the seemingly chaotic buying practices in some international markets, media costs are indeed a great challenge in executing cost-effective advertising campaigns.

The Regulatory Challenge in Advertising

The regulatory restrictions on international advertising are many and varied, reflecting diverse cultural values, market by market. The range and specificity of regulation can be

EXHIBIT 7.13

Summary of world advertising expenditures. Figures are in millions of U.S. dollars.

Major Media*	1996	1997	1998	1999	2000
North America	105,569	112,583	118,904	124,898	131,167
Europe	72,923	78,606	83,421	87,700	92,165
Asia/Pacific	61,702	67,226	67,226	70,362	73,996
Latin America	21,051	24,214	26,741	29,614	33,127
Africa/M East	5,281	6,123	6,809	7,570	8,437
Sub Total	**266,525**	**288,751**	**303,100**	**320,143**	**338,891**
Direct Mail					
North America	31,990	33,621	35,303	37,107	38,888
Europe	29,786	31,395	32,996	34,613	36,274
Japan	2,711	2,860	2,969	3,082	3,165
Miscellaneous Media**					
USA	33,369	35,037	36,789	38,592	40,367
Japan	10,052	10,605	11,008	11,426	11,735
Total	**374,434**	**402,269**	**422,165**	**444,962**	**469,320**

*TV, Print, Radio, Cinema, and Outdoor
**Includes point-of-sale/sales promotion expenditure
Source: *Advertising Expenditures Forecast* (Zenith Media, July 1998).

19. Joy Dietrich, "Multichannel Ad Revenues up 23% in '98," *Ad Age International,* June 1999, 21.

aggravatingly complex. Tobacco and liquor advertising are restricted (typically banned from television) in many countries, although several lift their ban on liquor after 9:00 or 10:00 P.M. With respect to advertising to children, Austria, Canada, Germany, and the United States have specific regulations. Other products and topics monitored or restricted throughout the world are drugs (Austria, Switzerland, Germany, Greece, and The Netherlands), gambling (United Kingdom, Italy, and Portugal), and religion (Germany, United Kingdom, and The Netherlands).

This regulatory complexity, if anything, continues to grow. Generally, advertisers must be sensitive to the fact that advertising regulations can, depending on the international market, impose limitations on the following:

- The types of products that can be advertised
- The types of appeals that can be used
- The times during which ads for certain products can appear on television
- Advertising to children
- The use of foreign languages (and talent) in advertisements
- The use of national symbols, such as flags and government seals, in advertisements
- The taxes levied against advertising expenditures

In short, just about every aspect of advertising can be regulated, and every country has its own peculiarities with respect to ad regulation. More examples of the regulatory differences among nations are featured in Exhibit 7.14. An excellent resource for keeping up with regulations around the world is the European Association of Advertising Agencies (EAAA). The EAAA Web site (http://www.eaa.be) has hot links to advertising associations around the world.

CHALLENGES IN INTERNATIONAL SALES PROMOTION, DIRECT MARKETING, AND E-COMMERCE

There are a wide range of challenges to using sales promotion, direct marketing, and e-commerce in foreign markets. But despite these challenges, firms have experienced great success in using a variety of sales promotion tools. Philips Electronics set up barber's chairs and sinks in shopping malls and cinemas in Belgium to introduce a new shaving product called Philishave Cool Skin. The 4,600 trials during the event translated into a 25 percent purchase rate.[20] Pepsi and Visa have used event sponsorships, particularly rock concerts, across Europe to give their brands name recognition. Häagen-Dazs used heavy sampling as a way to crack the tough European market. DaimlerChrysler, BMW, and General Motors are each investing more than $250 million to sponsor teams in the European Grand Prix racing circuit.[21]

In China, where television advertising is still highly regulated by the government owned TV stations, marketers have found that brand placements within Chinese daytime "soaps" work extremely well. In a single episode of the highly popular program *Love Talks,* the female star is shown using Pond's Vaseline Intensive Care Lotion, applying Maybelline lipstick in a cab, and then borrowing a Motorola mobile phone from a handsome stranger. That's one promotion point each for Dutch-Anglo firm Unilever SA, Paris-based L'Oréal, and Motorola of the United States.[22]

Direct marketing also has the potential to be a successful promotional tool in several world markets. In Europe, the other leading region in the world for direct

20.   John Seeley, "Step Right Up for a Shave, Sir!" *Ad Age International,* November 1999, 13.
21.   Oliver Edwards, "Detroit Moves In to Replace Tobacco," *EuroBusiness,* June 1999, 23.
22.   Peter Wonacott, "In Chinese Soaps, It's Lights, Camera, Maybelline Lipstick!" *The Wall Street Journal Europe,* January 26, 2000, 1.

United Kingdom	No television advertising for cigarettes, politics, hypnotists, gambling, religion, or charities. The Independent Broadcasting Authority (IBA) carefully monitors television advertising for "appropriateness." Recently, the major independent television network, ITV, has decided to start running liquor ads. This reverses a long-standing policy.[1]
France	No television advertising for tobacco, alcohol, margarine, or diet products. Tourism outside the country cannot be promoted. Children may be used only in ads for children's products. Supermarket advertising is discouraged (though not illegal) for fear that traditional food shops will suffer.
Germany	There are several volumes of regulation published by the German Advertising Federation (ZAW). Advertising cannot instill fear or promote superstition or discrimination. Children may not be used to promote products. Product claims must be carefully documented. No television advertising for cigarettes, religion, charities, narcotics, or prescription drugs. No advertising of any kind for war-related toys. The German regulatory system can act swiftly and effectively. An advertising campaign (for the Italian clothing firm Benetton) that featured child laborers and an oil-soaked seabird was deemed morally offensive because it exploited "pity for commercial purposes." The ads were immediately banned from print publication.[2]
Italy	Italy is one of the few international markets in which comparative ads are allowed. Testimonial statements must be authenticated. No television advertising for cigarettes, gambling, jewels, furs, clinics, or hospitals.
Sweden	Regulatory constraints in Sweden are hard to pin down. First, the two government-controlled television stations and the three government-controlled radio stations do not accept advertising. The independent media are just starting to evolve within the country, and cable broadcasts are being sent from outside the country. The Swedes do not allow the use of young, attractive models in cigarette advertising.
Brazil	Price advertising is carefully regulated by the Brazilian government. Restrictions on television advertising include no advertising for alcohol, cigarettes, or cigars until after 9 P.M. Nudity in Brazilian ads is unregulated. The Brazilian government is committed to economic growth, and the new, more stable currency is causing tremendous change in the consumption culture. While there are good markets for many U.S. goods, Brazilians frown on ads made by U.S. agencies.
Australia	Restrictions on Australian advertising are fairly basic, with one major exception—the Australian government has mandated that 80 percent of all advertising running in Australia must be created by Australian companies. Deception is subject to regulation. Cigarettes are banned from television advertising.
Japan	For a country of strict rules and regulations, there is much flexibility in the interpretation of advertising regulation—with the exception of comparison and hard-sell advertising. As long as good taste prevails, nudity is permitted. There are no laws governing the use of a product by a spokesperson. The one area of high scrutiny is exaggeration of claims.
China	As we have seen recently with copyright infringement and intellectual property disputes, the regulatory system for commercial transactions in China is still in a state of infancy. The "regulation" of advertising has much more to do with understanding traditions and complying with standard business practice. For example, many media organizations will discriminate against advertisers who use an agency, in an attempt to circumvent agency commissions. Some have been known to refuse to execute a media plan submitted by an agency. Specific restrictions are placed on comparative ads and "slanderous propaganda."

1. Laurel Wentz, "UK TV to Accept Liquor Ads," *Advertising Age*, June 5, 1995, 8.
2. Brandon Mitchener, "German Court Rules against Benetton," *International Herald Tribune*, July 7, 1995, 13.

EXHIBIT 7.14

Sample advertising regulations around the world. To get current information on regulations around the world, visit the European Association of Advertising Agencies Web site at http://www.eaaa.be, *which has hot links to ad associations around the world.*

marketing activities next to the United States, programs are running behind developments in the United States, although the gap is rapidly closing. The world's second-largest direct-marketing market is the United Kingdom, where 90 percent of the industry's annual sales of $6.1 billion is generated by just five big companies. These companies, which started after World War I to sell to the working class on credit, still cater to lower-income households. This has created a vast market of upscale consumers left untapped for marketers to target. British firms should realize great success since the current global trend is to target affluent consumers with direct-marketing promotions. Japan has the technological and cultural prerequisites to evolve into a key market for direct marketing, but their long tradition of distribution via multilayered channels still dominates the market. Acceptance of direct marketing in Japan is coming about slowly, as young consumers shed their loyalty to the traditional department store retail structure in Japan and order products such as casual-wear clothing through direct-marketing channels like catalogs.

Within many developed-country markets, there is a trend for fast-moving consumer goods companies to move more of their promotional budget out of advertising to other activities such as public relations and direct marketing. In France, Nestlé has successfully launched Le Relais bébé, rest-stop structures along the highways where French families on vacation can stop to feed their babies and change their diapers. Each summer, 64 hostesses welcome 120,000 baby visits, and dispense 600,000 samples of baby food and free disposable diapers. Creating a database from the visitors that notes the date of the baby's birth allows Nestlé to send messages over time that track the development and growth of the baby, offering information and product advice to parents. They even send a Mother's Day mailing, "signed" from baby to Mama. As a result, Nestlé's share of the market has increased by 24 percent over the past years, in spite of being outspent seven-to-one in advertising by the market leader Blédina.[23]

E-commerce is evolving and developing so rapidly that generalizations are hard to come by, but here are a few current observations from around the world. Marketers in Brazil are finding that e-commerce selling is highly successful in a market characterized by busy two-breadwinner households and a relatively unprofessional retailing environment.[24] Commerce commissioners in Europe are feeling the pressure to catch up with the United States and are discussing ways the Internet infrastructure can be bolstered to support more e-commerce.[25] But in Mexico, the attitude toward the Internet and e-commerce is less than enthusiastic. When the head of Infosel, the Mexican subsidiary of the Spanish Internet company Terra Networks, made his Internet pitch to a group of equity brokers in Mexico City, the response was less than enthusiastic. Although they noted the robust growth of the Internet in the United States, the brokers commented that "the U.S. is different. Not in Mexico."[26]

As in the United States, sales promotions, direct marketing, and the Internet are appealing to consumers around the world, but not uniformly and not universally. The issues related to using sales promotion, direct marketing, and e-commerce in international markets focus on characteristics of the product being promoted, level of economic development, structure of the trade channel, and regulations.

23.   "Nestlé Banks on Databases," *Advertising Age,* October 25. 1993, 16.

24.   Dana James and Kathleen V. Schmidt, "Brazil Net: Growing Demand Tempered by Privacy Regulations," *Marketing News,* September 27, 1999, 40–41.

25.   Deborah Hargreaves, "Brussels Sets Urgent Agenda to Pass E-Commerce Laws," *Financial Times–London,* January 27, 2000, 1.

26.   Andrea Petersen, "Terra Networks' Man In Mexico Finds the Net a Tough Sell," *The Wall Street Journal Europe,* January 25, 2000, 1.

CAREERPROFILE

Name:	*Abby Leibel*
Title:	*National Coordinator*
Organization:	*Association for Marketing Communications in Israel, a division of Coast 2 Coast Communications, Ra'Anana, Israel, http://www.amci.co.il*
Education:	*B.A., Social Studies*

Not many recent college graduates get to influence the development of marketing communications in another country. Abby Leibel, an American who graduated from the University of Maryland, is doing just that. She is the National Coordinator of the Association for Marketing Communications in Israel (AMCI), a professional organization for Israeli marketing communications practitioners.

"The idea is to give members of the association the opportunity to stay as up-to-date and competitive in their field as possible," explains Abby. "My job is to make the Association bigger, better and better known." To help accomplish this goal, she writes and edits the monthly AMCI newsletter, *MarCom Matters*, as well as a monthly column about marketing communications for the Jerusalem Post (visit http://www.virtualjerusalem.com to read some of her articles). Abby is also in charge of the AMCI Web site and scheduling and promoting AMCI meetings and educational workshops.

Although Hebrew is the official language of Israel, Abby says most of AMCI's communications activities and programs are conducted in English because 90 percent of members are native-English speakers. A large percentage are also Americans. She says English is also the language of choice for many marketing communications programs developed by Israeli companies. "Marketing communications is the eye to the 'outside world' for Israeli companies and most of the outside world understands English," explains Abby.

Abby reports that many AMCI members tell her that marketing communications is still in its infancy in Israel. "Many members say that the field seems to be underrecognized and underappreciated by their companies," she explains.

Abby is proud to be part of an organization helping to improve the image of marketing communications in Israel. "I never imagined that at the age of 25 I would be given an entire association to mold and create and grow with. It's an amazing opportunity and very exciting."

To learn more about international marketing communications, visit these Web sites:

International Advertising Association
http://www.iaaglobal.org

Technology and International Marketing Communications
http://www.atalink.co.uk/iaa2000/html/welcome.html

Characteristics of the Product

Product prevalence and use key determinants are of the potential for different promotions in world markets. A product category may be firmly entrenched and widely known in one market but virtually unknown in another. The story earlier of General Mills and Nestlé attempting to introduce American-style cold cereals into the European market is an example. Another example is luxury cars. While most countries in the world have discovered luxury cars, they are only now being introduced into the Chinese market.[27] When a product category is new to a market, broad-based awareness needs to be created and many different sales promotion tools can be effective in this regard. In addition, heavy trade promotions may be necessary to convince distributors and retailers to carry the product category.

Second, as the competitive environment becomes more complex, advertising designed to differentiate brands will become more predominant. Products moving into the growth stage of the product life cycle will need to be differentiated and positioned, and that is primarily the role of advertising. But as products become mature in markets, various promotions will manifest themselves again. Promotions that encourage brand switching, typically couponing or sampling, will become valuable. Conversely, promotions that encourage brand loyalty like event sponsorships or in-package coupons will be necessary to try to prevent brand-switching behavior.

Level of Economic Development

As discussed earlier, level of economic development is a basic consideration in understanding the nature of a market. This factor influences the use of sales promotions as well. In the highly industrialized markets discussed earlier, all forms of promotion and direct marketing are available to marketers and hold promise for successful communication. But in less developed countries or newly industrialized markets, some promotions may be inappropriate or simply not possible.

In less developed countries, the sheer lack of a wide range of consumer goods and the low income levels make promotions pretty much a

27. Normandy Madden, "GM's Buick Rides Luxury into China," *Advertising Age*, June 21, 1999, 16.

nonissue. People can barely afford the staples in life. Few competitors serve these markets, and "brand battles" that typically rely heavily on promotions are just not happening. In addition, low literacy levels in many less developed countries make communicating difficult with print media, which is how many promotions—for example, coupons—are distributed. The other problem in less developed countries is the low penetration of most media vehicles. Without television, radio, and newspaper, direct marketing is undermined. In addition, an unsophisticated mail system makes shipping of products promoted though direct marketing inefficient and prone to high loss rates.

Newly industrialized markets provide a much better environment for promotional tools, but each market must be managed carefully. As consumer incomes rise, more consumer goods are introduced and succeed. As media proliferate, sales promotions and direct-marketing efforts can be introduced based on a market-by-market assessment.

Structure of the Trade Channels

Markets vary with respect to the extent and sophistication of trade channels. In highly developed distribution and retailing systems, marketers will find that trade channel members will demand support for carrying the marketers brand. Much like the situation in the United States, trade allowances, incentives, point-of-purchase displays, and sampling may be expected (or demanded) by trade channel members. In addition, the highly developed trade channel structure will have the means to handle coupon redemption or premium distributions.

In less developed trade channels, marketers may not be able to use traditional promotional techniques. The trade channels in many countries are fragmented without dominant retailers that have distribution across many markets. This fragmentation makes implementation and coordination of campaigns difficult, if not impossible. These retailers have no mechanism (and very little interest, actually) in handling coupons. In addition, shops in countries like China and India are so small that there is no room to accommodate P–O–P materials or end-of-aisle displays. But the innovative user of promotional tools can have great success in less developed markets. Power House Health Club in South Delhi used small stickers and tent cards placed around town to attract 200 new members to the club—all on a $330 budget.

One of the most important promotional tools for the trade channel throughout the world is the trade show. Huge trade shows, or trade fairs as they are sometimes called outside the United States, offer marketers the chance to contact hundreds of potential customers in a short period of time. For example, the Frankfurter Buch Messe (Frankfurt Book Fair) is the largest book fair in the world and has been held every October for the last fifty years. Every important publisher in the world attends the five-day event. Often the trade show allows the use of other promotional tools like brochures, premiums, and contests—all designed to create awareness and a positive attitude toward a brand.

Regulations

As with advertising, the regulation of promotion, direct marketing, and e-commerce varies widely from market to market. Most sales promotion tools, like premiums, free products, mail-in offers, cents-off coupons, and multipack offers, are legal across Europe, except in Germany where each of these promotions is illegal. In fact, the only fully permitted promotion in Germany is an in-store demonstration. Sweepstakes are either banned or heavily regulated in all European markets. In Japan, the value of a premium offered with a product is limited to 10 percent of the value of the original product.

In China, the government suddenly passed legislation banning all forms or direct selling. Marketers like Avon, Amway, and Mary Kay were caught off guard since they had been doing business in China using the "party method" of marketing and distribution for years. But some firms had set up pyramid schemes, and the government reacted by enacting a sweeping ban on all forms of direct sales.[28] The Chinese government is also very anxious about the security of the Internet. Because of recent activities on the Internet of radical political groups, new rules have just been published making Internet companies responsible for policing their own content. Many observers feel that the new rules will dampen the development of e-commerce in the country.[29]

In Brazil and Europe, the governments are drafting legislation to protect the privacy of citizens using the Internet. The legislation is designed to require Internet firms to inform individuals about the type of information it collects, how it is collected, the information's purpose, and the types of organizations to which the information could be disclosed—all of which could put a damper on the development of direct marketing and e-commerce strategies in the countries affected.[30]

The examples discussed here are obviously not meant to provide an exhaustive list of regulations affecting the use of sales promotions or direct marketing in foreign markets, but rather signal an alert that such regulations are varied and extensive. Using promotions and direct marketing in foreign markets requires careful evaluation before implementation.

CHALLENGES IN INTERNATIONAL PUBLIC RELATIONS

Exxon's Valdez oil spill, or Union Carbide's tragic accident at its plant in Bhopal, India, create situations that affect a company's image worldwide. Negative publicity is not just limited to companies. The Sicilian Wine Growers Association produces some excellent red and white wines, yet has problems in distributing the wines or gaining consumer acceptance because of the negative publicity stemming from the mafia's presence on the island. Usually, companies have less control over global publicity relative to domestic situations, and no corporations are powerful enough to control a host country's media.

Such was the case with Coca-Cola's runaway public relations problem in Belgium. Several hundred school children in Belgium became ill after drinking Coke products in the summer of 1999. The story hit the press like a ton of bricks, and Coke found that its flagship global brand was not only being shunned in Belgium—shopkeepers literally threw away thousand of bottles of Coke—but merchants in the rest of Europe were refusing to sell Coke. So Coke had to go on the offensive, launching a widespread public relations campaign to try to get customers back that included giving away free bottles of Coke and distributing coupons all across Europe for discounts on Coke products.[31]

At best, attempts are made to provide positive information about the company that is directed at influential targets such as members of the broadcasting media, editors, or journalists. For example, to reduce the trend of "Japan bashing" in the early 1990s in the United States, Japanese corporations have made use of PR firms who assist in developing positive publicity regarding the companies' philanthropic activities in America.

28. Normandy Madden, "China's Direct Sales Ban Stymies Marketers," *Advertising Age,* May 18, 1998, 56.
29. James Kynge, "China Cracks Down on Burgeoning Internet Use," *Financial Times–London,* January 27, 2000, 20.
30. James and Schmidt, "Brazil Net," 40.
31. William Echikson, "Have a Coke and a Smile—Please," *Business Week,* August 16, 1999, 18.

PROMOTION AGENCIES AROUND THE WORLD

An experienced and astute agency can help a marketer deal with the challenge of conceiving and executing the proper promotional campaign in foreign markets. In Brazil, using a local agency is essential to get the creative style and tone just right. In Australia, Australian nationals must be involved in certain parts of the production process. And in China, trying to work through the government and media bureaucracy is nearly impossible without the assistance of a local agency.

Marketers in the United States have three basic alternatives in choosing an agency to help them prepare and place promotion in other countries: They can use a global agency, an international affiliate, or a local agency.

The Global Agency

The consolidation and mergers taking place in the promotion industry are creating more and more **global agencies,** or worldwide agencies. Most of these global organizations continue to show healthy revenue growth, as marketers attempt to extend their reach to consumers worldwide. As you might expect, New York, London, Tokyo, Chicago, and Paris have become the promotion capitals of the world.

The great advantage of a global agency is that it will know the marketer's products and current promotion programs (presuming it handles the domestic promotion duties). With this knowledge, the agency can either adapt domestic campaigns for international markets or launch entirely new campaigns. This is a tremendous advantage from the standpoint of creating integrated marketing communications on a global basis. Another advantage is the geographic proximity of the advertiser to the agency headquarters, which can often facilitate planning and preparation of ads. The size of a global agency can be a benefit in terms of economies of scale and political leverage.

Their greatest disadvantage stems from their distance from the local culture. Exporting meaning is never easy. This is no small disadvantage to agencies that actually believe they can do this. Most, however, are not that naive or arrogant (some are), and they have procedures for acquiring local knowledge.

The International Affiliate

Many agencies do not own and operate worldwide offices, but rather have established foreign-market **international affiliates** to handle clients' international promotion needs. Often, U.S. agencies will set up joint ventures with local agencies as a way to effectively serve clients, as the Global Issues box discusses. Many times these agencies join a network of foreign agencies or take minority ownership positions in several foreign agencies. The benefit of this arrangement is that the marketer typically has access to a large number of international agencies that can provide local market expertise. These international agencies are usually well established and managed by foreign nationals, which gives a local presence in the international market, while avoiding any resistance to foreign ownership. This was the reasoning behind Coca-Cola's decision to give local creative responsibility for advertising its Coke Classic brand in Europe to the French agency Publicis SA.[32] Although Coke Classic is a global brand, Coke felt that the French agency was better suited to adapt U.S. ad campaigns to the European market.

The risk of these arrangements is that while an international affiliate will know the local market, it may be less knowledgeable about the marketer's brands and competitive strategy worldwide. The threat is that the real value and relevance of a brand will not be incorporated into the foreign campaign and that promotions from

---

32. Daniel Tilles, "Publicist Gets a Sip of Coke Account," *International Herald Tribune,* July 7, 1995, 13.

market to market will not be managed in true integrated marketing communications style. But in a break with traditional wisdom, Pepsi has chosen an international affiliate, CLM/BBDO, to create an international campaign aimed at teenagers around the world.[33] Up to that point, Pepsi's main global agency, BBDO Worldwide in New York, had centrally prepared all the brand's global campaigns to insure the IMC effect of the campaigns.

GLOBAL ISSUES

GOOD EEEEEEEVENING VIETNAM!!

After nearly a decade of lobbying by international ad agencies, a proposal to allow Saatchi & Saatchi to create the first foreign-backed advertising agency joint venture in Vietnam has won the support of three Vietnamese ministries. The government is under great pressure to stimulate the country's crisis-ridden economy. Direct foreign investment is down nearly 50 percent from the mid-1990s, and Vietnam's ministries of planning and investment, culture, and information and trade are all recommending that the government approve changes in advertising laws that would allow such a partnership.

Currently in Vietnam, advertising agencies can only operate what are referred to as "representative offices" rather than a complete agency. With the joint venture, agencies will have greater powers to cultivate customers and place ads in local media. The international agencies are cautiously optimistic. But the reaction of local ad agencies has not been favorable. They argue that politicians and foreign agencies bend or flout laws and avoid dealing with local suppliers. And they claim they keep local hires from maturing rapidly by failing to teach management skills and give them technology training. As one U.S. agency representative said, however, "the move to joint ventures has still got to get full government approval," so don't look for that Robin Williams salutation just yet.

Source: Harry Knowles, "Vietnam Nears Approval of Int'l Agency Ventures," *Advertising Age International,* September 1999, 13.

The Local Agency

The final option is for a firm to choose a **local agency** in every foreign market where promotion will be carried out. Local agencies have the same advantages as the affiliate agencies just discussed: They will be knowledgeable about the culture and local market conditions. Such agencies tend to have well-established contacts for market information, production, and media buys. But the advertiser that chooses this option is open to administrative problems. There is less tendency for standardization of the creative effort; each agency in each market will feel compelled to provide a unique creative execution. This lack of standardization can be expensive and potentially disastrous for brand imagery when the local agency seeks to make its own creative statement without a good working knowledge of a brand's heritage.[34] Of course, this means that the threat of lack of integrated communications is even greater as each agency tries to make its mark. Finally, working with local agencies can create internal communication problems because of a lack of physical proximity, which increases the risk of delays and errors in execution.

STANDARDIZED VERSUS CUSTOMIZED PROMOTIONAL CAMPAIGNS ❹

Marketers must determine the extent to which a campaign will be standardized across international markets versus customized for individual markets. **Standardized campaigns** (also referred to as globalized campaigns) use the same appeal and creative execution across all (or most) international markets. The French ad for

---

33. Laurel Wentz and Joy Dietrich, "Pepsi Breaks First International Campaign Created Outside the U.S.," *Ad Age International,* March 8, 1999, 12.
34. Leon E. Wynter, "Global Marketers Learn to Say No to Bad Ads," *The Wall Street Journal,* April 1, 1998, B1.

EXHIBIT 7.15

This ad for French spring water Evian is a global ad because it can run virtually unchanged all over the world. Why is that?

Evian spring water in Exhibit 7.15 can run around the world essentially unchanged. By contrast, **customized campaigns** (also referred to as localized campaigns) involve preparing creative executions for each market a firm has entered.

Those who favor the standardized campaign assume that similarities as well as differences between markets should be taken into account. They argue that standardization of messages and promotion materials should occur whenever possible, adapting the message only when absolutely necessary. For example, Mars's U.S. advertisements for Pedigree dog food have used golden retrievers, while poodles were deemed more effective for the brand's positioning and image in Asia. Otherwise, the advertising campaigns were identical in terms of basic message appeal.[35] Overall, a brand and its international marketing situation are well suited for a standardized approach when:

- Communication about the brand can occur using primarily or exclusively a visual appeal, thus avoiding the problem of multiple language translations. The Evian ad in Exhibit 7.15 does precisely this.
- Communication about a brand relies on such "culture-less," universal appeals as power, health, sex or, wealth.
- Brands that are in high-technology product categories where the product use and value is standardized across cultures.
- Products have a global reputation based on country of origin like French champagne, German automobiles, or Swiss watches.

Those who argue for the customized approach see each country or region as a unique communication context, and they claim that the only way to achieve promotional success is to develop separate campaigns for each market.

The two fundamental arguments for standardized campaigns are based on potential cost savings and creative advantages. Just as organizations seek to gain economies of scale in production, they also look for opportunities to streamline the communication effort. Having one standard theme to communicate allows a company to focus on a uniform brand image and promotional strategy worldwide, develop promotional materials more quickly, and make maximum use of good ideas. Thus, while Gillette sells hundreds of different products in more than 200 countries around the world, its corporate philosophy of standardization is expressed in the "Gillette—the Best a Man Can Get" theme. This theme is attached to all ads and promotional materials, like coupons or premiums for men's toiletry products, wherever they are sold.[36]

35. Zachary Schiller and Rischar A. Melcher, "Marketing Globally, Thinking Locally," *International Business Week,* May 13, 1991, 23.
36. Mark Maremont, "Gillette Finally Reveals Its Vision of the Future, and It Has 3 Blades," *The Wall Street Journal,* April 14, 1998, A1.

EXHIBIT 7.16

This British ad demonstrates that demographic and social trends—two breadwinner households and fewer kids—are spreading worldwide. This ad could easily be run in the U.S. market and communicate quite effectively.

The Environment for Standardized Promotion

In recent years, several aspects of the global marketplace have changed in such a way that the conditions for standardized campaigns are more favorable. Specifically, the conditions fostering the use of such campaigns are:[37]

- *Global communications media.* Worldwide cable and satellite networks have resulted in television becoming a truly global communications medium. The 200 European advertisers on MTV almost all run English-language-only campaigns in the station's 28-nation broadcast area. These standardized messages will themselves serve to homogenize the viewers within these market areas. Beyond traditional media, the global communications afforded by the Internet also allows for globalized campaigns that can be customized, as Reebok International's e-commerce strategy demonstrates in the New Media box.

- *The global teenager.* It is argued that global communications, global travel, and the demise of communism have created common norms and values among teenagers around the world. One advertising agency videotaped the rooms of teenagers from twenty-five countries, and it was hard to tell whether the room belonged to an American, German, or Japanese teen. The rooms had soccer balls, Levi jeans, NBA jackets, and Sega video games.[38] In response to such similarity, Swatch has created a worldwide campaign aimed at teenagers that uses the same image in all international markets and merely changes the copy in print ads to adapt to language differences.

- *Universal demographic and lifestyle trends.* Demographic and lifestyle trends that emerged in the 1980s in the United States are manifesting themselves in markets around the world. More working women, more single-person households, increasing divorce rates, and fewer children per household are now widespread demographic phenomena that are affecting lifestyles. Look at the British ad in Exhibit 7.16. It reflects the same lifestyle values we hold in the United States.

- *The Americanization of consumption values.* Perhaps of greatest advantage to U.S. advertisers is the Americanization of consumption values around the world. American icons are gaining popularity worldwide, especially due to the exportation of pop culture fueled by the U.S. entertainment industry. This trend has become so pervasive that some countries are seeking ways to shield themselves from U.S. entertainment exports. A recent meeting of culture ministers from nineteen nations, including Canada, Britain, Mexico, and Sweden, discussed proposals for exempting cultural "products" from international free-trade pacts. The ultimate target of this discussion by these czars of local culture was undeniably "Made in the USA" entertainment products.[39]

37. This list was adapted from Henry Assael, *Consumer Behavior and Marketing,* 5th ed., (Cincinnati, OH: South-Western College Publishing, 1995), 491–494.
38. Shawn Tully, "Teens: The Most Global Market of Them All," *Fortune,* May 16, 1994, 90.
39. Terry Teachout, "Cultural Protectionism," *The Wall Street Journal,* July 10, 1998, 11.

http://www.yokohamatire.com

EXHIBIT 7.17

Using standardized campaigns for global brands is difficult. This Italian Yokohama ad may suit Italian sensibilities, but how will it play in Peoria? Many American tire ads stress safety (for example, the ad showing a baby securely nestled in a solid, sensible tire), and performance in adverse weather, not a torrid romance with the road. Might this be a consequence of differences in who buys tires? When both mom and dad drive (and take for service) their own cars, the whole of the family's considerations come into play.

All these forces are creating an environment where a common message across national boundaries becomes more possible. To the extent that consumers in various countries hold the same interests and values, standardized images and themes can be effective in advertising.

Finally, global marketers need to distinguish between strategy and execution when using a standardized approach to promotion. The basic need identified may well be universal, but style of communication about the product or service may be strongly influenced by cultural values in different markets and may work either for or against standardization. For another example, take a look at Exhibit 7.17. What do you think of this Italian ad for Yokohama tires? Would it play in Peoria? But what about the Spanish ad for Telefonica in Exhibit 7.18? Does it seem to be more culturally universal?

THE CHALLENGES IN DEVELOPING AND MANAGING A GLOBAL SALES FORCE

Earlier in the chapter, we talked about the need to recognize and minimize one's self-reference criteria and consider local cultural and market conditions in creating promotional communications. No place is this more true than in personal selling. As the world becomes more interdependent, and as companies become more

THIRD IN SALES BUT FIRST IN E-COMMERCE

Even though Nike and adidas-Salomon have more worldwide sales, Reebok International leads the race for getting customers through global e-commerce. By developing dedicated microsites for thirty-six countries within the main corporate site (http://www.reebok.com), Reebok is reaching a global customer base in a way that is unrivaled by its wealthy competitors.

Through these subsites, "local" customers can purchase Reebok shoes, clothes, and equipment using five new dedicated e-commerce services formed around activities. These services represent buying "communities" where buyers share an interest not just in athletic gear, but also in an athletic lifestyle. In the words of Roger Wood, Reebok's VP of global e-commerce and direct marketing, "We're looking for communities by activity, not just by country. The idea is to cater to that constituency within the culture of the country."

The thirty-six cyber store countries, including the United States, were chosen from the seventy markets where Reebok has direct-marketing operations including mail-order services. The main criterion for choosing these markets for e-commerce was that each has relatively well-developed Internet services and fast growth in households being wired. The e-commerce program is being managed from five regional centers in Amsterdam, Hong Kong, New York, Boston, and New Delhi. And in true integrated "international" marketing communications style, each Reebok microsite will have a common look and feel but will feature the favorite national sport of a country—cricket in India, rugby in the United Kingdom, and baseball in the United States.

Source: Juliana Koranteng, "Reebok Takes the Early Lead in E-commerce Competition," November 1999, *Ad Age International*, 3.

dependent on foreign earnings, there is a growing concern within many companies for developing cultural awareness in all aspects of their operations. More and more, annual reports from multinational corporations are mentioning their firm's cultural diversity as a "soft resource" they intend to develop and use as a strategic weapon to create long-term and sustainable competitive advantages. While this new sense of awareness should take place at all levels within the organization, it is perhaps most critically needed during the ongoing processes of interaction between a company and its clients—that is, during the personal selling process. The activities involved in developing and then managing a global sales force bring a new set of complex challenges to international managers managing the promotional mix.

Developing a Global Sales Force

There are two fundamental approaches used in establishing a sales force in international markets. The first approach involves the use of someone else's sales representatives—such as import firms, or wholesalers operating in a region or country. For many small and medium-sized companies with a limited product line, this arrangement is the most feasible. The firm gets a sales force, but doesn't employ or control the salespeople.

An alternative strategy, which is more common among larger multinationals, is to service foreign markets with sales personnel from other company operations. For example, many British textbook publishers send sales representatives to the European continent for sales calls that last from one to three weeks. Once sales reach a certain volume in a new market, the decision may be made to set up a sales office in a particular country to serve that market.

Regardless of which approach a company uses to establish their own sales force, they will have to make some decisions regarding the selection of personnel. Personnel for sales forces in global markets can be comprised of expatriates, local nationals, or third-country nationals. Each nationality type brings its own set of potential advantages and problems to international selling.

Expatriate Personnel. An **expatriate** is an employee working in a country other than his or her home country, such as a Dutch citizen working for Unilever in Chile. A firm might make use of an expatriate with proven managerial talents to

Lazos de unión.

En Telefónica llevamos años trabajando

para ofrecer mejores comunicaciones.

Nuevas tecnologías. Mayores recursos.

Años de esfuerzo dedicados a una sola cosa.

Que hoy y siempre, puedas estar mejor

comunicado. Todo esto es lo que nos une a ti.

Telefónica

EXHIBIT 7.18

Do you think this ad for the telephone company in Spain would do better than the Yokohama ad in Exhibit 7.17 as a globalized campaign? Why or why not?

establish a new local operation and to hire and train a local sales force. For some types of projects, technical expertise may be critical to the sales effort, and an expatriate may be the person best suited for the project. For example, when the German computer company Siemens Nixdorf sold a computerized system to run all aspects of Singapore's new "Dragon World Park" theme park, the sales effort involved technically trained German sales personnel working closely with Chinese construction workers and technicians.[40]

For American companies in particular, the use of expatriates has been a traditional practice. Expatriates with years of proven sales talent may be especially useful in the start-up phase of establishing and training local sales personnel, but they typically do not have the deep understanding of local culture required for effectively communicating in the local market. In fact, these cultural aspects present subtle but potentially damaging challenges in global sales. For example, who among us is fully aware that in some countries, leaving something on your dinner plate is a way to show your appreciation of a meal? Or that direct eye contact in some countries is considered confrontational and challenging? Or that even placing a hand on a foreign client's shoulder would be considered a totally unacceptable invasion of private, personal space?[41] These are all elements of the communications environment that expatriates struggle with.

Local Nationals. Local nationals are sales employees based in their home country. A Thai who sells Honda automobiles in Thailand is a local national salesperson. The trend recently has been toward using local nationals in global business, in particular for personal selling. Understanding the cultural and social norms of a country with respect to selling is key to the process of selecting effective salespeople in global markets. In countries with rich ethnic compositions like Brazil, Malaysia, or Indonesia, or in regions with highly proscribed social norms of behavior like the Middle East, the hiring of local nationals to manage the sales operation is more likely to be necessary than in countries where selling practices share a highly similar cultural context with the home country. Large differences in languages (and acceptable dialects!), social customs and the scope of personal influence, as well as government regulations will sometimes dictate the wisdom of local hiring. Simply put, local nationals bring a superior understanding of local market conditions. Their ability to work within its cultural and social norms while pursuing the company's sales objectives very often makes them the most effective and economically efficient choice.

Third-Country Nationals. Third-country nationals are usually employees who are citizens of one country, employed by a corporation from a second country, and working for that corporation in a third country. A German manager who supervises the retail sales operations of the Anglo-Dutch Shell Oil Company in

---

40.   Siemens Nixdorf I.T. World News, *The Economist,* February 22, 1992, 58.
41.   Erika Rasmusson, "International Intelligence," *Sales and Marketing Management,* September 1999, 144.

South Africa is a third-country national. The distinct features of these managers has more to do with their ability to operate easily and effectively in a variety of situations than with the combination of nationality, employer, and work location that go into the definition of a third-country national. The increase in global trade has led to an increase in the demand for cosmopolitan-minded managers with a broader worldview. Typically, managers of this type are at the upper-middle management level or higher. They are managers with a highly developed sense of cultural empathy for both their company's clients and employees. They are managers who are often fluent or comfortable with three or four languages, and who have advanced training in either technical or management studies. They are also well versed in the cultural subtleties of communication and can manage a sales presentation in complex situations.

Managing the Global Sales Force

The tasks involved in managing a sales force in the global context are not fundamentally different in scope from the management tasks in the domestic setting. What does change from managing a sales force domestically is the nature of the activities within a task area. Below are discussions of the differences for two areas where the most significant differences exist: training and motivation/compensation programs.

Training. The process and nature of a training program for global sales personnel will depend in large part on whether the training is intended for expatriates or foreign personnel. Expatriate training will mostly focus on the customs and special conditions of acculturation and selling that will be encountered in their new assignment. Foreign national personnel training will place more emphasis on the company and its products, selling methods, and procedures. In short, training for expatriates is intended to familiarize personnel with the country culture where they will be working so that communication can be effective and appropriate. This orientation may range from following video lectures and taking language classes, having the employee and his or her family visit the country for a few weeks, or receiving training to enhance one's awareness of their self-reference criteria and increase sensitivities to the culture where they will be working.

Training for foreign personnel tends to focus on the corporate or internal culture with which the salesperson will interact on a regular basis. Apart from the basics relating to selling the company's brands and teaching them company procedures, the real value in training programs for foreign personnel is to cultivate within that group a sense of identification with the company. Just as expatriates are captives of their own habits and patterns of behavior when moving abroad, foreign personnel live and work in their own local environment, where their local habits and customs are continually reinforced. Regular training and social contacts between foreign markets and the home office may be important simply because of the lack of routine contact with the parent company and its marketing personnel.

Motivation and Compensation. Just as sales personnel need to take their clients' norms and cultural values into account in the design and execution of communications, companies must likewise consider culture in the design and execution of programs for compensating and motivating their global sales force. Developing an equitable and functional compensation plan that motivates a sales force is difficult enough in a domestic market situation. It becomes even more of a challenge when the company operates in a number of countries, when individuals work in a number of countries, and when the sales force is comprised of expatriate and foreign national personnel who have regular contact with each other.

A common guideline in developing a package of compensation is to examine carefully the way firms operating in other markets are compensating people. What is relevant here in the United States may be far from appropriate in foreign markets. Notice that the key word in the discussion is *package* of compensation. In high tax-rate countries, sales personnel press for packages that include more liberal expense accounts and fringe benefits that are nontaxable, instead of direct income and financial bonuses tied to performance which are also subject to high taxes. Cost-of-living allowances, private school tuition for school-age dependents, home-leave travel for a manager, and contributions to domestic benefits plans or retirement programs can all be part of the expatriate's compensation package, which can increase total expenses 200 to 300 percent of the base salary. These costs, coupled with the strong belief that local nationals can more effectively operate in a local sales environment, largely explains the trend for hiring locals.

Personal selling is hard, competitive work regardless of the cultural setting in which it takes place. International sales managers work hard, travel extensively, and deal with a wide variety of day-to-day challenges. All these activities require support from the home office and a constant flow of inspiration in order for salespeople and managers to keep functioning at an optimal level. Salary, expense accounts, and fringe benefits are an important part of the motivational process in any sales management effort.

In closing, it should be noted that one of the trends that began in the 1990s to help work out the most effective communication techniques for a global sales force is using training programs developed by expert consultants. Global companies regularly hire outside consultants and firms to run cultural sensitivity seminars for their sales teams who regularly come in contact with clients and coworkers from other cultures. International project teams comprised of managers from a variety of countries are also growing in popularity. These teams are designed to increase cultural understanding of management issues within the company. They meet periodically to exchange ideas and experiences and work on regional or global projects that require coordination.

SUMMARY

1 Understand that international communications is about cultures, not nations.

Culture is the total life ways of a people, the social legacy the individual acquires from his or her group. Culture is typically invisible to those who are immersed within it, which makes communicating across cultures difficult. Promotion, and particularly advertising, is a cultural product; it means nothing outside the culture within which it was created. Culture surrounds promotion, informs it, and gives it meaning.

Promotion depends on effective communication, and effective international communication depends on creating shared meaning between cultures. The degree of shared meaning is significantly affected by cultural membership.

As communications technology has progressed in the latter half of the twentieth century, international communication, and particularly commercial communications, has become extremely important. International scholars point out that the importance and complexity of international communications can be understood by assessing the complex social, economic, and political changes that affect the international communications environment.

2 Explain the different types of cross-cultural research that can provide key information to the process of effective communication in international markets.

We all wear cultural blinders, and as a result we must overcome substantial barriers in trying to communicate with people from other countries. This is a major problem for international marketers as they seek to promote their brands around the world. To overcome this problem and avoid errors in promotional planning, cross-cultural audience analysis is needed. Such analyses involve evaluation of economic conditions, demographic characteristics, customs, values, rituals, and product use and preferences in the target countries.

3 Identify three distinctive challenges that complicate the execution of advertising as a promotional tool in international settings.

Worldwide marketers face three distinctive challenges in executing their advertising campaigns. The first is a creative challenge that derives from differences in experience and meaning among cultures. Even the pictures featured in an ad may be translated differently from one country to the next. The second is a media challenge. Media availability, media coverage, and media costs vary dramatically around the world, adding a second complication to international advertising. Finally, the amount and nature of advertising regulation vary dramatically from country to country and may force a complete reformulation of an advertising campaign.

4 Discuss the advantages and disadvantages of standardized versus customized promotional campaigns.

An ongoing concern for international promotion entails the degree of customization a marketer should attempt in campaigns designed to cross national boundaries. Standardized campaigns use virtually the same message and creative execution in all markets, whereas customized campaigns feature heavy customization for each market. Standardized messages bring tremendous cost savings and create a common brand image worldwide that enhances integrated marketing communications, but they may miss the mark with consumers in different nations. As consumers around the world become more similar, standardized campaigns are likely to become more prevalent. Teenagers in many countries share similar values and lifestyles and thus make a natural target for globalized campaigns.

5 Discuss the development and management of an international sales force.

The development and management of an international sales force to achieve effective international communications requires assembling the proper type of salespeople and then effectively training and motivating them. In terms of assembling a sales force, the choice must be made with respect to expatriates, local nationals, or third-country nationals. An expatriate is an employee working in a country other than his or her home country. Local nationals are sales employees based in their home country. Third-country nationals are usually employees who are citizens of one country, employed by a corporation from a second country, and working for that corporation in a third country.

With respect to training a global sales force, the emphasis in training will change depending on the personnel. Expatriates need more training on cultural sensitivities to effectively communicate in foreign markets. Local nationals and third-country nationals need more training on the firm and its brands and the value delivered. Motivation and compensation are highly dependent on the market within which the salesperson is working. In high tax-rate markets, nonsalary compensation of various types can be highly motivating and rewarding.

KEY TERMS

international promotion, 227
culture, 227
ethnocentrism, 230
self-reference criteria (SRC), 230
secondary data, 232
primary data, 232
less developed countries, 233
newly industrialized countries, 233

highly industrialized countries, 233
cultural values, 234
rituals, 235
ethnographic research, 235
picturing, 237
global agencies, 249
international affiliates, 249
local agency, 250

standardized (globalized) campaign, 250
customized (localized) campaign, 251
expatriate, 254
local national, 255
third-country national, 255

QUESTIONS FOR REVIEW AND CRITICAL THINKING

1. What are ethnocentrism and self-reference criteria? Why are they a threat to effective international promotion decision making?

2. In this chapter, we discuss the challenges advertisers face in Asia when it comes to representing husbands and wives in ads for products such as laundry detergents and vacuum cleaners. Why is this a challenging issue in Asia today? Would you expect that advertisers face this same challenge in other parts of the world? Where?

3. What factors should be examined in each country when doing cross-cultural research?

4. Explain the appeal of new media options such as direct broadcast by satellite and the Internet for marketers who have created globalized promotion campaigns.

5. Compare and contrast the advantages of global versus local ad agencies for implementing international promotion.

6. Identify several factors or forces that make consumers around the world more similar to one another. Conversely, what factors or forces create diversity among consumers in different countries?

7. Teens and retired people are two market segments found worldwide. If these two segments of European consumers were each being targeted for new promotion campaigns, which one would be most responsive to a globalized promotion campaign? Why?

8. What are the different choices in selecting personnel for a global sales force?

EXPERIENTIAL EXERCISES

1. **In-class exercise.** How many of you have lived or traveled in a foreign country? What types of promotional tools did you encounter? Were there cultural differences that were reflected in the way a product was used?

2. **Out-of-class exercise.** As discussed in the chapter, it is extremely important to understand cultural differences before developing advertising for foreign countries. For example, personal-care products seem to be a preoccupation of consumers in the United States. Write a report on how consumers in Russia, Brazil, and France appear to differ from their U.S. counterparts when it comes to the use of personal-care products. Explain how these differences will affect American advertisers developing ads for personal-care products in these countries. You may wish to talk with someone who is familiar with advertising in these countries, or go to the university or local library and browse through consumer magazines published in these countries to see which products are being advertised and which are not.

USING THE INTERNET

Exercise 1

While English might be the most common language of the World Wide Web, there are a great many non-English Web pages, and a means for machine translation of Web pages would seem to be a good thing. AltaVista launched one: "Babelfish" (named for a creature from Douglas Adams's *Hitchhiker's Guide to the Galaxy*). This service endeavors to translate text in any of a variety of languages into any of the others. Try translating text from English into a foreign language with which you're familiar, or select some foreign language text from a Web site for conversion into English. (Another trick is to try translating English language text into a foreign language, then back to English.)

Altavista.com: http://www.babelfish.altavista.com

1. How faithful does the translation seem to be? In some cases, even a bad translation can be helpful—for example, the man shouting "Combustion! Combustion!" in a crowded French theater might get his point across, even before you smell the smoke. But as discussed in the text, an advertisement's message might miss its point, if not become nonsensical.

2. How effective do you think Altavista's Babelfish might be in translating advertising text?

3. What sorts of copy might convey cultural meaning best?

4. What would suffer the most in the translation process?

Exercise 2

A great many Web sites have, as their audience, groups in one country interested in information about another. Coming2America.com wants to be a cross-cultural portal site for anyone headed for the United States, while Craighead.com goes in the other direction: helping its visitors (presumably more likely Americans than anyone else) to gather information on other countries. The Embassy.org site is more a gathering of the community of nations represented by the foreign embassies in Washington, DC; each has its own ideas as to what to put forward, and whom it's trying to educate and serve.

Coming2America.com
http://www.coming2america.com

Craighead.com
http://www.craighead.com

Embassy.org
http://www.embassy.org

1. How do the Web sites define their audiences, and let you know if this is the right site for you?

2. How do the sites address language issues?

3. What are the sites' relationships with commercial advertisers?

PART 3

THE TOOLS OF PROMOTION AND IMC

This is the part of the book where the practical application of promotion takes place. The emphasis here is to first identify the inherent nature of each promotional tool, then examine in detail the communications features of the tool, and finally discuss the value that each tool can add to the IMC effort. Each of the tools of promotion is covered with the same level of intensity reflecting the core perspective that promotion is truly a blend of many different communications efforts. The diversity of applications in promotion can be intimidating. From multimedia advertising through the Internet, sales promotion, public relations, and personal selling, a wide array of opportunities to communicate exists. Aside from the diversity across promotional tools, we will consider new media applications within every promotional tool. The Internet is not just relevant to advertising and e-commerce. Literally every promotional area can find effective applications for new media, and these applications are highlighted throughout the chapters in this section.

8

Advertising: Message and Media Strategies pays proper homage to the advertising process. The chapter begins with a definition of advertising, the key parties involved in its conception, and the scope of advertising. The distinguishing feature of advertising among the promotional tools is the creative execution, so the chapter explores message strategies that make advertising stand out as a creative effort. The chapter concludes with a review of the media-planning process and an overview of the media vehicles that maximize the advertiser's objective.

9

Internet Advertising introduces Web-based advertising and the use of various advertising options including banner ads, pop-up ads, e-mail, and corporate home pages. Next, the chapter presents issues involved in establishing and maintaining a Web site and the challenges of establishing a brand in the "e-community." Finally, the chapter explores how Internet advertising can be a highly successful component of an IMC campaign.

10

Direct Marketing and E-Commerce identifies how firms can manage traditional and e-commerce direct marketing opportunities present in the marketplace. Specifically, this chapter examines the growing field of direct marketing and the explosive growth of direct marketing through e-commerce. The goal is to understand how they both may be used as part of the promotional mix in a firm's IMC program.

11

Sales Promotion: Consumer, Trade, and Business Market Techniques highlights the fact that sales promotions such as contests, sweepstakes, sponsorships and merchandise giveaways attract attention and give new energy to the promotional effort. The emphasis of this chapter is that sales promotion has proven to be a popular complement to mass media advertising because it accomplishes things advertising cannot. Both consumer *and* trade techniques in sales promotion are covered in this chapter.

12

Sponsorship, Point-of-Purchase, and Supportive Communication reflects the extraordinary range of options available to today's advertiser, from billboards and transit advertising to event sponsorship, point-of-purchase advertising, and the most elaborate online services. In addition, this chapter points out that a marketer must understand and take advantage of the nonmedia supportive communications opportunities inherent in the brand name, logo and slogan as well as packaging, labeling and word of mouth tactics.

13

Public Relations and Corporate Advertising considers the tools and objectives of public relations and corporate advertising. While public relations and corporate advertising are rarely the foundation tools of a promotional mix and IMC program, they do represent key tactics under certain conditions. We explore the nature of these two specialized promotional tools and the conditions under which they are ideally suited for the IMC program.

14

Personal Selling and Sales Management concludes the discussion of promotional tools. This chapter considers the nature of personal selling as another valuable tool in the promotional effort. We first examine the role of personal selling, the types of personal selling, and the challenge of establishing personal selling objectives. Then, we examine the process of personal selling and learn how technology is enhancing the personal selling effort. The chapter concludes with a review sales management's role in maximizing the personal selling effort.

After reading this chapter, you will be able to:

1 Make the distinction between advertising, an advertisement, and an advertising campaign.

2 Identify the most common message strategy objectives in advertising.

3 Identify the methods used to pursue advertising message strategy objectives.

4 Detail the important components of the media-planning process.

5 Identify the main considerations in devising media strategy.

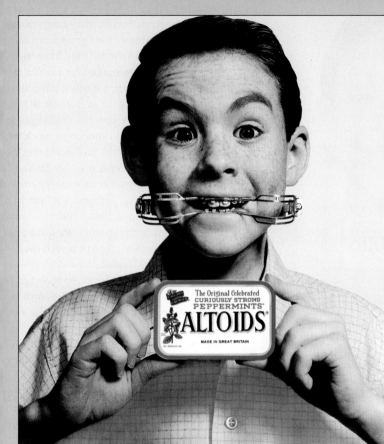

Here's an advertising opportunity for all you budding creatives and brand managers. The brand you can take over is 200 years old, made in Britain, and has a market share too small to detect. Oh, you also get to go up against big names like Procter & Gamble, Mars candies, and Warner-Lambert. And just to make things interesting, let's say your advertising budget is limited to, how about $1 million.

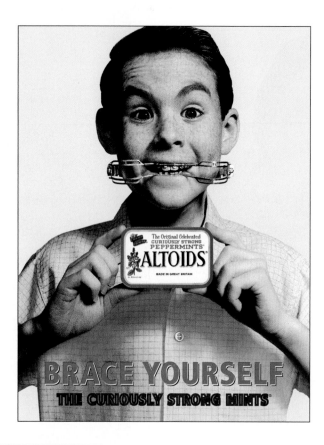

EXHIBIT 8.1

Leo Burnett creative Steffan Postaer used a series of retro images like this one to appeal both to loyal users of Altoids and gain broad awareness in the market for a brand that used to have minuscule market share.

So, what do you think? You want to take on the challenge? Most brand managers and their agency creative partners would probably burst out laughing at the prospect. But the brand managers at Kraft Foods and the creatives at Leo Burnett didn't laugh at all. This was precisely the challenge they had to take on with Altoids, now widely know, as the "Curiously Strong Mint."

As product categories go, breath mints isn't one that will get the heart rate up at most agencies. After all, what can you say about a breath mint? But when British confectioner Callard & Bowser, the makers of Altoids, was bought by Kraft Foods, marketing manager Mark Sugden was sure the brand could grow from its nonexistent market share. He had the fan mail from loyal Altoids users to prove it. So he persuaded his bosses at Kraft to let him hire Leo Burnett for a modest advertising campaign.

The creative team at Burnett did not spurn the opportunity. But they saw the challenges as well—no market share and only $1 million to work with. Realizing that a big part of the loyalty to Altoids was its low profile, the team, led by new wave creative Steffan Postaer, rejected the idea of TV commercials used by the big competitors Tic Tac and Certs.[1] Instead, the ads had to raise broad awareness without being too mainstream. "We didn't want to betray those who were already committed. The key was to remain consistent with everything [the brand] stood for," said Sugden.[2]

Postaer went to work to leverage the $1 million as much as possible and come up with a distinctive campaign. What he came up with is the now widely known "Curiously Strong Mint" campaign build on retro images and featuring the traditional Altoids tin box (see an example in Exhibit 8.1). The original campaign was executed only through a limited magazine placement and posters. Now the campaign has broadened its magazine presence and spread to billboards and even some limited TV spots.[3] The results have been stunning. At the beginning of the campaign, sales totaled about $7 million and the market share wasn't even a blip on the radar. Now sales have grown to over $60 million, and market share is nearing 25 percent. And that $1 million budget? It's grown a little—to about $20 million.

1. Anthony Vagnoni, "The Next Wave," *Advertising Age*, January 17, 2000, 16.
2. Pat Wechsler, "A Curiously Strong Campaign," *Business Week*, April 21, 1997, 134.
3. "1999 Agency Reviews," *Advertising Age*, January 31, 2000, S12.

INTRODUCTION

Advertising is the granddaddy of all the promotional tools. It's the most conspicuous, the most scrutinized, and the most controversial. It's the place where more money is spent than any other way of communicating about a brand—$220 billion in the United States and nearly $500 billion worldwide on media alone.[4] Add in agency revenues and spending on production and the spending goes over $1 trillion easily. But as prevalent and obvious as it is, advertising means different things to different people. It's a business, an art, an institution, and a cultural phenomenon. To the CEO of a multinational corporation, advertising is an essential marketing tool that helps create brand awareness and loyalty and stimulates demand. To Mark Sugden of Altoids, it was a way to get the word out about a brand he knew could succeed. To a local restaurant owner, advertising is the way to communicate to the neighborhood. To the art director in an ad agency, advertising is the creative expression of a concept. To a media planner, advertising is the way a marketer uses the mass media to communicate to current and potential customers. To scholars and museum curators, advertising is an important cultural artifact, text, and cultural record.

Our study of advertising will focus on the full range of what advertising is and how it can contribute to the promotional process. We will begin with a definition of advertising and the key parties involved in its conception. Next we will clarify the scope of advertising and the target audiences advertising can reach. The distinguishing feature of advertising among the promotional tools is the creative execution. We will look at message strategies that make advertising stand out as a creative effort. Finally, we will turn our attention to the media through which advertising is transmitted to the target audiences.

THE NATURE AND SCOPE OF ADVERTISING

As we discussed above, advertising means different things to different people. In fact, sometimes determining just what is and what is not advertising is a difficult task. Keeping all that in mind, consider this straightforward definition: Advertising is a paid, mass-mediated attempt to persuade.

As direct and simple as this definition seems, it is loaded with distinctions. Advertising is paid communication by a company or organization that wants its information disseminated. In advertising language, the company or organization that pays for advertising is called the **client** or **sponsor.**

First, if communication is not paid for, it's not advertising. For example, a form of promotion called publicity is not advertising because it is not paid for. Let's say Bruce Willis appears on the *Late Show with David Letterman* to promote his newest movie. Is this advertising? No, because the producer or film studio did not pay the *Late Show with David Letterman* for airtime. But when the film studio produces and runs ads for the newest Bruce Willis movie on television and in newspapers across the country, this communication is paid for by the studio, and is most definitely advertising.

For the same reason, public service announcements (PSAs) are not advertising either. True, they look like ads and sound like ads, but they aren't ads. They are not commercial in the way an ad is because they are not paid for like an ad. They are offered as information in the public (noncommercial) interest. When you hear a message on the radio that implores you to "Just Say No" to drugs, this sounds very much like an ad, but it is a PSA. Simply put, PSAs are excluded from the definition of advertising because they are unpaid communication.

---

4.   "100 Leading National Advertisers," *Advertising Age,* September 2000.

Second, advertising is mass mediated. This means it is delivered through a communication medium designed to reach more than one person—or mass of people. Advertising is widely disseminated through familiar means—television, radio, newspapers, and magazines—and other media such as direct mail, billboards, the Internet, and videocassettes. The mass-mediated nature of advertising creates a communication environment where the message is not delivered face-to-face. This distinguishes advertising from personal selling as a form of promotion.

Third, all advertising includes an attempt to persuade. To put it bluntly, ads are communication designed to get someone to do something. Even an advertisement with a stated objective of being purely informational still has persuasion at its core. The ad informs the consumer for some purpose, and that purpose is to get the consumer to like the brand and because of that liking to eventually buy the brand. In the absence of this persuasive intent, a communication might be news, but it would not be advertising.

At this point, we can say that for a communication to be classified as advertising, three essential criteria must be met:

1. The communication must be paid for.
2. The communication must be delivered to an audience via mass media.
3. The communication must be attempting persuasion.

It is important to note here that advertising can be persuasive communication not only about a product or service but also about an idea, a person, or an entire organization. When Colgate and Honda use advertising, this is product advertising and meets all three criteria. Likewise, when Dean Witter, Delta Air Lines, Terminix, or your dentist runs advertisements, it is service advertising and meets all three criteria. Idea advertising occurs in various situations, but is most prevalent in political advertising. Finally, when is a person advertised? How about when Ricky Martin does a concert or when Zig Zigler gives a speech? Here, people are being advertised as the "brand" that consumers will pay for.

Advertising, Advertisements, and Advertising Campaigns

Now that we have a working definition of advertising, we turn our attention to other important distinctions in advertising. Specifically, the distinction between an advertisement and an advertising campaign. An **advertisement** refers to a specific message that has been placed to persuade an audience. An **advertising campaign** is a series of coordinated advertisements that communicate a reasonably cohesive and integrated theme. The theme may itself be made up of several claims or points but should advance an essentially singular theme. Successful advertising campaigns can be developed around a single advertisement placed in multiple media, or they can be made up of several different advertisements (more typically) with a similar look, feel, and message. The Slates® ads in Exhibits 8.2 and 8.3 represent an excellent use of similar look and feel to create an advertising campaign. If we took away the brand name, you would still be sure that both ads were part of the same campaign. Advertising campaigns can run for a few weeks or for many years. The advertising campaign is, in many ways, the most challenging aspect of advertising execution. It requires a keen sense of the complex environments within which a marketer must communicate to different audiences and of how these messages interact with one another and an audience.

The vast majority of ads you see each day are part of broader campaigns. And most individual ads would make little sense without the knowledge audience members have about ads for this particular brand or the product category in general. Ads are interpreted by consumers through their experiences with the product and with

EXHIBITS 8.2 AND 8.3

Advertising campaigns feature a series of advertisements with a similar feel and theme. The Slates® Clothing campaign by Levi Strauss is an excellent example of a campaign that achieves a distinctive look and feel and promotes a single theme. Each ad was designed to run as two consecutive right hand pages, with the still life as the first page and the portrait as the second page.

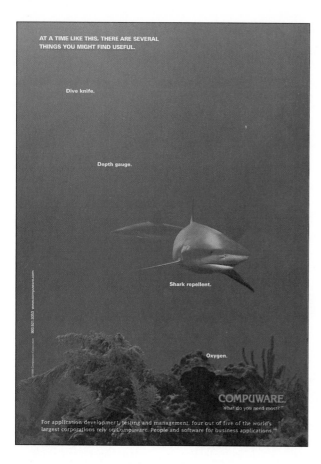

AT A TIME LIKE THIS, THERE ARE SEVERAL
THINGS YOU MIGHT FIND USEFUL.

Dive knife.

Depth gauge.

Shark repellent.

Oxygen.

COMPUWARE.
What do you need most?

For application development, testing and management, four out of five of the world's
largest corporations rely on Compuware. People and software for business applications.

EXHIBIT 8.4

Advertising can be directed at several different categories of audiences from household consumers to government officials. This advertisement for software Compuware is directed at members of business organizations who make decisions about software applications. The ad ran in business publications like Fortune *and* Business Week.

previous ads for the brand. When you see a new Coca-Cola ad, you make sense of the ad through your history with Coca-Cola and its previous advertising. Even ads for a new brand or whole new product are situated within audiences' broader knowledge of products, brands, and advertising. After years of viewing ads and buying brands, each member of the audience brings a rich history and knowledge to every communications encounter.

Audiences for Advertising

In Chapter 2, we had a brief encounter with audiences as the last (and critical) link in the structure of the advertising industry. In advertising, audiences are a very important topic indeed. In the language of advertising, an **audience** is a group of individuals who receive and interpret messages sent from marketers through mass media. In advertising, audiences are often targeted. A **target audience** is a particular group of consumers singled out for an advertisement or advertising campaign. In Chapter 4, we talked about target markets in STP marketing. The target market is the target *audience* in the lingo of advertising. Target audiences are always *potential* audiences because advertisers can never be totally sure that the message will actually get through as intended. While advertisers can identify dozens of different target audiences, five broad audience categories are commonly described: household consumers, members of business organizations, members of the trade channel, professionals, and government officials and employees.

Audience Categories. **Household consumers,** who buy goods and services for their personal use, are the most conspicuous audience for advertising in that most mass-media advertising is directed at them. Unilever, Miller Brewing, Saturn, The Gap, and Nationwide Insurance have products and services designed for the consumer market, and so their advertising targets household consumers. The most recent information indicates that there are about 101.5 million households in the United States and approximately 273 million household consumers.[5] Total yearly retail spending by these households is about $3 trillion.[6] This huge audience is typically where the action is in advertising. Under the very broad heading of "consumer advertising," very fine audience distinctions are made by advertisers. Target audience definitions—such as men, 25 to 45, college educated, living in metropolitan areas, with incomes greater than $50,000 per year—are common.

Members of business organizations are the focus of advertising for firms that produce business and industrial goods and services, such as office equipment, production machinery, supplies, and software. While products and services targeted to this audience often require personal selling, advertising is used to create an awareness and a favorable attitude among potential buyers. Gateway, the maker of PCs that

5.   "1999 Survey of Buying Power," *Sales and Marketing Management,* September 1999, 58.
6.   Ibid.

come in the funny cowhide-looking boxes, has always had great success selling to household consumers. Now the firm has targeted business organizations and is using a $50 million multimedia advertising effort to boost its awareness among business organizations.[7] Exhibit 8.4 is an example of an ad directed at members of business organizations by another computer industry marketer, Compuware.

Members of a trade channel include retailers, wholesalers, and distributors; they are an audience for producers of both household and business goods and services. As we have discussed before, unless a producer can obtain adequate retail and wholesale distribution through a trade channel, a marketer's brands will not reach customers. Therefore, it is important to direct advertising at the trade level of the market. While other tools in the promotional mix are key to communicating with the trade, advertising can play an important role. Members of the trade are always impressed when a marketer puts big advertising dollars behind a brand to stimulate demand—which will ultimately benefit the members of the trade.

Professionals form a unique target audience and are defined as doctors, lawyers, accountants, teachers, or any other careerpeople who have received special training or certification. This audience warrants separate classification because its members have distinct needs and interests. The language and images used in advertising to this target audience tend to rely on the esoteric terminology and unique circumstances that members of professions readily recognize.[8]

Government officials and employees constitute an audience in themselves due to the large dollar volume of buying that federal, state, and local governments do. Government organizations such as schools and road maintenance operations buy huge amounts of various products. Producers of items such as furniture, construction materials, vehicles, fertilizers, computers, and business services all target this group with their advertising. Advertising to this audience group is dominated by direct-mail advertising."

Audience Geography. It is important to recognize that audiences for advertising can be thought of in geographic terms. As we saw in Chapter 7, very few ads can be effective for all consumers worldwide. However, recall that **globalized advertising** occurs when the same fundamental message is used in markets around the world with few if any variations. These are typically brands that are considered citizens of the world and whose manner of use does not vary tremendously by culture. Even though cultures vary significantly in their view of time and men's jewelry, Exhibits 8.5 and 8.6 show extremely similar executions of a Rolex ad in different countries. Firms that market brands with cross-cultural appeal, such as Singapore Airlines, IBM, Levi's, Sony, and Pirelli, attempt to develop and place advertisements with a common theme and presentation in all markets around the world. Global placement is possible only when a brand and the messages about that brand have a common appeal across diverse cultures.

International advertising occurs when firms prepare and place different advertising in different national markets. As we also saw in Chapter 7, when cultural variations produce differences in values or product usage, each international market requires unique or original advertising. Unilever prepares different versions of ads for its laundry products for nearly every international market due to differences in the way consumers in different cultures approach the laundry task. Consumers in the United States use large and powerful washers and dryers and lots of hot water. Households in Brazil use very little hot water and hang clothes out to dry. Very few firms enjoy the luxury of having a brand with truly cross-cultural appeal and global

---

7. Beth Snider, "Gateway Pursues Business PC Buyers," *Advertising Age,* January 3, 2000, 1, 34.
8. Amy Barrett, "Why Drugmakers Prescribed an Ad Blitz," *Business Week,* March 22, 1999, 95.

„Voller Einsatz. Anders kann ich nicht Tennis spielen."

Jim Courier gilt als ausgesprochen kämpferischer und entschlossener Gegner auf den Courts. Und doch zugleich als einer, der sich eine bemerkenswert souveräne Einstellung gegenüber seinem Sport bewahrt hat.

„Wenn einer kommt, der besser spielt als ich – kein Problem. Ich versuche einfach, mich das nächste Mal zu steigern."

Seine Fähigkeit, unter wachsendem Druck besser zu werden, hat Jim Courier bereits vier Grand Slam-Titel eingebracht. Vor allem in Australien ist er der dominierende Spieler. Dort gewann er gleich zwei Australian Open hintereinander. Dieser

Triumph war die Krönung einer erstaunlichen Siegesserie in 32 Spielen. „Wenn er in Bestform ist, verbinden sich bei Courier Kraft und Ausdauer auf eine Art, die geradezu unheimlich ist", schreibt *Tennis Week* über ihn.

Ob es ein Spiel in fünf Sätzen auf dem schwierigen Rotsandboden in Paris ist oder in glühender Hitze auf den Plätzen in Melbourne, Courier spielt sein bestes Tennis, wenn es hart auf hart geht.

Es überrascht also kaum, daß er eine Uhr gewählt hat, deren Qualitäten ebenso unübertroffen sind. **ROLEX**

Rolex GMT-Master Chronometer in Stahl
Rolex Uhren GmbH. Postfach 10 30 41, 50470 Köln. Schreiben Sie uns. Wir senden Ihnen Broschüren.

"Bisogna essere fortissimi per raggiungere il 'centrale'. Ed imbattibili per rimanerci."

"Prendere possesso del "centrale" di Wimbledon è una delle emozioni più grandi nella vita di un tennista. Perchè è il torneo più importante e di maggior prestigio, quello che ogni giocatore sogna di vincere.

Avevo sedici anni quando venni a Wimbledon la prima volta per seguire un incontro sul "centrale". Ero emozionatissimo. Ed anche oggi, quando ci gareggio io, provo lo stesso brivido.

È una sensazione che ti prende negli spogliatoi, dove il giocatore si concentra prima di affrontare quello che sicuramente sarà uno degli incontri più importanti della sua carriera.

Raggiungo il rettangolo da gioco, e sen-

to appena gli applausi del pubblico. Raccolgo tutte le mie forze e mi dico che posso farcela. A questo punto l'incanto si rompe e sento un'enorme carica di energia e di stimoli. Sono pronto.

È meraviglioso sollevare il trofeo sul "centrale" di Wimbledon dove è già un grande successo essere ammessi e dove, secondo me, il tennis è nato."

Jim Courier

Jim Courier e l'organizzazione di Wimbledon hanno scelto Rolex. La precisione e l'affidabilità di Rolex sono le qualità richieste affinchè il grande meccanismo di Wimbledon possa funzionare proprio come un orologio. Una scelta condivisa da molti altri campioni. **ROLEX** Ginevra

CRONOMETRO ROLEX DAY-DATE IN ORO GIALLO 18 CT. DISPONIBILE ANCHE IN ORO BIANCO 18 CT. E IN PLATINO.

EXHIBITS 8.5 AND 8.6

Advertising outside your domestic market is a challenge. If the brand has cross-cultural appeal and universal use—like a watch—a marketer can prepare highly similar (standardized) ads for many markets. These two ads for Rolex from Germany and Italy show how global advertising can be done when similarity of product use is a key factor.

recognition. Since this is true, most firms must pursue other-nation markets with international advertising rather than global advertising.

National advertising reaches all geographic areas of one nation. National advertising is the term typically used to describe the kind of advertising we see most often in the mass media in the domestic U.S. market. **Regional advertising** is carried out by marketers—producers, wholesalers, distributors, and retailers—who concentrate their efforts in a relatively large, but not national, geographic region. Best Buy, a regional consumer electronics and appliance chain, has distribution confined to a few states. Because of the nature of the firm's market, it places advertising only in regions where it has stores.

Local advertising is much the same as regional advertising. **Local advertising** is directed at an audience in a single trading area, either a city or state. Retail shopkeepers of all types rely on local media to reach customers in their small geographic trading area. This includes local firms like restaurants, hair salons, tanning and nail boutiques, and tax advisors. Under special circumstances, national advertisers will share advertising expenses in a market with local dealers to achieve specific advertising objectives. This sharing of advertising expenses between national advertisers and local merchants is called **cooperative advertising** (or co-op advertising). Exhibit 8.7 illustrates a co-op advertisement run by TUMI luggage and one of its retailers, Shapiro.

http://www.tumi.com

EXHIBIT 8.7

National advertisers will often share advertising expenses with their trade channel partners. This is called co-op advertising. Here, TUMI luggage is featured in advertising by a local retailer, Shapiro. And the Web provides an ideal medium in which to expand promotional favors: The TUMI Web site provides an exhaustive yet easily searched roster of retailers who carry TUMI. The TUMI site doesn't play favorites in delivering customers to particular retailers, does it?

ADVERTISING MESSAGE STRATEGIES ② ③

Message strategy is the essence of the power and distinctiveness of advertising as a promotional tool. A **message strategy** consists of the objectives to be pursued and methods used in an advertisement or advertising campaign. It defines the goals of the advertiser and how those goals will be achieved. This section offers nine message strategy objectives and discusses and illustrates the methods often used to pursue them. This is not an exhaustive list, but it covers the most common and important message strategy objectives. Exhibit 8.8 summarizes the nine message strategy objectives presented here.

Promote Brand Recall

Since the very beginning, a major goal of marketers has been to get consumers to remember the brand's name. This is typically referred to as the brand recall objective. Of course, marketers not only want consumers to remember their name, but also want it to be the *first* name consumers remember. Marketers want their brand name to be "top of mind" or at least in the evoked set—a small list of brand names (typically less than five)—that come to mind when a product or service category

Objective: What the Advertiser Hopes to Achieve	Method: How the Advertiser Plans to Achieve the Objective
Promote brand recall: To get consumers to recall its brand name(s) first; that is, before any of the competitors' brand names	Repetition ads Slogan and jingle ads
Link a key attribute to the brand name: To get consumers to associate a key attribute with a brand name and vice versa	Unique selling proposition (USP) ads
Instill brand preference: To get consumers to like or prefer its brand above all others	Feel-good ads Humor ads Sexual-appeal ads
Scare the consumer into action: To get consumers to buy a product or service by instilling fear	Fear-appeal ads
Change behavior by inducing anxiety: To get consumers to make a purchase decision by playing to their anxieties; often, the anxieties are social in nature	Anxiety ads
Transform consumption experiences: To create a feeling, image, or mood about a brand that is activated when the consumer uses the product or service	Transformational ads
Situate the brand socially: To give the brand meaning by placing it in a desirable social context	Slice-of-life ads Light fantasy ads
Define the brand image: To create an image for a brand by relying predominantly on visuals rather than discourse	Image ads
Persuade the consumer: To convince consumers to buy a product or service through high-engagement discourse	Reason-why ads Hard-sell ads Comparison ads Information-only ads Testimonial ads Demonstration ads Advertorial
Invoke a direct response: To get consumers to take immediate buying action, typically by providing a toll-free number	Call or click now ads Infomercials

(for example, airlines, soft drinks, photographic film) is recalled. In the case where consumers perceive homogeneity between brands (for example, laundry soaps) and other "low-involvement" goods and services, the first brand remembered is often the most likely to be purchased. First-remembered brands are often the most popular brands. Consumers may infer popularity, desirability, and even superiority from the ease with which they recall brands. So, how do marketers promote easy recall? There are several methods.

Repetition. As simple as it sounds, repetition is a tried-and-true way of gaining easier retrieval from memory. This is done not only through buying a lot of ads (although that certainly helps), but also by repeating the brand name within the ad copy itself. The idea is that things said more often will be remembered more easily than things said less frequently. When the consumer stands in front of the laundry detergent aisle, you can't expect deliberate and extensive consideration of product attributes: Just the recall of a name, a previous judgment, or (most often) habit drives the purchase decision. This type of advertising tries to keep existing users as much as it tries to get new ones, usually more so.

Slogans and Jingles. Slogans are linguistic devices that link a brand name to something memorable, due to the slogan's simplicity, meter, rhyme, or some other factor. Jingles do the same thing, just set to music. Examples are numerous: "Bud-Weis-Er"; "You Deserve a Break Today"; "Tide's In, Dirt's Out"; "The Best Part of Waking Up Is Folgers in Your Cup"; "You're in Good Hands with Allstate." No doubt you've heard a few of these before. Slogans and jingles allow for rehearsal and often rely on things that can enhance retrieval, such as metaphors and similes. Ultimately, a slogan or jingle creates a mnemonic, or memory cue, so that the consumer can recall the brand name easily.

Link a Key Attribute to the Brand Name

Sometimes marketers want consumers to remember a single attribute along with the brand name. If done well, ads employing this message strategy achieve an echo effect: The attribute helps in the recall of the brand name, and the brand name is linked to one key attribute. This type of advertising is most closely identified with the famous adman from the 1950s, Rosser Reeves, who coined the term "unique selling proposition" (USP) method of advertising.

EXHIBIT 8.9

When a brand has the benefit of a distinct feature to offer consumers, the marketer can use a "unique selling proposition" method of advertising. Lucky Jeans touts its "heavy duty" workwear feature as a unique selling proposition.

Unique Selling Proposition. Unique selling propositions (USP) emphasizing one and only one brand attribute are a very good idea. Ads that try to link several attributes to a brand while working to establish recall often fail. Good examples of successful ads of this sort are "All-Temp-a-Cheer" and the USP offered in Exhibit 8.9, a good example of this approach—no beautiful models, no style, no prestige, just tough jeans.

Instill Brand Preference

The brand-preference objective is fairly universal. Marketers want consumers to like (and better yet, prefer) their brand. Liking gets you closer to preference than does not-liking. So, liking the brand is good. Liking is different from awareness or top-of-mind recall. Liking is measured in attitudes and expressed as a feeling. There are many approaches to getting the consumer to like one's brand. Let's look at some of the general approaches.

Feel-Good Ads. These ads are supposed to work through "affective association." In the language of psychology, *affective* means liking. Feel-good ads are supposed to link the good feeling elicited by the ad with the brand: You like the ad, you like the brand. While the actual theory and mechanics of this seemingly simple reflex are more complex (and more controversial) than you might think, the basic idea is that by creating ads with positive feelings, marketers will lead consumers to associate those positive feelings with the advertised brand, leading to a higher probability of purchase. As Steve Sweitzer of the Hal Riney and Partners advertising agency said:

[C]onsumers want to do business with companies they LIKE. If they LIKE us, they just may give us a try at the store. What a concept. Sometimes just being liked is a strategy.[9]

The evidence on how well this method works is mixed and equivocal. It may be that positive feelings are transferred to the brand, or it could be that they actually interfere with remembering the message or the brand name. Liking the ad doesn't necessarily mean liking the brand. But message strategy development is a game of probability, and liking may, more times than not, lead to a higher probability of purchase. For example, the long-running and apparently successful Chevrolet truck television campaign "Like a Rock" features the music of Bob Seger and scenes of hardworking, patriotic Americans and their families. It seems to work for a lot of consumers. The good feeling it produces may be the result of widely shared patriotic associations and the celebration of working-class Americans evoked by the advertising.

GLOBAL ISSUES

WHAT'S SO FUNNY ABOUT ICED COFFEE?

How absurd. Advertising iced coffee in Great Britain? The land of tea? That was the theme of an advertising campaign used in the U.K. by a subsidiary of U.S.-based Starbucks for its iced Frappuccino. The drink has been a huge hit in the United States for years. But, hey, we drink iced tea over here. Would anybody in Britain even care? Well, they did more than care. The ad campaign was a big hit, and Brits have discovered iced coffee.

Starbucks launched the drink in the summer of 1999 based on a mythical employee named Billy. Billy came up with this iced coffee idea and was ridiculed by his coworkers for the stupidity of coming up with such a concoction. But the drink becomes a big success, and Starbucks and all the employees have to apologize to Billy in subsequent spots. The spots plead with Billy, "Billy, we're sorry we said it was a stupid idea. Please come back to work," and "The work of a genius, not a loser." The main campaign was run in magazines and then supported by billboards and T-shirts worn by store employees.

The humor in the campaign struck a chord with the Brits. They were not used to iced coffee, but Brits love a good bit of humor, and the campaign delivered on that note. Starbucks' U.K. marketing manager Helen Benedict said, "In bringing the brand into Britain, we've stressed the experience—that it's all about tasting it, feeling it, touching it. We've also tried to emphasize the people side of the business, and the Billy campaign shows that we can poke a little fun at ourselves."

Source: Charles Goldsmith, "Starbucks Hits a Humorous Note in Pitching Iced Coffee to Brits," *The Wall Street Journal*, September 1, 1999, B7.

Humor Ads. The goal of a humor ad is pretty much the same as that of feel-good ads, but humor is a different animal altogether. The goal of humor in advertising is to create in the receiver a pleasant and memorable association with the product. Recent advertising campaigns as diverse as those for Budweiser beer ("Waaazzz Up?"), Electronic Data Systems (herding cats), and Little Caesar's ("Pizza-Pizza") have all successfully used humor as the primary message theme. But research suggests that the positive impact of humor is not as strong as the intuitive appeal of the approach. Quite simply, humorous versions of advertisements often do not prove to be more persuasive than nonhumorous versions of the same ad—or research is simply inadequate to detect the difference.

How many times have you been talking to friends about your favorite ads, and you say something like, "Remember the one where the guy knocks over the drink,

9.   The One Club E-mail Discussion, July 27, 1997, as published in *One: A Magazine for Members of the One Club for Art and Copy,* vol. 1, no. 2 (Fall 1997), 18.

and then says. . . ." Everybody laughs, and then maybe someone says something like, "I can't remember who it's for, but what a great ad." Wrong; this is not a great ad. You remember the gag, but not the brand. Not good. Why is it that with some funny ads you can't recall the brand, but with others you can? Research offers us several cautions when it comes to the use of humor:

- Humorous messages may adversely affect comprehension (you can't remember the brand).
- Humorous messages can wear out as quickly as after three exposures, leaving no one laughing, especially the marketer.[10]
- Humorous messages may attract attention without increasing the persuasive impact of an advertisement.

Currently, many of the new dot-com companies are using humor to attract attention to the brand, but fail to show the payoff for the brand. These are the kinds of ads where the humor is remembered and the brand is forgotten. And humor just may be the universal language, as the Global Issues box highlights.

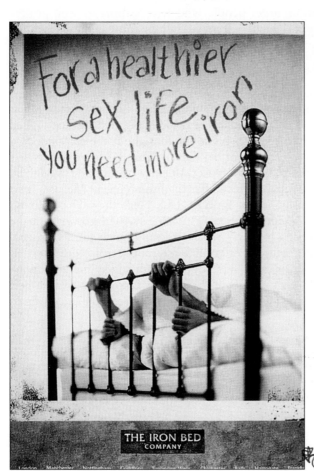

EXHIBIT 8.10

Using sex appeal is one of the ways to pursue the objective of instilling brand preference. This ad for The Iron Bed Company uses a mild sex appeal (with a bit of humor thrown in).

Sex Appeal. Because they are directed toward humans, ads tend to focus on sex from time to time. Not a big surprise, but does sex sell? In a literal sense, the answer is no, because nothing, not even sex, can make someone want what their lifestyle or circumstance or cultural context doesn't make them want. However, sexual appeals are attention getting, which may affect how consumers feel about a brand.

Can you use sex to help create a brand image? Sure you can. Calvin Klein and many other marketers have used sexual imagery successfully to mold brand image. But these are for products such as clothes and perfumes, which emphasize how one looks, feels, and smells. Does the same appeal work as well for cars, telephones, computer peripherals, or file cabinets? How about breakfast cereals? In general, no. But because humans are complex and messy creatures, we cannot say that sex-appeal ads never work in such categories. Sometimes they do. In 1993, the print ads rated most successful in Starch Tested Copy were ads using muted sexual appeal.[11] The ad shown in Exhibits 8.10 uses a muted sex appeal. What do you think? Will it sell beds?

Scare the Consumer into Action

Sometimes the idea is simply to scare consumers or create enough anxiety so that they take action—that is, buy your brand to relieve the fear and anxiety. Fear and anxiety are powerful emotions and may be used to get consumers to take some very important action. However, it must be used strategically and judiciously to work well—or even work at all.

---

10. This claim is made by Video Storyboards Tests, based on its extensive research of humor ads, and cited in Kevin Goldman, "Ever Hear the One About the Funny Ad?" *The Wall Street Journal,* November 2, 1993, B11.
11. Leah Richard, "Basic Approach in Ads Looks Simply Superior," *Advertising Age,* October 10, 1994, 30.

Fear-Appeal Ads. A fear appeal highlights the risk of harm or other negative consequences of not using the advertised brand or not taking some recommended action. The intuitive belief about fear as a message tactic is that fear will motivate the receiver to buy a product that will reduce or eliminate the portrayed threat. For example, Radio Shack spent $6 million to run a series of ads showing a dimly lit, unprotected house, including a peacefully sleeping child, as a way to raise concerns about the safety of the receiver's valuables, as well as his or her family. The campaign used the theme "If security is the question, we've got the answer." The ad closed with the Radio Shack logo and the National Crime Prevention Council slogan, "United against Crime."[12]

The contemporary social environment has provided marketers with an ideal context for using fear appeals. In an era of drive-by shootings, carjackings, and gang violence, Americans fear for their personal safety. Manufacturers of security products such as alarm and lighting security systems play on this fearful environment.[13] Other marketers have recently tried fear as an appeal. One such advertiser, the Asthma Zero Mortality Coalition, urges people who have asthma to seek professional help and uses a fear appeal in its ad copy: "When those painful, strained breaths start coming, keep in mind that any one of them could easily be your last." The creator of the ad states, "Sometimes you have to scare people to save their lives."[14]

Social psychologists and marketing researchers have disagreed on the effectiveness of a fear-based appeal. Traditional research wisdom indicates that intense fear appeals may actually short-circuit persuasion and result in a negative attitude toward the advertised brand. It seems that receivers get so anxious about the fear-inducing message that they focus on the fear and not on overcoming it. Other researchers argue that the tactic is beneficial to the advertiser. But fear works best when the advertising threatens the receiver's loved ones rather than the receiver and uses mild fear, like the ad for Conseco Insurance in Exhibit 8.11. Here the fear of leaving one's loved ones destitute is an attention-getter. The ad may then go on to make explicit suggestions for avoiding the threat—like buying insurance from Conseco, for example. Using fear messages without offering a way out seems more likely to fail than does inducing moderate levels of fear coupled with suggesting an actionable behavior promised to reduce or eliminate the danger. Unfortunately, the best academic research does not provide a clear conclusion on the potential effectiveness of fear as a method.[15]

Anxiety-Inducing Ads. Like fear, anxiety is not pleasant. Most people try to avoid feeling anxious. As a way of coping, people may buy or consume things to help them in their continuing struggle with anxiety. They might buy mouthwash, deodorant, condoms, a safer car, or even open a retirement account as a way to relieve anxiety—and marketers know this.

Marketers use many settings to demonstrate why you should be anxious and what you can do to alleviate the anxiety. Social, medical, and personal-care products frequently use anxiety ads. The message conveyed in anxiety ads is that (1) there is a clear and present danger, and (2) the way to avoid this danger is to buy the advertised brand. When Head & Shoulders dandruff shampoo is advertised with the theme "You never get a second chance to make a first impression," the audience

12. Jeffery D. Zbar, "Fear!" *Advertising Age,* November 14, 1994, 18.
13. Ibid.
14. Emily DeNitto, "Healthcare Ads Employ Scare Tactics," *Advertising Age,* November 7, 1994,
15. Irving L. Janis and Seymour Feshbach, "Effects of Fear Arousing Communication," *Journal of Abnormal Social Psychology* 48 (1953), 78–92; and Michael Ray and William Wilkie, "Fear: The Potential of an Appeal Neglected by Marketing," *Journal of Marketing,* vol. 34, no. 1 (January 1970), 54–62.

EXHIBIT 8.11

Fear and anxiety appeals are designed to scare the consumer into action. This ad for Conseco offers a bit of fear and anxiety, but also a solution.

realizes the power of Head & Shoulders in saving them the embarrassment of having dandruff.

The danger is also often portrayed as being subject to negative social judgment. One of the more memorable Procter & Gamble (a frequent purveyor of anxiety) social anxiety ads is the scene where husband and wife are busily cleaning the spots off the water glasses before dinner guests arrive because they didn't use P&G's Cascade dishwashing product, which, of course, would have prevented the glasses from spotting and saved them the social embarrassment.

Transform Consumption Experiences

You know how sometimes it's hard to explain to someone else just exactly why a certain experience was so special, why it felt so good? It wasn't just this or that; it was that the entire experience was somehow better than the sum of the individual facets. That feeling of overall satisfaction is at least partly due to your expectations of what something might be like, your positive memories of previous experiences, or both. Sometimes marketers try to provide that very anticipation and/or familiarity, bundled up in a positive memory of an advertisement, to be activated during the consumption experience itself. It is thus said to have "transformed" the consumption experience, in part through advertising, and this is a very powerful thing.

Transformational Ads. The idea behind transformational advertising is that it can actually make the consumption experience better. For example, after years of advertising by McDonald's, the experience of eating there is actually transformed or made better by virtue of what you know and feel about McDonald's each time you walk in. **Transformational advertising messages** attempt to create a brand feeling, image, and mood that are activated when the consumer uses the brand. Transformational ads that are acutely effective are said to connect the experience of the advertisement so closely with the brand that consumers cannot help but think of the advertisement (or more accurately, be informed by the memory of many ads), when they think of the brand.

Situate the Brand Socially

Maybe you haven't given it much thought, but if you're ever going to understand advertising, you have to get this: Objects have social meanings. While it applies to all cultures, this simple truth is at the very center of consumer cultures. In consumer cultures such as ours, billions of dollars are spent in efforts to achieve specific social meanings for advertised brands. Marketers have long known that by placing their product in the right social setting, their brand takes on some of the characteristics of the surroundings. In advertising, a brand is placed into a custom-created social setting perfect for the brand. A setting in which the brand excels. Hopefully, this becomes the way in which the consumer remembers the brand, as fitting into this manufactured, very favorable social reality.

**Got a life?
Gotta ask for Scotchgard.**™

Her dolly's thirsty and only juice will do. So don't leave the store without buying a carpet with genuine Scotchgard protection. Nothing protects better or lasts longer. No wonder Scotchgard products are used to take care of more carpet than any other brand. So whether you walk on it, sit on it or wear it, make sure to ask for Scotchgard protection.

There's protection. Then there's Scotchgard™ Protection.

3M *Innovation*

EXHIBIT 8.12

Slice-of-life as an advertising method attempts to situate the brand in a common social context that is relevant to the target audience. This is a familiar scene for anyone who has had kids.

Slice-of-Life Ads. By placing a brand in a social context, it gains social meaning, and relevance, by association. **Slice-of-life advertisements** depict a common scene from common life and suggest gaining benefits and satisfaction from using the brand. Exhibit 8.12 shows a common (and recurring) scene for anyone who has kids. (Note: Not only is this a slice-of-life ad, it is also a "pull" strategy ad—check out Chapter 3 again on promotional planning.)

Light Fantasy. Some ads use a form of light fantasy. These ads allow receivers to pretend a little and think about themselves in the position of the rich, the famous, or the accomplished. For example, the average guy wearing a particular athletic shoe can feel like an NBA all-star. Or what about all that lottery advertising that shows us the wonderful results of winning the lottery? Chances are you're not going to win, but it sure is fun to think about the possibilities while you wait to hear someone else's number drawn.

Define the Brand Image

Wayne Gretzky has an image; Britney Spears has an image; so do Saab and Pepsi. Just like people, brands have images. Images are the most apparent and most prominently associated characteristics of a brand—if a marketer is lucky (and good). Image is the strongest impression consumers associate with a brand, even though it is nearly impossible for consumers to articulate that impression. Marketers are in the business of creating, adjusting, and maintaining images—in other words, they often engage in the define-the-brand-image objective.

Image Ads. Image advertising means different things to different people. To some, it means the absence of hard product information. To others, it refers to advertising that is almost exclusively visual. This is an oversimplification, but it is true that most image advertising tends toward the visual. In both cases, it means an attempt to link certain attributes to the brand, rather than to engage the consumer in any kind of discourse. Sometimes these linkages are quite explicit, such as using a tiger to indicate the strength of a brand. Other times, the linkages are implicit and evoke feelings, like the Harley-Davidson ad in Exhibit 8.13. Read the copy in this ad—you can almost feel the wind in your face.

Persuade the Consumer

Advertising that attempts to persuade is high-engagement advertising. Its goal is to convince the consumer, through a form of commercial discourse, that a brand is superior. The persuasion objective requires a significantly high level of cognitive engagement with the audience. The receiver has to think about what the advertiser is saying. The receiver often engages in a form of mental argument with the commercial. For example, an ad says, "In a Mercedes, you wouldn't get stuck behind a Lexus on the road. . . . Why would you get stuck behind one at your dealer?" You

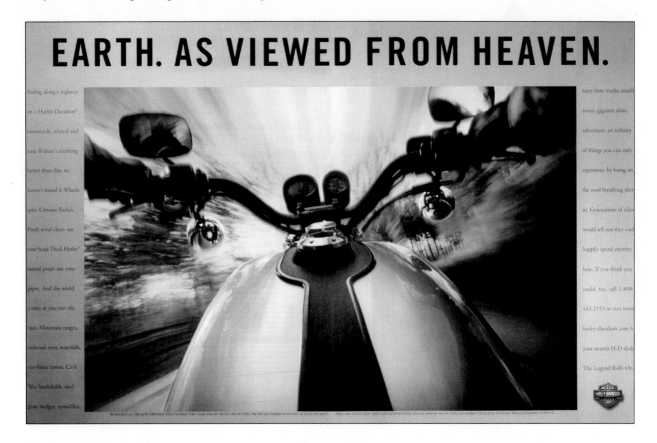

EXHIBIT 8.13

Image advertising creates and maintains a favorable mental impression for receivers. There are few ads that execute as well as this Harley-Davidson ad on creating an image—can you hear the pipes roar?

might read that and say to yourself, "Hey, what's wrong with Lexus? I think Lexus is great. Forget this." Or you might say, "Yeah, if I could afford a Mercedes, I'd buy a really great car." Or maybe you would say to yourself, "Hey, that's right. . . . You know, maybe I should consider a Mercedes next time. They're probably not much more than a Lexus." The point is that in a persuasion ad, there is an assumed dialogue between the ad and the receiver.

Persuading the consumer is the strategy that marketing managers like the best. The methods used in persuasion advertising always feature the brand, frequently feature brand attributes, and always highlight the brand name—all the things that make marketing managers sleep well. Because of this preference in the managerial ranks, there are multiple methods for implementing the persuade-the-consumer strategy objective.

Reason-Why Ads. In a reason-why ad, the advertiser reasons with the consumer. The ad points out to the receiver that there are reasons why this brand will be satisfying and beneficial. Marketers are usually relentless in their attempt to reason with consumers when using this method. They begin with some claim like "Seven great reasons to buy Brand X," and then proceed to list all seven, finishing with the conclusion (implicit or explicit) that only a moron would, after such compelling evidence, do anything other than purchase Brand X.

Hard-Sell Ads. Hard-sell ads are characteristically high pressure and urgent. Phrases such as "act now," "limited time offer," "your last chance to save," and

http://www.glad.com

EXHIBIT 8.14

When you're the little guy in market share, using comparison as method can be very persuasive. That's what Glad is doing against the market leader Tupperware. Glad's Web site, though, won't bother to mention Tupperware—once you've arrived there, probably better to list benefits than invite comparisons (and suggest links away from http://www.glad.com). One place where brands do entangle on the Web is on search sites, where companies can buy the opportunity to have their brands' banner ads appear when users query for a competitor's product. Where might one find product comparisons on the Web?

"one-time-only sale" are representative of this method. The idea is to create a sense of urgency so consumers will act. Of course, many consumers have learned how to decode and otherwise discount these messages, decreasing their effectiveness and persuasive power.

Comparison Ads. Comparison advertisements are ads in which a brand's ability to satisfy consumers is demonstrated by comparing its features to those of competitive brands. Comparisons can be an effective and efficient means of communicating a large amount of information in a clear and interesting way, or they can be extremely confusing. Comparison as a technique has traditionally been used by marketers of convenience goods, such as pain relievers, laundry detergents, and household cleaners. More recently, marketers in a wide range of product categories have tried comparison as their main message method. Even luxury car makers BMW and Lexus have recently targeted each other with comparative claims.[16] In one ad, BMW attacks the sluggish performance of Lexus with the message, "According to recent test results, Lexus' greatest achievement in acceleration is its price." Because of the popularity of comparison advertising by marketers, there has been some fairly extensive research on the method that has identified key aspects to successfully using comparison. Exhibit 8.14 is a comparison ad that follows most of the rules and was probably pretty effective.

- Direct comparison by a *low*-share brand to a high-share brand increases the attention on the part of receivers and increases the purchase intention of the low-share brand.
- Direct comparison by a *high*-share brand to a low-share brand does not attract additional attention and increases awareness of the low-share brand.
- Noncomparative claims by high-share brands are more effective than either direct or indirect comparison at enhancing purchase intention.

- Indirect comparison by moderate-share brands to either high- or low-share brands is more effective than direct comparison at enhancing the purchase intention of moderate-share brands.
- Direct comparison is more effective if members of the target audience have not demonstrated clear brand preference in their product choices.
- Direct comparison is more effective if the television medium is employed to make the comparison.[17]

There is also evidence that comparison advertising is *not* appropriate and will not be effective when one or more of the following are true:

- The fundamental brand appeal is emotional rather than logical.
- The brand is a new product in the product category.
- The product category is characterized by insignificant functional differences between brands, thus making comparisons trivial.
- The competition has powerful counterclaims that can be made in retaliation to the original comparison.
- The brand has distinctive features that can differentiate it from the competition in the absence of comparison.[18]

There are some risks to the advertiser with the use of the comparison tactic. The firm sponsoring a comparative ad is sometimes perceived as less trustworthy, and comparative ads are sometimes evaluated as more offensive and less interesting than noncomparative ads.

Information-Only Ads. First, there is really no such thing as an "information-only" ad. All ads exist to persuade in one way or another. An information-only ad presents facts about a brand, but these facts are not randomly selected. They are chosen for persuasive reasons. A brand with distinctive features can use the information-only message tactic to great advantage. These ads often use a visual to help the audience identify the product features being highlighted.

Testimonial Ads. A frequently used message tactic is to have a spokesperson who champions the brand in an advertisement, rather than simply providing information. When an advocacy position is taken by a spokesperson in an advertisement, this is known as a **testimonial.** The value of the testimonial lies in the authoritative presentation of a brand's attributes and benefits by the spokesperson. There are three basic versions of the testimonial message strategy:

- The most conspicuous version is the **celebrity testimonial.** Sports stars such as Michael Jordan (McDonald's) and Arnold Palmer (Pennzoil, Cadillac) are favorites of marketers. Actresses such as Jamie Lee Curtis (Sprint) and supermodels such as Cindy Crawford (Pepsi) are also widely used. The belief is that a celebrity testimonial will increase an ad's ability to attract attention and produce a desire in receivers to emulate or imitate the celebrities they admire.[19] And

17. Conclusions on this list are drawn from William R. Swinyard, "The Interaction Between Comparative Advertisements and Copy Claim Variation," *Journal of Marketing Research,* 18 (May 1981), 175–186; Cornelia Pechmann and David Stewart, "The Effects of Comparative Advertising on Attention, Memory, and Purchase Intentions," *Journal of Consumer Research* (September 1990), 180–191; and Sanjay Petruvu and Kenneth R. Lord, "Comparative and Noncomparative Advertising: Attitudinal Effects Under Cognitive and Affective Involvement Conditions," *Journal of Advertising* (June 1994), 77–90.

18. In general, comparative advertisements are not more effective than noncomparative ads when the intention is to affect brand attitude. For a current review of literature on conditions related to the effectiveness of comparative advertising, see Cornelia Pechmann and David Stewart, "The Psychology of Comparative Advertising," in *Attention, Attitude, and Affect in Response to Advertising,* E. M. Clark, T. C. Brock, and D. W. Steward, eds. (Hillsdale, NJ: Erlbaum, 1994), 79–96.

19. Kevin Goldman, "Year's Top Commercials Propelled by Star Power," *The Wall Street Journal,* March 16, 1994, B1.

testimonials don't have to be just in advertising, as the IMC in Practice discussion points out. Of course, there is the ever-present risk that a celebrity will fall from grace, as several have in recent years, and potentially damage the reputation of the brand for which he or she was once the champion.

- **Expert spokespersons** for a brand are viewed by the target audience as having expert product knowledge. The GM Parts Service Division created an expert in Mr. Goodwrench, who was presented as a knowledgeable source of information. A spokesperson portrayed as a doctor, lawyer, scientist, gardener, or any other expert relevant to a brand is intended to increase the credibility of the message. There are also real experts. Advertising for The Club, a steering-wheel locking device that deters auto theft, uses police officers from several high-crime U.S. cities to demonstrate the effectiveness of the product. Some experts can also be celebrities. This is the case when Michael Jordan gives a testimonial for Nike basketball shoes.

- There is also the **average-user testimonial.** Here, the spokesperson is not a celebrity or portrayed as an expert but rather just an average user speaking for the brand. The idea here is that the target market can relate to this person. Solid theoretical support for this testimonial approach comes from reference group theory—consumers may rely on opinions from people they consider similar to themselves, rather than on objective product information. Simply put, the consumer's logic in this situation is "That person is similar to me and likes that brand; therefore, I will also like that brand." In theory, this sort of logic frees the receiver from having to pore over detailed product information by simply substituting the reference group information. Of course, in practice, the execution of this strategy is nowhere near that easy. Consumers are pretty savvy at detecting this attempt at persuasion.

Demonstration. How close an electric razor shaves, how green a fertilizer makes a lawn, or how easy an exercise machine is to use are all product features that can be demonstrated by using a method known simply as the demonstration ad. "Seeing is believing" is the motto of this school of advertising. When it's done well, the results are striking.

Advertorial. An **advertorial** is a special advertising section designed to look like the print publication in which it appears. Advertorials are so named because they have the look of the editorial content of a magazine or newspaper, but really represent a long and involved advertisement for a brand. *The Wall Street Journal, Redbook, Fortune,* and *New York* magazine have all carried advertorials. *Sports Illustrated* has inserted advertorials for the Kentucky Derby and the Indianapolis 500. The potential effectiveness of this technique comes from the increased credibility of the look and length of the advertisement. These features have, however, raised controversy. Some critics believe that most readers aren't even aware they're reading an advertisement because of the similarity in appearance to the publication.[20]

Invoke a Direct Response

A direct-response advertising appeal implores the receiver to act immediately. It's a blend of hard selling and impulse buying. Price appeals associated with special sales or the convenience of ordering from the comfort of one's home form the basis of the direct-response objective. National direct merchants such as L. L. Bean and J. Crew are the most frequent users of this message strategy. The main characteristic

---

20. Cynthia Crossen, "Proliferation of 'Advertorials' Blurs Distinction Between News and Ads," *The Wall Street Journal,* April 21, 1998, 33.

of all direct-response (sometimes called direct-action) ads, however, is encouraging the audience to respond immediately. Ads in traditional media encourage consumers to call or mail in a coupon. Internet advertising wants us to "click now" to take advantage of offers. The other form of direct response is the **infomercial,** which is an elaborate version of the direct-response message strategy.

IN PRACTICE

TAKING IT IN THE SHORTS

For a brand that has been associated for decades with youthful rebellion, Levi's has an interesting problem: teenage indifference. While Levi's has successfully followed baby boomers into adulthood and middle age with jeans tailored to a changing body and new "casual" clothes like Dockers, the firm has lost its grip on teenagers. The firm completely missed the baggy rebellion of youth—including the droopy shorts.

The problem is not minimal. Levi's market share among kids is down from 33 to 26 percent. By 1999, the firm was experiencing double-digit sales declines with teens turning to private label brands like JCPenney's Arizona and The Gap as well as spending more on designer jeans from Calvin Klein and Tommy Hilfiger. What was worse was the way kids were talking about Levi's. Company executives were forced to endure video after video of focus group sessions in which teens talked about Levi Strauss as if it were a has-been—saying the jeans were uncool or only suited for their parents or older brothers and sisters. As one consultant put it, Levi Strauss was zagging while the world was zigging. But Levi Strauss does have a response. The company's SilverTab brand is very popular among more stylish young consumers. The brand has a median age of 18 for purchasers. It has a baggier fit and is on the right side of the fashion line.

So how does Levi's take advantage of this brand opportunity? By developing an exciting and effective integrated marketing communications program. Along with traditional magazine and television advertising—the mainstays of marketing clothes to teens—the firm has a wide array of new and different ways to reach teens. First, the company is sponsoring concerts by up-and-coming bands that play "electronica" music. Next, characters on new, hot, teen-oriented shows such as *Friends* and *Beverly Hills 90210* are outfitted in SilverTab jeans. Another piece of the communications puzzle is to make sure that Levi's retailers maintain stylish presentation so that all aspects of the SilverTab communication are consistent and hip.

The use of various tools beyond major advertising is a way to reinforce the advertising themes and reach teens in different and interesting ways—classic integrated marketing communications. The trick will be to keep the company name viable among the Bob Dylan set.

Sources: Linda Himelstein, "Levi's Is Hiking Up Its Pants," *Business Week*, December 1, 1997, 70, 75; and Alice Z. Cuneo, "Levi's $75 mil TV Account in Review," *Advertising Age*, January 31, 2000.

Call, Mail, or Click Now. Direct-response ads have become more prevalent in recent years for several reasons. First, many direct-response messages feature a price-oriented appeal. In today's era of value-oriented, price-conscious consumers, direct-response messages provide an ideal opportunity for offering consumers a discount via a mail-in coupon or special television offer that is a price-based appeal. Second, firms have developed sophisticated databases that allow them to specifically target well-defined customer groups. Such databases can be tailored to geographic areas, demographic characteristics of audiences, or past product use as ways to target different audiences. With Internet profiling techniques, surfing behavior can be tracked to offer consumers brands that fit their interest areas. With database information, the marketer can then send a specific and different message to each target audience. Third, marketers are demanding more evidence that the dollars they spend on advertising are having an impact. Ad agencies have found that direct-response messages offer the most tangible evidence of advertising impact, and they are using the technique as a means of accountability. The BOSE ad in Exhibit 8.15 is an interesting example because it gives the consumer the choice of calling, mailing, or clicking.

Infomercials. With the infomercial, a marketer buys from five to sixty minutes of television time and runs a documentary/information/entertainment program that is really an extended advertisement. Real estate investment programs, weight-loss and fitness products, motivational programs, and cookware have dominated the infomercial

20 engineers, 18 months, and the result doesn't really look or sound any different from the original.

Now that's a success story.

It was a tall order, even for Bose® engineers: take the most highly reviewed radio regardless of size or price—what Radio World called "simply amazing...a genuine breakthrough." Now make it even better. Add a CD player. Match the award-winning sound of the original Wave® radio. Go to any lengths necessary—but don't increase the size of the radio by more than a quarter inch.

The result: the new Bose Wave radio/CD. To keep it small and sleek, like its predecessor, we made room for a compact disc player by redesigning the patented acoustic waveguide speaker. Listen and you'll hear full, natural bass and clean sound that no conventional radio can produce. Naturally, the new Wave radio/CD offers all the convenience of the original, and then some. The remote, in addition to adjusting the volume and changing stations, also lets you control the CD player from across the room. There are even dual alarms that can wake you to your favorite CD track.

Insert disc. Press play. Be impressed. The new Wave radio/CD is available for $499 directly from Bose. If you prefer, you can make six interest-free payments. Listen for 30 days. The Wave radio/CD is unlike any conventional radio you've heard before. If you don't agree, return it for a full refund—no questions asked. Call Bose today and find out why we think we've created the world's best-sounding radio. Twice.

1-800-375-2073, ext. T2559
For information on all our products: **www.bose.com/t2559**
Please specify color when ordering.
Wave radio/CD $499: ☐ Platinum White only
Wave radio $349: ☐ Platinum White or ☐ Graphite Gray

Name _____ Address/City/State/Zip
Day Phone _____ Evening Phone
Mail to: Bose Corporation, Dept. CDD-T2559, The Mountain, Framingham, MA 01701-9168.

Wave Radio/CD $499   **Wave Radio** $349

BOSE
Better sound through research.

© 2000 Bose Corporation. Covered by patent rights issued and/or pending. Bose and the Wave radio design are registered trademarks of Bose Corporation. Installment payment plan not to be combined with any other offer and available on credit card orders only. Payment plan subject to change without notice. Frank Beacham, Radio World, 1/3/96.

http://www.bose.com/t3584; http://www.digimarc.com

EXHIBIT 8.15

Direct-response advertising tries to get the consumer to take immediate action. This BOSE *ad uses all the direct-response techniques available— call, mail, or click now. Note the use of a code in the Web address:* BOSE *also wants to know how you arrived there, and the code provides a no-mistake way to log exactly which ad pulled you in. New technologies are intended to make it even easier to get from here to there: Digimarc has a scheme that embeds scannable codes in print ads, to let those consumers with scanning tools "zap" on an ad and be whisked straight to an advertiser's Web site. What direct-response techniques do you think work best?*

format. A 30-minute infomercial can cost from $50,000 to $1.2 million to put on the air. The program usually has a host who provides information about a brand and typically brings on guests to give testimonials about how successful they have been using the brand. Most infomercials run on cable stations, although networks have sold early-morning and late-night time slots as well. Recently, big firms have used infomercials. Philips Electronics has had great success with a 30-minute adventure-like infomercial for its compact disc interactive (CD–I) player. Philips spent nearly $20 million to produce and buy prime-time media for the infomercial but contends the infomercial had much more impact than the print advertising it replaced.[21]

Message strategy is where the advertising battle is usually won or lost. It's where real creativity exists. It's where the agency has to be smart and figure out just how to turn the wishes of the client into effective advertising. It is where the creatives have to get into the minds of consumers, realizing that the advertisement will be received by different people in different ways. Great messages are developed by people who can put themselves into the minds of their audience members and anticipate their response, leading to the desired outcomes. They create social texts that resonate with the lived experience of their consumers.

But even the greatest ad ever conceived will be powerless without the right media placement. If an ad reaches the wrong target audiences, not only will it not impress them, it might even offend them. To avoid this, the creatives turn the process over to the media planners, who can identify the media mix that will reach target audiences effectively and efficiently.

The Media-Planning Process ④

The wealth of media options demands incredible attention to detail in the media-planning process. As we saw in Chapter 1, one of the reasons firms are putting so much emphasis on IMC is because of the proliferation of media—both traditional media and new media.

In order to appreciate the importance of media planning, we will look at the way marketers and their agencies put together a media plan. But first, we're going to have to get down some basic terminology to understand this process. A **media plan** specifies the media in which advertising messages will be placed to reach the desired target audience. A **media class** is a broad category of media, such as television, radio, or newspapers. A **media vehicle** is a particular option for placement within a media class. For example, *Newsweek* is a media vehicle within the magazine media class.

A media plan includes objectives, strategies, media choices, and a media schedule for placing a message. Exhibit 8.16 shows the specific components of a media plan. Notice

21.   Kevin Goldman, "Philips Infomercial Does Its Thing in Popular TV Watching Hours," *The Wall Street Journal,* September 23, 1993, B6.

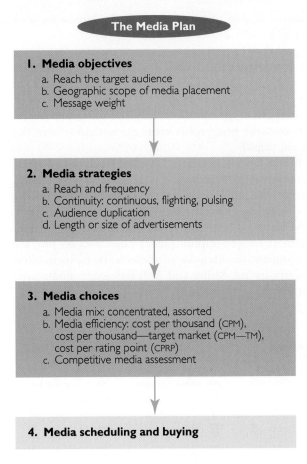

The Media Plan

1. Media objectives
   a. Reach the target audience
   b. Geographic scope of media placement
   c. Message weight

2. Media strategies
   a. Reach and frequency
   b. Continuity: continuous, flighting, pulsing
   c. Audience duplication
   d. Length or size of advertisements

3. Media choices
   a. Media mix: concentrated, assorted
   b. Media efficiency: cost per thousand (CPM),
      cost per thousand—target market (CPM—TM),
      cost per rating point (CPRP)
   c. Competitive media assessment

4. Media scheduling and buying

EXHIBIT 8.16

The media planning process

that media planners set media objectives, identify strategies, make media choices, and finally set a media schedule, including the media-buying process. We need to discuss each stage of the media-planning process.

Media Objectives

Media objectives set specific goals for a media placement: Reach the target audience, determine the geographic scope of placement, and identify the message weight, or the total mass of advertising delivered against a target audience.

Reach. The first and most important media objective is that the media chosen reach the target audience. Recall that the definition of a target audience can be demographic, geographic, or based on lifestyle or attitude dimensions. The target may be a consumer audience or a business audience. In many cases, media planners are placed in the awkward situation of trying to put together a media plan based only on weak secondary data provided by media companies—usually only demographic data.

If marketers are willing to spend extra money, however, there are media research organizations that provide detailed information on the media habits and purchase behaviors of target audiences. This information can greatly increase the precision of media choices. The two most prominent providers of demographic information that is correlated with product usage data are Mediamark Research, Inc. (MRI) and Simmons Market Research Bureau (SMRB). An example of the type of information supplied is shown in Exhibit 8.17, where market statistics for four brands of men's aftershave and cologne are compared: Eternity for Men, Jovan Musk, Lagerfeld, and Obsession for Men. The most revealing data are contained in columns C and D. Column C shows each brand's strength relative to a demographic variable, such as age or income. Column D provides an index showing that particular segments of the population are heavier users of a particular brand. Specifically, the number expresses each brand's share of volume as a percentage of its share of users. An index number above 100 shows particular strength for a brand. The strength of Eternity for Men as well as Obsession for Men is high in both the 18–24 and the 25–34 age cohorts.

Recently, even more sophisticated data have become available. Research services such as ACNielsen's Home★Scan and Information Resources' BehaviorScan are referred to as **single-source tracking services,** which offer information not just on demographics but also on brands, purchase size, purchase frequency, prices paid, and media exposure. BehaviorScan is the most comprehensive, in that not just brand behavior but also exposure to particular television programs, magazines, and newspapers can be identified. With demographic, behavioral, and media-exposure correlations provided by research services like these, marketers and media planners can answer really tough questions that up until now, they had no clue about:

- How many members of the target audience have tried our brand, and how many are brand loyal?
- What affects brand sales more—more advertising or changes in advertising copy?
- What other products do buyers of the our brand purchase regularly?

- What television programs, magazines, and newspapers reach the largest number of people in the target audience?[22]

Geographic Scope of Media Placement. Another critical element in setting advertising objectives is determining the geographic scope of media placement. In some ways, this is relatively easy: just identify the media that cover the same geographic area as the marketer's distribution system. Obviously, spending money on the placement of ads in media that cover geographic areas other than where the marketer's brand is distributed is, ah, stupid.

But it's not always that easy. When factors like brand market share or competitors' activities are taken into account, media objectives for geographic scope get a little more complicated. For example, the strength of microbreweries in the northeastern and northwestern United States has forced major national brewers such as Miller Brewing and Anheuser-Busch (A–B) not only to develop specialty beers, such as Red Wolf, but also to alter their geographic media objectives to provide different coverage based on the competitive intensity of these markets. In markets where microbreweries are particularly strong, Miller and A–B buy extra media time or run special promotions to combat the competition.

BASE: MEN	TOTAL U.S. '000	ETERNITY FOR MEN A '000	B % DOWN	C % ACROSS	D INDEX	JOVAN MUSK A '000	B % DOWN	C % ACROSS	D INDEX	LAGERFELD A '000	B % DOWN	C % ACROSS	D INDEX	OBSESSION FOR MEN A '000	B % DOWN	C % ACROSS	D INDEX
All Men	92674	2466	100.0	2.7	100	3194	100.0	3.4	100	1269	100.0	1.4	100	3925	100.0	4.2	100
Men	92674	2466	100.0	2.7	100	3194	100.0	3.4	100	1269	100.0	1.4	100	3925	100.0	4.2	100
Women	–	–			–	–			–	–			–	–			–
Household Heads	77421	1936	78.5	2.5	94	2567	80.4	3.3	96	1172	92.4	1.5	111	2856	72.7	3.7	87
Homemakers	31541	967	39.2	3.1	115	1158	36.3	3.7	107	451	35.5	1.4	104	1443	36.8	4.6	108
Graduated College	21727	583	23.7	2.7	101	503	15.8	2.3	67	348	27.4	1.6	117	901	23.0	4.1	98
Attended College	23842	814	33.0	3.4	128	933	29.2	3.9	113	*270	21.3	1.1	83	1283	32.7	5.4	127
Graduated High School	29730	688	27.9	2.3	87	1043	32.7	3.5	102	*460	36.3	1.5	113	1266	32.2	4.3	101
Did not Graduate High School	17374	*380	15.4	2.2	82	*715	22.4	4.1	119	*191	15.0	1.1	80	*475	12.1	2.7	65
18-24	12276	754	30.6	6.1	231	*391	12.2	3.2	92	*7	0.5	0.1	4	747	19.0	6.1	144
25-34	20924	775	31.4	3.7	139	705	22.1	3.4	98	*234	18.5	1.1	82	1440	36.7	6.9	162
35-44	21237	586	23.8	2.8	104	1031	32.3	4.9	141	*311	24.5	1.5	107	838	21.3	3.9	93
45-54	14964	*202	8.2	1.4	51	*510	16.0	3.4	99	*305	24.0	2.0	149	481	12.3	3.2	76
55-64	10104	*112	4.6	1.1	42	*215	6.7	2.1	62	*214	16.9	2.1	155	*245	6.2	2.4	57
65 or over	13168	*37	1.5	0.3	10	*342	10.7	2.6	75	*198	15.6	1.5	110	*175	4.4	1.3	31
18-34	33200	1529	62.0	4.6	173	1096	34.3	3.3	96	*241	19.0	0.7	53	2187	55.7	6.6	156
18-49	62950	2228	90.4	3.5	133	2460	77.0	3.9	113	683	53.9	1.1	79	3315	84.5	5.3	124
25-54	57125	1563	63.4	2.7	103	2246	70.3	3.9	114	850	67.0	1.5	109	2758	70.3	4.8	114
Employed Full Time	62271	1955	79.3	3.1	118	2141	67.0	3.4	100	977	77.0	1.6	115	2981	76.0	4.8	113
Part-time	5250	*227	9.2	4.3	163	*141	4.4	2.7	78	*10	0.8	0.2	14	*300	7.7	5.7	135
Sole Wage Earner	21027	554	22.5	2.6	99	794	24.9	3.8	110	332	26.2	1.6	115	894	22.8	4.3	100
Not Employed	25153	*284	11.5	1.1	42	912	28.6	3.6	105	*281	22.2	1.1	82	643	16.4	2.6	60
Professional	9010	*232	9.4	2.6	97	*168	5.3	1.9	54	*143	11.3	1.6	116	504	12.8	5.6	132
Executive/Admin./Managerial	10114	*259	10.5	2.6	96	*305	9.6	3.0	88	*185	14.6	1.8	134	353	9.0	3.5	82
Clerical/Sales/Technical	13212	436	17.7	3.3	124	*420	13.2	3.2	92	*231	18.2	1.7	128	741	18.9	5.6	132
Precision/Crafts/Repair	12162	624	25.3	5.1	193	*317	9.9	2.6	76	*168	13.2	1.4	101	511	13.0	4.2	99
Other Employed	23022	631	25.6	2.7	103	1071	33.5	4.7	135	*261	20.6	1.1	83	1173	29.9	5.1	120
H/D Income $75,000 or More	17969	481	19.5	2.7	101	*320	10.0	1.9	52	413	32.5	2.3	168	912	23.2	5.1	120
$60,000 - 74,999	10346	*368	14.9	3.6	134	*309	9.7	3.0	87	*142	11.2	1.4	100	495	12.6	4.8	113
$50,000 - 59,999	9175	*250	10.2	2.7	103	*424	13.3	4.6	134	*153	12.1	1.7	122	*371	9.4	4.0	95
$40,000 - 49,999	11384	*308	12.5	2.7	102	*387	12.1	3.4	99	*134	10.6	1.2	86	580	14.8	5.1	120
$30,000 - 39,999	12981	*360	14.6	2.8	104	542	17.0	4.2	121	*126	10.0	1.0	71	*416	10.6	3.2	76
$20,000 - 29,999	13422	*266	10.8	2.0	75	*528	16.5	3.9	114	*164	12.9	1.2	89	*475	12.1	3.5	84
$10,000 - 19,999	11867	*401	16.3	3.4	127	*394	12.3	3.3	96	*67	5.3	0.6	41	*481	12.3	4.1	96
Less than $10,000	5528	*31	1.3	0.6	21	*291	9.1	5.3	153	*69	5.4	1.2	91	*194	4.9	3.5	83

Source: Mediamark Research Inc., Mediamark Research Men's, Women's Personal Care Products Report (Mediamark Research Inc., Spring 1997), 16. Reprinted with permission.

EXHIBIT 8.17

Commercial research firms can provide marketers with information about a brand's strength in a demographic market relative to the competition. This data table is typical of the information available from one such firm, Mediamark Research, and shows how several men's fragrance brands perform in different demographic segments.

22. Donaton and Sloan, "Control New Media," 8; Alasdair Reid, "P&G Will Make Use of Any New Medium That Proves Effective," ASAP, September 18, 1998, 28.

Some analysts suggest that when certain geographic markets demonstrate unusually high purchasing tendencies of a product category (like barbecue sauce in Texas or white wine in California) or by brand, then geotargeting should be the basis for the media placement decision. **Geotargeting** is placing advertisements in geographic regions where higher purchase tendencies for a product category or brand are evident. For example, in one geographic area the average consumer purchases of Prego spaghetti sauce were 36 percent greater than the average consumer purchases nationwide. With this kind of information, media buys can be geotargeted to reinforce high-volume users.[23] This is called investing into your strength.

Message Weight. The final media objective is message weight, the total mass of advertising delivered. **Message weight** is the gross number of advertising messages or exposure opportunities delivered by the vehicles in a schedule. An important issue in message weight is that the measurement includes **duplication of exposure**—that is, an individual may be counted more than one time in a message weight calculation. **Unduplicated audience measurement,** known as reach, is discussed in the next section. Media planners are interested in the message weight of a media plan because it provides a simple indication of the size of the advertising effort being placed against a specific market. (The word "against" means "invest in," basically. It is a special word that advertising people use all the time for some reason, and no one has ever been able to figure out how it got started.)

Message weight is typically expressed in terms of gross impressions. **Gross impressions** are the sum of exposures to the vehicles in a media plan. Planners often distinguish between two types of exposure possibilities. **Potential ad impressions,** or opportunities to be exposed to ads, are the most common and refer to exposures by the media vehicle carrying advertisements (for example, a TV program or magazine). **Message impressions,** on the other hand, refers to exposures to the ads themselves. Information on ad exposure probabilities can be obtained from a number of companies, including Nielsen, Simmons, Roper-Starch, Gallup & Robinson, Harvey Research, and Readex. This information can pertain to particular advertisements, campaigns, media vehicles, product categories, ad characteristics, and target groups. To be honest, the most reasonable measure is the message impression. Do we really care about "potential impressions"?

For example, consider a media plan that, in a one-week period, placed ads on three television programs and in two national newspapers. The sum of the exposures to the media placement might be as follows:

		Gross Impressions	
		Potential Ad Impressions	**Message Impressions**
Television:	Program A audience	16,250,000	5,037,500
	Program B audience	4,500,000	1,395,000
	Program C audience	7,350,000	2,278,500
Sum of TV exposures		28,100,000	8,711,000
Newspapers:	Newspaper 1	1,900,000	376,200
	Newspaper 2	450,000	89,100
Sum of newspaper exposures		2,350,000	465,300
Total gross impressions		30,450,000	9,176,300

23. This section and the example are drawn from Erwin Ephron, "The Organizing Principle of Media," *Inside Media,* November 2, 1992.

CAREER PROFILE

Name: Sharie Lesniak
Title: Copywriter
Company: Addis Group, Berkeley, Calif., http://www.addis.com
Education: B.B.A., Marketing

When Sharie Lesniak was struggling to decide what she wanted to do after graduation, she made a list of all the things she enjoyed most. Topping the list were writing, art, music, and working with people. Was there any type of job that would let her combine all of these things? The answer, Sharie discovered, was advertising copywriting. "I love my job," says Sharie. "I feel sorry for people who don't do something they enjoy as much as I do."

As a copywriter, Sharie has been involved with developing media messages for clients as diverse as Nissan, Smith & Hawkins, Absolut Vodka, and pharmaceutical maker Merck & Co. According to Sharie, the most successful promotional campaigns start with what she calls "the Big Idea." The goal is to distill the essence of a product down to a one-word concept which then leads to the big idea. "If you get the right idea, it's not hard to make it work across the board, whether you're writing a print ad, a television commercial, or some other type of promotional piece," she explains. "The most important thing a copywriter should be able to do is recognize a good idea, whether it comes from them, the client, or the office receptionist."

At Addis, developing the right message for effective campaigns is always a team effort. An account executive, art director, and copywriter meet with the client to ask questions and discuss objectives. During these meetings, Sharie listens closely. "The more information I can get, the better my chances of discovering a gem for a successful campaign," she says. Later, the Addis team meets to develop a creative strategy for getting the client's message across in words and visuals. "In most cases, the words come first and then we decide how to tie into the idea visually," says Sharie. Although many advertising agencies use separate media planning departments, at Addis media decisions are made by the account executive, with input from other team members. "Working together, both within the agency and with the client, is the strongest way to develop something that works," says Sharie.

To learn more about copywriting and media planning visit these Web sites:

USCreative.com
http://www.uscreative.com

Advertising Age magazine
http://www.adage.com

Adweek Online
http://www.adweek.com

The Advertising Media Internet Center
http://www.amic.com

Here's another thing we have to be aware of. This does not mean that 30,450,000 separate people were exposed to the programs and newspapers or that 9,176,300 separate people were exposed to the advertisements. Some people who watched TV program A also saw program B and read newspaper 1, as well as all other possible combinations. This is called **between-vehicle duplication.** It is also possible that someone who saw the ad in newspaper 1 on Monday saw it again in newspaper 1 on Tuesday. This is **within-vehicle duplication.** That's why we say that the total gross impressions number contains *audience duplication.* Data available from services such as SMRB report both types of duplication so that they can be removed from the gross impressions to produce the unduplicated estimate of audience, called reach. (You should know, however, that the math involved in such calculations is fairly complex.)

The message weight objective provides only a broad perspective for a media planner. What does it mean that a media plan for a week produced more than 30 million gross impressions? It means only that a pretty large number of people were sitting around watching TV or reading newspapers and magazines and just *might* be exposed to the brand's message. This does not mean that message weight is unimportant. It does give the marketer a general point of reference. When Toyota Motors introduced the Avalon in the U.S. market, the $40 million introductory ad campaign featured 30-second television spots, newspaper and magazine print ads (see Exhibit 8.18), and direct-mail pieces. The highlight of the campaign was a nine-spot placement on a heavily watched Thursday evening TV show, costing more than $2 million. The message weight of this campaign in a single week was enormous—just the type of objective Toyota's media planners wanted for the brand introduction.[24]

Media Strategies ⑤

The true power of a media plan is in the media strategy. The strategy is expressed in decisions made about each media vehicle's reach and frequency, the continuity of media placement, the audience duplication, and the length and size of

24. Bradley Johnson, "Toyota's New Avalon Thinks Big, American," *Advertising Age,* November 14, 1994, 46.

EXHIBIT 8.18

When Toyota introduced the Avalon, they used a media mix that included TV spots, magazine and newspaper print ads, and direct-mail pieces. Toyota was trying to create a heavy "message weight" by using several media.

advertisements. Good media strategy decisions help ensure that good messages get placed in the right media so they can have as much impact as possible.

Reach and Frequency. As we just saw in media objectives, **reach** refers to the number of people or households in a target audience that will be exposed to a media vehicle or schedule at least once during a given period of time. It is often expressed as a percentage. If an advertisement placed on the hit network television program *ER* is watched at least once by 30 percent of the advertiser's target audience, the reach is said to be 30 percent. Media vehicles with broad reach are ideal for consumer convenience goods, like toothpaste, soft drinks, snack foods, and cold remedies. These are products with fairly simple features, and they are frequently purchased by just about everybody in America. Broadcast television, cable television, and national magazines have the largest and broadest reach of all the media, so they get the nod when reach is the main goal.

Frequency is the average number of times an individual or household within a target audience is exposed to a media vehicle in a given period (typically a week or a month). For example, say a marketer places an ad on a weekly television show with a 20 rating (20 percent of households) for four weeks in a row. The show has an (unduplicated) reach of 43 (percent) over the four-week period. So, frequency is then equal to $(20 \times 4)/43$, or 1.9. This means that an audience member had the opportunity to see the ad an average of 1.9 times.

An important measure for media planners related to both reach (r) and frequency (f) is gross rating points (GRP). **Gross rating points** is the product of reach times frequency (GRP $= r \times f$). When media planners calculate the GRP for a media plan, they multiply the rating (reach) of each vehicle in a plan times the number of times an ad will be inserted in the media vehicle and sum these figures across all vehicles in the plan. Exhibit 8.19 shows the GRP for a combined magazine and television schedule.

The GRP number is used as a relative measure of the intensity of one media plan versus another. Whether a media plan is appropriate or not is ultimately based on the judgment of the media planner. Is the media plan in Exhibit 8.19 better than some other plan that could achieve the same 362 GRP? Maybe. Maybe not. This is where the judgment comes in.

Marketers often struggle with the dilemma of increasing reach at the expense of frequency, or vice versa. At the core in this struggle are the concepts of effective frequency and effective reach. **Effective frequency** is the number of times a target audience needs to be exposed to a message before the objectives of the advertiser are met—either communications objectives or sales impact. Many factors affect the level of effective frequency. New brands and brands laden with features may demand high frequency. Simple messages for well-known products may require less frequent exposure for consumers to be affected. While most analysts agree that one exposure will typically not be enough, there is debate about how many exposures are enough. A common industry practice is to place effective frequency at three exposures, but analysts argue that as few as two or as many as nine exposures are needed to achieve effective frequency.[25]

Effective reach is the number or percentage of consumers in the target audience that are exposed to an ad some minimum number of times. The minimum-number estimate for effective reach is based on a determination of effective frequency. If effective reach is set at four exposures, then a media schedule must be devised that achieves at least four exposures over a specified time period within the target audience.

EXHIBIT 8.19

Gross rating point (GRP) summary for a media plan

Media Class/Vehicle	Rating (reach)	Number of Ad Insertions (frequency)	GRP
Television			
ER	25	4	100
Law & Order	20	4	80
Good Morning America	12	4	48
Days of Our Lives	7	2	14
Magazines			
People	22	2	44
Travel & Leisure	11	2	22
U.S. News & World Report	9	6	54
Total			**362**

25. For a complete discussion of the evolution of the concepts of effective reach and effective frequency, see Jack Z. Sissors and Lincoln Bumba, *Advertising Media Planning,* 5th ed. (Lincolnwood, IL: NTC Business Books, 1996), 115–147.

A final word on the concept of reach is necessary in the interest of total honesty and full disclosure. It may have occurred to you during this whole discussion of reach that there is a somewhat *massive* assumption being made. Namely, that if a message "reaches" a household, the assumption is that someone actually paid attention to it. Recall our discussion in Chapter 5 about the communication process and selective attention. Just because an ad appears on a television screen or in a magazine doesn't mean the receiver paid any attention to it. Implicitly, the concept and calculations of reach assume that those ads are "reaching" (that is, are seen by) a receiver. You need to know this.

Continuity. The second important strategic decision in the media plan is about continuity. **Continuity** is the pattern of placement of advertisements in a media schedule. There are three strategic scheduling alternatives: continuous, flighting, and pulsing. **Continuous scheduling** is a pattern of placing ads at a steady rate over a period of time. Running one ad each day for four weeks during the soap opera *General Hospital* would be a continuous pattern. Similarly, an ad that appeared in every issue of *Spin* magazine for a year would also be continuous. Flighting is another media-scheduling strategy. **Flighting** is achieved by scheduling heavy advertising for a period of time, usually two weeks, then stopping advertising altogether for a period, only to come back with another heavy schedule.

Flighting is often used to support special seasonal merchandising efforts or new product introductions, or as a response to competitors' promotions. The financial advantages of flighting are that discounts might be gained by concentrating media buys in larger blocks. Communication effectiveness may actually be increased because a heavy schedule will cause the repetition necessary to achieve consumer awareness.

Finally, **pulsing** is a media-scheduling strategy that combines elements from the continuous and flighting techniques—advertisements are scheduled continuously in media over a period of time, but with periods of much heavier scheduling (the flight). Pulsing is most appropriate for products that are sold fairly regularly all year long but have certain seasonal spikes, like clothing.

Length or Size of Advertisements. Beyond whom to reach, how often to reach them, and in what pattern, media planners must make strategic decisions regarding the length of an ad in electronic media or the size of an ad in print media. Certainly, the marketer, creative director, art director, and copywriter have made determinations in this regard as well. Television advertisements (excluding infomercials) can range from ten to sixty seconds, and sometimes even two minutes, in length. Is a sixty-second television commercial always six times more effective than a ten-second spot? Of course, the answer is no. Is a full-page newspaper ad always more effective than a two-inch, one-column ad? Again, not necessarily. Marketers use full-page newspaper ads when some product claim warrants it.

The decision about the length or size of an advertisement depends on the creative requirements for the ad, the media budget, and the competitive environment within which the ad is running. From a creative standpoint, ads attempting to develop an image for a brand may need to be longer in broadcast media or larger in print media to offer more creative opportunities. On the other hand, a simple, straightforward message announcing a sale may be quite short or small, but it may need heavy repetition. From the standpoint of the media budget, shorter and smaller ads are, with few exceptions, much less expensive. If a media plan includes some level of repetition to accomplish its objectives, the lower-cost option may be mandatory. From a competitive perspective, matching a competitor's presence with messages of similar size or length may be essential to maintain the share of mind in a target audience. Once again, the size and length decisions are a matter of judgment between the creative team and the media planner, tempered by the availability of funds for media placement.

Media Choices

The next stage of the media-planning process focuses on media selection. Exhibit 8.20 gives general assessment of the advantages and disadvantages for the major media. We'll evaluate the Internet separately in the next chapter. The marketer and the agency team together will determine which media class is appropriate for the current effort. Media choice addresses three distinct issues: media mix, media efficiency, and competitive media assessment.

Media Mix. In making specific media choices for placing advertisements, media planners have to decide what sort of media mix to use. The **media mix** is the blend of different media that will be used to effectively reach the target audience. There are two options for a media planner with respect to the media mix: a concentrated media mix or an assorted media mix.[26] A **concentrated media mix** focuses all the media placement dollars in one medium. The rationale behind this option is that it allows an advertiser to have great impact on a specific audience segment. A highly concentrated media mix can give a brand an aura of mass acceptance, especially within an audience with restricted media exposure.[27] The range of benefits possible from a concentrated media mix are as follows:

- It may allow the advertiser to be dominant in one medium relative to the competition.

EXHIBIT 8.20

Advantages and disadvantages of major media classes

Medium	Advantages	Disadvantages
Television	Multisensory: sight and sound Broad reach Low cost per contact Prestigious Image builder	Fleeting messages Low selectivity High absolute cost High clutter
Magazines	High selectivity High-quality reproduction Can be information intensive Long life Pass-along readership	Narrow reach Long lead times for placement Clutter Sight only
Newspapers	Credibility Local coverage Short lead times for placement Timeliness Low cost Good for coupon distribution	Creative limitations Low selectivity Short life Readers skim pages Few national newspapers
Radio	Broad reach local coverage Low cost Flexible placement Good for repetition	Moderate selectivity Few national networks Creative limitations Fleeting message Poor audience attention
Outdoor	Geographic selectivity Repetition	Poor attention environment Severe creative limitations Environment scourge Poor image
Direct Mail	High selectivity Information intensive	High cost per contact Poor image as "junk mail"

26. Arnold M. Barban, Steven M. Cristol, and Frank J. Kopec, *Essentials of Media Planning: A Marketing Viewpoint,* 3rd ed. (Lincolnwood, IL: NTC Business Books, 1993), 76–80.
27. Leo Bogart, *Strategy in Advertising,* 2nd ed. (Lincolnwood, IL: NTC Business Books, 1984), 147.

- Brand familiarity might be heightened, especially within target audiences that have a narrow range of media exposure.
- Concentrating media buys in high-visibility media, such as prime-time television or large advertising sections in premium magazines, can create enthusiasm and loyalty in a trade channel. Distributors and retailers may give a brand with heavily concentrated media exposure preferential treatment in inventory or shelf display.
- Concentration of media dollars may result in significant volume discounts from media organizations.

An **assorted media mix** employs multiple media alternatives to reach target audiences. The assorted mix can be advantageous to an advertiser because it facilitates communication with multiple market segments. By using a mix of media, an advertiser can place different messages for different target audiences in different media. In general, the advantages of an assorted media mix are as follows:

- A marketer can reach different target audiences with messages tailored to each target's unique interests in the product category or brand. To reach women with an interest in fitness, major publishers Time and Condé Naste have launched new titles like *Sports Illustrated for Women* and *Women's Sport and Fitness.*[28] These publications allow marketers to reach specialized targets.

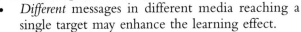

- *Different* messages in different media reaching a single target may enhance the learning effect.
- The *same* message placed in different media reaching a single target audience can also enhance the learning effect—this is called **audience duplication** and is a good thing. Heineken ran a very heavy television/magazine schedule for the "It's all about the beer" campaign with great success. The closing shot of the television ads was featured as a full-page magazine ad (see Exhibit 8.21). The "duplication" of the image has a powerful effect on consumer memory.
- Mulitmedia placement will increase the reach of a message, compared to concentrating placement in one medium.
- The probability of reaching audiences who use diverse media is greater with an assorted media mix.

One caution should be offered with the assorted media mix approach. Since different media placements often require different creative and production efforts, the cost of preparing advertisements can increase dramatically. Preparing both print and broadcast versions of an ad may drain media funds quickly, which can compromise other important goals, such as gross impressions or GPR.

EXHIBIT 8.21

"Audience duplication" is a technique where the same target audience receives the same basic advertisement—but in two different media. Here is the print version of a Heineken ad that used the same imagery of the bottle with the tag line "It's all about the beer" as the closing shot of an extensive television campaign.

Media Efficiency. Each medium under consideration in a media plan must be scrutinized for the efficiency with which it performs. In other words, which media deliver the largest target audiences at the lowest cost? A common measure of media efficiency is cost per thousand. **Cost per thousand (CPM)** is the

28.   Ann-Christine P. Diaz, "Women's Sports Titles Re-emerge," *Advertising Age,* February 7, 2000, 28.

dollar cost of reaching 1,000 (the M in CPM comes from the roman numeral for 1,000) members of an audience using a particular medium. The CPM calculation can be used to compare the relative efficiency of two media choices within a media class (magazine versus magazine) or between media classes (magazine versus radio). The basic measure of CPM is fairly straightforward; the dollar cost for placement of an ad in a medium is divided by the total audience and multiplied by 1,000. Let's calculate the CPM for a full-page black-and-white ad in the Friday edition of *USA Today*:

$$\text{CPM} = \frac{\text{Cost of media buy}}{\text{total audience}} \times 1000$$

$$\text{CPM for } USA\ Today = \frac{\$72,000}{5,206,000} \times 1,000 = \$13.83$$

These calculations show that *USA Today* has a CPM of $13.83 for a full-page black-and-white ad. But this calculation also shows the cost of reaching the *entire* readership of *USA Today*. If the target audience is restricted to male college graduates in professional occupations, then the **cost per thousand–target market (CPM–TM)** calculation will be much higher for a general publication such as *USA Today* than for a more specialized publication such as *Fortune*:

$$\text{CPM–TM for } USA\ Today = \frac{\$72,000}{840,000} \times 1000 = \$85.71$$

$$\text{CPM–TM for } Fortune = \frac{\$54,800}{940,000} \times 1,000 = \$58.30$$

You can see that the relative efficiency of *Fortune* is much greater than that of *USA Today* when the target audience is specified more carefully and a CPM–TM calculation is made.

Information about ad cost, gross impressions, and target audience size is usually available from the media company. Detailed audience information to CPM–TM–target market analysis also is available from media research organizations, such as Simmons Market Research Bureau (for magazines) or ACNielsen (for television). Cost information also can be obtained from Standard Rate and Data Service (SRDS) and Bacon's Media Directories, for example.

Another measure of media efficiency is cost per rating point, which is used to judge the efficiency of a broadcast media schedule (although it is used almost exclusively to judge television schedules). Like CPM, a **cost-per-rating-point (CPRP)** calculation provides relative efficiency comparison options. In this calculation, the cost of a media vehicle, such as a spot television program, is divided by the program's rating. (One rating point is equivalent to 1 percent of the television households in the designated rating area tuned to a specific program.) Like the CPM calculation, the CPRP calculation gives a dollar figure, which can be used for comparing media efficiency. The calculation for CPRP is as follows, using television as an example.

$$\text{CPRP} = \frac{\text{dollar cost of ad placement on a program}}{\text{program rating}}$$

For example, an advertiser on WLTV (Univision 23) in the Miami–Ft. Lauderdale market may wish to compare household CPRP figures for 30-second announcements in various dayparts on the station. The calculations for early news and prime-time programs are as follows.

$$\text{CPRP for WLTV early news} = \frac{\$2,205}{9} = \$245$$

$$\text{CPRP for WLTV prime time} = \frac{\$5,100}{10} = \$510$$

In this example, an early news daypart program delivers households more efficiently at $245 CPRP, less than half the cost of prime time, with approximately 90 percent of the typical prime-time rating.

It is important to remember that these efficiency assessments are based solely on costs and coverage. They say nothing about the quality of the advertising and can't be used as a measure of *advertising* effectiveness, only media efficiency. When media efficiency measures such as CPM and CPM–TV are combined with an assessment of media objectives and media strategies, they can be quite useful. Taken alone and out of the broader campaign-planning context, you'll end up with a lot of cheap time and space that doesn't even come close to fulfilling the objectives for a campaign. And there's another thing to think about. As new technologies make it possible for consumers to block TV advertising with smart new VCR type machines, the whole concept of media measurement, including efficiency, is thrown into turmoil (see the New Media box for a discussion).

ARE NEW DEVICES SMARTER THAN ADVERTISING?

Advertisers are diligent in scrutinizing their media schedules for reach and frequency. They press their media buyers for numbers on cost per thousand and cost and effective reach. But there are some Silicon Valley gadgets that, if they catch on, throw that whole debate out the window. The ability to measure reach, frequency, and cost per thousand will get much more complicated.

These new gadgets go by a lot of different names—personal video recorder (PVR), personal TV (PTV), TVHD (television hard disk), and DVR (digital video recorders). What they're called doesn't matter much. What matters is what they do. These devices come as a set-top box that is fairly nondescript and sells for about $500. It's sort of a cross between a PC and a VCR, without any of the complexity of either one. These DVRs incorporate a hard disk drive, a modem, and some Silicon Valley magic circuitry. The magic part converts the TV signal coming into your home (broadcast, cable, dish, it doesn't matter) into digital bits that the hard drive can store for you to watch at your convenience.

That doesn't sound a lot different from a VCR, and that part is not. What is different is that when you are watching live TV, the DVR can make it seem like you are making time stand still. Let's say you're watching your favorite prime-time sitcom and the phone rings. No problem; just "pause" the broadcast and pick it up after your conversation—the hard drive has been storing it.

The problem for advertisers, as you have probably figured out, is that DVRs will let you skip commercials with ease. And if marketers think this won't be a big problem, they better think again. Forrester Research of Cambridge, MA, predicts that 13 percent of all U.S. households will have one of these boxes by 2004. This is an adoption rate faster than the VCR. Advertisers will once again have to rethink how to get consumers to view ads when they have the chance to skip them.

Source: Brent Schlender, "Goodbye to TV As We Know It," *Fortune*, August 2, 1999, 219–220.

Competitive Media Assessment.

Keeping an eye trained on the competition is always useful. While media planners don't base an overall media plan on how much or where competitors are spending their money, a competitive media assessment can provide a useful perspective. Competitive media assessment is particularly important for product categories in which all the competitors are focused on a narrowly defined target audience. This happens in categories where heavy-user segments dominate consumption: snack foods, soft drinks, beer and wine, and chewing gum are examples. Brands of luxury cars and financial services also compete for common-buyer segments.

When a target audience is narrow and attracts the attention of several major competitors, a marketer must assess its competitors' spending and the relative share of voice its brand is getting. **Share of voice** is the calculation of any one marketer's expenditures on a brand's advertising relative to the overall ad spending in a product category:

$$\text{share of voice} = \frac{\text{one brand's advertising expenditures in a medium}}{\text{total product category advertising expenditures in a medium}}$$

We can do this calculation for all advertising by a brand compared to all advertising in a product category, or we can do it as a way to compare our advertising against a competitor. For example, sport shoe and apparel marketers spend about $380 million per year in measured advertising media. Nike and Reebok are the two top brands, with approximately $198 million and $60 million respectively in annual expenditures in **measured advertising media.** The share-of-voice calculations for both brands follow.

$$\text{share of voice, Nike} \quad = \frac{\$198 \text{ million}}{\$380 \text{ million}} \times 100 = 52.16\%$$

$$\text{share of voice, Reebok} = \frac{\$60 \text{ million}}{\$318 \text{ million}} \times 100 = 15.7\%$$

Together, both brands dominate the product category advertising with a nearly 70 percent combined share of voice. Yet Nike's share of voice is nearly three times that of Reebok.

Research data, such as that provided by Competitive Media Reporting, can give an assessment of share of voice in up to ten media categories. A detailed report shows how much a brand was advertised in a particular media category versus the combined media category total for all other brands in the same product category. Knowing what competitors are spending in a medium and how dominant they might be lets a marketer consider how to strategically schedule within a medium. Some strategists believe that scheduling in and around a competitor's schedule can create a bigger presence for a small advertiser.[29]

Media Scheduling and Buying. Media scheduling and buying are activities that take place throughout the planning effort. Media scheduling focuses on several issues related to timing and impact. All aspects of timing, and the strategies set for reach, frequency, and competitive media assessment, are evaluated during the scheduling phase. In addition, the total media schedule is evaluated with respect to CPM or gross impressions to gauge the impact the entire schedule delivers in each time frame. Seasonal buying tendencies in the target segment also have a major impact on scheduling. Scheduling media more heavily when consumers show buying tendencies is referred to as **heavy-up scheduling.**[30]

Once an overall media plan and schedule are in place, the focus must turn to media buying. **Media buying** entails securing the media time and space needed by the schedule. The current technological media environment has made media buying a strategic challenge.[31] An important part of the media-buying process is the agency of record. The **agency of record** is the advertising agency chosen by the marketer to purchase time and space. The agency of record coordinates media discounts and negotiates all contracts for time and space. Any other agencies involved in the advertising effort submit insertion orders for time and space within those contracts.

---

29.   Andrea Rothman, "Timing Techniques Can Make Small Ad Budgets Seem Bigger," *The Wall Street Journal*, February 3, 1989, B4; also see Robert J. Kent and Chris T. Allen, "Competitive Interference Effects in Consumer Memory for Advertising: The Role of Brand Familiarity," *Journal of Marketing* (July 1994): 97–105.
30.   Sissors and Bumba, *Advertising Media Planning*, 309–310.
31.   Rebecca Cox, "Buyer's Market," *Critical Mass*, Fall 1999, 68–70.

Rather than using an agency of record, some marketers use a **media-buying service** (recall our discussion in Chapter 2), which is an independent organization that specializes in buying large blocks of media time and space and reselling it to marketers. Some agencies have developed their own media-buying units to control both the planning and the buying process.[32] Regardless of the structure used to make the buys, media buyers evaluate the audience reach, CPM, and timing of each buy. The organization responsible for the buy also monitors the ads and estimates the actual audience reach delivered. If the expected audience is not delivered, then media organizations have to **make good** by repeating ad placements or offering a refund or price reduction on future ads. For example, making good to marketers because of shortfalls in delivering 1998 Winter Olympics prime-time spots cost CBS an estimated 400 additional 30-second spots.[33]

SUMMARY

1 Make the distinction between advertising, an advertisement, and an advertising campaign.

Advertising is the overall process of communicating with a marketer's target audience(s) and is defined as "a paid, mass-mediated attempt to persuade." An advertisement refers to a specific message that has been placed to persuade an audience. An advertising campaign is a series of coordinated advertisements that communicate a reasonably cohesive and integrated theme. These are three closely related but distinct elements of the concept of advertising.

2 Identify the most common message strategy objectives in advertising.

There are nine message strategy objectives that are most commonly pursued: Promote brand recall, link a key attribute to the brand name, instill brand preference, scare the consumer into action, transform the consumption experience, situate the brand socially, define the brand image, persuade the consumer, and invoke a direct response. Each of these message strategy objectives pursues a very different effect with advertising.

3 Identify the methods used to pursue advertising message strategy objectives.

For each advertising message strategy objective, there are one or methods that can be used to pursue the objective:

Promote brand recall:
- Repetition ads
- Slogan and jingle ads

Link a key attribute to the brand name:
- Unique selling proposition

Instill brand preference:
- Feel-good ads
- Humor ads
- Sex appeal ads

Scare the consumer into action:
- Fear-appeal ads
- Anxiety ads

Transform the consumption experience:
- Transformational ads

Situate the brand socially:
- Slice-of-life ads
- Light fantasy ads

Define the brand image:
- Image ads

Persuade the consumer:
- Reason-why ads
- Hard-sell ads
- Comparison ads
- Information-only ads
- Demonstration ads
- Advertorials

Invoke a direct response:
- Call, mail, or click-now ads
- Infomercials

32. Joe Mandese, "Ayer Adjusts to Complex Media Buys," *Advertising Age,* December 12, 1994, 6.
33. "CBS Faces Olympics Make-Goods." Available online at http://www.adage.com/, February 19, 1998.

Detail the important components of the media-planning process.

A media plan specifies the media vehicles that will be used to deliver the advertiser's message. Developing a media plan entails setting objectives such as effective reach and frequency and determining strategies to achieve those objectives. Media planners use several quantitative indicators, such as CPM and CPRP, to help them judge the efficiency of prospective media choices. The media-planning process culminates in the scheduling and purchase of a mix of media vehicles expected to deliver the advertiser's message to specific target audiences at precisely the right time to affect their consumption decision.

 Identify the main considerations in devising media strategy.

Media strategy is where the true power of the media plan lies. The strategy is expressed in decisions made about each media vehicle's reach and frequency, gross rating points, the continuity of media placement (including flighting and pulsing), the audience duplication, and the length and size of advertisements. Good media strategy decisions help ensure that good messages get placed in the right media so they can have as much impact as possible.

KEY TERMS

advertising, 265
client, or sponsor, 265
advertisement, 266
advertising campaign, 266
audience, 268
target audience, 268
household consumers, 268
members of business organizations, 268
members of a trade channel, 269
professionals, 269
government officials and employees, 269
globalized advertising, 269
international advertising, 269
national advertising, 270
regional advertising, 270
local advertising, 270
cooperative advertising, 270
message strategy, 271
slogans, 273
unique selling proposition (USP), 273
transformational advertising

messages, 277
slice-of-life advertisements, 278
comparison advertisements, 280
testimonial, 281
celebrity testimonial, 281
expert spokespersons, 282
average-user testimonial, 282
advertorial, 282
infomercial, 283
media plan, 284
media class, 284
media vehicle, 284
media objectives, 285
single-source tracking services, 285
geotargeting, 287
message weight, 287
duplication of exposure, 287
unduplicated audience measurement, 287
gross impressions, 287
potential ad impressions, 287
message impressions, 287
between-vehicle duplication, 288
within-vehicle duplication, 288

reach, 289
frequency, 289
gross rating points (GRP), 290
effective frequency, 290
effective reach, 290
continuity, 291
continuous scheduling, 291
flighting, 291
pulsing, 291
media mix, 292
concentrated media mix, 292
assorted media mix, 293
audience duplication, 293
cost per thousand (CPM), 293
cost per thousand–target market (CPM–TM), 294
cost per rating point (CPRP), 294
share of voice, 295
measured advertising media, 296
heavy-up scheduling, 296
media buying, 296
agency of record, 296
media-buying service, 297
make good, 297

QUESTIONS FOR REVIEW AND CRITICAL THINKING

1. What is the relationship between an advertisement and an advertising campaign? Is every advertisement part of a campaign?

2. Identify the different audiences for advertising. Why is it important to separate audiences into categories?

3. Explain the difference between brand recall and brand preference as message strategies. Which is the more difficult objective to pursue? Why?

4. Humor and fear are popular methods in advertising. Are these good methods? Which do you think is better?

5. Review the do's and don'ts of comparison advertising. Decide which of the following pair of brands would be a good pair for comparison and which would not: Lexus and Mercedes, Tylenol and Advil, Calvin Klein jeans and Ralph Lauren jeans, Chanel No. 5 and Charlie, Contempo Casuals and The Limited.

6. Have you ever responded to a banner ad on an Internet site and "clicked now." What made you respond to this direct-response ad? If you have never responded to one, why not?

7. Carefully watch one hour of television and record the time length of each advertisement. Using your perceptions about the most and least persuasive ads during this hour of television, develop a hypothesis about the value of long versus short advertising messages. When should an advertiser use long instead of short ads, to accomplish what goals?

8. Review the mathematics of the CPM and CPRP calculations, and explain how these two indicators can be used to assess the efficiency and effectiveness of a media schedule.

9. Assume that you are advising a regional snack-food manufacturer whose brands have a low share of voice. Which pattern of continuity would you recommend for such an advertiser? Would you place your ads in television programming that is also sponsored by Pringles and Doritos? Why or why not?

10. Media strategy models allow planners to compare the impact of different media plans, using criteria such as reach, frequency, and gross impressions. What other kinds of criteria should a planner take into account before deciding on a final plan?

EXPERIENTIAL EXERCISES

1. **In-class exercise.** Choose a position: Sex appeals in advertising work, or sex appeals in advertising don't work. Defend your position (and be sure to define what you mean by it "works").

2. **Out-of-class exercise.** Find an example of an advertorial. Identify the publication where the ad appeared. Examine the ad and describe what the organization is trying to do with the message. Was there a call to action in the ad?

USING THE INTERNET

Exercise 1

Select some of your favorite Web sites that carry banner advertising, and spend some time on the sites, noting how many different banners you see and how often banners are repeated. To some extent what you see will depend on the technology and providers behind the site: a "low-tech" site might use a fixed banner, perhaps for the single sponsor the site has signed itself, while a site using one of the banner ad networks (DoubleClick, Engage Media, Burst! Media, etc.) will display ads selected and flighted by the network according to its own calculations. Some sites that have invested in ad management applications can control their own advertising. Check out some of the ad networks as if you were a prospective advertiser looking to make an ad campaign purchase.

DoubleClick: http://www.doubleclick.com

Engage Media: http://www.engage.com/engagemedia/

Burst! Media: http://www.burstmedia.com

1. What sort of control do the services offer over the sorts of audience your ads will reach?

2. What sort of reporting would you be able to receive on your ad campaign?

3. What sort of technologies do the services employ to more accurately target advertising?

4. Do any of the services provide for guaranteed results?

Exercise 2

Advertisers use a variety of message strategies and methods for accomplishing their strategic goals. Visit the following sites:

Clinique: http://www.clinique.com

Ragu: http://www.eat.com

Sprint: http://www.sprint.com/college

For each site, answer the following questions:

1. Is there a big idea behind the site?

2. What is the fundamental message objective?

3. How have the site designers used creativity to achieve this objective?

After reading this chapter, you will be able to:

1 Identify the basic components of the Internet.

2 Identify the Internet media available for communicating over the World Wide Web.

3 Describe the different types of search engines used to surf the Web.

4 Describe the different advertising options on the Web.

5 Discuss the issues involved in establishing a site on the World Wide Web.

6 Discuss the integrated marketing communications aspects of coordinating a firm's Web activities with other promotional activities.

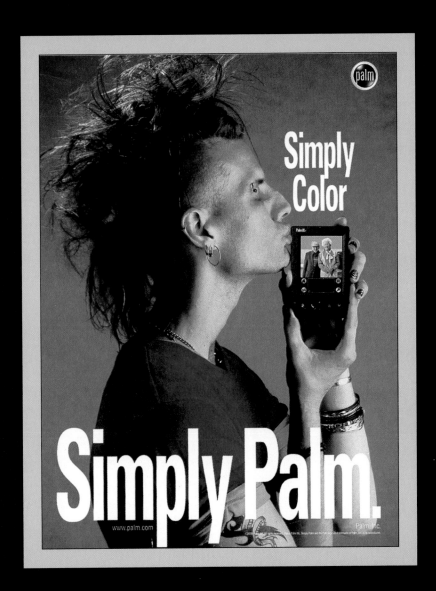

When executives at RCA records started plotting the promotional strategy for Christina Aguilera's debut album, they knew the Internet would play a crucial role in the introductory campaign. Most important, they understood that the teen target audience was skeptical and not receptive to traditional marketing tactics. In the words of one Internet marketing strategist, "they have their B.S. detectors on 11."[1] With that knowledge, RCA put into motion an Internet-based advertising/word-of-mouth strategy to create an Internet buzz around Ms. Aguilera and her new album that would end up being so successful that the album, self-titled *Christina Aguilera,* soared to number one when it debuted.

The first step in using the Internet in the promotional mix was to hire Electric Artists, a small New York Internet marketing firm that specialized in music marketing. Ken Krasner and Marc Schiller had a four-stage plan for using the Internet to promote Aguilera's album:

- *Stage 1:* To learn what teens already knew about Aguilera and what they were saying, Electric Artists began monitoring popular teen sites like http://www.alloy.com and http://www.gurl.com (see Exhibit 9.1) as well as sites created for other teen stars like the Backstreet Boys and Britney Spears. The firm compiled some important information about fans' reactions to Aguilera's single "Genie in a Bottle" and also learned that there was a budding rivalry between Aguilera fans and Spears fans.

- *Stage 2:* Electric sent a team of cybersurfers to popular sites to start chatting up Aguilera, her single, her past, and the rumor of her new album. The surfers posted messages on sites or e-mailed individual fans with comments like "Does anyone remember Christina Aguilera—she sang the song from *Mulan* called 'Reflection'? I heard she has a new song out called 'Genie in a Bottle' and a new album is supposed to be

EXHIBIT 9.1

In an effort to create a "buzz" around the release of Christina Aguilera's first album, Internet advertising agency Electric Arts hired surfers to post messages on sites like gurl.com and alloy.com. The strategy was a great success. The album debuted at number one.

EXHIBIT 9.2

After the successful launch of Christina Aguilera's first album, RCA set up a Web site for her fans to chat, send her e-mail, and, of course, buy merchandise. Notice that the site also provides information on upcoming concerts and a photo gallery.

1. Erin White, "'Chatting' a Singer Up the Pop Charts," *The Wall Street Journal,* December 5, 1999, B1, B4.

out this summer."[2] Krasner says, "It's kids marketing to each other. We call it viral marketing. We didn't break Christina, but we helped accelerate the process by putting the music in the hands of kids and watching them talk about it.[3]

- *Stage 3:* The promotional strategy ascended to a new level as Electric shifted the emphasis of its Internet communication from Aguilera's single to the album itself. One challenge included motivating teen fans to go from a $1.98 purchase to a $16.00 purchase. Another hurtle was to convince the big music retailers like Amazon.com and CDNow that Aguilera deserved prominent visibility on their Web sites. To complement these strategies, Electric ensured that the album cover and album name were highly memorable to parents who were shopping for their teenagers.
- *Stage 4:* To retain the momentum gained from the initial Internet promotional effort, Electric continued to strengthen and broaden Aguilera's fan base using a

variety of additional Internet strategies. The continuously updated Web site offered, and continues to offer, teen audiences access to concert and TV appearances, chats, fan club information, merchandise, and e-mail (see Exhibit 9.2). Electric also continues to monitor teen interest in competitors like Mariah Carey and Whitney Houston to stay connected to the broader teen music scene.

The result of this Internet-based promotional campaign was a number-one album and eventually the "Best New Artist" Award at the Grammys in Los Angeles. The story of Christina Aguilera shows that the power of Internet advertising lies in its ability to target and communicate in very specific language to an audience. That is the distinguishing feature of the Internet as a promotional mix alternative. The Aguilera story demonstrates that Internet advertising is much more than just banner ads.

INTRODUCTION

Technology changes everything—or at least it has the power and potential to change everything. When it's communications technology, it can change something very fundamental about human existence. The connected consumer is connected to other consumers in real time and with connection comes community, empowerment, even liberation. Or in the case of Christina Aguilera, a communication buzz that led to huge success. Is the Internet a revolution in communication?

Well, "revolutions" are more common than they used to be. Still, what is truly revolutionary about the Internet is its ability to alter the basic nature of communication within a commercial channel. And if you want a revolutionary perspective on the Internet and advertising, consider the short history of communication in this channel.[4] In 1994, marketers began working with Prodigy and CompuServe, the first Internet service providers (ISPS). These marketers had the idea that they would send standard television commercials online. Well, the technology was not in place back then for that to work. The standard PC at that time had modem speeds of only 2,400 bits per second, nowhere near the speed needed for audio/visual transmission. That technological fact sent the marketers and the ISPs back to the drawing board. With the emergence of more commercial ISPs like America Online (AOL), the new Web browsers were worth exploring as a way to send commercial messages. The first Web browser was Mosaic, the precursor to Netscape 1.0., and the first ads began appearing in *HotWired* (the online version of *Wired*) in October 1994. The magazine boasted twelve advertisers including MCI, AT&T, Sprint, Volvo, and Club Med. Each marketer paid $30,000 for a 12-week run of online banner ads with no guarantee of the number or profile of the viewers.

2.   Ibid., B1.
3.   Christopher John Farley and David E. Thigpen, "Christina Aguilera: Building a 21st Century Star," *Time*, March 6, 2000, 70–71.
4.   Gene Koprowski, "A Brief History of Web Advertising," *Critical Mass*, Fall 1999, 8–14.

The rest, as they say, is history. Now the Internet is being accessed worldwide by about 300 million users.[5] Advertising revenues on the Internet were estimated at about $4 billion in the year 2000 and are expected to grow to over $30 billion by the year 2004.[6] This technology really could change everything, and this chapter explores the change that the Internet is bringing about in the world of advertising. The chapter begins with an overview of cyberspace and some of the basics of the way the Internet works. Then we will consider the different types of advertising that can be used and some of the technical aspects of the process. We will look at the issues involved in establishing a Web site and developing a brand in the "e-community." Finally, we will explore the IMC challenges of Internet advertising. We will save the issue of measuring the impact of Internet advertising until Chapter 15, where all the promotional tools are evaluated.

Country	Number Online	Percent of Total Population
Europe:		
Austria	442,000	5.5
Belgium	2.0 million	19.6
Czech Republic	292,000	2.8
Denmark	1.7 million	34.0
Finland	1.6 million	32.0
France	6.2 million	12.9
Germany	15.9 million	21.0
Hungary	500,000	5.0
Italy	9.0 million	15.9
Netherlands	3.8 million	24.1
Norway	1.8 million	41.3
Spain	3.1 million	8.7
Sweden	3.9 million	44.3
Switzerland	1.2 million	16.2
Latin America	9.0 million	6.0
Japan	21.0 million	20.2
Russia	5.4 million	3.7
United Kingdom	13.9 million	23.6
United States	125.0 million	47.0
Worldwide Total	285.0 million	6.6

Source: Data taken from NUA Internet Surveys accessed at http://www.nua.net/surveys accessed on March 20, 2000

EXHIBIT 9.3

Estimates of Internet users worldwide as of 2000

5.   NUA Internet Surveys, accessed at http://www.nua.net/surveys/ on March 20, 2000.
6.   "Advertising That Clicks," *The Economist,* October 9, 1999, 71–72.

AN OVERVIEW OF CYBERSPACE

We refer to the Internet casually because it has become so prominent in the technological landscape. But just what is this thing called the Internet? The **Internet** is a global collection of computer networks linking both public and private computer systems. It was originally designed by the U.S. military to be a decentralized, highly redundant, and thus reliable communications system in the event of a national emergency. Even if some of the military's computers crashed, the Internet would continue to perform. Today the Internet comprises a combination of computers from government, educational, military, and commercial sources. In the beginning, the number of computers connected to the Internet would nearly double every year, from 2 million in 1994 to 5 million in 1995 to about 10 million in 1996. But beginning in 1998, the top blew off Internet use with around 90 million people connected in the United States and Canada, and 155 million people worldwide. Exhibit 9.3 shows that Internet access around the world has continued its accelerated rate of increase, with nearly 300 million current users. As you can see, the United States, Japan, and Western Europe account for most of the "worldwide" Web traffic. Internet users are, at present, disproportionately affluent white American males, but usage in the United Kingdom, Western Europe, parts of Southeast Asia, and Latin America is growing in both absolute and relative terms.[7] Like many communication technologies, the Internet started rather upscale, but is now broadening to middle- and lower-income consumers with the advent of affordable PCs and WebTV.

E-MAIL FROM NEARLY ANY PHONE FOR ONLY $9.95/MONTH.
No more phone jacks. No more expensive wireless services. Now with a simple toll free call you can send and retrieve unlimited e-mails for only $9.95/month. PocketMail® devices by SHARP® and JVC® available at Staples®, OfficeMax® and Office Depot®. Call 1-877-EMAILHERE or visit us at www.pocketmail.com

COMPOSE MESSAGE   DIAL 800-POCKETM   **PocketMail®**

EXHIBIT 9.4

The 24/7, come-as-you-are convenience of Internet access is of tremendous value to consumers.

The Basic Parts ❶

While many of you are frequent and savvy Web users, you may never have had the chance to explore the foundations of the Internet. Let's take some time to look at the basic parts of the Internet that allow us to surf and gives marketers the opportunity to use the Web as another tool in the promotional mix. There are four main components of the Internet: electronic mail, IRC, Usenet, and the World Wide Web. **Electronic mail (e-mail)** allows people to send messages to one another. In 2000, there were over 1.5 trillion e-mails sent from within the United States, which may explain the proliferation of services, technologies, and devices that support electronic messaging and the advertising associated with them—an example of which is seen in Exhibit 9.4. **Internet Relay Chat (IRC)** makes it possible for people to "talk" electronically in real time with each other, despite their geographical separation. For people with common interests, **Usenet** provides a forum for sharing knowledge in a public "cyberspace" that is separate from their e-mail program. Finally, with the **World Wide Web (WWW)**, people can access an immense database of information in a graphical environment through the use of programs called Web

---

7. Jeffery D. Zbar, "Web Hot: Net Marketing Surges in Latin America," *Advertising Age,* February 14, 2000, 28.

browsers (such as Netscape and Internet Explorer). Many Web sites are still listed with the prefix http://, which stands for hypertext transfer protocol, or rules of interaction between the Web browser and the Web server that are used to deal with hypertext. Currently, many Web browsers assume the file will be in hypertext, so they don't require users to type out the prefix.

To use the Internet, the user's personal computer must be connected to the network in some way. The most common way to access the Internet is by using a modem to call a host computer, which then provides the client computer access to the Internet. The four most common access options are through a commercial online service, such as America Online or Juno; a corporate gateway, such as AT&T's WorldNet Service; a local Internet service provider; or an educational institution. In addition to using one of these networks, a personal computer needs software, such as a Web browser and/or e-mail application, to communicate and move

Term	Definition
Applet:	A Java program that can be inserted into an HTML page (see definition for HTML below).
Banner ad:	An advertisement, typically rectangular in shape, used to catch a consumer's eye on a Web page. Banner ads serve as a gateway to send a consumer to an expanded Web page for a firm or a product where more extensive information is provided. Many include an electronic commerce capability where a product or service can be ordered through the banner itself.
Bandwidth:	The capacity for transmitting information through an Internet connection. Internet connections are available through phone lines, cable, or various wireless options.
Baud:	A measure of data transmission speed, typically referring to a modem.
Click-through:	The process of a Web site visitor clicking on a banner ad and being sent to a marketer's home page for further information. Ad banner click-through rates average about 1 percent.
Cookie:	A piece of information sent by a Web server to a Web browser that tracks Web page activity. Because they identify users and their browsing habits, cookies are at the center of Web privacy issues.
CPM:	Cost per thousand impressions, the long-standing measure of advertising rates used in traditional media and now carried over as a standard for the Internet.
Domain name:	The unique name of a Web site chosen by a marketer. There are five designations for domain names after the unique name chosen by the marketer: .com and .net refer to business and commercial sites; .org refers to an institution or nonprofit organization; .gov identifies government Web sites; .edu refers to academic institutions.
E-mail:	Text message exchanged via computer, WebTV, and various wireless devices like Palm Pilots and cell phones.
HTML:	An acronym that stands for "hypertext markup language," which is used to display and link documents to the Web.
Interstitial:	Pop-up ads that appear when a Web user clicks on a designated (or not designated) area of a Web page.
Intranet:	An online network *internal* to a company that can be used by employees. Intranets are even showing up in some households.
Spam:	"Junk" e-mail sent to consumers who haven't requested the information. Not an acronym the Internet term is said to have derived from a Monty Python skit about a restaurant where everything comes with Spam—the Hormel lunch meat, that is.

EXHIBIT 9.5

An Internet glossary of basic terminology

around while online. For example, if one is interested in the graphic-oriented World Wide Web, software such as Netscape Navigator or Microsoft Internet Explorer is needed. If one is interested only in e-mail, a program such as Eudora will suffice. A new option for novice users and those not in need of computing capability is WebTV. With a simple keyboard and Internet connection, the user's television provides access to the World Wide Web. The user can then surf Web sites and send and receive e-mail. It's not exactly computing, but it is a connection to the Web.

While much of the vocabulary of the Web is common knowledge or intuitive, some of the language of the Web is, well, a mystery. The short glossary in Exhibit 9.5 defines some of the terms you have heard dozens of times, but had no idea what they really meant.

Internet Media

Internet media for advertising consist of e-mail (including listservs), Usenet, and the World Wide Web. Internet advertising tactics differ in the degree to which the advertisement is "pushed" onto or requested ("pulled") by the consumer. Internet advertising that uses a **push strategy** is akin to traditional advertising: The marketer delivers the communication to the consumer at the marketer's choosing, retaining control over when, where, and how the advertising message is delivered. Advertising delivered via e-mail and Usenet typically involves push strategies. As will be discussed, if such strategies are done improperly, it can lead to considerable backlash. With **pull tactics,** consumers have control over advertising exposure. That is, consumers seek information at their own convenience. This strategy is most common on the World Wide Web.

E-mail is frequently used by marketers to reach potential and existing customers. A variety of companies collect e-mail addresses and profiles that allow marketers to direct e-mail to a specific group. The DM Group (http://www.dm1.com) maintains a list of e-mail groups and has reportedly collected hundreds of thousands of e-mail addresses. Widespread, targeted e-mail advertising is just now materializing through organizations like exactis.com (http://www.exactis.com) due to significant consumer resistance to marketers' direct mailing to personal e-mail addresses (see Exhibit 9.6). Exactis.com will target, prepare, and deliver e-mails to highly specific audiences for marketers. As techniques and guidelines are better established for direct e-mail advertising, it may become more accepted in the future. Many believe it's only a matter of time because, historically, marketers have rarely worried about being too intrusive.

People who wish to discuss specific topics through the Internet often join electronic mailing lists, or **listservs.** Thousands of mailing lists are available on an incredible variety of topics. A message sent to the list's e-mail address is then re-sent to everybody on the mailing list. A niche for commercial services that collect and sell listservs certainly exists and is already attracting attention. Buying lists from these organizations is inexpensive. Unlimited access to lists through organizations like L-Soft International (http://www.lsoft.com) can be downloaded for a few thousand

EXHIBIT 9.6

Several Internet service firms have emerged to help marketers place highly targeted e-mail messages on the Internet that serve as customized one-on-one advertising.

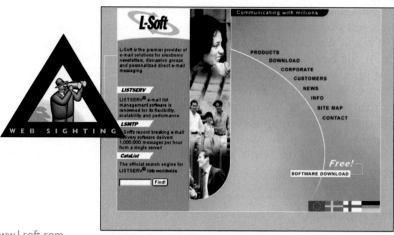

http://www.Lsoft.com

EXHIBIT 9.7

L-Soft sells the tools for managing e-mail lists. Vendors like L-Soft have dramatically lowered the bar to even small and niche sites, offering as much interactivity as major corporate destinations, and they have kept e-mail in the running as one of the Net's most important applications. How many sites have you seen that include e-mail subscription as an option? What functions can such lists be used for? Have you ever used the "e-mail this article to a friend" feature of some sites?

dollars (see Exhibit 9.7). Marketers need to use discretion when buying and using listervs. It is currently considered in very bad taste to openly sell products via listservs, particularly when there is no apparent connection between the mailing list's theme and the advertised product. Product information shared through these mailing lists is similar to traditional word-of-mouth communications and is, at the moment, still in the hands of users. This is why Electric Artists hired "surfers" to go to the listservs frequented by teens to spread the word on Christina Aguilera rather than the agency or RCA itself posting information.

As we saw earlier, Usenet is a collection of discussion groups in cyberspace. People can read messages pertaining to a given topic, post new messages, and answer messages. For marketers, this is an important source of consumers who care about certain topics. For example, the Usenet group alt.beer is an excellent place for a new microbrewery to promote its product. Marketers can also use Usenet as a source of unobtrusive research, getting the latest opinions on their products and services. Television shows such as *The X-Files* often monitor Usenet groups, such as alt.tv.x-files, to find out what people think about the show. Usenet is also used as a publicity vehicle for goods and services. It represents a relatively self-segmented word-of-mouth channel.

Uninvited commercial messages sent to listservs, Usenet groups, or some other compilation of e-mail addresses is a notorious practice known as **spam.** In one instance, more than 6 million people were spammed at a cost of only $425. In retaliation, such organizations as the Coalition Against Unsolicited Commercial E-mail (http://www.cauce.org) have compiled resources for fighting spam as well as a blacklist of marketers who have used spam. For an ambitious and gutsy marketer, such a tactic could prove an enormously cost-effective advertising buy, or it could provoke a great deal of hate mail, resentment, or even more dire consequences, including a loss of business reputation. Loss of reputation is a distinct possibility because surveys of consumers find that they trust the government more than they trust e-mail marketers to regulate the use of e-mail as a communications medium.[8] Again, the point is for marketers to make sure they are at least wanted guests and not despised intruders into what often amount to valuable virtual communities.[9]

Finally, this phenomenon we know as the World Wide Web is the universal database of information available to most Internet users, and its graphical environment makes navigation simple and exciting. Of all the options available for Internet

---

8.   "No Taste for Spam," *Promo,* May 2000, 57–58.
9.   For a discussion of spamming versus targeted e-mail pitches, see Dana Garber, "Spam Has Choicer Cuts," *CNN Interactive* (August 10, 1998), accessed at http://cnn.com/tech/computing/9808/10/tastyspam.idg/ on March 28, 1999.

marketers, the Web holds the greatest potential. It allows for detailed and full-color graphics, audio transmission, delivery of in-depth messages, 24-hour availability, and two-way information exchanges between the marketer and customer. For some people, spending time on the Web is replacing time spent viewing other media, such as print, radio, and television. There is one great difference between the Web and other cyberadvertising vehicles: It is the consumer who actively searches for the marketer's home page. Of course, Web marketers are attempting to make their pages much easier to find and, in reality, harder to avoid.

Surfing the World Wide Web ❸

By using software such as Netscape, consumers can simply input the addresses of Web sites they wish to visit and directly access the information available there. However, the Web is a library with no card catalog. There is no central authority that lists all possible sites accessible via the Internet. This condition leads to **surfing**—gliding from home page to home page. Users can seek and find different sites in a variety of ways: through search engines, through direct links with other sites, and by word of mouth.

A **search engine** allows an Internet user to type in a few keywords, and the search engine then finds all sites that correlate with the keywords. Search engines all have the same basic user interface but differ in how they perform the search and in the amount of the Web that is accessed. There are four distinct styles of search engines: hierarchical, collection, concept, and robot. There are also the special cases of Web community sites and mega-search engines called portals.

Hierarchical Search Engines. Most of you are familiar with Yahoo! Yahoo! is an example of a search engine built on a hierarchical, subject-oriented guide (see Exhibit 9.8). In a **hierarchical search engine,** all sites fit into categories. For example, Nike is indexed as Business and Economy>Companies>Apparel>Footwear>Athletic Shoes>Brandnames. Users are thus able to find and select a category as well as all the relevant Yahoo! sites. Going to Business and Economy>Companies>Sports>Snowboarding>Board Manufacturers, for instance, gives a list of nearly sixty companies that sell snowboards on the Web. By checking these sites, a person could find a snowboard company and buy a snowboard over the Web. Although hierarchical sites like Yahoo! are great for doing general searches, they do have some significant limitations. For example, Yahoo!'s database of Web sites contains only submissions. That is, Yahoo! does not actually search the Web but only its database of sites that users have told it about. Because of this, Yahoo! omits a significant portion of the vast information available on the Web.

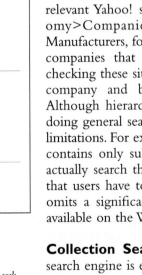

EXHIBIT 9.8

Big Internet sites like Yahoo! offer Internet users a hierarchical search engine to seek out information on the Internet. Notice also that sites like Yahoo!, Lycos, and Excite provide all sorts of links for travel, games, chat, e-mail, and news and sports information.

Collection Search Engines. A second type of search engine is exemplified by AltaVista. **Collection search engines** use a **spider,** which is an automated program that "crawls" around the Web and collects information. By mid-2000, the collection of Web pages indexed by AltaVista stood at over 3 million. With AltaVista, a person can perform a text search on all these sites, resulting in access to literally tens of billions of words. For example, the search for the phrase "alpine skiing" returned 22,493 pages that contain this exact phrase. By comparison, the same phrase entered in a Yahoo! search turned up only 128 category matches.

Because of the sheer quantity of Web pages, AltaVista ranks the best matches first. The relatively large amount of information available on AltaVista mandates that users know what they are really interested in; otherwise, they will be flooded with useless information.

Concept Search Engines. Excite is a concept search engine. With a **concept search engine,** a concept rather than a word or phrase is the basis for the search. Using the alpine skiing example, the top sites with the concept alpine skiing are listed in an Excite search. To narrow the search, simply clicking on one of the sites found in the original search with the Excite icon enables another search based on the selected link. The percentage key gives the user an idea of how close a particular site is to the concepts. This is a very efficient way of searching, producing relatively focused results compared to AltaVista and with the added ability of using the results of a search to further modify the search. The downside is that concept search engines such as Excite lack the comprehensiveness of collection search engines. Ask Jeeves, another concept search engine, allows users to conduct searches using natural-language questions such as, "Who was the fourteenth president of the United States?" (Answer: Franklin Pierce, 1853–1857.)

Robot Search Engines. The newest technique employs **robots** ("bots") to do the legwork for the consumer by roaming the Internet in search of information fitting certain user-specified criteria. For example, there are shopping robots that specialize in finding the best deals for your music needs (see Exhibit 9.9), insurance needs (http://www.insuremarket.com/), or traveling needs (http://www.travelocity.com/). Web retailers concerned that such robots will result in an electronic marketplace governed entirely by price rather than brand loyalty have designed their sites to either refuse the robot admission to the site or to confuse the robot.[10] Still, there are analysts who believe that future e-commerce will be governed by "shopbots," and that loyalty will shift to the shopbot sites rather than retail brand names. We will explore this issue in great detail in Chapter 10 on direct marketing and e-commerce.

Portals. Portal is the most overused, misused, abused, and confused term in Internet vocabulary. A **portal** is a starting point for Web access and search. Portals can be vertical (serving a specialized market or industries, like Chemdex for the chemical industry, http://www.chemdex.com), horizontal (providing access and links across industries like VerticalNet, with 53 different business trade communities, http://www.verticalnet.com), or they can be ethnic (http://www.latina.com) (see Exhibit 9.10) or community based.[11] Several of the large search engines, such as Yahoo! and Lycos, are focusing their attention on becoming portals for Internet exploring. In addition to providing its own content, AOL serves as a convenient and well-organized entrance to the Web. From AOL a Web surfer can jump to many locations highlighted by AOL, particularly commercial sites that are partnering with AOL and have paid a fee for preferred placement on the site.[12] Portals are interested in channeling surfers to particular sites, especially commercial ones.

10. *The Wall Street Journal,* September 3, 1998, B1, B8.
11. Mougayar Walid, "The New Portal Math," *Business 2.0,* January 2000, 245.
12. Chip Bayers, "Capitalist Econstruction," *Wired,* March 2000, 211–218.

EXHIBIT 9.9

The newest way to search the Internet is with "shopbots" or "bots." These are automated Internet search engines that take directions on what to search for and then deliver it automatically back to the user. With BizBuyer.com, you can send shopbot Bernie out to find quotes on a wide range of business products and services.

EXHIBIT 9.10

Community portals like Latina.com offer the opportunity to visit a site that matches surfers interests for information on a variety of topics from politics to culture to entertainment.

The portal wars are already hot, with each portal trying to provide access and incentive for using their service as a gateway to the Internet or commerce. Each is trying to top the other in monthly traffic and advertising revenue. This battle is only going to get hotter in the near term as portals vie for superiority and dominance in the wireless Web. In 1999, 3.6 million households had wireless Web browsing capability. By 2003, this number is expected to grow to over 40 million.[13]

Other Ways to Find Sites. Many people have created their own Web pages, which list their favorite sites. This is a fabulous way of finding new and interesting sites—as well as feeding a person's narcissism. For example, the Web address for this book, http://semenik.swcollege.com, is a resource for information about advertising that includes hotlinks to a wide range of industry resources. Since this page is maintained, updated, and checked regularly, it is a good resource for someone interested in advertising. Although most people find Web pages from Internet resources (over 80 percent of respondents in a 1998 survey find Web pages from search engines or other Web pages), sites can also be discovered through traditional word-of-mouth

13.   Patricia Riedman, "Portals Find More Wars to Wage on Wireless Web," *Advertising Age,* March 6, 2000, s34.

communications. Internet enthusiasts tend to share their experiences on the Web through discussions in coffeehouses, reading and writing articles, Usenet, and other non-Web venues. In fact, over two-thirds of respondents in the 1998 survey reported learning of Web pages from friends or from printed media. Moreover, a recent survey reveals that including the company's URL in print advertisements is becoming an increasingly common practice, especially in business and computer magazines.[14] There are also Web community sites such as http://www.theglobe.com, and mega-search engines—those that combine several search engines at once (http://www.dogpile.com).

ADVERTISING ON THE INTERNET

In 1995, $54.7 million was spent advertising on the Internet. Spending in 1996 was around $300 million. In 1997, it jumped to just around $1 billion, and in 1998, it was somewhere around $2 billion; the year 2000 logged in at just over $3 billion. Advertising revenues on the Internet are expected to reach $33 billion by 2004— an astronomical growth rate.[15] At the same time, the cost of advertising on the Internet is falling; it dropped about 6 percent in 1998 alone and has continued to fall. So as demand for cyberadvertising goes up, apparently so does supply. Furthermore, don't let the big numbers impress you too much. Internet advertising still represents only about 1.5 percent of all United States advertising; counting all promotion dollars, it's less than half of 1 percent. In other words, as one researcher said, "For AT&T, the Web budget is a rounding error."[16] That's for the time being, however. As new and better ways of advertising are discovered, the nature and cost of Web advertising could change significantly.

There are a wide range of issues associated with using the Internet for advertising purposes. This section begins by exploring the advantages of this kind of advertising. Then we'll look at who is advertising on the Internet, the costs associated with it, and the different types of Internet advertising.

The Advantages of Internet Advertising

Internet advertising has emerged as a legitimate option for marketers—and not just because the Web represents a new and different technological option. There are several unique advantages to Internet advertising over traditional forms.

Target Market Selectivity. The Web offers marketers a new and precise way to target market segments. Not only are the segments precisely defined (you can place an ad on the numismatist society page), but the Internet allows forms of target that truly enhance traditional segmentation schemes like demographics, geographics, and psychographics. (By the way, a numismatist is a coin collector.) Marketers can focus on specific interest areas, but they can also target based on geographic regions (including global), time of day, computer platform, or browser.

Tracking. The Internet allows marketers to track how users interact with their brands and to learn what interests current and potential customers. Banner ads and

14. Ann E. Schlosser and Alaina Kanfer, "Current Advertising on the Internet: The Benefits and Usage of Mixed-Media Advertising Strategies," in D. Schumann and E. Thorson, eds., *Advertising and the World Wide Web* (Mahwah, NJ: Lawrence Erlbaum Associates, 1999), 41–60.
15. "Advertising That Clicks," *The Economist,* October 9, 1999, 71–72.
16. K. Hafner and J. Tanaka, "This Web's for You," *Newsweek,* April 1, 1996, 75.

http://www.airclic.com; http://www.scan.com

EXHIBIT 9.11

A decade ago, the Internet was still largely confined to universities and clunky workstations; now you can take it with you in your pocket. The availability of wireless access is increasing and prices are dropping. With a range of small "personal digital assistants" on the market from the likes of Palm and Handspring, companies are rushing to deliver wireless versions of their services, or purely wireless plays, such as shopping comparison ventures AirClic and Scan.com. How well does the Net work when you remove the wires?

Web sites also provide the opportunity to measure the response to an ad (number of hits), a feature that is unattainable in traditional media. Recall our discussion in Chapter 8 on the imprecision of the "exposure" measure in traditional media.

Deliverability and Flexibility. Online advertising is delivered twenty-four hours a day seven days a week for the convenience of the receiver. Whenever the receiver is logged on and active, advertising is there and ready to greet them. As importantly, a campaign can be tracked on a daily basis and be updated, changed, or replaced almost immediately. This is a dramatic difference from traditional media, where changing a campaign might be delayed for weeks given media schedules and the time needed for production of ads. A perfect example of this kind of deliverability and flexibility is GMbuy.com (http://www.gmbuy.com). And, as mentioned earlier, as Web delivery goes wireless, there will be even more flexibility and deliverability for Web communications (see Exhibit 9.11).

Interactivity. A lofty and often unattainable goal for a marketer is to engage a prospective customer with the brand and the firm. This can be done with Internet advertising in a way that just cannot be accomplished in traditional media. A consumer can go to a company Web site (or **click-through** from a banner ad) and take a tour of the brand's features and values (presuming the Web site is well designed). Software is a perfect example of this sort of advantage of the Web. Let's say you are looking for software to do your taxes. You can log onto http://taxes.Yahoo.com, where (through H&R Block Tax Consulting) you will find all the software, tax forms, and online information you need to *prepare* your taxes. Then you can actually *file* your taxes with both the IRS and your state tax agency! And this sort of interactivity is not reserved for big national companies. Try this as an exercise. Find a sign company in your local phone directory. It is likely one will have a Web site where you can design your own sign, order it, and ask for it to be delivered. You have complete interaction with the firm and its product without ever leaving your computer.

Cost. While the cost-per-thousand numbers on reaching audiences through the Web are still relatively high (see the next section) compared to radio or television, the cost for producing a Web ad is relatively low. This includes both banner ads and Web sites. Banner ads are very cheap at a few hundred or few thousand dollars to produce and place. Web sites can be expensive—tens or even hundreds of thousands of dollars to develop—but the cost maybe fixed for a long period of time. More on cost of Web advertising shortly.

Integration. Web advertising is easily integrated with other forms of promotion. In the most basic sense, all traditional media advertising being used by a marketer can carry the Web site URL. Web banner ads can highlight themes and images from television or print campaigns. Special events or contests can be featured in banner ads and on Web sites. Overall, the integration of Web activities with other components of the marketing mix is one of the easiest integration tasks in the

EXHIBIT 9.12

Top advertisers on the Web ranked by impressions

Top Advertisers on the Web Ranked by Impressions			
Rank	**Company Name**	**Impressions**	**Unique Audience**
1	TRUSTe	683,741,385	14,518,289
2	Amazon	136,164,042	16,920,128
3	Yahoo!	132,226,705	13,112,965
4	America Online	107,050,620	16,141,691
5	Microsoft	76,669,124	13,260,472
6	SexTracker	70,873,985	3,419,758
7	Barnes and Noble	70,791,551	9,658,516
8	Next Card	69,331,559	11,311,527
9	E*TRADE	68,288,105	2,452,851
10	Netscape	62,833,283	10,321,849
11	Datek	61,209,107	2,655,590
12	WebSideStory	43,072,008	5,240,341
13	Ad Council	41,790,825	3,300,938
14	Morgan Stanley Dean Witter	40,982,929	754,595
15	Fidelity	36,692,432	2,155,281
16	Proflowers	36,472,688	7,743,014

Source: AdAge Data Place, http://www.adage.com, accessed via the Internet on March 20, 2000.

IMC process. This is due to the flexibility and deliverability of Web advertising discussed earlier. The concluding section of the chapter deals with the IMC aspects of Internet advertising in great detail.

Who Advertises on the Internet?

The charts in Exhibits 9.12 and 9.13 demonstrate that advertising on the Web, compared to television and magazines, for example, is highly concentrated among a very few marketers with similar business model profiles. You can see that the big spenders on the Web are Internet companies themselves. The top advertisers based on both impressions and the most viewed banner ads are either exclusively Web organizations or those with significant Web presence. This will have to change if the Web is to really challenge traditional media.

The Cost of Internet Advertising

On a cost-per-thousand (CPM) basis, the cost of Web ads is beginning to compare favorably with ads placed in traditional media. Exhibit 9.14 shows the steady drop in CPM for Web advertising in recent years to about $33.00 per thousand. For reference, the cost for a 30-second TV spot on network news is about $5.42 per thousand—much cheaper than the Internet. But for a full-color, national magazine, it's about $43.55 per thousand—about a third more. The real attraction of the Internet is not found in raw numbers and CPMs, but rather in highly desirable, highly segmentable, and highly motivated audiences (Exhibit 9.15). The Internet is ideally suited for niche marketing—that is, for reaching only those consumers most likely to buy what the marketer is selling. This aspect of the Internet as an advertising option has always been its great attraction—the ability to identify segments and

EXHIBIT 9.13

Top banner advertisers ranked by unique audience and reach.

Top Internet Banner Ads			
Rank	Company Name	Unique Audience	Reach Percentage
1	Bonzi Software	4,531,875	8.2
2	AmeriDebt	3,097,561	5.6
3	Capital One	2,924,063	5.3
4	Red Cross	2,201,503	4.0
5	ClassMates	2.055,752	3.7
6	Next Card	2,008,862	3.6
7	GetSmart	1,888,421	3.4
8	HealthQuick	1,872,918	3.4
9	@Backup	1,830,461	3.3
10	GetSmart	1,820,243	3.3
11	Next Card	1,808,998	3.3
12	Rocketlinks	1,791,674	3.2
13	Audio Book Club	1,757,908	3.2
14	@Backup	1,740,497	3.1
15	Uproar	1,698,569	3.1

Source: AdAge Data Place, http://www.adage.com, accessed via the Internet on March 20, 2000.

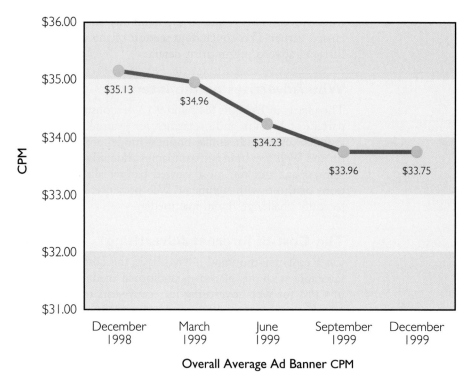

Overall Average Ad Banner CPM

Comment: Rates are averages of all Planner sites reporting CPM rates, and they are as stated on rate cards.
Key finding: During the last year, CPM rates have stabilized. The average CPM rate decreased by 4 % in 1999, about 1% per quarter.

Source: AdKnowledge System

EXHIBIT 9.14

The cost per thousand (CPM) for banner ads has been falling steadily over the last several years.
However, compared to television or radio broadcasts, banner ad CPM is still relatively high.

deliver almost customized (or in the case of e-mail, actually customized) messages directly to them, one by one.

The current Internet audience is relatively affluent, so it does have the means to buy. In the cases where there is an active search for product or service information on the Internet, there is also a predisposed and motivated audience. This makes the Internet fairly special among advertising-supported vehicles. On the other hand, there are enormous audience measurement problems; we don't really know with much certainty who sees or notices Internet advertising. So marketers don't know exactly what they are buying. This bothers them. Further, there is some evidence that audience tolerance for Web advertising is actually declining. Recent studies find that Web surfers are even less tolerant of advertising then average consumers. The number of Web users who say they actively avoid the ads is up, and the number who say they notice ads is down.[17] This is consistent with the experience of advertising history in general: As advertising becomes more common, fewer ads are noticed, fewer are accepted, and fewer make any impact at all. Ads thus become less powerful as they become more common, familiar, and annoying. Advertising has always had a way of being a victim of its own success. What's more, Internet advertising comes into an already crowded and highly cluttered media and information environment.

17.   "Advertising That Clicks," *The Economist,* October 9, 1999, 71–72.

TAKE YOUR FRIENDS' ADVICE ON MEN.
NOT DOCTORS.

CASE# 8779

The first place you turn for a doctor referral is your friends. But what makes you think they know any better than you do? Ask an expert. Visit HealthGrades.com. A free, objective source for ratings on doctors, hospitals and health plans nationwide. Now you can make your medical decisions informed ones.

©1999, HealthGrades.com, Inc.

health grades .com
The Healthcare Rating Experts

EXHIBIT 9.15

One of the key advantages of the Internet is that Web sites provide very specific information tailored to the needs of narrowly defined segments.

Regardless of the lack of effective measurement and evaluation of reach, the narrow audience composition, and the unknown impact of Web advertising, companies seem to be afraid of being left behind. Apparently, there is some prestige attached to advertising on the WWW, or at least a feeling of inadequacy to not be there. In addition, most marketers want to have a well-established Web image in the future, so getting involved now makes sense even if the best strategy for doing so is unclear. Keeping on eye on the future seems like a good idea, too. By the year 2005, it is expected that there will be 77 million Internet users under the age of eighteen. This means that a new generation of Net surfers and users will be emerging will be searching the Web with ease.[18]

Types of Internet Advertising 4

There are several ways for marketers to post advertising messages on the Web. The most basic route is by establishing a corporate home page. These pages clearly identify the company and the brand that supports the site. The style of sites ranges from those explicitly focused on the presentation of specific product benefits, to those based on special interests or lifestyle topics (which indirectly push the product), to those that actually let the consumer purchase the product.

Another way for marketers to advertise on the Web is through ads on entertainment, media, or corporate sites. Besides the actual ad purchased on a media company's Web site, the marketer can also get a link to its own home page. So if a consumer is browsing on Yahoo! and sees a Toyota banner ad, he or she can click on the ad and be taken straight to Toyota's home page. A different version of the banner ad is the pop-up. The most highly customized and targeted form of "advertising" on the Internet is through e-mail.

Banner Ads. Banner ads are paid placements of advertising on other sites that contain editorial material. An additional feature of banner ads is that consumers not only see the ad but also can make a quick trip to the marketer's home page by clicking on the ad (this is the "click-through" defined earlier). Thus, the challenge of creating and placing banner ads is not only to catch people's attention but also to entice them to visit the marketer's home page and stay for a while. Many high-traffic Web sites that provide information content have started to rely on marketers to support their services. Sites such as Yahoo! and HotWired will have banner advertisements as well as specialized sites like golf.com that attract a well-defined target audience.

A high-traffic site offers a relatively high level of exposure (remember the problems with the definition of "exposure" from Chapter 8) to an advertising message. Much like placing advertisements within traditional print media such as newspapers and magazines, marketers can purchase space on sites providing a diversity of

---

18.   Bernadette Burke, "Meeting Generation Y," *NUA Internet Surveys,* July 19, 1999, accessed at http://www.nua.net/surveys/ on March 22, 2000.

editorial content, such as *The New York Times,* the *Chicago Tribune,* the *Los Angeles Times, The Wall Street Journal,* USA *Today, Newsweek, U.S. News & World Report, Car and Driver, Atlantic Monthly,* Time Warner Communications, and ESPN.

A more targeted option is to place banner ads on sites that attract specific market niches. For example, a banner ad for running shoes would be placed on a site that offers information related to running. This option is emerging as a way for marketers to focus more tightly on their target audiences. Currently, marketers consider WWW users to be a focused segment of their own. However, as the Web continues to blossom, marketers will begin to realize that, even across the entire Web, there are sites that draw specific subgroups of Web users. These niche users have particular interests that may represent important opportunities for the right marketer.

A pricing evaluation service for banner ads is offered by Interactive Traffic. The I-Traffic Index computes a site's advertising value based on traffic, placement and size of ads, ad rates, and evaluations of the site's quality.[19] Forrester Research assesses the costs of banner ads on a variety of sites and what marketers get for their money, as shown in Exhibit 9.16. Complicating the matter now is the fact that consumer resistance to banner ads is increasing. First, most online consumers do not click on Web banner ads. For example, one survey found that only 1 percent of surfers click on banner ads.[20] Second, many consumers resent banner ads, which they see as intrusive and annoying and which increase Web page load times due to their complex graphics and animation. Supporting this trend are fixes called ad blockers, which allow consumers to screen out such ads. For example, one ad blocker program called AdWipe allows a surfer to load pages sans banner ads.[21] At the same time, the banner advertisement should be designed with downloading time in mind.

There is currently wide debate about the value and even the future of banner ads. Banner ads drew over $1 billion in business in 1999, but they are the most reviled of all elements of online marketing.[22] One Web site, Mediconsult.com, announced that it was abandoning banner ads altogether after completing extensive

Site	Rate	Deliverables
ESPN SportsZone	$100,000/quarter; $300,000/year	Estimated 542,000 users/week; 20.5 million hits/week; exclusive and rotating placement
HotWired	$13,000–$15,000/month	Minimum 100,000 banner views guaranteed; weekly traffic reports; discounts for *Wired* advertisers
Netscape	$30,000/month	Estimated 1 million impressions; estimated CPM of $25–$30
Pathfinder	$30,000/quarter	Free position in Pathfinder marketplace; weekly tracking reports
Yahoo! search page	$20,000/1 million impressions	Estimated 2.9 million hits/month; 135 million search results (cumulative)

Source: Forrester Research and *Advertising Age,* January 8, 1996, 25. Reprinted with permission of Forrester Research, Inc.

EXHIBIT 9.16

Advertising cost and audience delivered for various Web sites

19. K. Cleland, "SRDS, I Join Interactive Frenzy," *Advertising Age,* October 16, 1995, 22.
20. *The Economist,* September 26, 1998.
21. *San Francisco Chronicle,* August 26, 1998.
22. Kim Cross, "Whither the Banner," *Business 2.0,* December 1999, 137.

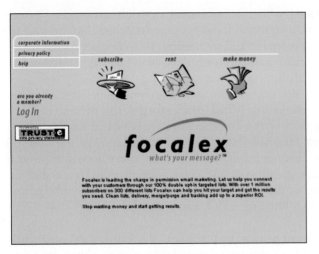

EXHIBIT 9.17

E-mail as an advertising alternative can meet with some heavy resistance from Web users. One way to avoid the resistance is to use a permission marketing firm. These firms have lists of consumers who "opt in," or agree to have e-mail sent to them by commercial sources.

focus group surveys with its users. The 3.5 million annual visitors to the site now surf banner free.[23] On the plus side, banner ads are accounting for about 60 percent of all online spending by companies trying to use the Web as part of their promotional mix. This, of course, accounts for most of the revenue of the pure online promotion organizations. In addition, a study shows that recall for a single banner ad exposure is about 12 percent, which compares favorably with the 10 percent recall for a single exposure to a television ad.

On the negative side of the argument, eMarketer estimates that 99 percent of all banner ads don't get clicked. In addition, eMarketer estimates that 49 percent of Web surfers don't even look at a banner ad while they surf, and in order to develop any brand recognition a consumer would have to be exposed to a banner ad twenty-seven times—not a good combination of statistics. The current thinking is that most users of banner advertising will shift their Web spending from banners to strategic partnerships and sponsorships.[24]

Pop-up Ads. The only thing surfers hate more than banner ads is pop-up Internet ads. The idea is borrowed from TV. A **pop-up ad** is an advertisement that appears as a Web site page is loading or after a page has loaded. A surfer wants to go to a certain site but has to wade through an ad page first, just as a television viewer must watch a commercial before seeing a favorite show. It is often not merely a word from a sponsor, but invitations to link to another related site. A pop-up ad opens a separate window. The more times people click on these ads, the more money can be charged for the privilege of advertising. If the future of banner ads is uncertain, then the future of pop-ups must be doomed. But as long as marketers are willing to give pop-up ads a try, we'll all have our pleasant surfing interrupted with unwanted commercial messages.

E-mail Communication. As mentioned earlier, e-mail communication may be the Internet's most advantageous application. Through e-mail, the Internet is the only "mass" medium capable of customizing a message for thousands or even millions of receivers. The message is delivered in a unique way, one at a time, which no other medium is capable of doing. E-mail advertising is expected to grow from about 3 percent of total Web advertising in 1999 to about 15 percent of the total in 2003.[25] The attitude toward e-mail varies, of course, depending on whether people are "spammed" with unwanted e-mail or they have signed up and given permission for e-mail to be delivered. When Web users agree to receive e-mails from organizations, it is called **permission marketing.** There are Web firms, like focalex.com (see Exhibit 9.17), that specialize in developing what are called "opt-in" lists of Web users who have agreed to accept commercial e-mails.

The data on permission-based e-mailing versus spamming are compelling. Sixty-six percent of Web users who give their permission to have e-mail sent to them indicate that they are either eager or curious to read the e-mail. This compares

23. Ibid.
24. "Consumer Attitudes Toward Web Marketing," eMarketing Report published July 7, 1999, accessed at http://www.emarketing.com on March 22, 2000.
25. "E-Mail Marketing Report," January, 2000, *eMarketer,* accessed at http://www.emarketer.com/stats/ on March 22, 2000.

to only 15 percent of Web users who receive e-mail through spamming.[26] And e-mail advertisers are turning to some traditional message strategies, like humor, to make the e-mail messages more palatable and interesting. BitMagic, an Amsterdam-based Web advertising specialty firm, has Web users download software containing a joke, cartoon, or game along with the e-mail message.[27]

And don't forget that, as in the case of Christina Aguilera, e-mail and listservs marketers can encourage viral marketing. **Viral marketing** is the process of consumers marketing to consumers over the Internet through word of mouth transmitted via e-mails and listservs. Hotmail (http://www.hotmail.com) is the king of viral marketing. Beginning as an undercapitalized start-up, every e-mail by every Hotmail subscriber concludes with the tag line "Get your private, free e-mail at http://www.hotmail.com." So far, the viral marketing program has helped sign up 12 million subscribers with 150,000 being added every day.[28]

Corporate Home Pages. A **corporate home page** is a Web site where a marketer provides current and potential customers detailed information about the firm. The best corporate home pages not only provide corporate and product information, but also offer other content of interest to site visitors. The Toshiba site (http://www.toshiba.com) in Exhibit 9.18 allows people to find out about the extensive Toshiba line of consumer and business products, pricing, specifications, and the closest dealers. This product-oriented site also allows consumers to request brochures, communicate their comments and questions to the Toshiba corporation, and find a dealer when they are ready to make a purchase. A corporate site that focuses on the lifestyle end of the spectrum is the Crayola site (http://www.crayola.com) displayed in Exhibit 9.19. Rather than showcasing its famous product, the company decided to emphasize the needs of the parents and children that use Crayola crayons. Visitors can read bedtime stories, search for local child-care providers, discover hints on getting kids to help with housework, or browse movie reviews for family-oriented flicks. And, of course, there are links to areas where kids can create art with computerized Crayolas.

A variation on the corporate Web site is setting up a site and placing it inside a virtual mall. A **virtual mall** is a gateway to a group of Internet storefronts that provide access to mall sites by simply clicking on a category of store, as shown in the Mall.com site in Exhibit 9.20. Notice that many of the resident stores at the Mall.com Web site have their own corporate Web sites and home pages but have chosen to also set up a site in the virtual mall. Mall visitors can be led directly to the corporate site. Having this additional presence just gives stores like The Gap and J. Crew more exposure.

EXHIBIT 9.18

Some corporate Web sites are developed as purely information sites. The Toshiba site provides extensive product information for the full line of the company's business products.

26.   Ibid.
27.   Kathryn Kranhold, "Internet Advertisers Use Humor in Effort to Entice Web Surfers," *The Wall Street Journal,* August 17, 1999, B9.
28.   Steve Jurvetson, "Turning Customers into a Sales Force," *Business 2.0,* March 2000, 231.

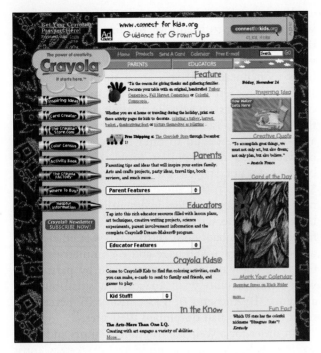

EXHIBIT 9.19

In contrast to purely information sites, other Web sites are more "lifestyle" sites. The Crayola site offers parents, educators, and kids all sorts of interesting, entertaining, and educational options.

EXHIBIT 9.20

Virtual malls provide advertisers another way to reach surfers. Malls like this one provide links to corporate Web sites that consumers might not go to directly.

The nature of virtual malls varies widely. Compared with Mall.com, the MetroWest's Virtual Mall (http://www.virtmall.com) features a more local orientation from west Boston. The advantage of malls for a marketer is the opportunity to attract browsers to its site, much as window shopping works in the physical world. Check out CyberShop: The online mall allows virtual shoppers to browse by department or brand. Offerings range from gourmet food stuffs to housewares to women's accessories, and include constantly updated sale items. Found at: http://www.cybershop.com.

ESTABLISHING A SITE ON THE WORLD WIDE WEB ⑤

While setting up a Web site can be done fairly easily, setting up a commercially viable one is a lot harder and a lot more expensive. The top commercial sites today cost $1 million to develop, about $4.9 million for the initial launch, and about $1.8 million per year to maintain.[29] The 100 leading e-commerce sites actually spend much more—an average of $8.6 million a year on marketing alone.[30] Setting up an attractive site costs so much because of the need for specialized designers to create—and, most important, to constantly update—the site. The basic hardware for a site can be a personal computer, and the software to run the site ranges from free to several thousand dollars, depending on the number of extras needed. A site anticipating considerable traffic will need to plan for higher-capacity connections—and hence, a bigger phone bill.[31]

29. Kim Cross, "Web Development Spending," *Business 2.0,* October 1999, 244.
30. G. Beato, "Web-O-Matic," *Business 2.0,* October 1999, 190–196.
31. *Information Week,* December 7, 1998, G2–G3.

EXHIBIT 9.21

One of the biggest challenges facing Web marketers is making a site "sticky." A sticky site gets consumers to stay long and come back often. Notice that at the iwon.com site you not only have a chance to win big money on a daily basis and bigger money on a monthly basis, but you also have access to all sorts of options like checking sports scores, sending greeting cards, or visiting a chat room.

But what if you're not a big IPO Internet firm with $8 million to spend for the first year of operating of a Web site? Not to fear. There are actually some very inexpensive ways of setting up a site and finding hosts to maintain it if you are a small or medium-sized business and want an Internet presence. Some of the big players are actually coming to the rescue of the little guys. Yahoo!, AT&T, Intel, MindSpring, and others have begun to offer low-cost hosting and browser-based development tools that allow small business to get started on the Internet for about $300 a month.[32] But there is even better news. A new class of Web builders is emerging with an even better deal. One start-up based in Emeryville, California, freemerchant.com (http://www.freemerchant.com) will set up a Web page and e-commerce site for free. The company makes its revenue by partnering with vendors who want to reach a small-business audience. By the end of 1999, nearly 37 percent of small businesses had developed Web sites.[33]

In order for a Web site to attract visitors and build consumer loyalty and confidence, marketers must conceive a Web strategy that addresses the issues raised in the next section.

Getting Surfers to Come Back

Once a site is set up, getting those who spend considerable time on the Internet (**netizens,** as they are commonly called) to spend time at the site and to come back often is a primary concern. When a site is able to attract visitors over and over again and keep them for a long time, it is said to be a **sticky site;** or to have features that are "sticky." A site with pages and pages showing the product and its specifications may have no appeal beyond a single visit. Even a quick tour of various home pages reveals countless boring corporate Web pages. According to recent research, most Web sites merely include rich product descriptions that simply mimic printed brochures.[34] Although such Web sites might satisfy the needs of netizens searching for specific product information, they are unlikely to attract and capture the interest of surfers enough to get them to return. The whole idea is to satisfy visitors and get them to come back. The New Media box points out ten Web design goofs that can alienate visitors.

To make a site sticky, a marketer should incorporate engaging, interactive features into the site. For the major hosting sites and portals, recurring information like the weather, late-breaking news, sports scores, and stock quotes are key to attracting visitors daily or even several times a day. In an effort to break into the world of portals, iwon.com (http://www.iwon.com) offers all sorts of links to current information—as well as the chance to win $10,000 a day or $1 million each month for using the site. Pretty much an all-out assault to try to get surfers to return (see

32.   G. Beato, "Web-O-Matic," *Business 2.0,* October 1999, 190.
33.   "Small Biz Web Sites on the Rise," Prodigy Communications Corporation, accessed at http://www.prodigy.com on March 17, 2000.
34.   Schlosser and Kanfer, "Current Advertising on the Internet," 41–60.

N E W MEDIA

TEN WEB DESIGN GOOFS THAT CAN BE FATAL TO A WEB SITE

1. *Don't Be a "Back" Breaker* Your Web site will be a "back breaker" for users if you commit one of these Web design sins: Open a new browser window with a Back return; every time the user clicks back, the browser returns to a page that bounces the user forward to an undesired location; a back click requires a fresh trip to the server.

2. *Don't Do New Windows* Don't pollute a Web site with new windows as a surfer maneuvers the site. If users want a new window, they should be able to choose when to access one.

3. *No Weird Widgets* Consistency is one of the most highly prized features of a Web site by users. The worst consistency violations on the Web are found in the use of graphical user interfaces (GUI) widgets such as radio buttons and checkboxes.

4. *Don't Hide* Even the earliest Web studies showed that users want to know the people behind the information on the Web. Photographs of corporate personnel or biographies of authors at information sites, but satisfy users' desires for accountability.

5. *Don't Lock Up the Archives* Old information is often valuable information to users—especially those using the Web for research purposes. Maintaining archives may add 10 percent to the cost of maintaining a site, but can increase the usefulness of a site up to 50 percent in the eyes of users.

6. *Don't Switch URLs* Anytime a page moves, you make the user exert extra effort and you break any incoming links from other sites.

7. *Write Your Own Headlines* Headlines on the Web are not like headlines in traditional media. A Web headline provides a user interface and may guide visitors through the site. Web headlines should accomplish two basic goals: (1) to tell visitors what's at the other end and (2) to protect users from following the link if they would not be interested in the destination page.

8. *Beware the Buzzword* The Web is awash in site buzzwords. There is no substitute for spending the time, money, and management bandwidth on a useful site with good ergonomics.

9. *Improve Your Serve* Users don't care why the response time is slow at your site. All they know is that the site doesn't offer good service. Invest in a fast server, and get the performance architecture and code quality right to optimize response times.

10. *Looks Like an Ad? It's Bad.* Web users have stopped paying attention to ads that get in the way of goal-driven surfing. It is best to avoid *any* design that looks like an advertisement. The best recommendations are: (1) Users never fixate on anything that looks like a banner ad. Avoid everything that is rectangular in shape. (2) Users have learned "animation avoidance" and ignore everything that flashes and blinks. Avoid everything that flashes and blinks. (3) Users have learned to close "pop-up" windows before they even fully load. Avoid everything that requires a pop-up presentation.

Source: Jakob Nielsen, "Designing for Disaster," *Business 2.0*, December 1999, 159.

Exhibit 9.21). For home pages or Web sites, entertaining features such as online games or videos can also get surfers to stay at a site and get them to come back.[35] One area in the Cartoon Network (http://www.cartoonnetwork.com) site allows kids to help direct the action in a special made-for-the-Web interactive cartoon called *Robot Frenzy*. Thus, it is important for marketers to learn about their customers before setting up a site. Good consumer and communications research can be useful in this context.

A well-developed site can keep customers coming back for more. A good example is the New Jersey Devils Web page (http://www.newjerseydevils.com). Visitors can do more than just read how their favorite NHL team did the night before. They can read in-depth interviews with players, coaches, and even team trainers. Visitors compete for fan-of-the-month awards, while younger fans get a chance to be sportswriters. Tickets, schedules, and team merchandise are readily available. And, of course, no visit to the New Jersey Devils site is complete without a rousing game of Zamboni Master, where players race around the Devils' arena in a Zamboni, repairing damage inflicted by invasions of opposing teams. These features give people multiple reasons to continue to visit the site. This approach to Web-presence design, called **rational branding,** stresses the need for a brand's Web site to provide some unique informational resource to justify visiting it. These features give people multiple reasons to continue to visit the site. There are firms that provide marketers with all the tools they need to develop a sticky site.

35. Anne E. Schlosser and Alaina Kanfer, "Culture Clash in Internet Marketing," in M. J Shaw, R. Blanning, T. Strader, and A. Whinston, eds., *Handbook on Electronic Commerce* (New York: Springer-Verlag, 1999).

EXHIBIT 9.22

Marketers can turn to firms like ScreamingMedia (http://www. screamingmedia.com) to help them develop sites that attract Web surfers and keep them coming back.

Screaming Media (http://www.screamingmedia.com) is one such firm and provides design and features for Web sites to attract visitors and keep them coming back (see Exhibit 9.22).

One crucial Web site feature (regardless of whether consumers are searching for specific information or browsing the Web) is the presence of multiple navigational tools; the more such tools available, the more the visitor will like the site.[36] Navigational tools help guide the visitor around the site; examples include home and section icons, a search engine that is specific to the site, and a site index. Just as consumers need a cable guide to help them enjoy their cable services, so too do consumers need resources to help them realize and enjoy all the possibilities of the site. Remodeling a site is a costly investment: According to Forrester Research, adding search and other personalization features to a site can cost $300,000 to $425,000. Many argue that such an investment is worthwhile, since the consequences of a poorly designed site include lost revenues and the erosion of brand image.

Thus, the objective of having repeat customers depends on substance, ease of use, and entertainment value. Netizens are discriminating in that while nice pictures are interesting, sites that have considerable repeat users offer something more. This can be product information and ongoing technical support, or it can be general news about a product, original writing, or the latest or most comprehensive information about just about anything. At the same time, the company should ensure that the advertising information and graphics can be easily downloaded by their consumers. Above all, it has to satisfy the consumer's goal for visiting the site—pure and simple. In the words of one Web development consultant, "To stay on a Website, customers need incentive, convenience, and competitive prices."[37]

Purchasing Keywords and Developing a Domain Name

Online search engines such as Yahoo! sell keywords. A marketer can purchase a keyword so that its banner appears whenever users select that word for a search. For example, when a user searches for a keyword such as "inn" on the search engine Lycos, he or she will see an ad from a directory for bed-and-breakfast inns. Keyword sponsorship on Lycos costs around five cents per impression ($50 CPM). Sponsorship on Yahoo! costs a bit more.[38] These search engines let marketers pay a flat monthly fee or a per-impression fee (based on how many people see the ad). Thus, getting a popular word may result in a considerable number of impressions and a higher bill. The other factor is effectiveness. The Infoseek search engine claims buy

36. Schlosser and Kanfer, "Current Advertising on the Internet," 41–60.
37. Anu Shukla, "Sticking to the Basics," *Business 2.0,* March 2000, 129.
38. J. Hodges, "Words Hold the Key to Web Ad Packages," *Advertising Age,* January 15, 1996.

A breakthrough in getting
customers to your website.

http://www.realnames.com

EXHIBIT 9.23

While Internet domain names are convenient for computers, they're often awkward—and, at times, downright ugly—for consumers. RealNames thinks it has a better mousetrap: It maintains a mapping of more human-friendly keywords and phrases to domain names, and has even negotiated to have its keywords recognized by Microsoft's Web browser. AOL offers something very similar—short navigational keywords, like "BN" for Barnes & Noble's cobranded area—within its own service. What challenges might companies offering alternative citation systems like RealNames' and AOL's keywords face?

rates from 2 to 36 percent, while other engines claim that keyword ads do not significantly differ from the banner ads in effectiveness. However, keyword ads are a great way to get a product in front of someone interested in that general category.

Purchasing keywords helps consumer find your site while they search for information. But before purchasing a keyword, a marketer must decide on a domain name that establishes the basis for the keyword. A **domain name** is the unique URL through which a Web location is established. If you are The Gap or Sony, your domain name is your corporate name and consumers know how to search for your location. But for thousands of Web start-ups that provide specialized Web products and services, the domain name issue is a dilemma. You want the name to be descriptive but unique, intuitive but distinctive.[39] That was the strategy used by Dennis Scheyer when he recommended that GoToTix.com, a ticketing and entertainment site, stick with its original name. The name was intuitive and easy to remember. But the firm insisted on running a consumer contest to rename the company. Scheyer said of the names that made the final cut, "One sounded like a breakfast cereal you wouldn't eat. One sounded like a cough medicine. And one sounded like a prophylactic." In the end, the firm chose Acteva.com (we suspect this is Scheyer's cough medicine entry) because "Act conveys activity. E signifies E-commerce and 'va' has that international flavor."[40] Fortunately, there are companies out there like RealNames (http://www.realnames.com) that help firms identify and register Internet keywords (see Exhibit 9.23).

Promoting Web Sites

Building a Web site is only the first step; the next is promoting it. Throughout the text, you have seen advertising by companies promoting their Web sites. Several agencies, including BBDO Wieden & Kennedy, and Ogilvy One, specialize in

39.   Clay Timon, "10 Tips for Naming" *Business 2.0,* March 2000, 151.
40.   Laurie Freeman, "Domain-Name Dilemma Worsens," *Advertising Age,* November 8, 1999, 100.

promoting Web sites. The quickest and lowest-cost way to promote a Web site is to notify appropriate Usenet groups. The other key method is to register the site with search engines such as Yahoo! and AltaVista. With Yahoo!, because it is a hierarchical search engine, it is important to pick keywords that are commonly chosen, yet describe and differentiate that site. Other places to register are with the growing Yellow Pages on the Internet (for example, http://www.bigyellow.com) and with appropriate listserv groups. It is also important to send out press releases to Internet news sites. E-mail as a form of direct mail is another method to promote the site.

But the dot-com companies have found the allure of traditional mass media irresistible. Exhibit 9.24 shows spending by Web companies on traditional media with online brokerages leading the way. Offline ad spending by online companies topped $1 billion in 1999 and is expected to grow steadily over the next several years. About half of the $1 billion was spent on television advertising and the bulk of the remainder on magazine ads (see Exhibit 9.25).

What is interesting about dot-com spending on TV advertising is that they are relying on many traditional techniques to achieve brand name awareness and recognition. As you probably know just from seeing the ads yourself, humor is a preferred technique for many of the Web firms that choose television. Others are turning to celebrity spokespersons like William Shatner (priceline.com) and Rodney Dangerfield (BargainBid.com) as a way to attract attention offline.[41] If a marketer wants to

EXHIBIT 9.24

Here is a list of the leading dot-com spenders ranked by spending on traditional media advertising.

Rank	Marketer	Annualized Spending
1	Charles Schwab (online business) Agency: BBDO Worldwide, New York, and Sansome Group, San Francisco; in-house (online)	$300,000,000
	E*Trade Group Agency: Goodby, Silverstein & Partners, San Francisco	$300,000,000
3	Ameritrade Holdings Corp. Agency: OgilvyOne, Chicago (Ameritrade), DDB Worldwide, Chicago (OnMoney)	$200,000,000
4	HomeGrocer.com Agency: Wieden & Kennedy, Portland, Ore.	$120,000,000
5	AltaVista (CMGI) Agency: Wieden & Kennedy, Portland, Ore.	$100,000,000
	TD Waterhouse Group Agency: Emmerling Post, New York	$100,000,000
	Value America Agency: Stevens Reed Curcio & Co., Alexandria, VA; (offline), in-house (online)	$100,000,000
	Webvan Group Agency: Publicis & Hal Riney, San Francisco	$100,000,000
9	NBCi (Snap.com, Xoom.com) Agency: NBC in-house productions	$95,000,000
10	Datek Online Agency: Bozell Worldwide, New York	$80,000,000

Source: AdAge Data Place, http://www.adage.com, accessed via the Internet on March 22, 2000.

41. Jennifer Gilbert, "Celebrity Pitchpersons Build Instant Brands for dot-coms," *Advertising Age,* November 8, 1999, 100, 110.

draw people to its Web site as one of the goals of a television commercial, the address should be visible on the screen long enough for viewers to capture and actually remember the site address. The necessary length of time can range from three to five seconds, depending on the length and memorability of the address. Whatever traditional advertising vehicle is used, it is important that the product advertised in traditional media is easily found at the promoted Web site.[42]

Security and Privacy Issues

Any Web user can download text, images, and graphics from the World Wide Web. Although marketers place trademark and copyright disclaimers on their online displays, marketers on the Web have to be willing to accept the consequence that their trademarks and logos can be copied without authorization. Currently, there is no viable policing of this practice by users. Thus far, marketers have taken legal action only against users who have taken proprietary materials and blatantly used them in a fashion that is detrimental to the brand or infringes on the exclusivity of the marketer's own site. This may change.

EXHIBIT 9.25

Many dot-com companies have discovered the power of traditional of-fline media in building awareness for their online brands. This ad for BrassRing.com appeared in Time *magazine.*

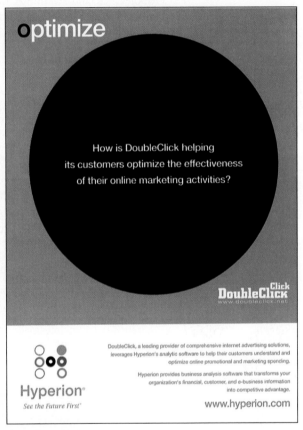

EXHIBIT 9.26

The firestorm around privacy on the Internet, unfortunately, has focused mostly on one firm—DoubleClick and its Hyperion division. In an effort to assure surfers that they are not trying to find out and use personal information, DoubleClick has adopted a privacy policy and appointed a Chief Privacy Officer.

42. Schlosser and Kanfer, "Current Advertising on the Internet," 41–60.

In Chapter 6, we discussed privacy as an ethical and regulatory issue. At this point, we can consider privacy from a strategic management standpoint. Also, as we saw in Chapter 6, the privacy issues are a very complex and sensitive topic. Discussions at the highest levels focus on the extent to which regulations should be mandated for gathering and disseminating information about Web use. The concern among marketers are not just the regulatory aspects of the issue. In addition, consumers are expressing concerns about using the Internet for fear of invasion of privacy—clearly a strategic management issue. A recent survey found that a whopping 78 percent of consumers surveyed were either very or somewhat concerned that a company would use their personal information to send them unwanted information. This is up from 65 percent two years earlier.[43]

Ground zero in this debate is the Web research and profiling firm DoubleClick (http://www.doubleclick.net). DoubleClick is in the business of helping Web companies identify and understand customer groups to better develop and target marketing efforts (see Exhibit 9.26). Using DoubleClick's Hyperion division, companies like 3Com can keep track of the buying habits and traffic patterns of the 30 million people who visit the 3Com Web site each week. But as we learned in Chapter 6, this sort of profiling has come under intense scrutiny. In response, profiling research firms like DoubleClick and Avenue A have issued privacy statements and even appointed Chief Privacy Officers as a way to assure consumers (and regulators) that consumer profile information is used strictly to improve the service to customers and not to dig into (or

EXHIBIT 9.27

CASIE, the Coalition for Advertising Supported Information and Entertainment, has issued a set of goals for advertisers on the Internet.

1. We believe it is important to educate consumers about how they can use interactive technology to save time and customize product and service information to meet their individual needs. By choosing to share pertinent data about themselves, consumers can be provided the product information most relevant to them and can help marketers service them more economically and effectively.

2. We believe any interactive electronic communication from a marketer ought to disclose the marketer's identity.

3. We believe that marketers need to respect provacy in the use of "personal information" about individual consumers collected via interactive technology. "Personal information" is data not otherwise available via public sources. In our view, personal information ought to be used by a marketer to determine how it can effectively respond to a consumer's needs.

4. We believe that if the marketer seeks personal information via interactive electronic communication, it ought to inform the consumer whether the information will be shared with others. We also believe that before a marketer shares such perosnal information with others, the consumer ought to be offered an option to request that personal information not be shared. Upon receiving such a request, the marketer ought to keep such personal information confidential and not share it.

5. We believe consumers ought to have the ability to obtain a summary of what personal information about them is on record with a marketer that has solicited them via interactive electronic communication. In addition, a consumer ought to be offered the opportunity to correct personal information, request that such information be removed from the marketer's database (unless the marketer needs to retain it for generally accepted and customary accounting and business purposes), or request that the marketer no longer solicit the customer.

Source: Coalition for Advertising Supported Information and Entertainment. Available online at http://www.casie.com/guide1/priv.html. Accessed March 28, 2000.

43. Heather Green, et al, "It's Time for Rules in Wonderland," *Business Week,* March 20, 2000, 82–96.

sell) information about consumers' private affairs.[44] This would seem to be the right approach because consumers claim that with some assurance of privacy their concerns about surfing or shopping the Web are greatly diminished.[45] With respect to consumer privacy, the Coalition for Advertising Supported Information and Entertainment, (CASIE) has suggested five goals for marketers, which we've reproduced in Exhibit 9.27. Striving for these goals will certainly contribute to consumers' loyalty toward and confidence in a brand. Privacy is a legitimate concern for Internet users and will likely continue to be one for civil libertarians and regulators as well.

MANAGING THE BRAND IN AN E-COMMUNITY

The Internet, in addition to providing a new means for marketers to communicate to consumers, also provides consumers a new and efficient way to communicate with one another. In fact, the social aspect of the Internet is one of the most important reasons for its success. Via Usenet newsgroups, e-mail, IRC and even Web pages, consumers have a new way to interact and form communities. Sometimes communities are formed online among users of a particular brand. Such groups behave much like a community in the traditional sense, such as a small town or ethnic neighborhood. They have their own cultures, rituals, and traditions. Members create detailed Web pages devoted to the brand. They even feel a sense of duty or moral responsibility to other members of the community. For example, among many Volkswagen drivers, it is a common courtesy to pull over to help another VW broken down on the side of the road. Harley-Davidson riders feel a similar sense of obligation to help others who use the same brand when they are in trouble.

In most respects, such communities are a good thing. One of the reasons members of these communities like to get together is to share their experiences in using the brand. They can share what they like about the brand and what it means to them, or suggest places to go to buy replacement parts or have the product serviced. However, marketers need to be careful not to alienate members or turn them off of the brand. These consumers can also share their dislikes about recent changes in the brand and its advertising, rejecting them if severe enough. Since the Internet makes it easier for members of these communities to interact, brand communities are likely to proliferate in coming years. Consequently, dealing effectively with these communities will be one of the challenges facing marketers. Several firms have emerged to facilitate the community interaction process by providing shared access to a site that promotes communication between members (see Exhibit 9.28).

EXHIBIT 9.28

Building an e-community with great loyalty to a site is a tall task. Tools provided by companies like MyEvents.com help advertisers develop a site that is interesting, attractive, and worth coming back to again and again.

44. "DoubleClick Appoints Chief Privacy Officer and Privacy Advisory Board Chairman," *Company Press Release,* March 8, 2000, accessed at http://biz.yahoo.com on March 17, 2000.
45. Heather Green, et al, "It's Time for Rules in Wonderland," *Business Week,* March 20, 2000, 84.

Of course, this creates new management issues as well. One of the most intriguing ideas for marketers has been how to access and use consumer word of mouth. The Internet has made the collection and management of this data much easier.

BRANDING AND THE WEB'S GLOBAL PRESENCE

Arthur Andersen is a $7.3 billion professional services and consulting firm that helps clients navigate through the complexities of new economic realities around the world. But the company itself recently woke up to new reality—its brand was mired in an old business model with a market perception that was fading into a conservative and staid image. This definitely did not match the company's current objective, which was to be viewed as a global expert on the "new economy." What made things worse is that Arthur Andersen regional operations around the world were pursuing their own individual strategies. In the words of Matthew Gonring, global managing partner of communications and integrated marketing, "The way we went to market was confusing and diluting the brand. We had to go to one Arthur Andersen master brand around the world."

To reverse the slide and rejuvenate the brand image, the company devised a new promotional program that relied heavily on the Web and attacked the image problem in a way that would provide not only a contemporary look, but also a global presence. The first step was to redesign the Arthur Anderson Web site. Ogilvy Interactive was the agency called on to revamp and redesign the site. They immediately cut more than half the content and added new updated material on the firm's services (http://www.arthurandersen.com). The site also highlighted a new brand logo and bold language—"maverick and inventive"—to describe the company's services. Then 13,000 direct mail pieces were sent to executives worldwide containing miniature CD-ROMs that guided both existing clients and potential customers to the new Web site.

Remember that all this reinventing and redesigning was undertaken for arguably the most recognized and respected brand in corporate consulting. But in Gonring's words, "While we recognized that the Arthur Andersen brand is one of the strongest, the brand research was saying that if we wanted to capture the new business . . . tweaking the status quo wasn't going to get us there."

Source: Amanda Beeler, "Arthur Andersen Takes Wraps off Global Image," *Advertising Age*, February 14, 2000, 24.

Marketers can monitor Usenet discussions, develop proprietary search engines that scour the Web to find who is saying what about new products, and so on—just as Electric Artists did in building a buzz around Christina Aguilera. Another firm that relied exclusive on the Web to build awareness of its brand was the Israeli company ICQ (formally known as Mirabilis). This company never spent a dime on traditional promotional tools. Rather, it used only "word of mouse" to spread the word on its chat and instant messaging technology. Two years after launching a chat room/ Usenet-only campaign, the company had 30 million users worldwide, and America Online bought the firm for $400 million.[46]

We also need to realize that using the Web as a brand builder is not reserved just for consumer brands. Business products marketers are discovering the power of the Web for brand building as well. Plus, from a corporate perspective, the Web is an ideal global medium, as Arthur Andersen, the global consulting firm, discovered when it set out to revamp its brand image.[47] The Global Issues box tells the whole story.

IMC AND INTERNET ADVERTISING ⑥

Marketers are starting to rethink their strategies for Web-based advertising. They have come to realize that Internet advertising cannot simply be a transfer of advertising from other media. For example, a television campaign that is designed to generate a mood or image for a brand does not work well on the Internet, nor does simply transferring magazine ad images over to a Web site. The Internet has its own strengths and weaknesses, like all other media.

---

46.   Tania Hershman, "Word of Mouth," *Business 2.0,* December 1999, 371.
47.   Amanda Beeler, "Arthur Andersen Takes Wraps off Global Image," *Advertising Age,* February 14, 2000, 24.

IN PRACTICE

SMALL BUSINESSES GET STAMPED

E-Stamp Corp., the pioneer in distributing postage over the Internet, relied on offline promotional techniques to spread the word about the company and its service. The goal of the campaign was to establish E-Stamp as *the* Internet postage provider for small office and home office (SOHO) businesses.

The company has become known for its commitment to leadership in this industry. In a bold promotional move, E-Stamp spent 65 percent of the money it raised in an IPO—$126 million—on branding, marketing, and customer acquisition activities. The integrated marketing communications campaign used to heighten awareness in the SOHO segment used a wide array of promotional tools. These included national spot television ads, business and trade print advertising, banner advertising, online sweepstakes and promotions, direct marketing, and in-store point-of-purchase displays at retail stores.

E-Stamp worked with its advertising agency, Butler, Shine, and Stern of Sausalito, California, to develop a creative national television and cable advertising campaign that would appeal to its target audience of SOHO businesspeople. The broad media schedule included national network and cable prime-time news shows ranging from CNBC and CNN to the Discovery Channel. The campaign theme highlighted the convenience and time-saving aspects of Internet postage access as opposed to those "adventurous" trips to the post office. The national television advertising was supported by radio, print, and banner advertising, which supported the themes of convenience, choice, and ease of use. The direct-marketing and radio campaigns focused on E-Stamp's top ten geographic markets: San Francisco, Washington, D.C., New York, Seattle, Baltimore, Boston, Los Angeles, Chicago, San Jose, and Denver. The online banner advertising supported the direct-marketing promotions and was designed to drive traffic and customer sign-up at http://www.e-stamp.com.

Nicole Eagan, Senior Vice President of Sales and Marketing, described the campaign in this way: "Our approach has always been characterized by execution and by our ability to listen and respond to the needs of our SOHO customers. We're in the business of making their lives easier. One way we can do this is by making it more convenient for them to buy postage." The entire focus of the IMC campaign was directed to these core values of the E-Stamp program.

Source: "E-Stamp Launches Integrated Marketing Campaign Aimed at Small Office/Home Office Customers," *Business Wire*, October, 25, 1999, accessed at http://biz.yahoo.com/ on November 11, 1999.

It is great for providing detailed information that is beyond the scope of other media. With the Internet's interactive and high-speed nature, data about a brand's performance or technical specifications in various categories can be highly organized and quickly accessible. Given this strength, it can play a pivotal role in an IMC campaign: Media such as television and print ads can be used to create a powerful image, while the Web site can provide detailed information on the product and help close the sale.

Many Web firms are indeed using traditional media for image building, and then the Internet site follows through with information, entertainment, or community interaction.[48]

E-Stamp, the pioneer of Internet postage, used a fully integrated set of promotional tools in its initial brand-recognition campaign. The promotional mix included national television spots, print advertising, direct marketing, and online activities.[49] The IMC in Practice box gives the details of the campaign. Saturn uses a similar multimedia strategy. It promotes its Web site with quirky image ads in TV and print, such as the one in which a college student orders a Saturn over the Internet and has it delivered, much the same way a pizza is delivered. The print and TV ads build an image for the brand and refer consumers to the corporate Web page. Once there, consumers can learn more about the product, put together a package that satisfies their particular needs, calculate lease rates and monthly payments, and get in contact with a Saturn dealer in their vicinity. As a result of Saturn's integrated campaign, traffic to the Saturn Web site tripled, and the company now receives 80 percent of its sales leads from the Internet.[50]

48. Kim Girard, "Companies Bank on Ad Campaigns to Build Internet Image," CNET News.com, October 11, 1999, accessed at http://technews.netscape.com on March 28, 2000.

49. "E-Stamp Launches Integrated Marketing Campaign Aimed at Small Office/Home Office Customers," *Business Wire,* October, 25, 1999, accessed at http://biz.yahoo.com/ on November 11, 1999.

50. *San Francisco Chronicle,* August 26, 1998.

CAREERPROFILE

Name: *David Murcek*
Title: *Group Account Director*
Company: *Qfactor.com, Bethesda, MD*
(http://www.Qfactor.com.com)

When David Murcek first thought about a career in advertising, he leaned toward becoming a copywriter. One of his professors, however, urged him to consider becoming an account executive (AE) instead. "He thought I'd be a better fit as an AE because I could be involved with the whole process," says David.

After working as an AE at traditional advertising agencies, David is now Group Account Director at webnet-marketing, one of the largest independent interactive advertising agencies in the country. The agency helps clients like Network Solutions, WashingtonPost.com, and BabySuperCenter.com plan and implement banner advertising campaigns.

While the Internet is a relatively new advertising medium, David says traditional marketing principles still apply. "Internet advertising has to be part of the whole marketing program," he says. "You still have to think about your brand and make sure your online efforts are in tune with the image you want to portray. The banner's tone, placement, and Web site are a window on that brand." David works closely with the client's marketing team and webnet-marketing's media and creative departments to make sure that the Web sites chosen as ad sites match marketing objectives.

Since the purpose of online banner ads is to get viewers to visit a specific Web site, David must also evaluate the effectiveness of each client's site. "We could get a million impressions of a banner ad, but if people click on that banner to go the Web site and they get an error message or the site doesn't do a good job of selling, then spending the client's money on banner advertising isn't going to be very worthwhile," he says.

If you're interested in a career in Internet advertising, David advises that you bring a passion for the medium to the job. "You have to believe in the Internet and its ability to communicate and market," he says. He also notes that Internet advertising jobs require analytical skills. "You should be number oriented and willing to spend time pulling together data and analyzing results." Most important, he says, is flexibility. "This is still very much a new and evolving field," he says.

To learn more about Internet advertising, visit these Web sites:

Internet Advertising Resource
http://www.admedia.org

Internet Advertising Bureau
http://www.iab.net

Channel Seven.com
http://www.channelseven.com

But integrating Internet advertising into the overall promotional mix is much more than integration with other advertising media. True integration means coordinating Web advertising and corporate Web sites with other promotional mix tools as well. Let's take a look at the way the Internet can be used with some different forms of promotion.

Coupons

Companies such as e-centives (see Exhibit 9.29) distribute coupons via the Internet and via the sites of other commercial online services. E-centives simply allows users to print coupons on their home printers and then take them to the store for redemption. The company charges clients anywhere from $3 to $15 per thousand coupons distributed. The average cost to manufacturers for coupons distributed via freestanding inserts is $7 per thousand. However, only a small portion of those coupons are even clipped (2 to 3 percent redemption rate), whereas with online coupons the manufacturer is paying only per thousand clipped, or in this case printed, by consumers.

Contests

We have already talked about sites like iwon.com and LuckySurf.com that run ongoing contests to try to gain the loyalty of Web users. Another form of promotion using contests is common on the Web. Traditional firms like Pepsi or Web firms like MyFamily.com will partner with big portals like Yahoo! and traditional firms like Disney to run contests that draw attention to the brand over the Web along with similar promotions being run offline. Pepsi partnered with Yahoo! for an under-the-bottle-cap promotion called Stuff.com. The promotion allowed users to earn points or discounts from under the cap awards on bottles of brands across the Pepsi line. The contest was also launched on network TV and local spot radio. Drinkers of Pepsi brands were able to redeem points online and accumulate enough points to purchase goods or get discounts from merchants like Sony Music and Foot Locker.[51]

51. "Pepsi Links with Yahoo! for Promotion," AdAge.com, March 22, 2000, accessed at http://www.adage.com/interactive on March 22, 2000.

EXHIBIT 9.29

The Internet is ideally suited to be integrated with other promotional tools so a marketer can truly pursue integrated marketing communications. Companies like e-centives help marketers deliver coupons over the Web. Notice that e-centives is a permission based organization of the type discussed earlier.

To explain how these programs are put together, consider this example. MyFamily.com, an online community dedicated to connecting families on the Web, teamed up with Walt Disney Co. to promote Disney's animated feature film *The Tigger Movie*. The partnership was arranged in this way: Disney and MyFamily.com entered into a barter arrangement whereby MyFamily featured *The Tigger Movie* in its advertising, and all Disney advertising for the film listed the URL for MyFamily and directed ad viewers to the Web community's home page. The campaign by both firms features a sweepstakes with a grand prize of a 25-person family reunion at Walt Disney World in Orlando, Florida.[52] Both partners benefit in that Disney gets highly targeted exposure for the film and MyFamily.com gets a boost from affiliating with a high-profile, family-oriented entertainment conglomerate.

Event Marketing

The Web is also an avenue for ties to event and sports marketing. For instance, the Super Bowl, the Oscars, and every event on the PGA golf tour have Web sites to provide real-time interaction with viewers. The site is promoted during the television

52. Cara Beardi, "MyFamily, Disney Link for 'The Tigger Movie,'" *Advertising Age,* February 14, 2000, 50.

broadcast, and sponsors get their logos on the site, have links to their own home pages prominently displayed, and have an opportunity to offer editorial content for the event site.

Public Relations and Publicity

Companies can use the Web to disseminate information about the firm in a classic public relations sense. Web organizations like Business Wire (http://www.businesswire.com) and PR Newswire (http://www.prnewswire.com) offer services where firms can request the dissemination of a press release over the Internet. These are often highly targeted press releases. Business Wire Connect Software gives its clients easy point-and-click access to its services and allows them to transmit news directly into the company's system at any modem speed up to 56K bps. Cost of the service varies by topic category—business, entertainment, news, or sports. Generally, a domestic national press release is $525 for 400 words and $135 for a 100-word release. Global distribution is $1,995. Businesslike is also able to provide targeted e-mail distribution of the release for 50 cents per destination—a little pricey for most companies to consider.

Aside from press releases, which are controllable, firms are, of course, subject to publicity over the Web that is totally uncontrollable. Any site, from digizines to news services like CNN, can run a story about a firm. There are also a host of news organizations like Reuters and Associated Press that will pick up news stories. Dealing with unfavorable publicity is a topic for Chapter 13.

Sales Support

Internet advertising can be coordinated with sales force support in several ways. The Internet equivalent to 800 numbers and mail-in information cards is e-mail. Home pages have the ability to provide an e-mail option for those who visit the site to respond to the marketer and ask for further information. As with 800 numbers, a marketer has to make sure that the e-mail account is adequately staffed to respond to queries in a timely manner. In addition, e-mail and Web site inquiries can be turned over to field sales staff who can use old-fashioned methods of communication like a phone call or sales call. The full story on the use of interactive tools in contemporary selling is told in Chapter 14.

THE FUTURE OF INTERNET ADVERTISING

When it comes to the Internet, talking about the future is usually futile. The future seems to come with every new issue of *Business Week, Fortune, Wired,* or *Business 2.0.* But the future of the Internet and the advertising that gets placed there seems unavoidably linked to two types of technology: wireless communication and video. The AOL/Time Warner merger signals the future direction for the Web and Web advertising. Time Warner brought to this merger all of its movie studio properties as well as an emerging Internet movie business and digital delivery of Warner Bros. movies on demand. Time Warner also has Time Warner cable television. What AOL brought to the merger, of course, was its online service including Netscape, CompuServe, MovieFone, and Instant Messenger e-mail service. Oh, did I forget to mention AOL's nearly 30 million members? Together, AOL and Time Warner can offer speedier and more diverse Internet and interactive TV services using Time Warner's cable lines.[53]

53. Maryanne Murray Buechner, et. al., "Happily Ever After?" *Time,* January 24, 2000, 39–44.

Mergers and partnerships of broadcast and Internet firms are one side of the story. On the other side, marketers and advertising agencies are preparing for new opportunities with "broadcast Web." For example, Sears Roebuck & Company and Forbes are testing a new technology that can instantly connect TV sets to specific Internet sites. With this technology, TV watchers can click on an icon during a television program and be connected to Web sites pertaining to the nature of the programming—sports, entertainment, news, and so forth.[54] Not only does this technology merge the Net with television programming, it can provide advertisers with general demographic and preference data about its registered users without resorting to names or e-mail addresses—the crux of the privacy concerns we have discussed. In the words of one agency executive, "This will revolutionize advertising on the Web because it establishes accountability and connection. I know that every one of our clients that has been shown this technology has been blown away."[55] And there may be some good reasons to get excited. In an Arbitron Internet Information Services/Edison Media research study, "streamies" (the nickname for Webcast viewers and online radio listeners) were twice as likely as general online users to click on banner ads or buy from a Web site, with 40 percent reporting they had made a purchase online.[56]

Does this mean that in the near future every television ad is really a Web ad? Well, maybe it won't be that extreme, but it does appear that the technology is available to provide direct links to Web sites for information and purchasing through television ads—a huge opportunity and potential. The possibilities are attracting all the big players—Microsoft, ABC, CBS and Warner Brothers Online, to name just a few. They all see video streaming as another piece of this Web broadcast puzzle.[57] Of course, this next step in the evolution of the Internet and its potential as an advertising alternative depends on the consumer's willingness to allow the communication to occur. Some things never change.

---

54. Diane Mermigas, "Net Technology Connects Data with Marketers," *Advertising Age,* January 17, 2000, 2.
55. Ibid.
56. Amanda Beeler, "Marketers Find Lucrative Audience in 'Streamies,'" *Advertising Age,* February 21, 2000, 48.
57. Dana Blankenhorn, "Where TV, Net Link," *Advertising Age,* January 17, 2000, s20.

SUMMARY

❶ Identify the basic components of the Internet.

There are four main components of the Internet: electronic mail IRC, Usenet, and the World Wide Web.

1. Electronic mail (e-mail) allows people to send messages to one another using the Internet.
2. Internet Relay Chat (IRC) makes it possible for people to "talk" electronically in real time with each other, despite their geographical separation.
3. For people with common interests, Usenet provides a forum for people with common interests to share knowledge in a public "cyberspace" that is separate from their e-mail program.
4. The World Wide Web (WWW) allows people to access an immense database of information in a graphical environment through the use of programs called Web browsers (such as Netscape and Internet Explorer). Many Web sites are still listed with the prefix http://, which stands for hypertext transfer protocol, or rules of interaction between the Web browser and the Web server that are used to deal with hypertext.

❷ Identify the Internet media available for communicating over the World Wide Web.

As described above, e-mail is an Internet function that allows users to communicate much as they do using standard mail. Some marketers have used this function of the Internet to communicate with potential consumers. A variety of companies collect e-mail addresses and profiles that allow marketers to direct e-mail to a specific group.

People who wish to discuss specific topics through the Internet often join electronic mailing lists, or listservs. Thousands of mailing lists are available on an incredible variety of topics. A message sent to the list's e-mail address is then re-sent to everybody on the mailing list. Product information shared through these mailing lists can be likened to traditional word-of-mouth communications and is, at the moment, still in the hands of users.

Usenet is a collection of discussion groups in cyberspace. People can read messages pertaining to a given topic, post new messages, and answer messages. For marketers, this is an important source of consumers who care about certain topics and therefore provide an ideal targeted audience for advertising messages. Usenet is also used as a publicity vehicle for goods and services. Usenet represents a relatively self-segmented word-of-mouth channel.

The World Wide Web is the universal database of information available to most Internet users, and its graphical environment makes navigation simple and exciting. Of all the options available for Internet marketers, the WWW holds the greatest potential as an advertising medium. It allows for detailed and full-color graphics, audio transmission, delivery of in-depth messages, 24-hour availability, and two-way information exchanges between the marketer and customer. For some people, spending time on the Web is replacing time spent viewing other media, such as print, radio, and television.

❸ Describe the different types of search engines used to surf the Web.

- *Hierarchical search engines.* In a hierarchical search engine, all sites are fit into categories. Although hierarchical sites like Yahoo! are great for doing general searches, they do have some significant limitations. For example, Yahoo!'s database of Web sites contains only submissions from consumers. That is, Yahoo! does not actually search the Web, but only its own database of sites that users have told it about. Because of this, Yahoo! omits a significant portion of the vast information available on the Web.
- *Collection search engines.* This second type of search engine is exemplified by AltaVista. Collection search engines use a spider, an automated program that crawls around the Web collecting information. Because of the sheer quantity of Web pages, collection search engines rank the best matches first. The relatively large amount of information available on the Web mandates that users know what they are really interested in; otherwise, they will be flooded with useless information.
- *Concept search engines.* Here, a concept rather than a word or phrase is the basis for the search. The top sites with the concept are listed in order after a search. To narrow the search, simply clicking on one of the sites found in the original search enables another search based on the selected link. The percentage key gives the user an idea of how close a particular site is to his or her concepts. This is a very efficient way of searching, producing relatively focused results compared to other search engines.
- *Robot search engines.* The newest technique employs robots ("bots") to do the legwork for the consumer by roaming the Internet in search of information fitting certain user-specified criteria.
- *Portals.* A portal is a starting point for Web access and search. Portals can be vertical (serving a specialized market or industries), horizontal (providing access and links across industries), or ethnic or community based. Several of the large search engines, such as Yahoo! and Lycos, are focusing their attention on becoming portals for Internet exploring.

4   Describe the different advertising options on the Web.

- *Banner Ads.* Banner ads are paid placements of advertising on other sites that contain editorial material. With banner ads, consumers not only see the ad but also can make a quick trip to the marketer's home page by clicking on the ad (called "click-through"). Thus, the challenge of creating and placing banner ads is not only to catch people's attention but also to entice them to visit the marketer's home page and stay for awhile.
- *Pop-up ads.* Based on an idea borrowed from TV, a pop-up ad is an advertisement that appears as a Web page is loading or after a page has loaded.
- *E-mail communication.* E-mail communication may be the Internet's most advantageous application. Through e-mail, the Internet is the only "mass" medium capable of customizing a message for thousands or even millions of receivers. The message is delivered in a unique way, one at a time, which no other medium is capable of doing.
- *Corporate home pages.* A corporate home page is a Web site where a marketer provides current and potential customers information about the firm in great detail. The best corporate home pages not only provide corporate and product information, but also offer other content of interest to site visitors. A variation on the corporate Web site is setting up a site and placing it inside a virtual mall. A virtual mall is a gateway to a group of Internet storefronts that provide access to mall sites by simply clicking on a category of store.

5   Discuss the issues involved in establishing a site on the World Wide Web.

There are three key issues to successfully establishing and maintaining a site on the World Wide Web:
- *Getting surfers to come back.* Once a site is set up, getting those who spend considerable time on the Internet to spend time at the site and to come back often is a primary concern. When a site is able to attract visitors repeatedly and keep them for a long time, it is said to be

a sticky site or have features that are "sticky." To make a site sticky, a marketer should incorporate engaging, interactive features into the site.
- *Purchasing keywords and developing a domain name.* Online search engines such as Yahoo! sell keywords. A marketer can purchase a keyword that will ensure its banner appears whenever users select that word for a search. Purchasing keywords helps consumers find your site while they search for information. But before purchasing a keyword, a marketer must decide on a domain name, which establishes the basis for the key word. A domain name is the unique URL through which a Web location is established.
- *Promoting Web sites.* Building a Web site is only the first step; the next is promoting it. The quickest and lowest-cost way to promote a Web site is to notify appropriate Usenet groups. The other key method is to register the site with search engines such as Yahoo! and AltaVista. Many new Internet companies have chosen to invest heavily in television advertising.

6   Discuss the integrated marketing communications aspects of coordinating a firm's Web activities with other promotional activities.

The Internet is great for providing detailed information that is beyond the scope of other media. With the Internet's interactive and high-speed nature, data about a brand's performance or technical specifications in various categories can be highly organized and quickly accessible. Given this strength, the Internet can play a pivotal role in an IMC campaign: Media such as television and print ads can be used to create a powerful image, while the Web site can provide detailed information on the product and help close the sale. Many Web firms are indeed using traditional media for image building, and then the Internet site follows through with information, entertainment, or community interaction. Strategies for contests, sweepstakes, couponing, public relations and publicity, and sales force support can all be enhanced by using the Internet as supportive communication for the main promotional mix tool.

KEY TERMS

Internet, 305
electronic mail (e-mail), 305
Internet Relay Chat (IRC, 305)
Usenet, 305
World Wide Web (WWW), 305
push strategy, 307
pull tactics, 307
listservs, 307
spam, 308
surfing, 309

search engine, 309
hierarchical search engine, 309
collection search engine, 309
spider, 309
concept search engine, 310
robots, 310
portal, 310
click-through, 314
banner ads, 317

pop-up ad, 319
permission marketing, 319
viral marketing, 320
corporate home page, 320
virtual mall, 320
netizens, 322
sticky site, 322
rational branding, 323
domain name, 325

QUESTIONS FOR REVIEW AND CRITICAL THINKING

1. In the face of considerable uncertainty about audience size, audience composition, and cost-effectiveness, marketers have nonetheless been flocking to the World Wide Web (WWW). What is it about the Web that marketers have found so irresistible?

2. How can an understanding of search engines and how they operate benefit an organization initiating an ad campaign on the WWW?

3. Explain the two basic strategies for developing corporate home pages, exemplified in this chapter by Toshiba and Crayola.

4. Niche marketing will certainly be facilitated by the WWW. What is it about the WWW that makes it such a powerful tool for niche marketing?

5. Visit some of the corporate home pages described in this chapter, or think about corporate home pages you have visited previously. Of those you have encountered, which would you single out as being most effective in giving the visitor a reason to come back? What conclusions would you draw regarding the best ways to motivate repeat visits to a Web site?

6. Why is an agreement between AOL and Time Warner such big news for marketers with an interest in the WWW? Regarding the agreement between the two, what new opportunities do you see for marketers to use advertising on the Internet?

7. The Internet was obviously not conceived or designed to be an advertising medium. Thus, some of its characteristics have proven perplexing to marketers. If advertising professionals had the chance to redesign the Internet, what single change would you expect they would want to make to enhance its value from an advertising perspective?

EXPERIENTIAL EXERCISES

1. **In-class exercise.** What do you think about the proposition that television will eventually have an icon that will allow you to click through to a Web site? Do you think this will give a boost to Internet advertising, or will consumers ignore it?

2. **Out-of-class exercise.** Television commercials often end with a Web site address. After viewing a television ad, go to the Web site address given. Are the television and Web site messages coordinated, showing an IMC orientation? Is there a synergy between the two messages? Does the Web site refer to the television ad or to any print ads?

USING THE INTERNET

Exercise 1

How much is an Internet domain name worth? Given that there are only so many ways you can slice and dice a few dozen letters (and still mean something, and not pick something that someone else has got), some particularly attractive ones have commanded a pretty penny. Currently, "business.com," sold for a reported $7.5 million, holds the record. Digital Equipment Corporation (later acquired by Compaq) paid a reported several million dollars for "altavista.com," after its AltaVista search engine became a runaway success (no doubt to the delight of the smaller company that owned the most appropriate domain name for it). Most domain name sales, though, don't break into these stratospheric numbers.

Think up some possible domain names for a new Net venture, and check their availability at Network Solutions, Register.com, or one of the other domain name registration sites:

Network Solutions
http://www.networksolutions.com

Register.com
http://www.register.com

Visit some of the domain name brokers and appraisal sites listed at:

DN Resources
http://www.dnresources.com

1. How easy is it to find an untaken domain name?

2. What sorts of domain names are available from brokers?

3. Someone approaches your business with a request to buy your domain name. What issues will you need to consider?

Exercise 2

To learn more about banner ad services, visit these Web sites:

DoubleClick
http://www.doubleclick.com

Engage Media
http://www.engage.com/engagemedia/

Link Exchange
http://www.linkexchange.com

Imagine that you represent a company with a community Web site, dedicated to home improvement, yard landscaping, and gardening, looking to secure banner advertisers and other site sponsorship.

1. What requirements would your site need to meet to be of interest to these ad services?

2. What functions do the services perform, and what would you, as the affiliate, or publisher, need to perform?

3. What discretion would you have to accept or reject certain types of advertising, or specific advertisers? (And why might you want to?)

Now imagine you're developing an advertising campaign for a horticultural nursery, and are considering Web-based advertising.

1. What factors would go into a decision as to whether or not to advertise on such a Web site?

2. What functions would the banner ad services perform, and what would you be responsible for?

After reading this chapter, you will be able to:

1 Describe the relationship between direct marketing and e-commerce.

2 Identify the three primary purposes of direct marketing.

3 Identify the dimensions of database marketing and its applications.

4 Describe a model of e-commerce.

5 Discuss the integrated marketing communications issues related to direct marketing and e-commerce.

CHAPTER 10

Dana Youngren walked into The Gap at her local mall and was interested in a casual but stylish black pullover shirt. Unfortunately, the $19 item was nowhere to be found in her size. Undaunted, Dana simply went back to her office, logged on to gap.com, and bought the item there instead (see Exhibit 10.1). With a few clicks, she was assured the item was properly ordered and on its way via a second-day UPS shipment. Ever since that initial experience, Ms. Youngren has been getting personalized e-mails from The Gap about twice a month letting her know about specials on items in her size. And Youngren estimates that she has been spending about 10 to 15 percent more of her clothing dollars at The Gap ever since discovering the Web site.

Consumers like Dana Youngren are just what The Gap envisioned when it launched its Web site (http://www.gap.com/) in late 1997. The Gap was one of the first major retailers to add the electronic retailing format to its overall marketing strategy at a time when selling clothing online seemed revolutionary if not just plain dumb. But by late 2000, online sales at The Gap exceeded $200 million, and while this is still a tiny fraction of the $10 billion in annual sales generated by the company's 2,600 retail stores, the trend line is very positive.[1]

Merging e-commerce online sales with traditional operations and promotions is exactly what Jeanne Jackson, chief executive of Gap Inc. Direct, had in mind. At the core of her strategy is the conviction that The Gap's

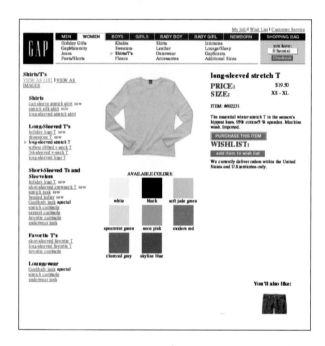

EXHIBIT 10.1

The Gap has successfully made the transition from pure bricks and mortar to a "clicks-and-mortar" firm. Blending traditional retail with e-commerce, "e-tail" is a transition many firms are finding challenging.

EXHIBIT 10.2

There are many e-commerce firms that do not have traditional retail operations. Platform.net (http://www.platform.net) is one of these firms that are often referred to as pure-play e-tailers.

1. Louise Lee, "'Clicks and Mortar' at Gap.Com," *Business Week,* October 18, 1999, 76–78.

network of retail outlets can be turned into an advantage relative to pure-play clothing e-tailers like Platform.net (http://www.platform.net/, see Exhibit 10.2). By aggressively promoting both the stores and the Web site, Jackson is convinced that both will flourish. She appears to be right. Among the top fifteen online apparel retailers (The Gap ranks second behind LandsEnd.com), not a single pure-play apparel e-tailer is ranked.[2]

But success at The Gap is due to more than just the fact that it is a "click and mortar" operation as opposed to a pure online merchant. The careful integration of promotion across both online and offline operations is the secret to its success. The Web site is promoted at every cash register, in every traditional media Gap advertisement, and most recently in the in-store window displays with the slogan "surf.shop.ship." Clerks are trained to refer shoppers to The Gap Web site. Also, in several high-traffic Gap and GapKids stores, the company has installed "Web lounges" that welcome shoppers with comfortable couches and a direct connection to gap.com.

Make no mistake about it, The Gap's careful coordination of Web, retail, and promotion is designed to achieve one objective—beat the Net-only marketers. And the stakes are indeed high. While online apparel sales reached only $1.4 billion in 1999, that number is expected to triple by 2004. Furthermore, among core Gap target markets, teenagers and women, the potential is even more compelling. By 2002, kids from five to eighteen will spend about $1.5 billion online of the $150 billion they pump into the U.S. economy. Analysts expect this Web-savvy group to shift much more of that total to the Web over the next several years.[3] And females placed over 58 percent of the online orders. Of course, pure-play e-tailers are not going to sit back and watch the click-and-mortar giants craft their heavyweight marketing and promotional strategies without a response. Online merchants are coming up with their own offline/online options for shoppers. For example, eBay (http://www.ebay.com/) is holding real-world auctions and other community-building events, and Gateway (http://www.gateway.com/), the direct and online computer merchant, is opening retail shops.[4]

The battle between online, offline, and multichannel retailers will continue to unfold throughout the decade of the '00s. Predictions put online spending on a steep upward trajectory reaching about $184 billion by 2004.[5] Other predictions decry the "death of retail," and still others shout about the inevitable shakeout among e-tailers.[6] One thing is sure: Organizations like The Gap with well-conceived strategies and smart managers will not only survive but likely flourish in a complex direct-marketing and e-commerce environment.

INTRODUCTION

One reason The Gap is expected to be successful in its e-commerce ventures is that the firm is relying on a highly diverse but integrated promotional effort to promote both its offline and online business, allowing each to leverage the strengths of the other. As we saw in the introductory scenario, The Gap uses television and print advertising, in-store promotions, in-store events, window displays, and personal selling as tools in the promotional mix for both Gap stores and gap.com. Just how a firm, like The Gap, can manage the direct-marketing opportunities present in the marketplace—both the traditional and e-commerce opportunities—is the focus of this chapter. Specifically, this chapter examines the expanding field of direct marketing and its explosive growth through e-commerce. Our goal is to understand how both may be used as part of the promotional mix in a firm's IMC program. When direct marketing and e-commerce are carefully coordinated with other tools in the promotional mix, as demonstrated by The Gap, great success in the marketplace is often the result.

2.   Julie Skur Hill, "Online Selling Puts Dent in Stores, Catalogs," *Advertising Age,* September 27, 1999, S18.
3.   Roger O. Crockett, "Forget the Mall. Kids Shop on the Net," *Business Week E-Biz,* July 26, 1999, EB14.
4.   Janet Ginsburg and Kathleen Morris, "Xtreme Retailing," *Business Week,* December 20, 1999, 120–128; and Jane Hodges, "Bricks for Branding," *Business 2.0,* February 2000, 95–96.
5.   Jeffrey Davis, "Chasing Retail's Tail," *Business 2.0,* January 2000, 172.
6.   The death of retail is discussed in Erika Rasmusson, "The Death of Retail?" *Sales and Marketing Management,* March 1999, 17; on the other hand, the death of e-tailers is discussed in International Data Corporation, "Pure Play Dotcoms Will Disappear This Year," January 11, 2000, at http://www.nua.net/surveys/ accessed on January 13, 2000.

First, we consider the relationship between direct marketing and e-commerce. Since e-commerce is a phenomenon of the last five or six years, its scope and nature need to be considered in the broader context of the direct-marketing effort. Next, we discuss direct marketing specifically. This area of marketing and promotion has grown over the years to become a key element in the marketing strategy of many firms. We look at the popularity of direct marketing, its purposes, and the media used to carry it out. An essential discussion regarding direct marketing is the development and management of databases.

Finally, we examine the new and expanding world of e-commerce. Fueled by consumer and business access to the Internet, e-commerce has become a key issue for both promotion and, quite frankly, overall marketing strategy. We look at a model of e-commerce that describes how the process works, and then we discuss the various participants in the e-commerce process and the role each plays in making e-commerce a viable marketing and promotional channel.

THE RELATIONSHIP BETWEEN DIRECT MARKETING AND E-COMMERCE ❶

Before any confusion sets in (or maybe it already has), let's clarify the relationship between direct marketing and e-commerce. **Direct marketing** is the traditional promotional/marketing process whereby marketers use direct contact with consumers or business buyers with the intent of communicating information or bringing about a transaction. The direct contact can take place by telephone, through the mail, or through major mass media from the seller's side. From the buyer's side, contact with the seller has traditionally taken place through the mail or by phone. If you have called a toll-free number and ordered something from a television, radio, or magazine advertisement, that was direct marketing. Similarly, if you filled out an order form that you got in the mail or clipped from a newspaper, or mailed in an order from a catalog, that was direct marketing too. Oreck, the famed direct marketer of vacuum cleaners, has for many years used a direct-marketing approach. Notice that the Oreck ad in Exhibit 10.3 offers you the chance to respond either by phone or by mail (we'll get to the Web site listing in a minute). And if the phone rang during dinner and you ordered tickets to the symphony, that was a direct-marketing experience, too.

The scope and nature of e-commerce are almost exactly the same as direct marketing. In using an **e-commerce** structure and methods, marketers make direct contact with consumers and business buyers, they intend to communicate information, and they hope to bring about a transaction through the contact. While we might think that e-commerce is limited to communicating to target markets by electronic means, like a banner ad or a Web site, that is not *necessarily* a condition for e-commerce. As the Oreck ad in Exhibit 10.3 shows, consumers can be brought into an e-commerce transaction through more traditional direct-marketing media like a magazine ad.

So what's the difference between direct marketing and e-commerce? There are actually two key differences. First, and most important, is the mode of the transaction. The transaction in direct marketing takes place through traditional means of contact between buyers and sellers—phone or mail. In e-commerce, the transaction is electronic and typically takes place by computer and the Internet, although wireless devices will become a common means of conducting transactions as well.

The second key difference is that all transactions in e-commerce are direct-marketing transactions, but not all direct-marketing transactions are e-commerce. In other words, e-commerce is an electronic version of direct marketing. To summarize the nature of the relationship, the similarities and differences are:

http://www.digitalisland.com

EXHIBIT 10.3

Direct marketing as a promotional tool attempts to create an interactive communication with a consumer. This Oreck ad provides the consumer with information but also allows communication via telephone, mail, or the company's Web site.

EXHIBIT 10.4

It's important to remember that Cyberspace isn't just a single new dimension into which commerce is projected, but a multidimensional landscape of time (it's the height of the business day on the Net somewhere in the world, every minute of the day) and geographic and demographic reach. Companies like Digital Island help their e-tailer customers to make it appear that that product is a quick click away. What companies are providing the connectivity and services behind your favorite e-commerce sites?

- Direct marketing and e-commerce use different methods to communicate with consumers and business buyers.
- Direct marketing and e-commerce are both techniques used to bring about a transaction with consumers and business buyers, thus making direct marketing a distribution program as well as a communications effort.
- Direct marketing uses traditional print and broadcast media.
- E-commerce uses traditional print and broadcast media to communicate with consumers but also uses electronic media such as the Internet and e-mail.
- In direct marketing, consumers and business buyers respond through traditional communications means such as by telephone and by mail.
- In e-commerce, consumers and business buyers respond by electronic means through the Internet and e-mail and culminate a transaction and, potentially, delivery through electronic means (see Exhibit 10.4).
- All e-commerce communications and transactions are direct marketing, but not all direct-marketing communications and transaction are e-commerce.

So we can see that the relationship between direct marketing and e-commerce is very close. They serve the same broad customer groups and share the same intentions. The main differences relate to the media through which the communication takes place and the way a transaction is culminated.

DIRECT MARKETING

We will discuss direct marketing first since it is the traditional method of direct contact with the target markets. Let's turn to the official Direct Marketing Association (DMA) definition to gain an appreciation for the scope and characteristics of direct marketing: "Direct marketing is an interactive system of marketing which uses one or more advertising media to effect a measurable response and/or transaction at any location."[7]

First, note that direct marketing is interactive in that a marketer is attempting to develop an ongoing dialogue with the customer. Direct-marketing programs are commonly planned with the notion that one contact will lead to another and then another, so that the marketer's promotional message can become more focused and refined with each interaction.

The DMA's definition also notes that multiple advertising media can be used in direct-marketing programs. This is an important point for two reasons. First, we do not want to equate direct mail and direct marketing. As discussed earlier, any medium can be used in executing direct-marketing programs, not just the mail.

Another key aspect of direct-marketing programs is that they almost always are designed to produce some form of immediate, measurable response. Direct-marketing programs can produce an immediate sale. The customer might be asked to return an order form with $49.99 to get a copy of Zelda 64 by Nintendo, or to call an 800 number with a credit card handy to get twenty-two

IN PRACTICE

RULE NO. 1: GET PEOPLE TO OPEN THE ENVELOPES

If direct marketing is a tool to "close the sale," then consumers have to cooperate in a most basic way. In the words of Andrew Morrison, founder and president of Nia Direct, a New York–based direct-marketing agency, rule number 1 is to "Get people to open the envelopes." Morrison's company specializes in ethnic direct-marketing programs. Nia brings direct-marketing programs into 3 million African-American homes annually through coupons and other direct-mail promotions. The firm culls names and information from lists provided by African-American fraternities and sororities, churches, and other nonprofit organizations. Then Morrison and his staff run the list data against data from the Bureau of Labor Statistics and the U.S. Census Bureau.

Morrison says, "I look at current responders to African-American direct marketing programs and build a profile of those individuals. Then I go out and find similar consumers and match the data." But the direct-marketing effort goes beyond simply matching demographic and geographic profiles. The essence of an effective campaign is to profile behavioral data as well. This includes the kind of products and services purchased as well as the devices that motivated targeted customers to "open the envelopes." This data includes the type of mailing (bulk or first class), the personalization of the message, the "teaser" on the outside of the envelope, and any incentive offer to the customer, such as a discount or premium offered with the original purchase.

Direct-marketing firms like Nia Direct help marketers weave direct marketing into the overall IMC program. They can educate their clients on the spending habits of customers, but they also offer a value-added asset: information on closing the sale based on the devices that get that envelope opened in the first place.

Source: Eileen P. Gunn, "Special Delivery," *Advertising Age*, October 19, 1999, s1, s5.

7.   Bob Stone, *Successful Direct Marketing Methods* (Lincolnwood, IL: NTC Business Books, 1994), 5.

timeless hits on a CD called *The Very Best of Tony Bennett.* Because of this emphasis on immediate response, direct marketers are always in a position to judge the effectiveness of a particular program.

The final phrase of the DMA's definition notes that a direct-marketing transaction can take place anywhere. The key idea here is that customers do not have to make a trip to a retail store for a direct-marketing program to work. Follow-ups can be made by mail, over the telephone, on the Internet, or via an express delivery service. As we will discuss in the e-commerce section of the chapter, pure-play e-tailers who are also pure direct marketers, such as Amazon.com or CDnow.com may pose a real threat to those who have made their living operating a traditional retail outlet.[8] On the other hand, these same e-tailers are nervous about big, mortar-only retailers, like Wal-Mart, that are learning about Internet e-commerce and converting to clicks and mortar like The Gap.[9]

The Role of Direct Marketing in Promotion and IMC ❷

Direct marketing is rooted in the legacy of mail-order giants and catalog merchandisers such as L. L. Bean, Lillian Vernon, Publishers Clearing House, and JCPenney. Today, however, direct marketing has broken free from its mail-order heritage to become a promotional tool used by all types of organizations throughout the world. Although many types of businesses and not-for-profit organizations are making use of direct marketing, it is common to find that such direct-marketing programs are not carefully integrated with an organization's other advertising and promotional efforts. Integration should be the goal for advertising, promotional and direct-marketing; impressive evidence supports the thesis that integrated programs are more effective than the sum of their parts.[10]

With the defining features of the DMA definition in mind, we can see that direct-marketing programs are commonly used for three primary purposes: closing a sale, identifying prospects for future programs, and engaging the customer as a means of enhancing both the promotional and marketing effort.

Closing the Sale. As you might imagine, the most important purpose of direct marketing as a promotional tool is to close a sale with a customer. This can be done as a stand-alone program, or it can be carefully coordinated with a firm's other promotional efforts. Telecommunications companies such as MCI have made extensive use of the advertising/direct-marketing combination in promotional programs.[11] For example, MCI has spent heavily on TV advertising to promote its Friends & Family discount calling program. The advertising was used to familiarize consumers with the program and was then followed up with both direct-mail and telemarketing campaigns to convert customers to the program. Closing the sale is the main objective of New York–based Nia Direct, as explained in the IMC in Practice box.

Identifying Prospects. A second purpose for direct-marketing programs is to identify prospects for future contacts and, at the same time, provide in-depth information to selected customers. Since dialogue and interactivity are at the heart of successful direct-marketing programs, it will come as no surprise that direct marketers are eager to adapt their methods to the Internet, as we will see in the

---

8. Patrick M. Reilly, "In the Age of the Web, a Book Chain Flounders," *The Wall Street Journal,* February 22, 1999, B1, B4.
9. Wendy Zellner, "When Wal-Mart Flexes Its Cybermuscles . . . ," *Business Week,* July 26, 1999, 82–84.
10. Ernan Roman, *Integrated Direct Marketing* (Lincolnwood, IL: NTC Books, 1995).
11. Kate Fitzgerald, "AT&T, MCI Ringing Up Bigger Cash Lures," *Advertising Age,* May 8, 1995, 6.

We've survived three Woodstocks.

Not once. Not twice. But thrice. Ours was
the sound that rocked the largest concerts
of all time. And if we can do that,
imagine what we could do in your living
room. For more information, contact
1.800.336.4JBL or www.jbl.com.

JBG   JBL
the sound of woodstock

H A Harman International Company

EXHIBIT 10.5

One of the goals of direct marketing as a promotional tool is to establish a dialogue with current and prospective customers. Even a simple print ad can motivate dialogue between a customer and the firm. In what way does this JBL ad try to stimulate a dialogue?

e-commerce section.[12] Even a simple print ad like that in Exhibit 10.5 is designed as a marketer's attempt to induce a dialogue (notice the line "For more information, contact . . .") with a prospective customer through toll-free telephone or Web-based contact.

Engaging the Customer. Direct-marketing programs are also initiated as a means to engage customers, seek their advice, furnish helpful information about using a product, reward customers for using a brand, and, in general, foster brand loyalty, as the direct-mail promotion for Infiniti in Exhibit 10.6 illustrates. As another example, the manufacturer of Valvoline motor oil seeks to build loyalty for its brand by encouraging young car owners to join the Valvoline Performance Team.[13] To join the team, young drivers just fill out a questionnaire that enters them into the Valvoline database. Team members receive posters, special offers on racing-team apparel, news about racing events in which Valvoline has provided sponsorship, and promotional reminders at regular intervals that reinforce the virtues of Valvoline for the driver's next oil change.

The Popularity of Direct Marketing

The growth in popularity of direct marketing is due to a number of factors. Some of these have to do with changes in consumer lifestyles and technological developments that in effect create a climate more conducive to the practice of direct marketing. In addition, direct-marketing programs offer unique advantages vis-à-vis conventional mass-media advertising, leading many organizations to shift more of their marketing budgets to direct-marketing activities.

Overall, direct marketing has experienced strong and steady growth due to the desire for convenience among consumers, more liberal attitudes toward credit, developments in technology, and the desire on the part of marketers for more measurable results from their promotional programs.

Consumers' Desire for Convenience. From the consumer's standpoint, direct marketing's growing popularity might be summarized in a single word: convenience. Dramatic growth in the number of dual-income and single-person households has reduced the time people have to visit retail stores. Direct marketers provide consumers access to a growing range of products and services in their homes, thus saving many households' most precious resource—time.

Attitudes Toward Credit. More liberal attitudes about the use of credit and the accumulation of debt have also contributed to the growth of direct marketing. Credit cards are the primary means of payment in most direct-marketing

---

12. Rebecca Quick, "Direct Marketing Association to Merge with Association of Interactive Media," *The Wall Street Journal,* October 12, 1998, B6.
13. Edward Nash, "The Roots of Direct Marketing," *Direct Marketing,* February 1995, 38–40.

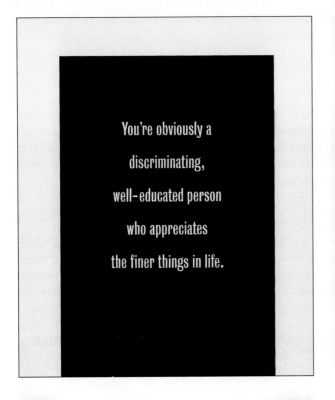

EXHIBIT 10.6

Database marketing is dependent on input from the consumer. This Infiniti ad has as a major purpose gathering information from consumers to help develop the firm's database. Notice the questions also engage the consumer and encourage a relationship with a firm.

transactions. The widespread availability of credit cards makes it ever more convenient to shop from the comfort of home.

Changes in Technology. Developments in telecommunications have also facilitated the direct-marketing transaction. After getting off to a slow start in the late sixties, toll-free 800 (now including 888 and other variations) numbers have exploded in popularity to the point where it is hard to find a product or a catalog that does not include an 800 number for interacting with the manufacturer. And whether one is ordering a twill polo shirt from Eddie Bauer, or inquiring about an OzziRoo mountain bike shown in Exhibit 10.7, a preferred mode of access for many consumers has been and remains the toll-free 800 number.

Another technological development having a huge impact on the growth of direct marketing is the computer. Did you know that your parents' new Buick has more computer power than the Apollo spacecraft that took astronauts to the moon? The incredible diffusion of computer technology through all modern societies has been a tremendous boon to direct marketers. The computer now allows firms to track, keep records on, and interact with about 5 million customers for what it used to cost to track a single customer in 1950![14] As we will see in an upcoming

EXHIBIT 10.7

The toll-free 800 number has been a major factor in making direct marketing such a popular marketing and promotion tool for both companies and consumers.

14. Don Peppers and Martha Rogers, "The End of Mass Marketing," *Marketing Tools,* March/April 1995, 42–51.

discussion, the computer power now available for modest dollar amounts is fueling the growth of direct marketing's most potent tool—the marketing database.

Interactive television also promises to be an attractive vehicle for intensified direct marketing. Companies such as Time Warner, Spiegel, Sharper Image, The Nature Company, Warner Brothers Studio Store, Williams-Sonoma, and Chrysler are working together to develop the technical capabilities to deliver a wide array of interactive services through consumers' TV sets.[15] The day is coming when marketers of all sorts will be able to carry on interactive dialogues with consumers in their homes via the television.

Measurability of Direct Marketing. The appeal of direct marketing is enhanced further by the persistent emphasis on producing measurable effects, which we saw as motivation for broadening the promotional mix in Chapter 1. For instance, in direct marketing, it is common to find calculations such as **cost per inquiry (CPI)** or **cost per order (CPO)** being featured in program evaluation. These calculations simply divide the number of responses to a program by that program's cost. When calculated for each and every program an organization conducts over time, CPI and CPO data quickly help an organization appreciate what works and what doesn't work in its promotional execution.

This emphasis on producing and monitoring measurable effects is realized most completely through an approach called **database marketing.** Working with a database, direct marketers can target specific customers, track their actual purchase behavior over time, and experiment with different programs for affecting the purchasing patterns of these customers.[16] Obviously, those programs that produce the best outcomes become the candidates for increased funding in the future. Let's look into database marketing as a key aspect of direct marketing.

Database Marketing

If any ambiguity remains about what makes direct marketing as a promotional tool different from other promotional tools, that ambiguity can be erased by the database. The one characteristic of direct-marketing promotion that clearly distinguishes it from other tools is its emphasis on database development. Knowing who the best customers are along with what and how often they buy is a direct marketer's secret weapon. This knowledge accumulates in the form of a database.

Databases used as the centerpieces in direct-marketing campaigns take many forms and can contain many different layers of information about customers. At one extreme is the simple mailing list that contains nothing more than the names and addresses of current and potential customers; at the other extreme is the customized marketing database that augments names and addresses with various additional information about customers' characteristics, past purchases, and product preferences. Understanding this distinction between mailing lists and marketing databases is important in appreciating the scope of database marketing.

Mailing Lists. A **mailing list** is simply a file of names and addresses that an organization might use for contacting current, prospective or prior customers. Mailing lists are plentiful, easy to access, and inexpensive.[17] For example, CD–ROM phone directories, now available for less than $200, provide a cheap and easy way to generate mailing lists. More targeted mailing lists are available from a variety of suppliers. These suppliers offer lists such as the 107,521 active members of the

15. Lindsey Kelly, "Interactive TV's Rough Road," *Advertising Age,* March 13, 1995, S12–S16.
16. Don E. Schultz and Paul Wang, "Real World Results," *Marketing Tools,* April/May 1994, 40–47.
17. John Kremer, *The Complete Direct Marketing Sourcebook* (New York: John Wiley & Sons, 1992).

EXHIBIT 10.8

This subscription response card from Spin *is another way companies gather information from customers for database development.*

Association of Catholic Senior Citizens; the 174,600 Kuppenheimer male-fashion buyers; the 825,000 subscribers to *Home*; and the 189,000 buyers of products from the Smith & Hawken gardening catalog.[18]

Each time you subscribe to a magazine, order from a catalog, register your automobile, fill out a warranty card, redeem a rebate offer, apply for credit, join a professional society, or log in at a Web site, the information you provide about yourself goes on another mailing list. This is exactly what the publishers of *Spin* do when you fill out the subscription card like the one shown in Exhibit 10.8. These lists are freely bought and sold through many means, including the Internet. Sites such as http://www.worldata.com and http://www.ira-ondemand.com allow one to buy names and addresses after sorting on demographic and zip-code information for about 15 cents per record.

Two broad categories of lists should be recognized: the internal, or house list, versus the external, or outside list. **Internal lists** are simply an organization's records of its customers, subscribers, donors, and inquirers. **External lists** are purchased from a list compiler or rented from a list broker. At the most basic level, internal and external lists facilitate the two fundamental activities of the direct marketer: Internal lists are the starting point for developing better relationships with current customers, whereas external lists help an organization cultivate new business.

18. Ibid.

List Enhancement. Name-and-address files, no matter what their source, are merely the starting point for database marketing. The next step in the evolution of a database is mailing-list enhancement. Typically, this involves augmenting an internal list by combining it with other, externally supplied lists or databases. External lists can be appended or integrated with a house list.

One of the most straightforward list enhancements is simply adding more names and addresses to an internal list. Proprietary name-and-address files can be purchased from other companies that operate in noncompetitive businesses.[19] With today's computer capabilities, adding these additional households to an existing mailing list is simple. Many well-known companies such as Sharper Image, American Express, Bloomingdale's, and Hertz sell or rent their customer lists for this purpose.

A second type of list enhancement involves incorporating information from external databases into a house list. Here the number of names and addresses remains the same, but an organization ends up with a more complete description of who its customers are. Typically, this kind of enhancement includes any of four categories of information that we learned about in Chapter 4 when we were considering the role of market segmentation in promotion:

- Demographic data are the basic descriptors of individuals and households available from the Census Bureau.
- Geodemographic data provide information that reveals the characteristics of the neighborhood or region in which a person resides.
- Psychographic data are data that allow for a more qualitative assessment of a customer's general lifestyle, interests, and opinions.
- Behavioral data provide information about other products and services a customer has purchased; prior purchases can help reveal a customer's preferences.[20]

List enhancements that require merging existing records with new information rely on software that allows the database manager to match records based on some piece of information the two lists share. For example, matches might be achieved by sorting on zip codes and street addresses.

Many suppliers gather and maintain databases for the sole purpose of list enhancement. Infobase Premier is an enhancement file offered by Infobase Services and is particularly notable for its size and array of available information. Infobase Premier contains 170 different pieces of information about 200 million American consumers. Because of its massive size, this database has a high match rate (60 to 80 percent) when it is merged with clients' internal lists.[21] A more common match rate between internal and external lists is 45 to 60 percent. As with most things, list enhancement services are now available on the Web at sites such as http://www. imarketinc.com. For its product named MarketPlace Pro, iMarketinc. promises match rates of 50 to 75 percent.

The Marketing Database. Mailing lists come in all shapes and sizes, and by enhancing internal lists they obviously can become rich sources of information about customers. But for a mailing list to qualify as a marketing database, one important additional type of information is required. Although a **marketing database** can be viewed as a natural extension of an internal mailing list, a marketing database also includes information collected directly from individual customers.[22] Developing a marketing database involves pursuing dialogues with customers and learning about their individual preferences and behavioral patterns. This is exactly what American Express does with its database marketing program. Using its database

---

19. Terry G. Vavra, "The Database Marketing Imperative," *Marketing Management 2,* no. 1 (1993): 47–57.
20. Ibid.
21. Ibid.
22. Herman Holtz, *Databased Marketing* (New York: John Wiley & Sons, 1992).

CAREERPROFILE

Name:	Jeff Yowell
Title:	President and Chief Executive Officer
Company:	DATACORE, Inc., Kansas City, Missouri
	http://www.datacoremarketing.com
Education:	B.S., Business with a concentration in marketing, Trinity University, San Antonio, Texas; M.A., Marketing, University of Missouri at Kansas City

Jeff Yowell was a recent college graduate working for a Kansas City advertising agency when he was asked to solve a client's problem. The direct-marketing campaign that the agency had recently created for a manufacturer was overwhelming the client with sales leads. Using his knowledge of computers, Jeff helped the manufacturer build a database to track information about each customer.

Soon after, Jeff decided that other firms needed similar assistance. At 25, he was knocking on the doors of corporate executives trying to sell the services of his fledgling database marketing firm, DATACORE. At first, potential customers were skeptical when he explained that he could help improve their marketing effectiveness by integrating information about their customers into their promotional efforts. "Most of the companies already had data about their customers' preferences, behavior, and needs in their computer databases, but they weren't using it for marketing purposes," says Jeff. "I had to convince them that using that information could help them communicate with customers in a much more personal way." Today, eight years later, DATACORE has grown into a $8.5 million-a-year business, with clients like American Express Incentive Services, Bayer Corporation, and Sprint Communications.

When Jeff begins working with a new customer, the first step is to understand the client's marketing issues. "We sit down and discuss their marketing objectives. Are they trying to build loyalty? Reach end users? Develop a sales channel? Then we look at every piece of data they have about their customers and compile it into a marketing database that will support those objectives," he explains.

Jeff believes effective promotion still comes down to basics. "You have to understand core marketing principles like consumer behavior and market segmentation in order to use information and technology effectively," he says. "When I'm hiring employees, I don't look at their tech skills, I look at their ability to use marketing concepts."

To learn more about database marketing and direct marketing, visit these Web sites:

Database Marketing Institute
http://www.dbmarketing.com

Direct Marketing Association
http://www.the-dma.org

of millions of cardmembers, American Express generates specific marketing programs almost person by person. Some of the offers that AmEx sends out with its bill statements each month go to as few as 20 people.[23] This remarkable capability to sort through millions of customer records and speak to individuals is made possible by a marketing database.

State-of-the-art direct marketing today has database development as its defining feature. According to one survey of marketing practitioners, 56 percent of retailers and manufacturers have database development under way, another 10 percent will soon begin development, and a whopping 85 percent believe that a marketing database will be a requirement to remain competitive after the year 2000.[24] A marketing database represents an organization's collective memory, which allows the organization to give customers the personalized attention that once was characteristic of the corner grocer in small-town America.

While you might find this concept of cybernetic intimacy a bit far-fetched, it certainly is the case that a marketing database can have many valuable applications. Before we look at some of these applications, let's review the terminology introduced thus far. We now have seen that direct marketers use mailing lists, enhanced mailing lists, and/or marketing databases as the starting points for developing many of their programs. The crucial distinction between a mailing list and a marketing database is that the latter includes direct input from customers. Building a marketing database entails pursuing an ongoing dialogue with customers and continuously updating records with new information. While mailing lists can be rich sources of information for program development, a marketing database has a dynamic quality that sets it apart. A marketing database can be an organization's living memory of who its customers are and what they want from the organization.

Marketing Database Applications. Many different types of customer-communication programs are driven by marketing databases. One of the greatest benefits of a database is that it allows an organization to quantify how much business the organization is actually doing with

23. Jonathan Berry, "Database Marketing," *Business Week,* September 5, 1994, 56–62.
24. Ibid.

EXHIBIT 10.9

Once a database has been developed, firms need to come up with ways to take advantage of the knowledge they have about customers. Here, Saturn uses a newsletter that is mailed to Saturn owners as a way to maintain and strengthen the relationship with customers.

its current best customers. A good way to isolate the best customers is with a recency, frequency, and monetary (RFM) analysis.[25] An **RFM analysis** asks how recently and how frequently a specific customer is buying from a company, and how much money he or she is spending per order and over time. With these transaction data, it is a simple matter to calculate the value of every customer to the organization and identify those customers that have given the organization the most business in the past. Past behavior is an excellent predictor of future behavior, so yesterday's best customers are likely to be any organization's primary source of future business.

RFM analysis allows an organization to spend marketing dollars to achieve maximum return on those dollars. Promotions targeted at the best customers will typically pay off with handsome returns. For example, Claridge Hotel & Casino uses its frequent-gambler card—CompCard Gold—to monitor the gambling activities of its 350,000 active members.[26] Promotions such as free slot-machine tokens, monogrammed bathrobes, and door-to-door limo services are targeted to these best customers. Such promotional expenditures pay for themselves many times over because they are carefully targeted to people who spend freely when they choose to vacation at Claridge's resort hotels.

A marketing database can also be a powerful tool for organizations that seek to create a genuine relationship with their customers. The makers of Ben & Jerry's ice cream use their database for two purposes: to find out how customers react to potential new flavors and to involve their customers in social causes.[27] In one recent program, their goal was to find 100,000 people in their marketing database who would volunteer to work with Ben & Jerry's to support the Children's Defense Fund. Jerry Greenfield, cofounder of Ben & Jerry's, justifies the program as follows: "We are not some nameless conglomerate that only looks at how much money we make every year. I think the opportunity to use our business and particularly the power of our business as a force for progressive social change is exciting."[28] Of course, when customers feel genuine involvement with a brand like Ben & Jerry's, they also turn out to be very loyal customers.

Reinforcing and recognizing preferred customers can be another valuable application of the marketing database. This application may be nothing more than a simple follow-up letter that thanks customers for their business or reminds them of the positive features of the brand to reassure them that they made the right choice. As illustrated in Exhibit 10.9, GM's Saturn division uses its "branded" newsletter to continuously remind owners of the joys of driving a Saturn.

25. Rob Jackson and Paul Wang, *Strategic Database Marketing* (Lincolnwood, IL: NTC Business Books, 1994).
26. Berry, "Database Marketing," op. cit.
27. Murray Raphel, "What's the Scoop on Ben & Jerry?" *Direct Marketing,* August 1994, 23–24.
28. Joseph Pereira, "The Web @Work/Ben & Jerry's Homemade, Inc.," *The Wall Street Journal,* March 27, 2000, B6.

To recognize and reinforce the behaviors of preferred customers, marketers in many fields are experimenting with **frequency-marketing programs** that provide concrete rewards to frequent customers. Frequency-marketing programs have three basic elements: a database, which is the collective memory for the program; a benefit structure, which is designed to attract and retain customers; and a communication strategy, which emphasizes a regular dialogue with the organization's best customers.[29] Spectrum Foods, a San Francisco–based company with fifteen upscale restaurants in California, has had considerable success with its frequency-marketing program known by diners as Table One.[30] Table One members earn points each time they dine. They can earn $25 award certificates; $250 shopping sprees at Nordstrom; or, for really frequent diners, trips to Italy and Mexico. Spectrum's program also includes free benefits such as valet parking, preferred reservations, and exclusive invitations to wine tastings and special dinners. Spectrum Foods has received a positive response to this program. Table One members dine at Spectrum's restaurants more often, spend more money each time they dine, and recommend the program to their friends—which has helped Spectrum grow its business at twice the industry average.

Another common application for the marketing database is cross-selling. Since most organizations today have many different products or services they hope to sell, one of the best ways to build business is through **cross-selling**—identifying customers who already purchase some of a firm's products, and creating promotional programs aimed at these customers but featuring other brands in the firm's product line. If they like our ice cream, perhaps we should also encourage them to try our frozen yogurt. If they have a checking account with us, can we interest them in a credit card? If customers dine in our restaurants on Fridays and Saturdays, perhaps, with the proper promotional incentives, we can get them to dine with us midweek, when we really need the extra business. A marketing database can provide a myriad of opportunities for cross-selling.

A final application for the marketing database is a natural extension of cross-selling. Once an organization gets to know who its current customers are and what they like about various products, it is in a much stronger position to go out and seek new customers. Knowledge about current customers is especially valuable when an organization is considering purchasing external mailing lists to append to its marketing database. If a firm knows the demographic characteristics of current customers—what they like about products, where they live, and insights about their lifestyles—then the selection of external lists will be much more efficient. The basic premise here is simply to try to find prospects who share many of the same characteristics and interests with current customers. And the best vehicle for coming to know the current, best customers is the marketing database.

Media Applications in Direct Marketing

While mailing lists and marketing databases are the focal point for originating most direct-marketing campaigns, a successful promotional effort still depends on communicating persuasively to target audiences. As we saw in the definition of direct marketing earlier in this chapter, multiple media can be deployed in campaign implementation, and some form of immediate, measurable response is typically an overriding goal. The immediate response desired may be an actual order for services or merchandise, a request for more information, or the acceptance of a free trial offer. Exhibit 10.10 shows the tremendous growth rate and enormous dollar volume of sales through the various direct-marketing media. Notice also that direct marketing is by no means only a consumer market medium. While direct-marketing sales

29.   Richard Barlow, "Starting a Frequency Marketing Program," *Direct Marketing,* July 1994, 35.
30.   Greg Gattuso, "Restaurants Discover Frequency Marketing," *Direct Marketing,* February 1995, 35–36.

	1994	1998	1999	2000	2004	Compound Annual Growth 94–99	99–04
Direct Mail	$305.9	$439.6	$479.1	$520.7	$723.8	9.4%	8.6%
Consumer	197.3	274.4	297.2	320.2	430.6	8.5%	7.7%
Business-to-Business	108.6	165.3	181.9	300.6	293.3	10.9%	10.0%
Telephone Marketing	339.0	492.3	538.3	585.9	811.2	9.7%	8.5%
Consumer	156.1	213.1	230.0	247.0	328.6	8.1%	7.4%
Business-to-Business	183.0	279.2	308.3	338.9	482.6	11.0%	9.4%
Newspaper	140.4	198.0	215.8	234.1	314.4	9.0%	7.8%
Consumer	93.6	128.4	139.1	149.5	193.7	8.2%	6.8%
Business-to-Business	46.7	69.6	76.7	84.6	120.7	10.4%	9.5%
Magazine	51.8	74.6	80.9	87.5	118.0	9.3%	7.8%
Consumer	28.4	39.4	42.4	45.4	59.4	8.3%	7.0%
Business-to-Business	23.4	35.2	38.5	42.1	58.6	10.5%	8.8%
Television	64.2	95.8	105.8	115.5	159.8	10.5%	8.6%
Consumer	39.7	57.6	63.2	68.5	92.5	9.7%	7.9%
Business-to-Business	24.5	38.2	42.6	47.0	67.2	11.7%	9.5%
Radio	22.6	36.7	41.1	45.0	63.2	12.7%	9.0%
Consumer	13.1	20.9	23.2	25.2	34.9	12.1%	8.5%
Business-to-Business	9.4	15.8	17.8	19.7	28.3	13.6%	9.7%
Other	46.6	66.9	73.4	83.3	146.5	9.5%	14.8%
Consumer	31.3	43.6	47.6	51.5	68.1	8.7%	7.4%
Business-to-Business	15.3	23.2	25.8	31.8	78.4	11.0%	24.9%
Total	970.5	1,403.8	1,534.4	1,672.0	2,336.9	9.6%	8.8%
Consumer	559.5	777.3	842.8	907.4	1,207.7	8.5%	7.5%
Business-to-Business	410.9	626.6	691.6	764.6	1,129.1	11.0%	10.3%

Note: These numbers have not been inflation adjusted—they represent current (nominal) dollars. Due to rounding, total may not exactly equal the sum of each column.

Source: Direct Marketing Association accessed at http://www.the-dma.org, accessed on April 15, 2000

EXHIBIT 10.10

Direct-marketing sales and growth rates by medium (in millions of dollars)

to consumers reached over $900 million in the year 2000, business-to-business sales topped $1.1 billion. We will see an even greater dominance of B2B sales in the e-commerce section of the chapter.

As you probably suspect, direct mail and telemarketing are the direct marketer's prime media. However, all conventional media, such as magazines, radio, and television, can be used to deliver direct-response messages. And nowadays, we are finding that e-mail can serve as an effective catalyst for direct response, which we'll discuss in the next section on e-commerce. In addition, a dramatic transformation of the television commercial—the infomercial—has become especially popular in direct marketing. Let's begin our look at these media options by considering the advantages and disadvantages of the dominant devices—direct mail and telemarketing—and then we'll consider catalogs, the infomercial, and other media tools.

Direct Mail. Direct mail communicates and attempts to create transactions by sending printed matter to target markets. Direct mail has some notable faults as a promotional medium, not the least of which is cost. It can cost fifteen to twenty times more to reach a person with a direct mail piece than it would to reach that person with a television commercial or newspaper advertisement.[31] Additionally, in a society where people are constantly on the move, mailing lists are commonly

31. Stone, *Successful Direct Marketing Methods,* 362.

plagued by bad addresses. Each bad address represents promotion dollars wasted. And direct-mail delivery dates, especially for bulk, third-class mailings, can be unpredictable. When the timing of a promotional message is critical to its success, direct mail can be the wrong choice.

There will be times, however, when direct mail is definitely the right choice. Direct mail's advantages stem from the selectivity of the medium, its flexibility, and (believe it or not) consumer preference for some types of communication through direct mail.

Selectivity. When an advertiser begins with a database of prospects, direct mail can be the perfect vehicle for reaching those prospects with little waste. Also, direct mail is a flexible medium that allows message adaptations on literally a household-by-household basis.[32] For example, through surveys conducted with its 15 million U. S. subscribers, *Reader's Digest* has amassed a huge marketing database detailing the health problems of specific subscribers.[33] In the database are 771,000 arthritis sufferers, 679,000 people with high blood pressure, 206,000 with osteoporosis, 460,000 smokers, and so on. Using this information, *Reader's Digest* sends its subscribers disease-specific booklets containing advice on coping with their afflictions, wherein it sells advertising space to drug companies that have a tailored message that they want to communicate to those with that particular problem. This kind of precise targeting of tailored messages is the hallmark of direct marketing.

Direct mail as a medium also lends itself like no other to testing and experimentation. For example, with direct mail it is common to test two or more different appeal letters using a modest budget and a small sample of households.[34] The goal is to establish which version effects the largest response. When a winner is decided, that form of the letter is backed by big-budget dollars in launching the organization's primary campaign.

Flexibility. In addition, with direct mail, the choice of formats an organization can send to customers is virtually limitless. It can mail large, expensive brochures; videotapes; computer disks; or CDs. It can use pop-ups foldouts, scented strips (see Exhibit 10.11), or simple postcards. If a product can be described in a limited space with minimal graphics, there really is no need to get fancy with the direct-mail piece. The double postcard (DPC) format has an established track record of outperforming more expensive and elaborate direct-mail packages.[35] Moreover, if an organization follows U.S. Postal Service guidelines carefully in mailing DPCs, the pieces can go out as

EXHIBIT 10.11

One of the advantages of direct mail as a direct marketing medium is the flexibility it provides in the materials that can be sent to consumers.

---

32. Jack Z. Sissors and Lincoln Bumba, *Advertising Media Planning* (Lincolnwood, IL: NTC Business Books, 1994).
33. Sally Beatty, "Drug Companies Are Minding Your Business," *The Wall Street Journal,* April 17, 1998, B1, B3.
34. Pamela Sebastian, "Charity Tries Two Letters to Melt Cold Hearts," *The Wall Street Journal,* November 22, 1994, B1.
35. Michael Edmondson, "Postcards from the Edge," *Marketing Tools,* May 1995, 14.

first-class mail for reasonable rates. Since the Postal Service supplies address corrections on all first-class mail, using DPCs usually turns out to be a winner on either CPI or CPO measures, and DPCs can be an effective tool for cleaning up the bad addresses in a mailing list!

Consumer Preference. While direct mail is often referred to as "junk mail," there are several conditions under which consumers actually prefer to receive communication and promotion through the mail. In a survey of consumers by the Direct Marketing Association, 52 percent preferred to receive information about grocery, health, and beauty care products through the mail as opposed to information from other media such as television (27 percent), magazines (20 percent), or in-package information (23 percent). Similarly, when asked how they would prefer to receive product samples of grocery of health and beauty products, a vast majority (70 percent) preferred to receive them in the mail rather than in the store (46 percent) or delivered to the house with a newspaper (43 percent).[36]

Telemarketing. **Telemarketing** creates a phone contact between buyer and seller initiated by either party for the purposes of communication or the initiation of a transaction. Telemarketing is probably the direct marketer's most potent tool. As with direct mail, contacts can be selectively targeted, the impact of programs is easy to track, and experimentation with different scripts and delivery formats is simple and practical. And because telemarketing involves real, live, person-to-person dialogue, no medium produces better response rates.[37] Telemarketing shares many of direct mail's limitations. Telemarketing is very expensive on a cost-per-contact basis, and just as names and addresses go bad as people move, so too do phone numbers. It is typical in telemarketing programs to find that 15 percent of the numbers called are inaccurate.[38] Further, telemarketing does not share direct mail's flexibility in terms of delivery options. When you reach people in their home or workplace, you have a limited amount of time to convey information and request some form of response.

If you have a telephone, you already know the biggest concern with telemarketing: It is a powerful yet highly intrusive medium that must be used with discretion. High-pressure telephone calls at inconvenient times can alienate customers. Telemarketing gives its best results over the long run if it is used to maintain constructive dialogues with existing customers and qualified prospects.[39]

For example, Kayla Cosmetics of Burbank, California, uses telemarketing to generate 93 percent of its sales from a marketing database of 19,000 customers.[40] Kayla's phone operators maintain ongoing dialogues with customers, and even though it may be months between contacts, each customer always works through the same personal operator when placing orders with Kayla. When that customer calls or is contacted by Kayla, her records, with purchase histories and personal details, appear immediately on the operator's computer screen. The first comment the customer hears from a Kayla operator is *not* "What item did you want to buy today?" but rather something like "What did you name your new baby?" Using technology and well-trained employees to add a personal touch to telemarketing efforts is a good way to get the most from this medium.

Catalogs. Catalogs go back to the very beginnings of the direct marketing process. In 1667 the first catalog—a gardening catalog—was published by William

---

36. *Cox Direct 20th Annual Survey of Promotional Practices* (Largo, FL: Cox Direct, 1998), 25, 27.
37. Sissors and Bumba, *Advertising and Media Planning.*
38. Ibid.
39. Stone, *Successful Direct Marketing Methods,* Chapter 14.
40. William Dunn, "Building a Database," *Marketing Tools,* July/August 1994, 52–59.

EXHIBIT 10.12

Value of U.S. catalog sales
(in billions of dollars)

	1994	1998	1999	2000	2004	Compound Annual Growth 94–99	Compound Annual Growth 99–04
Total	$61,687	$85,237	$93,272	$99,840	$125,130	8.6%	6.1%
Consumer	38.316	52.281	57.115	60.908	75.468	8.3%	5.7%
Business	23.371	32.956	36.157	38.932	49.662	9.1%	6.6%

Source: Direct Marketing Association accessed at http://www.the-dma.org, accessed on April 15, 2000

Lucas, an English gardener.[41] The catalog business has grown dramatically through the centuries, with department store merchants like Sears and Montgomery Ward getting their start with catalogs. In recent times, specialty catalogers like L. L. Bean and Cabella's sell hundreds of millions of dollars of merchandise without a storefront—strictly through catalogs. And as Exhibit 10.12 shows, the catalog industry is bigger than all of the rest of the direct marketing industry *combined*. Consumer sales via catalogs totaled over $60 billion dollars in 2000, with business catalog buying reaching nearly $40 billion. Each year, about 15 billion catalogs are distributed to consumers and business buyers. A key advantage of catalogs is that they can be tailored to any demographic or lifestyle segment from home improvement catalogs to the catalog sent out by The Pleasant Company, which targets seven- to twelve-year- olds with its American Beauty line of dolls. One issue with respect to catalogs is the extent to which consumer and business affinity for the Internet (and e-commerce) will radically affect consumers' use of catalogs. Most catalog merchants believe that there can be a synergistic and complementary relationship between online shopping and offline catalog direct marketing.[42]

Infomercials. The infomercial is a novel form of direct-response promotion that merits special mention. An **infomercial** is fundamentally just a long television advertisement made possible by the lower cost of ad space on many cable and satellite channels. Infomercials range in length from 3 to 60 minutes, but the common length is 30 minutes. Although producing an infomercial is a lot like producing a television program, infomercials are all about selling. There are several keys to successful use of this unique vehicle.

A critical communication factor are testimonials from satisfied users. Celebrity testimonials can help catch the viewer who is channel surfing past the program, but celebrities aren't necessary and, of course, they add to production costs. Whether testimonials are from celebrities or from folks just like you and me, one expert summarizes matters this way: "Testimonials are so important that without them your chances of producing a profitable infomercial diminish hugely."[43]

Another important point to remember about infomercials is that viewers are not likely to stay tuned for the full 30 minutes. An infomercial is a 30-minute direct-response sales pitch, not a classic episode of *Seinfeld* or *The Simpsons*. The implication here is that the call to action should come not just at the end of the infomercial—most of the audience is likely to be long gone by minute 28 into the show. A good rule of thumb in a 30-minute infomercial is to divide the program into

41. "Grassroots Advocacy Guide for Direct Marketers," the Direct Marketing Association, 1993.
42. William J. Lansing, "Sellers to Take Back Seat as Buyer's Market Emerges," *Marketing News,* December 6, 1999, 19.
43. Herschell Gordon Lewis, "Information on Infomercials," *Direct Marketing,* March 1995, 30–32.

MEDIA

TELEVISION ADVERTISING IS DIRECT-RESPONSE ADVERTISING

By the year 2010, television is going to become a direct-response medium in a way none of us can fully appreciate right now. This doesn't mean we're going to be inundated with plaintiff lawyer ads for personal injury cases (we hope not!) or hours of psychic hotline ads. Nor does it mean that 30-second brand-building spots will disappear completely. But there is going to be a significant shift toward 1-800 and dot-com spots designed to achieve all sorts of responses— an order, request for more information, or a visit to a Web site.

This possibility is not a dot-com pipe dream. The roots of this transformation for television are already in place. While the dot-coms are currently fascinated with who can make the funniest spot, that will change in the near future to a preference for a more serious (and more useful) ad where direct response is the main theme. These television ads will be longer spots that better explain the site and offer and provide more screen time for the Web site address. They will begin to use incentives and special promotions to increase back-end sales. And the dot-coms will learn to better use direct-response media strategies like cable, dayparts, late night, and weekends instead of SuperBowl ads.

The reason for this transformation is rooted not so much in a new sophistication by dot-coms, but rather in the fact that the dot-coms will no longer be satisfied with mere site visits. For them, the site visit has to be a direct-marketing experience, not just a casual (and nonproductive) site tour. The managers of major Internet companies are already complaining about the lack of seriousness of surfers' site visits. Direct-response techniques will help on-site purchasing behavior as well.

In addition to the sheer motivation of Web-based merchants to make television advertising direct-response advertising, the evolution of the cable industry is providing an assist as well. New cable stations continue to proliferate, but in a good way. For years, many marketers steered away from direct-response ads because they were seen as a shotgun approach in a world of targeted media options. Now, new cable stations provide the "narrow casting" needed for targeted specialized direct-response offers. Does this really mean that all advertising will be direct response? Most likely not. But with the combination of Internet access, highly motivated dot-com managers, and more precise cable segmentation, get ready for a huge increase in direct-response TV ads.

Source: Ron Bliwas, "TV Becomes Direct Response," *Advertising Age*, February 21, 2000, 30.

10-minute increments and close three times.[44] Each closing should feature the 800 number that allows the viewer to order the product or request more information. And an organization should not offer information to the customer unless it can deliver speedy follow-up; same-day response should be the goal in pursuing leads generated by an infomercial.

Many different types of products and services have been marketed using infomercials, and now via Internet extensions such as http://www.iqvc.com. Self-help videos, CD players, home exercise equipment, kitchen appliances, and hair restoration treatments have all had success with the infomercial. And while it is easy to associate the infomercial with things such as the Ronco Showtime Rotisserie & BBQ (yours for just four easy payments of $39.95!), large, sophisticated marketers like Cadillac have also had success in this format. When Cadillac was looking for a way to take buyers away from Lexus, Mercedes, and BMW, they turned to a 30- minute infomercial titled "The Challenge of Change." Cadillac executives added the infomercial to a more traditional print campaign because they needed a more elaborate message environment to explain the technical features of the STS model. The direct response? Viewers were urged to call a toll-free number to request print materials and special offers.[45]

Direct Marketing in Other Media. Direct marketers have experimented with many other methods in trying to convey their appeals for a customer response. Using magazines, a popular device for executing a direct marketer's agenda are **bind-in insert cards,** those little postcard-size inserts in

---

44. Ibid.
45. Dave Guilford, "Cadillac Takes New Route for Seville STS: Infomercial," *Advertising Age,* August 23, 1999, 8.

Just another lonely, isolated dandruff sufferer
who called for a free sample.

The freedom will go to your head.

Nizoral
A-D

Anti-
Dandruff
Shampoo

Try the only shampoo made with the #1 prescribed ingredient for dandruff. Just shampoo twice
a week with the rich, great-smelling lather of Nizoral® A.D.

FOR YOUR FREE SAMPLE, CALL 1-888-NIZORAL (649-6725).

EXHIBIT 10.13

Various media can be used to elicit a direct response from consumers. This ad for Nizoral offers not only direct contact with a toll-free number but also a free sample.

magazines that give you the chance to subscribe to magazines or order merchandise or get a free sample.[46] Thumb through a copy of any magazine and you will see how effective these light cardboard inserts are in stopping the reader and calling attention to themselves. Insert cards not only promote their products but also offer the reader an easy way to order a pair of Optek sport sunglasses or select those ten free CDs that will make the reader a member of the BMG Music Club.

Another critical medium for direct response that has been referenced several times is the toll-free number. When AT&T introduced the first 800 service in 1967, it simply could not have known how important this service would become to direct marketing. Newspaper ads from *The Wall Street Journal* provide toll-free numbers for requesting everything from package delivery (1-800-PICK-UPS) to notebook PCs (1-800-TOSHIBA). If you watch late-night TV, you already know the 800 number to call to order the Grammy-winning CD by Walter Ostanek and his polka band. IDS Financial Services, a division of American Express, featured its 800 number in radio ads as part of a two-step offer designed to generate prospects for its financial planning business. IDS operators took the caller's name, address, phone number, and age to input into a marketing database, and they offered to book the caller for a consultation. The company found this radio-based campaign more than twice as profitable as the direct-mail promotional campaigns it had used previously.[47]

Magazine ads are also commonly used to provide an 800 number to initiate contact with customers. The ad in Exhibit 10.13 not only attempts to initiate contact, it also provides a method for consumers to acquire a free sample (and end up in the company's database). As these diverse examples indicate, toll-free numbers make it possible to use nearly any medium for direct-response purposes. And there are those who believe that all television advertising will become direct-response advertising with emerging changes in technology, as the New Media box explains.

E-COMMERCE

Direct marketing, as we have just discussed it, has long been a foundation tool in the promotional process of many firms. In 1995, when Internet access and applications became a reality, the direct-marketing world went through seismic change. A completely new approach to the process was suddenly a possibility. This is not to say that the very nature of direct marketing has been changed—quite the contrary. If you review the earlier discussion of the popularity of direct marketing, you will see that those same principles explain the popularity and growth of e-commerce.

---

46.   Stone, *Successful Direct Marketing Methods,* 250–252.
47.   Nancy Coltun Webster, "Radio Tuning In to Direct Response," *Advertising Age,* October 10, 1994, S14–S15.

http://www.jcpenney.com; http://www.amazon.com

EXHIBIT 10.14

Convenience is one of the foundations of the popularity of direct marketing. Note how Amazon.com emphasizes this feature of Web shopping with the "Anything, Anytime, Everywhere" appeal. How does Amazon.com compare with a local store, or with a "bricks-and-clicks" store, like JCPenney, with both physical stores and a Web presence?

Convenience (see Exhibit 10.14), acceptance of credit, changes in technology, and measurability of results all apply to e-commerce—in spades. And remember from the introductory discussion of the relationship between direct marketing and e-commerce: All e-commerce is direct marketing, but not all direct marketing is e-commerce.

E-commerce is a world unto itself when it comes to the technology of communications and transactions. Exhibit 10.15 is a brief glossary of e-commerce terminology that is an essential starting point for our discussion. Notice that much of this terminology has to do with the technical infrastructure of the Internet that facilitates e-commerce communication and transactions. If you think this is irrelevant to your knowledge of promotion, think again. When an organization decides to add an e-commerce component to its promotional mix, this terminology suddenly becomes part of daily conversation—not so much regarding the strategic application of e-commerce in the promotional mix, but rather with the dozens of organizations that a firm will rely on to make e-commerce a successful reality for the firm. We will examine in detail shortly just what kinds of facilitating organizations (called "enabling firms") are needed to establish an e-commerce operation.

In our discussion of e-commerce, we will begin with a look at the two main areas—business to consumer and business to business. Then we will turn our attention to the way e-commerce works and examine what it takes to set up a successful e-commerce system. Finally, we will consider the issue of coordinating both directing marketing and e-commerce into an IMC program.

Business-to-Consumer and Business-to-Business E-Commerce

While e-commerce has not changed the fundamental nature of direct marketing as a promotional tool, what does represent a seismic change in direct marketing is the massive amount of business-to-business (B2B) commerce being carried out. We tend to be more familiar with business-to-consumer (B2C) e-commerce because firms like Amazon.com and eBay serve our consumer needs. But the true power of

A Brief Glossary of e-Commerce Terms

ASP:	(Application Service Provider) Refers to companies that rent software over the Internet. Rather than buying a copy of Microsoft Office, you pay a monthly fee based on your use of it or other programs piped to your computer over the Web.
B2B:	Abbreviation for business-to-business transactions conducted over the Internet. A large number of firms specializing in both business products (PurchasePro.com, Intel) and Internet-related hardware (Cisco, Nortel Networks) and services (Bowstreet, UUNet are vying for the trillions of dollars of B2B transactions over the Web.
B2C:	Abbreviation for business-to-consumer transactions conducted over the Internet. Also referred to as "e-tail." Traditional firms like The Gap and JCPenney have e-tail operations. There are also "pure-play" e-tailers like furniture.com and Boo.com (sportswear) and service providers like owners.com (home listing and selling services).
Bandwidth:	The maximum speed at which data can be transmitted between computers in a network.
Broadband:	High-speed Internet access technology that provides large amounts of space to accommodate huge applications companies wish to send to users. The delivery of broadband can take place either through DSL, which uses phone lines, or cable now used to bring television programming to homes.
Browser:	An application program that interprets HTML and presents the final Web page. It is used to "surf the WWW." Examples include Internet Explorer, Netscape Navigator, and Mosaic.
Cookie:	A file that is written to your hard disk when you access certain Web pages. The file contains certain information, often data that you entered when you displayed the page. The next time you access this page, a check is done to see if the cookie exists. The information within the cookie may well influence what happens next. Cookies are used by firms to profile Web surfers for the purposed of targeting banner advertising and e-mail communicators.
Convergence:	The merging of all forms of media and technology wired together by the Internet. For example, television, stereo, and computer will combine to provide video conferences, on-demand films, and self-programmed Internet radio stations.
DSL:	Digital Subscriber Line, which uses standard phone lines to send high-speed Internet transmissions.
E-Tail:	The combination of electronic and retail to designate the selling of goods and services over the Web to consumers.
Fat Pipe:	A more hip term for broadband. The suggestion here is that more data can move through the connection as opposed to the "narrow" pile of a standard dial-up.
Firewall:	A combination of specialized hardware and software designed to keep unauthorized users from accessing information from certain designated (firewalled) parts of a networked computer system.

continued

EXHIBIT 10.15

A brief glossary of e-commerce terminology

e-commerce is in the B2B market. Exhibit 10.16 on page 366 shows the both the dramatic growth of e-commerce overall and the total domination of B2B e-commerce over B2C e-commerce.

There are several important aspects of e-commerce revealed in Exhibit 10.16. First, notice in comparing B2C and B2B that e-commerce between businesses is not only about 10 times greater than consumer e-commerce, but it is also expected to grow at a much greater rate. By the year 2003, B2C e-commerce is projected to reach about $110 billion, whereas B2B will exceed $1.3 *trillion*. Next, look carefully at the set of bar charts that show e-commerce as a proportion of all commerce in the United States. In the year 2000, e-commerce was hardly a blip on the radar, but by the year 2003, we should see e-commerce transactions making up almost

A Brief Glossary of e-Commerce Terms, *continued*

Gateway:	A device that connects different networks together. It handles the transfer of data between networks and any conversion required to enable the data that has been extracted from one network to be read in another network.
HTML:	Hypertext markup language. The text-based language used to construct WWW pages and is interpreted by Web Browsers.
HTTP:	(Hypertext transmission protocol) A protocol that computers on the Internet use to communicate with each other.
Internet Appliance:	Any device, other than a computer, that connects to the Web. Wireless phones, electronic organizers and devices like GM's "On-Star" Web-enabler installed in certain cars are examples of Internet appliances.
Java:	First seen in 1995, Java is a modern programming language used to bring Web pages to life. It is an interpreted, object-orientated program language with a syntax and structure similar to C++, designed specifically for the Internet by Sun Microsystems. Java programs are referred to as applets. One huge plus for Java is that its programs can run on many different types of computer (e.g., IBM, PC, Apple Macintosh).
Linux:	A variant of the Unix operation system developed by the Finnish programmer Linus Torvalds. Linux is a system that some believe will challenge the Microsoft Windows operating system. The proper pronunciation of Linux rhymes with "cynics."
Network:	A network is basically a series of wires and cables that connects a number of computers. Data is exchanged between computers via these cables. The maximum speed at which the data can be transmitted is called the bandwidth.
MP3:	The informal name for the audio files that play CD-quality sound over a computer. MP3 players can download dozens of songs and play them in the order you program them. It is expected that in the near future, stereo system will have an Internet jack to download MP3 files.
SOHO:	(Small Office Home Office) Describes those businesses that are either run from home or in a small office. You may well ask why have we gone to the trouble of including this definition in a Glossary of e-Commerce terminology. The reason is that software and hardware companies will promote their products as being suitable for the SOHO market.
Smart Card:	A card with a computer chip instead of a magnetic strip. This sort of card has been used for several years in Europe but has never caught on in the U.S. A smart card can store all of your passwords and login information providing hacker-proof online access.
Smart Phone:	A wireless phone that connects to the Internet. Also called a Web phone or WAP (wireless application protocol) phone. Most use a program called WAP that translates picture-laden Internet transmissions into simple text messages.
URL:	(Uniform Resource Locater) How documents of the WWW are referenced. In plain language, this is the name that follows the www. in an Internet address.

10 percent of all commercial transactions in the United States. If we refine the total transactions by industry, we can see that computing and electronics (not surprisingly) will be the leading e-commerce industries, but you may be surprised to see that chemicals and utilities rank second and third. The reason for these seemingly "anonymous" industries turning to e-commerce has to do with the way transactions can be structured in e-commerce, which happens to ideally suit these industries. (We'll see how this works in the next section.)

Currently, there is a fairly vigorous debate about the future of the Internet as a B2C direct-marketing tool versus its B2B potential. The numbers in Exhibit 10.16 certainly tell an interesting tale about the dominance of B2B. But what about the future of B2C e-commerce? There are those who argue that B2C commerce has

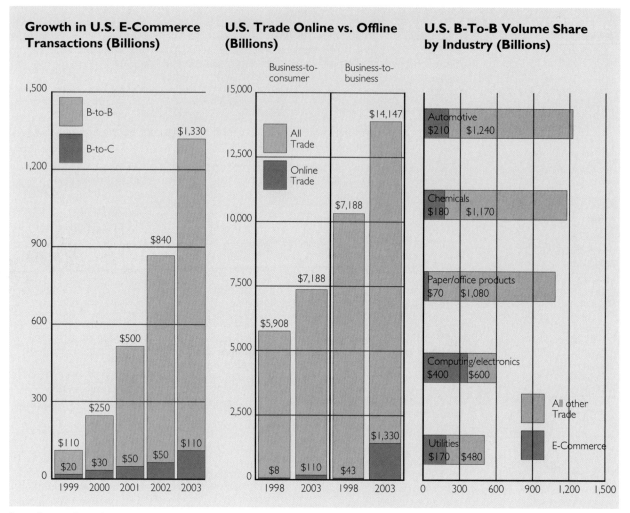

Growth in U.S. E-Commerce Transactions (Billions)

U.S. Trade Online vs. Offline (Billions)

U.S. B-To-B Volume Share by Industry (Billions)

Source: Forrester Research

EXHIBIT 10.16

While business-to-consumer e-commerce gets a lot of press, the value and future growth of e-commerce really lies with business-to-business transactions.

just as much potential as B2B. As an example, online toy sales represented only 2 percent of all toy sales in the year 2000, but that represented a tenfold increase.[48] The other aspect of B2C that is underrepresented in assessing its potential relative to B2B transactions is the way in which relationships are formed on the Web by consumers. Yahoo! and Disney make online shopping an *experience,* not just a transaction. Relationship building has long-term payoffs. Finally, by the year 2003, about 60 percent of all U.S. households will be wired to the Web, and almost 10 percent of the world will have direct access, making for a truly large and global marketplace.[49]

48. Rick Aristotle Munarriz, "B2B or B2C: The Bear Argument," Fool.com News and Commentary, March 15, 2000, accessed at http://www.fool.com on March 16, 2000.
49. "Net by Number," *Business 2.0,* January 2000, 182.

http://www.nextcard.com

EXHIBIT 10.17

Is e-commerce really going to make us all "Kiss the Mall Good-Bye"? Clearly, some products are more amenable to online shopping than others, and going to the mall has always been a bit more than just swapping cash for consumables. NextCard wants you to imagine that shopping online is the future (since you've effectively got to have a credit card to shop that way); it's also promoted itself heavily online, as one of the foremost buyers of banner advertising on networks like DoubleClick and Engage's Flycast. How does NextCard Concierge make online shopping easier?

Those who see e-commerce being almost exclusively a B2B environment have some pretty compelling arguments as well. First, there are the raw growth numbers we saw earlier. Second, some well-financed and well-managed e-tailers like Peapod, the online grocer, are teetering on the brink (and may be gone by the time you read this). Peapod is in trouble despite heavy financing, $58 million, and a good management team.[50] Analysts who follow e-commerce closely are predicting a massive shakeout among B2C marketers. A main part of the problem is the poor performance of e-tailers in serving customers. For example, during the 1999–2000 holiday season, only 35 percent of sales made by pure-play e-tailers were delivered on time in the United States. By comparison, click-and-mortar merchants like The Gap and BarnesandNoble.com delivered orders as promised 80 percent of the time.[51] Failing to deliver in a timely manner is a fatal error in an environment where the consumer has to assume multiple risks for the value of convenience. E-tailing in Europe has problems just as serious. A survey of European consumers found that of European homes with Internet access, only 10 percent purchased goods online. Fully two-thirds also indicated that they preferred to see and touch goods in stores before buying, and most expressed concerns about privacy and security—not an ideal environment for succeeding.[52] The Global Issues box has some suggestions on how to manage an e-tailing operation in Europe.

Finally, the most basic argument against e-tailing is the nearly total lack of barriers to entry. As one critic of B2C commerce sarcastically pointed out, he was able to set up the fully functional B2C shopping site "PetPeeves.com" in all of three minutes.[53] With low barriers to entry, sites like eToys and priceline.com will face extensive competition and cannot hope to hold the line on profit margins. This is quite the turnaround from the late 1990s, when traditional retailers were being warned that they needed to reinvent themselves or face certain distinction.[54] So what do you think, is it time to "Kiss the Mall Goodbye"? (See Exhibit 10.17.)

Setting Up and Managing an E-Commerce Operation ④

To this point, we have shown that e-commerce is part promotion, part marketing strategy, and part distribution. What we want to do now is dive into the workings of an e-commerce system and understand how one is set up and managed. This sort

50.   Darnell Little, "Peapod Is in a Pickle," *Business Week,* April 3, 2000, 41.
51.   Bradley Johnson, "Massive E-Tailer Shakeout Foreseen," *Advertising Age,* January 10, 2000, 34.
52.   "Europeans Slow to Shop Online," Forrester Research, February 24, 2000, accessed at http://www.nua.net on March 20, 2000.
53.   Munarriz, "B2B or B2C: The Bear Argument."
54.   Gary Hamel and Jeff Sampler, "The E-Corporation," *Fortune,* December 7, 1998, 80–92.

of examination will reveal the communication aspects of e-commerce relative to the marketing and distribution aspects.

Exhibit 10.18 shows the stages of operation of a typical e-commerce system. This model applies to either a B2C or B2B system. One of the things you will learn about setting up and managing an e-commerce operation is that it is not so much a matter of learning about how e-commerce works, per se, as it is learning to set up and manage relationships with facilitators. There are hundreds of companies out there ready and able to help a firm at each stage of its e-commerce operation. In the language of e-commerce, these firms are called "enabler" companies.[55] At each stage of an e-commerce operation, enabler service firms are available to make the hardware, software, tools, and transaction platforms that build the infrastructure of an e-commerce operation. We will consider each stage of the e-commerce model and discuss the types of enabler firms available to help set up and manage an e-commerce operation.

Identify Customers. As in any form of promotion, the first step in an e-commerce system is identifying target customers. In Chapter 3, we learned that effective promotion is highly dependent on careful planning. The same is true for an e-commerce operation. A situation analysis, not unlike the one described in Chapter 3, is necessary. In the case of e-commerce, identifying customers is a twofold process. First, there is the need to understand the values customers are seeking from a brand. This would be a standard assessment no matter what promotional tool is being used. Second, there is the need to understand why and how a target segment would seek to discover and acquire the brand through e-commerce. Here, specific consumer behavior analysis relative to e-commerce is necessary.

We do know certain general tendencies with respect to consumer

GLOBAL ISSUES

E-TAILING IN EUROPE? HERE ARE SOME RULES

The European Union and growing Internet access throughout Europe are creating huge potential for U.S.-based Internet e-tailers. But there are some simple rules that will greatly increase the probability of success for U.S. merchants hoping to tap Europe's potential.

1. Proven and profitable merchandise that sells well in the United States may not sell in Europe. Even if it is the Internet, cultural differences in product preferences and uses (and everything else discussed in Chapter 7) still hold.
2. The site needs to be easily navigated by non-English-speaking consumers. While the language of business has become predominantly English, the language of shopping is still culturally bound.
3. Ensure domestic assistance from local marketing experts to make certain that offline promotions like direct mail, billboards, and magazine spots are properly targeted to generate traffic to the site. Hardly anyone finds a site by accident. As the discussion in Chapter 9 highlighted, dot-coms have to go offline to get people online, and that holds in Europe, too.
4. Ensure that your infrastructure is in place in Europe before you launch the Web site. Fulfillment processes like warehouses, local sources of supply, and toll-free/multilanguage telephone support need to be fully aligned before you start generating demand online.
5. Test the service for at least four weeks before the official launch. Possible slip-ups include e-mail routing that does not reach customer service people, suppliers unable to fill orders locally in a timely fashion, and Web navigation glitches.

Source: Allyson L. Stewart-Allen, "Coordinate Logistics When E-Tailing to Europe," *Marketing News*, November 22, 1999, 18.

behavior on the Web. Given the nature of e-commerce as a direct-marketing system, we are aware that consumers seek the convenience that the Web offers. Specific studies of online shopping show the following characteristics about the average e-tail Web shopper:[56]

55. Jeffrey Davis, "How It Works," *Business 2.0,* February 2000, 2112–114.
56. CNNfn, "Convenience, Bargains Motivate Online Shoppers—Study," May 18, 1999, accessed at http://www.cnnfn.com on January 19, 2000; Boston Consulting Group, "E-commerce Sites Still Failing Shoppers," NUA Internet Surveys, March 8, 2000, accessed at http://www.nua.com on March 17, 2000.

- Is female
- Belongs to a high-income household
- Is likely to make impulse purchases
- Uses both online and traditional retailers for shopping and buying
- Conducts ten transactions on the Internet a year
- Spends $460 per transaction
- Expects to wait no longer than 13.2 seconds for a home page to load
- Expects to spend no longer than 5.8 minutes to find a product
- Expects to spend no longer than 4.5 minutes to complete an order
- Expects to receive delivery in 6.4 days

Consumer behavior analysis also shows that online consumers are often frustrated with their e-commerce experience. In a survey of frequent online shoppers, 48 percent said sites take too long to load and 45 percent felt that sites were so poorly designed that products could not be found.[57]

There is no similar profile available for the B2B buyer. But as we saw in Chapter 5, the typical business buyer, traditional or e-commerce, is likely going to focus on the information and pricing aspects of an e-commerce opportunity. Because of

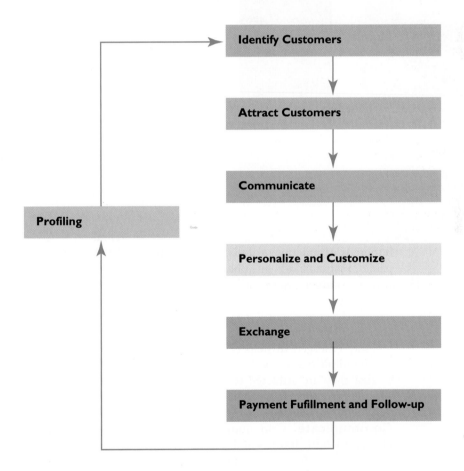

EXHIBIT 10.18

A model of the stages in an e-commerce operation

57. Boston Consulting Group, "E-commerce Sites Still Failing Shoppers," NUA Internet Surveys, March 8, 2000, accessed at http://www.nua.com on March 17, 2000.

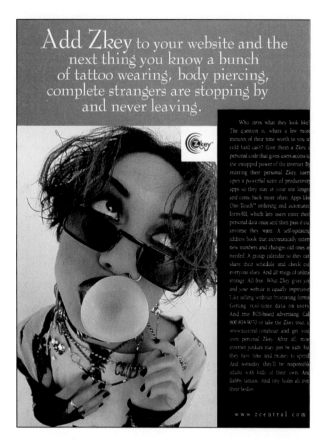

Add Zkey to your website and the next thing you know a bunch of tattoo wearing, body piercing, complete strangers are stopping by and never leaving.

www.zcentral.com

EXHIBIT 10.19

One of the great challenges of managing an e-commerce operation is getting consumers to come back again and again to your Web site. So called "enabler" firms like Zkey help e-commerce companies develop systems that attract and retain customers.

the nature of business buyers generally and the kinds of problems that plague e-tail shoppers on the Web, Herman Miller, the furniture manufacturer located in Holland, Michigan, has devised the SQA division to build and manage their e-commerce system. SQA stands for "Simple, Quick, Affordable," and the company is linking all purchasing, sales, and shipping information through the Internet to ensure a positive experience for customers. One indication of the results is a sign that hangs outside one of the Herman Miller plants boasting that the workers there haven't been late in shipping a single order in seventy days.[58]

Attract Customers. One unchangeable fact of commercial life—traditional or e-commerce—is that nothing can happen without customers. In the e-commerce environment, firms are going to have to attract customers to their Web site or into an electronic marketplace if they want to sell them a product or service. There are all sorts of new services and technologies that can deliver targeted audiences to e-commerce sites. Some, like LinkExchange and BeFree, manage affiliation programs that create partnerships among companies trying to attract customers. One affiliate program partnered ActionAce, an entertainment and community portal, with Yahoo!Geocities. With the BeFree affiliation, ActionAce's site was ultimately placed on 45,000 BeFree affiliate sites as a main method of attracting customers.

As we saw in Chapter 9, there are several media organizations Web companies can use to drive traffic to a Web site. Offline advertising in traditional media has been heavily relied on by Web firms. Beyond the hundreds of millions of dollars invested in television advertising by dot-com companies, magazine ads in publications like *Cooking Light* and *National Geographic* for B2C e-commerce sites and *Business Week* and *Business 2.0* for B2B target customers are used to "drive traffic." Recall also that targeted e-mail can be sent through firms like NetCreations, and listservs can be used for direct communication as a way to encourage prospective customers to visit a site. Other types of facilitators have also recently emerged to help e-commerce firms attract and keep customers. Service organizations like Zkey (see Exhibit 10.19) provide a suite of services to customers so that they are attracted to the site and continue to return for the services and applications available.

Communicate. Communicating through an e-commerce site offers sellers a chance to both inform and persuade. Once customers are driven to a Web site, they expect to find information suited to their needs and desires, and judge a site as much for its information value as the offering contained at the site itself.[59] There are dozens of companies ready to create platforms for serving customers' information and ordering needs. This is a critical part of the e-commerce process. Recall

58. David Rocks, "Reinventing Herman Miller," *Business Week e.biz,* April, 3, 2000, 89–96.
59. Steve Mott, "Winning One Customer at a Time," *Business 2.0,* March 2000, 269–273.

that many Web firms are struggling with providing information quickly enough to suit consumer desires. Similarly, the majority of Web e-tailers have failed to deliver goods on time during critical holiday shopping seasons.

In an effort to build a completely integrated system that would provide both communication and service to Web customers, one company, W. W. Grainger, turned to two Web specialty firms—OnDisplay and Requisite Technology. W. W. Grainger is a 75-year-old catalog merchant that developed e-commerce operations in 1997. In the beginning, Grainger was updating product and customer information by hand, resulting in data being entered twice and endless phone calls and faxes between suppliers and Grainger branches. That's when the company turned to OnDisplay (http://www.vignette.com), an online content manager that helps businesses update and manage Web site information content. OnDisplay configured a system whereby Grainger could plug into 2,000 supplier databases, translate product data into XML or HTML for Web delivery to customers, aggregate the data for quick download and delivery, and provide a secure system for round-the-clock access to customers.[60] Then Grainger enlisted the help of Requisite Technology (http://www.requisite.com) to install a search engine *inside* the Grainger site for quicker and easier navigation for customers. The end result of the communication system: Grainger operates and manages three different Web sites and generates about $180 million a year in e-commerce. Other enabler companies at this stage of the e-commerce operation are CardoNet (http://www.cardonet.com) and Vignette (http://www.vignette.com).

Personalize and Customize. One of the great promises of the Internet for marketers is the ability to personalize communications and customize product offerings. We have already learned that with profiling (which we will visit again shortly), customized e-mails can be sent to highly targeted audiences. In addition, banner ads relevant to a consumer's interests (based on past Web surfing behavior) can appear at sites frequented by the consumer. In a similar way, another of the great promises of e-commerce is customized products and services—a promise that is becoming a reality. As consumers configure and assemble combinations of components and options that go into everything from PCs to tractors, their demand for customization is growing. The reality of customization lies in "configuration engines," which now allow this mix-and-match process by enhancing databases with digital logic and rules capable of ensuring that everything the customer wants can indeed be ordered, assembled, paid for, and delivered.

Acumin Corporation, a manufacturer of custom-blended vitamin formulas, launched a Web site designed to educate consumers as well as allow them to customize their own vitamins. Managers at Acumin enlisted the help of enabler company Frontier Media Group (http://www.frontiermedia.com) to meet the objectives of communication and customization. The resulting Web site (http://www.acumins.com) allows consumers to create specialized mixes of vitamins that fit their individual goals. Customers do so by answering a set of questions within the Web site called "Smart Select." The results of the questioning are searched against 1 million different vitamin formulas—essentially a database of virtual vitamin options. Part of the customization process is that none of the 1 million formulas actually exists in Acumin's inventory. Rather, once the vitamin survey and ordering process is completed, Acumin uses its highly sophisticated manufacturing technology to build the vitamin product that matches each customer's needs as specified by the survey responses.[61] Six months after installing the Frontier Media system, 50 percent

60. Alicia Neumann, "A Better Mousetrap Catalog," *Business 2.0,* February 2000, 117–118.
61. Jay Winchester, "Formula for Success," *Sales and Marketing Management,* February 2000, 76.

of Acumin's sales were transacted over the Web. Other enabling firms in the e-commerce customization business are Calico Commerce (http://www.calico.com), FirePond (http://www.firepond.com), and Selectrica (http://www.selectrica.com).

Exchange. In the end, an e-commerce system is about creating exchanges between buyers and sellers. As we have seen, the dollar amount of transactions in the B2B market dwarf the B2C market. At the center of e-commerce transactions are market-making mechanisms called "platforms." **Platforms** represent the way in which e-commerce transactions are initiated and culminated—direct purchase, catalogs, auctions, e-malls, and barter models. Regardless of the specific platform, the idea is to provide a marketplace (now referred to as an e-market) that is accessible and services the needs of a targeted customer group. In just a few short years, more than 750 B2B market places have been established around the world.[62] To be a player in e-commerce, it is becoming more and more necessary to be part of an e-marketplace. Current estimates predict that by 2004, 53 percent of the $2.7 trillion in e-commerce will take place in e-marketplace platforms. In electronics, shipping and warehousing, and utilities, over 70 percent of exchanges will be e-market transactions.[63]

We're all familiar with eBay and Travelocity in the e-tail exchange, but consider how the new e-market exchange platforms work for B2B marketers like the alcoholic beverage industry. Indianapolis-based National Wine & Spirits needed to be on the Internet. A raft of upstart dot-coms were on the verge of taking large portions of National's business. J. S. Wallin, the owner, formed eSkye.com (http://www.eskye.com) as a national marketplace platform for beverage makers, distributors, and retailers to buy and sell online (see Exhibit 10.20). Platform marketplaces like eSkye.com operate as intermediaries between suppliers and customers and charge a small percentage on each transaction for maintaining the hardware, software, and servers that run the site. These exchange marketplaces are being formed with blinding speed as small companies like Wallin's and giants like GM, Ford and DaimlerChrysler look for greater proficiency in their procurement.[64] The auto giants are collaborating on an exchange for auto parts suppliers that is expected to transact $100 billion worth of business in a few short years. Leaders in the area of developing and managing exchange platforms are Ariba (http://www.ariba.com) in shared e-commerce service, CommerceOne (http://www.commerceone.com) in procurement and vertical platforms, and TradingDynamics (http://www.tradingdynamics.com) in online auction and exchange markets.

Payment, Fulfillment, and Follow-Up. Once the online transaction occurs, the goods and services must be paid for using either credit, debit, or barter. Payment and financing functions have opened the door for firms like eCredit.com (http://www.ecredit.com), which develops real-time credit underwriting software, and Paylinx (http://www.cybersource.com), which offers payment server solutions whereby an exchange can operate and maintain a dedicated payment transaction server.

After payment comes production and delivery. In the world of e-commerce, delivery is still delivery, but the process is now called **fulfillment.** Most e-commerce vendors are turning to supply-chain management systems for order fulfillment rather than trying to manage this part of the e-commerce operation. As Tom Stevens, director of business process development at Sun Microelectronics, put it, "the most interesting thing about our supply chain is that we're not in it."[65] This

62. "Seller Beware," *The Economist,* accessed at http://www.economist.com/editorial/ on March 6, 2000.
63. Forrester Research, "B2B to Be Marked by New eMarketplaces," accessed at http://www.nua.net/surveys on February 20, 2000.
64. Robert D. Hof, et. al., "E-Malls for Business," *Business Week,* March 13, 2000, 32–34.
65. Sean Donahue, "Supply Traffic Control," *Business 2.0,* February 2000, 130.

EXHIBIT 10.20

Virtual marketplaces are emerging in many industries. eSkye.com is the marketplace for manufacturers, distributors, buyers, and sellers of alcoholic beverages. Interestingly, this site was started by an "old-line" distributor rather than one of the new, heavily financed dot-com start-up companies.

is the way it works at Sun Microelectronics. The company contracts work to outside manufacturers, who in turn rely on components from their own subcontracted suppliers. All totaled, it's a supply chain with 150 links, with users and producers in places like Canada, Japan, Taiwan, and the United Kingdom. No hard goods ever sit in Sun's inventory system or touch the hands of any of Sun's 29,000 employees—amazing.

The fulfillment operations of e-commerce are referred to as **back-end networks.** Companies like Sun rely on an enabler company like i2 Technologies to develop large-scale supply-chain forecasting and fulfillment software. The way it works for Sun is that they will gather chip demand forecasts based on projected OEM (original equipment manufacturers) sales and load these data into i2 software. Then every supplier in the Sun system has access to the forecasts. This way, each supplier can monitor Sun's expected needs and ramp up their own inventory and production scheduling. Sun needs only one employee to manage the i2 system, which can run different demand scenarios and automatically handle large-scale computations involved in demand planning.[66]

Follow-up begins once fulfillment is complete. In the world of e-commerce, delayed support and unanswered e-mail are now as intolerable as an inattentive salesperson. Any e-merchant that fails these standards will sooner rather than later be left out of the system. While e-tailers have struggled with follow-up (as of 2000 only 1.3 percent of e-tailers' business came from repeat customers), and no one is sure how B2B merchants are doing, there is good news on the software front for ensuring that current customers are satisfied and happy enough to consider buying again. For example, the Lands' End Web site incorporates a "live help" button that initiates a Web-based chat between a customer and a live support person. Through the software made by WebLine Communications, customers can also choose to have

66. Ibid.

EXHIBIT 10.21

At the stage of an e-commerce operation where payment, fulfillment, and follow-up need to take place, firms must ensure that customer satisfaction is maintained. Companies like iSky help e-merchants handle this stage of the operation. By the way, iSky has no relationship to the enabling firm eSkye from Exhibit 10.20.

a company representative call them directly.[67] Other firms like iSky are providing a full range of customer service after the transaction to ensure satisfaction and communication at this stage (see Exhibit 10.21). Either way, the customer can get immediate assistance as good as an offline store often provides. Enabler firms providing expertise in payment, fulfillment, and follow-up include eCredit.com, Celarix (http://www.celarix.com), and Manugistics (http://www.manugistics.com).

Profiling. We have examined the issue of profiling several times but always in the context of privacy issues. **Profiling** is the process of tracking and cataloging the behavior of customers in an e-commerce setting. The sites visited, purchases made, and information gathered all provide a profile of preferences for site visitors. Each time customers click into an e-commerce site, the site has a chance to learn something. Technologies like "data mining" software capture all this customer data and analyze patterns of behavior. With these data, the e-commerce firm can make the next interaction that much more personal and satisfying.

To appreciate the value of data mining software and the profiling it can produce, consider the situation facing online movie superstore Reel.com (http://www.reel.com), a subsidiary of offline company Hollywood Entertainment. When Reel.com announced a sale on a video, it could never figure out how many first-time customers were likely to come back and buy again. Nor could the company understand which customers were price sensitive and therefore higher prospects for future sales.

Frustrated by these questions, Reel.com turned to the enabler firm Verbind (http://www.verbind.com). Verbind provided tracking software that would let Reel.com answer all its questions on sale items—and more. The first test was when Reel announced a $12.50 sale on the sci-fi blockbuster movie *The Matrix* on DVD. The day the sale went online, a Verbind data agent was standing by to watch customers' moves. The results were immediate. The new profiling software was able to distinguish price-sensitive buyers from the frequent shoppers and the preorder types from other types of customers. Then tracking was initiated on customers who jumped for big sales and those who wouldn't buy no matter what the incentive was. Verbind's software, called LifeTime, then went beyond mere tracking and started to predict consumer behavior based on past behaviors. Reel began saving money in promotions and making money on sales immediately by being able to target offers much more efficiently and effectively. The system can handle 2 million transactions per hour across a customer base of 12 million. The typical user of this kind of software can reduce database costs by 20 percent. The increase in effectiveness from more careful targeting is hard to estimate, but it is powerful. Other firms in the profiling and data-mining business include DataSage (http://www.datasage.com),

67. Kim Cross, "@ Your Service," *Business 2.0,* March 2000, 427.

E.piphany (http://www.epiphany.com), and Personify (http://www.personify.com).

At the end of data mining and profiling, the system restarts. Firms are able to identify customers, attract them or keep them coming back, communicate, and so on. The world of e-commerce is indeed complex. The click-and-mortar competitors like The Gap, Wal-Mart, and IBM are learning lessons and learning them fast. The pure-play e-commerce companies are also learning. They are learning that their "old economy" and "old technology" competitors are no slouches when it comes to setting up and managing an e-commerce operation. In fact, analysts are now saying that in order to effectively compete for the long term, pure e-commerce players will likely have to establish some sort of offline merchandising presence.[68]

COORDINATING DIRECT MARKETING AND E-COMMERCE IN THE IMC PROGRAM ❺

As you have seen in previous chapters, the wide variety of promotional tools available to a marketer poses a tremendous challenge with respect to coordination in the IMC program. Organizations are looking to achieve the synergy that can come when various promotion options reach the consumer with a common and compelling message. However, to work effectively with various promotional tools, functional specialists both inside and outside an organization need to be employed. It then becomes a very real problem to get the promotions manager, special events manager, sales promotion manager, and now direct marketing and e-commerce managers to work in harmony. And as we have seen in the e-commerce operation, there are many enabling organizations that are critical to setting up and managing the e-commerce operation.

The evolution and growing popularity of direct marketing and e-commerce raise the challenge of achieving integrated marketing communications to new heights. In particular, the development of marketing databases and the strategic applications available through profiling and data mining commonly lead to interdepartmental rivalries and can create major conflicts between the promotional managers. And the diversity of tools can put a strain on a company's relationship with its main promotion agencies as well. The marketing database is a powerful source of information about the customer; those who do not have direct access to this information will be envious of those who do. Additionally, the growing use of direct-marketing campaigns and e-commerce operations will likely mean that someone else's budget is being cut. Typically, direct-marketing programs and e-commerce operations come at the expense of conventional advertising campaigns that might have been run on television, in magazines, or in other mass media.[69] Since direct marketing and e-commerce take dollars from those activities that have been the staples of traditional ad agency business, it is easy to see why advertising agencies view these forms of promotion with some resentment.[70] Similarly, it is easy to see why large advertising agencies are interested in buying up smaller, fast-growing direct-marketing and e-commerce enabler companies.[71] If you can't beat 'em, buy 'em!

There are no simple solutions for achieving integrated marketing communications, but one approach that many organizations are experimenting with is

---

68. Richard Wise and Richard Christner, "On Again, Off Again," *Business 2.0,* February 2000, 257.
69. Kate Fitzgerald, "Beyond Advertising," *Advertising Age,* August 3, 1998, 1, 14.
70. Jim Osterman, "This Changes Everything," *Adweek,* May 15, 1995, 44–45.
71. Sally Goll Beatty, "Interpublic Group Considers Move into Hot Field of Direct Marketing," *The Wall Street Journal,* April 19, 1996, B3.

the establishment of a marketing-communications manager, or marcom manager for short.[72] A **marcom manager** plans an organization's overall communications program and oversees the various functional specialists inside and outside the organization to ensure that they are working together to deliver the desired message to the customer.

One company that has experimented with this marcom manager system is AT&T. Like its telecommunications rivals, AT&T makes heavy use of direct-marketing programs, e-commerce, and mass-media advertising to reach out and touch its customers. George Burnett, the company's marcom manager, explains the value of integrating direct mail and advertising this way: "Honestly, I think it is simplicity and clarity. . . . That is one of the goals of integrated communications, because in this complicated world, adding complication on top of the competitiveness is really not in our customers' interest."[73]

Burnett adds emphasis to a theme that has been developed throughout this book. Perhaps the major challenge in the world of promotion today is to find ways to break through the clutter of competitors' promotion, get customers' attention, and make a point with them. If the various programs an organization employs are sending different messages or mixed signals, the organization is only hurting itself. To achieve the synergy that will allow it to overcome the clutter of today's marketplace, an organization has no choice but to pursue integrated marketing communications.

From the standpoint of direct marketing and e-commerce, the firm must ensure that these programs follow through on the synergy of one-voice communication. This can be difficult because, as we have seen, direct marketing and e-commerce are only partly about communication. They also constitute an important transaction program for a firm. To carefully coordinate communication and transaction goals with the overall promotional program is indeed a challenging task in integrated marketing communications.

---

72. Don E. Schultz, Stanley I. Tannenbaum, and Robert F. Lauterborn, *Integrated Marketing Communications* (Lincolnwood, IL: NTC Business Books, 1993).
73. Gary Levin, "AT&T Exec: Customer Access Goal of Integration," *Advertising Age,* October 10, 1994, S1.

SUMMARY

1 Describe the relationship between direct marketing and e-commerce.

Direct marketing is the traditional promotional/marketing process whereby marketers use direct contact with consumers or business buyers with the intent of communicating information or bringing about a transaction. The direct contact can take place by telephone, through the mail, or through major mass media from the seller's side. From the buyer's side, contact with the seller has traditionally taken place through the mail or by phone. The scope and nature of e-commerce is almost exactly the same as direct marketing. In using an e-commerce structure and methods, marketers make direct contact with consumers and business buyers; they intend to communicate information, and they hope to bring about a transaction through the contact. There are actually two key differences. First, and most important, is the mode of the transaction. The transaction in direct marketing takes place through traditional means of contact between buyers and sellers—phone or mail. In e-commerce, the transaction is electronic and typically takes place by computer and the Internet, although wireless devices will become a common means of conducting transactions as well. The second key difference is that all transactions in e-commerce are direct-marketing transactions, but not all direct-marketing transactions are e-commerce. In other words, e-commerce is an electronic version of direct marketing.

2 Identify the three primary purposes served by direct marketing.

Many types of organizations are increasing their expenditures on direct marketing. These expenditures serve three primary purposes: potent tools for closing sales with customers, identifying prospects for future contacts, and for offering information and incentives that help foster brand loyalty. The growing popularity of direct marketing can be attributed to several factors. Direct marketers make consumption convenient: Credit cards, 800 numbers, and now the Internet take the hassle out of shopping. Additionally, today's computing power, which allows marketers to build and mine large customer information files, has enhanced direct marketing's impact. The emphasis on producing and tracking measurable outcomes is also well received by marketers in an era when everyone is trying to do more with less.

3 Identify the dimensions of database marketing and its applications.

A marketing database is a natural extension of a firm's internal mailing list, but includes information about individual customers and their specific preferences and purchasing patterns. A marketing database allows organizations to identify and focus their efforts on their best customers. Recognizing and reinforcing preferred customers can be a potent strategy for building loyalty. Cross-selling opportunities also emerge once a database is in place. In addition, as marketers gain more information about the motivations of current best customers, insights usually emerge about how to attract new customers.

4 Describe a model of e-commerce.

E-commerce can be described in a model that represents seven stages in an e-commerce operation:

- Identifying customers
- Attracting customers
- Communication
- Personalize and customize
- Exchange
- Payment, fulfillment, and follow-up
- Profiling

Setting up and managing an e-commerce operation is not so much a matter of learning about how e-commerce works, per se, as it is learning to set up and manage relationships with facilitators. There are hundreds of companies out there ready and able to help a firm at each stage of its e-commerce operation. In the language of e-commerce, these firms are called "enabler" companies. At each stage of an e-commerce operation, enabler service firms are available to make the hardware, software, tools, and transaction platforms that build the infrastructure of an e-commerce operation.

5 Discuss the integrated marketing communications issues related to direct marketing and e-commerce.

Direct marketing and e-commerce constitute a special challenge for firms when it comes to integrating these promotional tools into the overall IMC program. First, direct marketing and e-commerce often draw funds away from the advertising effort, creating a strain on the relationship with a firm's advertising agency. Second, direct marketing and e-commerce are only partly about communication. They also constitute an important transaction program for a firm. To carefully coordinate communication and transaction goals with the overall promotional program is indeed a challenging task in integrated marketing communications.

KEY TERMS

direct marketing, 344
e-commerce, 344
cost per inquiry (CPI), 351
cost per order (CPO), 351
database marketing, 351
mailing list, 351
internal lists, 352

external lists, 352
marketing database, 353
RFM analysis, 355
frequency-marketing programs, 356
cross-selling, 356
direct mail, 357
telemarketing, 359

infomercial, 360
bind-in insert cards, 361
platforms, 372
fulfillment, 372
back-end networks, 373
profiling, 374
marcom manager, 376

QUESTIONS FOR REVIEW AND CRITICAL THINKING

1. Direct marketing is defined as an interactive system of marketing. Explain the meaning of the phrase "interactive system." Give an example of a noninteractive system. How would such a system be helpful in the cultivation of brand loyalty?

2. For the next ten days, identify ten direct-marketing materials you encounter. This can include direct mail sent to you as well as magazine, television, or radio direct-response ads. Now, visit some Web sites that offer you both information and the opportunity to buy products. Which method of direct marketing do you prefer?

3. Review the major forces that have promoted the growth in popularity of direct marketing. Can you come up with any reasons why its popularity might be peaking? What are the threats to its continuing popularity as a marketing tool?

4. Describe the various categories of information that a credit card company might use to enhance its internal mailing list. For each category, comment on the possi-

ble value of the information for improving the company's market segmentation strategy.

5. Discuss the different media applications in direct marketing. Which medium seems to be have the most advantages?

6. How do business-to-consumer and business-to-business e-commerce compare? Do you regularly buy items over the Internet? How big do you think B2C e-commerce will be?

7. Go to a Web site that offers you the opportunity to place an order with the firm. How do you rate the design of the site? Did the page load quickly? Was the site easy to maneuver? Were you able to make contact by phone as well as electronically? Was the site good enough so that you would feel comfortable placing an order?

8. Now that you have learned about profiling as both a privacy issue and a strategic issue, what are your thoughts about it? Do you believe it should be restricted or regulated?

EXPERIENTIAL EXERCISES

1. **In-class exercise.** Divide the class in half. One half takes the position that direct marketing and e-commerce are promotional tools. The other half takes the position that they are really alternative distribution systems. What general conclusions can you draw from the debate?

2. **Out-of-class exercise.** Spend an hour watching television, with the goal of viewing an advertisement by a direct marketer. What product was offered? Was the offer unique? Can the product be found in stores in your area? Describe what immediate action the advertiser wants you to take.

USING THE INTERNET

Exercise 1

A great many companies rushed into the Internet-based home fulfillment market, trying to be the one-stop shop for household groceries and like products. Some are managing; others have already been acquired or have gone out of business. Whole Foods Markets (which owns several chains of organic/healthy food stores, under various brands) launched and then shut down a Web site aimed at home fulfillment, abandoning online sales in favor of partnering with another company, Gaiam.com, already experienced with mail-order sales. Visit some or all of the following sites:

WebVan
http://www.webvan.com

NetGrocer
http://www.netgrocer.com

Kozmo
http://www.kozmo.com

Drugstore.com
http://www.drugstore.com

Peapod.com
http://www.peapod.com

Streamline.com
http://www.streamline.com

Gaiam.com
http://www.gaiam.com

1. How do the various ventures differ in their targeted markets?

2. To which consumer needs do the services attempt to appeal?

3. How does each site use its home page to convince you to walk in the "virtual door"?

Exercise 2

In the war for customers' attention, Internet-based businesses have used two direct-advertising weapons: targeted e-mail and personalized Web site advertising. As every new offense helps new defenses evolve (and vice versa), various companies have provided antidotes to both.

While one person might appreciate targeted e-mail (especially where they've "opted in" to receiving it, for example, by checking off a box on a site subscription form, to be notified of special offers), another might consider it spam. Similarly, some Web users are bothered by the near ubiquitous advertising (especially distracting animated banners).

Several companies have developed tools to let users filter out spam, or block out the banner ads appearing on Web pages. Visit:

AdSubtract
http://www.adsubtract.com

Junkbusters
http://www.junkbusters.com

1. How does the Internet differ from other media (broadcast, television, and print, in particular) in how it permits end consumers to filter the advertising content out of what they absorb?

2. What sort of legal or intellectual property issues might arise around the process of "stripping" content of its ads?

After reading this chapter, you will be able to:

1. Explain the importance and growth of sales promotion as a promotional mix tool.

2. Describe the main sales promotion techniques used in the consumer market.

3. Describe the main sales promotion techniques used in the trade and business markets.

4. Explain how new media, including the Internet, are affecting the use of sales promotion.

5. Identify the risks of using sales promotion.

CHAPTER 11

"WHY IS OUR AWARD PROGRAM SO POPULAR WITH FREQUENT TRAVELERS? WE'RE IN EVERY CITY THEY FREQUENT."

As a business traveler you earn free vacations faster with Marriott's Honored Guest Award program. With over 250 locations worldwide, we're doing business wherever you're doing business. To join the program call 1-800-648-8024. For reservations, call your travel agent or 1-800-228-9290.

Marriott
HOTELS · RESORTS · SUITES

WE MAKE IT HAPPEN FOR YOU™

Video games, skateboards, dollhouses—this is all fun and games. Not quite. In the $23-billion-a-year toy industry, the stakes are too high for competitors to have much fun at all. And the challenges are particularly tough for industry leader Toys "R" Us. Everyone is out to get an industry leader, and Warren Kornblum, senior VP and chief marketing officer, is using all forms of promotion to protect the company's leadership position.

The need to rely on broad-based promotions can be traced back to the early 1990s. At that time, Toys "R" Us watched its market share get sniped at by formidable foes. Wal-Mart expanded its toy departments and made toys a key draw for shoppers at the Wal-Mart Super-Centers that were being put in place. Kmart reconfigured its stores and gave more shelf space to toys. And upstart K-B Toys used an arsenal of tiny shops to divert billions of dollars of toy spending into its coffers.

Toys "R" Us was shell-shocked. The toy giant's first competitive reaction was to tweak the merchandise and fiddle with the store layouts. But that wasn't good enough. Between 1990 and 1997, market share fell from 25 percent to 18 percent. To add insult to injury, in 1998, Wal-Mart officially became the largest toy retailer in the United States—ouch! The loss of industry leadership motivated Kornblum to look for a more aggressive response to competition. That response was a new marketing plan that was anchored primarily in new and innovative promotions.

The first step was to rein in the scattered marketing effort and create fewer but more robust promotional campaigns. As

an example, Toys "R" Us teamed with Buzz Lightyear and was a key partner in the launch of the movie *Toy Story 2*. The main strategy in this promotion was an innovative "scan and win" promotion that lured shoppers to Toys "R" Us stores and got them interacting with the *Toy Story* characters. This is how it worked. Toys "R" Us distributed 250 million unique UPC (universal product code) game pieces through newspaper inserts. Buzz Lightyear and Woody encouraged consumers to stop by Toys "R" Us stores and scan in. When they arrived armed with their UPC game piece, players held the UPC up to scanners placed throughout the store to see if they had won. Prizes included a $1 million grand prize, trips to Disney World, Chevy Astro Vans, and $1,000 Toys "R" Us shopping sprees. The results were powerful. One million consumers scanned in to see if they had won a prize, and store traffic increased dramatically.[1]

But in-store promotions were only the first in a series of sales promotion techniques used by Toys "R" Us to help bolster sagging market share. Other techniques included sponsorship of major league baseball's Diamond Skills campaign aimed at developing youth baseball skills. Stores featured promotions with prizes like the chance to throw out the ceremonial first ball at the All-Star Game. Another sales promotion was sponsorship of the Fox Kids World Tour, a traveling interactive theme park that showcased the Fox Kids Network shows. Promotions like these are helping Toys "R" Us reclaim its leadership in the toy industry (see Exhibit 11.1).

EXHIBIT 11.1

Toys "R" Us began relying heavily on sales promotion as a way to recapture its leadership in the toy industry.

1.   Dan Hanover, "The Real Toy Story," *Promo*, April 2000, 84–88.

INTRODUCTION

Sales promotion is a key alternative for marketers within the promotional mix. As the Toys "R" Us example highlights, sales promotions like contests, sweepstakes, sponsorships, and merchandise giveaways can attract attention and give new energy to the promotional effort. In contrast, mass-media advertising suffers from having effects that are hard to measure in the short run. This is not the case with sales promotion. Sales promotion is conspicuous and designed to make things happen in a hurry. Used properly, sales promotion is capable of almost instant demand stimulation—as Toys "R" Us realized with the "scan and win" promotion. Sales promotion is also emerging as a global force as firms try to introduce U.S. brands into distant markets. The "message" in a sales promotion features price reduction (or free sample), a prize, or some other incentive for consumers to try a brand or visit a retailer. Sales promotion has proven to be a popular complement to mass-media advertising because it accomplishes things advertising cannot.

Formally defined, **sales promotion** is the use of incentive techniques that create a perception of greater brand value among consumers, the trade, and business buyers. The intent is to create a short-term increase in sales by motivating trial use and encouraging larger or repeat purchases. Consumer-market sales promotion includes coupons, price-off deals, premiums, contests and sweepstakes, sampling and trial offers, brand (product) placements, rebates, loyalty/frequency programs, phone and gift cards, and event sponsorship. All are ways of inducing household consumers to purchase a firm's brand rather than a competitor's. Notice that some incentives reduce price, offer a reward, or encourage a trip to the retailer. Trade-market sales promotion uses point-of-purchase displays, incentives, allowances, or cooperative advertising as ways of motivating distributors, wholesalers, and retailers to stock and feature a firm's brand in their merchandising programs. Sales promotions designed to cultivate business buyers include trade shows, premiums, incentives, and loyalty/ frequency programs.

THE IMPORTANCE AND GROWTH OF SALES PROMOTION

Sales promotion is designed to affect demand differently from advertising. As we have learned throughout the text, most advertising is designed to have awareness-, image-, and preference-building effects for a brand over the long run. The role of sales promotion, on the other hand, is primarily to elicit an immediate purchase from a customer. Coupons, samples, rebates, sweepstakes, and similar techniques offer a consumer an immediate incentive to choose one brand over another, as exemplified in Exhibit 11.2, which shows Pepsi logo items as a form of premium available to consumers.

Other sales promotions, such as brand placements (getting the company's brand placed in a movie or on a TV show) and frequency programs (for example, frequent-flyer programs), provide an affiliation value with a brand, which increases a consumer's ability and desire to identify with a particular brand. Sales promotions featuring price reductions, such as coupons, are effective in the convenience goods category, where frequent purchases, brand switching, and a perceived homogeneity among brands characterize consumer behavior.

Sales promotions are used across all consumer goods categories and in the trade market as well. When a firm determines that a more immediate response is called for—whether the target customer is a household, business buyer, distributor, or retailer—sales promotions are designed to provide the incentive. The goals for sales

EXHIBIT 11.2

Sales promotion techniques, like these premiums from Pepsi, give a consumer a reason to choose one brand versus another.

promotion versus advertising are compared in Exhibit 11.3. Notice the key differences in the goals for these different forms of promotion. Sales promotion encourages more immediate and short-term responses, while the purpose of advertising is to cultivate loyalty and repeat purchases over the long term.

The Importance of Sales Promotion

The importance of sales promotion in the United States should not be underestimated. Sales promotion may not seem as stylish and sophisticated as mass media advertising, but expenditures on this tool are impressive. In recent years, sales promotion expenditures have grown at an annual rate of about 9 to 12 percent, compared to a 6 to 8 percent rate for advertising.[2] By 1999, the investment by marketers in sales promotions reached nearly $95 billion.[3] Add to that figure consumer savings by redeeming coupons and rebates and the figure exceeds $150 billion.[4] Exhibit 11.4 shows the spending, percentage increase, and proportion of total sales promotion spending for the most frequently used sales promotion techniques.

It is important to realize that full-service advertising agencies specializing in advertising planning, creative preparation, and media placement typically do not prepare sales promotion materials for clients. These activities are normally assigned to sales promotion agencies that specialize in couponing, event management, premiums, or other forms of sales promotion that require specific skills and creative preparation.

2.   Russ Brown, "Sales Promotion," *Marketing and Media Decisions,* February 1990, 74.
3.   Peter Breen, "Seeds of Change," *Promotion Trends 2000,* Annual Report of the Promotion Industry Report compiled by *Promo,* May 2000, A3.
4.   Betsy Spethmann, "So Much for Targeting," *Promo,* April 2000, 69.

Purpose of Sales Promotion	Purpose of Advertising
Stimulate short-term demand	Cultivate long-term demand
Encourage brand switching	Encourage brand loyalty
Induce trial use	Encourage repeat purchases
Promote price orientation	Promote image/feature orientation
Obtain immediate, often measurable results	Obtain long-term effects, often difficult to measure

EXHIBIT 11.3

Sales promotion and advertising serve very different purposes in the promotional mix. How would you describe the key difference between the two based on the features listed here?

The development and management of an effective sales promotion program requires a major commitment by a firm. Procter & Gamble estimates that during any given year, 25 percent of sales force time and 30 percent of brand management time are spent on designing, implementing, and overseeing sales promotions.[5] The rise in the use of sales promotion and the enormous amount of money being spent on various programs make it one of the most prominent forms of marketing activity. But again, it must be undertaken only under certain conditions and then carefully executed for specific reasons.

Growth in the Use of Sales Promotion

Marketers have shifted the emphasis of their promotional spending over the past decade. Most of the shift has been away from mass-media advertising and toward consumer and trade sales promotions. Currently, the budget allocation stands at

EXHIBIT 11.4

There are several different sales promotion techniques relied on by marketers. This list shows spending on those techniques as well as the amount spent on promotion agency services and research.

Promotion Industry Gross Revenues (in millions)			
Segment	1999 Revenues	Increase	% of Total
Premium Incentives	$26,300	5.2%	28.1%
Ad Specialties	14,800	12.1%	15.8%
P-O-P	14,400	5.1%	15.4%
Sponsorships	7,600	11.8%	8.1%
Coupons	6,980	8.2%	7.5%
Printing	6,200	10.7%	6.6%
Licensing	5,500	5.0%	5.9%
Fulfillment	3,297	20.1%	3.5%
Agency	2,178	49.2%	2.3%
Interactive	1,471	44.2%	1.6%
Sweeps	1,380	15.0%	1.5%
Research	1,340	8.9%	1.4%
Sampling	1,120	10.9%	1.2%
In-store	870	8.7%	0.9%
Total	$93,436	9.4%	

Source: Promo Magazine May 2000, A5

5.   Robert D. Buzzell, John A. Quelch, and Walter J. Salmon, "The Costly Bargain of Sales Promotion," *Harvard Business Review* (March/April 1990), 141–149.

about 46 percent for advertising, 29 percent for trade promotions, and 25 percent for consumer promotions.[6] There are several reasons why many marketers have shifted their funds from mass media advertising to sales promotions, as follows.

Demand for Greater Accountability. In an era of cost cutting and downsizing, companies are demanding greater accountability across all functions, including marketing, advertising, and promotions. When activities are evaluated for their contribution to sales and profits, it is often difficult to draw specific conclusions regarding the effects of advertising. Conversely, the immediate effects of sales promotions are typically easier to document. Another plus for the accountability of sales promotion is that ACNielsen and IPSOs–ASI research firms have developed Market Drivers, a new research program that evaluates the effects of sales promotions.[7] The program combines Nielsen's store sales data with the IPSOs–ASI copy-testing measures to identify the effects of sales promotions versus ads in communicating to target segments. But this measurement is not cheap. The companies estimate that using the Market Drivers program runs about $100,000 per project.

Short-Term Orientation. Several factors have created a short-term orientation among managers. Pressures from stockholders to produce better quarter-by-quarter revenue and profit per share is one factor. A bottom-line mentality is another. Many organizations are developing marketing plans—with rewards and punishments for performance—based on short-term revenue generation.[8] This being the case, tactics that can have short-term effects are sought. Nabisco found that a contest directed at kids had just the sort of short-term effect the firm was looking for. In its "Don't eat the winning Oreo" promotion, which featured a Volkswagen Beetle filled with Oreos, sales jumped 29 percent during the time the promotion was running.[9]

Consumer Response to Promotions. The precision shopper of the nineties is demanding greater value across all purchase situations, and the trend is "battering overpriced brands."[10] These precision shoppers search for extra value in every product purchase. Coupons, premiums, price-off deals, and other sales promotions increase the value of a brand in these shoppers' minds. This positive response goes beyond value-oriented consumers. For consumers who are not well informed about the average price in a product category, a brand featuring a coupon or price-off promotion is sensed to be a good deal and will likely be chosen over competitive brands.[11] Overall, consumers report that coupons, price, and good value for their money influence 75 to 85 percent of their brand choice decisions.[12] (Be careful here—coupons, price, and value, in particular, do not necessarily mean consumers are choosing the *lowest*-price item, only that these sales promotion techniques act as an incentive to purchase the brand using the promotion.)

Proliferation of Brands. Each year, thousands of new brands are introduced into the consumer market. The drive by marketers to design products for specific market segments to satisfy ever more narrowly defined needs has caused a proliferation of brands that creates a mind-dulling maze for consumers. At any point in time, consumers can choose from approximately 64 spaghetti sauces, 103 snack chips,

6. Breen, "Seeds of Change."
7. James B. Arndorfer, "ACNielsen Market Drivers Will Gauge Promos' Punch," *Advertising Age,* February 23, 1998, 8.
8. "What Happened to Advertising," *Business Week,* September 23, 1991, 66.
9. Stephanie Thompson, "Nabisco Stuffs More into Oreo Promotion," *Advertising Age,* January 10, 2000, 8.
10. Rahul Jacob, "Beyond Quality and Value," *Fortune,* Autumn/Winter 1993, 8–11.
11. Leigh McAlister, "A Model of Consumer Behavior," *Marketing Communications,* April 1987, 26–28.
12. *Cox Direct 20th Annual Survey of Promotional Practices,* Chart 22, 1998, 37.

EXHIBIT 11.5

As you can see by this shelf of spaghetti sauces, getting the consumer to pay attention to any one brand is quite the challenge. This proliferation of brands in the marketplace has made marketers search for ways to attract attention to their brands, and sales promotion techniques often provide an answer. Notice the point-of-purchase promotion attached to the shelves.

54 laundry detergents, 91 cold remedies, and 69 disposable diaper varieties.[13] As you can see in Exhibit 11.5, gaining attention in this blizzard of brands is no easy task. Often, marketers turn to sales promotions—product placements, contests, coupons, and premiums—to gain some recognition in a consumer's mind and stimulate a trial purchase.

Increased Power of Retailers. Retailers such as Home Depot, The Gap, Toys "R" Us, and the most powerful of all, Wal-Mart, now dominate retailing in the United States. These powerful companies have responded quickly and accurately to the new environment for retailing, where consumers are demanding more and better products and services at lower prices. Because of the lower-price component of the retailing environment, these companies are demanding more deals from manufacturers. Many of the deals are delivered in terms of trade-oriented sales promotions: P–O–P displays, slotting fees (payment for shelf space), case allowances, and cooperative advertising allowances. In the end, manufacturers use more and more sales promotion devices to gain and maintain good relations with the new, powerful retailers—a critical link to the consumer.

Media Clutter. A nagging and traditional problem in the advertising process is clutter. Many advertisers target the same customers because their research has led them to the same conclusion about whom to target. The result is that advertising

13.   Gabriella Stern, "Multiple Varieties of Established Brands Muddle Consumers, Make Retailers Mad," *The Wall Street Journal,* January 24, 1992, B1, B9.

media are cluttered with ads all seeking the attention of a common target. One way to break through the clutter is to feature a sales promotion. In print ads, the featured deal is often a coupon. In broadcast advertising, sweepstakes and premium offers can attract listeners' and viewers' attention. The combination of advertising and creative sales promotions has proven to be a good way to break through the clutter.[14]

SALES PROMOTION IN THE CONSUMER MARKET

It is clear that U.S. consumer-product firms have made a tremendous commitment to sales promotion in their overall marketing plans. During the 1970s, consumer goods marketers allocated only about 30 percent of their budgets to sales promotion, with about 70 percent allocated to mass-media advertising. Today, some estimates show that for many consumer goods firms, the percentages are just the opposite, with nearly 75 percent being spent on sales promotions.[15] With this sort of commitment to the sales promotion process in the promotional mix, let's examine in detail the objectives for sales promotion in the consumer market and the wide range of techniques used.

Objectives for Consumer-Market Sales Promotion

To help ensure the proper application of sales promotion, specific strategic objectives should be set. The following basic objectives can be pursued with sales promotion in the consumer market:

Stimulate Trial Purchase. When a firm wants to attract new users, sales promotion tools can reduce the consumer's risk of trying something new. A reduced price or offer of a rebate may stimulate trial purchase. When Keebler wanted to attract trial use in eight key Hispanic markets, it created the Keebler Kids Club, which featured giveaways and the Keebler Kids Quiz Show, which gave Spanish-speaking youngsters the chance to win college scholarships.[16] Exhibit 11.6 shows an attempt to stimulate trial use.

Stimulate Repeat Purchases. In-package coupons good for the next purchase, or the accumulation of points with repeated purchases, can keep consumers loyal to a particular brand. The most prominent frequency programs are found in the airline industry, where competitors such as Delta, American, and United try to retain their most lucrative customers by enrolling them in frequency programs. Frequent flyers can earn free travel, hotel stays, gifts, and numerous other perks through the programs. Recently, fast-food chains such as McDonald's have started frequency programs (the McExtra card) to keep customers coming back in the brand switching–prone fast-food industry.[17]

Stimulate Larger Purchases. Price reductions or two-for-one sales can motivate consumers to stock up on a brand, thus allowing firms to reduce inventory or increase cash flow. Shampoo is often double-packaged to offer a value to consumers. Exhibit 11.7 is a sales promotion aimed at stimulating a larger purchase.

Introduce a New Brand. Because sales promotion can attract attention and motivate trial purchase, it is commonly used for new brand introduction. When the

14. Kate Fitzgerald, "Sega Screams Its Way to the Top," *Advertising Age,* March 20, 1995, S2.
15. *Cox Direct 20th Annual Survey,* Chart 24, 1998, 39.
16. "Best in the World," *Promo,* November 1995, 39.
17. Louise Kramer, "McD's Eyes Rollout of Loyalty Card," *Advertising Age,* April 27, 1998, 3.

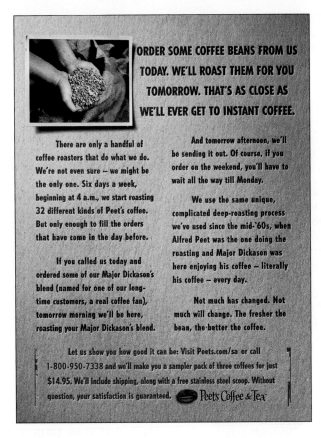

EXHIBIT 11.6

One objective for sales promotion in the consumer market is to stimulate trial use. Here, Peets Coffee & Tea is encouraging consumers to try their product by offering a sample pack available through the Web or toll-free number.

EXHIBIT 11.7

Sales promotions are often used to encourage larger purchases. This coupon for Spaghettios offers consumers the chance to stock up on three cans.

makers of Curad bandages wanted to introduce their new kid-size bandage, 7.5 million sample packs were distributed in McDonald's Happy Meal sacks. The promotion was a huge success, with initial sales exceeding estimates by 30 percent.[18]

Combat or Disrupt Competitors' Strategies. Because sales promotions often motivate consumers to buy in larger quantities or try new brands, they can be used to disrupt competitors' marketing strategies. If a firm knows that one of its competitors is launching a new brand or initiating a new advertising campaign, a well-timed sales promotion offering deep discounts or extra quantity can disrupt the competitors' strategy. Add to the original discount an in-package coupon for future purchases, and a marketer can severely compromise competitors' efforts. *TV Guide* magazine used a sweepstakes promotion to combat competition. In an effort to address increasing competition from newspaper TV supplements and cable-guide magazines, *TV Guide* ran a Shopping Spree Sweepstakes in several regional markets. Winners won $200 shopping sprees in grocery stores—precisely the location where 65 percent of *TV Guide* sales are realized.[19]

Contribute to Integrated Marketing Communications. In conjunction with advertising, direct marketing, public relations, and other programs being

---

18. Glen Heitsmith, "Still Bullish on Promotion," *Promo,* July 1994, 40.
19. "TV Guide Tunes in Sweepstakes," *Promo,* November 1995, 1, 50.

carried out by a firm, sales promotion can add yet another type of communication to the mix. Sales promotions suggest an additional value, with price reductions, premiums, or the chance to win a prize. This is an additional and different message within the overall communications effort.

MEDIA

COUCH POTATO COUPON FESTIVAL

Couch potatoes are always portrayed as inactive, passive, and generally out of it. No more. Now couch potatoes can become active consumers without ever putting down the remote control. Enhanced TV now offers consumers promotions that can be redeemed via the remote control—coupons, special offers, free products—just like going out and really shopping! The technique is catching on with automakers, financial services firms, and restaurants.

The interactive promotional system is offered by RespondTV and Wink Communications and works this way. Internet-based technology is used to seed URL addresses as triggers for communication in television programming. Each URL "trigger" appears as an icon on viewers' screens. The viewers click their remotes on the icon to see the offer—information, a coupon, or a product sample—and respond to a menu of choices. Domino's Pizza ran an interactive promotion during a *Star Trek* Marathon on UPN network's San Francisco affiliate station. Domino's nine ads during the programming were tagged with offers for free pizza and soft drinks, and 150 viewers responded.

Analysts predict that there will be set-top boxes—appliances that route Internet access through TV cables—in about 30 million homes by 2004. (They're in about a million homes now.) Richard Fisher, the director of RespondTV, feels that when 3 to 5 million set-top boxes are installed, marketers will get excited about this new media distribution method for coupons and special offers. Until then, technology providers will work on refining the fine art of couch-potato promotions.

Source: "Talking Back to the TV," *Promo*, April 2000, 56–57.

Consumer-Market Sales Promotion Techniques ❷

Several techniques are used to stimulate demand and attract attention in the consumer market. Some of these are coupons, price-off deals, premiums and advertising specialties, contests and sweepstakes, sampling and trial offers, phone and gift cards, brand (product) placement, rebates, frequency (continuity) programs, and event sponsorship.

Coupons. A **coupon** entitles a buyer to a designated reduction in price for a product or service. Coupons are the oldest and most widely used form of sales promotion. The first use of a coupon is traced to around 1895, when the C. W. Post Company used a penny-off coupon as a way to get people to try its Grape-Nuts cereal. Annually, about 300 billion coupons are distributed to American consumers, with redemption rates ranging from 2 percent for gum purchases to nearly 45 percent for disposable diaper purchases. Exhibit 11.8 shows coupon redemption rates for several product categories. In 1999, marketers invested $6.9 billion in coupons as a sales promotion technique.[20] And they are finding new and innovative ways to reach consumers with coupons, as the New Media box highlights.

There are five advantages to the coupon as a sales promotion tool:

- They make it possible to give a discount to a price-sensitive consumer while still selling the product at full price to other consumers. A price-sensitive customer takes the time to clip the coupon and carry it to the store; a regular consumer merely buys the product at full price.
- The coupon-redeeming customer is often a competitive-brand user, so the coupon can induce brand switching.

20. "Back to Basics," *Promotion Trends 2000,* Annual Report of the Promotions Industry compiled by *Promo,* May 2000, A20.

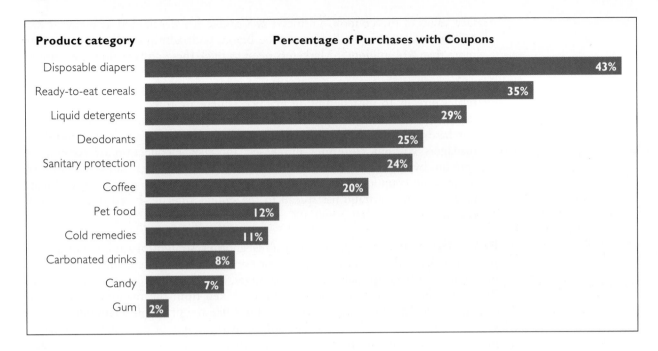

Product category   **Percentage of Purchases with Coupons**

Product category	Percentage
Disposable diapers	43%
Ready-to-eat cereals	35%
Liquid detergents	29%
Deodorants	25%
Sanitary protection	24%
Coffee	20%
Pet food	12%
Cold remedies	11%
Carbonated drinks	8%
Candy	7%
Gum	2%

EXHIBIT 11.8

Percentage of purchases made with coupons in various product categories.

- A manufacturer can control the timing and distribution of coupons. This way a retailer is not implementing price discounts inappropriately.
- A coupon is an excellent method of stimulating repeat purchases. Once a consumer has been attracted to a brand, with or without a coupon, an in-package coupon can induce repeat purchase. The long-standing belief is that in-package coupons stimulate greater brand loyalty than media-distributed coupons. While an in-package coupon is designed to encourage repeat purchase and brand loyalty, retailers believe that coupons attached to the store shelf and distributed at the point of purchase are the most effective.[21]
- Coupons can get regular users to trade up within a brand array. For example, users of low-price disposable diapers may be willing to try a premium variety with a coupon.

The use of coupons is not without its problems. There are administrative burdens and risks with coupon use:

- While coupon price incentives and the timing of distribution can be controlled by a marketer, the timing of redemption cannot. Some consumers redeem coupons immediately; others hold them for months. Expiration dates printed on coupons help focus the redemption time but may compromise the impact of coupons.
- Coupons do attract competitors' users and some nonusers, but there is no way to prevent current users from redeeming coupons with their regular purchases. Heavy redemption by regular buyers merely reduces a firm's profitability. This has led some firms to consider eliminating coupons from their arsenal of marketing tools.[22]
- Couponing entails careful administration. Coupon programs include much more than the cost of the face value of the coupon. There are costs for production and distribution and for retailer and manufacturer handling. In fact, the cost for handling, processing, and distribution of coupons is equal to about two-thirds of the

21. Data displayed in *Advertising Age,* May 10, 1993, S-5.
22. "P&G to Experiment with Ending Coupons," *Marketing News,* February 12, 1996, 11.

face value of the coupon.[23] Procter & Gamble has distributed as many as 773 million coupons for its Folgers coffee brand, with administrative costs totaling more than $14 million.[24] Marketers need to track these costs against the amount of product sold with and without coupon redemption.

- Fraud is a chronic and serious problem in the couponing process. The problem relates directly to misredemption practices. There are three types of misredemption that cost firms money: redemption of coupons by consumers who do not purchase the couponed brand; redemption of coupons by salesclerks and store managers without consumer purchases; and illegal collection or copying of coupons by individuals who sell them to unethical store merchants, who in turn redeem the coupons without the accompanying consumer purchases. Unfortunately, this sort of fraud has spread to the online, Internet-based distribution of coupons.[25]

Price-Off Deals. The price-off deal is another straightforward technique. A **price-off deal** offers a consumer cents or even dollars off merchandise at the point of purchase through specially marked packages. The typical price-off deal is a 10 to 25 percent price reduction. The reduction is taken from the manufacturer's profit margin rather than the retailer's. Manufacturers like the price-off technique because it is controllable. Plus, the price-off, judged at the point of purchase, can effect a positive price comparison against competitors. Consumers like a price-off deal because it is straightforward and automatically increases the value of a known brand. Regular users tend to stock up on an item during a price-off deal. Retailers are less enthusiastic about this technique. Price-off promotions can create inventory and pricing problems for retailers. Also, most price-off deals are snapped up by regular customers, so the retailer doesn't benefit from new business.

Premiums and Advertising Specialties. **Premiums** are items offered free, or at a reduced price, with the purchase of another item. Many firms offer a related product free, such as a free granola bar packed inside a box of granola cereal. Service firms, such as a car wash or dry cleaner, may use a two-for-one offer to persuade consumers to try the service.

There are two options available for the use of premiums. A **free premium** provides consumers with an item at no cost; the item is either included in the package of a purchased item or mailed to the consumer after proof of purchase is verified. The most frequently used free premium is an additional package of the original item or a free related item placed in the package. Some firms do offer unrelated free premiums, such as balls, toys, and trading cards. These types of premiums are particularly popular with cereal manufacturers.

A **self-liquidating premium** requires a consumer to pay most of the cost of the item received as a premium, as shown in Exhibit 11.9. Self-liquidating premiums are particularly effective with loyal customers. However, these types of premiums must be used cautiously. Unless the premium is related to a value-building strategy for a brand, it can, like other sales promotions, serve to focus consumer attention on the premium rather than on the benefits of the brand. Focusing on the premium rather than the brand erodes brand equity.

Advertising specialties have three key elements: a message, placed on a useful item, and given to consumers with no obligation. Popular advertising specialties are baseball caps, T-shirts, coffee mugs, computer mouse pads, pens, and calendars. Industry sources estimate that firms spend between $11 and 14 billion on advertising

23. *1998 Annual Report of the Promotion Industry,* S37.
24. "Coffee's On," *Promo,* February 1996, 48–49.
25. Michael Scroggie, "Online Coupon Debate," *Promo,* April 2000, 53.

EXHIBIT 11.9

One form of premium is the "self-liquidating" premium. What makes this offer by Jell-O a self-liquidating premium (no pun intended!)?

EXHIBIT 11.10

Instant winner sweepstakes are popular with consumers and generate excitement at the point of purchase.

specialties a year.[26] The Promotional Products Association International (http://www.promotion-clinic.ppa.org) puts promotional products into seventeen different categories ranging from buttons/badges/bumper stickers to jewelry and watches.[27]

Contests and Sweepstakes. Contests and sweepstakes can draw attention to a brand like no other sales promotion technique. Technically, there are important differences between the two. A **contest** has consumers compete for prizes based on skill or ability. Winners in a contest are determined by a panel of judges or based on which contestant comes closest to a predetermined criterion for winning, such as picking the total points scored in the Super Bowl. Contests tend to be somewhat expensive to administer because each entry must be judged against winning criteria.

A **sweepstakes** is a promotion in which winners are determined purely by chance. Consumers need only to enter their names in the sweepstakes as a criterion for winning. Official entry forms are often used as a way for consumers to enter the sweepstakes. Other popular types of sweepstakes use scratch-off cards. Instant-winner scratch-off cards tend to attract customers. Exhibit 11.10 shows an instant-winner sweepstakes run by Gillette. Gasoline retailers, grocery stores, and

---

26. "The Digital Sales Pitch," *Promotion Trends 2000,* Annual Report of the Promotions Industry compiled by *Promo,* May 2000, A19.
27. Dan S. Bagley III, *Understanding and Using Promotional Products* (Irving, TX: Promotional Products Association International, 1999), 6.

CAREERPROFILE

Name: Todd Holscher
Title: Assistant Brand Manager
Company: SC Johnson, Racine, WI, http://www.scjohnson.com
Education: B.S., Journalism/M.B.A., Advertising

Next time you see squeaky clean windows, think of Todd Holscher. Todd is an assistant brand manager for the Windex brand at SC Johnson. His job is planning and implementing marketing and sales promotion strategies for the brand.

"A lot of what I do involves trying to understand what's going on with consumer behavior," he says. "The first step in any sales promotion program is getting a clear picture of our current situation in the market." Using internal sales reports and standardized data from external sources, Todd looks for trends and changes that signal whether current strategies are working as planned or need to be refined. He might, for example, work with an advertising agency to develop and place freestanding inserts (FSIs) in local newspapers that include a coupon or other incentives to entice buyers. "One thing you have to think about with FSIs is whether your goal is to just deliver a coupon, to advertise the brand, or both," says Todd. "If you're launching a new product, the goal might be to build awareness and get trial. If it's an established brand, the FSIs main purpose may just be to deliver the coupon."

Often, sales promotional activities also have to be coordinated with external factors, such as the season. "There are definitely times of the year when consumers are more likely to purchase cleaning supplies," he explains. "We have to be cognizant of the timing of our promotions."

Todd also works hand-in-hand with SC Johnson's sales department to coordinate incentives and promotions for retailers. "In general, any type of sales promotion we can do to help consumers to feel strongly about our product fits the trade as well. They're interested in the same thing we are: satisfying consumers and increasing sales."

Finding the right mix of sales promotional tools can be challenging. "In an established business like ours, you are always looking for those marketing nuggets and tools that will make a big enough difference so that you'll become the preferred product in consumers' minds," he says. "Luckily, SC Johnson is a very innovative company that really works from an underlying desire to understand and satisfy consumers. That makes marketing's job much easier."

To learn more about sales promotion, visit these Web sites:

Sales Promotion magazine
http://www.sp-mag.com

Creative magazine
http://www.creativemag.com

Promo magazine
http://www.promomagazine.com

fast-food chains commonly use scratch-off card sweepstakes as a way of building and maintaining store traffic. Sweepstakes can also be designed so that repeated trips to the retail outlet are necessary to gather a complete set of winning cards. Research indicates that for contests and sweepstakes to be effective, marketers must design them in such a way that consumers perceive value in the prizes and find playing the games intrinsically interesting.[28]

Contests and sweepstakes can span the globe. British Airways ran a contest with the theme "The World's Greatest Offer," in which it gave away thousands of free airline tickets to London and other European destinations. While the contest increased awareness of the airline, a spokesperson said there was definitely another benefit: "We're creating a database with all these names. All those people who didn't win will be getting mail from us with information on other premium offers."[29]

Contests and sweepstakes often create excitement and generate interest for a brand, but the problems of administering these promotions are substantial. Primary among them are the regulations and restrictions on such promotions. Advertisers must be sure that the design and administration of a contest or sweepstakes complies with both federal and state laws. Each state may have slightly different regulations. The legal problems are complex enough that most firms hire agencies that specialize in contests and sweepstakes to administer the programs.

Another problem is that the game itself may become the consumer's primary focus, while the brand becomes secondary. The technique thus fails to build long-term consumer affinity for a brand. This problem is inherent in most forms of sales promotion, not just contests and sweepstakes.

The final problem with contests and sweepstakes relates to the IMC effort a firm may be attempting. It is hard to get any message across in the context of a game. The consumer's interest is focused on the game, rather than on any feature or value message included in the contest

28. James C. Ward and Ronald Paul Hill, "Designing Effective Promotional Games: Opportunities and Problems," *Journal of Advertising*, vol. 20, no. 3 (September 1991), 69–81.
29. Thomas R. King, "Marketers Bet Big with Contests to Trigger Consumer Spending," *The Wall Street Journal*, April 4, 1991, B8.

or sweepstakes communication. A related problem is that if a firm is trying to develop a quality or prestige image for a brand, contests and sweepstakes may contradict this goal.

Sampling and Trial Offers. Getting consumers to simply try a brand can have a powerful effect on future decision making. **Sampling** is a sales promotion technique designed to provide a consumer with an opportunity to use a brand on a trial basis with little or no risk. Saying that sampling is a popular technique is an understatement. Estimates suggest that nearly 90 percent of consumer-product companies use sampling in some manner and invest approximately $1.12 billion a year on the technique.[30] A recent survey shows that consumers are very favorable toward sampling, with 43 percent indicating that they would consider switching brands if they liked a free sample that was being offered.[31] Sampling is particularly useful for new products, but should not be reserved for new products alone. It can be used successfully for established brands with weak market share in specific geographic areas. Kraft recently put its sampling program "on tour" and handed out free samples of items from its existing product lines at Vince Gill concert sites.[32] Six techniques are used in sampling:

- **In-store sampling** is popular for food products and cosmetics. This is a preferred technique for many marketers because the consumer is at the point of purchase and may be swayed by a direct encounter with the brand. Increasingly, in-store demonstrators are handing out coupons as well as samples.
- **Door-to-door sampling** is extremely expensive because of labor costs, but it can be effective if the marketer has information that locates the target segment in a well-defined geographic area. Some firms enlist the services of newspaper delivery people, who pack the sample with daily or Sunday newspapers as a way of reducing distribution costs.
- **Mail sampling** allows samples to be delivered through the postal service. Again, the value here is that certain zip-code markets can be targeted. A drawback is that the sample must be small to be economically feasible. Specialty-sampling firms, such as Alternative Postal Delivery, provide targeted geodemographic door-to-door distribution as an alternative to the postal service.
- **Newspaper sampling** has become very popular in recent years and 42 percent of consumers report having received samples of health and beauty products in this manner.[33] Much like mail sampling, newspaper samples allow very specific geographic and geodemographic targeting.
- **On-package sampling,** a technique in which the sample item is attached to another product package, is useful for brands targeted to current customers. Attaching a small bottle of Ivory conditioner with a regular-sized container of Ivory shampoo is a logical sampling strategy.
- **Mobile sampling** is carried out by logo-emblazoned vehicles that dispense samples, coupons, and premiums to consumers at malls, shopping centers, fairgrounds, and recreational areas. Marketers at Pennzoil are finding that intercepting prospects while they're at play or engaged in activities that complement product use is a good way to influence awareness, use, and preference.[34]

Of course, sampling has its critics. Unless the product has a clear value and benefit over the competition, simple trial of the product is unlikely to persuade a

---

30. "Sampling Continues to Be a Popular Choice," *Advertising Age,* May 16, 1993, 2; and "Give and Take," *Promotion Trends 2000,* Annual Report of the Promotion Industry compiled by *Promo,* May 2000, A36.

31. *Cox Direct 20th Annual Survey,* 1998, 28.

32. Kate Fitzgerald, "Samples Go on Tour," *Advertising Age,* May 5, 1997, 37.

33. *Cox Direct 20th Annual Survey,* 1998, 27.

34. Jean Halliday, "Pennzoil Hits Road with Promotion for New Motor Oil," *Advertising Age,* June 15, 1998, 32.

consumer to switch brands. This is especially true for convenience goods because consumers perceive a high degree of similarity among brands, even after trying them. The perception of benefit and superiority may have to be developed through advertising in combination with sampling. In addition, sampling is expensive. This is especially true in cases where a sufficient quantity of a product, such as shampoo or laundry detergent, must be given away for a consumer to truly appreciate a brand's value. In-store sampling techniques are being devised that can reduce the cost of traditional sampling methods.[35] Finally, sampling can be a very imprecise process. Despite the emergence of special agencies to handle sampling programs, a firm can never completely ensure that the product is reaching the targeted audience.

Trial offers have the same goal as sampling—to induce consumer trial use of a brand—but they are used for more expensive items. Exercise equipment, appliances, watches, hand tools, and consumer electronics are typical of items offered on a trial basis. Trials offers can be free for low-priced products, as we saw in Exhibit 11.6. Or trials can be offered for as little as a day to as long as ninety days for more expensive items like vacuum cleaners or computer software. The expense to the firm, of course, can be formidable. Segments chosen for this sales promotion technique must have high sales potential.

Phone and Gift Cards. Phone and gift cards represent a new and increasingly popular form of sales promotion. This technique could be classified as a premium offer, but it has enough unique features to warrant separate classification as a sales promotion technique. The use of phone and gift cards is fairly straightforward. Manufacturers or retailers offer either for free or for purchase debit cards that provide the holder with either minutes of phone time or some preset spending limit in the case of a gift card. The cards are designed to be colorful and memorable. A wide range of marketers, from luxury car manufacturers like Lexus to retailers like The Gap, have made effective use of phone and gift cards.[36] In Exhibit 11.11, Oldsmobile is trying to lure shoppers to dealerships with a $50 gift card to Blockbuster Video.

Brand (Product) Placement. **Brand placement** (often erroneously referred to as product placement) is the sales promotion technique of getting a marketer's brand featured in movies and television shows. The use of a brand by actors and actresses or the mere association of a brand with a popular film or television show can create a positive image or, occasionally, a demonstrated sales impact for a brand. Marketers and advertisers used to think brand placements affected only consumers' perceptions of a brand, much like advertising. But recent brand placements have shown that the technique can have a sales impact like a traditional sales promotion. For example, consider these results:

- When British agent 007, James Bond, switched from his traditional Aston-Martin sports car to the new BMW Z3, a brand placement in the Bond film *Goldeneye,* along with a tightly coordinated dealer promotion program, resulted in 6,000 predelivery orders for the Z3.
- Sales of Nike sneakers and apparel jumped after the release of the hit movie *Forrest Gump.* The film featured star Tom Hanks getting a pair of Nike running shoes as a gift, which his character, Gump, believes is "the best gift anyone could get in the whole wide world." Later in the film, Gump wears a Nike T-shirt during a cross-country run.

35. Debbie Usery, "What's In-Store," *Promo,* May 2000, 54.
36. Carolyn Shea, "Calling All Cards: Pre-Paid Phone Cards are Racking Up Sales," *Promo,* March 1995, 42.

Every member of your family will want to get their hands on this.

WEB SIGHTING

Get a free $50 BLOCKBUSTER GiftCard when you test drive any new Silhouette or Oldsmobile.
And just like the GiftCard, the Silhouette will keep your family entertained with luxury features like dual climate controls, flip-and-fold seats with leather trim** and only on the Premiere, a built-in video entertainment system.
For more details, head to www.silhouettevan.com or call 1-800-395-5999.

start discovering **SILHOUETTE** | Oldsmobile.

http://www.flooz.com

EXHIBIT 11.11

Phone and gift cards have emerged as a popular new sales promotion device among a wide range of marketers. The new Internet economy is allowing all sorts of new instruments to stand in for cash, making it possible to give gifts or compensation (for example, prizes awarded by a Web site to random visitors) in ways that promote selected vendors. Flooz is an "online gift currency" that can be sent via e-mail. How does it differ from a traditional store gift certificate?

- When Jennifer Gray danced in retro oxford sneakers in the film *Dirty Dancing,* the shoe's manufacturer, Keds, saw a huge increase in sales.
- One of the biggest beneficiaries of a brand placement was Bausch and Lomb. Tom Cruise wore distinctive Bausch and Lomb Ray-Ban sunglasses in the film *Risky Business,* and the glasses were featured on the movie poster as well. Ray-Ban sales rocketed to all-time highs after the film's release.[37] More recently, Cruise sparked a wave of interest in Oakley's X-Metal Romeo glasses after wearing them in the beginning of the film *Mission Impossible 2.* Obviously, Tom is the king of sunglasses brand placement.
- In an episode of *Friends,* Phoebe and Rachel spent most of the show discussing the merits of the Pottery Barn, a retailer of home accessory items. While there is no estimate of the sales effect on the retailer, "Pottery Barn" was uttered by the two stars at least 50 times.

The newfound power of brand placement has been surprising, but the process is relatively simple. Once a movie studio or television production team approves a script and schedules production, placement specialists, either in-house or working for

37. Blair R. Fischer, "Making Your Product the Star Attraction," *Promo,* July 1996, 58.

"WHY IS OUR AWARD PROGRAM SO POPULAR WITH FREQUENT TRAVELERS? WE'RE IN EVERY CITY THEY FREQUENT."

As a business traveler you earn free vacations faster with Marriott's Honored Guest Award program. With over 250 locations worldwide, we're doing business wherever you're doing business. To join the program call 1-800-648-8024. For reservations, call your travel agent or 1-800-228-9290.

Marriott
HOTELS · RESORTS · SUITES
WE MAKE IT HAPPEN FOR YOU

EXHIBIT 11.12

Frequency (continuity) programs build customer loyalty and offer opportunities for building a large, targeted database for other promotions.

specialty agencies, go to work. They send the script to targeted companies in an effort to sell the placement opportunities. If a company agrees, then little more is involved than having the brand sent to the studio for inclusion in the film or program. Marketers such as BMW and Coke play a more formative role, but they are exceptions.

Brand placement, like any other communications effort, shows varying results. If the brand name is spoken aloud, such as when Gene Hackman tells Tom Cruise to help himself to a Red Stripe beer during the film *The Firm,* the impact can be dramatic. Similarly, prominent use by a celebrity of a featured brand, such as Mel Gibson clearly drinking a Dr. Pepper or Dennis Quaid eating at McDonald's, can achieve 40 to 50 percent recognition within an audience. Less obvious placements, such as when Bond smashes a car into a Heineken beer truck—referred to as background placements—are considered by some to be a waste of money.[38]

Rebates. Rebates started in the mid-1970s when auto dealers feared price freezes would be imposed by the government as a means to curb inflation. Auto dealers discovered that a rebate on the purchase price of a car was a way around the impending freeze. The price freeze never materialized, but the rebate survived as a sales promotion technique. A **rebate** is a money-back offer requiring a buyer to mail in a form requesting the money back from the manufacturer rather than the retailer (as in couponing). The rebate technique has been refined over the years and is now used by a wide variety of marketers. A recent survey of packaged goods companies revealed that 76 percent had used a money-back offer.[39] Rebates are particularly well suited to increasing the quantity purchased by consumers, so rebates are commonly tied to multiple purchases.

Another reason for the popularity of rebates is that few consumers take advantage of the rebate offer after buying a brand.[40] The best estimate of consumer redemption of rebate offers by the research firm Market Growth Resources is that only 5 to 10 percent of buyers ever bother to fill out and then mail in the rebate request.

Frequency (Continuity) Programs. In recent years, one of the most popular sales promotion techniques among consumers has been frequency programs. **Frequency programs,** also referred to as continuity programs, offer consumers discounts or free product rewards for repeat purchase or patronage of the same brand or company. These programs were pioneered by airline companies. Frequent-flyer programs such as Delta Air Lines' SkyMiles, frequent-stay programs such as Marriott's Honored Guest Award program, and frequent-renter programs such as Hertz's #1 Club are examples of such loyalty-building activities. But frequency

38.   "Motion Pictures, Moving Brands," *Promo,* January 1996, 44.
39.   William M. Buckley, "Rebates' Secret Appeal to Manufacturers: Few Consumers Actually Redeem Them," *The Wall Street Journal,* February 10, 1998, B1.
40.   Ibid.

programs are not reserved for big national airline and auto-rental chains. Chart House Enterprises, a chain of 65 upscale restaurants, successfully launched a frequency program for diners, who earned points for every dollar spent. Frequent diners were issued "passports," which were stamped with each visit. Within two years, the program had more than 300,000 members.[41] Exhibit 11.12 features Marriott's frequency program.

Event Sponsorship. When a firm sponsors or cosponsors an event, such as an auto race, charity marathon, or rock concert, the brand featured in the event immediately gains credibility with the event audience. The audience attending (or participating) in an event already has a positive attitude and affinity for the context—they chose to attend or participate voluntarily. When this audience encounters a brand in this very favorable reception environment, the brand benefits from the already favorable audience attitude.

Advocates of events as a promotional tool point to the fact that entertainment tie-ins touch consumers in a way that advertising cannot. When Nissan launched its Xterra SUV, the firm decided that the best way to demonstrate the powers of the vehicle to a demand audience was to assume the title sponsorship of a series of off-road, extreme competitions. The fit was good and the audience was a perfect target.[42] Sponsorship has grown to be the fourth most popular form of promotion used by U.S. firms, with about $7.6 billion invested annually and a growth rate exceeding 11 percent per year.[43]

The most preferred venue for sponsorship is, not surprisingly, sporting events, which attract about $5 billion in sponsorship dollars. The next most popular activities for attracting sponsors are entertainment tours at about $800 million, festivals and fairs at $740 million, causes and fund raisers with $700 million, and art events

GLOBAL ISSUES

THE BIGGEST EVENT OF ALL

You've finally reached that pinnacle of performance that so many dream about, but so few actually achieve. The endless hours of work and dedication, away from the family on weekends, no time to yourself, finally pay off in your chance to show the world that you are the best in the world at what you do. This is the Olympic Games. And you are an Olympic sponsor. Is there any event bigger than the Olympic Games? When it comes to sponsorships and promotions for marketers, the answer is no—not even close.

The Olympic Games is a key sponsorship opportunity for many global firms like Kodak, General Motors, and Home Depot. But for Visa International, the Olympics always holds special promise. Each year the Olympics are staged as a chance for Visa to tout, once again, that its sponsorship means that it is the only card accepted at the games, a promotional message the firm relishes in its competition with MasterCard and American Express.

Visa used a multifaceted promotional campaign in the months leading to the 2000 Summer Games in Sydney, Australia. To drive home the point that Visa was a sponsor and the exclusive card at the games, banks issued Olympic-themed credit cards beginning in January 2000. Within Australia, the company developed several promotions around the campaign theme "Dream with No Boundaries." The centerpiece of the promotion was the "Dream Trips Sweepstakes," in which cardholders were entered to win one of five Games travel packages every time they made a purchase. The sweepstakes was touted on Visa's Web site, via billing statement inserts, and through P-O-P signage in retail shops. Yet another sweepstakes called "Your Dream Your Team" offered ten winners $5,000, with Visa donating a matching amount to the U.S. Olympic team of the winners choice.

At the games themselves, Visa used tie-ins with local merchants at the point of purchase. Michael Lynch, the VP for event and sponsorship marketing for Visa, explained that the firm worked with local merchants as a way to "customize programs specific to their marketplace needs to build their profitability." This might include Visa promotional tie-ins or even appearances by athletes.

While promotions are important to many firms across a wide variety of applications, the Olympics offers a special opportunity. Few firms have taken advantage of an opportunity as well as Visa International takes advantage of its Olympic opportunities.

Source: Bob Woods, "They Got Games," *Promo,* April 2000, 79–82.

41. Kerry J. Smith, "Building a Winning Frequency Program—the Hard Way," *Promo,* December 1995, 36.
42. Kate Fitzgerald, "Events Offer New Level of Brand Immersion," *Advertising Age,* April 17, 2000, 22.
43. "Record Growth, Without Gold," Promotion Trends 2000, Annual Report of the Promotions Industry compiled by *Promo,* May 2000, A23.

at about $500 million in sponsorship spending.[44] But don't conclude that sponsorships are a popular sales promotion tool only in the United States. The Global Issues box shows that firms have found this sales promotion technique effective as a global strategy as well.

SALES PROMOTION IN THE TRADE AND BUSINESS MARKETS

Sales promotions can also be directed at members of the trade—wholesalers, distributors, and retailers. For example, Compaq Computer designs sales promotion programs for its retailers like Circuit City in order to ensure that the Compaq line gets proper attention and display. But Compaq will also have sales promotion campaigns aimed at business buyers like Andersen Consulting or IHC HealthCare. The purpose of sales promotion as a tool does not change in the trade market. It is still intended to stimulate demand in the short term and help *push* the product through the distribution channel or cause business buyers to act more immediately and positively toward the marketer's brand.

Effective trade promotions can generate enthusiasm for a product and contribute positively to the loyalty distributors show for a brand. In the business market, sales promotions can mean the difference between landing a very large order and missing out entirely on a revenue opportunity. With the massive proliferation of new brands and brand extensions, manufacturers need to stimulate enthusiasm and loyalty among members of the trade and also need a way to get the attention of business buyers suffering from information overload.

Objectives for Promotions in the Trade Market

As in the consumer market, trade-market sales promotions should be undertaken with specific objectives in mind. Generally speaking, when marketers devise incentives for the trade market, they are executing a **push strategy**—that is, sales promotions directed at the trade help push a product into the distribution channel until it ultimately reaches the consumer. Four primary objectives can be identified for these promotions, as follows.

Obtain Initial Distribution.
Because of the proliferation of brands in the consumer market, there is fierce competition for shelf space. Sales promotion incentives can help a firm gain initial distribution and shelf placement. Like consumers, members of the trade need a reason to choose one brand over another when it comes to allocating shelf space. A well-conceived promotion incentive may sway them.

Bob's Candies, a small, family-owned business in Albany, Georgia, is the largest candy cane manufacturer in the United States. But Bob's old-fashioned candy was having trouble keeping distributors. To reverse the trend, the company designed a new name, logo, and packaging for the candy canes. Then each scheduled attendee at the All-Candy Expo trade show in Chicago was mailed three strategically timed postcards with the teaser question "Wanna Be Striped?" The mailing got a 25 percent response rate, and booth visitations at the trade show were a huge success.[45]

Increase Order Size.
One of the struggles in the channel of distribution is over the location of inventory. Manufacturers prefer that members of the trade maintain large inventories so the manufacturer can reduce inventory-carrying costs.

---

44. Ibid.
45. Lee Duffey, "Sweet Talk: Promotions Position Candy Company," *Marketing News,* March 30, 1998, 11.

Conversely, members of the trade would rather make frequent, small orders and carry little inventory. Sales promotion techniques can encourage wholesalers and retailers to order in larger quantities, thus shifting the inventory burden to the channel.

Encourage Cooperation with Consumer-Market Sales Promotions. It does a manufacturer no good to initiate a sales promotion in the consumer market if there is little cooperation in the channel. Wholesalers may need to maintain larger inventories, and retailers may need to provide special displays or handling during consumer-market sales promotions. To achieve synergy, marketers often run trade promotions simultaneously with consumer promotions. As it turned out, when Toys "R" Us ran its "scan and win" promotion, they actually ran out of several very popular toy items during the critical holiday buying season because distributors (and Toys "R" Us) were unprepared for the magnitude of the response to the promotion.

Increase Store Traffic. Retailers can increase store traffic through special promotions or events. Door-prize drawings, parking-lot sales, or live radio broadcasts from the store are common sales promotion traffic builders. Burger King has become a leader in building traffic at its 6,500 outlets, with special promotions tied to Disney movie debuts. Beginning in 1991 with a *Beauty and the Beast* tie-in promotion, Burger King has set records for generating store traffic with premium giveaways. The *Pocahontas* campaign distributed 55 million toys and glasses. Most recently, a promotion tie-in with Disney's huge success *Toy Story* resulted in 50 million toys, based on the film's characters, being given away in $1.99 Kid Meals.[46]

Manufacturers can also design sales promotions that increase store traffic for retailers. A promotion that generates a lot of interest within a target audience can drive consumers to retail outlets. A good example of this is shown in Exhibit 11.13. Jelly Belly jelly beans ran this giveaway of a new VW Bug as a way to attract attention to the brand. But notice the copy in the ad: "To enter, visit your nearest participating retailer and ask for your 'Very Cherry Sweepstakes' entry form . . ." Supporting retailer traffic in this way creates strong and lasting relationships between marketers and their trade channel partners.

EXHIBIT 11.13

One of the objectives for sales promotion at the trade market level is to build store traffic. While retailers often use sales promotion techniques to do so, occasionally a manufacturer will try to stimulate store traffic for a retailer, as the Very Cherry Sweepstakes attempts to do.

Trade-Market Sales Promotion Techniques ❸

When marketers devise incentives to encourage purchases by members of the trade, they are executing a push strategy; that is, sales promotions directed at the trade help push a product into the distribution channel until it ultimately reaches consumers. The sales promotion techniques used with the trade are point-of-purchase displays, incentives, allowances, trade shows, sales training programs, and cooperative advertising.

46.   Editors' Special Report, "Having It Their Way," *Promo*, December 1995, 79–80.

EXHIBIT 11.14

Point-of-purchase displays attract shoppers' attention to a marketer's brand. But with the advent of online shopping, more retailers are using P-O-P a technique for making the in-store experience more entertaining and satisfying for consumers.

Point-of-Purchase Displays. Product displays and information sheets are useful in reaching the consumer at the point of purchase and often encourage retailers to support one's brand. P-O-P promotions can help win precious shelf space and exposure in a retail setting. From a retailer's perspective, a P-O-P display should be designed to draw attention to a brand, increase turnover, and possibly distribute coupons or sweepstakes entry forms. Exhibit 11.14 shows a typical P-O-P display. Advertisers invested $14.4 billion on P-O-P materials in 1999. This is more than was spent on either magazine or radio advertising.[47]

In an attempt to combat the threat of losing business to online shopping, retailers are trying to enliven the retail environment, and P-O-P displays are part of the strategy. Both brand marketers and retailers are trying to create a better and more satisfying shopping experience. The president of a large display company says that "We're trying to bring more of an entertainment factor to our P-O-P programs."[48]

Incentives. Incentives to members of the trade include a variety of tactics not unlike those used in the consumer market. Awards in the form of travel, gifts, or cash bonuses for reaching targeted sales levels can induce retailers and wholesalers to give a firm's brand added attention. The incentive does not have to be large or expensive to be effective. Weiser Lock offered its dealers a Swiss Army knife with every dozen cases of locks ordered. The program was a huge success. A follow-up promotion featuring a Swiss Army watch was an even bigger hit.

Another form of trade incentive is referred to as push money. **Push money** is carried out through a program in which retail salespeople are offered a monetary

47. "Retailtainment Today," *Promotion Trends 2000,* Annual Report of the Promotions Industry compiled by *Promo,* May 2000, A16.
48. Ibid.

reward for featuring a marketer's brand with shoppers. The program is quite simple. If a salesperson sells a particular brand of refrigerator for a manufacturer as opposed to a competitor's brand, the salesperson will be paid an extra $50 or $75 "bonus" as part of the push money program.

One risk with incentive programs for the trade is that salespeople can be so motivated to win an award or extra push money that they may try to sell the brand to every customer, whether it fits that customer's needs or not. Also, a firm must carefully manage such programs to minimize ethical dilemmas. An incentive technique can look like a bribe unless it is carried out in a highly structured and open fashion.

Allowances. Various forms of allowances are offered to retailers and wholesalers with the purpose of increasing the attention given to a firm's brands. Allowances are typically made available to wholesalers and retailers about every four weeks during a quarter. **Merchandise allowances,** in the form of free products packed with regular shipments, are payments to the trade for setting up and maintaining displays. The payments are typically far less than manufacturers would have to spend to maintain the displays themselves.

In recent years, shelf space has become so highly demanded, especially in supermarkets, that manufacturers are making direct cash payments, known as **slotting fees,** to induce food chains to stock an item. The proliferation of new products has made shelf space such a precious commodity that these fees now run in the hundreds of thousands of dollars per product. Another form of allowance is called a bill-back allowance. **Bill-back allowances** provide retailers a monetary incentive for featuring a marketer's brand in either advertising or in-store displays. If a retailer chooses to participate in either an advertising or display bill-back program, the marketer requires the retailer to verify the services performed and provide a bill for the services. A similar program is the **off-invoice allowance,** where marketers allow wholesalers and retailers to deduct a set amount from the invoice they receive for merchandise. This program is really just a price reduction offered to the trade on a particular marketer's brand. The incentive for the trade with this program is that the price reduction increases the margin (and profits) a wholesaler or retailer realizes on the off-invoiced brand.

Sales-Training Programs. An increasingly popular trade promotion is to provide training for retail store personnel. This method is used for consumer durables and specialty goods, such as personal computers, home theater systems, heating and cooling systems, security systems, and exercise equipment. The increased complexity of these products has made it important for manufacturers to ensure that the proper factual information and persuasive themes are reaching consumers at the point of purchase. For personnel at large retail stores, manufacturers can hold special classes that feature product information, demonstrations, and training about sales techniques.

Another popular method for getting sales-training information to retailers is the use of videotapes and brochures. Manufacturers can also send sales trainers into retail stores to work side by side with store personnel. This is a costly method, but it can be very effective because of the one-on-one attention it provides.

Cooperative Advertising. Cooperative (Co-op) advertising as a trade promotion technique is referred to as vertical cooperative advertising. (Such efforts are also called vendor co-op programs.) Manufacturers try to control the content of this co-op advertising in two ways. They may set strict specifications for the size and content of the ad and then ask for verification that such specifications have been met. Alternatively, manufacturers may send the template for an ad, into which retailers merely insert the names and locations of their stores. Such an ad is featured in Exhibit 11.15. Notice that the James Bond and Omega watch components are national, with the co-op sponsorship of the Hawaiian retailer highlighted in the lower right.

Business-Market Sales Promotion Techniques

Often the discussion of sales promotion focuses only on consumer and trade techniques. It is a major oversight to leave the business buyer market out of the discussion. The Promotional Product Association estimates that several billion a year in sales promotion is targeted to the business buyer.[49]

Trade Shows. At **trade shows,** related products from many manufacturers are displayed and demonstrated to members of the trade. Literally every industry has trade shows, from gourmet products to the granddaddy of them all—COMDEX. COMDEX is the annual computer and electronics industry trade show held in Las Vegas that attracts over a quarter of a million business buyers.

At a typical trade show, company representatives are on hand manning a booth that displays a company's products or service programs. The representatives are there to explain the products and services and perhaps make an important contact for the sales force. The use of trade shows must be carefully coordinated and can be an important part of the business market promotional program. Trade shows can be critically important to a small firm that cannot afford advertising and has a sales staff too small to reach all its potential customers. Through the trade-show route, salespeople can make far more contacts than would be possible with direct sales calls.

Trade shows are also an important route for reaching potential wholesalers and distributors for a company's brand. But the proliferation of trade shows has been so extensive in recent years that the technique is really more oriented to business buyers these days.

Business Gifts. Estimates are that nearly half of corporate America gives business gifts.[50] These gifts are given as part of building and maintaining a close working relationship with suppliers. Business gifts that are part of a promotional program may include small items like logo golf balls, jackets, or small items of jewelry. Extravagant gifts or expensive trips that might be construed as "buying business" are not included in this category of business market sales promotion.

Premiums and Advertising Specialties. As mentioned earlier, the key chain, ball cap, T-shirt, mouse pad, or calendar that reminds a buyer of a brand name and slogan can be an inexpensive but useful form of sales promotion. A significant portion of the $14 billion premium and advertising specialty market is directed to business buyers. While business buyers are professionals, they are not immune to the value perceptions that an advertising specialty can create. In other words, getting something for nothing appeals to business buyers as much as it does to household consumers. Will a business buyer choose one consulting firm over another to get a sleeve of golf balls? Probably not. But advertising specialties can add to the satisfaction of a transaction nonetheless.

Trial Offers. Trial offers are particularly well suited to the business market. First, since many business products and services are high cost and often result in a

---

49.   Bagley, *Understanding and Using Promotional Products,* 5.
50.   Ibid.

EXHIBIT 11.15

Here is a classic example of co-op advertising between manufacturer and retailer. Omega is being featured by this Hawaiian retailer in a magazine ad. Is there another form of sales promotion going on here as well?

EXHIBIT 11.16

Business products often require a large time and money commitment. A risk-free trial offer, like this one for GoldMine software, allows business buyers the chance to try something new at a very low risk.

significant time commitment to a brand (that is, many business products and services have a long life), trial offers provide a way for buyers to lower the risk of making a commitment to one brand over another. Second, a trial offer is a good way to attract new customers who need a reason to try something new. The GoldMine software offer in Exhibit 11.16 is a perfect demonstration of these points. Software installation and use requires both a time and money commitment on the part of a business buyer. And using software for sales force team communications and planning may be new to many organizations. The chance to try a new product for 30 days with no financial risk can be a compelling offer.

Frequency Programs. The high degree of travel associated with many business professions makes frequency programs an ideal form of sales promotion for the business market. Airline, hotel, and restaurant frequency programs are dominated by the business market traveler. But frequency programs for the business market are not restricted to travel-related purchases. Retailers of business products like Staples, Office Max, and Costco have programs designed to reward the loyalty of the business buyer. Costco has teamed with American Express to offer business buyers an exclusive Costco/American Express credit card. Among the many advantages of the card is a rebate at the end of the year based on the level of buying—the greater the dollar amount of purchases, the greater the percentage rebate. The IMC in Practice box discussion gives an example of how frequency programs can be used in the professional business market.

IN PRACTICE

HOW TO BUILD A FREQUENCY PROGRAM FOR THE BUSINESS MARKET

Most of us are used to frequency programs where a company will reward us for being loyal to their brands. From multinational airline companies to the local bagel shop, we can get our frequency card punched and reap rewards. But what about a frequency program targeted to the business market? Sure, business travelers will rack up points with favorite airlines and hotels, but can loyalty/frequency programs be used in any other product categories?

As far as the marketing manager at Bell Atlantic is concerned, the answer is absolutely yes! Steve McVeigh, senior marketing manager at Bell Atlantic, believes that to most business users, telephone service is a commodity—everybody is going to offer the same services and options. That's why Bell Atlantic started Business Link, a frequency program for corporate customers. Companies enrolled in the program can save roughly 15 percent on their direct-dial calls when their monthly usage exceeds a set amount. They can also earn points based on how much they use certain specified Bell Atlantic services.

Kodak has a similar program called ProRewards. This is a points-based program for professional photographers. With their accumulated points, photographers can get discounts on a wide array of items—except film. As a Kodak spokesperson so succinctly put it: "What we want to do is get them to *buy* the film."

A real payoff for both firms is that once they have business users enrolled in the frequency programs, a database is developed of these loyal customers. With the database, specialized product promotions can be developed and mailed to these frequent buyers and loyal customers. To get the most from a loyalty/frequency program in the business market, the following guidelines are offered:

• Give rewards or discounts only to those who spend enough to make the discounts profitable.

• Track buying habits and customer information to create targeted marketing programs and to develop special offers.

• Offer your best customers special rewards—an exclusive customer service phone number, e-mail bulletins, or early release of products—that show you recognize their value to your company.

Source: Chad Kaydo, "How to Build a B-to-B Frequency Program," *Sales and Marketing Management,* April 1999, 79.

SALES PROMOTION, THE INTERNET, AND NEW MEDIA ❹

Sales promotion has entered the era of new media as well. Marketers are expanding their use of sales promotion techniques in the consumer, trade, and business markets by using the Internet and other new media options. There are two parts to the issue of sales promotion in new media applications. First, there is the *use by* Internet and new media companies of sales promotion techniques. Second, there is the *use of* the Internet and new media to implement various sales promotion techniques.

The Use of Sales Promotion by Internet and New Media Organizations

The new titans of technology—AOL, Yahoo!, Network Associates—have discovered a new way to generate revenue fast: They give their products away. More specifically, they have discovered the power of sales promotion in the form of distributing free samples. These fast-growing, highly successful companies have discovered an alternative to advertising—sales promotion.

Of course, giving away free samples, as we have seen, is not a new sales promotion technique. But giving away intellectual property, such as software, is new, and America Online is the Godzilla of giveaways (see Exhibit 11.17). With each new release AOL blankets the United States with diskettes and CD-ROMs offering consumers a free one-month trial of its Internet services. No distribution channel is left untapped in trying to reach consumers with the free diskettes. They have been stashed in boxes of Rice Chex cereal, in United Airlines in-flight meals, and in packages of Omaha Steaks—not to mention inside the plastic sack along

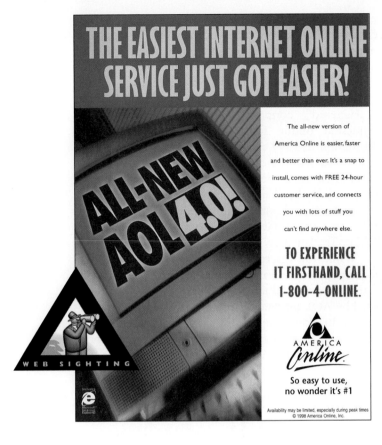

THE EASIEST INTERNET ONLINE
SERVICE JUST GOT EASIER!

ALL-NEW
AOL 4.0!

WEB SIGHTING

The all-new version of
America Online is easier, faster
and better than ever. It's a snap to
install, comes with FREE 24-hour
customer service, and connects
you with lots of stuff you
can't find anywhere else.

**TO EXPERIENCE
IT FIRSTHAND, CALL
1-800-4-ONLINE.**

AMERICA
Online

So easy to use,
no wonder it's #1

Availability may be limited, especially during peak times
© 1998 America Online, Inc.

http://www.aol.com

EXHIBIT 11.17

*AOL is the 800-pound gorilla of the free promotional diskette (and
now CD-ROM). While you can find other networks' start-up diskettes
at the checkout counters of computer stores, AOL's free CDs have
appeared in everything from breakfast cereals to business magazines.
While you might not be able to roof a whole house with AOL CDs,
you could certainly scrounge around and amass enough free hours (at
100 per each a CD) to never have to pay to get online again—how
does AOL actually make money?*

with your local Sunday paper that the neighborhood
kid delivers.

What makes sampling so attractive for AOL is that
it helps takes all the risk away from consumer trial.
Consumers with computers, of course, can give AOL
or Yahoo! a try without investing a penny or making
a long-term commitment to a piece of software. If
they like what they see, they can sign up for a longer
period of time. The technology companies have
embraced the concept and accepted the main liabilities of sampling—cost and time.[51]

But sampling is not the only sales promotion tool
discovered by the dot-coms. In their desire to create
"sticky" Web sites, Internet firms have relied heavily
on incentives as a way to attract and retain Web
surfers. Many of them are offering loyalty programs,
and others have devised offers to make members out
of visitors. In an attempt to make the incentive programs more interesting, many of the Web companies
allow participants to review their standings in contests
and then take a virtual tour of prizes—including
exotic travel destinations that typically constitute a
grand prize.[52]

These technology companies have discovered that
sales promotion can be a valuable component of the
overall promotional program—and that the potential
impact of sales promotion is quite different from
advertising. As we saw in Chapters 9 and 10, Internet
and new media companies are investing heavily in
advertising as a way to develop brand recognition.
Now they have discovered sales promotion as a way
to help drive revenues.

The Use of the Internet and New Media
to Implement Sales Promotions

It is interesting to see Internet and new media companies rely on traditional sales promotions. But it is
also interesting to see how companies of all types are
learning to use the Internet and new media to implement sales promotion techniques. In a survey of firms using various promotional techniques, over half
responded that the Internet and new media were having a large impact on their
promotional planning. Estimates are that the marketers invested about $926 million
in Web-based promotions in 1999, ranging from online sweepstakes and couponing
to loyalty and sampling programs.[53]

There are a variety of ways in which the Internet is being used to implement
sales promotions. First, companies like Starbelly.com (http://www.starbelly.com) are
emerging that increase the efficiency of the sales promotion process. Starbelly.com

51. Patricia Nakache, "Secrets of the New Brand Builders," *Fortune,* June 22, 1998, 167–170.
52. "Motivating Matters," *Promotion Trends 2000,* Annual Report of the Promotions Industry compiled by *Promo,*
May 2000, A13.
53. "Internet Invasion," Promotion Trends 2000, Annual Report of the Promotions Industry compiled by *Promo,*
May 2000, A30.

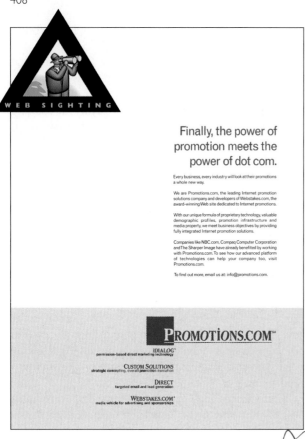

Finally, the power of
promotion meets the
power of dot com.

Every business, every industry will look at their promotions
a whole new way.

We are Promotions.com, the leading Internet promotion
solutions company and developers of Webstakes.com, the
award-winning Web site dedicated to Internet promotions.

With our unique formula of proprietary technology, valuable
demographic profiles, promotion infrastructure and
media property, we meet business objectives by providing
fully integrated Internet promotion solutions.

Companies like NBC.com, Compaq Computer Corporation
and The Sharper Image have already benefited by working
with Promotions.com. To see how our advanced platform
of technologies can help your company too, visit
Promotions.com.

To find out more, email us at: info@promotions.com

PROMOTIONS.COM℠

iDIALOG™
permission-based direct marketing technology

CUSTOM SOLUTIONS
strategic concepting, overall promotion execution

DIRECT
targeted email and lead generation

WEBSTAKES.COM™
media vehicle for advertising and sponsorships

http://www.promotions.com

EXHIBIT 11.18

*New Internet companies like Promotions.com assist in the planning
and execution of Web- and e-mail-based promotions. As with many
other services (hosting, managed e-mail, fulfillment, etc.), one can use
these sorts of providers to whip together a Web-based venture in short
order—the Web is a grand experiment in outsourcing. What are some
of the advantages of working with an implementer like Promotions.com,
beyond saving you the time of learning about customer behavior, and
stocking up on prizes?*

operates online promotional "stores" for corporate customers. Other online companies help firms determine how to use the Internet to implement sales promotion programs (see Exhibit 11.18).[54] Second, the Internet is being used as a distribution system for couponing. In the packaged goods area, Internet –"triggered" coupons (either printed from or requested online for mail delivery) increased to 14 million in 1999. As an example, PetsMart launched a PetsMart.com Store Savings Center. Site visitors enter their zip code and then print out coupons to redeem at their neighborhood PetsMart Store.[55] Finally, sweepstakes are highly popular on the Web, as we have seen. A General Motors game for the new Chevy Tracker drew 1.3 million Web-based entries.

While the Internet attracts most of the attention for sales promotion implementation, new media applications are also taking hold. The CD–ROMs distributed by AOL represent one form of new media application. In-store coupon dispensers is another. Finally, interactive kiosks in retail locations that provide both information and incentives are being developed.

THE RISKS OF SALES PROMOTION ⑤

Sales promotion can be used to pursue important sales objectives. As we have seen, there are a wide range of sales promotion options for both the consumer and trade markets. But there are also significant risks associated with sales promotion, and these risks must be carefully considered.

Creating a Price Orientation. Since most sales promotions rely on some sort of price incentive or giveaway, a firm runs the risk of having its brand perceived as cheap, with no real value or benefits beyond low price. Creating this perception in the market contradicts the concept of integrated marketing communication. If advertising messages highlight the value and benefit of a brand only to be contradicted by a price emphasis in sales promotions, then a confusing signal is being sent to the market.

Borrowing from Future Sales. Management must admit that sales promotions are typically short-term tactics designed to reduce inventories, increase cash flow, or show periodic boosts in market share. The downside is that a firm may simply be borrowing from future sales. Consumers or trade buyers who would have purchased the brand anyway may be motivated to stock up at the lower price. This results in reduced sales during the next few time periods of measurement. This can play havoc with the measurement and evaluation of the effect of advertising campaigns or

54. Peter Breen, "Straight from the Source," *Premiums*, April 2000, S4–S9.
55. "Back to Basics," A20.

other image-building communications. If consumers are responding to sales promotions, it may be impossible to tease out the effects of advertising.

Alienating Customers. When a firm relies heavily on sweepstakes or frequency programs to build loyalty among customers, particularly their best customers, there is the risk of alienating these customers with any change in the program. Airlines suffered just such a fate when they tried to adjust the mileage levels needed for awards in their frequent-flyer programs. Ultimately, many of the airlines had to give concessions to their most frequent flyers as a conciliatory gesture.

Time and Expense. Sales promotions are both costly and time-consuming. The process is time-consuming for the marketer and the retailer in terms of handling promotional materials and protecting against fraud and waste in the process. As we have seen in recent years, funds allocated to sales promotions are taking dollars away from advertising. Advertising is a long-term, franchise-building process that should not be compromised for short-term gains.

Legal Considerations. With the increasing popularity of sales promotions, particularly contests and premiums, there has been an increase in legal scrutiny at both the federal and state levels. Legal experts recommend that before initiating promotions that use coupons, games, sweepstakes, and contests, a firm should check into lottery laws, copyright laws, state and federal trademark laws, prize notification laws, right of privacy laws, tax laws, and FTC and FCC regulations.[56] The best advice for staying out of legal trouble with sales promotions is to carefully and clearly state the rules and conditions related to the program so that consumers are fully informed.

THE COORDINATION CHALLENGE— SALES PROMOTION AND IMC

There is an allure to sales promotion that must be put into perspective. Sales promotions can make things happen—quickly. While managers often find the immediacy of sales promotion valuable, particularly in meeting quarterly sales goals, sales promotions are rarely a viable means of long-term success. But when used properly, sales promotions can be an important element in a well-conceived IMC campaign. Key to their proper use is coordinating the message emphasis in advertising with the placement and emphasis of sales promotions. When advertising and sales promotion are well coordinated, the impact of each is enhanced—a classic case of synergy.

Message Coordination

The typical sales promotion should either attract attention to a brand or offer the target market greater value: reduced price, more product, or the chance to win a prize or an award. In turn, this focused attention and extra value acts as an incentive for the target market to choose the promoted brand over other brands. One of the coordination problems this presents is that advertising messages, designed to build long-term loyalty, may not seem totally consistent with the extra-value signal of the sales promotion.

This is the classic problem that marketers face in coordinating sales promotion with an advertising campaign. First, advertising messages tout brand features or emotional attractions. Then, the next contact a consumer may have with the brand

---

56.   Maxine S. Lans, "Legal Hurdles Big Part of Promotions Game," *Marketing News,* October 24, 1994, 15.

is an insert in the Sunday paper offering a cents-off coupon. These mixed signals can be damaging for a brand.

Increasing the coordination between advertising and various sales promotion efforts requires only the most basic planning. First, when different agencies are involved in preparing sales promotion materials and advertising materials, those agencies need to be kept informed by the advertiser regarding the maintenance of a desired theme. Second, simple techniques can be used to carry a coordinated theme between promotional tools. The use of logos, slogans, visual imagery, or spokespersons can create a consistent presentation. As illustrated in Exhibit 11.18, even if advertising and sales promotion pursue different purposes, the look and feel of both efforts may be coordinated. The more the theme of a promotion can be tied directly to the advertising campaign, the more impact these messages will generally have on the consumer.

Media Coordination

Another key in coordination involves timing. Remember that the success of a sales promotion depends on the consumer believing that the chance to save money or receive more of a product represents enhanced value. If the consumer is not aware of a brand and its features and benefits, and does not perceive the brand as a worthy item, then there will be no basis for perceiving value—discounted or not. This means that appropriate advertising should precede price-oriented sales promotions for them to be effective. The right advertising can create an image for a brand that is appropriate for a promotional offer. Then, presented with a sales promotion, consumers will be impressed by the offer as an opportunity to acquire superior value. This is precisely why Internet firms began investing so heavily in advertising before turning to sales promotions as a way of attracting visitors. In coordinating online with offline media, the chief marketing officer of a high-tech promotions shop makes the observation that "Online promotions used to be ugly stepchildren. But brands are now starting to use the Web smartly. They're combining the media and no longer treating online and offline separately."[57]

Conclusions from Recent Research

The synergy theme prominent in the preceding discussion is not just a matter of speculation. Recent research using single-source data generated by ACNielsen reaffirms many of the primary points of this chapter.[58] John Philip Jones has reported the major conclusions of this research:

- The short-term productivity of promotions working alone is much more dramatic than that of advertising. Promotions that involve price incentives on average yield a 1.8 percent increase in sales for each 1 percent price reduction. A 1 percent increase in advertising yields just a 0.2 percent sales increase on average.
- The average cost of a 1 percent reduction in price is always far greater than the cost of a 1 percent increase in advertising. Thus, more often than not, sales promotions featuring price incentives are actually unprofitable in the short term.
- It is rare that a sales promotion generates a long-term effect. Hence, there are no long-term revenues to offset the high cost of promotions in the short run. Successful advertising is much more likely to yield a profitable return over the long run, even though its impact on short-run sales may be modest.

57. "Internet Invasion," A30.
58. John Philip Jones, *When Ads Work* (New York: Lexington Books, 1995).

- While both advertising and sales promotions may be expected to affect sales in the short run, the evidence suggests that the most powerful effects come from a combination of the two. The impact of advertising and promotions working together is dramatically greater than the sum of each sales stimulus working by itself.

According to Jones, "The strong synergy that can be generated between advertising and promotions working together points very clearly to the need to integrate the planning and execution of both types of activity: the strategy of Integrated Marketing Communications."[59]

SUMMARY

1 Explain the importance and growth of sales promotion as a promotional mix tool.

Sales promotions use diverse incentives to motivate action on the part of consumers, members of the trade channel, and business buyers. They serve different purposes from mass-media advertising, and for some companies, sales promotions receive substantially more funding than does mass-media advertising. The growing reliance on these promotions can be attributed to the heavy pressures placed on marketing managers to account for their spending and meet sales objectives in short time frames. Deal-prone shoppers, brand proliferation, the increasing power of large retailers, and media clutter have also contributed to the rising popularity of sales promotion.

2 Describe the main sales promotion techniques used in the consumer market.

Sales promotions directed at consumers can serve various goals. For example, they can be employed as a means to stimulate trial, repeat, or large-quantity purchases. They are especially important tools for introducing new brands or for reacting to a competitor's advances. Coupons, price-off deals, phone and gift cards, and premiums provide obvious incentives for purchase. Contests, sweepstakes, and product placements can be excellent devices for stimulating brand interest. A variety of sampling techniques is available to get a product into the hands of the target audience. Rebates and frequency programs provide rewards for repeat purchase.

3 Describe the main sales promotion techniques used in the trade and business markets.

Sales promotions directed at the trade can also serve multiple objectives. They are a necessity in obtaining initial distribution of a new brand. For established brands, they can be a means to increase distributors' order quantities or obtain retailers' cooperation in implementing a consumer-directed promotion. P–O–P displays can be an excellent tool for gaining preferred display space in a retail setting. Incentives and allowances can be offered to distributors to motivate support for a brand. Sales training programs and cooperative advertising programs are additional devices for effecting retailer support.

In the business market, professional buyers are attracted by various sales promotion techniques. Frequency (continuity) programs are very valuable in the travel industry and have spread to business product marketers. Trade shows are an efficient way to reach a large number of highly targeted business buyers. Gifts to business buyers are a unique form of sales promotion for this market. Finally, premiums, advertising specialties, and trial offers have proven to be successful in the business market.

4 Explain how new media, including the Internet, are affecting the use of sales promotion.

New media and the Internet are affecting the use of sales promotion in two ways. First, sales promotions of all types are being used by Internet and new media companies to help attract and keep customers—much like traditional firms have used sales promotion. Sampling and incentive programs are particularly popular with Internet and new media companies. Second, companies of all types are using the Internet and new media to implement sales promotions. Online promotional stores, "triggered" coupons, and sweepstakes are frequently used to enhance more traditional sales promotion efforts.

5 Identify the risks of using sales promotion.

There are important risks associated with heavy reliance on sales promotion. Offering constant deals for a brand is a good way to erode brand equity, and it may simply be borrowing sales from a future time period. Constant deals can also create a customer mindset that leads consumers to abandon a brand as soon as a deal is retracted. Sales promotions are expensive to administer and fraught with legal complications. They yield their most positive results when carefully integrated with the overall advertising plan.

59. Ibid., 56.

KEY TERMS

sales promotion, 383
coupon, 390
price-off deal, 392
premiums, 392
free premium, 392
self-liquidating premium, 392
advertising specialties, 392
contest, 393
sweepstakes, 393
sampling, 395

in-store sampling, 395
door-to-door sampling, 395
mail sampling, 395
newspaper sampling, 395
on-package sampling, 395
mobile sampling, 395
trial offers, 396
brand placement, 396
rebate, 398

frequency (continuity) programs, 398
push strategy, 400
push money, 402
merchandise allowances, 403
slotting fees, 403
bill-back allowances, 403
off-invoice allowances, 403
cooperative (co-op) advertising, 403
trade shows, 404

QUESTIONS FOR REVIEW AND CRITICAL THINKING

1. Compare and contrast sales promotion and mass-media advertising as promotional tools. In what ways do the strengths of one make up for the limitations of the other? What specific characteristics of sales promotions account for the high levels of expenditures that have been allocated to them in recent years?

2. What is brand proliferation, and why is it occurring? Why do consumer sales promotions become more commonplace in the face of rampant brand proliferation? Why do trade sales promotions become more frequent when there is excessive brand proliferation?

3. Pull all the preprinted and freestanding inserts from the most recent edition of your Sunday newspaper. From them find an example of each of these consumer-market sales promotions: coupon, free premium, self-liquidating premium, contest, sweepstakes, and trial offer.

4. In developing an advertising plan, synergy may be achieved through careful coordination of individual elements. Give an example of how mass-media advertising might be used with on-package sampling to effect a positive synergy. Give an example of how event sponsorship might be used with mobile sampling to achieve a positive synergy.

5. Consumers often rationalize their purchase of a new product with a statement such as, "I bought it because I had a 50-cent coupon and our grocery was doubling all manufacturers' coupons this week." What are the prospects that such a consumer will emerge as a loyal user of the product? What must happen if he or she is to become loyal?

6. Early in the chapter, it was suggested that large retailers like Wal-Mart are assuming greater power in today's marketplace. What factors contribute to retailers' increasing power? Explain the connection between merchandise allowances and slotting fees and the growth in retailer power.

7. In your opinion, are ethical dilemmas more likely to arise with sales promotions directed at the consumer or at the business market? What specific forms of consumer or business promotions seem most likely to involve or create ethical dilemmas?

8. Many marketers argue that consumer sales promotions do not work unless a great deal of time and money are first invested in advertising. What logic might you offer to support this contention? Why would advertising be required to make a sales promotion work?

EXPERIENTIAL EXERCISES

1. **In-class exercise.** Debate the issue that "Sales promotion erodes brand loyalty and creates a commodity perception of a brand." Does sales promotion make you switch brands, or are you loyal to certain brands no matter what incentive a marketer might offer?

2. **Out-of-class exercise.** Buy a Sunday newspaper. Make a list of the sales promotions offered by manufacturers, and attach a few examples. Make a second list of the sales promotions offered by retailers, and attach a few examples. Are there any other types of organizations that use sales promotion offers within the newspaper?

USING THE INTERNET

Exercise 1

The Internet's origins as a sort of "gift economy," where its builders freely shared basic software, and academic sources of content were offered without thought of generating revenue, have had a strong influence on "what works" in Internet commerce. Numerous business models are based on distributing free software or services, and deriving revenues in other ways.

Some services, such as Tripod (http://www.tripod.com) and GeoCities (http://www.geocities.com), offer consumers free Web pages.

1. How do these services make use of advertising to generate their revenue?

Qualcomm's Eudora (http://www.eudora.com) is one of the Internet's best-known e-mail products.

2. How does Qualcomm structure its product and service offerings to produce (eventually) revenue from paying customers?

HotMail (http://www.hotmail.com) demonstrated the wisdom of giving away e-mail for free, when the start-up company was bought by Microsoft for an estimated several hundred million dollars.

3. What sort of people would find HotMail a useful service?

4. What products and services might be best to advertise to HotMail customers?

Exercise 2

You're used to getting pounds of inserts in the Sunday paper, with page after page of coupons that may or may not be relevant—surely the Internet might allow for more efficiency and fewer dead trees, you might guess? A number of companies have moved into the online delivery of coupons, including Valassis Communications, which produces around half of all of the freestanding inserts in the offline, print world. Valassis has made strategic investments in online couponing start-ups like Save.com. Visit the following Web sites:

Valassis Communications
http://www.valassis.com

Save.com
http://www.save.com

Coupons.com
http://www.coupons.com

BrightStreet
http://www.brightstreet.com

1. How can online couponing improve on offline couponing?

2. What challenges do online couponing services face that offline ones don't?

3. Who provides the couponing services to PetsMart.com (http://www.PetsMart.com)?

After reading this chapter, you will be able to:

1 Explain the growing popularity of sponsorship as a promotional tool.

2 Describe the appeal of point-of-purchase promotions as a key element of IMC.

3 Discuss the role of supportive communications tools in the promotional mix.

4 Identify the challenges of coordinating the ever-expanding media options in the promotional mix.

CHAPTER 12

Kiehl's is a small, 48-year-old company that makes men's and women's hair and skin care products. Kiehl's is committed to an unusual marketing and promotional program. It shuns advertising, doesn't host a Web site, and packages its products with hard-to-read labels (see Exhibit 12.1). Even more unusual is that Kiehl's has only one retail outlet, in New York City, where employees are encouraged to *give* products away.

After everything we've studied, what would we expect? No communication means no awareness and no brand preference, right? Wrong. Kiehl's has developed a fierce brand following that makes the big spenders in the cosmetics industry like Clinique, L'Oréal, and Redken envious. Celebrities like Winona Ryder and Sarah Jessica Parker swear by Kiehl's products. Exclusive retailers like Bergdorf Goodman and Barney's carry the brand with no solicitation from Kiehl's. Fashion seekers from around the world converge on the firm's East Village shop. The big-name cosmetic firms have offered to buy Kiehl's, but management has no interest in selling.

Kiehl's offers a striking lesson in the world of glitzy, multimethod promotional programs. Instead of using glossy magazine ads and courting high-profile supermodels, the firm creates a positive buzz about the brand with other, more subtle types of communication. For example, magazines from *Vogue* to *Marie Claire* routinely list Kiehl's products as among the best. The managing editor of *In Style* estimates that Kiehl's has been mentioned in more than sixty articles in a two-year span. In turn, many fashion moguls are regular customers of the Kiehl shop, which, in turn, creates its own sort of buzz among the city's celebrity hairdressers. At the same time, Kiehl's rosewater facial freshener-toner and pineapple papaya facial scrub appear in trendy, upscale places like Manhattan's Soho Grand Hotel, even though Kiehl's did not sell directly to them. No beautiful models with beautiful hair in beautiful fashion magazines.

So just what *does* Kiehl's do to promote its brand? First, the company is extremely customer oriented. When a customer comes into the (only) shop, Kiehl's employees have been known to spend up to half an hour with a customer sampling products. Second, employees are encouraged to give away as many free samples as the customer desires. Finally, the firm has a liberal return policy. Even if a product is almost completely used, Kiehl's will replace it or give a full refund. The one concession the firm has made to modern promotion is a toll-free number to make it easy for customers to order the brand.

How has this low-key approach to promotion played out? Growth has been between 20 and 30 percent per year since the mid-1990s. Not only is this outstanding growth for any company, but it far surpasses the average growth rate in the cosmetics–personal care products industry. And this is an industry where the average marketer spends from 15 to 20 percent of sales on promotion. Perhaps the success of Kiehl's, in the absence of mainstream promotion, is best summed up by Jami Morris (who runs the company with her husband), who says, "Touching a person—that's the best way to make a business grow. Then you're convincing them. It's not just false hope or promises."[1]

EXHIBIT 12.1

Despite spending virtually nothing on promotional materials and using bland, almost generic packaging, Kiehl's has been able to successfully market its line of men's and women's hair and skin care products. The secret? A variety of supportive communications that have created positive word of mouth has propelled the brand to high stature and high annual sales growth.

1.   Hilary Stout, "Ad Budget: Zero. Buzz: Deafening," *The Wall Street Journal,* December 29, 1999, B1.

INTRODUCTION

The Kiehl's example is a fitting prelude to this chapter because it illustrates several of the chapter's basic themes. It makes the point that marketers are constantly on the lookout for new, cost-effective ways to break through the clutter of competitors' promotions to register their appeals with carefully targeted consumers. Although major advertising media and sales promotions will continue to draw the lion's share of promotional expenditures, many other options exist for communicating with consumers, the trade, and business buyers.

This chapter examines a set of promotional options relating to sponsorship, point-of-purchase (P–O–P)communications, and a wide range of techniques commonly referred to as supportive communications. Promotional alternatives in the areas of P–O–P advertising and sponsorship continue to produce impressive results and are receiving more and more funding from many marketers. Two types of supportive communications are discussed in this chapter: media based, and nonmedia based. Supportive communications that are media based such as signs and billboards and signage, have been around for many years but are enjoying renewed interest from marketers. Other media–based supportive communications include transit, aerial, and directory advertising. In addition, a marketer must understand and take advantage of the nonmedia supportive communications opportunities inherent in the brand name, logo, and slogan, as well as, packaging and labeling and word-of-mouth tactics. Remember, in a true integrated marketing communications sense, *every* contact with the brand adds to the communication environment for the target customer, and these nonmedia factors represent another communications contact.

SPONSORSHIP

Marketers large and small have realized that the effectiveness of traditional broadcast media continues to erode as media become more fragmented and consumers become more distracted by the clutter of advertising that appears in programming. No one knows this better than one of the world's biggest marketers—General Motors. GM spends more than $2 billion annually in traditional media such as TV, radio, and magazines.[2] But as indicated by Exhibit 12.2, growing expenditures in these media were not producing the desired impact on market share. In a statement very similar to the one made by Kiehl's managers, one GM executive said, "You have to find other ways to touch customers rather than hammering them with network television."[3]

GM has experimented with a number of ways to "get closer" to its prospective customers. Most entail sponsoring events that get consumers in direct contact with its vehicles, or sponsoring events that associate the GM name with causes or activities that are of interest to its target customers. For example, GM has sponsored a scholarship program for the Future Farmers of America and Seventh Avenue's "Week of Fashion" shows in New York City. The company has also launched a movie theater on wheels that travels to state fairs, fishing contests, and auto races to show its 15-minute "movie" about the Silverado pickup truck. Like many marketers large and small, GM is shifting more of its promotional budget into sponsorship.[4]

Sponsorship is often used to support or supplement other ongoing promotional efforts, particularly advertising. The main reason is that sponsorships can provide a base for effective synergies with other activities such as sales promotions and public relations. As always, the IMC challenge is to get multiple tactical alternatives

---

2.   Fara Warner, "Under Pressure, GM Takes Its Sales Show on the Road," *The Wall Street Journal,* November 4, 1998, B1.
3.   Ibid.
4.   Ibid.

GM Is Spending More on Ads . . .

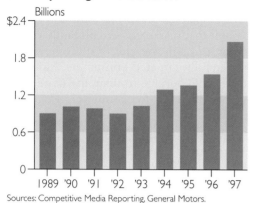

But Its Market Share Is Slipping

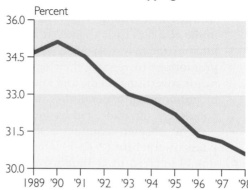

Sources: Competitive Media Reporting, General Motors.

EXHIBIT 12.2

While GM has been spending more and more on advertising, the auto giant has seen a steady decline in market share. The firm has decided to shift some of its promotional spending from advertising to sponsorships and supportive communications to see if these promotional tools can help reverse the trend.

working together to break through the clutter of the marketplace and register the message with the target customer. This is exactly what a new competitor to Altoids has done with a sponsorship series, discussed in the IMC in Practice box.

Who Uses Sponsorship?

A special and increasingly popular way to reach consumers, **sponsorship** involves a marketer providing financial support to help fund an event, such as a rock concert, auto race, golf tournament, or cultural event. In return, that marketer acquires the rights to display a brand name, logo, or advertising message on-site at the event. If the event is covered on television, the marketer's brand and logo may also receive exposure with the television audience. In 1999, marketers' expenditures for sponsorship reached $7.6 billion in the United States alone, with about two-thirds of this total coming from sports sponsorship. Spending is expected to continue to grow robustly for the next several years.[5]

Sponsorship can take many forms. The events can be international in scope, like the Olympics, or they may have a local flavor, like a chili cook-off in Amarillo, Texas. The events may have existed on their own with marketers offering funding after the fact, or marketers may literally create an event they can sponsor in hopes of engaging a segment of their customers. This is exactly what Mercedes-Benz did in the lucrative and high-margin SUV market. The company offered motorists the chance to compare the Mercedes SUV against rival SUVs in its "M-Class Power Trip" events.[6] Potential customers could directly compare the BMW X5, Lexus RX300 and Toyota LandCruiser against the new Mercedes M-Class 320 on incline and flat-track tests. Events like this provide a captive audience, may receive live coverage by radio and television, and are often reported in the print media. Hence, sponsorship can both yield face-to-face contact with consumers and receive follow-up publicity in the mass media.

The list of companies participating in sponsorships grows with each passing year. Sprint, Atlantic Records, Citibank, and a host of other companies have

---

5.   "Record Growth Without Gold," *Promotion Trends 2000,* Annual Report of the U.S. Promotion Industry, May 2000, A23.

6.   Jean Halliday, "Mercedes Brings Rivals on Road Trip," *Advertising Age,* March 20, 2000, 46.

IN PRACTICE

THE MINT WARS

As we saw at the beginning of Chapter 8, Altoids has established almost a cult following in the mint market with its "Curiously Strong" mint and an innovative advertising campaign. Well, a competitor has come up with a highly integrated marketing campaign that might just take some of the attention away from Altoids.

Botsford Group, the promotion agency for Mentos, has put together an exciting mix of events, media advertising, live telecasts, and Internet promotions to grab the attention of the hard-to-reach 18-to-24-year-old market. The centerpiece of the IMC campaign is "The Mentos Freshmaker Tour." This music tour will hit twenty-five college campuses with featured bands including Slow Children at Play, The Noyz, and Michelle Malone. The concert series will be supported with media advertising and live concert telecasts on College Television, which airs in college cafeterias and student unions. In addition, ads will be placed in *Link* student newspapers (http://www.eelink.net) and air on campus radio stations.

The Internet promotion offers a high degree of interaction and excitement for the target market. After logging onto http://www.mentos.com visitors can vote on which band should open the next tour stop, and register (remember that database thing?) to win concert tickets or inflatable Mentos whirlpool tubs.

To support the media and Internet promotions, retailers will be offered four different in-store promotions to complement the concerts. These include a mail-in offer for a free Freshmaker Tour CD, a contest offering a new CD a month for life, and a chance to sit on-stage at a concert in a La-Z-Boy recliner that will later be shipped to the winner's home.

This wide range of media advertising, consumer promotions, and trade support is just the kind of IMC campaign a new competitor needs to challenge an industry leader. David Botsford, president of the Botsford Group Agency, says "The Freshmaker Tour is a great way to extend Mentos' heavy media schedule and take the brand interaction to the next level."

Source: Stephanie Thompson, "Mentos' Music Tour Rolls; New Product Battles Altoids," *Advertising Age,* October 18, 1999, 26.

sponsored tours and special appearances for recording artists such as Brandy, Jewel, Elton John, and the Rolling Stones. Sprint reportedly paid $6 million to the Stones to fund their "Bridges to Babylon" tour, and as suggested by the ad in Exhibit 12.3, were grateful for the opportunity to be associated with "the World's Greatest Rock 'n' Roll Band." To capitalize on the growing popularity of women's NCAA college basketball, State Farm Insurance launched the Hall of Fame Tip-Off Classic.[7] If you have ever hit the beaches for spring break, you already know that companies such as Coca-Cola, MCI, and Sega will be there to greet you.

With the growing interest in stock-car racing and an expanded NASCAR circuit that includes races all over the United States, major brands such as Canon, Tide, Gillette, Winston, McDonald's, and Kodak are scrambling for the privilege of spending $4 million a year to sponsor their very own race car.[8] And the new Internet firms have also discovered the stock-car circuit, with Excite, Mall.com, and Northern Light all spending up to $50 million over five years to sponsor racers.[9] Andersen Consulting has dabbled in golf and auto racing funding, and was also a proud sponsor of the "Van Gogh Masterpieces" art exhibit at the National Gallery of Art in Washington, DC.[10] There can be no doubt that more marketers of all types will pursue sponsorship in the future.

The Appeal of Sponsorship

In the early days of sponsorship, it often wasn't clear what an organization was receiving in return for its sponsor's fee. Even today, many critics contend that sponsorship—especially of sporting events, which have seen fees shoot through the roof (or dome)—can be ego driven and thus a waste of money.[11] Company presidents

7. Patrick M. Reilly, "Rich Marketing Alliances Keep Music Stars Glowing," *The Wall Street Journal,* January 22, 1998, B1.
8. Chris Roush, "Red Necks, White Socks, and Blue-Chip Sponsors," *Business Week,* August 15, 1994, 74; and Alex Taylor III, "Can NASCAR Run in Bigger Circles?" *Fortune,* February 5, 1996, 38.
9. Chris Jenkins, "Search Engines, Dot-Com Firms Signing on at Indy," *USA Today,* May 26, 2000.
10. "Andersen Revamps Logo, Readies $100 Million," *Brandweek,* June 22, 1998, 1.
11. Peter Breen, "Getting Into the Game," *Promo,* November 1999, 69–71.

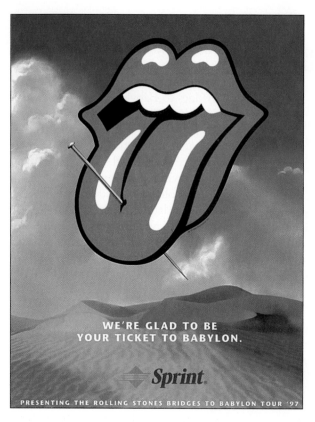

EXHIBIT 12.3

As corporations seek new and different ways to reach target markets with promotions, sponsorship has emerged as a key alternative. Sprint put up $6 million to be one of the lead sponsors of the Rolling Stones' Bridges to Babylon Tour in 1997.

are human, and they like to associate with sports stars and celebrities. This is fine, but when sponsorship of a golf tournament, for example, is motivated mainly by a CEO's desire to play in the same foursome as Jack Nicklaus or Tiger Woods, the company is really just throwing away promotional dollars.

One of the things fueling the growing interest in sponsorship is that many companies are now finding ways to make a case for the effectiveness of their sponsorship dollars. Boston-based John Hancock Mutual Life Insurance has been a pioneer in developing detailed estimates of the value of its sponsorships.[12] The firm began sponsoring a college football bowl game in 1986 and soon after had a means to judge the value of its sponsor's fee. Hancock employees scoured magazine and newspaper articles about their bowl game to determine name exposure in print media. Next they'd factor in the exact number of times that the John Hancock name was mentioned during television broadcast of the game, along with the name exposure in pregame promos. In 1991, Hancock executives estimated that they received the equivalent of $5.1 million in advertising exposure for their $1.6 million sponsorship fee. One John Hancock executive called this result "an extraordinarily efficient media buy."[13] However, as the television audience for the John Hancock Bowl dwindled in subsequent years, Hancock's estimates of the bowl's value also plunged. Subsequently, Hancock moved its sports sponsorship dollars into other events, such as the Winter Olympics from Lillehammer, Norway, and the U.S. Gymnastics Championships.

Other research is also providing hard evidence for the value of sponsorship.[14] Studies conducted with various types of sports fans by Performance Research of Newport, Rhode Island, indicate that fan loyalty can be converted to sales. Among stock-car racing fans, 70 percent say they frequently buy the products they see promoted at the racetrack. For baseball, tennis, and golf, these commitment levels run at 58 percent, 52 percent, and 47 percent, respectively.[15] These findings suggest that racing fans in particular have specific product preferences that marketers can identify and appeal to, and explain why marketers are flocking to the racetrack to get their brand names on the hood of a stock car or on the cap of a stock-car driver.

These research results are behind the reasons why a company like Procter & Gamble would sponsor the Tide Car in NASCAR events. Lots of women are NASCAR fans, and lots of women buy Tide. Additionally, P&G's own research jibes with that mentioned in the previous paragraph: NASCAR fans really are loyal to the brands that sponsor cars and have absolutely no problem with marketers plastering their logos all over their cars and their drivers. This translates into incredible visibility and exposure for the Tide brand during a race and in subsequent race coverage.

12.   Michael J. McCarthy, "Keeping Close Score on Sports Tie-Ins," *The Wall Street Journal,* April 24, 1991, B1.
13.   Ibid.
14.   T. Bettina Cornwell and Isabelle Maignan, "An International Review of Sponsorship Research," *Journal of Advertising,* vol. XXVII, no. 1 (Spring 1998), 1–21.
15.   Roush, "Red Necks, White Socks, and Blue-Chip Sponsors," 74.

Indeed, when it comes to TV exposure, NASCAR's average per-event TV ratings are second only to NFL football, and without a doubt, brands are truly the stars of the show during any NASCAR event.[16] When asked directly how they value the nationally telecast images of driver Ricky Rudd in his Tide jumpsuit standing in the winner's circle next to his screaming orange Tide Car, a tight-lipped P&G spokesperson would only say: "We have had the Tide race car as part of the Tide marketing program for many years, so obviously, we think it's a good way to reach consumers."[17] Obviously.

Sponsorship can furnish a unique opportunity to foster brand loyalty at other kinds of events as well. When marketers connect their brand with the potent emotional experiences often found at rock concerts, in sport stadiums, or on Florida beaches in mid-March, positive feelings may be attached to that brand. As part of its spring break promotion, Coca-Cola sponsors dance contests on the beach, where it hands out thousands of cups of Coke and hundreds of Coca-Cola T-shirts each day. The goal is to build brand loyalty with those 18-to-24-year-old students who've come to the beach for fun and sun. As assessed by one of Coke's senior brand managers, "This is one of the best tools in our portfolio."[18] Likewise, the brand may serve as a lasting reminder that links an individual to a special experience. Additionally, since various types of events attract well-defined target audiences, marketers can and should choose to sponsor just those events that help them reach a desired target. Such is the case with the sponsorships shown in Exhibit 12.4. Notice that JBL electronics is teaming up with TREK to sponsor nationwide mountain biking events. These so-called gravity sports events are particularly effective with cynical teens who reject traditional media advertising and are even starting to reject other forms of promotion. But in the words of one teen attending a BMX bike competition, "It's cool."[19]

Sponsorship is a particularly favored promotional activity in foreign markets. For instance, a "who's who" of the European brewing industry lines up to sponsor professional soccer teams such as Britain's Chelsea football club. Brewers such as Bass PLC and Carlsberg AS want to reach beer-drinking soccer fans in hopes that the fans will become as loyal to their beers as they are to their favorite soccer team. Heineken, based in the Netherlands, has a multiyear deal with the International Tennis Federation both because its managers want the international exposure and because they believe that perceptions of tennis as a more civilized sport better match the refined imagery they try to convey to the "sophisticated" beer drinker.[20] However, in 1998, Heineken relented,

EXHIBIT 12.4

One of the attractions of sponsorships is the ability to reach highly targeted audiences in a favorable reception environment. Here, JBL and TREK are sponsors of a mountain bike racing tour that reaches the media-skeptical 12-to-24-year-old male market.

---

16. Sam Walker, "NASCAR Gets Coup as Anheuser Is Set to Raise Sponsorship Role," *The Wall Street Journal,* November 13, 1998, B6.

17. Jeff Harrington, "P&G Bubbling over Tide Car's NASCAR Win," *Cincinnati Enquirer,* August 10, 1997, I1.

18. Bruce Horovitz, "Students Get Commercial Crash Course," *USA Today,* March 22, 1995, B1–B2.

19. Laura Petrecca, "Defying Gravity: NBC, Peterson Connect with Cynical Teens via Sports Fest," *Advertising Age,* October 11, 1999, 36.

20. Tara Parker-Pope, "Brewers' Soccer Sponsorships Draw Fire," *The Wall Street Journal,* February 27, 1995, B1.

EXHIBIT 12.5

Guidelines for using event sponsorship effectively

Guidelines for Event Sponsorship

1. Match the brand to the event. Be sure that the event matches the brand personality. Stihl stages competitions at Mountain Man events featuring its lumbering equipment, Would the Stihl brand fare as well sponsoring a boat race or a triathalon? Probably not.

2. Tightly define the target audience. Closely related to point number one is the fact that the best event in the world won't create impact for a brand if it's the wrong target audience. Too often the only barometer of success is the number of bodies in attendance. Far more important is the fact that the brand is getting exposure to the right audience. This is what JBL and trek accomplished with the mountain bike tour sponsorship.

3. Stick to a few key messages. Most event try to accomplish too much. People are there to experience the event and can only accommodate a limited amount of persuasion. Don't overwhelm them. Stick to a few key messages and repeat them often.

4. Develop a plot line. An event is most effective when it is like great theater or a great novel. Try to develop a beginning, a middle, and an exciting ending. Sporting events are naturals in this regard, which explains much of their popularity. In non-sporting events, the plot line needs to be developed and delivered in small increments so the attendees can digest both the event and the brand information.

5. Deliver exclusivity. If you staging a special event, make it by invitation only. Or, if you are a featured sponsor, invite only the most important customers, clients, or suppliers. The target audience wants to know that this event is special. The exclusivity provides a positive aura for the brand.

6. Deliver relevance. Events should build reputation, awareness, and relationships. Trying to judge the success of an event in terms of sales is misleading and short-sighted. Don't make the event product-centric; make it a brand-building experience for the attendees.

7. Use the Internet. The Internet is a great way to promote the event, maintain continuous communication with the target audience, and follow up with the audience after an event. Plus, it's a good way to reach all the people who can't attend the event in person. pga.com gets viewers involved with each event on the tour and gives sponsors another chance to reach the target audience.

8. Plan for the before and after. Moving prospects from brand awareness to trial to brand loyalty doesn't happen overnight. The audience needs to see the event as part of a broad exposure to the brand. This is the synergy that needs to be part of the event-planning process. The event must be integrated with advertising, sales promotions, and advertising specialty items.

Source: Laura Shuler, "Make Sure to Deliver When Staging Events," Marketing News, September 13, 1999, 12.

at least temporarily, as it ran a number of local promotions in conjunction with Holland's entry in the World Cup Soccer Championships. Given the incredible fan support generated for a World Cup team, Heineken simply could not pass on this loyalty-building opportunity. Hup Holland!

Seeking a Synergy Around Sponsorship

As we have seen, one way to justify sponsorship is to calculate the number of viewers who will be exposed to a brand either at the event or through media coverage of the event, and then assess whether the sponsorship provides a cost-effective way of reaching the target segment. This approach assesses sponsorship benefits in direct comparison with traditional advertising media. Some experts now maintain, however, that the benefits of sponsorship can be fundamentally different from anything that traditional media might provide. These additional benefits can take many forms.

Events can be leveraged as ways to entertain important clients, recruit new customers, motivate the firm's salespeople, and generally enhance employee morale. Events provide unique opportunities for face-to-face contact with key customers.[21] Marketers commonly use this point of contact to distribute specialty-advertising items so that attendees will have a branded memento to remind them of the rock concert or soccer match. Marketers may also use this opportunity to sell premiums such as T-shirts and hats, administer consumer surveys as part of their marketing research efforts, or distribute product samples. As you will see in the next chapter, a firm's event participation may also be the basis for public relations activities that then generate additional media coverage.

John Hancock Mutual Life has shown remarkable creativity in maximizing the benefits it derived from the $24 million it spent for its five-year sponsorship of the Olympic Games.[22] Of course, association with a high-profile event such as the Summer Games in Atlanta yields broad exposure for the John Hancock name, but the company has also been skillful in taking advantage of its sponsor status with local programs. For instance, in conjunction with the Winter Games, Hancock sponsored hockey clinics featuring Olympians from the 1980 gold medal–winning team. Children and their parents turned out in droves. While the clinics were designed for children, the parents who brought them became immediate prospects for Hancock sales representatives. It is this sort of synergy between sponsorship and local selling efforts that organizations often fail to strive for in maximizing the benefits of their sponsorship expenditures. To create synergy and impact, experts offer guidelines for making the most of sponsorships, and these are listed in Exhibit 12.5.

POINT-OF-PURCHASE ❷

Point-of-purchase (often described as **point-of-purchase advertising**) refers to materials used in the retail setting to attract shoppers' attention to a marketer's brand, convey primary brand benefits, or highlight pricing information. It can take many forms. In-store displays, banners, shelf signs, wall units, and floor stands are traditional and economical means of drawing attention to a brand in a retail setting. As we briefly discussed in Chapter 11, P–O–P displays may also feature price-off deals or other consumer sales promotions. A corrugated cardboard dump bin and an attached header card featuring the brand logo or related product information can be produced for pennies per unit. When they fill such units with a brand and place them as a freestanding display at retail, marketers often experience short-term sales gains—(referred to as "lift" in the industry (see Exhibit 12.6).

From 1981 to 1999, marketers' annual expenditures on P–O–P advertising rose from $5.1 to $14.4 billion per year.[23] Why this dramatic growth? First, consider that P–O–P is the only medium that places promotion, products, and a consumer together in the same place at the same time. Then think about these results.

- Research conducted by the Point-of-Purchase Advertising Institute (POPAI at http://www.popai.com) discovered that 70 percent of all product selections involve some final deliberation by consumers at the point of purchase.[24]

21. Susan Sloves, "Do Sponsorships Provide a Gold Mine or a Black Hole?" *Marketing News,* February 2, 1998, 9.
22. William M. Buckeley, "Sponsoring Sports Gains in Popularity, John Hancock Learns How to Play to Win," *The Wall Street Journal,* June 24, 1994, B1.
23. Lisa Z. Eccles, "P–O–P Scores with Marketers," *Advertising Age,* September 26, 1994, P1–P4; Leah Haran, "Point of Purchase: Marketers Getting with the Program," *Advertising Age,* October 23, 1995, 33; "The 1998 Annual Report of the Promotion Industry," in *Promo's 6th Annual SourceBook '99* (Stamford, CT: *Promo* magazine, 1999), 10, 11; and "Retailtainment Today," *Promotion Trends 2000,* Annual Report of the U.S. Promotion Industry, May 2000, A16.
24. Data cited in POPAI *U.S. Consumer Buying Habits Study,* 1995, pp.17–18. Conducted by POPAI in conjunction with Meyers Research Center.

EXHIBIT 12.6

The effective development and use of point-of-purchase materials will often result in short-term spikes in sales.

- A joint study sponsored by Kmart and Procter & Gamble found that P–O–P advertising boosted the sales of coffee, paper towels, and toothpaste by 567 percent, 773 percent, and 119 percent, respectively.[25]

- In a large study of 4,200 consumers in fourteen cities involving over 30,000 shopping choices related to point-of-purchases materials, researchers found that 59 percent of the purchases were unplanned (that is, the shoppers were motivated to buy, at least in part, by the P–O–P materials), consumers were more likely to make an unplanned decision when the product was displayed at the end of an aisle or at the cash register, and in-store decisions were greater for larger households with higher incomes.[26]

- Point-of-purchase display materials were found to increase sales in the carbonated soft drink and salt snack food categories in 13 weeks of a 20-week study period.[27]

With results like these, it is plain to see why P–O–P advertising is one of the fastest-growing categories in today's marketplace.

The Value of Point-of-Purchase

While we tend to think of P–O–P materials as providing value strictly to marketers as a promotional tool, there are values of in-store point-of-purchase to retailers and consumers as well. From the marketer's perspective, the most important effect of P–O–P materials is that they can have an impact on sales, as the research results cited above indicate. But there is more to the effect of P–O–P than the potential for a sales "lift." In-store displays can also make the brand name more prominent in a cluttered retail shopping environment. And with proper design and coordination, P–O–P materials can reinforce other promotional tools such as sales promotions or even media advertising.[28] The in-store Tommy Hilfiger displays for Tommy Fragrances uses placards that are reproductions of the magazine ads run for the brand, thus reinforcing consumers' exposure to media advertising.

Several advantages of point-of-purchase accrue to retailers who maintain in-store displays. Well-designed and creative in-store materials can make the shopping experience easier and more entertaining for consumers. The president of one display provider notes that "Brand marketers and retailers are trying to create a better shopping experience for consumers."[29] The better the shopping experience, the more time consumers will spend in a store and the more likely they are to increase their

25. Eccles, "P–O–P Scores with Marketers," P1–P4; Haran, "Point of Purchase: Marketers Getting with the Program," 33.

26. J. Jeffrey Inman and Russell S. Winer, "Where the Rubber Meets the Road: A Model for In-Store Consumer Decision Making," *Marketing Science Institute Working Paper Report No. 98-122,* October 1998, v.

27. "Establishing Point-of-Purchase Advertising as a Measured Medium," reported in a Pilot Study developed by the Point of Purchase Advertising Institute and The Advertising Research Foundation, March 16, 2000.

28. Doug Leeds, "Accountability Is In-Store for Marketers in '94," *Brandweek,* March 14, 1994, 17.

29. "Retailtainment Today," May 2000, A16.

spending. Further, the design of P–O–P materials can make the retailer's job easier. Well-designed in-store displays increase the revenue-generating space in a store by providing more effective shelf space. In addition, displays can help retailers maintain and track inventory.

Finally, there are values of point-of-purchase materials to consumers. First, all forms of in-store display provide information to consumers. Some of the information is functional, offering product use or application advice. Other information is more persuasive and emotional, alerting consumers to the availability of the brand. Second, P–O–P materials can make the shopping experience easier for the consumer. Well-designed displays help a consumer locate and easily acquire items. Making the shopping experience more pleasant and convenient for consumers will be positive for the consumer, but will also benefit the marketer and retailer.

EXHIBIT 12.7

This is a point-of-purchase display unit known as a "dump bin." Notice that the product is easily accessible to consumers from the "bin," while the display itself serves to attract shoppers' attention.

Types of P-O-P Displays

A myriad of displays and presentations are available to marketers wanting to use P–O–P as part of the promotional mix. Point-of-purchase materials generally fall into two categories: **Short-term promotional displays,** which are used for six months or less, and **permanent long-term displays,** which are used for more than six months.[30] Within these two categories, marketers have a wide range of choices with these general categories:[31]

- *Window and door signage:* Any sign that identifies and/or advertises a company or brand or gives directions to the consumer.
- *Counter/shelf unit:* A smaller display designed to fit on counters or shelves.
- *Floorstand:* Any P–O–P that stands independently on the floor.
- *Shelf talker:* A printed card or sign designed to mount on or under a shelf.
- *Mobile/banner:* An advertising sign suspended from the ceiling of a store or hung across a large wall area.
- *Cash register:* P–O–P signage or small display mounted on a cash register designed to sell impulse items like gum, lip balm, or candy.
- *Full-line merchandiser:* A unit that provides the only selling area for a manufacturer's line. Often located as an end-of-aisle display.
- *End-of-aisle display/gondola:* Usually a large display of products placed at the end of an aisle.
- *Dump bin:* A large bin with graphics or other signage attached. A dump bin with tower display for Nabisco's Barnum's Animals crackers is shown in Exhibit 12.7. This 76-inch-tall cardboard tower spent fourteen weeks in design before being mass produced and rolled out across the country. The gorilla towers, along with their tiger and elephant predecessors, were the cornerstone of the promotional strategy for Barnum's.[32]
- *Illuminated sign:* Lighted signage can be used outside or in-store to promote a brand or the store itself.
- *Motion display:* Any P–O–P unit that has moving elements to attract attention.

30. *The Point-of-Purchase Advertising Institute's Retailer Guide to Maximizing In-Store Advertising Effectiveness* (Washington, DC: Point-of-Purchase Advertising Institute, 1999), 4.
31. Ibid, 5–7.
32. Yumiko Ono, "'Wobblers' and 'Sidekicks' Clutter Stores, Irk Retailers," *The Wall Street Journal,* September 8, 1998, B1.

- *Interactive unit:* A computer-based kiosk where shoppers get information like tips on recipes or how to use the brand. Also, a unit that flashes and dispenses coupons.
- *Overhead merchandiser:* A display rack that stocks product and is placed above the cash register. The cashier can reach the product for the consumer. The front of overhead merchandisers usually carry signage.
- *Cart advertising:* Any advertising message adhered to a shopping cart.
- *Aisle directory:* Used to delineate contents of a store aisle and also provide space for an advertising message.

This array of in-store options give both marketers and retailers the opportunity to attract shoppers' attention, enliven the shopping environment, and provide more convenience for consumers. The future of P–O–P is dependent on proper execution, however, as the following sections discuss.

Coordinating P-O-P with the Sales Force

Effective deployment of P–O–P advertising requires careful coordination with the marketer's sales force. Gillette found this out when it realized it was wasting money on lots of P–O–P materials and displays that retailers simply ignored.[33] Gillette sales reps visit about 20,000 stores per month and are in a position to know what retailers will and will not use. Gillette's marketing executives finally woke up to this fact when their sales reps told them, for example, that 50 percent of the shelf signs being shipped to retailers from three separate suppliers were going directly to retailers' garbage bins. Reps helped redesign new display cards that mega-retailers such as Wal-Mart approved for their stores and immediately put into use. Now, any-time Gillette launches a new P–O–P program, it tracks its success through the eyes and ears of twenty of its sales reps who have been designated as monitors for the new program. Having a sales force that can work with retailers to develop and deliver effective P–O–P programs is yet another critical element for achieving integrated marketing communications.

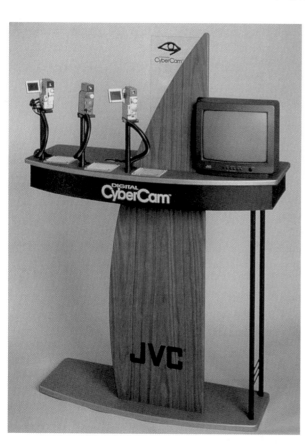

EXHIBIT 12.8

Technological advances are providing for more interactive P-O-P displays like this JVC CyberCam floor display.

Technology, E-Commerce, and P-O-P

Technological developments will have a major impact on the appeal of P–O–P advertising in the future. Interactive electronic displays, like the JVC Cyber-Cam floor display in Exhibit 12.8, remain expensive relative to traditional low-tech options. But as costs come down, high-tech displays are likely to see broader application because of both their information and entertainment value.

Warner-Lambert has shown good results from on-shelf computers placed in 600 Canadian drugstores.[34]

33. Nicole Crawford, "Keeping P–O–P Sharp," *Promo,* January 1998, 52, 53.
34. Lisa Z. Eccles, "Technology Gives P–O–P a New Look," *Advertising Age,* September 26, 1994, P6.

P-O-P GOES INTERACTIVE

Traditionally, point-of-purchase displays have offered customers an easy-to-spot, attractive product display, featured a two-for-one offer, or perhaps even dispensed a money-saving coupon. Well, P-O-P has leaped into the future with high-tech displays that not only make shopping more interesting for consumers, but also can generate valuable data for marketers.

Everbrite of Greenfield, Wisconsin, has introduced a line of interactive P-O-P units that provide a variety of services to both consumers and marketers. One unit prints coupons, product use recommendations, and prescription drug information. The real power of this type of unit lies in the fact that the display is linked to information sources by telephone lines. This means an advertiser can change or update the unit's output daily to provide unique and timely information to consumers.

Another high-tech P-O-P unit can link as many as thirty microcomputers. A host PC supplies the entire network with a database containing product information and graphic displays. When a customer interacts with the computer (which looks like a video display unit), the printer is programmed to print a coupon for the specific product in which the consumer is interested.

These new P-O-P units can also be used to gather information from consumers. A Toyota dealership in San Diego ran a direct-mail game. To find out if they won a prize, consumers had to visit the dealership and swipe the bar code of their game piece on a bar-code reader P-O-P display. The display also asked consumers, now identified by name and zip code location, their impressions of various Toyota products and programs. These data then were fed into the dealership's database for future direct-mail campaigns.

P-O-P displays are no longer the lifeless pyramid of products stacked at the end of an aisle. They can interact with consumers and gather data for marketers to produce better-integrated promotional programs. Audio chips, motion displays, and high-intensity lighting are also being employed to bring P-O-P displays to life. But the primary goal for P-O-P advertising never changes: to make your brand stand out in a crowd.

Sources: Kelly Shermach, "Great Strides Made in P-O-P Technology," *Marketing News*, January 2, 1995; "P-O-P Gains, But Girds for Tobacco Withdrawal," in *Promo's* 6th Annual SourceBook '99 (Stamford, CT: *Promo*, 1999), 14, 15.

At $250 per unit, these computers help consumers sort through the maze of over-the-counter cough, cold, and allergy remedies, leading them to select from Warner-Lambert brands such as Actifed and Benadryl. In the United States, interactive kiosks provide a similar function in more than 2,900 pharmacies across the country, generating an estimated minimum of 33 million customer contacts per year.[35] Advances in the materials used to construct traditional displays, such as new powder coatings that can give a cardboard display the look of chrome, zinc, or brass plating, will also keep the dollars flowing to P-O-P advertising.

These advances in technology have created both opportunities and concerns for P-O-P vendors and users. Developments in e-commerce have retailers concerned that they will start losing business in key product categories like personal care products, cosmetics, and over-the-counter pharmaceuticals as consumers turn to online shopping sites for these types of products. But technology also has the potential to transform the in-store P-O-P process. In the near future, consumers can expect to see in-store kiosks that will allow them to place orders for merchandise not available on-site in the store. In addition, the trend toward a more digital P-O-P world will offer consumers more creative and entertaining displays. For example, Helene Curtis has developed an in-store display for its Thermasilk brand shampoo that creates the illusion of a woman's hair being dried as the consumer walks past.[36] More efforts on the part of the industry are discussed in the New Media box.

35.   Kelly Shermach, "New CD Products Show Times Are A-Changin'," *Marketing News* March 27, 1995, 11.
36.   "Retailtainment Today," May 2000, A16.

SUPPORTIVE COMMUNICATIONS—MEDIA ③

This section will feature traditional supportive communications that are media based: outdoor signage and billboard advertising, transit and aerial advertising, and directory advertising. **Support media** are used to reinforce or extend a message being delivered via some other media vehicle; hence the name support media. They can be especially productive when used to deliver a message near the time or place where consumers are actually contemplating brand selections. Since these media can be tailored for local markets, they can have value to any organization that wants to reach consumers in a particular venue, neighborhood, or metropolitan area.

Outdoor Signage and Billboard Advertising

Billboards, posters, and outdoor signs are one of the oldest advertising forms.[37] Posters first appeared in North America when they were used during the Revolutionary War to keep the civilian population informed about the war's status. In the 1800s, they became a promotional tool, with circuses and politicians being among the first to adopt this new medium. With the onset of World War I, the U.S. government turned to posters and billboards to call for recruits, encourage the purchase of war bonds, and cultivate patriotism. Exhibit 12.9 shows one of the early uses of outdoor advertising. By the 1920s, outdoor advertising also enjoyed widespread commercial applications and, until the invention of television, was the medium of choice when an advertiser wanted to communicate with visual imagery.

While the rise of television stifled the growth of outdoor advertising, the federal highway system that was laid across the nation in the sixties pumped new life into billboards. The 40-foot-high burgers and pop bottles were inevitable, but throughout the seventies and eighties, billboards became an outlet for creative expression in advertising. One exceptional example of using the medium to its fullest was a Nike campaign run in the mid-eighties featuring high-profile athletes, such as Olympian Carl Lewis, performing their special artistry.[38] Today, the creative challenge posed by outdoor advertising is as it has always been—to grab attention and communicate with minimal verbiage and striking imagery, as do the billboards in Exhibits 12.10 and 12.11.

In excess of $4.8 billion was spent to deliver marketers' messages on the 400,000 billboards across the United States in 1999, and some of the most creative work in advertising is showing up on billboards.[39] It can be argued that outdoor advertising offers several distinct advantages relative to other promotion options.[40] This medium provides an excellent means to achieve wide exposure of a message in specific local markets. Their size is, of course, a powerful attraction, and when combined with special lighting and moving features, billboards can be captivating. Billboards created for Dayton Hudson in Minneapolis have even wafted a mint scent throughout the city as part of a candy promotion for

EXHIBIT 12.9

Outdoor signage is one of the oldest forms of supportive communication. This poster from the early 1900s features an appeal to patriotism from the U.S. Government.

37.   Ann Cooper, "All Aboards," *Adweek,* May 9, 1994, 3–10.
38.   Ibid.
39.   Ellen Neuborne, "Road Show: The New Face of Billboards," *Business Week,* May 8, 2000, 75.
40.   Jack Z. Sissors and Lincoln Bumba, *Advertising Media Planning* (Lincolnwood, IL: NTC Business Books, 1993).

**EXHIBITS 12.10
AND 12.11**

*Two key creative goals for
billboards are to attract attention and communicate with a
minimum of verbiage. There
are no better examples of accomplishing those goals than
these two billboards.*

Valentine's Day.[41] Billboards also offer around-the-clock exposure for an advertiser's message and are well suited to showing off a brand's distinctive packaging or logo.

Billboards are especially effective when they reach viewers with a message that speaks to a need or desire that is immediately relevant. For example, British Airways runs a single billboard in Manhattan along the freeway to JFK and LaGuardia airports, featuring a spectacular shot of its Concorde jet at takeoff.[42] The board simply reads "London Bridge" and provides a constant reminder that British Airways

41.   Ronald Grover, "Billboards Aren't Boring Anymore," *Business Week,* September 21, 1998, 88, 89.
42.   Cooper, "All Aboards."

should be in one's consideration set when traveling to Europe from New York City. This strategic reinforcement of a brand's presence and relevance represents the best that outdoor advertising has to offer.

Billboards have obvious drawbacks. Long and complex messages simply make no sense on billboards; some experts suggest that billboard copy should be limited to no more than six words.[43] Also, the impact of billboards can vary dramatically depending on their location, and assessing locations is tedious and time-consuming. To assess locations, companies typically must send individuals to the site to see if the location is desirable.[44] This activity (known in the industry as "**riding the boards**") can be a major investment of time and money. Moreover, the Institute of Outdoor Advertising rates billboards as expensive in comparison to several other media alternatives.[45] Considering that billboards are constrained to short messages, are often in the background, and are certainly not the primary focus of anyone's attention, their costs may be prohibitive for many marketers.

Despite the costs and the criticism by environmentalists that billboards represent a form of visual pollution, spending on outdoor advertising has been increasing, and because of important technological advances, the future looks secure for billboards.[46] The first of these advances combines the videotaping of billboard sites and their surroundings with software from International Outdoor Systems of London.[47] This tool reduces the amount of time and money that executives must spend riding the boards, and it helps them design boards to fit in with the surroundings at a particular location. The software package not only allows marketers to view billboard sites via videotape, but also lets them insert mock-ups of different billboard executions into the specific location pictured on their computer screen. This design tool and time-saving system should make outdoor advertising a more attractive option for many marketers.

Perhaps even more important to the future of billboard advertising is the development of computer-aided production technology for board facings.[48] Until a few years ago, billboard creation and painting was a labor-intensive process that could take a crew of workers several days to complete, and quality control from board to board was always problematic. Now, thanks to computer graphics, the biggest players are designing their boards digitally. One consequence of computer-aided design is that the time needed to get a campaign up and running on multiple boards has been reduced from months to days. Additionally, board facings can be produced in unlimited quantities with total quality control. The advent of computer-directed painting brings magazine-quality reproduction to billboards in any market. And digital design has set the stage for a major infusion of creativity in billboard advertising. If the designer can think it, he or she now can execute it on a billboard. The rapid deployment, quality control, and creative expression that now are possible in executing billboards and outdoor signage have attracted a whole new group of big-name marketers—such as Disney, Sony, Microsoft, America Online, and Amazon.com—to the great outdoors.[49]

Transit and Aerial Advertising

Transit advertising are ads placed on bus boards, taxis, and train and bus platforms primarily. Transit advertising is a close cousin to billboard advertising, and in many instances it is used in tandem with billboards. The phrase **out-of-home media** is

43. *Yellow Pages and the Media Mix* (Troy, MI: Yellow Pages Publishers Association, 1990).
44. Kevin Goldman, "Spending on Billboards Is Rising; Video Tool Makes Buying Easier," *The Wall Street Journal,* June 27, 1994, B6.
45. Sissors and Bumba, *Advertising Media Planning.*
46. Grover, "Billboards Aren't Boring Anymore."
47. Goldman, "Spending on Billboards Is Rising."
48. Cyndee Miller, "Outdoor Gets a Makeover," *Marketing News,* April 10, 1995, 26.
49. Grover, "Billboards Aren't Boring Anymore."

**EXHIBITS 12.12
AND 12.13**

*The phrase "out-of-home
media" is commonly used to
refer to the combination of
transit and billboard advertising, but as these two exhibits
show, the side of an old
building and the plywood
wall of a construction site
offer ideal space for out-of-
home media advertising.*

commonly used to refer to the combination of transit and billboard advertising, but
as illustrated in Exhibits 12.12, 12.13, and 12.14, out-of-home ads appear in many
venues, including on backs of buildings, at construction sites, and in sports stadiums.
Transit ads may appear as signage on terminal and station platforms, or actually
envelop mass-transit vehicles, as exemplified in Exhibit 12.15. Some cash-strapped
cities and towns even allow transit advertising on police cars, school buses, and
garbage trucks.[50]

50.   Douglas A. Blackmon, "New Ad Vehicles: Police Car, School Bus, Garbage Truck," *The Wall Street Journal,* February 20, 1996, B1.

EXHIBIT 12.14

As this Fenway Park scoreboard shows, signage and advertiser slogans are standard fare at the ballpark. Buy me some peanuts and Crackerjack, I don't care if I ever come back (and neither does Frito Lay, so long as I remember that brand!). None of these ads sport Web addresses . . . does it matter? Which might you decide you need more information on? Is donut selection predicated on nutritional research, or are they hoping you'll pick up a dozen on the way home from the park? Why do you think each chose to pick this particular place to advertise?

Transit advertising can be valuable when an advertiser wishes to target adults who live and work in major metropolitan areas.[51] The medium reaches people as they travel to and from work, and because it taps into daily routines repeated week after week, transit advertising offers an excellent means for repetitive message exposure. In large metro areas such as New York—with its 200 miles of subways and 3 million subway riders—transit ads can reach large numbers of individuals in a cost-efficient manner.

When working with this medium, an advertiser may find it most appropriate to buy space on just those trains or bus lines that consistently haul people from the demographic segment being targeted. This type of demographic matching of vehicle with target is always preferred as a means of deriving more value from limited ad budgets. Transit advertising can be appealing to local merchants because their message may reach a passenger as he or she is traveling to a store to shop. For some consumers, transit ads are the last medium they are exposed to before making their final product selection.

Transit advertising works best for building or maintaining brand awareness; as with outdoor billboards, lengthy or complex messages simply cannot be worked into this medium. Also, transit ads can easily go unnoticed in the hustle and bustle of daily life. People traveling to and from work via a mass-transit system are certainly one of the hardest audiences to engage with an advertising message. They can be bored, exhausted, absorbed by their thoughts about the day, or occupied by some

51. Sissors and Bumba, *Advertising Media Planning.*

http://www.converse.com
http://www.autowraps.com
http://www.freecar.com

EXHIBIT 12.15

This Dutch tram carries passengers and a commercial message (though maybe it'll inspire you to walk, and not take the bus!). These days, pretty much anything is fair game for transit advertising, from bumper stickers to whole cars—several companies will pay you to drive with corporate logos affixed to your car on thin film sheets, or even give you a car for free. How do you think those firms choose their drivers?

EXHIBIT 12.16

Aerial advertising offers marketers a unique way to communicate to consumers.

other medium. Given the static nature of a transit poster, breaking through to a harried commuter can be a tremendous challenge.

When an advertiser can't break through on the ground or under the ground, it may have to look skyward. **Aerial advertising** can involve airplanes pulling signs or banners, skywriting, or those majestic blimps and balloons (see Exhibit 12.16). For several decades, Goodyear had blimps all to itself; however, in the nineties, new blimp vendors came to the market with smaller, less expensive blimps that made this medium surge in popularity with other marketers.[52] Virgin Lightships now flies a fleet of small blimps that measure 70,000 cubic feet in size and can be rented for advertising purposes for around $200,000 per month. Not to be outdone, Airship International flies full-size blimps, about 235,000 cubic feet in size, which it promotes as offering 200 percent more usable ad space than the competition's minilimps.

Sanyo, Fuji Photo, MetLife, and Anheuser-Busch have clearly bought into the appeal of an airborne brand presence. The Family Channel has also been a frequent user of Virgin Lightships' miniblimps over sporting events such as the Daytona 500 NASCAR race. A recall study done after one such event showed that 70 percent of target consumers remembered the Family Channel as a

52. Fara Warner, "More Companies Turn to Skies as Medium to Promote Products," *The Wall Street Journal,* January 5, 1995, B6.

result of the blimp flyovers.[53] Blimps carrying television cameras at sporting events also provide game coverage that can result in the blimp's sponsor getting several on-air mentions. This brand-name exposure comes at a small fraction of the cost of similar exposure through television advertising.

Perhaps the best indication that blimp advertising does produce results is the growing blimp traffic over major sporting events. When a medium proves itself, more and more marketers will want it in their media plans. Of course, the irony is that as a medium becomes more attractive and hence cluttered, its original appeal begins to be diluted. We see this occurring with aerial advertising. With more and more blimps showing up at sporting events, networks can be choosy about which one gets the coveted on-air mention. Besides carrying an overhead camera for them, networks now demand that blimp sponsors purchase advertising time during the event if they want an on-air mention. Additionally, the sportscaster's casual banter about the beautiful overhead shots from so-and-so's wonderful blimp have now been replaced by scripted commentary that is written out in advance as part of the advertising contract.[54] As we've noted before, this cycle of uniqueness and effectiveness, followed by clutter and dilution of effectiveness, is one that repeats itself over and over again in the challenging world of promotion. But Pizza Hut may have found the ultimate solution to clutter, as the Global Issues box explains.

GL○BAL ISSUES

GLOBAL PROMOTION? HOW ABOUT INTERGALACTIC?

While most global promotions are pretty good and some are brilliant, they all suffer from one common drawback: They are all earthbound. Not so with a promotional plan by Pizza Hut. Global wasn't good enough for this promotion. This promotion ended up being intergalactic.

It all started when Pizza Hut strategists learned that they could buy the rights to paint the firm's newly redesigned logo on an unmanned Russian Proton rocket. The mammoth rocketing billboard was the centerpiece of a major space campaign by the company that included TV spots featuring the blastoff and a "galaxy" of in-store promotions.

The Proton section bearing the firm's logo would actually burn up in the atmosphere. But the prospect of a few seconds of intergalactic exposure was too much to turn down. Pizza Hut executives explained that "We needed a mythic symbol." Pizza Hut is not revealing the price tag on the logo launch, but did suggest that it was only about half the cost of a 30-second spot on the Super Bowl. That translates into about $1.5 million.

Actually, the Russian rocket was the company's *second* choice for interstellar exposure. Originally, the marketing group wanted to project the new logo onto the earth's moon. They called on officials from the Naval Observatory in Washington as well as the top experts at Hughes Space and Communications International, the Federal Aviation Administration, and scientists at the Hayden Planetarium in New York. But Pizza Hut hopefuls soon learned that the idea simply wouldn't work. First, the laser technology for projection would not be perfected for many years; second, the image would have to be as big as the state of Texas to be seen from Earth without a telescope. Finally, there was one minor problem that would nix the project even if the technical details could be worked out. It seems the light beam would have to be so bright that it might blind aircraft pilots and interfere with navigational equipment.

So, in the end, Pizza Hut had to settle for a few minutes of glory on the side of a Russian rocket. There is no word, as yet, what the next intergalactic promotion might be.

Source: Richard Gibson, "For Pizza Hut, a New Pie-in-the-Sky Ad Strategy," *The Wall Street Journal,* September 30, 1999, B1.

Directory Advertising

The last time you reached for a phone directory to appraise the local options for Chinese or Mexican food, you probably didn't think about it as a traditional support medium. However, yellow pages and other directory advertising play an important role in the media mix for many types of organizations,

53. Ibid.

54. Bill Richards, "Bright Idea Has Business Looking Up for Ad Blimps," *The Wall Street Journal,* October 14, 1997, B1.

as is evidenced by the $12.7 billion spent in this medium in 1999.[55] A wealth of current facts and figures about this media option are available at http://www.yppa.org.

A phone directory can play a unique and important role in consumers' decision-making processes. While most support media keep a brand name or key product information in front of a consumer, yellow pages advertising helps people follow through on their decision to buy. By providing the information that consumers need to actually find a particular product or service, the Yellow Pages can serve as the final link in a buying decision. Because of their availability and consumers' familiarity with this advertising tool, yellow pages directories provide an excellent means to supplement awareness-building and interest-generating campaigns that a marketer might be pursuing through other media.

On the downside, the proliferation and fragmentation of phone directories can make this a difficult medium to work in.[56] Many metropolitan areas are covered by multiple directories, some of which are specialty directories designed to serve specific neighborhoods, ethnic groups, or interest groups. Selecting the right set of directories to get full coverage of large sections of the country can be a daunting task. Additionally, working in this medium requires long lead times, and over the course of a year, information in a yellow pages ad can easily become dated. There is also limited flexibility for creative execution in the traditional paper format.

Because of emerging technologies, the phone directory of the future may evolve into a form that allows marketers considerably more room for creative execution. The Yellow Pages national organization has made a renewed commitment to providing a nationwide electronic directory system.[57] The system allows consumers to search for Chinese restaurants in Boston and retrieve current menu information online, along with photographs of the dining room and service staff. Bell Atlantic is also working with CD technology to deliver directory listings on television sets. The CD-based system can offer full-motion video and stereo sound, along with an interactive capability that could allow a customer to create a personalized map from home to the restaurant or retailer selected. A variation of this system is being tested with broadband and television delivery of the directory listings.

Additionally, many Web sites such as http://www.bigyellow.com and http://www.superpages.com now provide online access to yellow-page-style databases that allow for individualized searches at one's desktop. Exhibit 12.17 features the home page for BigYellow. Other high-profile Web players such as Yahoo! and Microsoft Network (http://national.sidewalk.msn.com) have also developed online directories as

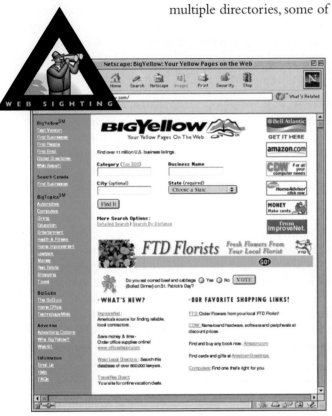

http://www.bigyellow.com; http://www.switchboard.com;
http://www.ftd.com

EXHIBIT 12.17

Certain categories of Web sites naturally attract sponsorship; directories, like BigYellow, Switchboard.com, and others, are one of them. Why might an ad for FTD Florists be appropriate for this site? Is a home mortgage loan ad equally appropriate? Who else might find it useful to put an ad on the BigYellow site?

55.   Yellow Pages Publishers Association: Industry Facts, accessed at http://www.yppa.com on May 28, 2000.
56.   *Yellow Pages and the Media Mix.*
57.   Comments made by John Greco, YPPA President and CEO, at the Annual ADM Conference, Hilton Head, SC, April 4, 2000, accessed at http://www.yppa.com

components of their service offerings for Web surfers. And Yahoo! has partnered with U.S. West to be the exclusive provider of Yellow Pages access. While the emergence of these Internet options cannot be a good thing for traditional yellow pages publishers, the threat they pose can be alleviated through the development of new business models. What those new models should be remains unclear, but most agree that simply dumping the traditional A-to-Z printed Yellow Pages onto the Internet is not the answer.[58] The key question is, when will marketers decide that they are better served by having their product or service described via an online directory rather than a paper directory? That day hasn't come yet, but if and when it does, the demand for yellow paper is going to go way down.

SUPPORTIVE COMMUNICATIONS—NONMEDIA

The nonmedia-based supportive communications are extremely important and can be very powerful in the overall promotional process. As we saw in the introductory scenario, Kiehl's uses no media-based promotional tools, but rather relies exclusively on nonmedia communications (and good press coverage) to carry the brand.

Branding, Logos, and Slogans

The name a company chooses for its brand, the logo, and any form of slogan to accompany the brand represents another form of supportive communication to consumers, the trade, and business buyers. What constitutes a good brand name, logo, or slogan is a matter more of art than science. But there are some basic insights on the communications potential of each of these product factors that can be considered.

Branding is establishing a name, term, symbol, or design that identifies a product with a particular seller and clearly distinguishes that product from products offered by competitors. A distinctive brand name or mark can help a company crystallize for a consumer the positive goodwill of a product. The brand can become a representation of satisfaction that influences a consumer to repeatedly choose a particular company's product over competitors' products. The more favorable and more powerful the positive associations are, the greater the sales potential for the product.

Positive brand associations in the mind of consumers may be the result of many factors. The design and function of the product itself are, of course, the most basic and straightforward way in which satisfaction and therefore positive brand associations can be achieved. The brand name may also have come to represent status and prestige (as do Mercedes for automobiles or Piaget for watches), thus providing a positive association in a less tangible fashion. Wolff Heinrichsdorff, the marketing vice president at Montblanc, explains that much of the power of the brand is in the image that comes from its French name even though the company is German (see Exhibit 12.18). He emphasizes this point by looking skyward, saying, "Can you imagine if [the company] was named after the highest mountain in Germany—Zugspitze?"[59]

A firm's **logo** is related to branding in that it is a visual symbol for a brand. Logos appear on the brand package, in advertising, in sales promotions, on advertising specialty items, and on corporate stationery and business cards. The logo can be a symbolic reminder of the brand name for consumers. Because of its ability to call to mind the brand name, the logo plays an important role in promotional communication.

---

58. *Yellow Pages: Facts and Media Guide 1998,* 4, 5.
59. Bridget Chapple, "Beautifully Crafted Marketing Slogans," *EuroBusiness,* June 1999, 147.

Branding is considered critically important to a firm's overall promotional strategy because consumers need to relate their consumption experiences to some tangible, visible markings. A brand name and logo together provide that tangible, visible representation for consumers to recall their experience with a particular brand from a particular manufacturer. Whether the experience was satisfying or dissatisfying, the consumer has an easily identifiable piece of information upon which to rely during the next buying decision process. If there were no name or symbol with which to associate the experience of, for instance, drinking a soft-drink, the consumer would find it difficult to repeat or to avoid the experience. Consider the unusual (or maybe silly) circumstance of encountering a soft drink vending machine where none of the buttons are labeled with brand names. You would have no way to choose the item you personally find most satisfying. Because manufacturers produce different products for different consumer tastes and preferences, brand names and symbols allow consumers to identify differences between those products and to choose the one they find most appealing and satisfying. Nike has done such a good job of associating the "swoosh" logo with the band name that most of the company's advertising now closes simply with the shot of the logo rather than the brand name.

EXHIBIT 12.18

A well-conceived brand name can contribute to the image of the brand and make promotion more effective and efficient. Even though the company is German based, strategist chose the "Montblanc" name for its prestige and quality image. Montblanc is the highest mountain in France. It does seem carry a better image than "Zugspitze" (the highest mountain in Germany), don't you think?

Promotional Effects of Branding. There are two key promotional effects from the effective use of branding and logos:

- *More efficient promotion.* Branding and logo development can greatly increase the efficiency of communications efforts. As consumers begin to relate the unique features and values of a product to a specific brand name and logo mark, it is easier and less costly for a firm to use various forms of promotion. Once a brand name and mark are established and recognized, a firm is able to communicate information to consumers simply by displaying the brand name or symbol. Mere exposure to the names BMW, Whirlpool, Crest, and McDonald's brings an image and meaning to the mind of consumers.

- *Broader distribution.* A well-established, successful brand will prompt wholesalers and retailers to carry and stock the item. When consumers demand a brand at the store level, retailers are compelled to keep the item in stock to satisfy their customers. Further, successful brands will generally command more retail shelf space, thereby aiding in-store identification of the brand within the clutter of all the other brands displayed.

Once retailers stock the brand because of consumer demand, then wholesalers are also required to carry the item to serve the demands of retailers. The distribution effect of branding, in general, is that it gives the manufacturer greater control over the channel of distribution as we saw in Chapter 2. With strong brand identity and preference among consumers, retailers and wholesalers find it in their best interest to stock the brand, thus taking some of the burden off the manufacturer to push the item through the channel.

CAREERPROFILE

Name:	*Kim E. Honda*
Title:	*Marketing Events and Communications Specialist*
Company:	*Home Director Inc., Morrisville, NC*
	http://www.homedirector.com
Education:	*B.A., Mass Communications,*
	M.S.M., Marketing Management

Imagine a home where you can direct everything from your satellite TV to your high-speed Internet connection from one central control panel. Home Director Inc., a company spun off from IBM in January 2000, is making this high-tech dream a reality with its home networking systems. As the company's Marketing Events and Communications Specialist, Kim Honda's job is to help make sure realtors, building contractors, and homebuyers understand the benefits of living in an "intelligent home."

Kim coordinates a variety of promotional events to get Home Director's message to its target audiences. She researches which technology trade shows will best promote the company's products and then negotiates sponsorships with show producers to make sure Home Director gets maximum visibility at each show. When the company moves into a new market, Kim sets up local launch parties, cobranding sponsorships, and speaking engagements for company executives.

"The projects I work on are always changing," says Kim. "I can start off the week putting together a promotional tent set-up at a local golf tournament and end it by planning a market launch party."

Recently, for example, Kim worked on a special event in Phoenix, Arizona. The goal? To educate local realtors about the latest home technology trends. Working closely with Home Director's sales and marketing executives, as well as the company's CEO, Kim chose a historical theater in Phoenix for the event's venue. She collaborated with a communications agency to develop a promotional plan to gain local media attention for the event while showcasing strategic partnerships with other businesses. She even arranged musical entertainment from the Four Tops.

Kim says staging a promotional event requires close attention to many behind-the-scenes details. "Project management skills and an ability to prioritize and juggle multiple projects are indispensable in this job," she says.

To learn more about promotional events planning, visit these Web sites:

International Association of Conference Centers
http://www.ises.com

***Special Events* Magazine**
http://www.specialevents.com

Meeting Professionals International
http://www.mpiweb.org

Evaluating Potential Brand Names. The issue was raised earlier that branding is more a matter of art than science. In fact, good brand names usually result when marketers let go of all the research and science and give way to the artistic side of the marketing process. But there are some guidelines that can be offered when evaluating potential brand names, and here are the traditional recommendations.

- *Be easy to pronounce and spell.* Short, easily identifiable brand names help the consumer recall and recognize the product. Names like Bold, Brim, Geo, and Dawn are examples.
- *Specify product use or benefit.* If a brand name can relate to the product's primary use, it will be more memorable and communicate valuable information to the buyer. Names like Easy-Off, Gleem, and Sof-Scrub all suggest the product's use and uniqueness.
- *Suggest an image.* A brand name will be more meaningful to consumers if it enhances the image of the firm or the product. Craftsman tools and Die Hard batteries are names that fulfill an image objective.
- *Clearly distinguish the brand name from the competition.* A brand name should be different enough from the competition that consumers can easily recognize it as being associated with a single source. Also, a distinctive brand name can avoid legal problems. Xerox and Coca-Cola are distinctive in highly competitive markets.
- *Be timely and adaptable.* A good brand name will avoid the pitfall of being bound to a unique period of time or single application. It should also be adaptable to a variety of packaging and promotional applications. Apple Computer has discovered that its "Apple" brand name was well suited to the primary and secondary school market, but is still not well received by various segments in the business market.

Like the brand name and logo, a slogan is an important supportive communication. A **slogan** is a short phrase used to help establish an image, identity, or position for a brand or an organization. The most important function of the slogan, however, is to increase the memorability of the brand name and logo. Often a slogan is described as a "brand promise" or a "brand positioning statement." A slogan is established by repeating the phrase in a firm's advertising and other promotional communications as well as through salespeople and event promotions. Slogans are often used as a headline or subhead in print advertisements, as the tag line at the conclusion of radio and television advertisements, and prominently displayed on banners, signage, and posters at events. Slogans typically appear directly below the brand or company name, as in all Lee jeans advertising: "The Brand That Fits." Some of the more memorable and enduring ad slogans are listed in Exhibit 12.19.

A good slogan can serve several positive purposes for a brand or a firm. First, it can be an integral part of a brand's image and personality. BMW's slogan, "The Ultimate Driving Machine," does much to establish and maintain the personality and image of the brand, as we saw in Chapter 1. Second, if a slogan is carefully and consistently developed over time, it can act as a shorthand identification for the brand and provide information on important brand benefits. The long-standing slogan for Allstate Insurance, "You're in Good Hands with Allstate," communicates the

Brand/Company	Slogan
Allstate Insurance	You're in Good Hands with Allstate.
American Express	Don't Leave Home Without It.
American Stock Exchange	The Smarter Place to Be.
AT&T (consumer)	Reach Out and Touch Someone.
AT&T (business)	AT&T. Your True Choice.
Beef Industry Council	Real Food for Real People.
Budweiser	This Bud's for You.
Chevrolet trucks	Like a Rock.
Cotton Industry	The Fabric of Our Lives.
DeBeers	Diamonds Are Forever.
Delta Airlines	You'll Love the Way We Fly.
Ford	Have You Driven a Ford Lately?
Goodyear	The Best Tires in the World Have Goodyear Written All over Them.
Lincoln	What a Luxury Car Should Be.
Microsoft (online)	Where Do You Want to Go Today?
Northwestern Mutual	The Quiet Company.
Panasonic	Just Slightly Ahead of Our Time.
Prudential Insurance	Get a Piece of the Rock.
Saturn	A Different Kind of Company. A Different Kind of Car.
Sharp	From Sharp Minds Come Sharp Products.
Toshiba	In Touch with Tomorrow.
Toyota	Everyday.
Visa	It's Everywhere You Want to Be.

EXHIBIT 12.19

Slogans help reinforce the brand name in the minds of consumers. Slogans are also often referred to as brand positioning statements or image statements. Here is a list of some of the most widely recognized and enduring slogans.

benefits of dealing with a well-established insurance firm. A good slogan also provides continuity across different media and between advertising campaigns. Microsoft's slogan—"Where do you want to go today?"—is all about freedom, and is included on all the promotional materials used by the firm.

Packaging and Labeling

A classic quote from one marketing consultant says that "Packaging is the last five seconds of marketing."[60] While the basic purpose of packaging seems fairly obvious, it can also make a strong positive contribution to the promotional effort. One of the best historical incidents of the power of packaging is when the candy company Just Born Inc. changed its old-fashioned-looking black-and-white packages to colorful new packaging featuring animated grapes and cherries. After the change, sales soared 25 percent in one year. A company marketing official said, "Kids say we went from dull to 'definitely awesome' without a single product or advertising change."[61] Additionally, the Point-of-Purchase Advertising Institute has research to show that more than 70 percent of supermarket purchases now result from in-store decisions.[62] This again suggests that packaging can play a communications role at the point of purchase.

In the simplest terms, **packaging** is the container or wrapping for a product. The package for a brand adds another strategic dimension and can serve an important role in communication It can also affect consumer behavior relating to brand evaluations and the level of use. The package provides strategic benefits to marketers as well as values to the trade and consumers.

Promotional Communication Benefits of Packaging to the Marketer.

Packaging provides several strategic benefits to the manufacturer. First, there is an effect on promotional strategy. The package carries the brand name and logo and communicates the name and symbol to a consumer. In the myriad of products displayed at the retail level, a well-designed package can attract a buyer's attention and induce the shopper to more carefully examine the product. Several firms attribute renewed success of their brands to package design changes. Kraft Dairy Group believes that significant package changes helped its Breyers ice cream brand make inroads in markets west of the Mississippi. A package consulting firm came up with a black-background package that was a radically different look for an ice cream product.

Additional value of packaging has to do with creating a perception of value for the product with the package. The formidable packaging surrounding computer software is made more substantial simply to add tangibility to an intangible product. Similarly, when consumers are buying image, the package must reflect the appropriate image. The color, design, and shape of a package have been found to affect consumer perceptions of a brand's quality, value, and image.[63] Perrier, one of the most expensive bottled waters on the market, has an aesthetically pleasing bottle compared to the rigid plastic packages of it competitors. Perfume manufacturers often have greater packaging costs than product costs to insure that the product projects the desired image.

61. Ibid.

60. Alecia Swasy, "Sales Lost Their Vim? Try Repackaging," *The Wall Street Journal,* October 11, 1989.

62. *An Integrated Look at Integrated Marketing: Uncovering P-O-P's Role as the Last Three Feet in the Marketing Mix* (Washington, DC: Point-of-Purchase Advertising Institute, 2000), 10.

63. Robert L. Underwood and Julie L. Ozanne, "Is Your Package an Effective Communicator? A Normative Framework for Increasing the Communicative Competence of Packaging," *Journal of Marketing Communications,* December 1998, 207–219.

Promotional Values of Packaging to the Trade. The distribution process is considerably aided by a well-designed package. Distributors and retailers are required to perform several functions that are facilitated by easy-to-store, easy-to-handle, and easy-to-display packages. Packages that are not designed for easy storage and handling result in increased expenses for resellers. Further, a package that does not adequately protect the product creates losses for members in the channel of distribution. Resellers are more prone to carry a firm's brand if its package serves their needs for handling, display, and protection.

Communication Values of Packaging to the Consumer. From a communications standpoint, the primary benefit of packaging to consumers is convenience. When a package clearly communicates the brand name and logo, consumers can more easily locate the brand in the shopping environment. This same effect is true when the consumer stores the brand at home. The package continues to communicate the brand name as well as a brand image.

Of course, there are a wide range of noncommunication values of packaging that are realized by consumers. Ease of use, economy of use, safety, and environmental benefits can all be built into package design. These factors go well beyond the communication and promotional role of packaging. Products that have pump applicators, pour spouts, and are easy to open are all more convenient for consumers and, therefore, more satisfying. Related to convenience is economy. Resealable and "no-spill" packages prevent waste. Reusable packages are also appealing from an environmental standpoint.

Closely related to both branding and packaging is the issue of labeling. The **label** is the wrapping on the product container that carries important product use information. The information contained on labels can also serve some important communications and promotional purposes. The label can contain very specific information regarding instructions for using the product. Firms have discovered that consumer dissatisfaction is often the result of improper product use. If a product is designed to function through a particular, precise application, the firm must ensure through label communications that the consumer is made aware of use procedures. Many firms have added toll-free 800 numbers and Web site addresses to help concerned or confused consumers with product use.

The label also provides a manufacturer with a method of communicating warranties. If the product is backed by a warranty, the label can explain its terms and conditions. Use hazards and warnings are also contained on the label. Products that are flammable or otherwise hazardous to use under certain conditions have warnings on the label. Over-the-counter medicines, for example, have historically stated that use is not suggested for certain individuals or in combination with other medicines.

Labels may be acquiring a new level of importance in the overall scheme of product strategies. As consumers are becoming more health and value conscious, they are scrutinizing product labels more. They are looking at nutritional information and scrutinizing labels for chemical additives. This trend will motivate marketers to make label information more precise and readable as consumers adopt the label as the source of information in the choice process—especially at the point of purchase discussed earlier.

Word-of-Mouth Communication

Often, word-of-mouth communication is not discussed as promotional communication for the simple reason that it tends to be out of the control of marketers. Unlike media advertising, promotions, sponsorships, a Web page, or even public relations, word of mouth acquires a life of its own. As we saw at the outset of the chapter, Kiehl's was the beneficiary of positive word of mouth from fashion experts and fashion expert wannabes. In fact, management at Kiehl's even admits that, "It sounds crazy, but it really is word of mouth."[64] In another instance of very beneficial word of mouth, Starbucks took advantage of the very cliquish Seattle coffee market to promote the firm when it began in 1971. Starting as a single shop in Seattle's Pike's Place Market, the firm promoted word of mouth by passing out free samples to passersby.[65] Now Starbucks has thousands of stores in several markets across the United States.

Despite the generally less-than-controllable nature of word of mouth, marketers should pay close attention to the communications potential of this social phenomenon. There are three areas where word-of-mouth communications represent opportunities for marketers in a promotional sense: new products, product categories prone to personal referrals, and the Internet. First, new, innovative products are prone to motivate word-of-mouth communications between individuals. The classic research on new products, which takes a diffusion-of-innovations perspective, shows that at various points in the diffusion of a new product, individuals turn to personal sources of information to learn about the new product.[66] These sources represent a somewhat formalized word-of-mouth communication system. In many new product categories, there is a tendency for certain individuals to come forward as innovators and act as opinion leaders regarding a new product. Opinion leaders are vocal about their experience and have a tendency to express their opinions widely. Based on research, it is possible to describe the characteristics of these opinion leaders. Opinion leaders tend to:[67]

- Live in urban areas and travel extensively.
- Rely on mass media for product information.
- Be more outgoing and have more social contacts than the average person.
- Have higher education.
- Have higher social class.
- Be generally more innovative.

Aside from innovative new products, there are many product choice situations where consumers are prone to rely on friends, neighbors, or relatives as sources of information. Examples of such product categories are books, movies, theater, and various medical service categories like physicians, dentists, and veterinarians. Consumers tend to trust the opinion of friends and relatives in these product categories rather than the information gained from the promotional efforts of firms or the service providers. When a product category is prone to word-of-mouth communication, marketers can "seed" the market by giving away free samples.[68] We saw this technique used by both Kiehl's and Starbucks to get the word out about their brands.

The consulting firm McKinsey & Co. has even developed an approach that explains how to recognize and then ignite explosive word-of-mouth momentum that can lead to what they call "Explosive Self-Generating Demand." McKinsey's program postulates that in order to realize widespread word of mouth and the demand it can generate, two conditions have to exist. First, the product has to be purchased for its social value. Consumers only want to talk about brands that have social meaning and provide social communication. Second, the product has to be "edgy." Word-of-mouth momentum cannot be generated for mundane products like toothpaste or shampoo.[69]

64. Stout, "Ad Budget: Zero. Buzz: Deafening."
65. Alice Z. Cuneo, "Starbuck's Word of Mouth Wonder," *Advertising Age,* March 7, 1994, 12.
66. Everett M. Rogers, *Diffusion of Innovations,* 4th ed. (New York: The Free Press, 1995). See especially Chapters 4 and 5.
67. Ibid.
68. Steve Gelsi and Matthew Grimm "Marketing by Seed," *Brandweek,* October 7, 1996, 20.
69. Renee Dye, "How to Create Explosive Self-Generating Demand," *Advertising Age,* November 8, 1999, s20.

Finally, the Internet offers new opportunities for "spreading the word" through word of mouth. As we saw at the outset of Chapter 9, the "buzz" created for Christina Aguilera's new album was fueled by placing messages on listservs and chatting up the album in chat rooms. The Internet's ability to reach a large number of people at very low cost makes it an ideal medium for creating positive word of mouth. Mass distribution of e-mails through listservs or a concerted effort in chat rooms offers marketers an opportunity to communicate to narrowly targeted audiences with an alterative to more mainstream promotional communications.

When Supportive Communications Are More Than Supportive Communication

There are going to be times when the capabilities and economies of supportive communications lead them to be featured in a firm's promotional plan. Obviously, in such instances, it would be a misnomer to label them as merely supportive. Out-of-home media used creatively and targeted in major metropolitan markets are especially compelling in this regard. A couple of examples should make this point clear.

There will be times when the particular advantages of transit advertising fit a marketer's communication objectives so perfectly that this medium will not be used merely as supportive communications, but instead as the primary means for reaching customers. Donna Karan's DKNY line of clothing, accessories, and cosmetics has relied heavily on transit advertising to reach its target audience in Manhattan.[70] For starters, the firm bought out the ten-car subway train that runs under Lexington Avenue on Manhattan's East Side and filled it with sophisticated image ads for DKNY. Not coincidentally, this particular subway train runs under the Bloomingdale's store on 59th Street, where DKNY has a supershop featuring all the products in its extensive line. DKNY ads have also appeared on the shuttles from Times Square to Grand Central Terminal, and at subway stations in the city. For the company, extensive advertising on and under the streets of New York City reflects its general strategy of using unconventional locations to create awareness and distinctive imagery for the DKNY product line.

One of the most creative and interesting examples comes from a long-standing brand that used a truly innovative supportive campaign. David Dorfman, co-owner of Insite Advertising, sells media space. But not just any media space. David and his partner Marc Miller sell access to the ad space in 250 restrooms of trendy bars, restaurants, and nightclubs throughout New York City. Marketers such as RJR Nabisco, the Joe Boxer Corporation, and Procter & Gamble have bought into Mr. Dorfman's program.[71]

Marketers of the Noxzema brand decided that women's restrooms throughout Manhattan were a place they wanted to be. The thinking was that Noxzema had been around forever, and it was time for a facelift. The company needed something fresh, edgy, unexpected, and new. It needed communication that would help it move up the hip scale and that would challenge women to think, "Whoa, what brand has the nerve to do and say that?" It needed to be in the restroom.

So, working with the company's ad agency, Noxzema brand managers created a series of small posters like those shown in Exhibit 12.20, featuring in-your-face humor such as "It's not the lighting" and "Did someone miss her beauty sleep?" with the common tag line "Next time Noxzema." These signs were hung in frames on the walls across from the mirrors in about 115 trendy restaurants and clubs in chic Manhattan neighborhoods. The signs were meant to be read in the mirror

---

70. Fara Warner, "DKNY Takes Upscale Ads Underground," *The Wall Street Journal,* October 6, 1994, B5.
71. Stuart Elliot, "P&G Takes a Most Unusual Tack with Its New, In-Your-Face Ads," *The New York Times,* June 3, 1998.

EXHIBIT 12.20

When Noxzema needed a facelift and a new edgy promotional campaign, these posters were developed and placed in restrooms in trendy clubs in Manhattan. All of these posters were meant to be read in the mirror.

exactly at that point in time when a woman might be thinking about her face and appearance before returning to the crowded dance floor. Perhaps, then, this is an example of being at the right place at the right time to deliver an in-your-face, "Hey, Look at Me" message, for a brand that had become a little too familiar, and a little too boring.

THE IMC COORDINATION CHALLENGE ❹

When we add sponsorship, point-of-purchase, and the supportive communications opportunities to the many options that have already been discussed in the promotional mix, we have an incredible assortment of choices for delivering messages to a target audience. And it doesn't stop there. As you have seen, marketers are constantly searching for new, cost-effective ways to break through the clutter and reach consumers. Important developments in information technologies will only accelerate this search for new options as the traditional mass media undergo profound changes.

In concluding this chapter, a critical point about this diversity in promotional options needs to be reinforced. Marketers have a vast and ever-expanding array of choices for delivering messages to their potential customers. From cable TV to national newspapers, from virtual billboards to logos to home pages on the World Wide Web, the variety is staggering. The keys to success for any promotional campaign are choosing the right set of options to engage a target segment and then coordinating the placement of messages to ensure coherent and timely communication. As we have seen repeatedly throughout the text, achieving this coordination is easier said than done.

Many factors work against coordination when it comes to sponsorship, point-of-purchase, and the wide array of supportive communications. As the promotional process has become more complex, organizations often become reliant on a large number of functional specialists. For example, an organization might have separate managers for sponsorship, billboards, point-of-purchase, or Web communications. Specialists, by definition, focus on their specialty and can lose sight of what others in the organization are doing. Specialists also want their own budgets and typically argue for more funding for their particular area. Internal competition for budget dollars often yields rivalries and animosities that work against coordination.

Coordination is also complicated by the fact that few ad agencies have all the internal skills necessary to fulfill clients' demands for integrated marketing communications. As an example, Coors Brewing employed Modem Media, an interactive-only ad agency based in Norwalk, Connecticut, to develop the Web site for its Zima brand.[72] Coors' traditional advertising agency, Foote, Cone & Belding, was not involved in this Internet project.

What we need to realize is that with each additional external organization employed to help develop promotional materials that deliver messages to customers, coordination problems will become more complicated and greater vigilance to the process will be needed.[73]

SUMMARY

❶ Explain the growing popularity of sponsorship as a promotional tool.

The list of companies sponsoring events grows with each passing year, and the events include a wide variety of activities. Of these activities, sports attract the most sponsorship dollars. Sponsorship can help build brand familiarity, it can promote brand loyalty by connecting a brand with powerful emotional experiences, and in most instances it allows a marketer to reach a well-defined target audience. Events can also facilitate face-to-face contacts with key customers and present opportunities to distribute product samples, sell premiums, and conduct consumer surveys.

❷ Describe the appeal of point-of-purchase promotions as a key element of IMC.

Expenditures on P–O–P advertising continue to grow at a rapid pace. The reason is simple: P–O–P can be an excellent sales generator when integrated with an overall advertising campaign. P–O–P displays may call attention to one's brand, remind consumers of key benefits provided by one's brand, or offer price-off deals as a final incentive to purchase. Retailers' cooperation is key in making P–O–P programs work; getting their cooperation requires diligent efforts from the marketer's sales force in the field. Due to advances in technology, online shopping and enhanced, interactive displays are boosting the appeal and effectiveness of P–O–P promotions.

❸ Discuss the role of supportive communications tools in the promotional mix.

There are two types of supportive communications: media based and nonmedia based. The traditional media-based supportive communications include out-of-home media along with billboard, transit, and directory advertising. Billboards and transit advertising are excellent means for carrying simple messages into specific metropolitan markets. Aerial advertising is becoming more prevalent and can be a great way to break through the clutter. Finally, directory

72. Joan E. Rigdon, "Hip Marketers Bypass Madison Avenue When They Need Cutting-Edge Web Sites," *The Wall Street Journal,* February 28, 1996, B1. For an in-depth description of the Zima Internet launch, see Cathy Taylor, "Z Factor," *Adweek,* February 6, 1995, 14–16.

73. Don E. Schultz, "New Media, Old Problem: Keeping Marcom Integrated," *Marketing News,* March 29, 1999, 11, 12.

advertising can be a sound investment because it helps a committed customer locate a marketer's brand easily and quickly. The nonmedia-based supportive communications include branding, logos, and slogans, packaging and labeling, and word-of-mouth communications. The brand, logo, and slogan all contribute to the overall information being received by consumers and also contribute to the image of the brand. The package and its labeling offer a marketer another opportunity to build awareness and an image both on the store shelf and in the consumer's own home as the consumer encounters the package over and over again in the cupboard. Finally, word-of-mouth communication, while generally uncontrollable, can work for or against a marketer's brand. New products are highly prone to word-of-mouth communication, and affecting opinion leaders' attitudes can stimulate positive word of mouth for a brand.

There are methods, particularly using the Internet, to stimulate positive word of mouth within targeted segments.

4 Identify the challenges of coordinating the ever-expanding media options in the promotional mix.

The tremendous variety of media options we have seen thus far represents a monumental challenge for a marketer who wishes to speak to a customer with a single voice. Achieving this single voice is critical for breaking through the clutter of the modern promotions environment. However, the functional specialists required for working in the various media have their own biases and subgoals that can get in the way of IMC. We will return to this issue in subsequent chapters as we explore other options available to marketers in their quest to persuade customers.

KEY TERMS

sponsorship, 418
point-of-purchase, or point-of-purchase advertising, 423
short-term promotional display, 425
permanent long-term displays, 425

support media, 428
riding the boards, 430
transit advertising, 430
out-of-home media, 430
aerial advertising, 433

branding, 436
logo, 436
slogan, 438
packaging, 440
label, 441

QUESTIONS FOR REVIEW AND CRITICAL THINKING

1. Explain the important advancements in technology that are likely to contribute to the appeal of billboards as an advertising medium.

2. Critique the out-of-home media as tools for achieving reach-versus-frequency objectives in a media plan.

3. Explain the unique role for directory advertising in a media plan. Given what you see happening on the Internet, what kind of future do you predict for traditional yellow pages advertising?

4. When would it be appropriate to conclude that tools such as transit or P–O–P advertising are serving more than just a supportive role in one's media plan? Give an example of each of these tools being used as the principal element in the promotion plan, either from your own experience or from examples that were offered in this chapter.

5. During your next visit to the grocery store, identify three examples of P–O–P advertising. How well were

each of these displays integrated with other aspects of a more comprehensive promotion campaign? What would you surmise are the key factors in creating effective P–O–P displays?

6. Present statistics to document the claim that the television viewing audience is becoming fragmented. What are the causes of this fragmentation? Develop an argument that links this fragmentation to the growing popularity of sponsorship.

7. Sponsorship can be valuable for building brand loyalty. Search through your closets, drawers, or cupboards and find a premium or memento that you acquired at a sponsored event. Does this memento bring back fond memories? Would you consider yourself loyal to the brand that sponsored this event? If not, why not?

8. Explain why new media contribute to the need for functional specialists in ad preparation. What problems do these and other functional specialists create for the achievement of integrated marketing communications?

EXPERIENTIAL EXERCISES

1. **In-class exercise.** Think about entertainment events you have attended in the last year—a concert, baseball game, soccer match, symphony, or modern dance concert. How many of them had corporate sponsorships? Was the event itself consistent with the product category of the sponsor? If you think some did not match up, think of a sponsor that would have been more appropriate for the event than the current sponsor.

2. **Out-of-class exercise.** In this chapter you learned about support media. When you are driving down a busy street, what types of commercial messages do you see? Which ones do you think are most effective, and why? How could an advertiser conduct formal, systematic research to determine whether its outdoor advertising messages are effective? What other traditional support media alternatives are available in your town? The next time you go to a movie, record the ways in which a marketer could get a message to you.

USING THE INTERNET

Exercise 1

"Brick, and mortar" stores have many advantages over Internet retailers in P–O–P advertising: among them, customers in physical stores can't be whisked away from making a purchase by an ill-considered link to something new. Note how Web-based retailers steer customers toward completion of a transaction. In a grocery store, register aisle displays provide a last chance to push products into the shopping cart—once the purchases are bagged and the clerk rings up the sale, the best one can do is give coupons for some future day's shopping. On the other hand, Web-based transactions could hand the customer off to additional sites ("Now that you've bought a widget, have you considered a widget cozy from Cozies.com?"), or piggyback future purchases on the customer's initial registration (and provision of all of the necessary credit card information).

1. How often do retail Web sites you've visited provide links *off* their site to others, while you're in their "shopping cart" pages?

2. What happens after you make purchases on those retail sites? Do they use the opportunity to merely thank you for your purchase, or do they take advantage of having gained your attention?

Exercise 2

Some outdoor signage has matured from plain old ad to cherished artifact. Mail Pouch Tobacco was one of the pioneers of paying people to sport a logo, offering to paint barns and other buildings for free in return for including the company's mark (while, as Exhibit 12.15 notes, we've gone from barns to BMWs, there's really nothing new under the sun, is there?). As with many historical phenomena, the Mail Pouch Tobacco barns are commemorated by a number of Web sites.

Use a Web search engine such as AltaVista or Google to look up "Mail Pouch Tobacco" to see some of these sites.

1. How extensive was Mail Pouch's outdoor advertising?

2. Why do you think Mail Pouch stopped the advertising campaign?

After reading this chapter, you will be able to:

1 Explain the role of public relations as part of a firm's overall promotional mix.

2 Detail the objectives and tools of public relations.

3 Describe how firms are using the Internet to assist their public relations activities.

4 Describe two basic strategic approaches to public relations activities.

5 Discuss the types of and objectives for corporate advertising.

CHAPTER 13

In 1995, Microsoft Corporation rolled out its Windows 95 operating system with tremendous fanfare and flair. A tightly coordinated global launch included a guest spot on *The Jay Leno Show*, a celebration for 3,500 people, a Ferris wheel, hot-air balloons, free copies of the software for dignitaries around the world, and a huge payment for the rights to use the Rolling Stones song "Start Me Up" as the product launch theme song. During the twelve months after the launch, Microsoft spent $200 million on advertising to support the introduction.

In 1998, Windows 98 was introduced with a low-key, waterfront, corporate affair in San Francisco attended by about 300 representatives from the press—no hot-air balloons, no Ferris wheel, no dignitaries, no Rolling Stones. Why the difference in intensity? As one journalist put it: "Windows 95—Jay Leno. Windows 98—Janet Reno?"[1] The reference, of course, is to the highly publicized investigation by the U.S. Justice Department into Microsoft's marketing and business practices regarding Windows software and the bundling of services within the basic operating system—specifically, its Internet Explorer program.

In 2000, the launch of Windows 2000 wasn't low key, it was more like no key. No special programs. No special promotions. Just a standard advertising program with few promotions. It appeared that the Justice Department investigation had worn down Microsoft to the point that management feared any broad-based promotional programs would be construed as "inappropriate" given the ongoing inquiries into the company's business practices.

The five-year Justice Department investigation has presented Microsoft with a public relations challenge of huge proportions. Literally every major business publication (*The Wall Street Journal, Business Week, Forbes, Fortune, Advertising Age*) has carried multiple stories about Microsoft's antitrust problems. Popular press from *USA Today* to *People* magazine to the local newspaper have followed the story. And, of course, the Internet has been buzzing with each new development. Coverage of the situation has often portrayed Microsoft as "predatory" and "anti-competitive," borrowing language that often appeared in Justice Department reports.

The low point in the negative publicity onslaught came in late 1997, when attorneys for Microsoft submitted a court filing in which they described Justice Department attorneys as "poorly informed lawyers [who] have no vocation for software design."[2] Microsoft executives regretted the statement and said the company should have been more respectful of the court. The official public reaction came from Microsoft's chief operating officer and executive vice president, Robert J. Herbold, who met with the press and offered the public relations understatement of the year, "We need to do a better job of toning down the rhetoric."[3]

Microsoft was clearly struggling. It had never faced a negative publicity challenge like this before, and it needed to respond to this challenge more effectively than it had been responding. Being a creative and astute organization, Microsoft crafted an interesting public relations and promotional response. First, the organization recognized that its efforts throughout the ordeal had been inadequate. A good public relations and corporate image campaign begins with full understanding and appreciation, drawing on the situation analysis discussed in Chapter 3.[4] Microsoft's

WINDOWS HELPS PEOPLE AND MACHINES UNDERSTAND EACH OTHER.

Where do you want to go today?® www.microsoft.com /windows/   **Microsoft®**

©1998 Microsoft Corporation. All rights reserved. Microsoft, Where do you want to go today?, the Windows logo and the Windows Start logo are either registered trademarks or trademarks of Microsoft Corporation in the United States and/or other countries. Windows is a registered trademark of Microsoft Corporation for its Windows brand operating systems.

EXHIBIT 13.1

As public relations problems continued to grow as a result of the Justice Department's antitrust case against Microsoft, the firm turned to corporate advertising to project a softer, gentler image to the public. Many of the ads featured kids and dogs as a way to buff the image of the firm.

1. Catalina Oritz, "Fed Lawsuit Offers Best PR for Microsoft's Windows 98," Associated Press, June 25, 1998.
2. Associated Press, January 9, 1998.
3. Ibid.
4. Geri Mazur, "Good PR Starts with Good Research," *Marketing News,* September 15, 1997, 16.

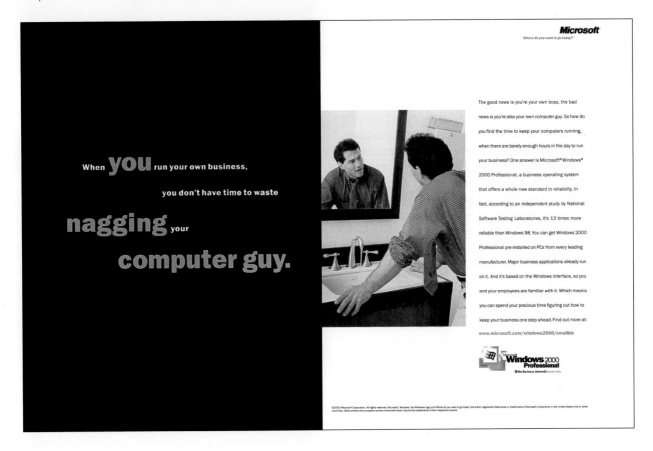

EXHIBIT 13.2

As the Justice Department case dragged on for more than five years, Microsoft continued to use a more casual and friendly approach in its corporate advertising.

own focus group research revealed that "bashing" Microsoft had become fashionable among information technology managers. Often, the first thing out of their mouths during a focus group session was "It's a monopoly."[5]

Once the firm had established an understanding of the situation, the next step was to evaluate the public persona it was presenting. The conclusion here was that Microsoft was indeed seen as a predatory giant seeking monopoly power. The solution was to recast the organization with a "kinder, gentler face" in its advertising and promotion campaigns. The firm set about doing this by carefully evaluating all promotional materials and recasting the organization in a more benign way. The main campaign for Windows 98 concentrated exclusively on consumer magazines such as *Bon Appétit, The New Yorker,* and *Time* (see Exhibit 13.1). The ads highlighted features and used such "friendly" headlines as "Shouldn't Your

Computer Be Smarter Than Your Dog?"[6] Another more friendly campaign was developed for the Microsoft-bashing information technology managers. In these ads, Microsoft offers such self-effacing revelations in the ad copy as "Apparently, there are those who do not subscribe to an all-Microsoft approach."[7]

But perhaps the most interesting, though not official, promotional/public relations response to the publicity-hostile environment was Bill Gates's decision to do an ad for Callaway Golf in which "Bill" reveals that he is a fairly poor golfer who is *really* trying hard to get better. Talk about your "kinder, gentler" faces. Here is Bill Gates (net worth about $43 billion with a reputation as a ruthless competitor) sheepishly admitting that he, golly gee, can't play golf very well. This is certainly a much more humanized version of Bill Gates than the Justice Department hearings ever showed.

5.   Bradley Johnson, "Microsoft Aims 3 Ad Drives at Small-Business Users," *Advertising Age,* February 16, 1998, 43.
6.   Bradley Johnson, "Microsoft's Win 98 Pitch Touts Product Advantages," *Advertising Age,* June 22, 1998, 4.
7.   Ibid.

In April 2000, Judge Thomas P. Jackson ruled that Microsoft had indeed used its position and power in a monopolistic way and bullied the best and brightest in the computer industry. Stellar firms like Compaq, Sun Microsystems, IBM, and Intel were all cited as having suffered as a result of Microsoft's software designs and access restrictions.[8] In response, Microsoft reacted with a variety of more subtle, public relations–oriented maneuvers. First, the Gates Foundation donated $10 million to the U.S. Capitol Visitors' Center as part of a multimillion-dollar donation effort to "worthy" causes. Next, the firm bolstered its in-house lobbying personnel (upping the staff to fourteen people from none in 1995) and spent an estimated $4.6 billion on lobbying over a 12-month period.[9] In tandem with the behind-the-scenes efforts, the firm started a pro-Microsoft trade association to support grassroots software development efforts, and Gates is featured in a new television advertising campaign—this time with Steve Ballmer, Microsoft's Executive VP of Sales and Support, showing that Microsoft really cares about its customers and the computer industry and the process of innovation. Magazine ads targeted both consumers and business buyers with more casual and friendlier language (see Exhibit 13.2). The architect of this broad-based public relations and corporate image campaign was Jack Krumholtz. Krumholtz is a casual 38-year-old who described the process simply as "Our goal is to get our message out and stop letting our competitors define us."[10]

Did Microsoft accomplish its goal of softening the blow of the decision? That remains to be seen. On June 7, 2000, the Supreme Court approved a Justice Department ruling to break the company into two parts: one part for the Windows operating systems and the other for all other Microsoft products including Word and MSN services.[11] Microsoft will appeal the decision, which will take up to two years to resolve.

INTRODUCTION

Microsoft used the tools of both public relations and corporate advertising to deal with negative publicity that was outside the firm's control. The challenge to the company's corporate structure will no doubt be chronicled as one of the longest and most severe PR challenges ever faced by a firm. As the introductory scenario shows, Microsoft used all forms of promotion in its normal approach to the market—advertising, special promotions, event sponsorship, support media, and trade programs. But once the environment turned hostile, the firm turned to a different set of communications tools—public relations and corporate advertising.

This chapter considers in detail the role of these two separate and important areas that must be part of a firm's overall integrated marketing communications effort: public relations and corporate advertising. Each has the potential to make a distinct and important contribution to the single and unified message and image of an organization, which is the ultimate goal of IMC. Each has the potential for effective and supportive communication, but they achieve this in different ways. Public relations is often a behind-the-scenes process, as the Microsoft example shows. We will discuss the many tools and objectives of public relations throughout this chapter. Corporate advertising uses major media to communicate its unique type of message, which is distinct from typical brand advertising a firm might do. While public relations and corporate advertising are rarely the foundation tools of a promotional mix and IMC program, they do represent key tactics under certain conditions. We will explore the nature of these two specialized promotional tools and the conditions under which they are ideally suited for the IMC program.

8. Business Week Editorial, "Does Microsoft Stifle Innovation?" *Business Week,* May 15, 2000, 198.
9. Dan Carney, et al., "Microsoft's All-Out Counterattack," *Business Week,* May 15, 2000, 103.
10. Ibid.
11. John Wilke, et al., "Judge's Breakup Order Stands to Transform Microsoft, Its Industry", *The Wall Street Journal,* June 8, 2000, A1, A10.

PUBLIC RELATIONS

Public relations is a marketing and management communications function that deals with the public issues encountered by firms across a wide range of constituents. An important component of public relations is **publicity**—news media coverage of events related to a firm's products or activities. Publicity presents both challenges (as Microsoft learned) and opportunities. News reports about problems, such as those Microsoft had to deal with, represent challenges. Large investment projects in facilities or new product discoveries represent opportunities for positive publicity.

Public relations problems can arise either from a firm's own activities or from external forces completely outside a firm's control. Let's consider two highly visible companies, Intel and Pepsi, and their public relations problems. In one case, the firm caused its own PR and publicity problems; in the other, an external, uncontrollable force created problems for the firm.

Intel is one of the great success stories of American industry. The company has risen from relative techno-obscurity as an innovative computer technology company to number thirty-nine on the Fortune 500 list. In just seventeen years sales have grown from $1.3 billion to more than $26 billion.[12] But all this success did not prepare Intel for the PR challenge it faced in late 1994. In early 1994, Intel introduced its new-generation chip, the Pentium, as the successor to the widely used line of X86 chips. The Pentium processor was another leap forward in computing speed and power. But in November 1994, Pentium users were discovering a flaw in the chip. During certain floating-point operations, some Pentium chips were actually producing erroneous calculations—albeit the error showed up in only the fifth or sixth decimal place. While this might not affect the average consumer who's trying to balance a checkbook, power users in scientific laboratories require absolute precision and accuracy in their calculations.

Having a defect in a high-performance technology product such as the Pentium chip was one thing; how Intel handled the problem was another. Intel's initial "official" response was that the flaw in the chip was so insignificant that it would produce an error in calculations only once in 27,000 years. But then, IBM, which had shipped thousands of PCs with Pentium chips, challenged the assertion that the flaw was insignificant, claiming that processing errors could occur as often as every twenty-four days. IBM announced that it would stop shipment of all Pentium-based PCs immediately.[13]

From this point on, the Pentium situation became a runaway PR disaster. Every major newspaper, network newscast, and magazine carried the story of the flawed Pentium chip. Even the cartoon series *Dilbert* got in on the act, running a whole series of cartoon strips that spoofed the Intel controversy (see Exhibit 13.3). One observer characterized it this way: "From a public relations standpoint, the train has left the station and is barreling out of Intel's control."[14] For weeks, Intel publicly argued that the flaw would not affect the vast majority of users, and the firm did nothing.

Ultimately, public pressure and user demands forced Intel to change its position. Consumers were outraged at Intel's initial policy of refusing to replace Pentium chips unless Intel thought the user needed one. Finally, in early 1995, Intel decided to provide a free replacement chip to any user who believed he or she was at risk. Andy Grove, Intel's highly accomplished CEO, in announcing the $475 million

12.   "The Fortune 500," *Fortune*, April 19, 2000, S1.
13.   Barbara Grady, "Chastened Intel Steps Carefully with Introduction of New Chip," *Computerlink*, February 14, 1995, 11.
14.   James G. Kimball, "Can Intel Repair the Pentium PR?" *Advertising Age*, December 19, 1994, 35.

DILBERT reprinted by permissin of the United Features Syndicate, Inc.

EXHIBIT 13.3

When Intel did not respond quickly and positively to problems with its Pentium chip, the press unloaded a barrage of negative publicity on the firm. Even Dilbert got into the act with this parody of Intel decision making.

Syringes Found in Two Cans Of Cola in Washington State

SEATTLE, June 13 (Reuters) — Hypodermic needles were found in two cans of Diet Pepsi in Washington State this week, prompting a Federal investigation and a warning from a bottling company that Pepsi drinkers should rattle their cans before taking a sip.

Preliminary Food and Drug Administration tests of the two cans revealed no contamination, the regional Pepsi bottler Alpac Corporation said. Alpac has not issued a recall.

The first syringe was found in a Diet Pepsi by an elderly couple in Tacoma. Earl and Mary Tripplett discovered the syringe and bent needle Wednesday rattling around in an empty can of Diet Pepsi which they had opened and drunk. They reported no illness.

Alpac said the second can was found by a resident of Federal Way, about 18 miles south of Seattle. It was collected Friday and turned over to the F.D.A.

In a television interview on Saturday, the president of the bottler, Karl Behnke, urged consumers to "rattle the cans a little bit" before drinking. Alpac supplies Pepsi to Washington, Alaska, Oregon, Hawaii and Guam.

EXHIBIT 13.4

Pepsi was confronted with a potential public relations disaster. Tampering at the retail level forced the company to deal with publicity like this news story.

program to replace customers' chips, admitted publicly that "the Pentium processor divide problem has been a learning experience for Intel."[15]

Intel's public relations and publicity problems were mostly of its own doing. But in many cases, firms are faced with PR crises that are totally beyond their control. One of these cases, which goes down in history as a classic, happened to Pepsi. In 1993, Pepsi had a PR nightmare on its hands. Complaints were coming in from all over the United States that cans of Pepsi, Diet Pepsi, and Caffeine Free Diet Pepsi had syringes inside them (see Exhibit 13.4). Other callers claimed their cans of Pepsi contained such things as a screw, a crack vial, a sewing needle, and brown goo in the bottom. Unlike Intel, Pepsi assembled a management team that was mobilized to handle the crisis. The team immediately considered a national recall of all Pepsi products—no matter what the cost. The Food and Drug Administration (FDA) told Pepsi there was no need for such action since no one had been injured and there was no health risk. The Pepsi team was sure that this was not a case of tampering in the production facility. A can of Pepsi is filled with cola and then sealed in nine-tenths of a second, making it virtually impossible for anyone to get anything into a can during production.

The president of Pepsi went on national television to explain the situation and defend his firm and its products. The company enlisted the aid of a powerful and influential constituent at this point—the Food and Drug Administration. The commissioner of the FDA, David Kessler, said publicly that many of the tampering claims could not be substantiated or verified. A video camera in Aurora, Colorado, caught a woman trying to insert a syringe into a Pepsi can. Pepsi was exonerated in the press, but the huge PR problem had significantly challenged the firm to retain the stature and credibility of a truly global brand.

15. Grady, "Chastened Intel Steps Carefully."

Pepsi is pleased to announce...
...nothing.

As America now knows, those stories about Diet Pepsi were a hoax. Plain and simple, not true. Hundreds of investigators have found no evidence to support a single claim.

As for the many, many thousands of people who work at Pepsi-Cola, we feel great that it's over. And we're ready to get on with making and bringing you what we believe is the best-tasting diet cola in America.

There's not much more we can say. Except that most importantly, we won't let this hoax change our exciting plans for this summer.

We've set up special offers so you can enjoy our great quality products at prices that will save you money all summer long. It all starts on July 4th weekend and we hope you'll stock up with a little extra, just to make up for what you might have missed last week.

That's it. Just one last word of thanks to the millions of you who have stood with us.

**Drink All The Diet Pepsi You Want.
Uh Huh®.**

DIET PEPSI and UH HUH are registered trademarks of PepsiCo Inc.

http://www.pepsi.com

http://www.urbanlegends.about.com/science/urbanlegends

EXHIBIT 13.5

Pepsi moves to head off trouble—in this case, all of the facts are on its side, as it quashes an apparent hoax. Some firms have found the Internet a challenge, as it gives a voice—and sometimes, unwarranted credibility—to virtually anyone who can slap up a Web page or broadcast e-mail. Some of the hoaxes, myths, and "urban legends" coloring the Internet have been documented on one of the About.com's many expert sites.

What happened to Intel and Pepsi highlights why public relations is such a difficult form of communication to manage. In many cases, a firm's PR program is called into action for damage control, as the Pepsi ad in Exhibit 13.5 illustrates. Intel and Pepsi had to be totally reactive to the situation rather than strategically controlling it, as with the other tools in the integrated communications process. But while many episodes of PR must be reactive, a firm can be prepared with public relations materials to conduct an orderly and positive goodwill and image-building campaign among its many constituents. To fully appreciate the role and potential of public relations in the broad communications efforts of a firm, we will consider the objectives of public relations, the tools of public relations, and basic PR strategies.

Objectives for Public Relations

The public relations function in a firm, usually handled by an outside agency, is prepared to engage in positive PR efforts and to deal with any negative events related to a firm's activities. Within the broad guidelines of image building and establishing relationships with constituents, it is possible to identify six primary objectives for public relations:

Promoting Goodwill. This is an image-building function of public relations. Industry events or community activities that reflect favorably on a firm are highlighted. When employees of General Electric participate in the Habitat for Humanity program, this event is newsworthy in a PR sense.

Promoting a Product or Service. Press releases or events that increase public awareness of a firm's brands can be pursued through public relations. Large pharmaceutical firms such as Merck and GlaxoWellcome issue press releases when new drugs are discovered or FDA approval is achieved.

Preparing Internal Communications. Disseminating information and correcting misinformation within a firm can reduce the impact of rumors and increase employee support. For events such as reductions in the labor force or mergers of firms, internal communications can do much to dispel rumors circulating among employees and in the local community.

Counteracting Negative Publicity. This is the damage control function of public relations. The attempt here is not to cover up negative events, but rather to prevent the negative publicity from damaging the image of a firm and its brands. When a lawsuit was filed against NEC alleging that one of its cellular phones had caused cancer, McCaw Cellular Communications used PR activities to inform the public and especially cellular phone users of scientific knowledge that argued against the claims in the lawsuit.[16]

Lobbying. The PR function can assist a firm in dealing with government officials and pending legislation. Recall that Microsoft reported spent $4.6 billion on such lobbying efforts. Industries maintain active and aggressive lobbying efforts at both the state and federal levels. As an example, the beer and wine industry has lobbyists monitoring legislation that could restrict beer and wine advertising.

Giving Advice and Counsel. Assisting management in determining what (if any) position to take on public issues, preparing employees for public appearances, and helping management anticipate the need for public reactions are all part of the advice and counsel function of public relations.

Tools of Public Relations

There are several vehicles through which a firm can make positive use of public relations and pursue the objectives just cited. The goal is to gain as much control over the process as possible. By using the methods discussed in the following sections, a firm can integrate its PR effort with other marketing communications.

Press Releases. Having a file of information that makes for good news stories puts the firm in a position to take advantage of free press coverage. Press releases allow a firm to pursue positive publicity from the news media. Exhibit 13.6 is a press release announcing the discovery by Myriad Genetics of a gene related to prostate cancer. Items that make for good public relations include the following:

- New products
- New scientific discoveries
- New personnel
- New corporate facilities
- Innovative corporate practices, such as energy-saving programs or employee benefit programs
- Annual shareholder meetings
- Charitable and community service activities

The only drawback to press releases is that a firm often doesn't know if or when the item will appear in the media. Also, the news media are free to edit or interpret a news release, which may alter its meaning. To help reduce these liabilities, consultants recommend carefully developing relationships with editors from publications the organization deems critical to its press release program.[17] And editors express a preference for information from firms that focuses on technical or how-to features and more case studies about company successes.[18]

Feature Stories. While a firm cannot write a feature story for a newspaper or televise a story over the local television networks, it can invite journalists to do an exclusive story on the firm when there is a particularly noteworthy event. A feature story is different from a press release in that it is more controllable. A feature story, as opposed to a news release, offers a single journalist the opportunity to do a fairly lengthy piece with exclusive rights to the information. Jupiter Communications, one of the leading research organizations that tracks Internet usage and generates

16.   John J. Keller, "McCaw to Study Cellular Phones as Safety Questions Affect Sales," *The Wall Street Journal,* January 29, 1993, B3.
17.   Adriana Cento, "7 Habits for Highly Effective Public Relations," *Marketing News,* March 16, 1998, 8.
18.   Chad Kaydo, "How to Boost Your Press Coverage," *Sales and Marketing Management,* July 1998, 76.

Tuesday June 6, 6:31 A.M. Eastern time
Company Press Release
Source: Myriad Genetics, Inc.

Myriad Genetics Discovers Novel Prostate Cancer Gene—Discovery Triggers $1 Million Payment

Salt Lake City, June 6 /PRNewswire/ -- Myriad Genetics, Inc. (Nasdaq: MYGN–News) today announced it has discovered a novel prostate cancer susceptibility gene, which resulted in a 41 million payment to Myriad from Schering-Plough Corporation under terms of the companies' 1997 research collaboration agreement.

To identify this gene, researchers at Myriad employed a proprietary form of linkage analysis that involves tracking a disease susceptibility gene to its location on a specific chromosome. Based on its analysis of prostate cancer families, Myriad determined that inherited mutations in this gene may significantly increase the risk of prostate cancer susceptibility test.

The discovery of this gene will allow Myriad scientists to more thoroughly investigate the full spectrum of genetic mutations associated with prostate cancer and the role they play in the development of the disease. Furthermore, the gene has been included in a ProNet® pathway discovery program to identify additional genes within the pathway that may provide drug development opportunities.

"The combination of elegant science and the company's vast genomic resources have again produced outstanding results," said Peter Meldrum, President and Chief Executive Officer of Myriad Genetics, Inc. "The delivery of this gene to Schering-Plough provides great potential for the development of both diagnostic and therapeutic products for a devastating disease, which kills 40,000 men a year."

Prostate cancer accounts for more than 35% of all cancer incidents in men. In excess of 200,000 new cases are diagnosed each year in the United States alone, of which 5–10% are thought to be genetically determined.

The alliance between Myriad and Schering-Plough was established specifically to uncover the genetic basis of prostate cancer. According to the agreement, Myriad retains all diagnostic product rights to this gene and will receive a royalty on all sales of relevant therapeutic products developed by Schering-Plough. United States and foreign patents have been filled for this newly discovered gene.

WEB SIGHTING

http://www.prnewswire.com

EXHIBIT 13.6

A press release is a good way to communicate positive information about a firm to a wide variety of constituents and stakeholders. Myriad Genetics has good news here—successful completion of genetic research. Myriad Genetics used PR Newswire to get out the good word. Wouldn't it have been sufficient just to put up the release on http://www.myriad.com*?*

statistics about the Internet, has a simple philosophy when it comes to using feature stories as a PR tool. The CEO says that "It is our goal to get every research project we do covered somewhere. We know this is the cheapest, and maybe most effective, way to market ourselves."[19]

Company Newsletters. In-house publications such as newsletters can disseminate positive information about a firm through its employees. As members of the community, employees are proud of achievements by their firm. Newsletters can also be distributed to important constituents in the community, such as government officials, the chamber of commerce, or the tourism bureau. Suppliers often enjoy reading about an important customer, so newsletters can be mailed to this group as well.[20] Firms are also discovering that the Internet is an excellent way to distribute

19. Andy Cohen, "The Jupiter Mission," *Sales and Marketing Management*, April 2000, 56.
20. Joanne Cleaver, "Newsletters Prove to be Both Effective and Cost-Effective," *Marketing News*, January 4, 1999, 6.

YOU HAVE (NEWSLETTER) E-MAIL

For nearly a year, 200,000 people have been getting small-business advice from Symantec Corporation via e-mail. This isn't the unwelcome company self-promotion disguised as e-mail we have come to know as spam. This is true managerial advice that has helped Symantec firmly establish its software brand online and sell its product to new customers.

The Symantec SmallBiz Newsletter is keyed off the company's database to reach customers who have recently bought the firm's ACT contact management program. More than 600 customers and potential customers join the opt-in program list a month. But the newsletter is more than just product information (remember our discussion of making a site "sticky" from Chapter 9). There are discount offers, sweepstakes, surveys, and news on how to use partnerships in a small-business setting. The Web site and newsletter have been so useful to Symantec that the company now allocates about 30 percent of its entire promotions budget to these communication tools.

Marketers from small software firms like Symantec to large corporations like IBM and Lands' End are taking advantage of the opt-in e-mail process to deliver messages on nearly a one-on-one basis. These electronic mail newsletters, or e-zines as they are called, are the latest in marketing/public relations on the Internet. The research director of the leading Internet research firm, Forrester Research, notes that online newsletters "are an effective tool in getting out information." More than 100,000 e-zines are published regularly, mostly by small and home-office marketers. But large marketers like Procter & Gamble also recognize the kind of "softer" voice an Internet newsletter offers to the promotional mix and IMC program. One Internet consultant noted: "Assuming that a big company doesn't mess it up by not communicating a friendly approach and personality, this is a very powerful, low-cost, high-return way for a company to get positive return."

Source: Jeffery D. Zbar, "Marketers Buoy Brands with E-mail Newsletters," *Advertising Age*, October 25, 1999, 74.

information that traditionally has been the focus of newsletters.[21] Procter & Gamble has done just that at http://www.clothesline.com/neighbor/ (see Exhibit 13.7). The New Media box describes how firms are using e-mail-based newsletters to great advantage.

Interviews and Press Conferences. As in the Pepsi tampering crisis, interviews and press conferences can be a highly effective public relations tool. Often, interviews and press conferences are warranted in crisis management. But firms have also successfully called press conferences to announce important scientific breakthroughs or explain the details of a corporate expansion. The press conference has an air of importance and credibility because it uses a news format to present important corporate information. New technology is fostering the use of press conferences as a means of getting the word out (see Exhibit 13.8).

Sponsored Events. In Chapter 12, sponsored events were discussed as a form of emerging support media. Sponsoring events can also serve as an important public relations tool. Sponsorships run the gamut from supporting local community events to sponsoring global events such as the World Cup soccer competitions. At the local level, prominent display of the corporate name and logo offers local residents the chance to see that an organization is dedicated to the community.

Another form of sponsorship is fund-raisers. Fund-raisers of all sorts for not-for-profit organizations give positive visibility to corporations. For many years, Chevrolet has sponsored college scholarships through the NCAA by choosing the offensive and defensive player of a game. The scholarships are announced weekly at the conclusion of televised games. This sort of notoriety for Chevrolet creates a favorable image for viewers.

One of the most difficult aspects of investing in sponsorships is determining the positive payoff the organization can expect from such an investment. Analysts are recommending that corporations (1) establish an evaluation procedure that tracks

21. Jeffery D. Zbar, "Marketers Buoy Brands with E-Mail Newsletters," *Advertising Age*, October 25, 1999, 74.

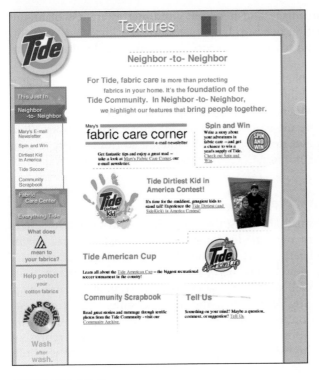

EXHIBIT 13.7

Companies have discovered that electronic distribution of newsletters is an efficient method to offer consumers information in a low-key way. Here, Procter & Gamble has created an electronic newsletter that not only gets information out about the Tide brand of laundry detergent, but also helps create a community around the product.

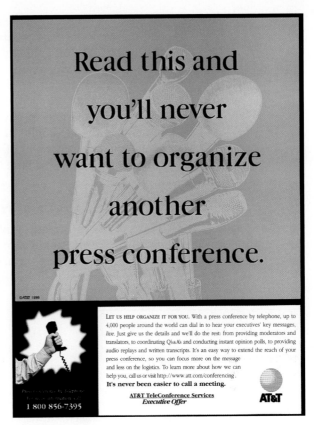

EXHIBIT 13.8

New technology is allowing firms to use press conferences more effectively.

awareness generated from sponsorships, (2) establish an event-tracking model that can identify target audience attitudes and purchase behavior, and (3) identify the components of the sponsorship that were most effective in achieving awareness and attitude goals.[22]

Publicity. Publicity is unpaid-for media exposure about a firm's activities or its products and services. Publicity is dealt with by the PR function but cannot, with the exception of press releases, be strategically controlled like other PR efforts. This lack of control was demonstrated earlier in the chapter with respect to the situations faced by Microsoft, Intel, and Pepsi. In addition, publicity can turn into a global problem for a firm. Benetton, the Italian sportswear maker, has learned this lesson (or maybe not) several times with its controversial advertising. In one instance, the firm ran an ad depicting a white child wearing angel's wings alongside a black child wearing devil's horns. In another campaign, the firm featured death row inmates to promote its clothing line, although company officials argued they were merely trying to raise public consciousness of the death penalty.[23] The reaction to such advertising was severe enough that at one point German retailers refused to carry the company's products.

Public relations professionals can react swiftly to publicity, as the team from Pepsi did, but they cannot control the flow of information. Despite the lack of

---

22.   Susan Sloves, "Do Sponsorships Provide a Gold Mine or a Black Hole?" *Marketing News,* February 2, 1998, 9.
23.   John Rossant, "The Faded Colors of Benetton," *Business Week,* April 10, 1995, 87, 90.

control, publicity can build an image and heighten consumer awareness of brands and organizations. An organization needs to be prepared to take advantage of events that make for good publicity and to counter events that are potentially damaging to a firm's reputation.

One major advantage of publicity—when the information is positive—is that it tends to carry heightened credibility. Publicity that appears in news stories on television and radio and in newspapers and magazines assumes an air of believability because of the credibility of the media context. Not-for-profit organizations often use publicity in the form of news stories and public interest stories as ways to gain widespread visibility at little or no cost.

Public Relations and New Media ❸

The fact that firms large and small are using the Internet to distribute newsletters reveals only one application of new media for public relations purposes. Firms are using the Internet for a variety of PR activities. Procter & Gamble, cited earlier for its use in distributing newsletters, has also created a special section at its Web site (http://www.pg.com/rumor) to battle nagging rumors that the firm has some sort of connection to satanic cults. The site offers facts about P&G's moon-and-stars logo (the thirteen stars represent the thirteen original colonies, not a satanic symbol). The site also carries testimonials posted from the Billy Graham Evangelistic Association. The rumors were being spread through the Web, so P&G is fighting fire with fire by using the Web for a PR counterattack.[24]

New Web companies are finding that their needs for public relations are just as great if not greater than established, non-Web-based firms. One Internet start-up, Digital Island, attributes most of its early success to the effects of proactive public relations strategies. One PR expert believes that "Every positive article is worth $1 million in valuation" to an Internet start-up. Further, analysts believe that without third-party endorsement (the press and industry analysts), it is doubtful that a start-up can be successful.[25]

The issue was raised before (Chapter 9) that new media can create a "buzz" through word-of-mouth that is more effective with certain target segments than any other tactic. In a noisy and crowded competitive environment, mainstream promotional tools like advertising, sales promotion, and sponsorships may get lost in the clutter. Public relations using new media, particularly Web sites, chat-room posts, and Web press releases can reach targeted audiences in a different way that carries more credibility than "in your face" company self-promotion.[26]

Finally, there is a major drawback to new media when it comes to public relations. Because of the

EXHIBIT 13.9

Companies often rely heavily on their PR firms to help them craft a proactive public relations strategy. Read the copy in this advertisement from Burson-Marsteller carefully. Can you find this firm's orientation to the PR process?

24. Nicholas Kulish, "Still Bedeviled by Satan Rumors, P&G Battles Back on the Web," *The Wall Street Journal,* September 21, 1999, B1.
25. "The Future of Public Relations Is the Internet," *The Strategist,* Spring 1999, 6–10.
26. Dana James, "Dot-Coms Demand New Kind of Publicity," *Marketing News,* November 22, 1999, 6, 11.

speed with which information is disseminated, staying ahead of negative publicity is indeed challenging. While word-of-mouth can be used to create a positive buzz, it can also spread bad news, or even worse, misinformation just as fast. When a crisis hits the Internet, one PR expert says that "act quickly becomes act *even more* quickly."[27] Acting quickly and responding with the right facts is the topic of the next section.

Basic Public Relations Strategies ❹

Given the breadth of possibilities for using public relations as part of a firm's overall integrated marketing communications effort, we need to identify basic PR strategies. Public relations strategies can be categorized as either proactive or reactive. **Proactive public relations strategy** is guided by marketing objectives, seeks to publicize a company and its brands, and takes an offensive rather than defensive posture in the public relations process. **Reactive public relations strategy** is dictated by influences outside the control of a company, focuses on problems to be solved rather than opportunities, and requires a company to take defensive measures.[28] These two strategies involve different orientations to public relations.

Proactive Public Relations Strategy. In developing a proactive public relations strategy, a firm acknowledges opportunities for it to use PR efforts to accomplish something positive. Companies often rely heavily on their PR firms to help them put together a proactive strategy. The advertisement in Exhibit 13.9 from the PR firm Burson-Marsteller discusses precisely this issue.

In many firms, the positive aspects of employee achievements, corporate contributions to the community, or the organization's social and environmental programs go unnoticed by important constituents. To implement a proactive public relations strategy, a firm needs to develop a comprehensive PR program. The key components of such a program are as follows:

1. *A public relations audit.* A public relations audit identifies the characteristics of a firm or the aspects of the firm's activities that are positive and newsworthy. Information is gathered in much the same way as information related to advertising strategy is gathered. Corporate personnel and customers are questioned to provide information. The type of information gathered in an audit includes descriptions of company products and services, market performance of brands, profitability, goals for products, market trends, new product introductions, important suppliers, important customers, employee programs and facilities, community programs, charitable activities, and the like.

2. *A public relations plan.* Once the firm is armed with information from a public relations audit, the next step is a structured PR plan. A **public relations plan** identifies the objectives and activities included in the public relations communications issued by a firm. The components of a public relations plan include the following:
   - *Current situation analysis.* This section of the public relations plan summarizes the information obtained from the public relations audit. Information contained here is often broken down by category, such as product performance or community activity.
   - *Program objectives.* Objectives for a proactive public relations program stem from the current situation. Objectives should be set for both short- and long-term opportunities. Public relations objectives can be as diverse and

27. Kathryn Kranhold, "Handling the Aftermath of Cybersabotage," *The Wall Street Journal,* February 10, 2000, B22.
28. These definitions were developed from discussions offered by Jordan Goldman, *Public Relations in the Marketing Mix* (Lincolnwood, IL: NTC Business Books, 1992), xi–xii.

CAREERPROFILE

Name:	*Debbie Davis*
Title:	*Director of Public Relations*
Company:	*Community Hospitals Indianapolis, Indianapolis, IN*
	http://www.ehealthindiana.com
Education:	*B.A., Journalism/Broadcasting*

One cold January afternoon, Debbie Davis received a phone call. A newborn infant had been found frozen to death in the parking lot of a Community hospital. As the media relations liaison for the hospital system, it was her job to make sure press coverage of the death didn't negatively impact the hospital's public image.

She arranged an on-site press conference. "We wanted to make sure that reporters knew that the baby hadn't been a patient at the hospital and that the baby was found in an area that was difficult to see so that our security wouldn't be questioned," says Debbie. "Then we wanted to point out solutions for people faced with a newborn they couldn't care for." The result? Media stories painted the hospital in a positive light, as a place people could turn to in times of trouble.

About 70 percent of Debbie's time is spent developing press releases, answering media inquiries, and handling crisis communications situations. "Making sure we present a consistent message to the press is an integral part of our marketing strategy," she says. "We want to get the story out that what we do is take care of our patients."

Debbie also manages the hospital's partnership with a local television station. The Community Hospitals provide health information and resources for news broadcasts and the station's Internet site. "We try to make sure that the partnership benefits both partners," she says. "I have to coordinate issues that are journalistically strong enough for them to cover but also fit with our promotional goals."

Another part of Debbie's job is keeping the hospital's Web site current with news about special events, personnel, and services. Recently, she also coordinated coverage of the first live-on-the-Internet in vitro fertilization. Internally, Debbie keeps employees informed about public relations activities via an employee newsletter, e-mail, and voice mail messages.

To learn more about public relations, visit these Web sites:

Public Relations Society of America
http://www.prsa.org

Council of Public Relations Firms
http://www.prfirms.org

The Institute of Public Relations
http://www.ipr.org.uk

About.com Public Relations page
http://publicrelations.about.com

---

complex as advertising objectives. And, as with advertising, the focal point is not sales or profits. Rather, factors such as the credibility of product performance (that is, placing products in verified, independent tests) or the stature of the firm's research and development efforts (highlighted in a prestigious trade publication article) are legitimate statements of objective.

- *Program rationale.* In this section, it is critical to identify the role the public relations program will play relative to all the other communication efforts—particularly advertising—being undertaken by a firm. This is the area where an integrated marketing communications perspective is clearly articulated for the public relations effort.

- *Communications vehicles.* This section of the plan specifies precisely what means will be used to implement the PR plan. The public relations tools discussed earlier in the chapter—press releases, interviews, newsletters—constitute the communications vehicles through which program objectives can be implemented. There will likely be discussion of precisely how press releases, interviews, and company newsletters can be used.[29]

- *Message content.* Analysts are now suggesting that public relations messages be researched and developed in much the same way that advertising messages are researched and developed.[30] Focus groups and in-depth interviews are being used to fine-tune PR communications. For example, a pharmaceutical firm learned that calling obesity a "disease" rather than a "condition" increased the overweight population's receptivity to the firm's press release messages regarding a new anti-obesity drug.[31]

A proactive PR strategy has the potential for making an important supportive contribution to a firm's IMC effort. Carefully placing positive information targeted to important and potentially influential constituents—such as members of the community or stockholders—supports the overall goal of enhancing the image, reputation, and perception of a firm and its brands.

Reactive Public Relations Strategy. A reactive public relations strategy seems a contradiction in terms. As stated earlier, firms must

---

29.   Ibid., 4–14.
30.   Mazur, "Good PR Starts with Good Research."
31.   Ibid.

implement a reactive PR strategy when events outside the control of the firm create negative publicity or circumstances. For firms such as Johnson & Johnson, swift and effective public relations can save an important brand from disaster. The makers of Tylenol had to rely heavily on reactive public relations in the infamous 1982 product-tampering case. Extra-Strength Tylenol that had been tampered with caused the deaths of several people. Within a week after the incident, Tylenol's market share had dropped from 35 percent to about 6 percent. Public relations people handled literally hundreds of inquiries from the public, distributors, the press, and police. The firm then quickly and carefully issued coordinated statements to the general public, the press, and government authorities to provide clarification wherever possible. The result was that through conscientious and competent PR activities, the firm came through the disaster viewed as a credible and trustworthy organization, and the brand regained nearly all its original market share within a year.

In a similar case, Coca-Cola was also able to rein in the publicity and negative public reaction by acting swiftly. Seven days after a bottling glitch at a European plant caused teens in Belgium and France to become sick after drinking Coke, the firm had pulled all Coca-Cola products from European shelves and the CEO issued an apology.[32] Because of the incident, the firm went from one of the most admired and trusted names in Europe to a company that ultimately had to start giving the product away to regain people's trust. The event was so catastrophic that Coke sales dropped 21 percent and earnings were pummeled. But Coke's President of the Greater Europe Group said that "We re-evaluated and re-tailored our marketing programs to meet the needs of consumers on a country-by-country basis and continue to reach out with marketing programs specifically designed to reconnect the brands with consumers."[33] The programs relied heavily on promotional strategies including free samples, dealer incentive programs, and beach parties featuring sound and light shows, live music DJs and cocktail bars with free Cokes to win back the critical teen segment.[34] By early in the year 2000, Coca-Cola was well on its way to recapturing the lost sales and market share.

It is much more difficult to organize for and provide structure around reactive public relations. Since the events that trigger the PR effort here are unpredictable as well as uncontrollable, a firm must simply be prepared to react quickly and effectively. Two steps help firms implement a reactive public relations strategy:

- *The Public Relations Audit.* The public relations audit that was prepared for the proactive strategy helps a firm also prepare its reactive strategy. The information provided by the audit gives a firm what it needs to issue public statements based on current and accurate data. For the Tylenol case and for the syringe-in-Pepsi scare, a current list of distributors, suppliers, and manufacturing sites allowed the firms to quickly determine that the problems were not related to the production process.

- *The Identification of Vulnerabilities.* In addition to preparing current information, the other key step in a reactive public relations strategy is to recognize areas where a firm has weaknesses in its operations or products that can negatively affect its relationships with important constituents. These weakness are called vulnerabilities from a PR standpoint. If aspects of a firm's operations are vulnerable to criticism, such as environmental issues related to manufacturing processes, then the public relations function should be prepared to discuss the issues in a broad range of forums with many different constituents. Leaders at Pepsi, Quaker Oats, and Philip Morris were taken somewhat by surprise when shareholders challenged the firms on their practices with respect to genetically

32.   Kathleen V. Schmidt, "Coke's Crisis," *Marketing News,* September 27, 1999, 1, 11.
33.   Amie Smith, "Coke's European Resurgence," *Promo,* December 1999, 91.
34.   Ibid.

modified foods. While the concern was among a minority of shareholders, there were enough concerned constituents to warrant a proxy vote on the genetically modified foods issue.[35]

Public relations is a prime example of how a firm can identify and then manage aspects of communication in an integrated and synergistic manner to diverse audiences. Without recognizing PR activities as a component of the firm's overall communication effort, misinformation or disinformation could compromise more mainstream communications such as advertising. The coordination of public relations into an integrated program is a matter of recognizing and identifying the process as an information source in the overall IMC effort.

NEED A HIGH PROFILE? GO CORPORATE.

More global marketers are shifting advertising dollars to corporate campaigns as the value of a broader-based image is being realized. Big-name global firms like Canon, Vivendi, and ABB are spending more money on corporate image ads to come up with a higher profile for the corporate brand. Canon, for example, has shifted 10 percent of its marketing budget in Europe to a corporate brand campaign. Best known for photocopiers, the firm wants to use its corporate advertising to help reposition the firm. Peter Kestern, Canon Europe's general manager, explained that "We would like people to see Canon as being a 'solutions provider' instead of just being a manufacturer of office automation machines. Canon is not well-known as a business partner in the information technology arena." To make the transition, Canon is using a corporate advertising campaign that carries the tag line "Created by . . ." with the visuals showing how Canon products stimulate consumers and companies to pursue their goals.

The Swiss engineering firm ABB had a different reason for investing in a corporate campaign. Bjorn Edlund, ABB's Director of Corporate Communications, explained that "We have to raise our profile, particularly in the United States where a California politician recently admitted he didn't know ABB had provided the mechanism by which the state was able to privatize its electricity grid." Basically, the campaign explains who ABB is and what it does.

These global firms are discovering that corporate campaigns that place a premium on image and broad information rather than specific brand features or performance characteristics are very successful in establishing the name of the firm in the minds of both consumers and corporate business buyers. Oh, what about Vivendi? Vivendi is the new corporate name for Compagnie Générale des Eaux, the French utility company. The former name literally meant "water company." The Chairman and CEO was looking for a more consumer-friendly name and launched a corporate campaign to introduce Vivendi to the public.

Source: Juliana Koranteng, "Corporate Campaigns Attract Bigger Slices of Advertising Pie," *Advertising Age International*, March 8, 1999, 2.

CORPORATE ADVERTISING ⑤

As we learned in Chapter 1, corporate advertising is designed not to promote a specific brand but to establish a favorable attitude toward a company as a whole. A variety of highly regarded and highly successful firms use corporate advertising to enhance the image of the firm and affect consumers' attitudes. This perspective on corporate advertising is gaining favor worldwide, as the Global Issues box describes. Firms with the stature of Toyota, Hewlett-Packard, Rockwell, and Coopers & Lybrand have recently invested in corporate advertising campaigns. The Coopers & Lybrand corporate campaign was conceived to show how the firm helps manage change in a dynamic, global environment. The goal was to establish the image of Coopers & Lybrand as a contemporary and visionary organization.[36] One of the ads from the Coopers & Lybrand campaign is shown in Exhibit 13.10.

The Scope and Objectives of Corporate Advertising

Corporate advertising is a significant force in the overall advertising carried out by organizations in the

35.   James Cox, "Shareholders Get to Put Bio-Engineered Foods to Vote," *USA Today*, June 6, 2000, 1B.
36.   Kevin Goldman, "Coopers & Lybrand TV Ads Paint Inspirational Image for Accounting," *The Wall Street Journal*, January 3, 1994, 12.

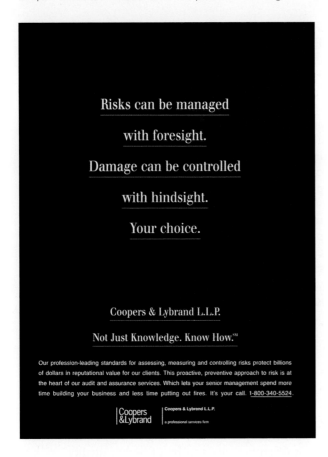

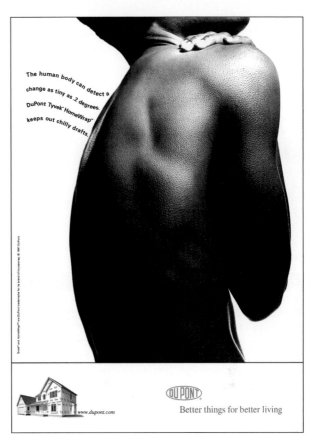

EXHIBIT 13.10

Coopers & Lybrand is an accounting firm, and this is one of the ads from their corporate image campaign. Does the headline remind you of public relations?

EXHIBIT 13.11

Corporate image advertising is meant to build a broad image for the company as a whole rather than tout the features of a brand. Does this ad qualify as a corporate image ad?

United States. The best estimates are that about 65 percent of all service companies, 61 percent of business goods manufacturers, and 41 percent of consumer goods manufacturers employ some form of corporate advertising as part of their overall marketing communications.[37] Billions of dollars are invested annually in media for corporate advertising campaigns. Interestingly, the vast majority of corporate campaigns run by consumer goods manufacturers are undertaken by firms in the shopping goods category, such as appliance and auto marketers. Studies have also found that larger firms (in terms of gross sales) are much more prevalent users of corporate advertising than are smaller firms. Presumably, these firms have broader communications programs and more money to invest in advertising, which allows the use of corporate campaigns. An example of a company using just such a campaign is shown in Exhibit 13.11. Here DuPont touts its image with a very stylish ad and makes only an oblique reference to a specific product in the DuPont line.

In terms of media use, firms have found both the magazine and television media to be well suited to corporate advertising efforts.[38] Corporate advertising appearing in magazines has the advantage of being able to target particular constituent groups with image- or issue-related messages. Hewlett-Packard chose to use both television

37.   David W. Schumann, Jan M. Hathcote, and Susan West, "Corporate Advertising in America: A Review of Published Studies on Use, Measurement, and Effectiveness," *Journal of Advertising,* vol. 20, no. 3 (September 1991), 38.
38.   Ibid., 40.

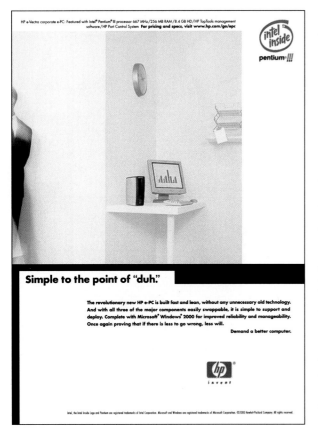

HP e-Vectra corporate e-PC: Featured with Intel® Pentium® III processor 667 MHz/256 MB RAM/8.4 GB HD/HP TopTools management software/HP Port Control System **For pricing and specs, visit www.hp.com/go/epc**

Simple to the point of "duh."

The revolutionary new HP e-PC is built fast and lean, without any unnecessary old technology. And with all three of the major components easily swappable, it is simple to support and deploy. Complete with Microsoft® Windows® 2000 for improved reliability and manageability. Once again proving that if there is less to go wrong, less will.

Demand a better computer.

EXHIBIT 13.12

The new CEO of Hewlett-Packard felt that the company's image had become fragmented. This is one of the ads in a new corporate image campaign designed to unify the image of the firm.

and magazine ads in its corporate campaign (see Exhibit 13.12).[39] The campaign was designed to unify the image of the firm after its new CEO, Carly Fiorina, determined the firm's image had become fragmented in the market. Magazines also provide the space for lengthy copy, which is often needed to achieve corporate advertising objectives. Television is a popular choice for corporate campaigns, especially image-oriented campaigns, because the creative opportunities provided by television can deliver a powerful, emotional message.

The objectives for corporate advertising are well focused. In fact, corporate advertising shares similar purposes with proactive public relations when it comes to what firms hope to accomplish with the effort. While corporate managers can be somewhat vague about the purposes for corporate ads, the following objectives are generally agreed upon to:

- Build the image of the firm among customers, shareholders, the financial community, and the general public
- Boost employee morale or attract new employees
- Communicate an organization's views on social, political, or environmental issues
- Better position the firm's products against competition, particularly foreign competition, which is often perceived to be of higher quality
- Play a role in the overall integrated marketing communications of an organization as support for main product or service advertising

Types of Corporate Advertising

Three basic types of corporate advertising dominate the campaigns run by organizations: image advertising, advocacy advertising, and cause-related advertising.

Corporate Image Advertising. The majority of corporate advertising efforts focus on enhancing the overall image of a firm among important constituents—typically customers, employees, and the general public. When IBM promotes itself as the firm providing "Solutions for a small planet" or when Toyota uses the slogan "Investing in the things we all care about" to promote its five U.S. manufacturing plants, the goal is to enhance the broad image of the firm. Bolstering a firm's image may not result in immediate effects on sales but, as we saw in Chapter 5, attitude can play an important directive force in consumer decision making. When a firm can enhance its overall image, it may well affect consumer predisposition in brand choice.[40] Exhibit 13.13 is an example of an image-oriented corporate ad. Here, Huntsman Chemical Corporation is using a quality theme to create a broad image for the firm, based on both the quality of its business practices and the philanthropy of the company founder.

39. Greg Farrell, "And Then There Was One H-P," *USA Today,* June 1, 2000, 5B.
40. For an exhaustive assessment of the benefits of corporate advertising, see David M. Bender, Peter H. Farquhar, and Sanford C. Schulert, "Growing from the Top," *Marketing Management,* vol. 4, no. 4 (Winter/Spring 1996), 10–19.

EXHIBIT 13.13

This corporate image ad for Huntsman Chemical Corporation highlights the quality orientation of its employees and its products.

EXHIBIT 13.14

Bayer used this corporate advertising campaign when the firm changed its name (from Miles Laboratories) and set out to reposition the company.

A distinguishing feature of corporate image advertising is that it is not designed to directly or immediately influence consumer brand choice. In the case of Bayer Corporation, its corporate advertising campaign launched in 1995 had two specific goals: first, to announce its name change from Miles Laboratories Inc. to Bayer Corporation; second, to change the perception of the company from that of an aspirin-product firm to that of a diverse, research-based international company with businesses in health care, chemicals, and imaging technologies. The ads show a wide range of nonaspirin and often nonconsumer products to demonstrate how Bayer regularly touches people's lives in meaningful ways. The target audience is business decision makers and opinion leaders. The media schedule reflects this nonconsumer target: *The Wall Street Journal* and *Business Week* in print and *Face the Nation* and *Meet the Press* in television. Exhibit 13.14 shows a print ad from this campaign.

While most image advertising intends to communicate a general, favorable image, several corporate image advertising campaigns have been quite specific. When PPG Industries undertook a corporate image campaign to promote its public identity, the firm found that over a five-year period, the number of consumers who claimed to have heard of PPG increased from 39.1 to 79.5 percent. The perception of the firm's product quality, leadership in new products, and attention to environmental problems were all greatly enhanced over the same period.[41] Another organization that has decided that image advertising is worthwhile is the national newspaper *USA Today*.[42] The newspaper has spent $1 million on print and outdoor ads that highlight the four color-coded sections of the newspaper: National, Money, Sports, and Lifestyle.

41.   Schumann, Hathcote, and West, "Corporate Advertising in America," 43, 49.
42.   Keith J. Kelly, "*USA Today* Unveils Image Ads," *Advertising Age,* February 6, 1996, 8.

Advocacy Advertising. **Advocacy advertising** attempts to establish an organization's position on important social, political, or environmental issues. Advocacy advertising is defined as "advertising that addresses and attempts to influence public opinion on issues of concern to the sponsor."[43] Exhibit 13.15 is an example of an advocacy corporate advertisement. Here, Chevron is touting its commitment to a clean environment. Typically, the issue is directly relevant to the business operations of the organization. Another company, W. R. Grace, which is a conglomerate in a variety of businesses, used to run advocacy ads warning the public about the disastrous effects of an ongoing federal government budget deficit. After one such campaign, the firm received 50,000 requests for its booklet on the issue.[44]

EXHIBIT 13.15

Firms can use corporate advertising to take an advocacy position on an important topic. Here Chevron is using corporate advertising to inform consumers of its environmental efforts.

Cause-Related Advertising. **Cause-related advertising** features a firm's affiliation with an important social cause—reducing poverty, increasing literacy, and curbing drug abuse are examples—and takes place as part of the cause-related marketing efforts undertaken by a firm. The idea behind cause-related marketing and advertising is that a firm donates money to a nonprofit organization in exchange for using the company name in connection with a promotional campaign. The purpose of cause-related advertising is that a firm's association with a worthy cause enhances the image of the firm in the minds of consumers. The Allstate ad in Exhibit 13.16 fits this definition perfectly. The firm is promoting responsible drinking and driving in partnership with MADD—Mothers Against Drunk Driving. The social cause of drinking and driving, however, also affects the company's business activities.

Cause-related advertising is thus advertising that identifies corporate sponsorship of philanthropic activities. Each year, *Promo* magazine provides an extensive list of charitable, philanthropic, and environmental organizations that have formal programs for corporations to participate in.[45] Most of the programs suggest a minimum donation for corporate sponsorship and specify how the organization's resources will be mobilized in conjunction with the sponsor's other resources.

Some high-profile firms have participated in cause-related marketing programs and have made extensive use of cause-related advertising. American Express first sponsored a major campaign as part of the restoration of the Statue of Liberty.[46] Next, it was the sole sponsor of a program in which the firm donated to a fight against hunger each time an American Express card was used for a purchase during the Christmas holidays. Another cause-related advertiser

---

43. Adapted from a definition offered by Karen Fox, "The Measurement of Issue/Advocacy Advertising Effects," *Current Issues and Research in Advertising,* vol. 9, no. 1 (1986), 62.
44. Bob Dietrich, "Mr. Nice Guy," *Madison Avenue,* vol. 26 (September 1984), 82.
45. For example, see the 1996 listing: "Causes That Move Cases," *Promo,* February 1996, 34–38.
46. Bill Kelley, "Cause-Related Marketing: Doing Well While Doing Good," *Sales and Marketing Management,* March 1991, 60.

http://www.allstate.com

http://www.madd.org

http://www.budweiser.com

http://www.heineken.com

EXHIBIT 13.16

Insurance company Allstate and advocacy organization MADD team up for cause-related advertising.
Clearly it's in Allstate's interests to see fewer alcohol-related accidents, and less alcohol consumption
wouldn't hurt; would MADD be as likely to share ad space with breweries like Budweiser or Heineken,
which also request that their patrons drink responsibly?

is Avon, the cosmetics firm, which has distributed more than 15 million brochures on breast cancer and underwritten a PBS special on the topic—all designed to encourage early detection of the disease.[47]

Firms are also finding that new media outlets such as the World Wide Web offer opportunities to publicize their cause-related activities. This is especially true for environmental activities that firms are engaged in. The higher-education, upscale profile of many Web users matches the profile of consumers that are concerned about the natural environment. When firms engage in sound environmental practices, the Web is a good place for them to establish a "green" presence. There are "green site" operators (http://www.greenmarketplace.com and http://www.envirolink.com are examples) that give firms a forum to describe their environmental activities.[48]

47. Sue Hwang, "Linking Products to Breast Cancer Fight Helps Firms Bond with Their Customers," *The Wall Street Journal,* September 21, 1993, B1.
48. Jacquellyn Ottman, *Marketing News,* February 26, 1996, 7.

IN PRACTICE

THIS CAMPAIGN FOR BRICKS IS NO BRICK

Ever heard the phrase during a basketball game that a player (most likely Shaquille O'Neal) "threw up a brick" to describe a bad free throw? Well, here's a story about a firm that really does throw bricks—but for a living.

Acme Brick of Fort Worth, Texas, has managed to make cause-related advertising the centerpiece of well conceived and highly successful IMC effort. Acme began doing brand development campaigns for its line of residential and commercial bricks decades ago. The company's $3 million annual promotions budget is spent pretty much as you would suspect, with substantial investment in trade industry ads, direct mail, and trade shows. But what you wouldn't suspect is that nearly half the budget is allocated to advertising in media directed primarily at consumers. And the bulk of that spending is devoted to cause-related ads.

The cause-related advertising program had an inauspicious start. When Troy Aikman, the Dallas Cowboys' highly revered quarterback, first came to Dallas, Acme struck a deal where Aikman would offer promotional services to the company in return for bricks to build the Aikman home. The relationship has grown significantly. Now every time a home is built with Acme Bricks, the company makes a contribution to the Troy Aikman Foundation for Children. This year, the firm estimates that more than 100 million advertising impressions about Acme's partnership with the Aikman Foundation will be made via television, billboards, and point-of-purchase materials. "We've found that cause-related marketing opens many avenues for us on the public relations front," says Bill Seidel, Acme's director of marketing.

And the $1.5 million a year investment in cause-related advertising and promotion is paying off. While it is always hard to trace advertising and promotion effects directly, consider these characteristics of Acme:

- Acme bricks command a 10 percent premium price in a market where the product is clearly perceived as a commodity by the average person.
- Acme has a 50 percent market share in its major Texas metropolitan markets and a 30 to 40 percent share in regional markets.

To appreciate the magnitude of these effects, you can look at the impact this way: approximately $20 million of Acme's $200 million in annual sales is at least in part the return on investment of the corporate cause-related campaign that cost about $1.5 million. That's a 13-fold return, and that's no brick.

Source: Bob Lamons, "Brick Brand's Mighty—Yours Can Be Too," *Marketing News,* November 22, 1999, 16.

While much good can come from cause-related marketing, there is some question as to whether consumers see it in a positive light. In a study by Roper Starch Worldwide, 58 percent of consumers surveyed believed that the only reason a firm was supporting a cause was to enhance the company's image.[49] The image of a firm as self-serving was much greater than the image of a firm as a philanthropic partner.

The belief among consumers that firms are involved with causes only for revenue benefits is truly unfortunate. Firms involved in causes do indeed give or raise millions of dollars for worthy causes. Consumers shopping at Eddie Bauer outlets or ordering from catalogs are encouraged by salespeople to "Add a dollar, plant a tree." With this program, the clothing retailer is helping to raise money for American Forests' Global ReLeaf Tree Project. So far, the program has raised more than $300,000, and Eddie Bauer has contributed another $75,000.[50] And, while there is some suspicion among consumers, there is growing evidence that cause marketing and advertising is particularly effective with teenagers. In a recent study, researchers found that 67 percent of teens shop for clothing and other items with a cause in mind, and more than half said they would switch to brands or retailers that were associated with a good cause.[51] In the words of one teen, "I bought a lot of my clothes at The Gap because they support the environment."[52]

Corporate advertising will never replace brand-specific advertising as the main thrust of corporate communication. But it can serve an important supportive role for brand advertising, and it can offer more

49. Geoffrey Smith and Ron Stodghill, "Are Good Causes Good Marketing?" *Business Week,* March 21, 1994, 64–65.
50. Daniel Shannon, "Doing Well by Doing Good," *Promo,* February 1996, 29–33.
51. Melinda Ligos, "Mall Rats with a Social Conscience," *Sales and Marketing Management,* November 1999, 115.
52. Ibid.

depth and breadth to an IMC program. One fundamental criticism corporate managers have of corporate advertising is the measurement of its specific effects on sales. If the sales effects of brand-specific advertising are difficult to measure, those for corporate advertising campaigns may be close to impossible to gauge. But one small firm has found that including corporate cause advertising in its IMC program has paid big benefits in revenue and market share, as the IMC in Practice box explains.

SUMMARY

① Explain the role of public relations as part of a firm's overall promotional mix

Public relations represents another aspect of an organization's IMC programming that can play a key role in determining how the organization's many constituents view the organization and its products. Public relations is a marketing and management communications function that deals with the public issues encountered by firms across a wide range of constituents. An important component of public relations is publicity—news media coverage of events related to a firm's products or activities.

② Detail the objectives and tools of public relations.

An active PR effort can serve many objectives, such as building goodwill and counteracting negative publicity. Public relations activities may also be orchestrated to support the launch of new products or communicate with employees on matters of interest to them. The PR function may also be instrumental to the firm's lobbying efforts and in preparing executives to meet with the press. The primary tools of public relations experts are press releases, feature stories, corporate newsletters, interviews, press conferences, and participation in the firm's event sponsorship decisions and programs.

③ Describe how firms are using the Internet to assist their public relations activities.

Firms are using the Internet for a variety of PR activities. The issue was raised earlier (Chapter 9) that new media can create a "buzz" through word-of-mouth that is more effective with certain target segments than any other tactic. In a noisy and crowded competitive environment, mainsteam promotional tools like advertising, sales promotion, and sponsorships may get lost in the clutter. Public relations using new media, particularly Web sites, chat-room posts, and Web press releases, can reach targeted audiences in a different way that carries more credibility than in-your-face company self-promotion.

New Web companies are finding that their PR needs are just as great as—if not greater than—established, non-Web–based firms. Analysts believe that without the third-party endorsement that PR provides from the press and industry analysts, it is doubtful that a start-up can be successful.

Finally, there is a major drawback to new media when it comes to public relations. Because of the speed with which information is disseminated, staying ahead of negative publicity is indeed challenging. While word-of-mouth can be used to create a positive buzz, it can also spread bad news—or, even worse, misinformation—just as fast.

④ Describe two basic strategic approaches to public relations activities.

When companies perceive public relations as a source of opportunity for shaping public opinion, they are likely to pursue a proactive public relations strategy. With a proactive strategy, a firm strives to build goodwill with key constituents via aggressive programs. The foundation for these proactive programs is a rigorous public relations audit and a comprehensive public relations plan. The plan should include an explicit statement of objectives to guide the overall effort. In many instances, however, PR activities take the form of damage control, and in these instances the firm is obviously in a reactive mode. While a reactive strategy may seem a contradiction in terms, it certainly is the case that organizations can be prepared to react to bad news. Organizations that understand their inherent vulnerabilities in the eyes of important constituents will be able to react quickly and effectively in the face of hostile publicity.

⑤ Discuss the types of and objectives for corporate advertising.

Corporate advertising is not undertaken to support an organization's specific brands, but rather to build the general reputation of the organization in the eyes of key constituents. This form of advertising uses various media—but primarily magazine and television ads—and serves goals such as image enhancement and building fundamental credibility for a firm's line of products. Corporate advertising may also serve diverse objectives, such as improving employee morale, building shareholder confidence, or denouncing foreign competitors. Corporate ad campaigns generally fall into one of three categories: image advertising, advocacy advertising, or cause-related advertising. Corporate advertising may also be orchestrated in such a way to be very newsworthy, and thus it needs to be carefully coordinated with the organization's ongoing public relations programs.

KEY TERMS

public relations, 453
publicity, 453
proactive public relations strategy, 461

reactive public relations strategy, 461
public relations plan, 461

advocacy advertising, 468
cause-related advertising, 468

QUESTIONS FOR REVIEW AND CRITICAL THINKING

1. Describe the two basic strategies a firm can select in determining its approach to the PR function. Which of these two strategies do you believe Microsoft operated under in dealing with the public relations challenges of the Justice Department case against it?

2. Review the criteria presented in this chapter and in Chapter 12 regarding the selection of events to sponsor. Obviously, some events will have more potential for generating favorable publicity than others. What particular criteria should be emphasized in event selection when a firm has the goal of gaining publicity that will build goodwill via event sponsorship?

3. Would it be appropriate to conclude that the entire point of public relations activity is to generate favorable publicity and stifle unfavorable publicity? What is it about publicity that makes it such an opportunity and threat?

4. There is an old saying to the effect that "there is no such thing as bad publicity." Can you think of a situation in which bad publicity would actually be good publicity?

5. Most organizations have vulnerabilities they should be aware of to help them anticipate and prepare for unfavorable publicity. What vulnerabilities would you associate with each of the following companies?

   R. J. Reynolds—makers of Camel cigarettes

   Procter & Gamble—makers of Pampers disposable diapers

   Kellogg's—makers of Kellogg's Frosted Flakes

   Exxon—worldwide oil and gasoline company

   McDonald's—worldwide restaurateur

6. Review the three basic types of corporate advertising, and discuss how useful each would be as a device for generating brand image. Is corporate image advertising necessarily the best image builder?

EXPERIENTIAL EXERCISES

1. **In-class exercise.** Obtain recent copies of popular business magazines like *Fortune, Forbes,* and *Business Week.* Look for "advocacy" and "cause-related" corporate ads. Bring the ads to class and explain how the positions and causes "fit" the corporations' main business areas?

2. **Out-of-class exercise.** Whatever happened to Coca-Cola in Europe? Track down news reports about the case in *The Wall Street Journal, Fortune,* and other business magazines and write a two-page summary of the final outcome.

USING THE INTERNET

Exercise 1

The Internet is an ideal medium for the dissemination of corporate public relations documents, and several companies have been formed to serve as channels. Visit:

Business Wire
http://www.businesswire.com

PR Newswire
http://www.prnewswire.com

A number of Web-based news services further "distribute" these releases through links on their own sites, for example, on the Yahoo! stock exchange quotes site (http://www.finance.yahoo.com).

1. What percentage of these press releases are business-oriented, as opposed to cause-related, news releases?

2. What sorts of biases does this news reflect?

The Center for Media & Democracy (http://www.prwatch.org) is an organization that challenges PR "spinmeisters" on their facts (or, perhaps, "facts").

3. In what ways does the Center take advantage of the Internet in its work?

The Internet is also a cheap medium for companies' opponents, for example, to disseminate rumors or even outright hoaxes, or to set up protest Web sites.

McSpotlight (http://www.mcspotlight.org) is a site dedicated to opposition to one corporate target: fast-food giant McDonald's.

4. How large an audience do you think this site has? How well is it reaching its target audience?

Exercise 2

In August 2000, Emulex, a manufacturer of computer network equipment, was the victim of a hoax: a former employee of an Interne-based newswire who was at risk of losing thousands of dollars shorting Emulex's stock, allegedly conned the newswire into accepting a fake press release from Emulex, announcing a restatement of earnings (to show huge losses) and the CEO's resignation. That release was picked up by other services, and Emulex's stock plummeted when the market opened; Emulex's market cap fell more than $2.5 billion. While the stock rebounded when the hoax was uncovered, investors who unloaded their stock on the way down lost money—lots of money—and several of the companies involved in disseminating the bogus "news" were sued.

You can find old news items about and press releases from Emulex on the Yahoo! Finance site (Emulex's stock ticker symbol is EMLX).

Yahoo! Finance
http://finance.yahoo.com

Internet Wire was the service that first disseminated the "news" of Emulex's "dire situation."

Internet Wire
http://www.internetwire.com

1. You're the CEO of a company and would like to avoid emulating Emulex. What sorts of precautions might you take?

After reading this chapter, you will be able to:

1 Explain why personal selling is the most important promotional tool in many corporations.

2 Discuss the variety of activities in addition to selling performed by salespeople.

3 Discuss the fact that setting objectives for personal selling goes beyond merely setting sales objectives and includes the identification of customer relationship objectives.

4 Outline the steps involved in the personal selling process.

5 Identify factors that contribute to a new environment for personal selling.

6 Discuss the wide range of responsibilities encompassed by the sales force management process.

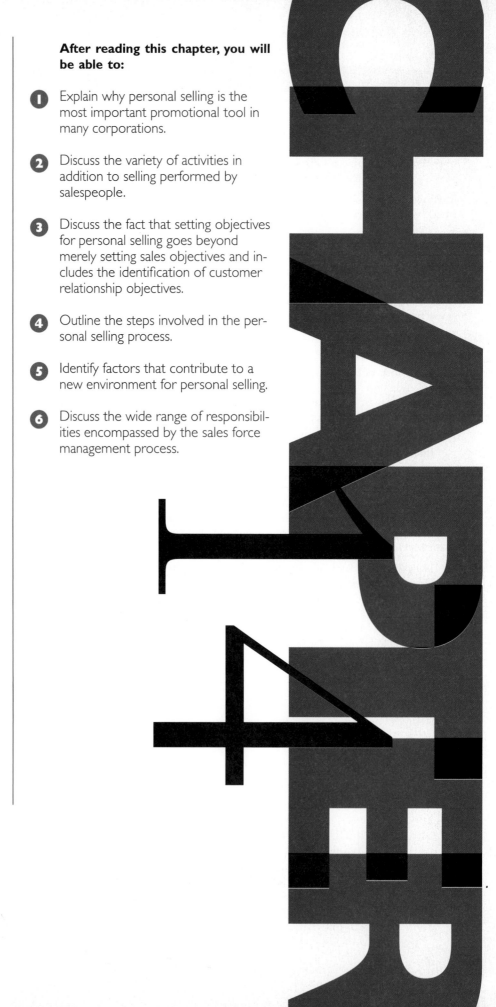

Private Business Inc., a $60-million-a-year business based in Nashville, Tennessee, has recently made it mandatory for its 200 salespeople to use an Internet-based program the company installed for managing the sales process. In the past, the sales reps were able to set up their own presentations and handle all the details of customer and prospect accounts. Now, the new centralized system, which is accessed from the road, allows for real-time updates on the time and location of each rep's next appointment. The system also provides market profiles and intelligence on the customers' businesses, and even gives directions to the customers' locations.

But the system does much more than act like an appointment book and pocket road map. Many of the routine and standardized aspects of the selling process are online and free the sales reps from a variety of mundane and burdensome tasks. The selling of repeat purchase items has been put online for customers. Catalogs, product information, and prices are also available online for both the reps and their customers. The system allows sales teams to spend less time on account maintenance tasks and more time on delivering high-level, strategic services to customers. There is a downside to the new system—at least as far as the sales reps are concerned. A highly automated sales assistance program like this takes the "gimme" orders out of the hands of the salespeople and forces them to show higher initiative—or risk a bad evaluation. "There was some irritation and complaining about the new system at first," says John Dodd, the vice president of Private Business. "But once they saw how much their close rates and commissions shot up, they stopped grumbling."[1]

http://www.dell.com

EXHIBIT 14.1

Dell originated in its founder's dorm room, with a field sales force of nil. The company has grown enormously since then, but it remains the premier Web-only source for PCs. Its Web site, allowing customers to mix and match and create the ensemble of pieces and parts that best meets their needs, does much of the selling, allowing the human sales force to be more selective in their targeting. Such a strategy can't work everywhere—why does it work well here, and where would it likely fail?

1.   Dana James, "Hit the Bricks," *Marketing News,* September 13, 1999, 1, 15.

Firms in all types of business-to-business selling are using the Internet to support the personal selling communication process. It's not just a matter of greater efficiency, however. As the CEO of a sale-productivity firm points out, "If you're a sales person who only *communicates* product value—'This is what we make, let me give you a presentation'— you're gone. But if you know how to *add* value, you're going to have a nice business as a consultive sales person."[2] In general, firms are finding that using e-commerce tools like the Internet give salespeople precious "face" time with customers for communicating complex information. Companies are setting up the electronic "shop" at their Web sites and giving customers passwords to access routine data. The process can also be used to request direct contact with a salesperson so the need for face-to-face contact can still be fulfilled.

The company that has invested most heavily in Internet-based support systems for the sales staff is Dell Computer Corporation. Dell initiated its Internet Store operation in 1996 and now does over $25 million. Dell expects 70 percent of its PC sales in Asia to be made over the Internet.[3] To foster customer use of the Internet, Dell has developed more than 14,000 secure, customized Web pages for their corporate and educational customers. Through these extranet sites, as they are called, Dell offers purchasing, order status, financial reporting, service consultation, and account team support (see Exhibit 14.1). How does the sales force at Dell feel about so much of the PC business moving to an Internet-based system? "They are finally freed up to do the things that Dell has always wanted them to," says Tina Juhl, the marketing manager for Dell's Relationship Online Group.[4] For example, Dell is starting to make new high-end servers, and the sales reps have to locate new prospective customers and educate them on Dell's new products—face-to-face. Also, the sales reps now sit down with clients to plan long-term strategies for their computing needs such as determining a schedule for the replacement of their PCs. Oh—one other thing about the Dell system that makes the reps feel pretty good about moving many customer activities, including some buying, to the Internet: The reps get a commission on *all* transactions by their clients, regardless of whether the transaction was completed in-person, by fax, or via the Internet.

One of the best ways for salespeople to flourish in the increasingly Internet-based world of sales is to be completely knowledgeable about what the Internet can and cannot do in the personal selling communications process. This means knowing when face-to-face communication is needed and what to focus on during those communications.[5] The other key to flourishing in a new media world is to specialize in a specific industry. By having in-depth knowledge of an industry and the needs of customers in the industry, a sales rep can deliver information that truly makes a sales call a value-added experience for customers.

INTRODUCTION

Despite the conspicuousness of advertising, sales promotion, sponsorships, and other tools in the promotional mix, personal selling is often the most important force for communication in many corporations. For firms like IBM, Xerox, State Farm Insurance, and a variety of retailing organizations like Dillard's and Nordstrom, the personal selling effort is primarily responsible for customer contact, communication, and culminating sales. The expense for personal selling can equal as much as 15 percent of gross revenue, and the average cost of a single sales call is about $169.64. Combine that cost with the fact that it takes, on the average, 3.7 calls to close a sale, and an organization is spending about $627.00 on average to get an order![6]

Aside from the sheer expense of the process, though, another measure of the importance of personal selling is the number of people employed in the profession. The most recent statistics from the U.S. Department of Labor put the number of people employed in sales jobs at about 9 million, or nearly 7 percent of the civilian labor force in the United States. Another view of the value of personal selling to

2. Ibid.
3. ON24 News, "Dell Predicts 70 Percent of Sales to Asia Over the Internet Next Year," accessed at http://biz.yahoo.com on June 10, 2000.
4. Dana James, "Hit the Bricks," 15.
5. Rochelle Garner, "The E-Commerce Connection," *Sales and Marketing Management,* January 1999, 40–46.
6. Michele Marchetti, "What a Sales Call Costs," *Sales and Marketing Management,* September 2000, 80.

Sales Occupations	Estimated Employment 1998	Percentange Change in Employment 1998-2008	Numerical Change in Employment Expected 1998-2008
Insurance Sales	387,000	2.2%	9,000
Parts Sales	300,000	1.2%	3,000
Sales Engineers	79,000	15.7%	12,000
Real Estate Agents, Brokers	347,000	9.8%	35,000
Retail Sales	4,056,000	13.9%	563,000
Securities and Financial Services Sales Reps	303,000	41.0%	124,000
Travel Agents	138,000	18.4%	25,000
All other sales	3,388,000	16.5%	558,000
Total sales employment	8,998,000	14.7%	1,330,000
Total U.S. enployment	140,514,000	14.4%	20,281,000

Source: U.S. Department of Labor, Bureau of Labor Statistics, accessed via the Internet at http://stats.bls.gov on June 10, 2000.

EXHIBIT 14.2

Personal selling employment in selected industries and as a percentage of overall U.S. employment

employment in the United States is provided in Exhibit 14.2. Here you can see that certain industries employ an enormous number of people in the personal selling process. Also, this exhibit shows the sales growth that is anticipated through the year 2008 for the various categories of selling professions. Notice that the Bureau of Labor statistics does not anticipate a decline in employment in such industries as travel sales and securities sales. This runs counter to some predictions that have suggested that these sales positions will be eliminated by consumers using the Internet for such services. Notice also that of the 20 million new jobs expected to be created over the ten-year period from 1998 to 2008, over 1.3 million will be in sales.

This chapter considers the nature of personal selling as another tool available to firms for the promotional effort. We first examine the role personal selling can play in the marketing effort and then more specifically with respect to promotional communications. After establishing the role, we identify the types of personal selling a firm can use. Next, the objectives for personal selling are considered. Recall that in Chapter 3 we identified objectives for the overall promotional effort. The objectives for personal selling tend to focus more on the sales aspect of those objectives than any other promotional tool we have examined so far. Then we examine the process of personal selling in great detail, including the stages of the personal selling effort. We also consider the new environment for personal selling and how new technologies are changing the way the selling effort is carried out. Finally, we look at sales management in order to understand what steps need to be taken to ensure that this promotional tool is used effectively and efficiently.

PERSONAL SELLING ❶

There are good reasons why personal selling is the dominant component in the promotional mix for many firms. The discussion of personal communication in Chapter 5 highlighted the potency of face-to-face communication. Products that are higher priced, complicated to use, require demonstration, are tailored to users needs, involve a trade-in, or are judged at the point of purchase are heavily dependent on personal selling. Household consumers and business buyers are frequently confronted with purchase decisions that are facilitated by interaction with a salesperson. In many decision contexts, only a qualified and well-trained salesperson can address the questions and concerns of a potential buyer.

The Role of Personal Selling ②

The importance of the role of personal selling is explained by the key fact that salespeople are often responsible for not just the selling effort but also implementing various aspects of marketing strategy. In a very real sense, the sales force is the embodiment of the entire marketing program for a firm. The responsibilities of salespeople have expanded to include a variety of activities associated with not just selling, but marketing per se. The role of the modern salesperson typically includes the following marketing strategy activities.

Market Analysis. Contact with customers allows salespeople to provide the firm with several different types of information related to market analysis. Feedback to the firm on trends in overall demand can be provided. Competitors' activities are detectable through regular contact with buyers who are also buying competitors' products. This information can be fed directly into the MkIS (Marketing Information System) system used for overall market planning.

Sales Forecasting. Related to the market analysis role is sales forecasting. Salespeople can give their estimates to marketing planners in the firm regarding sales potential for both the short and long term. Such estimates are based on the competitiveness of the firm's products as well as overall conditions in different customers' industries.

New Product Ideas. Salespeople are a direct source of new product ideas. Close contact with customers allows the sales force to detect unmet needs in the market and relay this information to the new product development function in the firm.

Buyer Behavior Analysis. The salesperson is in the best position to analyze buyer behavior tendencies. In negotiating sales with customers, the salesperson learns the criteria upon which different buyers are basing their decisions. Again, this information is fed back to the marketing strategists, who continuously adjust the marketing and promotion mixes.

Communications. To effectively inform and persuade customers, salespeople must be expert in communications methods. No matter how well the marketing mix is conceived, it is up to the sales force to effectively deliver the message to customers regarding the satisfaction to be gained from buying from the firm.

Sales Coordination. The salesperson must act as the coordinator between the firms' many marketing and sales activities and the buyer. The salesperson is often the leader of team selling efforts.

Customer Service. Customers are looking to the salesperson to provide a wide range of post-purchase service support. Salespeople can coordinate product delivery, installation, training, and financing.

Customer Relationship Management. As part of the whole "relationship marketing" movement, salespeople play an important role in building long-term

Worldtrak: Outlook on Steroids.

Imagine Microsoft® Outlook® as a full-fledged sales force automation program. Imagine Microsoft Outlook as the front office component of your *enterprise-wide* customer relationship management (CRM) solution. Imagine a CRM suite *actually designed for the Web*.

Worldtrak® is just that solution. It's an award-winning, browser-based CRM solution based on a platform your people already know and use — Microsoft Outlook. Worldtrak offers you the flexibility to build Outlook into an SFA program, *or* to build a comprehensive enterprise solution — using the Web to bring SFA, lead

management, call centers, marketing, inventory control, on-line order taking, e-commerce, and customer support into the ultimate CRM solution.

It's the one Web-enterprise solution both sales and IS people can really embrace. The only one built *natively* inside Microsoft Outlook, and the only CRM solution *natively* browser-based. That's significant – just ask your nearest IS professional. And best of all, total life-cycle costs for the Worldtrak solution are fully 50% less than the other guys.

So, get a whole new Outlook. Call 1-888-814-2880, or visit us at www.worldtrak.com.

Worldtrak® turns MS Outlook into a total field-sales solution.

CRM award winner 3 years running!

worldtrak
A New Outlook for Web-Based CRM

EXHIBIT 14.3

The sales force is key to the process of customer relationship management (CRM). Several firms have developed software to help manage the CRM process as the sales force level of the organization.

relationships with customers—referred to as **customer relationship management or CRM selling** (see Exhibit 14.3). As an example, Merck spends twelve months training its sales representatives not just in knowledge of pharmaceuticals, but also in trust-building techniques. And reps are required to take regular refresher courses. Similarly, General Electric went so far as to station its own engineers full-time at Praxair Inc., a user of GE electrical equipment, to help the firm boost productivity. As a GE manager put it, "Customers demand a new intimacy."[7] Furthermore, firms are discovering that CRM is a key strategy for gaining competitive advantage in foreign markets. [8] Recommendations for proceeding with CRMs in global markets are discussed in the Global Issues box.

Related to CRM, salespeople are also instrumental in ensuring total customer satisfaction. Since salespeople play a marketing strategy role as discussed above, they no longer simply approach customers with the intention of making a sale. Rather, they are problem solvers who work in partnership with customers. The salesperson is in the best position in the firm to analyze customer needs and propose solutions. By accepting this role, the sales force helps determine ways in which a firm can provide total customer satisfaction not just through the personal selling process but with the entire marketing mix.

Types of Personal Selling

Basically, every salesperson is engaged in personal communication, as we discovered in Chapter 5. But there are quite different types of selling. A salesperson can be engaged in order taking, creative selling, or supportive communication. The discussion that follows demonstrates that the communication task for each type of selling is vastly different.

Order Taking. The least complex type of personal selling is order taking. Its importance, however, should not be underestimated. **Order taking** involves accepting orders for merchandise or scheduling services either in written form or over the telephone. Order takers deal with existing customers who, as we have learned, are lucrative to the firm due to the low cost of generating revenue from this group. Order takers can also deal with new customers, which means that they need to be trained well enough to answer any questions a new customer might have about products or services. Order takers are responsible for communicating with buyers in such a way that a quality relationship is maintained. This type of selling rarely involves communicating large amounts of information. Nor does order taking typically warrant in-depth analysis of the customer.

The retail clerk who simply takes payment for products or services is considered an **inside order taker.** In this situation, the buyer has already chosen the product/ service and merely uses the salesperson to make payment. The person who runs the

7. Ibid.
8. Erika Rasmusson, "Going Global with CRM," *Sales and Marketing Management,* May 2000, 96.

WHEN IT COMES TO CRM, ONE SIZE DOES NOT FIT ALL

The advantages of customer relationship management (CRM) programs for U.S.-based customers are extensive and potent. The databases alone that developed from intimate knowledge of customers' buying patterns and preferences are worth the entire cost of a CRM program. But implementing CRM programs for global sales teams, while potentially equally beneficial as U.S. programs, presents challenges well beyond those of U.S.-based programs.

"The major thing is, 'One size fits all' is not true," says Jim Dickie, managing partner of Insight Technology Group and a CRM expert. Understanding what international sales reps need is an important first step in developing a successful program. "If you're really going to go international, you've got to do your homework," Dickie warns. The way to go about "doing your homework" involves several considerations. First, determine what functions to automate, and involve the sales force in the decision. Most firms fail to get input from the reps that are located outside the country and really know what the local situation needs. When Information Systems Marketing developed a CRM for a German biotech company, the firm formed two "super user-groups." One was made up of American and Australian reps with a European group leader. The other had European and Japanese reps with an U.S.-based project leader. Together, the groups were able to provide nearly global feedback on what sort of features the global CRM should have for both eastern and western territories.

The second issue focuses on researching the foreign market thoroughly in order to know the kind of sales relationship customers are likely to prefer. The method for doing research has two phases. First, research can be conducted from company headquarters and includes tapping into the U.S. Department of Commerce country trade reports and databases as a way to understand the challenges potential customers may be facing in their own country/product markets. This research is relatively inexpensive and can be conducted fairly quickly. The second phase of research is more costly and time-consuming. This phase entails doing in-country field research that usually involves focus groups and in-depth interviews. A company has to be an expert in a country's business environment by examining the political and social conditions, tariff and trade regulations, and corporate protocols and cultural tendencies.

When a firm does its homework, it can come up with an approach to CRM for its foreign customers that is customized to not only the firm itself, but the business environment of the country and region. Most definitely *not* a one-size-fits-all approach.

Sources: Erika Rasmusson, "Going Global with CRM," *Sales and Marketing Management*, May 2000, 96; Lambeth Hochwald, "Are You Smart Enough to Sell Globally?" *Sales and Marketing Management*, July 1998, 53–56.

cash register at a supermarket and the people manning the phones at an L. L. Bean catalog center are examples of inside order takers. The other type of order-taking task is performed by an outside order taker. An **outside order taker** typically calls on business buyers or members of the trade channel and performs relatively routine tasks related to orders for inventory replenishment or catalog orders. The customer accounts have been established, and the salesperson merely services them on a regular basis. Order takers act as an interface between a firm and customers, but do not engage in many of the marketing strategy activities discussed earlier. They are an important link for the firm to the market, however, in that they still help bring about customer satisfaction: courteous, timely, and attentive service by order takers helps increase the satisfaction a firm provides to its customers.

Creative Selling. Creative selling requires considerable effort and expertise. Situations where creative selling takes place range from retail stores through the selling of services to business and the sale of large industrial installations and component parts. **Creative selling** is the type of selling where customers rely heavily on the salesperson for technical information, advice, and service. At the retail level, stores that sell higher-priced items and specialty goods have a fully trained sales staff and emphasize customer and product knowledge. The services of an insurance agent, stockbroker, media representative, or real estate agent represent another type of creative selling. These salespeople provide services customized to the unique needs and circumstances of each buyer.

The most complex and demanding of the creative selling positions is in the business-to-business market. Many times, these salespeople have advanced degrees in technical areas like chemical engineering, computer science, or mechanical engineering. Business salespeople who deal in large-dollar purchases and complex corporate decisions for capital equipment, specialized component parts, or raw materials have tremendous demands placed on them. They are often called on to analyze the customer's product and production needs and carry this information back to the firm so that product design and supply schedules can be tailored for each customer. At MCI, sales representatives can spend weeks inside a customer's organization determining the precise mix of hardware and communications services needed to solve customer problems.

Three types of creative selling in the business market are worth particular attention: team selling, seminar selling, and systems selling. In **team selling,** a group of people from different functional areas within the organization are assembled as a team to call on a particular customer. Sales teams are prevalent in the areas of communications equipment, computer installations, and manufacturing equipment. This is how a sales team might work: A sales engineer is called on to analyze the customer's operations and design a product; a financial expert works out a purchase or lease agreement that fits the customer's financial situation; and a service representative participates with the team to ensure that delivery, installation, and any training that may be necessary are carried out properly. When IBM reoriented its personal selling effort in the late 1980s, it created selling teams deployed to implement the firm's new Information System Investment Strategies (ISIS) program. A marketing strategist, salespeople, and financial experts operated as a team that consulted customers such as G. Heilemann Brewing and Gulfstream Aerospace. The team spent several months interviewing customer management, touring facilities, analyzing operations, and looking at the customer's information systems. The team then built financial models of the customer's company six years out, with and without new investments in IBM computer software. The president of G. Heilemann Brewing reacted to IBM's team selling approach by saying the system turned complicated decisions about investing in computer systems "into terms that senior management can understand."[9]

Closely related to the team selling effort is seminar selling. **Seminar selling** is designed to reach a group of customers, rather than an individual customer, with information about the firm's products or services. The focus of seminar selling is not really selling at all. Rather, the intent is to educate customers and potential customers about various aspects of a company's market offerings. Seminar selling is a good way to begin the process of developing relationships with potential customers without the pressures of trying to close a sale.

The other noteworthy form of creative selling that has emerged in the last few years is system selling. **System selling** entails selling a set of interrelated components that fulfill all or a majority of a customer's needs in a product or service area. System selling has emerged as a form of selling because of the desire on the part of customers for "system buying." That is, large industrial and government buyers, in particular, have come to seek out one or a small number of suppliers that can provide a full range of product and service needed in an area and sell them an entire system of goods and services. Rather than dealing with multiple suppliers, these buyers then system buy from one source. This systems trend in both buying and selling emphasizes even more the CRM aspects of selling discussed earlier. Large government purchases in China and Eastern Europe for huge infrastructure projects like sea ports, airports, and communications systems demand that project engineering firms like Bechtel employ just such a systems selling approach.

Creative selling tasks call for high levels of preparation, expertise, and close contact with the customer and are primary to the process of relationship building. It is this sort of personal selling that assumes a comprehensive marketing strategy role within an organization. Exhibit 14.4 identifies the types of creative selling positions that are typically found in organizations.

9.   Patricia Sellers, "How IBM Teaches Techies to Sell," *Fortune,* June 6, 1988, 146.

Creative Selling Positions

Account Representative. This type of salesperson calls on large established accounts. Account representatives are used in industries like consumer packaged goods, textiles, clothing, bulk chemicals, and after-market auto parts. Account representatives sell to retailers, wholesalers, and distributors primarily, but may also sell to large manufacturing customers.

Detail Salesperson. The primary tasks undertaken by this type of salesperson are providing product information and introducing new products to potential customers. The pharmaceutical drug industry and the textbook publishing industry are the heaviest users of detail salespeople. Their tasks can be described generally as missionary selling and emphasize relationship building with customers.

Nontechnical Industrial Products Salesperson. This group sells all categories of nontechnical industrial products to end users. Examples of products this type of salesperson would handle are paper products, cleaning agents, lubricants, and office furniture.

Sales Engineers. These are industrial salespeople with specialized training in engineering or science. Products and services in the areas of communication, production, and computer applications (hardware and software) are handled by this type of salesperson.

Service Salesperson. Two types of salespeople actually fall into this category. First, there are the service sales reps who handle the postpurchase services associated with the sale of tangible product. They will handle delivery, installation, training, and product information needs of customers. The other type of service salesperson sells pure services such as a financial planner, real estate agent, or consultant.

System Salesperson. One of the most in demand of creative selling positions, the system salesperson must understand the needs and demands of large industrial and government buyers. System salespeople attempt to design an entire "system" of interrelated products and services for large-scale projects. Examples are integrated manufacturing facilities or government public works projects like airports and water treatment plants.

Team Salesperson. The distinguishing feature of this creative selling position is that the person is part of a team selling effort and perhaps only as a small part of his or her primary job. A team salesperson may be a financial analyst, an engineer, an accountant, or a salesperson per se. The important issue here is that this person performs an important role on a selling team that is assembled to deal with a customer's product and service needs.

EXHIBIT 14.4

Creative selling positions typically found in organizations

Supportive Communications. When a sales force is deployed with the purpose of supportive communications, it is not charged directly with generating sales. Rather, it is the objective of people in this sales area to provide information to customers, offer services, and generally create goodwill. Salespeople involved in supportive communications try to ensure that buyers are satisfied with the firm's product and services. Supportive communications takes place with two types of salespeople. The **missionary salesperson** calls on accounts with the express purpose of monitoring the satisfaction of buyers and updating buyers' needs. There may be some provision of product information after a purchase. Many firms have turned to telemarketing techniques, which use telephone, fax, and computer (e-mail and voice mail) communications as part of the supportive activities of missionary sales. The **detail salesperson** introduces new products and provides detailed product information to potential buyers without attempting to make a sale per se. Detail salespeople are widely used by large pharmaceutical firms to introduce new prescription drugs to physicians and provide information about the drug's application and efficacy.

Setting Objectives for Personal Selling ❸

The appropriate overall objective for any element of the promotional mix, including personal selling, is to communicate. As we have said many times before, the focus of the communication will be the "value" contained in a firm's brands and the satisfaction buyers will receive by purchasing them. Because several of the types of personal selling just discussed involve culminating a sale, reaching a sales objective is also primary. Because a salesperson is typically present when a contract is signed or an order is placed, the direct effect of personal selling on sales is more identifiable than the effect of other elements of the promotional mix.

But culminating a sale is not the only objective for the personal selling. Every encounter with potential buyers may be approached with different objectives in mind. The objectives a salesperson can pursue during a sales call are: create a profitable differential competitive advantage, accord uniqueness to each potential buyer, manage a set of buying-selling relationships for mutual profit, and control the communication without seeming to do so.

WANT TO SAVE TIME AND MONEY? GO VIRTUAL.

Face-to-face presentations are the ideal in many ways: an ideal location, entertaining visuals, firsthand information, the chance to network, and a keen eye trained on customer reactions. But when you dig into the costs of making face-to-face presentations, the ideal gets a little tarnished. Travel expenses, time out of the office, customer downtime at the presentation all add up so that a more efficient alternative is worth looking at. This is where the Internet provides yet another opportunity to effectively communicate with customers but save both the seller and potential buyer a lot of time and money.

One firm that has saved time and money with Web presentations is Sterling Software. Company executives turned to the Net when they came to the hard realization that they just couldn't afford to have people away from the office as much as they had been. And more importantly, they were finding that customers were unwilling to give a day or a portion of a day for the kind of presentation that Sterling needed to deliver. Managers at Sterling are quick to point out that virtual presentations are not just about saving time and money, though. There is a quality issue as well. The company explains that running seminars from remote locations has increased the ability to attract keynote speakers who otherwise would not have participated.

MCI is both a provider and a user of virtual presentations. The company's hourlong presentations cover such topics as e-commerce and investor relations. The presentations are free to MCI customers and prospective customers. The firm feels that it's a value-added service rather than just a sales pitch. To run a Web-based presentation using MCI as a service provider is priced on a per-connection basis. An event with up to ten web connections costs $180 per hour.

There are some situations where only a face-to-face environment will accomplish the objectives of a presentation. But if an analysis of the situation and an assessment of the audience suggest that Web-based communication can accomplish the desired result, then the savings and potential quality enhancements are worth the loss of personal contact.

Source: Erika Rasmusson, "The Value of Virtual Presentations," *Sales and Marketing Management*, November 1999, 113.

Create a Profitable Differential Competitive Advantage. Buyers will ultimately choose the product they perceive to be best suited to their needs. Stated in the context of the marketing concept, buyers are looking for satisfaction that is greater than the costs they will incur. In a personal selling situation, it is up to the salesperson to quickly understand what is best from the buyer's perspective. As discussed in Chapter 5, different buyers value different attributes of a product—functional, emotional, or self-expressive. Further, the services offered by an organization will also be factored into an assessment of satisfaction and value—delivery, installation, and repair services, for example. The salesperson must identify what is valued and then pursue the objective of demonstrating to the buyer that the firm's products and services match the buyer's needs more closely than competitors. In this way, a differential competitive advantage can be created as the buyer learns how the firm's products and services are superior to those of the competition.

Accord Uniqueness to Each Potential Buyer. A second objective is to grant the potential buyer unique status. This is accomplished by managing the communi-

EXHIBIT 14.5

One of the key objectives for personal selling is to manage the buying and selling relationship so well that loyalty between buyers and sellers develops. Several firms offer specialized sales force training designed to prepare salespeople for the task of managing the buying-selling relationship for mutual benefit.

cation process in such a way that a buyer does not feel like he or she is being "sold." Rather, a potential buyer must come away from the contact feeling like a decision to buy has been made. The salesperson who treats each buyer as unique will exert a powerful impact during the communication process. An important part of accomplishing this objective is for the salesperson to listen attentively. Good listening skills allow the salesperson to truly grant a buyer unique status by actually learning the buyer's individual needs and desires. This also allows a salesperson to shape the communication specifically to each buyer's unique desire for information, thus taking full advantage of one of the primary distinctions of personal communications over mass communication: tailoring the message to each receiver.

Manage a Set of Buying-Selling Relationships for Mutual Benefit. One of the greatest challenges facing a salesperson is determining how her/his firm is uniquely capable of satisfying customer needs. By matching what the firm is capable of doing with what a buyer desires allows both parties to enter a buying-selling relationship that is mutually beneficial. The salesperson must determine which of the following form the basis for providing satisfaction to individual buyers:

- Product superiority
- Service superiority
- Price superiority
- Source (company) superiority
- People superiority

Depending on the expression of needs by a buyer, a salesperson can determine what is most highly valued in the purchase decision from the list above. Once that decision is made, the salesperson can then emphasize the firm's unique capabilities in satisfying the customer. A sale can be negotiated emphasizing the ability of the firm to provide superior satisfaction on the desired factors. Over time, loyalty between organizations develops as firms begin to trust and rely on each other. Several firms offer specialized sales force training designed to prepare sales people for the task of managing the buying-selling relationship for mutual benefit (see Exhibit 14.5).

Control the Communication. On the surface, this objective may seem contrary to the spirit of effective communication. However, it is to the mutual benefit of both buyer and seller if the communication process is managed efficiently. The salesperson is in the best position to bring about effective and efficient information exchange by controlling the communication. If a salesperson can control the content and direction of the encounter, the potential buyer will be able to learn quickly and accurately what a firm has to offer. One way that firms are learning to communicate effectively and efficiently and to control the communication is by using "virtual presentations."[10] Virtual presentations rely on a variety of technologies that

10. Erika Rasmusson, "The Value of Virtual Presentations," *Sales and Marketing Management,* November 1999, 113.

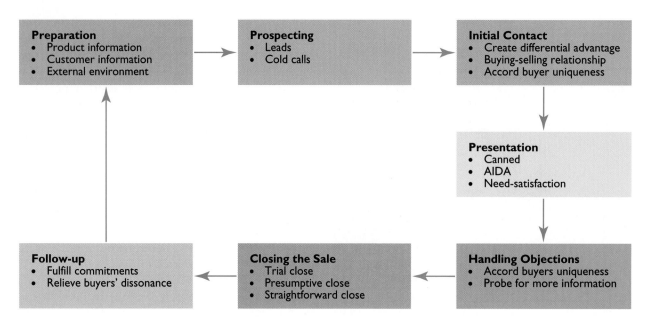

EXHIBIT 14.6

Activities in the personal selling process

let buyers send sellers information via computer and Internet methods. The techniques and the approach to making effective use of virtual presentations is discussed in the New Media box.

It is important to note that these objectives for personal selling are external in their orientation. Each focuses on the buyer. The emphasis of each objective is to understand the buyer's needs and with that understanding provide information on how the firm is capable of satisfying those needs. If these objectives are accomplished, the probability of a sale resulting from the contact increases greatly.

The Personal Selling Process ❹

Objectives for personal selling are only achievable in the context of a well-conceived and well-executed sales effort. In other words, time and care must be devoted to the process of personal selling itself. It is unreasonable and unrealistic to view personal selling as an isolated contact or series of contacts with buyers. It is essential to recognize the *buyer's state of mind* during a selling encounter. The selling process requires that salespeople attend to the need states of buyers individually (that is, accord them uniqueness) rather than treating all buyers as though they were the same. This orientation also takes advantage of the ability of personal communication to tailor a message specifically to an individual customer.

In order to fully adopt a "process" approach, the selling effort must be organized into a sequence of well-defined activities. The sales force must be able to understand characteristics of existing and potential customers, make a persuasive presentation, close a sale, and follow up the entire effort. Every organization has its own perspective on the steps required for an effective personal selling process. Generally, a well-conceived personal selling process involves seven distinct activities: preparation, prospecting, initial contact, presentation, handling objections, closing the sale, and follow-up. These activities are graphically depicted in Exhibit 14.6. We will discuss each of them separately.

Preparation. Preparation for a personal selling contact is really a very focused environmental analysis—not unlike one that a firm would do in developing overall marketing strategy. Preparation involves gathering relevant information about current customers, potential customers, product characteristics and applications, product choice criteria, corporate support activities (such as advertising and trade channel support), and competitors' products and activities. Further, economic and demographic trends that affect customers will also be analyzed. The firm that maintains an effective marketing information system greatly aids its salespeople in preparing for sales calls. An MkIS will contain data about purchasing behavior in the market as well as records relating to past behavior of current customers. Without comprehensive information in the areas just described, a salesperson cannot hope to accomplish sales objectives.

For example, a well-prepared salesperson may recognize that potential business buyers of drilling equipment have a general dissatisfaction with suppliers' ability to deliver on a dependable schedule. Recall from Chapter 5 that dependable delivery was a primary motive in business buyer behavior. Armed with such knowledge, the salesperson can approach a prospect with a sales presentation that highlights the reliability and dependability of the firm's distribution and delivery program.

Another important part of the preparation process is to recognize the extent to which the buying decision will be an individual decision versus a group buying decision. With individual buyers, the salesperson can tailor a very specific sales presentation to an individual. In group buying decisions, representatives from several different functional areas in the firm as well as pure administrators (like purchase agents) may be involved in the group effort. The communication at the group level must recognize the information needs of a wide range of constituents within the customer's organization. In fact, some experts recommend that salespeople actually encourage multiple decision makers within their customer firms. This is because if the salesperson is relying on one contact to champion a specific brand or buying project, the sale is dead in the water if that person leaves the customer firm or is transferred away from the buying decision.[11]

Overall, preparation involves knowing the firm's capabilities in all areas of the marketing mix, competitors' strengths and weaknesses, effects of the external environment, and customer choice criteria. With this information, the salesperson is prepared to deliver a selling message that is relevant and persuasive to buyers. How important is this preparation phase? The director of MIT's Entrepreneurship Center, Ken Morse, himself a former salesman, used to spend up to eight hours preparing for a fifteen-minute sales call.[12]

Prospecting. Much of the growth in total revenues for a firm depends on the sales force cultivating new customers. Therefore, primary in the selling process is for salespeople to prospect for new accounts. There are a variety of traditional methods for carrying out this activity. Successful prospecting is dependent on generating leads—that is, generating names of new potential buyers. Several sources can be tapped for leads. Current customers are an excellent source of leads since the salesperson benefits from a personal "introduction" to a potential customer. Advertising can create leads for the sales force with mail-in coupons placed in trade magazines. Mail-in coupons can be a particularly valuable source of leads since the person filling out the coupon normally provides the name of the proper contact including a current address and phone number. Telemarketing has increased the efficiency of the use of leads. Some firms maintain a full staff or outsource a call center operation to qualify sales leads. Leads can then be classified as either high or low potential, and nonproductive, expensive in-person sales calls can be avoided for those leads that seem to hold little promise.

11.   William Weeks, "Buying Decisions a Group Effort," *Marketing News,* December 6, 1999, 22.
12.   Ann Harrington, "I'll Take That Pitch with a Dash of Politesse," *Fortune,* June 12, 2000, 334.

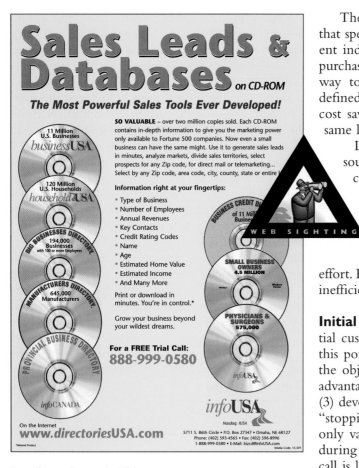

http://www.directoriesUSA.com

EXHIBIT 14.7

A critical activity in the personal selling process is prospecting for leads. Companies such as info-USA distill information from thousands of sources, then slice and dice the databases to produce specialized, targeted lists. It's now easy to fetch hundreds or thousands of prospects for less than the cost of a business flight. While that's cheap and easy, can you think of any drawbacks?

The newest source of leads is from companies that specialize in creating databases of firms in different industries (see Exhibit 14.7). The advantages of purchased database lists are that they can be a good way to get data on potential customers in well-defined target areas, and existing lists offer time and cost savings. But firms have to be aware that these same lists are readily available to competitors.[13]

Leads are the most valuable and effective source of prospecting, but salespeople still use the cold call as a prospecting method. Here, the salesperson will either telephone or actually visit a potential customer with whom there has been no previous contact. Normally, salespeople will use U.S. Government codes to better focus the cold-calling effort. Even with the SIC codes, cold calling is still an inefficient and rarely profitable approach, however.

Initial Contact. The initial contact with a potential customer is a critical step in the process. It is at this point that the salesperson must begin to address the objectives of (1) creating a profitable differential advantage, (2) according each buyer uniqueness, and (3) developing the buying-selling relationship. Merely "stopping by" to call on a potential customer with only vague notions of what might be accomplished during an initial contact is not a good idea. Such a call is likely to be viewed by a potential customer as an intrusion and a waste of time. A professional, well-planned, purposeful, and brief initial contact can establish the salesperson as a new and important source in the mind of the buyer. Reasonable activities in an initial contact can include leaving comprehensive information about the firm and its products, introducing the buyer to corporate selling programs, and gathering information about the buyer's organization and product needs.

The Presentation. The presentation is an important focal point of the personal selling process. On rare occasions, it will occur during the initial contact. Normally, it is a separately scheduled phase in the process. Presentations require great skill and preparation (see Exhibit 14.8). There are several ways in which a presentation can be carried out.

Some firms will require a **canned presentation.** This method has a salesperson recite, nearly verbatim, a prepared sales pitch. The reason some firms use a canned presentation approach is that it ensures important selling points are covered. It can also enhance the performance of marginally skilled salespeople. The drawback of the canned presentation is severe in that it undermines fundamental advantages of personal communication: tailoring the message to the buyer's unique needs and being able to respond to buyer feedback. Further, such an approach downplays the need

---

13.   Jamie Teschner, "Skill Workshop: Prospecting," *Selling Power,* March 2000, 34.

EXHIBIT 14.8

The presentation phase of the personal selling process requires great skill and preparation. Salespeople can be trained in presentation skills by firms like Miller Heiman that work closely with individual firms to ensure that sales force presentations focus on company objectives as well as customer needs.

to engage in comprehensive preparation as part of the selling process in that it presumes every buyer faces a similar buying situation.

An often implemented but marginally useful approach is **attention–interest–desire–action (AIDA).** In this form of presentation, the salesperson carefully structures the selling contact so that the first part of the presentation gains the buyer's **A**ttention. Then **I**nterest in the firm's offering is stimulated by touting product and service attributes. Next, the salesperson will try to stimulate a **D**esire on the part of the buyer by demonstrating how the firm's offering fulfills the buyer's needs. Finally, an attempt is made to close the sale, thus creating an **A**ction on the part of the buyer. The reason this approach is considered marginally effective is that it grants the buyer very little participation in the process. The salesperson dominates the communication (much more than merely controlling the communication), leading the buyer through the various stages of the AIDA system. The experienced buyer, after years of being subjected to this technique, will find it tiresome and obvious. It does have the advantage of controlling the communication, but goes too far in this regard to the detriment of the process.

A far more sophisticated and informed approach to the presentation is referred to as **need satisfaction.**[14] This is a customer-oriented approach that relies strictly on the marketing concept for its execution. With this technique, the salesperson recognizes that during every sales encounter, each buyer's need state must be assessed and the selling effort is then adjusted to that need state. Three different buyers' need states can be identified:

- *Need development.* These are potential customers who are beginning to form a recognition of the types of problems that exist in their organizations. With a buyer in this need state, the salesperson does very little talking and is monitoring feedback almost exclusively during the presentation. It is at this stage that the salesperson concentrates on according uniqueness to the buyer.
- *Need awareness.* This type of buyer is able to articulate specific needs in his or her organization. The salesperson who encounters this type of buyer can help define the buyer's needs relative to which of the firm's products and services address those needs.
- *Need fulfillment.* Here the buyer is fully aware of what products and services are needed and the salesperson assumes a dominant communication role by demonstrating how the firm and its products can fulfill the needs. It is with this sort of buyer that a salesperson must concentrate on creating differential competitive advantage.

The superiority of the need-satisfaction approach is that it explicitly recognizes that a sales presentation will emphasize different information depending on how

14. This section is based on an excellent discussion in Gary M. Grikscheit, Harold C. Cash, Cliff E. Young, *Handbook of Personal Selling* (New York: John Wiley & Sons, 1993), Chapter 1.

CAREERPROFILE

Name:	David Jahan
Title:	Account Executive
Company:	Gateway Computers, Lake Forest, CA
	http://www.gateway.com
Education:	B.S., Business

"When you're in sales, you're the key person between marketing and the customer," says David Jahan. In his job as an account executive with Gateway Computers, David handles telephone sales to small and mid-sized businesses. Each sales call is a little different, he says, because every customer has unique needs. His role is to uncover how Gateway computers can meet those needs. "I start by asking them specific questions to understand what they're looking to accomplish," he says. "Once I get an understanding of the organization, I begin to see how we can provide a solution that fits."

David sometimes encounters obstacles that must be overcome. "One of my biggest challenges is speaking to a client who is already dealing with another company," he says. "This is the perfect opportunity to turn that conversation around and ask where the current vendor may be lacking so we can come in and prove ourselves. As long as we can keep the client talking, we can start to build the credibility."

Gateway's salespeople get lots of support from marketing and other departments, says David. "We're kept informed as to what new products we have to offer and how they compete against our competitors' products through emails, marketing flyers, and by weekly sales training," he says. Additionally, Gateway salespeople can get instant information from the company's sales intranet, a private Internet site dedicated to keeping the sales force up-to-date. David also works closely with other sales team members, including his sales manager, to make sure customers are satisfied.

Before joining Gateway, David hadn't considered a career in sales. "I joined the Marine Corps after school and when I got out, I knew I wanted to work for an organization where I could have a great career path and good benefits," he says. "I started working for Gateway as a sales associate and realized that being in sales was challenging and exciting."

To learn more about sales careers and management, visit these Web sites:

The Wall Street Journal Career Journal—Sales
http://careerjournal.com/careers/resources/documents/cwc-sales.htm

National Association of Sales Professionals
http://www.nasp.com

SalesGuy.com
http://www.salesguy.com

The Sales Vault
http://www.salesvault.com

developed the buyer's need recognition is. Buyers in the need-awareness stage must be allowed to express themselves in relatively general terms. Buyers who have progressed to need awareness are ready to entertain propositions related to product solutions to their needs. The buyer who is at the need-fulfillment stage is aware of product solutions and is prepared to listen to detailed information about the selling firm's unique ability to satisfy those needs. It is possible that a salesperson can lead a buyer through all the need stages in a single presentation. More than likely, buyers will be encountered who are already at different levels, and the salesperson will be required to adjust the presentation accordingly. The need-satisfaction approach emphasizes the buyer and the buyer's state of mind. It also takes full advantage of direct feedback and tailoring the message according to that feedback.

It is also worth recognizing that there are two basic presentation formats available to salespeople for the presentation: face-to-face and telemarketing. Face-to-face presentation is self-explanatory. The salesperson and the prospect(s) are together, in person. The face-to-face format allows the salesperson to present materials or product examples. Additionally, the face-to-face format allows demonstrations of the product. Despite the efficiencies provided by new technologies for the selling effort, analysts suggest that face-to-face presentations are critical to recruiting new customers and maintaining good relationships with existing customers.[15] Often referred to as **consultive selling,** face-to-face sales presentations can be used by the sales force to create significant value for customers by helping them define their problems and design unique solutions.

The alternative to face-to-face sales is telemarketing. **Telemarketing** is a process whereby salespeople make their sales and information presentations over the telephone. Telemarketing offers an organization the chance to reach a much larger number of customers more often than consultive selling. For small accounts that wouldn't warrant a sales call because of expense, telemarketing offers the firm a way to maintain relationships with small customers. Union Pacific railroad serves its 20,000 smallest customers through telemarketing from a call center

15. Neil Rackham, "The Other Revolution in Sales," *Sales and Marketing Management,* March 2000, 34–36.

in Omaha.[16] And firms are finding that an efficient way to develop and maintain a global presence is to establish call centers that can reach a worldwide customer base regularly and efficiently.[17]

Handling Objections. During a presentation, especially with buyers in the need-fulfillment stage, objections on the part of the buyer are likely to surface. The most serious objections relate to the buyer's perception that the firm's product is not well suited to the need being discussed. The salesperson must be prepared to deal with objections. This is a highly sensitive situation that requires great skill. The salesperson must counter objections without seeming argumentative. Objections cannot be met with defensiveness or brushed aside as insignificant or irrational. Again, the buyer must be accorded uniqueness, which means *every* objection is legitimate and reasonable. The best method for handling objections is to probe for the exact nature of the obstacle and then try to lead the buyer to proposing a solution. In this way, the salesperson has created an alliance with the buyer, and the firms can work in partnership to solve the customer's problem. Another recommendation is to get customers away from a negative focus by asking them "What's the alternative?" This allows a customer to put an objection into perspective, and asks him or her to evaluate the firm's proposal on its merits relative to other solutions.[18]

Closing the Sale. After the presentation or perhaps several presentations, the time arrives when a salesperson needs to try to close the sale. Closing the sale is generally regarded as the most difficult part of the personal selling process—for good reason. This is the stage at which a salesperson is asking a buyer to incur costs—monetary, time, risk, opportunity, and, potentially, anxiety costs. The salesperson must ensure during closing that the buyer perceives that satisfaction can be obtained that will be greater than the costs being incurred. This is another reason why the need-satisfaction approach to the presentation can be so effective.

There are a variety of techniques recommended for effectively closing a sale. Critical to the process is that the salesperson actually ask for the order! Amazingly, some surveys indicate that about 60 percent of the time salespeople never ask for the order! They seem to rely on the customer to close the sale.[19] The first rule in closing, then, is to ask for an order. One technique in asking for the order is the **trial close.** Here the salesperson poses a question like "Would you like gray or oak finish?" or "Would you like this gift wrapped?" Another closing technique is the **presumptive close,** where the salesperson presumes a sale has been agreed upon and will ask something like "What address should appear on the invoice?" These techniques run the risk of being offensive and are, frankly, not very skillful.

The best approach to closing is for the salesperson to use a **straightforward close.** With this method, a salesperson must sense when to ask for an order in a straightforward, courteous manner—no tricks, no presumptions, no innuendo. If a salesperson has successfully achieved the objective of developing a buying-selling relationship for mutual profit, then a buyer will find this method most acceptable. This is the technique used by Ken Libman, founder of the architecture, engineering, and construction firm Libman Wolf Couples. Libman closes an astonishing 80 percent of all the new business he competes for. He explains his success by saying "I understand people; I put myself in their shoes."[20]

16.   Patrica Sellers, "How to Remake Your Sales Force," *Fortune,* May 4, 1992, 98–101.
17.   Erika Rasmusson, "Global Sales on the Line," *Sales and Marketing Management,* March 2000, 76–81.
18.   Gary Goldman, "Gary Goldman's 60 Second Salesman," (Paramus, NJ: Prentice-Hall, 1999) quoted in *Competitive Advantage a Newsletter for Sales and Marketing Professionals,* 1999, 8.
19.   Joseph P. Vaccaro, "Best Salespeople Know Their ABCs (Always Be Closing)," *Marketing News,* March 28, 1998, 10.
20.   Erika Rasmusson, "Image Is Everything," *Sales and Marketing Management,* December 1999, 25.

Follow-Up. Two distinct and very important activities occur after a sale has been made. First, a salesperson must ensure that all commitments of the negotiated sale are fulfilled. Shipping dates, installation, financing, and any training required can be monitored by the salesperson. Second, dealing with buyer postpurchase behavior is a critical follow-up activity. Relieving any cognitive dissonance being experienced by a buyer will make the purchase more satisfying and lay the foundation for future sales. Salespeople can address dissonance through direct communication, either written or oral. Salespeople at Nordstrom department stores send a handwritten and personalized note to customers within three days of a purchase. The note expresses appreciation for the purchase and encourages a recent buyer to contact the salesperson for any future clothing needs. Another important aspect of dealing with postpurchase behavior is for a salesperson to inquire about needs for related items. As the discussion of consumer behavior in Chapter 5 highlighted, many consumers, either out of enthusiasm or newly recognized needs, will purchase items that complement an initial purchase. For firms with broad product lines, a salesperson has an ideal opportunity to approach recent buyers with opportunities for additional purchases.

Viewing personal selling as a process that includes a series of related and integrated stages greatly enhances the performance of sales personnel. The process itself, however, must not become the overall goal. Rather, the potential impact of each stage in the process must be recognized and nurtured. Related to carrying out the process of personal selling is the environment within which salespeople operate. The contemporary selling environment has evolved and changed over the last several years.

The New Environment for Personal Selling ❺

Three changes in the broad business environment have created a significantly new environment for personal selling. First, the increased sophistication of marketing planning has greatly altered activities of salespeople. With more precise means of segmenting markets, efforts of the sales force are more tightly focused on very specific types of customers. Also, new marketing planning efforts are relying more on telemarketing techniques. This affects salespeople in two ways. Telemarketing helps qualify leads as mentioned earlier. It can also relieve the sales force of repeated calls on existing customers who now are serviced by phone rather than in person. In addition, greater efficiency is being achieved throughout the marketing process by virtue of enhanced marketing planning efforts. Salespeople are able to respond more quickly to customer requests because the market effort is more narrowly defined on a customer-by-customer basis. The effect of this greater efficiency has meant a reduction in the size of the sales force in several industries. As marketing efforts are better coordinated, the activities of salespeople can be made more efficient as well.

A second major change in the environment affecting salespeople has to do with sales force automation brought about by changes in technology. **Sales force automation (SFA)** is the result of the incorporation of computers, cell phones, pagers, the Internet, and other technologies to improve the efficiency and effectiveness of the personal selling process. Firms like salesforce.com have emerged to provide sales-automation software to help integrate the various technologies for communication between the sales force, the firm, and customers (see Exhibit 14.9).[21] Firms need to be careful not to adopt technology for technology's sake when considering how to automate the sales force. Clear objectives need to be set for the automation process that are consistent with the firm's customer needs and competitive situation.[22] And in order for SFA programs to be successful, managers need to be

21. Tim R. Furey, "Sales Rep Not Dead, Just Redefined," *Marketing News,* December 6, 1999, 16.
22. Steven J. Goldberg, "Make Sure Objectives Are Clear When Starting SFA Technology," *Marketing News,* November 8, 1999, 13.

http://www.salesforce.com

EXHIBIT 14.9

Sales force automation (SFA) describes all those technologies (cell phones, personal digital assistants, the Internet, etc.) used to improve the efficiency and effectiveness of the personal selling process. Firms like salesforce.com transfer many of the activities necessary to personal selling to the World Wide Web. What factors are encouraging rapid adoption of Web-based tools?

sure to involve the key users of the technology early in the process or the automated systems will be underused, thus defeating the main purpose of SFA programs.[23]

An important ramification of SFA is that the personal selling process is now database driven. Salespeople have come to rely on in-house MkIS systems to store knowledge about customers, markets, and company products. General advances in computer and communications technology have changed the way salespeople carry out their activities. Laptop computers and palm-size communicators are allowing salespeople to stay connected with their customer databases. These types of technological advances are powerful enough that salespeople can stay connected to their company's data sources on a global basis.[24] A salesperson can get ready for a sales call by entering pricing and sales forecast data. As orders are booked, the forecasts can be updated and, upon return to the office, downloaded to a desktop computer that is tied to the firm's MkIS system.

Communications technology provides salespeople with an arsenal of tools to communicate both to customers and back to the firm. Fax machines, cellular phones, videoconferencing, electronic data exchange, and voice mail all increase the efficiency and effectiveness of the sales force. The ability to manage data and information is greatly enhanced with these electronic wonders. Judicious use of such devices is paramount, however. If the only contact a customer has with a sales representative are voice mail messages or faxes, the lack of personal attention can strain an otherwise healthy relationship. These are tools through which the sales force can conduct its affairs more efficiently. They are not substitutes for the personal selling process and customer service.

As we saw in the chapter opening vignette, the Internet is a technology tool that can be very valuable to the overall personal selling effort. In a recent survey,

23. Jack Retterer, "Successful Sales Automation Calls for Incorporating People," *Marketing News,* November 8, 1999, 12.
24. Janet Guyon, "The World Is Your Office," *Fortune,* June 12, 2000, 227–234.

57 percent of managers use the Internet to generate leads for the sales force.[25] Most firms are using the Internet as a way for salespeople to communicate with the firm, but some are finding Internet firms are also offering ways to enhance the sales force automation process. Overall, experts suggest that the value of the Internet to the personal selling process relates to five factors:[26]

- Building customer loyalty
- Saving customers money
- Increasing the speed of the sales process
- Improving customer relationships with more frequent communication
- Lowering the sales cost

But experts also warn that there is a major threat to the selling process related to using the Internet. Specifically, firms fail to consider the impact of their Web strategies on compensation and incentive plans. If they feel threatened by the Internet, salespeople may try to dissuade customers from accessing the company site. The key to avoiding this liability is to involve salespeople early in the conversion to the Internet and, according to the experts, "clearly communicate exactly what the company is trying to achieve with its e-business strategy."[27] It is also recommended that the sales force be involved with the design of the compensation arrangements related to direct sales to customers versus Internet-originated sales. This issue was part of the reasoning behind Dell Computer's decision to give sales reps full commission on sales generated through the Internet.[28]

Finally, the third change in the broad business environment is that salespeople now deal with more demanding buyers. Buyers in both the trade channel and business sectors have become more sophisticated and demanding. While salespeople have benefited from readily available and larger amounts of information, so have buyers. Several years ago, Wolverine World Wide, the marketer of Hush Puppies and other footwear brands, had to respond to demands from JCPenney Co. Penney's wanted 24-hour inventory replenishment, direct computer hookup to Wolverine for reordering, and sophisticated financial analysis of each footwear category. Wolverine World Wide responded with just-in-time inventory procedures and a computer link to the firm.[29] The household consumer is also more knowledgeable by virtue of being exposed to more communication about brands through both traditional promotions and Web site information.

Another aspect of the demanding nature of buyers in the current environment is the increase in expectations buyers have of both products and the firms that provide them. Competitive pressures to satisfy customers have escalated the average level of both product performance and service, so that, sellers have to perform to higher standards than in years past. Salespeople are unavoidably affected by this increase in expectations. Both household and business consumers will expect the salesperson to provide timely and high-quality service and respond to specific requests.

SALES MANAGEMENT ❻

The *process* aspects of personal selling are critically important to the efficacy of the sales effort. Equally important, however, are the activities associated with *managing* the process. Salespeople are responsible for managing their own individual efforts. It is the sales management team, however, that is responsible for the overall

25.   Ginger Conlon, "Direct Impact," *Sales and Marketing Management,* December 1999, 58.
26.   Garner, "The E-Commerce Connection," 42.
27.   Melinda Ligos, "Clicks and Misses," *Sales and Marketing Management,* June 2000, 74.
28.   James, "Hit the Bricks."
29.   Christopher Power, Lisa Driscoll, and Earl Bohn, "Smart Selling," *Business Week,* August 3, 1992, 48.

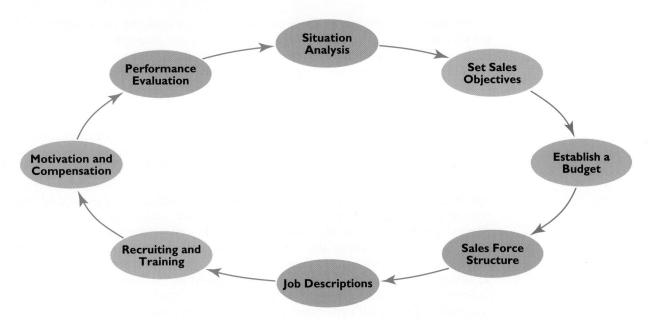

EXHIBIT 14.10

Areas of responsibility for sales management

performance of the entire sales force. **Sales management** is responsible for a wide range of factors related to the personal selling effort from establishing objectives for the selling effort to the creation of the sales staff through performance evaluation. Exhibit 14.10 identifies the areas of responsibility for sales management that are conceived to ensure that the sales force is effectively designed and efficiently deployed to carry out its role in the organization. Notice that areas of responsibility are depicted in Exhibit 14.10 in a circular fashion. This is because sales managers are constantly working on all phases of the management process simultaneously rather than in a hierarchical manner.

Situation Analysis

Managers of the sales process must engage in a comprehensive situation analysis. This situation analysis is very much like the one conducted for overall promotional planning. Here, however, the analysis is much more narrowly defined in that the selling effort is the focus. Both internal and external aspects of the situation facing the sales effort are analyzed. An **external situation analysis** identifies trends in the industry, technological advances in product categories, economic conditions that may be affecting the firm's customers, competitors' activities, and choice criteria being emphasized by buyers. The external situation analysis will also rely on an evaluation of the markets within which the firm has a significant competitive advantage. New product and market potentials are also estimated here.

An example of the impact of an external analysis is how such information was used by Apple Computer. The new head at Apple Computer needed to combat inroads made by competitor IBM into Apple's traditional market of schools and colleges. As part of an external situation analysis, Apple sent its sales force into the market to survey these customers to see what they wanted in new software and hardware. To better understand the higher-education market, teams of employees were sent to universities on "camping trips" to pick the brains of students and faculty."[30] The teams then relayed information back to sales management personnel in the organization to be incorporated into future product development and planning for the sales effort.

30.   Barbara Buell, et al., "Apple: New Team, New Strategy," *Business Week,* October 15, 1991, 93.

An **internal situation analysis** entails assessing the strengths and weaknesses of the sales force and corporate support for the selling effort. Strengths and weaknesses of the sales effort are determined by evaluating sales force performance in the context of the firm's overall marketing mix. Note from Exhibit 14.10 that performance evaluation feeds directly to this situation analysis. In addition, sales force knowledge and training can be examined relative to competition in the assessment of strengths and weaknesses. Corporate support for the sales force is evaluated by examining the nature of the marketing mix. Corporate activities regarding product development and positioning provide the sales force with it primary basis for competing in the market. The pricing component of the mix relates to the ability of the sales force to offer competitive prices on products as well as price incentives and financing options to customers. The distribution variable directly affects the sales force in that inventory levels and delivery schedules will affect the ability to serve customer demand quickly (time and place utility). Finally, the other variables in the promotional mix lend support to the sales staff by stimulating demand in the market through advertising, sales promotions, sponsorships, direct marketing, or publicity. As an example, when General Mills offered free Polaroid film with the purchase of Kix children's cereal, the firm was giving parents another reason to purchase Kix over competitive brands with the sales promotion. This promotion provided the sales force with a reason to encourage grocery store retailers to increase their order size for Kix in anticipation of greater demand for the cereal.

Set Sales Objectives

In the discussion of the personal selling process, it was emphasized that the objectives for personal selling must relate to communication: create profitable differential competitive advantage, accord each buyer uniqueness, manage the buying-selling relationship, and control the communication. At the level of sales management, however, setting objectives focuses on sales. Sales objectives are set at various levels. At the broadest level, total sales serve as a statement of sales objectives. The sales objective is determined by sales forecasts that draw on projections of total industry sales and the firm's estimate of its share of those sales. The next level of specificity is to estimate sales by territory or product category. Here, different geographic territories or product groups are evaluated for conditions that may affect the firm's ability to generate sales over a given time period. Different areas of the geographic market may have unique economic or competitive conditions, as will different product categories. These conditions may represent either significant challenges or opportunities to generating sales. Quarterly and annual sales objectives are set for territories and product categories.

The most specific level of setting objectives is by individual salesperson, and the most common method is to use sales quotas. A sales quota can be specified for each salesperson in several ways, but a percentage of prior years' sales (usually greater than 100 percent) is the most prevalent method. Factored into the quota determination are the effects of new products brought to the market, competitor's activities, economic conditions in the salesperson's territory, and nonselling tasks, such as postpurchase customer service demanded of the salesperson. A key to effectively setting sales quotas that are workable is involving the sales force in the process. The western advertising manager for CNet, a new media company, says that the key to using quotas for her seven sales reps is "all about communization, gathering information from your sales force and being on top of your business."[31] CNet's manager goes about the quota-setting process by first comparing CNet's revenue and market share to those of key competitors, and then examining the growth potential of each of her seven sales reps' territories.[32]

---

31. Michele Marchetti, "How High Can Your Reps Go?" *Sales and Marketing Management,* September 1998, 101.
32. Ibid.

Establish a Budget

A task that requires painstaking effort is establishing a budget for the overall personal selling effort. Normally, factors charged to the personal selling budget include:

- Recruiting costs
- Training costs
- Travel expenses
- Promotional materials—samples, catalogs, product brochures
- Salaries and benefits
- Incentive programs—bonuses, awards

Recruiting, training, travel, and salary, and benefit expenses are cost factors that are self-explanatory. Promotional materials relate to those materials from other promotional mix programs that are used by salespeople to support their own selling effort. For example, an auto parts sales rep may have a catalog of several thousand items that is provided to customers to facilitate the ordering process. In selling college textbooks, literally hundreds of samples of a new text will be mailed to prospective adopters at colleges and universities. College professors need a sample copy of the textbook in order to make an informed decision. The cost of sending samples to these professors can be tens of thousands of dollars. Normally, such costs are charged to the overall selling effort. The coordination of sampling, events, or supportive communications materials is managed by the sales force in consultation with the marketing manager. In the best spirit of IMC, any promotional program that will potentially affect the salesperson's job needs to be carefully coordinated with the sales effort.

The methods employed in establishing a budget for the personal selling effort are identical to several techniques discussed in Chapter 3 for setting the overall promotional budget:

- A **percentage-of-sales approach** can be used but suffers from a lack of recognition of unique challenges facing the sales force, such as introducing a new product or expanding into a new geographic territory.
- A **competitive-parity approach** can be used where a firm sets its personal selling budget (particularly salary, benefit, and bonus programs) relative to what other firms in the industry are doing. Again, this technique is inappropriate because the objectives of competitors and therefore the activities of their salespeople may be very different. Use of the competitive-parity approach can easily result in over- or underpaying salespeople.
- The **objective-and-task method** for budget determination is the most effective for personal selling, just as we found it to be for the overall promotional program. Management assesses the objectives that are established for the overall selling effort. Based on those objectives, tasks for the sales force are specified, as are compensation and incentive programs. All costs associated with the tasks are determined, and the budget is then projected. This method relates activities to costs and is the only rational and reasonable basis for establishing a budget.

Sales Force Structure

A critically important strategic decision for sales management is how the sales force will be structured to achieve the goals of market coverage and cultivation. A sales force can be structured around product lines, type of customer, or geographic territory.

When a sales force is structured by product lines, salespeople are assigned to handle only specific products. The most common reason for structuring the sales force around product lines has to do with the nature of the product. For products that are technologically complex, individual salespeople will need special training and experience to successfully sell the product. Conversely, nontechnical or standardized items require less expertise and can be handled by a different sales force. Pharmaceutical firms that manufacture both prescription and over-the-counter drug items often have a separate sales force for each product line based on the complexity of the product.

An alternative structure is to organize the sales effort around the type of customer. Customer groups can be segmented based on order size, position in the channel, or product use characteristics. Some firms employ a "key account" system where a separate sales staff will call on large buyers like Kmart and Wal-Mart. Similarly, one sales staff can be deployed to call on wholesalers while another calls directly on retailers. Pharmaceutical firms might use this structure rather than the product-line structure described earlier by having separate sales staffs call on physicians, pharmacists, and grocery store buyers.

Finally, the sales force can be structured by geographic territory. In this arrangement, salespeople are assigned a designated geographical territory. This structure requires that each salesperson call on all types of customers in the area and be prepared to sell the firm's entire product line. This deployment of the sales force is most appropriate for standardized items that are sold to a variety of different customers. Stanley Tools, for example, can have its sales force call on hardware stores, home improvement centers, and discount retailers with the firm's entire line of standardized items—hammers, screwdrivers, wrenches, and the like. These are simple, relatively standardized products that are packaged and distributed similarly to all different types of customers.

The decision on sales force structure is driven by two considerations: the nature of the product and the nature of the market. If products in the line are highly sophisticated or the line contains a wide range of different items, the product-line structure is most appropriate. These conditions will require special expertise and extensive product knowledge on the part of the sales staff so product-line emphasis is called for. Knowledgeable buyers and easily segmented customer groups facilitate a type of customer structure. This structure evolves quite naturally from the nature of the market. Product lines with standardized items that are sold without alteration to a variety of different customers suggests a geographic structure for the sales force. No specialized expertise is needed in the selling process based on the nature of the product, nor does the market itself suggest any natural basis for separate segments. Managers can draw on a variety of tools to help them make decisions about sales force structure and deployment that will optimize a firm's resources (see Exhibit 14.11).

Job Descriptions and Qualifications

The sales management task also includes hiring salespeople. Before recruiting can be undertaken, however, complete job descriptions and the qualifications an individual must have are prepared. The **job description** will identify all the tasks to be performed by salespeople. A job description cites both selling and nonselling tasks. The type of selling tasks that will be required depends on the type of product, the types of customers being called on, and the anticipated dollar volume a salesperson is expected to produce. Nonselling tasks involve the amount of paperwork required—invoice preparation, activity reports, expense reports—and service activities expected of the salespeople. Service activities may include point-of-purchase display maintenance, coordination and monitoring of delivery, and arranging financing or training for the customer. Depending on the mix of selling and nonselling tasks, very different job descriptions will be produced.

The tasks included in a job description translate directly into the **qualifications** of the individuals needed to fill positions—the combination of skills and training that relate to effective performance. Very different types of people will need to be recruited depending on the job requirements. Highly technical selling jobs will

EXHIBIT 14.11

In making the sales force structure decision, managers have a wide range of tools available to help deploy and manage the sales force.

require people with relevant technical training. Job descriptions that include significant nonselling tasks mean the firm will have to find people with training or experience to carry out the nonselling activities effectively. In technical product categories, firms often recruit people with engineering degrees. Conversely, in nontechnical product areas, people with backgrounds in marketing or communications are highly sought after. For jobs with both technical selling requirements and significant nonselling tasks, a technical background with an advanced business degree is a common statement of qualifications.

Firms also draw on their experience with current sales personnel in determining what qualifications are most directly related to success. Personal characteristics of individuals can also be included in a statement of qualifications. While legislation bars firms from including criteria in a job description related to age, sex, or race of an individual, research suggests that, compared with unsuccessful salespeople, a successful salesperson will be a good listener, enjoy social events, feel socially satisfied, and be more individualistic. They also tend to be more disciplined, aggressive, and creative than unsuccessful salespeople.[33] Today, recruiters say over and over that they are looking for (1) people with good written and oral communication skills and (2) people who are comfortable around other people and can be effective in a team setting.

---

33. Bradley D. Lockman and John H. Hallaq, "Who Are Your Successful Salespeople?" *Journal of the Academy of Marketing Science* (Fall 1982), 463–468; and Timothy J. Trow, "The Secret of a Good Hire: Profiling," *Sales and Marketing Management,* May 1990, 44.

Recruiting

Well-written job descriptions and statements of qualifications provide management with guidelines for both the type and number of salespeople needed. At this point, the firm can begin to recruit people to meet staffing needs. An important aspect of recruiting is that it should be a continuous process. A firm must seek out qualified people on a regular schedule so that a file of qualified applicants is available. The firm that begins to recruit only when a need arises may be tempted to accept unqualified or inappropriate people.

Sources of Applications. Successful recruiting procedures depend on identifying sources of qualified applicants and using effective screening and evaluation techniques. There are several sources that can be used to generate a pool of qualified applicants. College and university campuses offer a highly structured environment for recruiting. Firms can schedule recruiting visits and indicate what background, experience, and degree they require for the job. Employment agencies represent another useful source of recruits. Professional employment agencies charge individuals, firms, or both a fee to match individuals with jobs. Classified advertisements in the employment section of local newspapers can also be a source. Normally, applicants for selling jobs that require very little skill can be generated in this way. However, firms occasionally advertise much more highly skilled positions in local newspapers to fulfill equal employment opportunity requirements. Other outlets for advertising that have proven successful for some firms are trade publications. Trade publications subscribed to by members of a specific industry frequently carry employment ads. Finally, intrafirm recruiting has become more popular of late. Procter & Gamble regularly moves salespeople between its Noxell, Revlon, and Richardson-Vicks divisions. When IBM initiated a corporate restructuring program, the firm redeployed 21,500 employees. Of that total, 11,800 employees were shifted to the field sales force. Similarly, General Motors encourages employees outside their home departments to seek opportunities across the vast GM network of organizations.[34]

Attracting Applicants. Another component of effective recruiting is understanding the values that applicants bring to the recruiting process. In tight labor markets, which have persisted in the United States since the late 1990s, firms need to battle for top recruits. Winning the recruiting war will depend largely on offering top candidates what they want. Recent surveys suggest that candidates are coming well prepared for interviews in terms of knowing what they want. One candidate for a sales job with Computer Associates said flatly, "With a new baby, I really didn't want to have to travel fifty percent of the time. I expected a fair compensation level, but I really wanted something that fit my lifestyle."[35] Development Dimensions International, a recruiting research firm, has identified what highly successful firms have offered to lure top job candidates. In order of importance, firms reported that successful recruiting depends on:[36]

- Corporate reputation
- Benefits package
- Potential for advancement
- Corporate culture
- Salary scale
- Stock options

34. Sellers, "How to Remake Your Sales Force," 101; Erin Strout, "Finding Your Company's Top Talent," *Sales and Marketing Management,* May 2000, 113.
35. Geoffrey Brewer, "How to Win Today's Recruiting Wars," *Sales and Marketing Management,* March 2000, 85.
36. Ibid.

Notice that the corporate culture and reputation rank much higher than salary in the minds of modern recruits. A firm is well served if it carefully researches the candidate pool and then inquires of candidates what they value in the job setting.

Screening and Evaluating Applicants. To effectively and efficiently recruit the proper individuals, a firm can rely on several screening and evaluation techniques. A resume is valuable for assessing an individual's qualifications. Information on educational background, work experience, and references is useful in evaluating potential applicants. A variety of psychological tests can also be used to screen applicants. These tests are designed to identify personality and motivation characteristics that may be related to job success. Some firms will administer standardized psychological tests to their most successful salespeople and use those results as a benchmark for evaluating applicants' scores on the same tests. The logic is that similar scores should be an indicator of success for an applicant.

Finally, a personal interview can be invaluable as an evaluation technique for discovering attributes of an individual that a résumé or tests cannot identify. Traits such as personal appearance and verbal skills are discovered only through personal contact. But several firms are opting out of the face-to-face interview process and instead are placing more emphasis on telephone or videoconference interviews. At Capital One Financial, a holding company whose subsidiaries provide a variety of products and services to consumers using its proprietary information-based strategy, managers admit that "we try to minimize the traditional face-to-face interviews." Managers at Capital One explain that they have applied their data-driven approach used in product markets to the hiring process. The Capital One system relies on a battery of tests that measure everything from data analysis skills to reliability.[37] Video-conferencing is playing a part in the interview process because firms can get feedback about candidates more quickly and from more parts of the organization. Organizations like the National Career Center in Boulder, Colorado, offer video-conferencing rooms for about $150 per hour. Kinko's, the copy center firm, now rents rooms in about a quarter of its stores for videoconferencing.[38] Different parts of the organization can be tuned into the videoconference or a tape of the conference can be delivered to key decision makers. There are even Web-based firms that are starting to post video interviews on secure Web sites.[39] Overall, video conferencing offers a faster and lower-cost alternative to the traditional face-to-face interview.

Training

Whether a sales staff is being assembled or a new salesperson is being added to the existing staff, training individuals for the sales task is a critical sales management responsibility. The personal selling process is complex, as we discussed earlier in the chapter. Further, the personal selling effort is integral to achieving corporate revenue objectives. Because the selling effort is so important, the firm must have a well-planned sales training program. A number of decisions need to be made about training.

Content of the Program. The content of the training program will vary depending on the sales force structure, type of product, selling/nonselling tasks involved, and the objectives set for the selling effort. Product knowledge and choice criteria used by customers are required content in any program. Beyond these basics, industry trends and economic conditions affecting the firm's market may also

37. Mike McNamee, "We Try to Minimize Face-to-Face Interviews," *Business Week,* November 22, 1999, 176.
38. Dan Hanover, "Hiring Gets Cheaper and Faster," *Sales and Marketing Management,* March 2000, 87.
39. Ibid.

EXHIBIT 14.12

Firms are finding that they can move some or all of their sales force training materials to Web-based learning systems.

be included. Another decision here relates to the training techniques to be used. Role playing, classroom lectures, videotaping of presentations, computer simulations, and tours of corporate facilities are some of the techniques used by firms to train sales personnel. Sales trainers are also discovering that introducing humorous but challenging tasks into sales training is fostering creative problem solving among trainees. For example, Kraft Foods has run programs where they ask the sales trainees to think of ways to sell "unsellable" products like a ladder with no rungs or a shoe with no sole. Managers feel that such techniques foster improvisation and "Improvisation builds on skills such as active listening, developing commitment to reactivity and to respond to immediate needs."[40]

The new environment for personal selling discussed earlier requires that a broader range of topical areas be included in the training program. Team selling techniques should be part of an effective program. These include team building, team managing, and team membership skills. Similarly, seminar selling, which requires the ability to communicate to a larger group of participants with diverse interests, also requires the development of unique skills. Finally, the use of sales force automation tools requires that the sales force be trained in the use of those tools. SFA training includes both hardware and software training sessions.[41]

Duration of the Training. Firms must decide how long it will take to properly train individuals. At Procter & Gamble, the training period lasts twelve to eighteen months; at State Farm, training is a two-year stint; Dow Chemical requires thirty weeks; and Merck puts marketing reps through an initial training period of twelve months with frequent refresher courses. The duration of training depends on several factors. The complexity of the selling task and the company's product line are the overriding factors. The individual trainee's background and experience also dictate how long it will take for training to be completed.

Training Personnel. Many firms rely on experts outside the firm to conduct some or all of their training programs. There are professional organizations, like Learning International, whose sole business is to provide complete sales force training. Universities and colleges of business often have corporate training programs, many of which concentrate on selling tasks. Similarly, many firms have found that outsourcing the training program to specialized firms is a much more effective way of achieving training goals than trying to do all the training in-house. A recent survey has found that only 16 percent of companies are developing and executing their own training programs.[42] Alternatively, sales managers and highly successful members of the current sales staff can act as trainers. Occasionally, upper-level management will participate as well. Home Depot founder "Bernie" Marcus helped prepare

40. Vincent Alonzo, "When Sales Is a Laughing Matter," *Sales and Marketing Management,* April 2000, 50.
41. Retterer, "Successful Sales Automation Calls."
42. Erika Rasmusson, "Getting Schooled in Outsourcing," *Sales and Marketing Management,* January 1999, 49–53.

the sales training program for his home improvement products chain and often participates in training sessions. The sales staff is given extensive technical training—how to lay tile and do electrical installations, for example. But the staff is also trained in effective selling techniques like how to listen to customers' needs and walking customers through the store to find the materials they require.[43]

Location of the Training. The issue here is whether training is conducted in a laboratory/classroom setting or whether the trainees go out into the field for the learning experience. The laboratory/ classroom has the advantage of being a low-pressure environment where there are few consequences to the trainees' activities. Training in the field has the advantage of allowing the salesperson to encounter actual selling situations under the tutelage of an experienced salesperson. The drawbacks of the field are the mistakes a trainee might make with customers and the time drain on the salespeople who must supervise the field training. A new consideration for training is to post all or some of the training materials on the Web (see Exhibit 14.12).[44] The IMC in Practice box describes how some firms are using the Web for training—and eventually selling purposes.

Sales training should not be reserved for new salespeople. As the external environment changes, the firm develops new products and customer knowledge, and new selling techniques are discovered, members of the existing sales staff can benefit enormously from regular training sessions. These sessions would differ greatly from those conducted for new hires, but it is a mistake to presume that current salespeople do not need regular retooling.

Compensation and Motivation

Compensation schemes and motivation efforts may be the most challenging responsibilities of sales management. There are three basic compensation alternatives available for monetary remuneration of the sales staff: straight salary, straight commission, and some combination of the two. Exhibit 14.13 indicates the factors influencing the use of salary and commission alternatives.

If the sales staff is highly skilled, the selling effort is drawn out over a long period, there are time-consuming nonselling tasks, or a team selling approach is being used, then the most appropriate compensation method is straight salary. As the selling task becomes less complex and requires few service activities on the part of the sales force, then the commission approach is more feasible. Many firms use a

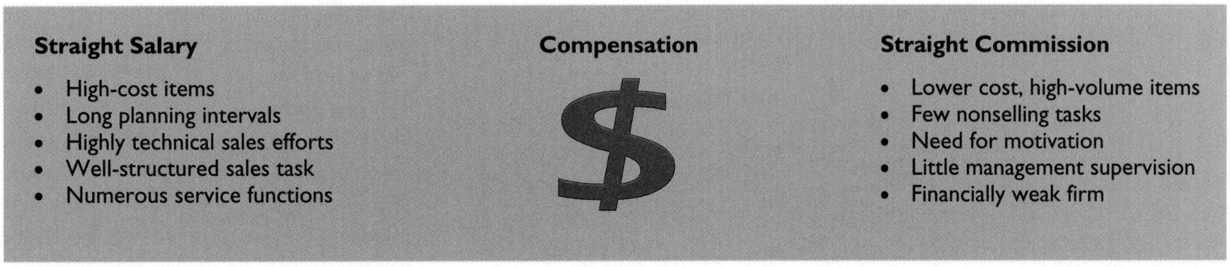

Straight Salary	Compensation	Straight Commission
• High-cost items • Long planning intervals • Highly technical sales efforts • Well-structured sales task • Numerous service functions		• Lower cost, high-volume items • Few nonselling tasks • Need for motivation • Little management supervision • Financially weak firm

EXHIBIT 14.13

Influences on sales force compensation alternatives

43.   Walecia Konrad, "Cheerleading, and Clerks Who Know Awls from Augers," *Business Week,* August 3, 1992, 51.
44.   Melinda Ligos, "Point, Click, and Sell," *Sales and Marketing Management,* May 1999, 51–56.

IN PRACTICE

CLASSROOM, SALES PRESENTATIONS AND EVENTS— ALL IN ONE BOX

How's this for a classroom: People show up at all times of the day and night, sometimes in their pajamas; they take a dozen breaks to call clients; and sometimes the family cat attends sitting on their laps. You've probably figured out that this is not a regular classroom. This is the classroom in a box—the Web box, to be specific. Firms are finding that posting sales training materials can be a highly effective way to get training delivered to a large number of employees.

Fisher Scientific, a New Hampshire-based chemical company, has been using the Internet to teach the majority of its salespeople in the privacy of their homes, cars, hotel rooms, or wherever else they bring their laptop computers. To get updates on pricing or to refresh themselves on a highly technical product feature, salespeople just log onto the Web, type in a URL, and select from a lengthy list of subjects in which they might need training or support. With the help of a Web-based product called Performance Learning System, they can get information on a new product, take an exam, or post messages for product experts—all without ever entering a traditional classroom.

But Web applications for sales communication go beyond sales training programs. In fact, in the selling area, the Web is kind of its own IMC program. Firms are discovering a wide range of communication applications using the Web to enhance many different aspects of the personal selling process. While Fisher Scientific is finding it useful to create a virtual classroom for employees, firms like Digital Equipment and Cisco are using the Web for other sales applications. Digital (now part of Compaq Computer Corp.) has been delivering sales presentations by combining teleconferencing with Web-based information transmission.

At Cisco, there are two attractions to using the Web as part of the personal selling process. First, the firm estimates it is saving about $1 million a month by holding sales meetings online. But cost savings is only the beginning. The company's program manager for distance learning says that "Our salespeople are actually meeting more online then they ever were face-to-face. That's very empowering for the sales reps, because they're able to make suggestions about where we're going with our sales and marketing strategies every step of the way."

As firms learn to combine the Web with other forms of communication, the applications to the personal selling process will surely continue to expand. There are some drawbacks to be overcome, however. Web-based communications come with their own, sometimes hefty, costs. The software can be expensive to buy and maintain. And to make Web-based communication attractive to the sales force, it has to be fast and easy, which means faster (and more expensive) computers. Also, nothing can be done to ensure that Web training or meetings are being attended by every individual. At some point, there is no substitute for in-person contact.

Source: Melinda Ligos, "Point, Click, Sell," *Sales and Marketing Management*, May 1999, 51–54.

combination plan since many selling efforts include features of both ends of the Exhibit 14.13 spectrum. An unfortunate circumstance arises when a firm relies on a commission compensation program but the selling task strongly warrants a salary arrangement. What tends to happen is that in their effort to generate sales and, therefore, income for themselves, the salespeople do not attend to important nonselling tasks like customer service, point-of-purchase display maintenance, or postsale follow-up. Such a conflict of interest on the part of salespeople usually spells disaster for the firm. Customers are dissatisfied and will seek alternative suppliers. Because customer satisfaction is so important to long-term success and profitability, firms like General Electric and AT&T are tying sales force compensation to customer satisfaction surveys.[45]

Compensation is itself motivational, but the issue of motivation is far more complicated than simple dollars-and-cents reward. The amount of satisfaction and sense of personal achievement individuals feel from performing tasks are also important to motivation. Several techniques can be used to increase the motivation of the sales staff that are not directly tied to the basic compensation program, as follows.

Task Clarity. Salespeople will be more motivated when their realm of responsibility is well defined. Further, clarification of the criteria upon which they will be evaluated will produce goal-oriented behavior. Clear criteria are motivational in that the salesperson will feel that there are attainable goals to be pursued. This appears to be particularly true of a new generation of tech-savvy employees who are demanding a more cooperative than adversarial

45.   Power, Driscoll, and Bohn, 48.

Now you can control sales behavior by pushing all the right buttons.

(recliner not included)

SC COMMISSION

Getting your sales force to push the right products to the right people has always been a challenge. Greater competition, changing sales channels, and more demanding customers can render your sales behavior erratic at best, leaving you with inconsistent performance and decreased profits. Because of this, implementing effective incentive programs has been prohibitively difficult. But not anymore. With Trilogy's SC Commission, you finally have a tool powerful enough to maximize your incentive dollars, effectively influence sales force behavior, and greatly improve your company's performance. SC Commission offers a rich set of incentive and reward components that gives you the flexibility to create and customize compensation programs to meet your own business needs. Create commissions that reward your sales force for selling your most profitable products to your most strategically important customers. Generate bonuses using

performance measures like profit margins, discounting, ranking within the organization, etc. And then, with your plan in place, communicate performance and earnings information to your sales force out in the field. In short, SC Commission gives you everything necessary to develop and implement comprehensive compensation programs to effectively control selling behavior. Trilogy's SC Commission. Now you can push all the right buttons and greatly improve your company's big picture.

SC Commission communicates up-to-the-minute performance and earnings information to your sales force out in the field.

TRILOGY

CONTACT US AT 1-800-843-0907 EXT. 806 OR VISIT OUR WEB SITE AT www.trilogy.com/sales
Circle # 103   or go to: www.salesandmarketing.com/saleslink

EXHIBIT 14.14

Automated compensation programs allow managers and the sales force to track their achievements against sales objectives.

relationship between managers and subordinates. Experts are recommending that managers consider themselves as "performance coaches" rather than overbearing intimidators. JCPenney learned that managers had complaints about the firm's brightest and most talented salespeople. The managers felt that they didn't know how to relate to the "twentysomethings" effectively. Task clarity and a more cooperative relationship turned out to be the key to the managers' new approach to these valued employees.[46]

Recognition of Goal Attainment. It is important for the organization to recognize the attainment of both short- and longer-term goals by salespeople. Short-term goal attainment, such as exceeding sales quotas, should be rewarded with incentive pay such as bonuses or stock options. Longer-term goal attainment, such as market or customer development, should be rewarded with status-enhancing recognition. Such recognition can come in the form of promotions or job titles. Recognition, however, also comes in the form of feedback. IBM found that launching a Web site for its 9,000 salespeople where they could check on their goal attainment was extremely important in keeping the sales force focused on the company goals. The site also provided immediate feedback for the sales reps on how their performance was matching up against objectives (see Exhibit 14.14). Brad Brown from the sales consulting firm Reward Strategies says that such systems are "important in terms of keeping salespeople motivated and focused on selling. These tools give reps instantaneous access to where they are versus their goals—it's like knowing the score of a ball game."[47]

Job Enrichment. There are a number of ways to motivate salespeople with job-enriching experiences. Many firms send sales people to professional conferences. Paid attendance at sales training programs is a similar reward. The firm can also consider allowing salespeople to participate in corporate planning sessions with management personnel. This can give the sales force a sense of "ownership" in the corporate strategies they will be asked to support. Of course, the most job-enriching experience is to offer people new tasks, responsibilities, and projects. When employees feel like they are constantly being challenged, they will be more motivated and more easily retained by a firm.[48]

Perquisites. In addition to compensation or bonuses, sales positions provide a firm an ideal opportunity to reward employees with "perks." A new car every year or so, membership at a health club, dinner at fine restaurants, or season tickets to sporting events are all legitimate business expense for cultivating sales. In turn, salespeople can enjoy these activities while doing business. Alternatively, compensation

46. Slade Sohmer, "Retention Getter," *Sales and Marketing Management,* May 2000, 80.
47. Michele Marchetti, "Helping Reps Count Every Penny," *Sales and Marketing Management,* July 1998.
48. Ibid.

experts have been advising firms to try to let people, as much as is legally and orga-nizationally possible, design their own compensation packages. Whereas one person may be very focused on salary as a main compensation issue, another may be far more motivated by a flexible work schedule. At one time, American Airlines used to rely on dedicated computers to dictate the travel rotation of their flight attendants and flight crews. Now, they have switched to systems that let their employees bid for routes on the basis of seniority and availability. The result has been that employees love the flexibility, and the systems are cheaper to implement and maintain.[49]

The motivational impact of the above factors is derived from both monetary incentives and public recognition of achievement and hard work. The rewards of motivation accrue not just to the salespeople. Well-conceived motivational programs should result in greater productivity from the sales force as well as lower turnover. Both of these factors translate directly into increased profitability for the firm.

Evaluation

Evaluating the performance of salespeople draws directly on the objectives set for the personal selling process and sales objectives. There are several objective and sub-jective criteria upon which sales staff members can be judged. We will go into great detail with respect to these evaluation criteria in the next chapter, where we con-sider ways to measure the success of the sales program as part of an overall assess-ment of the promotional mix and the IMC effort.

---

49. Michael Schrage, "Cafeteria Benefits? Ha! You Deserve a Richer Banquet," *Fortune,* April 3, 2000.

SUMMARY

1 Explain why personal selling is the most important promotional tool in many corporations.

Products that are higher priced and complicated to use, require demonstration, are tailored to users' needs, involve a trade-in, or are judged at the point of purchase are heavily dependent on personal selling. Household consumers and business buyers are frequently confronted with purchase decisions that are facilitated by interaction with a salesperson. In many decision contexts, only a qualified and well-trained salesperson can address the questions and concerns of a potential buyer.

2 Discuss the variety of activities in addition to selling performed by salespeople.

The modern salesperson is more like a one-person marketing strategy program. Aside from the direct tasks of personal selling, salespeople contribute to the overall marketing effort by providing information relevant to market analysis, sales forecasting, new product development ideas, buyer behavior analysis, communications, sales coordination, customer service, and customer relationship management (CRM).

3 Discuss the fact that setting objectives for personal selling goes beyond merely setting sales objectives and includes the identification of customer relationship objectives.

A salesperson in a contemporary selling environment doesn't just sell but rather manages a set of buying-selling relationships between the buyer and seller for mutual benefit. One of the greatest challenges facing a salesperson is determining how her/his firm is uniquely capable of satisfying customer needs. Matching what the firm is capable of doing with what a buyer desires allows both parties to enter a buying-selling relationship that is mutually beneficial. The salesperson must determine which features of a firm's products and services are most attractive and potentially satisfying. Depending on the expression of needs by a buyer, a salesperson can determine what is most highly valued in the purchase decision. Through such a determination, the salesperson can then emphasize the firm's unique capabilities in satisfying the customer. A sale can be negotiated emphasizing the ability of the firm to provide superior satisfaction on the desired factors.

4 Outline the steps involved in the personal selling process.

A well-conceived personal selling process involves seven distinct steps: preparation, prospecting, initial contact, presentation, handling objections, closing the sale, and follow-up.

5 Identify factors that contribute to a new environment for personal selling.

The key factors that have contributed to a new environment for personal selling are more sophisticated marketing planning techniques, information technologies (both hardware and software), communications technologies, the Internet, and more demanding and knowledgeable customers. Overall, the technological changes in the environment have put greater emphasis on sales force automation (SFA).

6 Discuss the wide range of responsibilities encompassed by the sales force management process.

The sales force management process includes the following areas of responsibility: situation analysis, setting sales objectives, establishing a budget for selling activities, identifying the proper sales force structure based on the situation analysis and budget, creating job descriptions, recruiting and training salespeople, motivating the sales force, creating compensation programs, and creating an evaluation procedure to judge the performance of salespeople.

KEY TERMS

customer relationship management
  or CRM selling, 480
order taking, 480
inside order taker, 480
outside order taker, 481
creative selling, 481
team selling, 482
seminar selling, 482
system selling, 482
missionary salesperson, 483

detail salesperson, 483
canned presentation, 488
attention-interest-desire-action
  (AIDA), 489
need satisfaction, 489
consultive selling, 490
telemarketing, 490
trial close, 491
presumptive close, 491
straightforward close, 491

sales force automation (SFA), 492
sales management, 495
external situation analysis, 495
internal situation analysis, 496
percentage-of-sales approach, 497
competitive-parity approach, 497
objective-and-task method, 497
job description, 498
qualifications, 498

QUESTIONS FOR REVIEW AND CRITICAL THINKING

1. The modern view of the role of personal selling recognizes that salespeople are essential to implementing marketing strategy. What types of activities do salespeople engage in, beyond selling, that are related to this modern view?

2. If support communications as a type of personal selling does not specifically identify sales as an objective, what purpose does such selling serve? Do you think it is worth deploying salespeople to engage in supportive communication?

3. Discussions in this chapter argue that both the buyer and the seller benefit if the salesperson "controls the communication" in a sales encounter. Do you agree or disagree with this position?

4. What are the areas of information that constitute proper preparation for the personal selling process?

5. Why is the AIDA approach considered outdated as a presentation technique? What approach is considered far superior and why?

6. In following up a successful sales effort, what two factors should a salesperson concentrate on to take advantage of opportunities at this stage of the selling process?

7. What has changed in the last several years to create a "new environment" for personal selling?

8. In sales force management, what are the three alternatives for sales force structure? What conditions suggest the use of each alternative?

EXPERIENTIAL EXERCISES

1. **In-class exercise.** How many of you have held sales positions? Describe your first experience with sales and how satisfied or dissatisfied you were with the experience. Was your first sales experience like the types of selling jobs described in this chapter?

2. **Out-of-class exercise.** Visit three businesses where salespeople are integral to the promotional process. Pick at least one business that is not household consumer oriented (for example, office equipment or business services organizations). Rate the salespeople you encountered as to their professionalism and skill level.

USING THE INTERNET

Exercise 1

One method of generating sales leads is to mine one's current customers. You've doubtless seen the "send this (article, photo, joke of the day . . .) to a friend" option on various Web sites—this is a clever means to have people who frequent your Web site invite others to join in, and to collect e-mail addresses for marketing. And certain Web sites collect e-mail addresses by their very nature. Blue Mountain was the Web's most popular site for online greeting cards and messages, where visitors could select from a range of graphical cards, add their own message, and have them delivered to friends, family, whomever, on birthdays, anniversaries, or whenever. Despite the fact that Blue Mountain never charged for the service, the site was snapped up by Excite.com, a search site company, in a billion-dollar stock deal. Excite wasn't after online card-creation technology—they wanted the vast community of Blue Mountain users and recipients, to blend into their own online communities.

Blue Mountain

http://www.bluemountain.com

1. Was Blue Mountain worth a billion dollars?

2. How is Excite.com using Blue Mountain today?

3. If Excite had asked you how they might profitably spend a billion dollars acquiring new customers, what might you have said?

Exercise 2

Tupperware is a case study in the issues surrounding personal selling's collision with World Wide Web technology. The company, which has been in existence for half a century, is based on direct selling, as a small army of consultants corrals homemakers for "Tupperware parties," working locally, and profiting, if not globally, at least nationally. With the arrival of the World Wide Web, there's every opportunity for individual agents to expand their reach . . . does it matter if, like Michael Dell, you're working out of a dorm room if you can attract attention and make a sale? Well, maybe so—allowing each Tupperware consultant to create his or her own Web site could wreak havoc in the organization, and raise issues of consultants poaching on each other's territory or dilution of the national brand by poorly executed Web sites. Tupperware frowned on this sort of chaos, discouraging individual Web page creation. Then in 1999, the company launched a corporate site through which it could make direct sales to consumers, to the detriment of its own field force—many of whom were highly critical of what looked like a play to gobble up the benefits those "high-touch" consultants had created in the market. Perhaps as a result of the backlash, in April 2000, Tupperware launched a new Web site, http://www.my.tupperware.com, to enable their 75,000 member U.S. direct sales force to create their own sites, tied into the corporate site to execute online sales (and presumably crediting the particular consultant who brought the sale).

Tupperware

http://www.tupperware.com

1. Using one of the search engine sites, query on the phrase "tupperware consultant." What sorts of pages do you turn up?

2. What do you think of Tupperware's compromise between its traditional strategy of relying solely on its field force, and the Dell "nothing but Net" Web-only sales strategy? Do you think Tupperware's sales force will grow or shrink as the result of the World Wide Web?

PART 4

EVALUATION AND MEASURING THE EFFECTIVENESS OF PROMOTION AND IMC

There may only be one chapter in this section, but it is loaded with information and recommendations. One of the reasons for the extensive growth in the use of promotional tools beyond advertising is that managers have been yearning for better accountability in the spending of promotional dollars. But we will also learn that there are many issues involved in trying to measure the effectiveness of such a vast array of promotional options. This chapter begins by considering issues related to the whole concept of measurement itself. Given the complex nature of communication in a promotional setting, there is a high degree of complexity and more than a little controversy with respect to measurement. Next, measuring the effectiveness of advertising is discussed in great detail. Maybe because it is so conspicuous, maybe because of the billions of dollars spent on production, or maybe because it relies so much more on creative execution, advertising has been and continues to be the subject of more measurement effort than any other promotional tool. This chapter then proceeds through discussions of every tool in the promotional kit as discussed in Part 3. Each tool is considered from an evaluation and measurement standpoint including recommendations on how measurement should be undertaken. Finally, evaluation and measure of the overall IMC program are considered.

15

Measuring the Effectiveness of Promotion and IMC concludes the textbook by presenting the complexity and occasional controversy in measuring the effectiveness of promotional options. First, we look at the options for measuring the effectiveness of advertising because of its dominance and visibility in promotional campaigns. Then we consider measurement options for Internet advertising, direct mail and e-commerce, sponsorship, point-of-purchase, supportive media, public relations, corporate advertising, and personal selling. Finally, the chapter concludes with a look at how the effectiveness of the overall IMC program can be measured.

After reading this chapter, you will be able to:

1 Discuss the issues related to the measurement of effectiveness of promotion and IMC.

2 Describe the complex and elaborate methods used to measure the effectiveness of advertising.

3 Describe the ways in which Internet advertising, direct marketing and e-commerce, sponsorships, point-of-purchase, public relations, and corporate advertising are judged for effectiveness.

4 Discuss the procedures used by sales managers in evaluating salespeople and judging the effectiveness of the personal selling effort.

5 Comment on the task of judging the effectiveness of the overall IMC effort.

CHAPTER 15
**Measuring the Effectiveness
of Promotion and IMC**

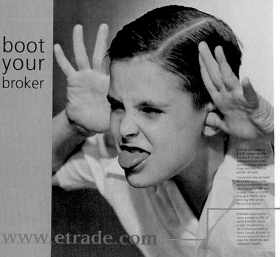

...essful new tire introductions of all time. Goodyear's ability to compete successfully against foreign competitors, particularly Michelin and Yokohama, was greatly enhanced by the Aquatred. It also contributed significantly to record levels of profits for Goodyear. Managers at the company attributed much of the initial success of the Aquatred to the introductory advertising campaign. This campaign featured "The Bucket"—a television commercial that showed how many buckets of water an Aquatred tire could disperse every mile.

Strategists at Goodyear believe "The Bucket" advertising was so successful because the ad went through extensive and rigorous testing before and during the brand's release. While the brand was being developed,

unique tread design with outstanding performance features would provide the basis for a compelling positioning strategy. Then, before the tire was ready for introduction, Goodyear and its advertising agency, Walter Thompson–Detroit, started researching several alternative television messages. First, the agency tested different basic message formats. One was a testimonial by a user (called "Richard on Aquatreds"); the other an ad that featured the tire's traction on wet, roads (called "Skiing"). Based on the results of the preliminary research, Goodyear and its agency concluded that a product performance ad emphasizing functional benefit positioning would be the best format for the introductory Aquatred campaign. The agency moved forward based on the research and developed "The Bucket" as an ad that specifically featured both the performance and demonstration dimensions. "Skiing" and "The Bucket" were aired during a four-week introductory period for Aquatred. Exhibit 15.1 shows the storyboard (the shot-by-shot sequence agencies use to plan scenes from a television ad) for "The Bucket."

Once the product was introduced, Goodyear tracked the effectiveness of "The Bucket" and "Skiing" using a persuasion rating system. These results were compared to the sales of Aquatred in various market areas. The firm discovered that both ads were having a significant and positive impact on sales; that "The Bucket" campaign was the most powerful; and that both ads became less effective after a four-week period. Goodyear also realized that the ads were contributing to a level of consumer demand beyond the firm's production capacity, so the advertising was actually scaled back to balance demand with supply.

Goodyear and its advertising agency used several different types of research to measure the potential, then actual effectiveness of the introductory adver...

(MUSIC) MAN: This is a Goodyear Aquatred

and this is a gallon of water.

At highway speeds in a rain storm

Goodyear Aquatred pumps a gallon of water every second

thanks to its computer designed deep groove Aqua Channel.

It channels water away as you drive

to keep more of the tire in contact with the road

for outstanding wet weather traction.

It's only from Goodyear

and it comes with a 60,000 miles tread life warranty.

The All Season Aquatred, try a set.

We like to say the best tires in the world have Goodyear written all over them. (MUSIC OVER)

INTRODUCTION

The experience of Goodyear highlights the role of measuring the effectiveness of a promotional effort. Managerial experience in a product category and a history of marketing to a particular target segment are extremely valuable but often insufficient to fully meet the challenges of judging how best to craft a message and assess its potential for effectiveness. By drawing on research, a marketer can better understand what tools are working in a promotional campaign. In a world of multimillion-dollar (or even billion-dollar) promotional budgets, managers are held responsible for verifying the effectiveness of all that spending.

In this chapter, we learn that there are many issues involved in measuring the effectiveness of such a vast array of promotional options. First, we need to consider issues related to the whole concept of measurement itself. Given the complex nature of communication in a promotional setting, there is a high degree of complexity and more than a little controversy with respect to measurement. Second, we consider measuring the effectiveness of advertising is great detail. Maybe because it is so conspicuous, maybe because of the billions of dollars spent on production, or maybe because it relies so much more on creative execution, advertising has and continues to be the subject of more poking and prodding measurement effort than any other promotional tool. This includes a heavy dose of measurement on a global scale, as the Global Issues box discusses.

Third, we look at each of the other promotional tools in the order we studied them in the text: Internet advertising, direct mail and e-commerce, sponsorship, P–O–P displays, supportive media, public relations, corporate advertising, and personal selling. These promotional tools either have a tendency to be subjected to less measurements, or the measurement is a more naturally an outgrowth of the execution of the campaign (that is, the number of phone calls received from a direct-mail piece or hits on a banner ad). Finally, we will conclude the chapter with a look at how the effectiveness of the overall IMC program can be measured.

GOING AFTER A GLOBAL VIEW

ACNielsen Corporation, the most widely known promotion and advertising research firm in the United States, is expanding its global services with new programs and better services for international marketers. Currently, Nielsen is known internationally for its AdEx International advertising spending measurement service and Peoplemeter TV audience measurement system. In adding to these existing international services, Nielsen will now offer better services through a new division called ACNielsen Media International. The goal of the new service is to provide global marketers with a method for measuring their multicountry programs through one organization.

Michael Connors, ACNielsen's chairman, says that "As clients begin to look more and more outside their countries' boundaries, we want to provide more than local solutions." The company's strategy for helping firms measure the effects of promotional programs across multiple country boundaries includes:

- More international television audience measurement programs
- Global and regional ad spending data to complement the firm's local ad spending data service
- Establishing a global Internet advertising measurement service
- Establishing a global e-commerce measurement service
- Adding Peoplemeter service in China, where there are 300 million TV homes and 900 television stations
  Currently ACNielsen can provide marketers with data from sixty-nine international markets. The expansion plans are designed to help marketers measure the performance of various aspects of their promotional programs in more markets and in more different ways.

Source: Juliana Koranteng, "ACNielsen Shoots for Global Growth," *Ad Age International*, December 1999, 29.

ISSUES IN MEASURING THE EFFECTIVENESS OF PROMOTION AND INTEGRATED MARKETING COMMUNICATIONS ❶

Several issues must be addressed regarding the process of measuring the effectiveness of the promotional tools and the overall IMC effort. First, what is the difference between marketing and promotion research? **Marketing research** is the systematic gathering, recording, and interpretation of information related to all marketing mix variables. **Promotion research** is a specialized form of marketing research that focuses on the development and performance of promotional materials.

Research comes into the promotional process at several points. It plays a role in helping strategists understand the audience members to whom the promotion will speak and which buttons to push. It is also used to make go/no-go decisions, to determine when to pull a promotion that is worn out (as Goodyear discovered), and to evaluate the performance of an advertising or promotion agency.

As you can see, promotion research is used to judge promotion, but who judges promotion research, and how? First of all, there is a chronic problem with not enough people in an organization questioning and judging research. Research is not magic or truth, and it should never be confused with such. Issues of reliability, validity, trustworthiness, and meaningfulness should be seriously considered when research is used to make important promotional decisions. **Reliability** means that the method generates consistent findings over time. **Validity** means that the information generated is relevant to the research questions being investigated. In other words, the research investigates what it seeks to investigate. **Trustworthiness** is a term usually applied to qualitative data, and it means exactly what it implies: Can one, knowing how the data were collected, trust them, and to what extent? Most difficult of all is the notion of **meaningfulness.** Just what does a piece of research really mean (if anything)? It is important for advertising professionals to take a moment (or several) to consider the limitations inherent in their data and in their interpretations. Too few take the time.

Account Planning Versus Measuring Effectiveness

Jon Steel, Director of Account Planning and Vice Chairman of Goodby, Silverstein, and Partners (their clients are Anheuser-Busch, California—"Got Milk?"—Milk Producers, Nike, Porsche, and Hewlett-Packard, among others), has called account planning "the biggest thing to hit American advertising since Doyle Dane Bernbach's Volkswagen campaign."[2] That may be stretching it a bit (it is), but account planning is a big story in the industry. What is it? Well, good question.

Account planning is defined in contrast to traditional promotion research. It differs mostly in three ways. First, in terms of organization, agencies that use this system typically assign an "account planner" to work as coequal with the account executive on a given client's business. Rather than depending on a separate research department's occasional involvement, the agency assigns the planner to a single client and has that planner stay with the project on a continuous basis. In the more traditional system, the research department would get involved from time to time as needed, and members of the research department would work on several different clients' promotional materials.

Another difference is that this organizational structure puts research and measurement in a different, and more prominent, role. In this system, researchers (or "planners") seem to be more actively involved throughout the entire promotional process and seem to have a bigger impact on it as well. Advertising and promotion

---

2. Jon Steel, *Truth, Lies & Advertising: The Art of Account Planning* (New York: John Wiley & Sons, 1998), jacket.

agencies that practice account planning tend to do more developmental research and less evaluative or measurement research. Third, "planning agencies" tend to do more qualitative and naturalistic research than their more traditional counterparts, who use quantitative techniques and models to measure effectiveness. **Naturalistic-inquiry** is a broad-based research approach that relies on data collection methods that are more qualitative than quantitative and include the use of videotape, audio-tape, and photography in an effort to investigate an issue more holistically.

Fundamental Issues in Message Evaluation

At the heart of any successful promotional campaign is the message that will be used to engage a target audience and give them a reason to believe in the brand. Advertising, Internet advertising, and corporate advertising, of course, have the most elaborate message development and execution. But direct marketing materials, point-of-purchase displays and brochures, sales promotion appeals, and public relations all have message content. Even sponsorships sent a "message" with respect to the image projected by the firm's affiliation with the event. For example, what sort of "message" does it send to an audience if a firm is a sponsor of a World Wrestling Federation event as opposed to being the sponsor of a fund-raiser for a children's hospital? Given the image effects and the meaning consumers take from messages, it should thus come as no surprise that much of the research conducted by promotion agencies and their clients deals with message testing. Message-testing research comes in two basic types: One occurs before a promotional campaign is executed (a pretest); the other occurs after a promotional campaign is placed (a posttest). There is no one right way to test messages that are used in a campaign, and as a result one can find conflicting advice about how to execute this type of measure of effectiveness. This diversity of opinion stems from multiple and sometimes competing testing criteria or outright confusion about what a promotion must do to be considered effective.

Motives and Expectations. Message testing can be a function of logic and adaptive decision making, or it may be driven by custom and history. In the best case, reliable, valid, trustworthy, and meaningful tests are appropriately applied. In the worst case, tests in which few still believe continue to thrive because they represent "the way we have always done things." More typically, however, industry practice falls somewhere in between. The pressure of history and the felt need for normative data (which allows comparisons with the past) partially obscure questions of appropriateness and validity. This makes for an environment in which the best test is not always done, and the right questions are not always asked.

This brings us to motives and expectations. Just what is it that marketers and agencies want out of their message tests? The answer, of course, depends on who you ask. Generally speaking, the account team wants some assurance that the promotional message does essentially what it's supposed to do. Many times, the team simply wants whatever the client wants. The client typically wants to see some numbers, generally meaning **normative test scores;** in other words, the client wants to see how well a particular advertisement or promotion scored against average campaigns of its type that were tested previously.

Whenever people begin looking at the numbers, there is a danger that trivial statistical differences can be made monumental. Other times, the required measure is simply inappropriate. Still other times, managers wishing to keep their jobs simply give the client what he or she wants, as suggested in Exhibit 15.2. If simple recall of an advertisement is what the client wants, then increasing the frequency of brand mentions might be the answer. If sales is what a client craves, then all sorts of short-term sales promotions (to the potential detriment of the brand) may be

Bob, a creative at a large agency, has learned from experience how to deal with lower-than-average day-after recall (DAR) scores. As he explains it, there are two basic strategies: (1) Do things that you know will pump up the DAR. For example, if you want high DARs, never simply super (superimpose) the brand name or tag at the end of the ad. Always voice it over as well, whether it fits or not. You can also work in a couple of additional mentions in dialogue; they may stand out like a sore thumb and make consumers think, "Man, is that a stupid commercial," because people don't talk that way. But it will raise your DARs. (2) Tell them (the account executive or brand manager and other suits) that this is not the kind of product situation that demands high DARs. In fact, high DARs would actually hurt them in the long run due to quick wearout and annoyance. Tell them, "You're too sophisticated for that ham-handed kind of treatment. It would never work with our customers." You can use the second strategy only occasionally, but it usually works. It's amazing.

EXHIBIT 15.2

Unfortunately, when clients demand numbers to verify the effectiveness of a promotional message, promotional planners can sometimes come up with ways to "pump up" the numbers a client is looking for.

proposed and executed. These tactics may not make good campaigns, but they may make for better scores and, presumably, a happy client in the short run.

Despite the politics involved, message-testing research is probably a good idea most of the time. Properly conducted, such research can yield important data that management can then use to determine the suitability of a promotional effort. It's far better to shelve an expensive commercial, direct-mail piece, or proposed sponsorship than execute something that will produce little good and may even do harm.

Dimensions of Message Assessment. There are many standards against which promotional messages are judged for effectiveness. One thing that managers need to avoid in judging messages is to go directly to sales as a single measure. Certainly a direct-action message that implores receivers to call in and order today can be evaluated for effectiveness on the basis of calls or even sales (if the price and distribution and brand features are right). But sales, as we learned in Chapter 3, are not always an appropriate objective or measure of effectiveness. Further, picking right criteria is not always an easy task, but it is the essence of effective message evaluation. A message like the one in Exhibit 15.3, which was used as a magazine ad, a direct-mail piece, and a P–O–P display, can be judged along many dimensions and with several criteria. We will discuss four basic dimensions on which a message can be evaluated: whether or not the message imparts knowledge about the brand, shapes attitudes and preferences, attaches feelings and emotions, or legitimizes the brand as one that is right for its target audience.

Impart Knowledge. It is commonly assumed that a promotional message generates thoughts, some of which are later retrieved and then influence a purchase. Some messages are judged effective if they leave this cognitive residue, or knowledge about the brand. This knowledge may take many different forms. It could be a jingle, a tag line, the recognition of a product symbol, or merely brand-name recognition at the point of purchase, for example. When McDonald's launched the "Two all-beef patties, special sauce, lettuce, pickles, onions on a sesame seed bun" Big Mac campaign, people had the jingle stuck in their heads for weeks! A more benign version of imparting knowledge is the careful development of a brand image that then

EXHIBIT 15.3

An advertisement like this one for Rogaine can be judged along several criteria for effectiveness. While sales during the campaign period is one way some managers might want to judge this ad, what are the communications criteria that can (and really should) be used to measure the effectiveness of an ad like this?

gets imparted through the brand logo like the Mercedes delta or the Nike swoosh. Generally, tests of recall and recognition are featured when knowledge generation is the marketer's primary concern.

Shape Attitudes. Attitudes can tell us a lot about where a brand stands in the consumer's eyes. Attitudes can be influenced by what people both know and feel about a brand. In this sense, attitude or preference is a summary evaluation that ties together the influence of many different factors. Marketers thus may view attitude shaping or attitude change as a key dimension for assessing advertising effectiveness. Message-testing research is frequently structured around the types of attitude measures discussed in Chapter 5. If a researcher asks how much you like or dislike Tide versus Bold versus Wisk laundry detergent, the research is focusing on a summary evaluation of attitude toward the brands.

Attach Feelings and Emotions. Marketers have always had a special interest in feelings and emotions. Ever since the 1920s, there has been the belief that feelings may be more important than thoughts as a reaction to certain messages. While this philosophy waxes and wanes, there has been a renewed interest in developing better measures of the feelings and emotions generated by promotional messages.[3] Measures typically used to measure feelings and emotions range from paper-and-pencil measures to dial-turning devices where those receiving a message turn a dial in either a positive or negative direction to indicate their emotional response to the message. Participants' responses are tracked by computer and can be aggregated and superimposed over the message during playback to allow brand managers to see the pattern of emotional reactions generated.

Legitimize the Brand. In a **resonance test,** the goal is to determine to what extent the message resonates or rings true with target-audience members.[4] This method fits well with consumer-experience research. The questions become, Does this message match consumers' own experiences? Does it produce an affinity reaction? Do consumers who view it say, "'Yeah, that's right; I feel just like that"? Do consumers receive the message and make it their own?[5] In the view of some, this is the direction in which message evaluation research needs to move. The assessment dimension here reflects the effectiveness of a message for legitimizing a brand within its target audience—legitimizing in the sense that receivers embrace the message as meaningful and relevant to their view of the world.

3.   Stuart J. Agres, Julie A. Edell, and Tony M. Dubitsky, eds., *Emotion in Advertising* (Westport, CT: Quorum Books, 1990). See especially Chapters 7 and 8.
4.   David Glenn Mick and Claus Buhl, "A Meaning-Based Model of Advertising Experiences," *Journal of Consumer Research,* vol. 19 (December 1992), 317–338.
5.   Linda Scott, "The Bridge from Text to Mind: Adapting Reader Response Theory for Consumer Research," *Journal of Consumer Research,* vol. 21 (December 1994), 461–486.

MEASURING THE EFFECTIVENESS OF ADVERTISING

As mentioned earlier, more effort is put into the measurement of the effects and effectiveness of advertising than for any other promotional tool. Over many years, a wide range of methods to measure the effectiveness of advertising have been developed. In general, these methods fall into three broad categories: pretest evaluations of advertising effectiveness, pilot testing of ads in the marketplace, and posttest evaluations of advertising effectiveness in the marketplace during or after a campaign.

Pretest Evaluations of Advertising Effectiveness

Because so much time, effort, and expense are involved in the development of advertising messages, most organizations pretest their messages to gauge consumer reaction *before* advertisements are placed. This is the attempt to save the firm the expense (or embarrassment) of running a series of ads that will not achieve the desired objectives. A variety of tools may be used in pretesting.

Communications Tests. A **communications test** simply seeks to see whether a message is communicating something close to what is desired. Communications tests are usually done in a group setting, with data coming from a combination of pencil-and-paper questionnaires and group discussion. Communications tests are done with one major thought in mind: to avoid a major disaster and to prevent communicating something the creators of the ad are too close to see but that is entirely obvious to those consumers first seeing the ad. This could be an unintended double entendre or an accidental sexual allusion. It could be an unexpected interpretation of the visual imagery in an ad as it is moved from country to country around the world. Remember, if the consumer perceives something in an ad, it doesn't matter whether it's intended or not—to the consumer, it's there and a meaningful part of the message. Cadillac embarrassed itself with an unfortunate bit of film for the new Cadillac Catera. In an effort to show consumers the handling capability of the "Cadillac that Zigs," one ad demonstrated the car's ability to pass on a curvy road—right over a double yellow line. It is highly likely that a communications test would have caught this unfortunate oversight.

Marketers should balance the risk of an error in an ad against the fact that communications test respondents feel a responsibility to be helpful, and thus they may try too hard to see things. This is another instance where well-trained and experienced researchers must be counted on to draw a proper conclusion from the testing.

Magazine Dummies. **Dummy advertising vehicles** are mock-ups of magazines that contain editorial content and advertisements, as a real magazine would. Inserted in the dummy vehicle are one or more test advertisements. Once again, consumers representing the target audience are asked to read through the magazine as they normally would. The test is usually administered in consumers' homes and therefore has some sense of realism. Once the reading is completed, the consumers are asked questions about the content of *both* the magazine and the advertisements as a way to divert heightened attention away from just the ads. Questions relating to recall of the test ads and feelings toward the ad and the featured brand are typically asked. This method is most valuable for comparing different message alternatives.

Theater Tests. Advertisements are also tested in small theaters, usually set up in or near shopping malls. Members of the theater audience have an electronic device through which they can express how much they like or dislike the advertisements shown. Simulated shopping trips can also be a part of this type of research. The problem with the **theater test** is that it is difficult to determine whether the respondent is really expressing feelings toward the ad or the brand being advertised. Given the artificial and demanding conditions of the test, experienced researchers are again needed to interpret the results.

This form of message pretesting has become quite common in the United States, and as a result, considerable data are available for judging the validity of this approach. John Philip Jones, a professor of communications at Syracuse University, has conducted analyses on these data and his conclusions are very supportive.[6] He contends that even if this form of message pretesting yields some incorrect predictions about ads' potential effectiveness (as it occasionally will), a marketer's success rate with a message is bound to improve relative to what would be realized without this sort of testing.

Thought Listings. It is commonly assumed that advertising generates thoughts, or cognitions, during and following exposure. Message research that tries to identify specific thoughts that may be generated by an ad is referred to as **thought listing,** or cognitive response analysis.

Here the researcher is interested in the thoughts that a finished or near-finished ad generates in the mind of the consumer. Typically, cognitive responses are collected by having individuals watch the commercial in groups and, as soon as it is over, asking them to write down all the thoughts that were in their minds while watching the commercial. The hope is that this will capture what the potential audience members made of the ad and how they responded, or talked back, to it.

These verbatim responses can then be analyzed in a number of ways. Usually, simple percentages or box scores of word counts are used. The ratio of favorable to unfavorable thoughts may be the primary interest of the marketer. Alternatively, the number of times the person made a self-relevant connection—that is, "That would be good for me" or "That looks like something I'd like"—could be tallied and compared for different ad executions.

Attitude-Change Studies. The typical **attitude-change study** uses a before-and-after ad exposure design. People from the target market are recruited, and their preexposure attitudes toward the advertised brand as well as toward competitors' brands are taken. Then they are exposed to the test ad, along with some dummy ads. Following this exposure, their attitudes are measured again. The goal, of course, is to gauge the potential of specific ad versions for changing brand attitudes.

Attitude-change studies are frequently conducted in a theater test setting. These tests often use a constant-sum measurement scale. A subject is asked to divide a sum (for example, 100 points) among several (usually three) brands. For example, they would be asked to divide 100 points among three brands of deodorants in relation to how likely they are to purchase each. They do this before and after ad exposure. A change score is then computed. Sometimes this change score is adjusted by the potential change, so as not to unfairly penalize established brands.

The reliability of these procedures is fairly high. Yet how meaningful are change scores? This is change premised on a single ad exposure (sometimes two) in an unnatural viewing environment. Many marketers believe that commercials don't register their impact until after three or four exposures. Still, a significant swing in before and after scores with a single exposure suggests that something is going on, and that some of this effect might be expected when the ad reaches real consumers in the comfort of their homes.

To test attitude change in regard to print ads, test ads can be dropped off at the participants' homes contained in test magazines. The test ads have been tipped in, or

6.   John Philip Jones, "Advertising Pre-Testing: Will Europe Follow America's Lead?" *Commercial Communications,* June 1997, 21–26.

EXHIBIT 15.4

Marketers often feel that hard science techniques, like measuring physiological responses, lends legitimacy to the message evaluation effort.

inserted into the magazine so the competitive environment for communication is more realistic. Subjects are told that the researcher will return the next day for an interview. They are also told that as part of their compensation for participating, they are being entered in a drawing. At that point, they are asked to indicate their preferences on a wide range of potential prizes. The next day when the interviewer returns, he or she asks for these preferences a second time. This is the postexposure attitude measure. There aren't many attitude-change studies in radio. This may be because most people consider radio as a medium best used for building awareness and recall, and not for the higher-order goal of attitude change.

Physiological Measures. Several message pretests use physiological measurement devices. **Physiological measures** detect how consumers react to messages, based on physical responses (see Exhibit 15.4). **Eye-tracking systems** have been developed to monitor eye movements across print ads. With one such system, respondents wear a gogglelike device that records (on a computer system) pupil dilations, eye movements, and length of view by sectors within a print advertisement. Another physiological measure is a **psychogalvanometer,** which measures galvanic skin response (GSR). GSR is a measure of minute changes in perspiration, which suggest arousal related to some stimulus—in this case, an advertisement. A new physiological measurement, borrowed from NASA research, is being applied to measure how effective banner ads are in causing an emotional response in Web users and how that response might translate into click-throughs and brand recall. The research employs brainwave tracking technology and is being tested by Capita Research Group.[7]

Voice response analysis is another high-tech research procedure. **Voice response analysis** measures inflections in the voice when consumers are discussing an ad that indicates excitement and other physiological states. In a typical applica-

7.   Jennifer Gilbert, "Capita Taps Brain Waves to Study Web Ads' Potency," *Advertising Age,* February 14, 2000, 55.

tion, a subject is asked to respond to a series of ads. These responses are tape-recorded and then computer analyzed. Deviations from a flat response are claimed to be meaningful. Other, less frequently used physiological measures record brain wave activity, heart rate, blood pressure, and muscle contraction.

All physiological measures suffer from the same drawbacks. While we may be able to detect a physiological response to an advertisement, there is no way to determine whether the response is to the ad or the brand, or which part of the advertisement was responsible for the response. In some sense, even the positive-negative dimension is obscured. Is excitement, increased heart rate, changes in blood pressure, or muscle contraction the result of a positive or negative reaction? Without being able to correlate specific effects with other dimensions of an ad, physiological measures are of minimal benefit.

Since the earliest days of advertising, there has been a fascination with physiological measurement. Advertising's fascination with science is well documented, with early attempts at physiology being far more successful as a sales tool than as a way to actually gauge ad effectiveness. There is something provocative about scientists (sometimes even in white lab coats) wiring people up; it seems so precise and legitimate. Unfortunately—or fortunately, depending on your perspective—these measures tell us little beyond the simple degree of arousal attributable to an ad. For most marketers, this minimal benefit usually doesn't justify the expense and intrusion involved with physiological measurement.

Commercial Pretest Services. Pretest message research can often be conducted by a marketer in conjunction with its advertising agency. However, several commercial pretesting services provide full-service pretesting for both television and print advertisements. Some of these service providers are described in Exhibit 15.5.

Marketplace Evaluation of Advertising: Pilot Testing

Before committing to the expense of a major campaign, marketers often take their message-testing programs into the field. Pursuing message evaluation with experimentation in the marketplace is known as **pilot testing.**

The fundamental options for pilot testing fall into one of three classes. **Split-cable transmission** allows testing of two different versions of an advertisement through direct transmission to two separate samples of similar households within a single, well-defined market area. This method provides exposure in a natural setting for heightened realism. Factors such as frequency of transmission and timing of transmission can be carefully controlled. The advertisements are then compared on measures of exposure, recall, and persuasion.

Split-run distribution uses the same technique as split-cable transmission, except the print medium is used. Two different versions of the same advertisement are placed in every other copy of a magazine. This method of pilot testing has the advantage of using direct response as a test measure. Ads can be designed with a reply card that can serve as a basis of evaluation. Coupons and toll-free numbers can also be used. The realism of this method is a great advantage in the testing process. Expense is, of course, a major drawback.

Finally, a **split-list experiment** tests the effectiveness of various aspects of direct-mail advertising pieces. Multiple versions of a direct-mail piece are prepared and sent to various segments of a mailing list. The version that pulls (produces sales) the best is deemed superior. The advantage of all the pilot-testing methods is the natural and real setting within which the test takes place. A major disadvantage is that competitive or other environmental influences in the market cannot be controlled and may affect the performance of one advertisement without ever being

Television Pretesting Services

Research Systems Corporation: ARS Persuasion System. This is the system Goodyear used to pretest its Aquatred advertisements. The ARS System employs 800 to 1,200 respondents in several market areas. These respondents view television ads embedded in television programs. Before and after viewing, respondents are asked to choose sets of products they would pick if they were chosen as a winner of a door prize. The persuasion measure is the number of respondents who choose the test product after exposure versus those who chose the product before exposure. Three days after exposure, a subsample is telephoned to measure recall and understanding of the test ad.

Gallup & Robinson InTeleTest. This test uses in-home viewing of a videotaped program with six test commercials and six normal commercials embedded. Testing is done in 10 different cities, with 150 male and female respondents. Respondents are told they are viewing a proposed new television program. The day after viewing the program, a researcher conducts a telephone interview and takes recall measures related to the advertising in the program. Later, respondents view a tape that contains only the test ads, and they then provide an evaluation of recognition, likability, and general reaction to each ad.

Video Storyboard Tests (VST). The VST is specifically designed to test rough versions of television ads. The ads are prepared from storyboards and music soundtracks by VST. One-on-one interviews are conducted after individual respondents are shown the storyboard ads on a television monitor. Respondents are asked questions relating to persuasion, liking, believability, and other features of the ad. VST can provide benchmark measures for other products in the category as a basis for rating the test ad.

Print Pretesting Services

Perception Research Services (PRS). PRS evaluates all types of print advertising using an eye-tracking camera that follows the respondent's eye movement around a print advertisement. Respondents that fit a target audience profile are allowed to view a print ad as long as they desire. The camera records the length of time for which and the sequence in which some ad elements are viewed, other elements are overlooked, and copy is read. A postsession interview identifies recall, likability of the ad, main idea perceptions, purchase interest, and product image.

ASI: Print Plus. ASI offers print ad pretesting through national magazines or its own dummy magazine vehicle, called *Reflections*. Testing is done in five markets in the United States. Test participants are told they are taking part in a public-opinion survey and are given a magazine to read in their home. A telephone interview is conducted the following day to determine recall and other dimensions of the test ad. Participants are asked to review four ads, after which a feature evaluation and product interest list is administered.

Video Storyboard Tests (VST). VST tests all forms of rough and fully finished print ads in its dummy vehicle magazine, called *Looking at Us*. Respondents are told they are examining a pilot issue of a new magazine. Individual interviews are conducted in shopping malls, where respondents rate ads on persuasion, product uniqueness, believability, competitive strength, likes and dislikes, and reactions to headlines.

Source: Adapted from descriptions in Jack Haskins and Alice Kendrick, *Successful Advertising Research Methods* (Chicago: NTC Business Books, 1993), 318–328.

EXHIBIT 15.5

There are several commercial services available to marketers for pretesting advertising effectiveness.

Television Pilot Testing

Gallup & Robinson: In-View. This service provides on-air testing of both rough and finished advertisements. One market area in the East, Midwest, and West is selected, and randomly selected samples of 100 to 150 subjects are targeted for the test. The test ad is aired on an independent network station with a former prime-time program now in syndication. Subjects are called *before* the program is aired and invited to watch for the purpose of evaluating the program itself. Researchers obtain day-after recall measures and ask questions regarding idea communication and persuasion for the test ad.

ASI: Recall Plus and Persuasion Plus. Unlike the Gallup & Robinson test, ASI uses cable transmission to test ads on a recruited audience. A standard random sample is 200 respondents drawn from a minimum of two test cities. In Recall Plus, respondents are called the day of the test and invited to preview a new television program. The program includes four noncompeting test advertisements and one filler nontest ad. Day-after recall and effectiveness measures are then taken. The Persuasion Plus test uses the same methods as Recall Plus, with the addition of brand-choice measures. More extensive screening of participants is done in the recruiting stage with respect to brand usage and preference. Then, within two hours after viewing the test program, Persuasion Plus respondents are interviewed and, in the context of prize drawing, asked to choose the brands they would most like to have. A "Tru-Share" persuasion score is calculated on the pretest and posttest brand preferences.

Print Pilot Testing

Gallup & Robinson: Rapid Ad Measurement (RAM). Regular readers of *Time* and *People* magazines are recruited in five metropolitan areas to participate in studies. Gallup & Robinson then offers advertisers the chance to buy advertising space in test issues of these magazines, which are delivered to 150 participants' homes in each test area. A telephone interview is conducted the day after delivery, and, after magazine reading has been verified, respondents are asked if they recall ads for a list of brands and companies. Detailed measures are obtained for recall, idea communication, and persuasion of the text ad.

Source: Adapted from descriptions in Jack Haskins and Alice Kendrick, *Successful Advertising Research Methods* (Chicago: NTC Business Books, 1993), 334–337.

EXHIBIT 15.6

Before an advertisement or campaign is scheduled for full roll-out, marketers can do pilot testing of the message in selected markets. Several well-known providers can help marketers conduct marketplace pilot testing.

detected by the researcher. Such effects provide an inaccurate comparison between test ads. Several well-known service providers are available to help marketers do pilot testing and are featured in Exhibit 15.6.

Marketplace Evaluation of Adverting: Posttesting

Posttest message tracking assesses the performance of advertisements during or after the launch of an advertising campaign. Common measures of an ad's performance are recall, recognition, awareness and attitude, and behavior-based measures.

Recall Testing. By far the most common method of advertising research is the **recall test**—the basic idea is that if the ad is to work, it has to be remembered. Following on this premise is the further assumption that the ads best remembered are the ones most likely to work. Thus the objective of these tests is to see just how much, if anything, the viewer of an ad remembers of the message. Recall is used in the testing of print, television and radio, and some supportive communications like billboard advertising.

In television, the basic procedure is to recruit a group of individuals from the target market who will be watching a certain channel during a certain time on a test date. They are asked to participate ahead of time, and simply told to watch the show. A day after exposure, the testing company calls the individuals on the phone and determines how much those who actually saw the ad can recall. The procedure generally starts with questions such as, "Do you remember seeing an ad for laundry detergent?" "If so, do you remember the brand?" If the respondent remembers, she or he is asked to replay the commercial; if not, further aids or prompts are given. The interview is generally tape recorded and transcribed. The verbatim interview is coded into various categories representing levels of recall, typically reported as a percentage. Recall testing for radio ads follows procedures similar to those for television.

In a typical print recall test, a consumer is recruited from the target market, generally at a shopping mall. He or she is given a magazine to take home. Many times the magazine is an advance issue of a real publication; other times it is a fictitious magazine created only for testing purposes. The ads are tipped in, or inserted into the vehicle. Some companies alter the mix of remaining ads; others do not. Some rotate the ads (put them in different spots in the magazine) so as not to get effects due to either editorial context or order. The participants are told that they should look at the magazine and that they will be telephoned the following day and asked some questions. During the telephone interview, **aided recall** is assessed. This involves a product-category cue, such as, "Do you remember seeing any ads for personal computers?" The percentage who respond affirmatively and provide some evidence of actually remembering the ad are scored as exhibiting aided recall. Other tests go into more detail by actually bringing the ad back to the respondent and asking about various components of the ad, such as the headline and body copy. Recall tests are more demanding for participants than are recognition tests, which are described next.

As we have discussed several times, there is an irrepressible urge to judge message effectiveness based on sales. Some research indicates there is little relation between recall scores and sales effectiveness.[8] But doesn't it make sense that the best ads are the ads best remembered? But "best" from a recall standpoint doesn't always mean that purchase motivation will follow. Recall the "Got Milk?" campaign where, despite near ubiquity of recall, the slide in milk consumption in the United States continued throughout the campaign. The history of advertising is littered with memorable campaigns that did not positively affect sales (remember ads by Dick?). This seemingly simple question has perplexed academics and practitioners for a long time.

Recognition Testing. Recognition tests ask magazine readers and television viewers whether they remember having seen particular advertisements and whether they can name the company sponsoring the ad. For print advertising, the actual advertisement is shown to respondents, and for television advertising, a script with accompanying photos is shown. For instance, a recognition test might ask, "Do you remember seeing the ad in Exhibit 15.7?" This is a much easier task than recall in that respondents are cued by the very stimulus they are supposed to remember, and they aren't asked to do anything more than say yes or no.

Companies that do this kind of research follow some general procedures. Subscribers to a relevant magazine are contacted and asked if an interview can be set up

8.   Rajeev Batra, John G. Meyers, and David A. Aaker, *Advertising Management,* 5th ed. (Upper Saddle River, NJ: Prentice-Hall, 1996), 469.

EXHIBIT 15.7

In recognition testing, consumers might be shown an ad like this one and asked "Do you remember seeing this ad?" Recognition testing is somewhat easier than recall testing for respondents because they are given the ad as a memory aid.

in their home. The readers must have at least glanced at the issue to qualify. Then each target ad is shown, and the readers are asked if they remember seeing the ad (if they noted it), if they read or saw enough of the ad to notice the brand name (if they associated it), and if they claim to have read at least 50 percent of the copy (if they read most of it). This testing is usually conducted just a few days after the current issue becomes available.

There is a longer history of recognition scores than of any other testing method. There are normative data on many types of ads. The biggest problem with this test is that of a yea-saying bias. In other words, many people say they recognize an ad that in truth they haven't actually seen. It's not that respondents are not telling the truth. Rather, there is a tendency for marketers who are marketing brands with similar features to prepare ads that are astonishingly similar. After a few days, do you really think you could correctly remember which of the three ads in Exhibits 15.8, 15.9 and 15.10 you actually saw, if you saw the ads under natural viewing conditions?

Recognition tests suffer from two other problems. First, because direct interviewing is involved, the test is expensive. Second, because respondents are given visual aids, the risk of overestimation threatens the meaningfulness of the collected data.

Awareness and Attitude Tracking. Tracking studies measure the change in an audience's brand awareness and attitude before and after an advertising campaign. This common type of advertising research is almost always conducted as a survey. Members of the target market are surveyed on a fairly regular basis to detect any changes. Any change in awareness or attitude is usually attributed (rightly or wrongly) to the advertising effort. The problem with this type of test is the inability to isolate the effect of advertising on awareness and attitude amid a myriad of other influences—media reports, observation, friends, competitive advertising, and so forth.

Behavior-Based Measures. The knee-jerk reaction to behavior-based posttest measures of advertising is that sales will be the sole "behavior" that is measured. When we get to direct marketing and e-commerce we will see that sales as a measure is a reasonable judgment criterion. But what about other measures of behavior that are relevant to the effectiveness of an advertising effort. Take, for example, major media advertising by Internet companies designed to drive traffic to the firm's Web site. This is certainly a meaningful and obtainable behavioral measure of advertising effectiveness. Take, for example, the multimillions of dollars spent by dot-coms on Super Bowl advertising. After Super Bowl 2000, E*Trade (one of the heaviest investors in traditional media advertising) found that its Super Bowl ad ranked as one of the best-liked ads aired during the game, but in the week following ad exposure, unique visitors (that is, individual visitor counts that eliminate multiple visits by the same person) to the E*Trade site fell 5.5 percent.[9]

9.   Jennifer Gilbert, "Top 10 Ads Score Raves, Not Hits Post-Super Bowl," *Advertising Age,* February 7, 2000, 63.

http://www.cadillac.com/catera/index.htm

EXHIBITS 15.8, 15.9, 15.10

All these ads are strikingly similar and do little to differentiate the product, make it memorable for the consumer, or promote the brand. If you actually saw one of these ads in a magazine, do you think you could really distinguish which one it was during a recognition test? General Motors' Cadillac Division tried to break out of the generic luxury car bin with its Catera model, a "Caddy that zigs!," with a cartoon duck mascot, with mixed results.

Another example of a behavior-based measure of effectiveness that is not based on sales comes from a campaign used by the Census Bureau. The Census Bureau used direct-response measures to judge the effectiveness of its "It's Your Future. Don't Leave It Blank" campaign for the 2000 Census. The campaign was designed to stem the tide of steadily declining response rates for mailing back census forms. The $103 million campaign is credited with generating a 66 percent mail-in rate, which was, in fact, an increased rate of return over previous censuses and 5 percentage points higher than the Census Bureau expected.[10]

So, while sales may be the most obvious behavioral measure of the effectiveness of advertising, there are certainly other behaviors that would suggest advertising has had an intended effect. Marketers need to be sensitive to behavioral measures other than sales that are related to the effectiveness of advertising.

Commercial Posttest Services. Exhibit 15.11 lists the most widely recognized commercial posttest message services. Overall, posttesting is appealing because of the

---

10.   Ira Teinowitz, "Census Bureau Counts Ad Effort a Success," *Advertising Age,* May 22, 2000, 8.

EXHIBIT 15.11

Commercial services available for posttest message research

Gallup & Robinson: Magazine Impact Research Service (MIRS). This service from Gallup & Robinson tests advertisements that appear in selected issues of major consumer magazines, including *Time, Playboy, Sports Illustrated, Business Week, Bon Appetit, People,* and others. Male and female respondents who have read at least two of the last four issues of one or more of the test magazines (but not the current issues used for the testing) are recruited in 10 metropolitan areas. Test magazines are delivered to participants, who are interviewed by phone the next day. Fifteen brand and product categories are examined, with questions relating to recall, idea communication, and persuasion.

ASI: Print Plus. This service is similar to ASI's pretesting service, discussed earlier. Male and female samples are drawn in five test markets for posttesting general consumer magazines. Participants are told they are in a public-opinion survey of magazines. A distinct feature of the ASI test is that brand attitude is measured before exposure to the test ad, in the context of a prize drawing for a dollar amount of a product (and brand) chosen by the participant. After delivery of the test magazines and verification of reading, recall and feature communication are tested. Re-exposure to four test ads is carried out to measure interest in the product. A postexposure brand preference is taken in the prize-drawing context for each category of advertisement tested. Pretest and posttest preference measures provide a persuasion index.

Starch INRA Hooper: Message Report Service. Starch provides the most extensive posttesting service available. Testing is available for 700 issues of all forms of magazines, including professional and trade publications. More than 75,000 subjects are interviewed each year by Starch. Starch draws samples from 20 to 30 urban locations for each test. Interviewers turn the pages of a publication and ask subjects about each ad under study. Along with demographic data on subjects, Starch produces the following evaluations for each ad:
- *Noted readers*—the percentage who remember having previously seen the ad in the issue being studied.
- *Associated readers*—the percentage who remember seeing the ad and are able to associate it with a brand or advertiser.
- *Read-most readers*—the percentage who read at least half of the material in the ad.

Starch INRA Hooper: Impression Study. This Starch service is designed to posttest ads that appear in print, television, and outdoor media. The measures are more qualitative and designed to identify the communication effects of advertising. Personal interviews are conducted in which subjects are shown an ad and then asked to describe in their own words their reactions with respect to the ad's meaning, the outstanding features of the ad, and the impressions formed from both the visual and written aspects of the ad.

Information Resources (IRI): Panel Data. While IRI's national sample of homes that maintain a diary on their purchases and media habits is not strictly designed to give detailed posttest message information, the panel data can provide some insights. The data from the households can be used to correlate promotional efforts with sales, which gives an indirect measure of message effectiveness. Of course, lack of control makes such a measure tenuous at best.

strong desire to track the continuing effectiveness of advertising in a real-world setting. However, the problems of expense, delay of feedback, and inability to separate sources of effect are compromises that need to be understood and evaluated when using this form of message testing.

A Final Thought on Measuring Advertising Effectiveness

None of the methods for measuring the effectiveness of advertising are perfect. There are challenges to reliability, validity, trustworthiness, and meaningfulness with all of them. Marketers sometimes think that consumers watch new television commercials the way they watch new, eagerly awaited feature films, or that they listen to radio spots like they listen to a symphony, or read magazine ads like a Steinbeck novel. Work by James Lull and other naturalistic researchers and ethnographers demonstrates what we as American consumers have known all along: We watch TV while we work, talk, eat, and study; we use radio as a night-light, background noise, and babysitter; we skim through magazines looking for content; and we whiz by billboards and hardly pay attention.[11] While these traditional methods of advertising evaluation have their strengths, more naturalistic methods, where researchers actually observe consumers observing advertising, are clearly recommended.

MEASURING THE EFFECTIVENESS OF INTERNET ADVERTISING ❸

When we discussed the privacy issues related to the Web in Chapters 6 and 9, the problem was that the consumers were concerned that marketers would know who they are and what sort of surfing behavior they were engaged in. Well, it turns out that the same system that causes the privacy concerns is the basis for measuring the effectiveness of Internet advertising.

The information a Web site typically gets when a user connects with a site is the Internet Provider (IP) address of the site that is requesting the page, what page is requested, and the time of the request. This is the minimum amount of information available to a Web site. If a site is an opt-in site and requires registration, then additional information (for example, e-mail address, zip code, gender, age, or household income) is typically requested directly from the user. Attempts at registration (and easy audience assessment) have been largely rejected by consumers because of the privacy concern, but plenty of service providers, such as Nielsen// NetRatings, are available to guide marketers through Web measurement options (see Exhibit 15.12).

Web Measurement Factors

Several terms, such as hits, click-throughs, pages, visits, users, and reach are used in Web audience measurement. We will consider the most meaningful of these measurement factors. **Hits** represent the number of elements requested from a given page and consequently provide almost no indication of actual Web traffic. For instance, when a user requests a page with four graphical images, it counts as five hits. Thus by inflating the number of images, a site can quickly pull up its hit count. Consider what might happen at the *Seventeen* magazine site (http://www.seventeen.com). The *Seventeen* site may get 3 million hits a day, placing it among the top Web sites. However, this total of 3 million hits translates into perhaps only 80,000 people daily. Thus, hits do not translate into the number of people visiting a site. Another measure of site effectiveness is the extent to which a site will motivate visitors to "click-through." A **click-through** is a measure of the number of page elements (hyperlinks) that have actually been requested (that is, "clicked through" from the banner ad to the link). It is typically 1 to 2 percent of hits. The click-through number (and percentage) is

---

11. James Lull, "How Families Select Television Programs: A Mass Observational Study," *Journal of Broadcasting*, vol. 26, no. 4 (1982), 801–811.

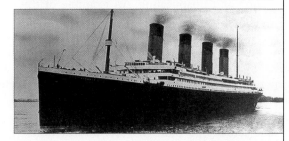

WITH A LITTLE BAD INFORMATION YOU COULD ACTUALLY GO DOWN IN HISTORY.

Keep your Internet strategies afloat with high-quality Internet audience research from Nielsen//NetRatings.

Bad information. It can lead to bad decisions and big disasters. Especially when it comes to Internet e-commerce, content or advertising strategies. To help you make the right decisions, Nielsen//NetRatings is dedicated to Information Quality.

Our secret? We capture comprehensive Internet user activity in real time from our representative panel of more than 38,000 Internet users: sites visited, ads viewed, media players used, purchasing activity and user connection speeds. It's a great way to know what's really happening on the Internet. How do we do it? Proprietary Internet measurement technology from NetRatings coupled with 50 years of proven research methods from Nielsen Media Research.

What's more, because we collect data in real time from our entire panel, nobody can provide it to you faster. Even overnight analysis is not a problem.

Another Nielsen//NetRatings advantage: our unique in-depth analysis. Nielsen//NetRatings team of analysts pinpoint emerging Internet trends, hot sectors and companies in weekly, monthly and quarterly reports–based on our rich database of user behavior.

Whenever you need high quality information and analysis to keep your head above water, count on Nielsen//NetRatings. In fact, call 1-888-634-1222 now for a free copy of our latest E-commerce Trends Report.

WEB SIGHTING

Nielsen//NetRatings
Your decisions are only as good as your data.

http://www.nielsen-netratings.com

EXHIBIT 15.12

Because of the nature of the Net, audience measurement can be far more precise and complete—Nielsen can "sit on your shoulder" as you surf and note every click, if you've opted to be one of their panelists. How do they recruit their panelists? Banner ads on popular Web sites?

the best measure of the effectiveness of banner advertising. If an ad is good enough to motivate a visitor to click on it and follow the link to more information, then that is verification that the ad was viewed and motivating. At 1 to 2 percent overall click-through rates, banner ads are not scoring too well on effectiveness as a group. This does not mean, however, that any particular banner ad could not achieve a much higher click-through percentage.

Pages (or **page views**) are defined as the pages (actually the number of HTML files) sent to the requesting site. However, if a downloaded page occupies several screens, there is no indication that the requester examined the entire page. Also, it "doesn't tell you much about how many visitors it has: 100,000 page views in a week could be ten people reading 10,000 pages, or 100,000 people reading one page, or any variation in between."[12] **Visits** are the number of occasions in which a user X interacted with site Y after time Z has elapsed. Usually Z is set to some standard time such as thirty minutes. If the user has not interacted with the site until after thirty minutes has passed, this would be counted as a new visit. **Users** (also known as unique visitors) are the number of different "people" visiting a site (a new user is determined from the user's registration with the site) during a specified period of time. Besides the address, page, and time, a Web site can find out the referring link address. This allows a Web site to discover what links people are taking to the site. Thus, a site can analyze which links do in fact bring people to the site. This can be helpful in Internet advertising planning. The problem is that what is really counted are similar unique IP numbers. Many Internet service providers use a dynamic IP number, which is different every time a given user logs in through their service: so "you might show up as 30 different unique visitors to a site you visited daily for a month."[13] *Advertising Age* provides a weekly overview of the visits to both Web sites and hits on banner ads. Notice that data are reported for unique visitors, which is the most reasonable measure of visits to a site (see Exhibit 15.13).

Web Measurement Tools

While marketers are embracing the Web as a new medium for advertising, they are simultaneously seeking new measurement systems that verify and justify their Web advertising investments. **Log analysis software** is measurement software that not only provides information on hits, pages, visits, and users, but also lets a site track audience traffic within the site. A site could determine which pages are popular and

---

12. "Let's Get This Straight: Reach for the Hits," at http://www.salonmagazine.com/21st/ rose/ther, an article that focuses exclusively on the measurement issue. See Allan L. Baldinger, "Integrated Communication and Measurement: The Case for Multiple Measures," in Esther Thorson and Jeri Moore, eds., *Integrated Communications* (Mahwah, NJ: Lawrence Erlbaum Associates, 1996), 271–283.
13. Ibid.

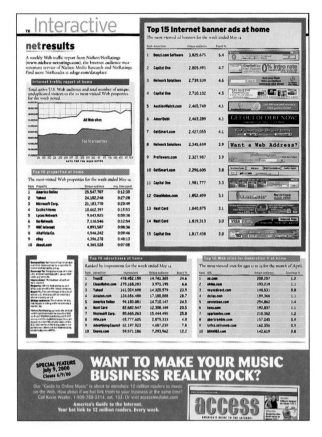

EXHIBIT 15.13

Advertising Age publishes a weekly summary of the performance of Web sites and banner ads.

expand on them. It is also possible to track the behavior of people as they go through the site, thus providing inferential information on what people find appealing and unappealing. An example of this software is MaxInfo's WebC, which allows marketers to track what information is viewed, when it is viewed, how often it is viewed, and where users go within a site.[14] A marketer can then modify the content and structure accordingly. It can also help marketers understand how buyers make purchase decisions in general.[15] It still isn't possible, however, to know what people actually do with Web site information.

There are plenty of companies such as I/PRO, NetCount, and Interse offering measurement services for interactive media. And, as exemplified in the New Media box, plenty of advice is available on how to do research on the Net. Yet there is no industry standard for measuring the effectiveness of one interactive ad placement over another. There also is no standard for comparing Internet with traditional media placements. Moreover, demographic information on who is using the WWW is severely limited to those consumers who have signed up for opt-in programs and, for example, allow targeted e-mails to be sent to them. Until these limitations are overcome, many marketers will remain hesitant about spending substantial dollars for advertising on the Web.

The new deal in town is the Media Metrix reach index (see Exhibit 15.14). Media Metrix and its competitors (for example, NetRatings, owned by Nielsen) are invoking older technology to measure Web ad effectiveness. This involves sampling through a "Nielsen family" model. Sampling is used to draw a representative set of families. Tracking software is installed on the users' computers, and then data are collected and transmitted back to the companies. These data are projected to the universe of Internet users. The figure that has become the standard is the reach figure; here it represents the percentage of these users who visit a site in any one-month period. Of course, there are systematic biases built in, such as undercounting of workplace surfing. Some critics simply have a problem with applying the reach concept to this new medium at all.

As a measure of Web use, reach is weighted toward the superficial: It favors sprawling sites with vast collections of largely unrelated pages (like, for instance, GeoCities, now owned by Yahoo!) over well-focused sites that collect specific groups of users with shared interests. Say one site has 200,000 loyal users who visit regularly; another has little regular traffic, but its wide variety of pages turn up in enough disparate search-engine results to attract brief visits during the course of a month from, say, 5 million visitors. The two sites may have identical page-view counts. The former site may actually have a more valuable franchise to sell to marketers or to hand over to e-commerce partners—but the latter site wins the reach contest by a landslide.[16]

14. Ibid.
15. Eric Johnson, "Microsoft Developing Oscar's Website," *Marketing Doctoral Consortium,* Wharton Business School, August 1995.
16. http://www.adage.com/interactive/articles/19961223/article1.html.

http://www.mediametrix.com

EXHIBIT 15.14

Firms like Media Metrix (a competitor of Nielsen//NetRatings) measure the Net activities of households that have opted into being monitored, using what they collect as statistically relevant samples. What other means are there to build snapshots of Web activities, or estimate the popularity of certain sites or services?

Technical Aspects of the Internet Measurement Problem

When a computer is connected to the Internet, it has a unique IP address, such as 204.17.123.5. When a link to a Web site such as http://www.yahoo.com is clicked on, a computer converts this textual representation into a number that is the unique IP address for Yahoo! This computer then requests from Yahoo! its home page, and in return it gives Yahoo! its unique IP address so Yahoo! knows the address of the requester. Thus the only information a computer at a site such as Yahoo! receives is an IP address, along with the material the user is actually requesting. Note that a textual IP address is not the same thing as an e-mail address. E-mail addresses are similar but follow a different protocol on the Internet.

A Web site log file contains the IP addresses of the computers requesting information. However, an IP address does not usually correspond to just one person. Many systems dynamically assign IP addresses to computers connected to the Internet. Therefore, a person visiting a site in two different sessions may have a different IP address each time. For a marketer, this means it is unclear exactly how many different people visited the site. Even if a requesting computer has a permanent static address, thus allowing a site to keep track of a specific computer, the site still doesn't know who is actually using the computer. The computer could be used by one graduate student in his or her apartment, or it could be in a computer lab where hundreds of different people have access to the same computer.

A Web site can track how many machines accessed the site, but this does not correspond to how many people actually visited the Web site. One estimate is that the number of visitors exceeds IP addresses by about 15 percent.[17] Thus it

17. J. Udell, "Damn Lies," *Byte,* February 1996, 137.

AN EMERGING SCIENCE IN INTERNET MEASUREMENT

Media Metrix (MM) of New York and RelevantKnowledge (RK) of Atlanta are two key players in the new business of Internet audience tracking. Both have gained notoriety as a result of their monthly top 25 most-visited site rankings, and each also offers other, more detailed reports about Internet audiences. For example, they can provide details about a site's penetration among all online households; how long surfers stay at a site per day; and gender, age, and other demographic statistics about Web surfers. Although there are notable differences in how each company goes about getting these data for Internet versus television or radio audiences, one thing is very much the same: A lot of people complain about the results.

One complainer—Rich LeFurgy, senior VP of Internet advertising at ESPN/ABC News—says to just have a look at their monthly top twenty five listings. It is common to find that as many as a third of the twenty five sites appearing in the two companies' lists don't overlap—an odd outcome, to be sure, when both companies claim to be ranking the same thing. LeFurgy also contends that both companies badly underestimate actual site visitations. In one count of ESPN page views, MM's estimate was 41 million and RK's was 94 million, but ESPN's internal logs showed 168 million. Obviously, Internet audience tracking is not an exact science.

On the other hand, executives at MM and RK are quick to defend their methods from critics such as Rich LeFurgy, and emphasize the superiority of their own methods versus the competitor's. MM says its data is more accurate than RK's because it draws on a much larger sample (30,000 versus 11,000) in conducting its surveys. MM president Mary Anne Packo claims: "The key difference is that our focus is on measuring the whole digital media space—not only Web sites but the online services and the non-Web services such as Pointcast." RK management counters that their method of sampling Internet users is superior, making raw sample size irrelevant. Clearly, both organizations are still learning how to cope with challenges posed by the new media. But then, who isn't?

The Net ratings issues is also taking on global proportions—as you might expect. Given the worldwide access to any Web site, it is obviously useful for firms to know the global reach of their Internet presence. Two firms—Xtreme Information in London, which has launched Xtreme Internet Ad Watch, and Nielsen//NetRatings, a U.S. company—now offer services that measure Web advertising in nineteen foreign markets.

Sources: Russell Shaw, "Online Ratings Are a Growing Business, with Firms Including RelevantKnowledge and Media Metrix," *Electronic Media*, March 2, 1998, 17; Jennifer Gilbert, "New Entries Join Global Race to Measure the Net," *Advertising Age*, September 17, 1999, 66.

is currently difficult to know exactly who is visiting a site, and if the visitors are revisiting. The only obvious enhancement would be implementing unique IDs in Web browsers. This would identify a specific computer visiting the site. However, this has not been seen as feasible due to current privacy concerns. It also leaves the possibility of many different people using the same computer, such as would occur in a computer lab.

The Caching Complication in Internet Measurement

To conserve resources on the Web, there is a system known as caching. **Caching** is an active memory in Web and computer technology. Once a page is downloaded, the cache on the computer saves that page so it can be immediately accessed. Commercial on line services such as America Online cache heavily trafficked sites on their computers so users get quicker response times when they request that page. Suppose a person first goes to a Web site's home page. After clicking on a link to go somewhere else, the user decides to go back to the home page. Instead of asking the Web site again for that home page, the cache will have stored it in anticipation of the user wanting it again. This conserves Internet re sources, commonly called bandwidth, because the user is not needlessly requesting the same material twice. However, this complicates matters in measuring activity at the site because once a person has cached a page, the Web site has no idea whether the user spent considerable time at the page in one visit, returned to the page several times, or immediately moved on.

Technological solutions can reduce the amount of caching, thus allowing sites better data on how often a page is viewed, but it comes with the cost of additional bandwidth for the site and a slower response time for the person viewing the site. Caching may result in fewer page requests to a Web site than have actually occurred. Moreover, if a person hits the reload button, a Web site will register more traffic than there actually is. While cache-busting technology (technology that allows sites to look inside users' computer caches to determine the true number of pages) does exist, its widespread use seems unlikely in the near future.

Internet Measurement and Payment

Internet marketers pay for ads in several ways, but they all, in one way or another, depend on the measurement of activity related to Web site visits where banner ads appear. Many pay in terms of impressions. It's supposed to mean the number of times a page with your ad on it is viewed; in reality these are roughly equivalent to hits, or opportunities to view. Often these are priced as flat fees—so many dollars for so many impressions. Others price with pay-per-click, which is in all reality the same as impressions. Others pay in click-throughs. Recall from our earlier discussion that a click-through "occurs when the visitor sees or reads the ad and clicks on it, taking them directly to the marketers Web site. . . . The overall average for click throughs for all web advertising is around 2 percent."[18] Others will buy on cost per lead (documented business leads) or cost per actual sale (very rare). A net rate refers to the 15 percent discounted rate given to advertising agencies, although direct deals with portals and browsers are very common.

MEASURING THE EFFECTIVENESS OF DIRECT MARKETING AND E-COMMERCE

Direct marketing and e-commerce are by far the easiest promotional techniques to measure for effectiveness. By their very nature, direct marketing and e-commerce are designed to stimulate action. In some cases, the action is a request on the part of a consumer or business buyer for information. In many cases, direct marketing and e-commerce promotions offer the audience the opportunity to place an inquiry or respond directly through a Web site, reply card, or toll-free phone number. An example of just such a promotion is displayed in Exhibit 15.15. An appeal that implores a behavioral response on the part of receivers allows for **inquiry/direct response measures.** These measures are quite straightforward. Promotions that generate a high number of inquiries, such as direct responses or orders or Web site visits, are deemed effective. Additional analyses may compare the number of inquiries or responses to the number of sales generated.

Aside from measuring just the inquiries or sales generated, direct marketing and e-commerce promotion allow for a more refined evaluation. Because these tools are primarily database driven for targeting audiences, then the inquiries and sales responses can similarly be partitioned with respect to the geodemographic nature of respondents. That is, marketers can compare one promotional campaign against another based on who responded, what region of the country they came from, and how quickly they responded. For example, telemarketing firms have historical data to show that a conversion rate in phone solicitations is about 2 to 4 percent. Various different scripts can be tested to see if any one particular message helps phone solicitors exceed the historical average. Armed with this geodemographic information, marketers can tailor different types of direct marketing and e-commerce messages to different target markets depending on historical response data.

Finally, the data-rich nature of direct marketing and e-commerce also allows for a profitability analysis of these tools that is typically not appropriate for more long-term-oriented promotional tools. Because of the fairly direct correlation with sales, a return on investment is quite easily calculated for direct marketing and e-commerce campaigns.

---

18.   E. Weise, "P&G Changes Way Ads Paid For," *Cincinnati Enquirer,* April 29, 1996, A3.

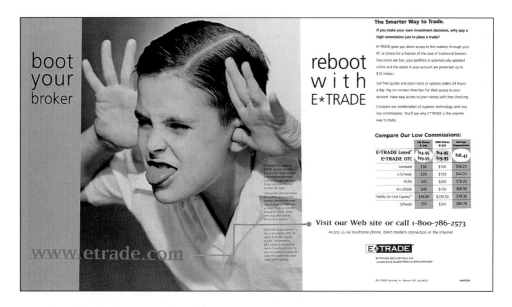

EXHIBIT 15.15

The effectiveness of direct marketing and e-commerce promotions is much easier to measure than other promotional tools. How would you measure the effectiveness of this promotion run by E*Trade?

MEASURING THE EFFECTIVENESS OF SALES PROMOTION

The approach to measuring the effectiveness of sales promotion is very similar to measuring the effectiveness of advertising. Sales promotion effectiveness can be carried out through pretesting and posttesting using techniques similar to those we discussed earlier regarding advertising.

Pretesting Sales Promotion with Consumers

Pretesting sales promotion focuses on measuring the consumer's perception of the value of a promotion. This means testing the perceived value of different levels of cents-off coupons, premiums, giveaways, frequency program, or contests. Each of these types of promotion will be assessed differently by consumers. For example, consumers need to weigh the perceived value of a 50-cents-off coupon for a brand they never use, versus paying 50 cents more for a brand they have been using regularly and find satisfying. Similarly, is it worth switching brands to enter a contest or sweepstakes? When it comes to premiums or bonus packs where the consumer can get a free product or extra quantity of a product, the perception of value of a brand-loyal customer is easy—more of a preferred brand at less cost. For the consumer contemplating trial use, however, getting an additional quantity of an unknown brand may be perceived as a liability since there is the risk the brand will not offer sufficient satisfaction. Each of the possibilities can be pretested with consumers using standard and fairly simple research methods like focus groups or a ballot method. A **ballot method** consists of mailing target consumers a list of promotional options and asking them to rank their preferences and mail the ballot back to the firm.

Pretesting Sales Promotion in the Trade Channel

There are two issues with respect to pretesting sales promotion in the trade channel. First, the effectiveness of consumer-oriented sales promotions are greatly compromised if members of the trade channel are not excited about the promotion and do not support it. If sweepstakes entries, coupons, or premium packs are not maintained by trade partners, the effectiveness of a sales promotion effort will be completely undermined. The best approach for pretesting consumer promotions with the trade channel is to meet with trade channel managers and work out the details of the execution with them.

The second issue in pretesting sales promotion in the channel has to do with trade-oriented sales promotions—that is, promotions directed at the channel members themselves. Here, the techniques used to pretest sales promotions with consumers are valuable as well. A survey of key retail partners in terms of what they would perceive as an energizing and high-value promotion will provide important feedback. The difference between allowances, which essentially lower the price, and sales contests or training programs is large. Getting a read on the channel's perceptions of value can mean the difference between motivating channel members and having them totally ignore a program.

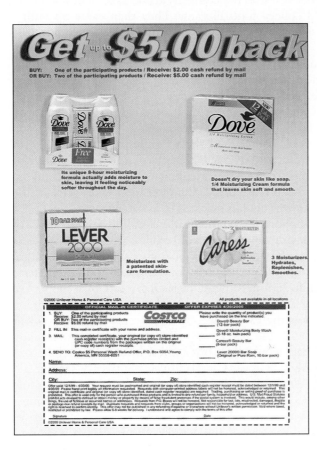

EXHIBIT 15.16

The effectiveness of sales promotion programs is typically done measures quantitatively. How would you measure the effectiveness of this Costco rebate program?

Posttesting Sales Promotion

Posttesting sales promotion is pretty much a matter of generating a quantified measure of the performance of a sales promotion device. In the broadest sense, changes in sales can be used with any sales promotion tool as a measure of effectiveness. But with contests and sweepstakes, another measure will be the number of consumer entries. With coupons and rebates, the number of coupons redeemed and rebate forms returned are additional quantitative measures. For example, Nestlé distributed coupon inserts for its Ortega salsa in Sunday papers slated to reach 50 million consumers. A reasonable measure of effectiveness would be tracking the redemption rate of that particular coupon.[19] In terms of working with trade channel partners, relying on sales measures time period by time period will allow a comparison of the effects of any sales promotion program. And you can be sure that the trade itself is focused on sales as a measure of a promotion's success. When Procter & Gamble introduced the Swiffer sweeper/duster, some retailers resisted carrying the brand because of the high price: $18.00 for the mop. But one supermarket buyer who had decided against carrying the product because of the high price said he might have to bow to consumer demand if P&G promotions were successful.[20] Some retailers are fairly aggressive at devising sales promotion programs and having ways of measuring their effectiveness (see Exhibit 15.16).

19. Stephanie Thompson, "Nestlé Tries Fresh Approach for Premium Ortega Salsa," *Advertising Age,* February 21, 2000, 16.
20. Jack Neff, "P&G Introduces Trio of Products in DMB&B Boon," *Advertising Age,* May 22, 2000, 77.

MEASURING THE EFFECTIVENESS OF SPONSORSHIP, POINT OF PURCHASE AND SUPPORTIVE COMMUNICATIONS

Sponsorship is one of those promotional tools that probably shouldn't even be measured. Sponsoring an event or community activity is meant to enhance the image of a brand and ultimately create a more positive attitude—which, in the long term, may have an effect on sales. But in an era of accountability, managers are usually pressed to come up with some measure of effectiveness for their sponsorship spending. Some simple quantitative measures are available. If the sponsorship is an event, the number of people attending the event is easily obtained. Similarly, if the event is televised, the number of viewers of the event gives a proxy measure of exposure to the brand. Remember from Chapter 12 that managers at John Hancock Insurance counted the number of times the company logo appeared on the television screen and the number of times the company name was mentioned during the telecast of a sponsored college football game. They then came up with a fairly elaborate model to translate those exposures into the equivalent of advertising dollars.[21]

Several research firms are now offering services to calculate the effects of sponsorship. Some specialize in performing sales audits in event areas, conduct exit interviews with attendees, and offer economic impact studies.[22] Others try to identify the impact of an event on the image of the firm, and some have tried to calculate the effects on sales—but with fairly strained methodologies.[23]

The success of P–O–P materials is measured almost exclusively on the basis of sales effects. Since the context for P–O–P materials offers little opportunity for "message" execution per se, changes in sales are a legitimate and appropriate measure of effectiveness. Also, since this promotional communication takes place at the point of behavior, the display material should play a role in catalyzing a sale.

Testing the effectiveness of supportive communications should rely on recall of the messages that appear in the major support media like billboards, transit, and aerial ads. It would be difficult to test for effectiveness of supportive communications tools like T-shirts, baseball caps, or calendars unless counting the number of items given away is deemed worthwhile and meaningful. In testing recall with supportive communications in billboards or aerial ads, researchers might make random phone calls in an area and ask, "Who was the twenty-second and twenty-fourth President of the United States?" Armed with the percentage of households who correctly answered the questions, researchers would then place a test message on a billboard or bus board or blimp stating simply, "Grover Cleveland was the twenty-second and twenty-fourth President of the United States." After the message has run for some designated time—usually two to four weeks—another random sample of households is surveyed. The difference in knowledge of the twenty-second and twenty-fourth President is then attributed to recall of the message. While that may seem to be a simple enough test of effectiveness, it does have a significant flaw. The message "Grover Cleveland was the twenty-second and twenty-fourth President of the United States" is so strange to passersby that it may be a very artificial measure of the effectiveness of various supportive communication vehicles.

There are, however, some supportive communication tools that can be tracked directly for effectiveness. John Deere relies heavily on a wide range of promotional tools to communicate with both its commercial and consumer target audiences. In one recent consumer promotion, the firm mailed videotapes to a select consumer

21.   Michael J. McCarthy, "Keeping Close Score on Sports Tie-ins," *The Wall Street Journal,* April 24, 1991, B1.
22.   B. Spethmann, "Sponsorships Sing a Profitable Tune in Concert with Event Promotions," *Brandweek,* January 1, 1994, 20.
23.   Scott Hume, "Sports Sponsorship Value Measured," *Advertising Age,* June 3, 1996, 46.

target group. The promotion not only doubled the response rate of previous campaigns (measured by inquiries), it was also credited with doubling sales—an obviously measurable result.[24]

MEASURING THE EFFECTIVENESS OF PUBLIC RELATIONS AND CORPORATE ADVERTISING

One attitude about measuring the effects of public relations and corporate advertising is that it really shouldn't even be tried. Since both public relations and corporate advertising have long-term image effects as primary objectives, trying to measure the effect of such programs at any one point in time seems, well, pointless. For example, just what would you be measuring if you attempted to measure the effectiveness of the Deloitte Consulting campaign featuring the ad shown in Exhibit 15.17? This is not an ad that focuses on the features of the service or distinctive characteristics of Deloitte as consulting firm—easy fodder for measurement. Rather, this is a beautifully creative piece that evokes feeling and more than likely will have a positive effect on brand image. But how does it affect brand image? And when? After a week, a month, five years? Just what would the measurement criteria be? Herein lies the problem with measuring the effects of public relations and corporate advertising.

But in an environment where promotional budgets are subject to heavy scrutiny, attempts are made to measure the effects of these types of subtle promotional efforts. One easy measure of the effects of public relations is to merely count the number of media exposures created by the PR program. Public relations firms often will present clients with a "clippings" book showing all the media that carried stories about the company, its employees, products, or events. But as we have discovered, equating placement with exposure is a tenuous link at best.

Another measure of the effects of either public relations or corporate advertising would be to measure changes in awareness or attitude. This would require original research that measures awareness and attitude before and then after a campaign has been carried out. Of course, it is likely that a firm will be running a wide range of promotional activities along with the PR and corporate campaign. This being the case, it would be almost impossible to separately measure the effects of public relations or corporate advertising from sales promotion, direct marketing, personal selling, mainstream media advertising, or even event sponsorship.

Given the broad and subtle effects of public relations and corporate advertising, it may be advisable to save the expense of the measurement process and

EXHIBIT 15.17

The effects of corporate advertising campaigns like this one for Deloitte Consulting are extremely hard to measure. Why?

24. Amanda Beeler, "Deere Goes Beyond Famed Brand to Cultivate Ties with Customers," *Advertising Age,* May 22, 2000.

have faith that these are important and useful forms of promotion and they are doing their behind-the-scenes job. Should such a perspective meet with resistance from managers, the best recommendation is to carry out pre- and postcampaign attitude and opinion tests and regularly monitor the image of the firm and each brand.

MEASURING THE EFFECTIVENESS OF SALESPEOPLE AND THE PERSONAL SELLING EFFORT ❹

Measuring the performance of salespeople draws directly on the objectives set for the personal selling process and sales objectives discussed in Chapter 14. There are several objective and subjective criteria upon which sales staff members can be judged.[25] Exhibit 15.18 outlines these criteria.

Objective	Subjective
1. Sales *Total dollar volume* *Total unit volume* *Percent of quota* *Dollars or units by product line* *Dollars or Units by territory* *Dollars or units by customer type*	1. Appearance
	2. Preparedness
	3. Customer relations
2. Profit (margin) generated *Total profit in dollars* *Average margin in percent* *Dollars or percent by product line* *Dollars or percent by territory* *Dollars or percent by customer type*	4. Attitude
	5. Product knowledge
	6. Team relationships
3. Orders *Number* *Size* *Returns*	
4. Sales calls executed	
5. Expenses generated	
6. Nonselling activities *Number and type of services rendered* *Display maintenance* *Follow-up*	
7. Customer satisfaction ratings	

EXHIBIT 15.18

Criteria used to measure sales force performance

25. For an extensive discussion of sales force evaluation procedures and criteria, see Gilbert A. Churchill, Jr., Neil M. Ford, Orville C. Walker, Jr., Mark W. Johnson, and John F. Tanner, *Sales Force Management,* 5th ed. (Burr Ridge, IL: Irwin Publishing, 2000), Chapter 16.

The objective criteria need to be carefully applied. For example, the total dollar volume of sales must be judged against the order size and expenses generated. A salesperson or an entire sales force might be rated highly on total dollar volume at the expense of many, repeated small orders at great cost to the firm. Also, depending on the specific objectives of the sales effort and the selling tasks involved, it may be that the nonselling tasks are critical to long-range plans even though current dollar volume sales are compromised. An important criterion in the contemporary measurement of the effectiveness of salespeople is customer satisfaction. As part of the whole process of relationship building, quantifiable customer satisfaction criteria can be of value to both management and the salesperson. Astute interpretation and application of the objective criteria are key to a useful evaluation.

The subjective criteria can be very difficult to operationalize. Being judgmental by nature, management must be willing to be flexible and allow individual styles to manifest themselves. The strength of any particular salesperson may lie in his or her unique style. Suppression of individual differences may be inefficient and demoralizing. The criteria related to team relationships is a difficult one as well. Teams often function in high-energy and high-stress situations. When people fail to cope with that stress, less than ideal performance results.

The measurement of the effectiveness of sales personnel is important for two reasons. First, salespeople need feedback on which they can base future efforts. An evaluation exercise can itself be motivational to the sales staff. The evaluation is also the basis on which management will make annual salary and bonus decisions. Second, the measurement of effectiveness of the staff is a primary source of information for an internal situation analysis. From this evaluation effort, managers can determine strengths and weaknesses in the sales staff, changes that need to be made in the nature of the selling task as it is currently conceived, and the level of corporate support needed for the sales staff.

MEASURING THE EFFECTIVENESS OF THE OVERALL IMC PROGRAM ❺

There are some basic approaches to measuring the effectiveness of the overall IMC program. One approach is to merely take on the measurement of each of the promotional tools used in a campaign, trying to measure the effectiveness of each and call it a day. This is viewed as a somewhat fragmented approach since there is no attempt to try to account for the synergies that are the hallmark of taking an IMC approach in the first place. The synergy of a coordinated, one-voice perspective in constructing the promotional mix and trying to execute the overall promotional effort in an integrated marketing communications fashion should produce synergy and an enhanced communication impact. That has been the philosophy throughout the text, and it has not changed at this point. But the limitations of measurement methodologies, which have been alluded to throughout this chapter, make that a difficult task indeed.

Consider the complexity of trying to measure the overall effect of a recent IMC campaign carried out by IBM. In September 1999, IBM launched a $30 million campaign called "Business Intelligence." The goal was to establish the company as a leader in developing solutions to gather, analyze, and manage data about a company's customers. The campaign had the following dimensions:[26]

- Print ads ran in high-profile publications including *The Wall Street Journal, USA Today, Business Week,* and *Forbes* designed to build widespread awareness.

26. Chad Kaydo, "Big Blue's Media Blitz," *Sales and Marketing Management,* December 1999, 80.

CAREERPROFILE

Name: Nicole Del Prato
Title: Program Manager
Company: J. Rice Communications, Santa Ana, CA
http://www.jricecomm.com

Nicole Del Prato says she was never exposed to the marketing role of trade shows in college. "There's a trade show for almost every type of product or service, from briefcases, to faucets, to video equipment. In four years of marketing classes, I don't recall ever receiving instruction on the importance of trade shows to a company's overall integrated marketing communications strategy, and how important it is to make sure trade show marketing is reflective of the whole communications plan." Nicole has spent most of her marketing career helping businesses achieve those goals.

Nicole is currently Program Manager at J. Rice Communications, a trade show marketing communications firm. She helps clients plan how they will communicate their marketing messages to potential customers before, during, and after a trade show. This can include exhibit and booth design, developing marketing brochures and direct-mail pieces, buying promotional items, and other marketing activities.

How is the effectiveness of these marketing communications programs measured? Before the show, questionnaires and surveys are used to benchmark the awareness of the client's target audience. Preshow mailings are sent to conference attendees to encourage them to stop by and visit a client's booth. Often, these mailings contain offers that can be redeemed at the trade show, providing a way to track their effectiveness at drawing customers. During the show, in-booth profiling questionnaires and drawings help determine visitor interest levels and planned buying activity. After the show, Nicole and her staff also conduct surveys to see how much actual buying activity has resulted from the show. "Based on the results of these measurements, we advise our clients as to which shows, programs, and communications media are producing the most value for their marketing dollar," she explains.

Nicole says trade show marketing can be exciting and challenging. Her advice if you're interested in a similar career? "Find a mentor who you can work side-by-side with to learn the ropes and get as much hands-on experience as possible."

To learn more about trade show marketing and management, visit these Web sites:

The Trade Show News Network
http://www.tsnn.com

Trade Show News
http://www.tradeshownews.com

Trade Show Jobs
http://www.tradeshowjobs.com

- Print ads were also placed in "vertical market" magazines that specifically targeted decision makers in the banking, retail, and insurance industries.
- Radio ads were run in the top ten North American markets.
- Television commercials were run during prime-time programs to also build awareness.
- Direct-mail pieces were sent to 250,000 executives in three main target industries. A week after the initial mailing, an additional 10,000 special mailers were sent to certain companies in the targeted industries that represented key "target accounts."
- Public relations initiatives included using IBM employees and local PR agencies to target analysts and industry publications.
- Banner ads were run on approximately forty Web sites, including several vertical industry sites and IT-related sites like ZDNet and CMPnet.

Whew! So how would you like to devise a measurement scheme for that campaign! This campaign targets a broad market, a narrow market, executives, IT managers, and on and on. The methodologies available pale in comparison to IMC campaigns like IBM's.

Single-Source Tracking Measures

Despite the methodological challenges, there are some recommendations on how to proceed with an evaluation of an overall IMC program like IBM's. One of these is to use single-source tracking measures, which identify the extent to which a sample of consumers has potentially been exposed to multiple promotional messages and the effect those messages have had on their behaviors. With the advent of universal product codes (UPCs) on product packages and the proliferation of cable television, research firms are now able to engage in single-source research that tracks the behavior of individuals in a respondent pool from television set to checkout counter. **Single-source tracking measures** provide information from individual households about brand purchases, coupon use, and television advertising exposure by combining grocery store scanner data and devices attached to the households' televisions (called peoplemeters), which monitor viewing behavior. These sophisticated measures are used to gauge the impact of

IN PRACTICE

JOINING FORCES TO MEASURE THE EFFECTS OF IMC PROGRAMS

The underlying thesis of IMC is that all the communication tools at a marketer's disposal can and should be used in combination to get the message across to the target segment. Direct marketing, sales promotion, event sponsorship, PR, and traditional broadcast advertising should be employed in an integrated program to reach the consumer. The hoped-for outcome is what Esther Thorson and Jeri Moore have referred to as "a synergy of persuasive voices." In combination, the various communication tools are supposed to produce an effect where the whole is greater than the sum of the individual parts. Sounds wonderful in theory, but how do we know that such synergies are actually being achieved in IMC campaigns? Can we measure the effects of all the individual parts and then quantify the synergistic effect due to them working in combination? Simply stated, we don't know, and we aren't even close to being able to validate the hoped-for synergistic effect. As represented by advertising researchers Helen Katz and Jacques Lendrevie, this is truly the search for IMC's Holy Grail.

But you have to start somewhere, and two advertising research companies have merged their evaluative know-how to begin the search. ACNielsen and IPSOs-ASI now offer a testing service they call "Market Drivers" to begin to sort out the joint effects of advertising and sales promotion. The fact that these former competitors joined forces to launch this service makes the point that the search for IMC's Holy Grail will require a new way of doing business. Market Drivers combines Nielsen's data on in-store sales with ASI's ad-testing capabilities to measure the joint effectiveness of advertising and sales promotion. The tool may be used in preparing a company's IMC plan or measuring the success of a program after it is launched. Expensive? Yes and no. The base price of $100,000 per project doesn't seem that bad if you think of it as a piece of the Holy Grail.

Sources: Helen Katz and Jacques Lendrevie, "In Search of the Holy Grail: First Steps in Measuring Total Exposures of an IMC Program," in Esther Thorson and Jeri Moore, eds., *Integrated Communication* (Mahwah, NJ: Lawrence Erlbaum Associates, 1996), Chapter 14; James B. Arndorfer, "ACNielsen Market Drivers Will Gauge Promos' Punch," *Advertising Age,* February 23, 1998, 8.

advertising and promotions on consumers' actual purchases. The main problem with these measures is that it is impossible to determine what aspects of advertising had positive effects on consumers. And while such a system is sophisticated and heavily endowed with technology, it really only focuses on television advertising and couponing—obviously not a comprehensive overview of all promotional tools. New methods are being worked on that try to integrate more forms of research in a final assessment. Some of these new approaches synthesize tracking data with mall-intercept and consumer survey research.[27] The IMC in Practice box raises additional considerations about the complications that can be anticipated in evaluating the various elements in an integrated marketing communications campaign in this manner.

Another approach is offered by industry practitioners Helen Katz and Jacques Lendrevie, who assert that "the ability to measure all communications elements is a prerequisite for an effective integrated program."[28] Katz and Lendrevie offer a measurement program that relies on a method that segments total exposures of an integrated program. Their orientation is that regardless of the promotional tools used in the promotional mix, communication will occur through media exposures, product impressions, or personal contacts:

- *Media exposure:* This component of measure includes all consumer exposures to the brand that take place through traditional media. Traditional media advertising in television, radio, newspapers, and magazines is one component. Another is all public relations and publicity that appear in mass media. A third dimension of media exposure is any sales promotion, like coupons, rebates, or special sales, announced through placement in major media (for example, free-standing inserts in the Sunday paper).

27.   Michael Hess and Robert Mayer, "Integrate Behavioral and Survey Data," *Marketing News,* January 3, 2000, 22.
28.   Helen Katz and Jacques Lendrevie, "In Search of the Holy Grail: First Steps in Measuring Total Exposures of an Integrated Communications Program," in Thorson and Moore, eds., *Integrated Communications,* 259–270.

- *Product (brand) impressions:* This component attempts to measure all target audience exposure to the brand itself.[29] Included here are in-store and in-home contact with the product. Contact with the product can also occur on the street, or while visiting friends and acquaintances, or in the workplace. Incidental exposure such as passing by a McDonald's and seeing the store sign and logo would also be included here as a product impression. Although the authors do not cite television or in-person exposure to the brand as a result of event sponsorship, it is presumed that such a major exposure would be included here as well.
- *Personal contacts:* There are a variety of personal contacts that create brand impressions. Salespeople at dealerships, conversations with friends, contact with opinion leaders, or the professional advice of a doctor, pharmacist, or hairstylist can all affect brand knowledge and awareness.

The above factors offer a good perspective on assessing the overall IMC program. Of course, in order for this evaluation program to be worthwhile, some approach to measurement of each criterion must be implemented. As discussed earlier, the methodologies for measurement are weak at best. Major media exposure is a matter of checking the media schedule for gross rating points and calculating impressions based on that figure. When it comes to measuring brand impressions and personal contacts, the authors of this model offer some tenuous and hypothetical approaches.[30]

Overall, the challenge of measuring the effectiveness of the total IMC effort is very, very difficult. As we have realized throughout the text, communication is a complex process that varies across times and places and varies from individual to individual. Testimony to the difficulty in measuring the effectiveness of the IMC effort is the almost total lack of literature devoted to the discussion.[31] This does not mean that measurement is not a good thing and should not be pursued. Rather, consider the lack of literature a signal of just how complex and fascinating the topic of integrated marketing communications is and will continue to be.

29.   We presume the authors really mean "brand" rather than "product" impressions. It does Honda or adidas little good if consumers encounter automobiles or sport shoes as a product category. The intent of the authors here would clearly seem to be that consumers encounter the "brand" in question not the broad product category.
30.   Katz and Lendrevie, 266–268.
31.   While there is extensive literature on measuring the effectiveness of *individual* elements of the promotional mix, aside from the Katz and Lendrevie article discussed, the author was only able to locate *one* other article that focuses exclusively on the measurement issue. See Allan L. Baldinger, "Integrated Communication and Measurement: The Case for Multiple Measures," in Thorson and Moore, eds., *Integrated Communications,* 271–283.

SUMMARY

1 Discuss the issues related to the measurement of effectiveness of promotion and IMC.

There are issues that need to be considered when exploring the issue of measuring the effectiveness of promotion and IMC:

a. The difference between marketing research and promotion research.

b. Judging research for reliability, validity, trustworthiness and meaningfulness.

c. Recognizing the differences between account planning and measuring effectiveness

d. Assessing the fundamental issues in measurement:
  - motives and expectations
  - basic dimensions of message assessment: imparting knowledge, shaping attitudes, attaching feelings and emotions, legitimizing the brand.

2 Describe the complex and elaborate methods used to measure the effectiveness of advertising.

Advertising is subjected to more measurement than other promotional tools because of its conspicuousness and the expense involved in preparing advertising materials. There are three basic ways in which advertising is measured for effectiveness:

a. Measures, which attempt to measure the effectiveness of advertising before it runs in the marketplace, include communications tests, magazine dummies, theater tests, thought listings, attitude change studies, and physiological measures.

b. Marketplace pilot testing tests advertising effectiveness in real market conditions by using split-cable transmission for television ads, split-run distribution for print ads, and split-list distribution for direct-mail advertising. Pilot testing of radio advertising is not a common practice.

c. Posttesting occurs after a campaign is running. The measurement devices are recall testing, recognition testing, and awareness and attitude tracking.

3 Describe the ways in which Internet advertising, direct marketing and e-commerce, sponsorships, point of purchase, public relations, and corporate advertising are judged for effectiveness.

Each of these tools of promotion is tested in different ways. Internet advertising is judged primarily on the visits to Web sites and hits on banner ads. New methods are being developed so that Internet advertising can be judged on unique visitors and impressions formed. Direct marketing and e-commerce are in many ways the easiest promotional tools to measure because sales is the primary intention for these forms of promotion. Aside from sales per se, the number of inquiries is another measurement criterion that can be used. Sponsorships can be measured by the number of people attending an event or the number of viewers of a televised event sponsored by the firm. Point-of-purchase promotion is also judged primarily by changes in sales. Public relations and corporate advertising are the most difficult tools to judge because their intended effects are subtle and long-term in nature. A firm can "count" the media mentions it gets as a basis for judging public relations.

4 Discuss the procedures used by sales managers in evaluating salespeople and judging the effectiveness of the personal selling effort.

Measuring the performance of salespeople draws directly on the objectives set for the personal selling process and sales objectives discussed in Chapter 14. There are several objective and subjective criteria on which sales staff members can be judged. The objective criteria have to do with quantifiable aspects of the sales force performance and include measurement variables like sales, sales per product line, sales per territory, profitability, and the like. Subjective criteria have to do more with the way a salesperson manages time and account relationships.

5 Comment on the task of judging the effectiveness of the overall IMC effort.

There are some basic approaches to measuring the effectiveness of the overall IMC program. One approach is to merely take on the measurement of each of the promotional tools used in a campaign, try to measure the effectiveness of each and call it day. This is viewed as a somewhat fragmented approach since there is no attempt to try to account for the synergies that are the hallmark of taking an IMC approach in the first place. Another approach is to use single-source tracking measures, which identify the extent to which a sample of consumers has potentially been exposed to multiple promotional messages. A third alternative has been proposed by practitioners which suggests measuring media exposures, product (brand) impressions, and personal contacts as a basis for determining the overall effect of an IMC program.

In the end, we need to realize that measuring the complex interaction of all the promotional mix elements is very, very complicated and may be beyond the methodological tools available at this time.

KEY TERMS

marketing research, 516
promotion research, 516
reliability, 516
validity, 516
trustworthiness, 516
meaningfulness, 516
account planning, 516
naturalistic inquiry, 517
normative test scores, 517
resonance test, 519
communications test, 520
dummy advertising vehicles, 520

theater test, 520
thought listing, 521
attitude-change study, 521
physiological measures, 522
eye-tracking systems, 522
psychogalvanometer, 522
voice response analysis, 522
pilot testing, 523
split-cable transmission, 523
split-run distribution, 523
split-list experiment, 523
posttest message tracking, 525

recall test, 525
aided recall, 526
hits, 530
click-through, 530
pages or page views, 531
visits, 531
users, 531
log analysis software, 531
caching, 534
inquiry/direct response measures, 535
ballot method, 536
single-source tracking measures, 542

QUESTIONS FOR REVIEW AND CRITICAL THINKING

1. Identify issues that could become sources of conflict between brand managers and promotion agency personnel in the message-pretesting process. What could go wrong if people in an agency take the position that what the client wants, the client gets?

2. Explain the key distinction between pretesting and pilot testing. What is it about direct-mail promotion that makes it so amenable to pilot testing? Do you think the ease of pilot testing has anything to do with the growing popularity of direct mail as a promotion option?

3. Attitude-change research is another versatile tool for message testing. Identify the key differences that distinguish an attitude-change study being conducted for pretesting purposes from an attitude-change study being conducted for posttesting purposes.

4. How would you explain the finding that ads that achieve high recall scores don't always turn out to do a good job in generating sales? Are there some features of ads that make them memorable but could also turn off consumers and dissuade them from buying the brand? Give an example from your experience.

5. How do marketers go about testing the effectiveness of sponsorship programs?

6. Identify and explain the different factors used to measure Internet advertising. What do these factors measure? Is it effectiveness?

7. If you were a marketing manager, would you insist that your organization measure the effectiveness of the firm's public relations and corporate advertising programs? Why or why not?

8. Discuss the methods that have been proposed for measuring the overall effectiveness of an IMC program. Do you think these are sufficient and would produce an accurate measure of the impact of an IMC program?

EXPERIENTIAL EXERCISES

1. **In-class exercise.** Describe a promotion that you believe truly affected your attitude toward a brand and ultimately your purchase behavior. Find out if anyone else in the class was affected the same way.

2. **Out-of-class exercise.** In this chapter, you learned about research methods that help managers avoid costly mistakes. Find an example of a print ad or describe a direct-mail piece you feel is truly awful. Explain your objections. Now imagine that you have the opportunity to conduct research before the ad actually runs. What type or types of research would you recommend that management conduct? Explain your recommendations and how the research might have changed the ad you selected.

USING THE INTERNET

Exercise 1

In the summer of 2000, a company called Digital Convergence launched the :CueCat, a device to let consumers scan bar codes in print ads and be whisked directly to advertisers' Web sites. The pitch to the end consumer is that the :CueCat simplifies the tedious process of remembering and typing long Web URLs, though obviously the reader also needs to have his or her computer nearby. The benefits to the advertiser are intended to include a lot more feedback on the consumers and their interest: Each :CueCat device has a unique number, so that dossiers can be compiled on their owners.

1. :CueCats were given out through a variety of means, for example, distributed free in Radio Shacks, or bundled with copies of *Forbes* magazine sent to subscribers. It wouldn't be possible to record who got each one, or to be sure one wasn't passed along to a friend. How can Digital Convergence best figure out the identity of a given :CueCat owner?

2. How might the :CueCat help you, as an advertiser in *Forbes,* better understand your advertising audience?

3. What privacy issues might the :CueCat raise, and how might consumer concerns be addressed?

Exercise 2

The Magellan Web search service (http://www.mckinley.com) offers "Search Voyeur," a snapshot of queries that other visitors to the site are performing (with some censoring of certain offensive terms).

Select the link to the Voyeur feature, and watch some of the queries being submitted—the list is refreshed every fifteen seconds.

1. What does such a random sampling suggest about what other people are using the Web for?

2. How often do you see typographical errors, or poor search terms?

3. How might search services turn all the transactions they process into a new revenue stream?

4. What limits or concerns might be inherent in such reuse of transactional data?

WEB SITE ADDRESSES

Abbot Wool's Market Segment Resource
http://www.awool.com/awool

About.com Public Relations Page
http://www.publicrelations.about.com

About.com
http://www.urbanlegends.about.com/science/urbanlegends

Acumin Corporation
http://www.acumins.com

Addis Group
http://www.addis.com

AdSubtract
http://www.adsubtract.com

Advertising Age
http://www.adage.com

Advertising Agencies
http://www.americanadagencies.com

The Advertising Media Internet Center
http://www.amic.com

Adweek Online
http://www.adweek.com

AirClic
http://www.airclic.com

All Advantage
http://alladvantage.com

Allstate Insurance
http://www.allstate.com

Alta Vista
http://www.altavista.com

Amazon.com
http://www.amzon.com

American Advertising Federation
http://www.aaf.org

American Association of Advertising Agencies
http://www.aaaa.org

American Demographics **magazine**
http://www.demographics.com

American Demographics
http://www.marketingtools.com

American Express
http://www.americanexpress.com

American Marketing Association Career Center
http://www.ama.org/jobs

Ameritrade
http://www.ameritrade.com

Anderson Travel & Cruises
http://www.andersontravel.com

AOL
http://www.aol.com

Apple
http://www.apple.com

Arent Fox Advertising Law Research Center
http://www.arentfox.com/quickGuide/businesslines/advert/advertisingLaw/advertisinglaw.html

Ariba
http://www.ariba.com

Arthur Andersen
http://www.arthurandersen.com

AskJeeves
http://www.askjeeves.com

The Association of Travel Marketing Executives
http://www.atme.org

AT&T
http://www.att.net/wns/maxim

Auto Wraps
http://www.autowraps.com

Avandia
http://www.avandia.com

Babelfish
http://www.babelfish.altavista.com

Better Business Bureau
http://www.bbbonline.org/business/code

BigYellow
http://www.bigyellow.com/

Blue Mountain
http://www.bluemountain.com

Blue Nile
http://www.bluenile.com

BMW
http://www.bmw.com

BOSE
http://www.bose.com/t3584

Bplans.com
http://www.bplans.com/marketing.htm

BrightStreet
http://www.brightstreet.com

Budweiser
http://www.budweiser.com

Burst! Media
http://www.burstmedia.com

Business Wire
http://www.businesswire.com

BuzzSaw
http://www.buzzsaw.com

Calico Commerce
http://www.calico.com

CardoNet
http://www.cardonet.com

Cartoon Network
http://www.cartoonnetwork.com

Celarix
http://www.celarix.com

Cellular Telecommunication Industry Association
http://www.wow-com.com

The Center for Media & Democracy
http://www.prwatch.org

Center for Media Education
http://www.cme.org

Cesare Catini
http://www.cesarecatini.com

Channel Seven.com
http://www.channelseven.com

Chemdex
http://www.chemdex.com

The Cincinnati Enquirer
http://www.cincinnati.com/
technology/

Citibank
http://www.citibank.com/us/cards/

Citysearch.com
http://national.sidewalk.msn.com

Clinique
http://www.clinique.com

CNET Computers.com
http://www.computers.com

CNET
http://www. cnet.com

Coalition Against Unsolicited Commercial Email
http://www.cauce.org

Coming2America.com
http://www.coming2america.com

CommerceOne
http://www.commerceone.com

Community Hospitals Indianapolis
http://www.ehealthindiana.com

comScore
http://www.comscore.com

Consumer Reports
http://www.consumerreports.com

Converse
http://www.converse.com

Cosmo (Hispanic/Latin America)
http://www.cosmohispano.com

Cosmo (Russian-language readers)
http://www.cosmopolitan.ru

Cosmo (US)
http://www.cosmo.women.com/cos/

Council of Public Realations Firms
http://www.prfirms.org

Coupons.com
http://www.coupons.com)

Crackerjack
http://www.crackerjack.com

Craighead.com
http://www.craighead.com

Crayola
http://www.crayola.com

Creative
http://www.creativmag.com

CyberShop
http://www.cybershop.com

CyberSource
http://www.cybersource.com

Database America
http://www.donnelleymarketing.com

Database Marketing Institute
http://www.dbmarketing.com

DataCore Marketing, Inc
http://www.datacoremarketing.com

DataSage
http://www.datasage.com

Datek Online
http://www.datek.com

Dell
http://www.dell.com

Diamond Information Center
http://www.adiamondisforever.com

Digimarc
http://www.digimarc.com

Digital Island
http://www.digitalisland.com

Direct Marketing Association
http://www.the-dma.org

Direct Media
http://www.directmedia.com

Discovery Communications
http://www.discovery.com

Disney
http://www.disney.com

DM Group
http://www.dm1.com

DN Resources
http://www.dnresources.com

Dogpile
http://www.dogpile.com

Double Click
http://www.doubleclick.com

Drugstore.com
http://www.drugstore.com

Dunkin donuts
http://www.dunkindonuts.com

E.piphany
http://www.epiphany.com

eBay
http://www.ebay.com/

e-Centives
http://www.ecentives.com

eCredit.com
http://www.ecredit.com

Edmund's Automobile Buyer's Guides
http://www.edmund.com

EE-link
http://www.eelink.com

Electric Artists
http://www.alloy.com
http://www.gurl.com

Electronic Privacy Information Center (EPIC)
http://www.epic.org

Embassy.org
http://www.embassy.org

Engage Media
http://www.engage.com/engagemedia

Entrepreneur
http://www.entrepreneurmag.com

Envirolink Network
http://www.envirolink.com

e-Satisfy
http://www.e-satisfy.com

eSkye.com
http://www.eskye.com

E-Stamp
http://www.e-stamp.com

E*Trade
http://www.etrade.com

European Association of Advertising Agencies
http://www.eaaa.be

European Union in the U.S.
http://www.eurunion.org

Exactis.com
http://www.exactis.com

Excite
http://www.excite.com

Experian
http://www.experian.com

Fashionmall.com
http://www.fashionmall.com

Federal Trade Commission
http://www.ftc.gov/

Fiorucci
http://www.fioruccisafetyjeans.com

FirePond
http://www.firepond.com

Flooz
http://www.flooz.com

Frankfurt Balkind
http://www.frankfurtbalkind.com

Free Car
http://www.freecar.com

FreeMerchant.com
http://www.freemerchant.com

Frontier Media Group
http://www.frontiermedia.com

FTD.com
http://www.ftd.com

Gaiam.com
http://www.gaiam.com

The Gap
http://www.gap.com/

Gateway
http://www.gateway.com

General Motors' Cadillac Division
http://www.cadillac.com/catera/index.htm

GeoCities
http://www.geocities.com

Glad
http://www.glad.com

Global System for Mobile Communicatons
http://www.gsm-pcs.org/

The Globe.com
http://www.theglobe.com

GMbuy.com
http://www.gmbuy.com

Google
http://www.google.com

GovCon
http://www.govcon.com

GreenMarketplace.com
http://www.greenmarketplace.com

Guerilla Marketing
http://www.gmarketing.com

Guess
http://www.guess.com

Hard Candy
http://www.hardcandy.com

Harvard
http://ksg.harvard.edu/project6/

HavenCo
http://www.havenco.com

Heineken
http://www.heineken.com

Home Director, Inc.
http://www.homedirector.com

HotBot
http://www.hotbot.com

HotMail
http://www.hotmail.com

IBM
http://www.ibm.com

infoUSA
http://www.directoriesUSA.com

Instinet
http://www.instinet.com

Insurance needs
http://www.insuremarket.com

The Institute of Public Relations
http://www.ipr.org.uk

Intel
http://www.intel.com

Inter-Continental Hotels and Resorts
http://www.interconti.com

International Advertising Association
http://www.iaaglobal.org

International Association of Conference Centers
http://www.ises.com

International Trade Administration
http://www.ita.doc.gov

Internet Advertising Bureau
http://www.iab.net

Internet Advertising Resource
http://www.admedia.org

Internet Wire
http://www.internetwire.com

Isuzu
www.isuzu.com

iWon
http://www.iWon.com

iwon.com
http://www.iwon.com

J. Rice Communications
http://www.jricecomm.com

J. Walter Thompson
http://www.jwtworld.com

JCPenney
http://www.jcpenney.com

Jeep
http://www.jeepunpaved.com

Jerusalem Post
http://www.virtualjerusalem.com

Jostens
http://www.jostens.com

Junkbusters
http://www.junkbusters.com

Kmart
http://www.bluelight.com
http://www.kmart.com

Know This-Marketing Careers
http://www.knowthis.com/careers/careersmkt.htm

KnowledgeBaseMarketing
http://www.ira-ondemand.com

Kozmo
http://www.kozmo.com

Lancôme
http://www.lancome.com

Latina
http://www.latina.com

Latino.com
http://www.latino.com

Leo Burnett
http://www.leoburnett.com

Libertel
http://www.libertel.com

Link Exchange
http://www.linkexchange.com

L-Soft International
http://www.lsoft.com

Luckysurf.com
http://www.luckysurf.com

Magellan
http://www.mckinley.com

Magnet Interactive
http://www.magnetinteractive.com

Mamma
http://www.mamma.com

Manugistics
http://www.manugistics.com

Marketing Communications
http://www.amci.co.il

Marketing
http://www.imarketing.com

Massive Media Group
http://www.massivemediagroup.com

McSpotlight
http://www.mcspotlight.org

Media Metrix
http://wwwmediametrix.com

Meeting Professionals International
http://www.mpiweb.org

Mentos
http://www.mentos.com

Message Media
http://www.messagemedia.com

MetroWest's Virtual Mall
http://www.virtmall.com

Modem Media.Poppe Tyson
http://www.poppe.com

Mother Against Drunk Driving
http://www.madd.org

Mountain Dew
http://www.mountaindew.com

MTV
http://www.mtv.com

National Association of Sales Professionals
http://www.nasp.com

Nature Conservancy
http://www.tnc.org

NBA
http://www.nba.com

NetGrocer
http://www.netgrocer.com

Network Solutions
http://www.networksolutions.com

New Jersey Devils
http://www.newjerseydevils.com

NextCard
http://www.nextcard.com

Nick.com
http://www.nick.com

Nielsen
http://www.nielsen-netratings.com

Noven Pharmaceuticals
http://www.noven.com

Ogilvy & Mather
http://www.ogilvy.com

Other World Bank
http://www.worldbank.org

Peapod.com
http://www.peapod.com

Pepsi
http://www.pepsi.com

Perdue Office
http://www.perdueoffice.com

Personify
http://www.personify.com

Petopia
http://www.Petopia.com

PetsMart
http://www.pets.com

Platform.net
http://www.platform.net/

Point of Purchase Advertising Institute
http://www.popai.org

PR Newswire
http://www.prnewswire.com

Procter & Gamble
http://www.pg.com

Promo
http://www.promomagazine.com

Promotional Products Association
http://www.promotion-clinic.ppa.org

Promotions.com
http://www.promotions.com

Proxicom
http://www.proxicom.com

Public Relations Society of America
http://www.prsa.org

QVC, Inc.
http://www.iqvc.com

Qfactor.com
http://www.qfactor.com

Qualcomm's Eudora
http://www.eudora.com

Ragu
http://www.eat.com

Real Media
http://www.realmedia.com

RealNames
http://www.realnames.com

Red Sky Interactive
http://www.redsky.com

Reebok International
http://www.reebok.com

Reel.com
http://www.reel.com

Register.com
http://www.register.com

Requisite Technology
http://www.requisite.com

Rhino Records
http://www.rhino.com

Russian Tea Room
http://www.russiantearoom.com

Sales Promotion
http://www.sp-mag.com

Sales Staffers International, Inc.
http://www.salesstaffers.com

Salesforce.com
http://www.salesforce.com

SalesGuy.com
http://www.salesguy.com

The Sales Vault
http://www.salesvault.com

Save.com
http://www.save.com

SC Johnson
http://www.scjohnson.com

Scan.com
http://www.scan.com

Screaming Media
http://www.screamingmedia.com

Selectrica
http://www.selectrica.com

Seventeen
http://www.seventeen.com

Silicon Valley Small Business Dev. Ctr
http://www.siliconvalley-sbdc.org

The Society for Consumer Psychology
http://www.consumerpsych.org

Special Events
http://www.specialevents.com

Sprint
http://www.sprint.com/college

Stamps.com
http://www.Stamps.com

Starbelly.com
http://www.starbelly.com

Streamline.com
http://www.streamline.com

Superpages.com
http://www.bigyellow.com

SwitchboardInc.
http://www.switchboard.com

Taxes
http://taxes.Yahoo.com

Technology and International Mktg. Comm.
http://www.atalink.co.uk/iaa2000/

Terra
http://www.terra.com

The Trade Show News Network
http://www.tsnn.com

Thermador
http://www.thermador.com

Toshiba
http://www.toshiba.com

TouchScape
http://www.touchscape.com

Trade Show Jobs
http://www.tradeshowjobs.com

Trade Show News
http://www.tradeshownews.com

TradingDynamics
http://www.tradingdynamics.com

Travel and Tourism Research Association
http://www.ttra.com

Travelocity.com
http://www.travelocity.com/

Tripod
http://www.tripod.com

TRUSTe
http://www.truste.org

TUMI
http://www.tumi.com

Tupperware
http://www.tupperware.com

U.S Marine Corps.
http://www.usmc.mil

United Nations
http://www.un.org

University of Texas Advertising Dept.
http://advertising.utexas.edu/world/Target.htm#Top

Urban Decay
http://www.urbandecay.com

USCreative.com
http://www.uscreative.com

Valassis Communications
http://www.valassis.com

Verbind
http://www.verbind.com

VerticalNet
http://www.verticalnet.com

Vignette
http://www.vignette.com

Vital Learning
http://vital-learning.com

The Wall Street Journal Career Journal
http://www.careerjournal.com

WebVan
http://www.webvan.com

Wilkinson
http://www.wilkinson-sword.com

Worldata
http://www.worldata.com

The X-Files
http://www.thex-files.com

Yahoo!
http://www.yahoo.com

Yahoo! Finance
http://finance.yahoo.com

Yellow Pages
http://www.bigyellow.com

Yokohama
http://www.yokohamatire.com

Zap Me
http://www.zapme.com

Zona Financiera
http://www.zonafinanciera.com

GLOSSARY

A

account planner A relatively recent addition to many advertising agencies; it is this person's job to synthesize all relevant consumer research and use it to design a coherent advertising strategy.

account planning In contrast to traditional promotional research, a system in which an "account planner" is assigned to work as coequal with the account executive on a client's business.

account services Group that identifies the benefits a brand offers, its target audiences, and the best competitive positioning, and then develops a complete promotion plan.

advertisement A specific message that an organization has placed to persuade an audience.

advertising agency An organization of professionals who provide creative and business services to clients related to planning, preparing, and placing advertisements.

advertising campaign A series of coordinated advertisements and other promotional efforts that communicate a single theme or idea.

advertising specialties Items used in advertising that have three key elements: a message, placement on a useful item, and as a gift to consumers with no obligation.

advertising substantiation program A 1971 program initiated by the FTC to ensure that advertisers make available to consumers supporting evidence for claims made.

advertising A paid, mass-mediated attempt to persuade.

advertorial A special advertising section designed to look like the print publications in which it appears.

advocacy advertising An attempt to establish an organization's position on important social, political, or environmental issues to influence public opinion on issues of concern to the sponsor.

aerial advertising Advertising that involves airplanes (pulling signs or banners), skywriting, or blimps.

affirmative disclosure An FTC action requiring that important material determined to be absent from prior ads must by included in subsequent advertisements.

agency of record The advertising agency chosen by the advertiser to purchase media time and space.

aided recall In advertising research, a technique of prompting consumers to remember an ad.

appropriation The use of pictures or images owned by someone else without permission.

aspirational groups Groups made up of people an individual admires or uses as role models but is unlikely to ever interact with in any meaningful way.

assorted media mix Multiple media alternatives combined to reach target audiences.

attention-interest-desire-action (AIDA) A method of sales in which the salesperson gains the buyer's Attention, encourages the buyer's Interest by touting product or service attributes, stimulates the buyer's Desire by showing how the firm's offering fulfills the buyer's needs, and creates an Action on the part of the buyer.

attitude An overall evaluation of any object, person, or issue that varies along a continuum, such as favorable to unfavorable or positive to negative.

attitude-change study A type of research that uses a before-and-after ad to determine consumers' feelings about a product or service based on exposure to a test ad and dummy ads.

audience duplication Enhancing the learning effect by placing the same message in different media reaching a single target audience.

audience A group of individuals who receive and interpret messages sent from advertisers through mass media.

average-user testimonial An advertisement that uses an ordinary person to convince consumers to purchase something, based on the theory that the average user will be similar to the consumer.

B

back-end networks The fulfillment operations of e-commerce.

bait-and-switch The practice of offering to sell an advertised product at an attractive price and then "switching" the consumer to a higher-priced item under the guise that the advertised item is sold out or unavailable.

ballot method A strategy of mailing target consumers a list of promotional options and asking them to rank their preferences and mail the ballot back to the firm.

banner ads An advertisement placed on World Wide Web sites that contain editorial material.

beliefs The knowledge and feelings a person has accumulated about an object or issue.

benefit positioning A positioning option that features a distinctive customer benefit.

benefit segmentation A type of market segmenting in which target segments are delineated by the various benefit packages that different consumers want from the same product category.

between-vehicle duplication Exposure to the same advertisement in different media.

bill-back allowances A form of trade incentive in which retailers are given money for featuring a marketer's brand in either advertising or in-store displays.

bind-in insert cards Postcard-size inserts in magazines that give readers the chance to subscribe to the magazine or order merchandise or get a free sample.

brand attitudes Summary evaluations that reflect preferences for various products and brands.

brand awareness An indicator of a consumer knowledge about the existence of the brand and how easily that knowledge can be retrieved from memory.

brand communities Groups of consumers who feel a commonality and a shared purpose grounded or attached to a consumer good or service.

brand equity The creation and maintenance of positive associations with a brand in the minds of consumers.

brand extension An adaptation of an existing brand to a new product area.

brand image The perception of a brand in the mind of consumers.

brand loyalty A decision-making mode in which consumers repeatedly buy the same brand of a product as their choice to fulfill a specific need.

brand placement The sales promotion technique of getting a market's brand featured in movies and television shows.

brand switching An advertising objective in which a campaign is designed to encourage customers to switch from their established brand.

branding The strategy of developing brand names so that manufacturers can focus consumer attention on a clearly identified item.

brand-loyal users A market segment made up of consumers who repeatedly buy the same brand of a product.

bribery The act of providing financial or other incentives in return for favorable treatment.

business markets The institutional buyers who purchase items to be used in other products and services or to be resold to other businesses or households.

buying center A purchasing concept in which one group may make the specifications, but several different people are involved in the buying decision.

C

caching An active memory in Web and computer technology.

canned presentation A sales method in which a salesperson recites, nearly verbatim, a prepared sales pitch; used to ensure that important selling points are always covered.

cause-related advertising An approach that features a firm's affiliation with an important social cause—reducing poverty, increasing literacy, and curbing drug abuse are examples.

cease-and-desist order An FTC action requiring an advertiser to stop running an ad within thirty days so a hearing can be held to determine whether the advertising in question is deceptive or unfair.

celebrity endorsements Advertisements that use an expert or celebrity as a spokesperson to endorse the use of a product or service.

celebrity testimonial An advertisement that uses a famous person to increase an ad's ability to attract attention and produce a desire in receivers to emulate or imitate the celebrity by purchasing the product.

channel length The number of levels of distribution a product passes through before it reaches the end user.

click-through The process of going from one Web site to another via links.

client or sponsor The company or organization that pays for advertising.

cognitive consistency impetus A mental state where a consumer is satisfied with an attitude and belief structure and the outcomes that produced them.

cognitive dissonance The anxiety or regret that lingers after a difficult decision.

collection search engine A mechanism that allows the user to search for information on the Web that was gathered by "spiders."

commission system A method of agency compensation based on the amount of money the advertiser spends on the media.

communication The concept of sending a message to a receiver.

communications test A measure of whether a message is imparting something close to what is desired.

community A group of people loosely joined by some common characteristic or interest.

comparison advertisements Advertisements in which an advertiser makes a comparison between the firm's brand and a competitor's brands.

competitive field The companies that compete for a segment's business.

competitive positioning A positioning option that uses an explicit reference to an existing competitor to help define precisely what the advertised brand can do.

competitive-parity approach An approach to establishing a budget for the personal selling effort in which a firm sets its budget relative to what other firms in the industry are doing.

concentrated media mix A media mix option that will be used to effectively reach the target audience.

concept search engine A mechanism that allows the user to search the Web for information using ideas rather than words or phrases as the basis for the search.

consent order An FTC action asking an advertiser accused of running deceptive or unfair advertising to stop running the advertisement in question, without admitting guilt.

conservative decision style A decision style characterized by an effort on the part of the buyer to minimize the risk in a purchase.

consideration set The subset of brands from a particular product category that becomes the focal point of a consumer's evaluation.

consultants A contracted group or individual who brings specialized expertise to the promotional process in a promotion.

consultive selling Face-to-face sales presentations used by the sales force to create significant value for customers by helping them define their problems and design unique solutions.

consumer behavior Those activities directly involved in obtaining, consuming, and disposing of products and services, including the decision processes that precede and follow these actions.

consumer markets The markets for products and services purchased by individuals or households to satisfy their specific needs.

consumer sales promotions Specialty promotions such as price-off deals, coupons, sampling, rebates, and premiums aimed at consumers.

consumerism The actions of individual consumers or groups of consumers designed to exert power in the marketplace.

contest A sales promotion that has consumers compete for prizes based on skill or ability.

continuity The pattern of placement of advertisements in a media schedule.

continuous scheduling A pattern of placing ads at a steady rate over a period of time.

convenience goods Frequently purchased, simple items characterized by brand switching.

cooperative (co-op) advertising The sharing of advertising expenses between national advertisers and local merchants.

corporate home page A site on the World Wide Web that focuses on a corporation and its products.

corrective advertising An FTC action requiring an advertiser to run additional advertisements to dispel false beliefs created by deceptive advertising.

cost per inquiry (CPI) The number of inquiries generated by a direct-marketing program divided by that program's cost.

cost per order (CPO) The number of orders generated by a direct-marketing program divided by its cost.

cost per rating point (CPRP) The cost of a spot on television divided by the program's rating; the resulting dollar figure can be used to compare the efficiency of advertising on various programs.

cost per thousand (CPM) The dollar cost of reaching 1,000 members of an audience using a particular medium.

cost per thousand–target market (CPM–TM) The cost per thousand for a particular segment of an audience.

coupon A type of sales promotion that entitles a buyer to a designated reduction in price for a product or service.

creative boutique An advertising agency that emphasizes copywriting and artistic services to its clients.

creative selling A type of selling where customers rely heavily on the salesperson for technical information, advice, and service.

creative services Group that devises the concepts that express the value of a company's brand in interesting and memorable ways.

cross-selling Identifying customers who already purchase some of a firm's products and creating promotional programs aimed at these customers but featuring other brands in the firm's product line.

cultural values Enduring beliefs about what is important to the members of a culture.

culture The total life ways of a people, the social legacy the individual acquires from his or her group.

customer relationship management (CRM) or CRM selling The salesperson's crucial role of building long-term relationships with customers.

customer satisfaction Good feelings that come from a favorable postpurchase experience.

customized (localized) campaign Campaigns created specifically for a particular market.

D

database agency An agency that provides a variety of direct-marketing services.

database marketing An approach in which marketers work with a database to target specific customers, track their actual purchase behavior over time, and experiment with different programs affect the purchasing patterns of these customers.

decision styles The approaches that business buyers typically take in going about the decision-making process.

defamation When a communication occurs that damages the reputation of an individual because the information in the communication is untrue.

demographic segmentation Market segmenting based on basic descriptors like age, gender, race, marital status, income, education, and occupation.

designers Those who help a firm create a logo.

detail salesperson One who introduces new products and provides detailed product information to potential buyers without attempting to make a sale per se.

direct mail A direct-marketing medium that involves using the postal service to deliver marketing materials.

direct marketing According to the Direct Marketing Association, "An interactive system of marketing which uses one or more advertising media to effect a measurable response and/or transaction at any location."

direct-marketing agency Same as database agency.

direct-response agency Another name for direct-marketing agency.

domain name The unique URL through which a Web location is established.

door-to-door sampling A type of sampling in which samples are brought directly to the homes of a target segment in a well-defined geographic area.

dummy advertising vehicles Mock-ups of magazines that contain editorial content and advertisements, as a real magazine would; distributed to consumers for testing purposes.

duplication of exposure The counting of an individual more than once in a message weight calculation.

E

e-commerce Business conducted between buyers and sellers using electronic exchange media.

e-commerce agency Company that handles a variety of planning and execution activities related to promotions using electronic commerce.

economies of scale The ability of a firm to lower the cost of each item produced because of high-volume production.

effective frequency The number of times a target audience needs to be exposed to a message before the objectives of the advertiser are met.

effective reach The number or percentage of consumers in the target audience that are exposed to an ad some minimum number of times.

effects Receivers' perception of message content, behavioral predisposition toward the product, and the amount and type of behavior actually stimulated by a communication.

electronic mail (e-mail) An Internet function that allows users to communicate electronically much as they do using standard mail.

emergent consumers A market segment made up of the gradual but constant influx of first-time buyers.

emotional benefits Those benefits not typically found in some tangible feature or objective characteristic of a product or service.

end-use segmentation Segmenting the market based on the final use or application of a product.

ethics Moral standards and principles against which behavior is judged.

ethnocentrism The tendency to view and value things from the perspective of one's own culture.

ethnographic research Depth interviewing and extended interaction with consumers in natural settings, intended to help marketers understand a culture's customs and rituals.

evaluative criteria The product attributes or performance characteristics on which consumers base their product evaluations.

event planning agency Company that specializes in finding locations, securing dates, and putting together a team of people to create a promotional event.

exclusive distribution Highly restricted placement of a product, typically requiring advertising to inform customers where it can be purchased.

executive summary A document that expresses the most important aspects of a promotion plan in brief, typically from two paragraphs to two pages in length.

expatriate An employee working in a country other than his or her home country.

expert spokespersons Doctors, lawyers, scientists, or other professionals who give an advertisement more weight through their standing as knowledgeable professionals.

extended problem solving A decision-making mode in which consumers are inexperienced in a particular consumption setting but find the setting highly involving.

external facilitators Organizations or individuals that provides specialized services to advertisers and agencies.

external information search A search for product information that involves visiting retail stores to examine alternatives, seeking input from friends and relatives about their experiences with the products in question, or perusing professional product evaluations.

external lists Mailing lists purchased from a list compiler or rented from a list broker and used to help an organization cultivate new business.

external position The competitive niche a brand pursues.

external situation analysis A technique of identifying trends in the sales industry, technological advances in product categories, economic conditions that may be affecting the firm's customers, competitors' activities, and choice criteria being emphasized by buyers.

eye-tracking systems Techniques that monitor eye movements across print ads to determine consumer attitudes.

F

fee system A method of agency compensation whereby the advertiser and the agency agree on an hourly rate for different services provided.

feedback In mass communication, information about the receivers of a message, its perceived content, reactions to it, and behavior stimulated by exposure to it.

flighting A media-scheduling pattern of heavy advertising for a period of time, usually two weeks, followed by no advertising for a period, followed by another period of heavy advertising.

free premium A sales promotion that provides consumers with an item at no cost; the item is either included in the package of a purchased item or mailed to the consumer after proof of purchase is verified.

free-enterprise economy An economy in which competition between organizations is fostered and encouraged.

frequency (continuity) programs A type of sales promotions that offers consumers discounts or free product rewards for repeat purchase or patronage of the same brand or company.

frequency The average number of times an individual or household within a target audience is exposed to a media vehicle in a given period.

frequency-marketing programs Direct-marketing programs that provide concrete rewards to frequent customers.

fulfillment centers Units within direct-marketing agencies that ensure customers will receive a product ordered through direct mail.

fulfillment In e-commerce, the process of delivering an ordered good or service.

full-service agency An advertising agency that typically includes an array of advertising professionals to meet all promotional needs of clients.

functional benefits Those benefits that come from the objective performance characteristics of a product or service.

funds available Also known as the "all-you-can-afford" approach, a strategy in which a promotional budget is restricted to the amount allocated for it.

G

gender The social expression of sexual biology or choice.

geodemographic segmentation A form of market segmentation that identifies neighborhoods (by zip codes) around the country that share common demographic characteristics.

geographic segmentation Marketing conducted that is within a country by region.

geotargeting The placement of ads in geographic regions where higher purchase tendencies for a brand are evident.

global agencies Advertising agencies with a worldwide presence.

globalized advertising Developing and placing advertisements with a common theme and presentation in all markets around the world where the firm's brands are sold.

government officials and employees One of the five types of audiences for advertising; includes employees of government organizations, such as schools and road maintenance operations, at the federal, state, and local levels.

gross impressions The sum of exposures to all the media placement in a media plan.

gross rating points (GRP) The product of reach times frequency.

H

habit A decision-making mode in which consumers buy a single brand repeatedly as a solution to a simple consumption problem.

heavy users Consumers who purchase one product or service much more frequently than they do others.

heavy-up scheduling Placing advertising in media more heavily when consumers show buying tendencies.

hierarchical search engine A mechanism that arranges information on the World Wide Web by subject and allows the user to search for it that way.

highly industrialized countries Countries with both a high GNP and a high standard of living.

hits The number of elements requested from a given Web page; considered an unreliable measure of actual Web traffic.

horizontal market segmentation The process of identifying potential customers across industries.

household consumers The most conspicuous of the five types of audiences for advertising; most mass media advertising is directed at them.

I

importance weights Indicators of the priority that a particular evaluative criterion receives in the consumer's decision-making process.

industry analysis In an advertising plan, the section that focuses on developments and trends within an industry and on any other factors that may make a difference in how an advertiser proceeds with an advertising plan.

inelasticity of demand Strong loyalty to a product, resulting in consumers being less sensitive to price increases.

infomercial A long advertisement that looks like a talk show or a half-hour product demonstration.

information intermediators A form of external facilitator that collects customer purchase transaction histories, aggregates them across many firms that have sold merchandise to these customers, and then sells the customer names and addresses back to the firms that originally sold to the customers.

information overload State of overexposure that make it impossible to process and integrate every promotional message to which a receiver is exposed.

in-house agency The advertising department of a firm.

inquiry/direct response measures Techniques for determining the results of requests for information by consumers on the Web.

inside order taker The retail clerk who simply takes payment for products or services.

in-store sampling A type of sampling that occurs at the point of purchase and is popular for food products and cosmetics.

integrated marketing communications (IMC) The process of using promotional tools in a unified way so that a synergistic communications effect is created.

intended behavioral effect How receivers respond to a communication.

intended message content The informational, persuasive, and visual content in a promotional communication.

intensity of distribution The total number of trade distributors and retailers that carry a product; a factor that affects promotional strategy.

intensive distribution The placement of a product in as many different types of outlets as possible.

interactive agency Advertising agency that helps advertisers prepare communications for new media like the Internet, interactive kiosks, CD-ROMs, and interactive television.

intergenerational effect When people choose products based on what was used in their childhood household.

internal information search A search for product information that draws on personal experience and prior knowledge.

internal lists An organization's records of its customers, subscribers, donors, and inquirers, used to develop better relationships with current customers.

internal position The niche a brand achieves with regard to other, similar brands a firm markets.

internal situation analysis A technique that entails assessing the strengths and weaknesses of the sales forcing and corporate support for the selling effort.

international advertising The preparation and placement of advertising in different national and cultural markets.

international affiliates Foreign-market advertising agencies with which a local agency has established a relationship to handle clients' international advertising needs.

international promotion Advertising that reaches across national and cultural boundaries.

Internet advertising A form of advertising in which the message is carried over the Internet rather than through traditional mass media.

Internet Relay Chat (IRC) A component of the Internet that makes it possible for users to "talk" electronically with each other, despite their geographical separation.

Internet A vast global network of scientific, military, and research computers that allows people inexpensive access to the largest storehouse of information in the world.

involvement The degree of perceived relevance and personal importance accompanying the choice of a certain product or service within a particular context.

J, L

job description An identification of all the tasks to be performed by salespeople.

label The wrapping on the product container that carries important product use information.

less developed countries Countries whose economics lack almost all the resources—capital, infrastructure, political stability, and trained workers—necessary for development.

libel Defamation that occurs in print, for example, in magazines, newspapers, direct mail, or Internet reports.

lifestyle segmentation, or psychographic segmentation A form of market segmenting that focuses on consumers' activities, interests, and opinions.

limited problem solving A decision-making mode in which consumers' experience and involvement are both low.

listservs Electronic mailing lists on the Internet.

local advertising Advertising directed at an audience in a single trading area, either a city or state.

local agency An advertising agency in a foreign market hired because of its knowledge of the culture and local market conditions.

local national A sales employee based in his or her home country—for example, a Thai who sells Honda automobiles in Thailand.

log analysis software Measurement programs for Web use that not only provide information on hits, pages, visits, and users, but also let a site track audience traffic within the site.

logo The graphic mark that identifies a company and other visual representations that promote a firm's identity.

M

mail sampling A type of sampling in which samples are delivered through the postal service.

mailing list A file of names and addresses that an organization might use for contacting prospective or prior customers.

make good A media buyer's promise to repeat ad placements, reduce the price on future ads, or offer a refund if the expected audience reach of and ad placement is not delivered.

marcom manager A marketing-communications manager who plans an organization's overall communications program and oversees the various functional specialists inside and outside the organization to ensure that they are working together to deliver the desired message to the customer.

market niche A relatively small group of consumers with a unique set of needs who are typically willing to pay a premium price to firms specializing in those needs.

market segmentation The breaking down of a large, heterogeneous market into submarkets or segments that are more homogeneous.

marketing database A mailing list that also includes information collected directly from individual customers.

marketing mix The blend of the four responsibilities of marketing—conception, pricing, promotion, and distribution—used for a particular idea, product, or service.

marketing research The systematic gathering, recording, and interpreting of information related to all marketing mix variables.

markup charge A percentage added by an agency to a bill to cover a variety of services purchased from outside suppliers.

meaningfulness In promotional research, the significance of the data gathered.

measured advertising media Media that are closely measured to determine advertising costs and effectiveness: television, radio, newspapers, magazines, and outdoor media.

media buying Securing the electronic media time and print media space specified in a given account's schedule.

media class A broad category of media, such as television, radio, or newspapers.

media mix The blend of different media that will be used to effectively reach the target audience.

media objectives The specific goals for a media placement: Reach the target audience, determine the geo-graphic scope of placement, and identify the message weight, which determines the overall audience size.

media organizations Groups that own and manage media access to consumers.

media plan A plan specifying the media in which advertising messages will be placed to reach the desired target audience.

media vehicle A particular option for placement within a media class (for example, *Newsweek* is a media vehicle within the magazine media class).

media-buying service An independent organization that specializes in buying media time and space, particularly on radio and television, as a service to advertising agencies and advertisers.

media-planning and -buying services Group that handles the placement task in the promotional effort.

medium The vehicle through which a message is transmitted to receivers.

members of a trade channel One of the five types of audiences for advertising; the retailers, wholesalers, and distributors targeted by producers of both household and business goods and services.

members of business organizations One of the five types of audiences for advertising; the focus of advertising for firms that produce business and industrial goods and services.

membership groups Groups an individual interacts with in person on some regular basis.

merchandise allowances A type of trade-market sales promotion in which free products are packed with regular shipments as payment to the trade for setting up and maintaining displays.

message impressions Actual exposure to ads.

message strategy A component of an advertising strategy; it defines the goals of the advertiser and how those goals will be achieved.

message The information designed to inform or persuade consumers and business buyers that a marketer's brand provides superior satisfaction.

message weight The gross number of advertising messages or exposure opportunities delivered by the media vehicles in a schedule.

missionary salesperson One who calls on accounts with the express purpose of monitoring the satisfaction of buyers and updating buyers' needs.

mixed economy An economy in which restrictions and guidelines have been imposed on fundamental economic processes, including promotion.

mobile sampling A type of sampling carried out by logo-emblazoned vehicles that dispense samples, coupons, and premiums to consumers at malls, shopping centers, fairgrounds, and recreational areas.

modified rebuy A recurring purchase in which product and vendor specifications can change over time, requiring that an information search be initiated.

monopoly power The ability of a firm to make it impossible for rival firms to compete with it, either through advertising or in some other way.

multiattribute attitude models (MAAMS) A framework and set of procedures for collecting information from consumers to assess their salient beliefs and attitudes about competitive brands.

N

national advertising Advertising that reaches all geographic areas of one nation.

naturalistic inquiry A broad-based research approach that relies on data collection methods that are more qualitative than quantitative and include the use of videotape, audiotape, and photography in an effort to investigate an issue more holistically.

need satisfaction A customer-oriented approach in which the salesperson recognizes that during every sales encounter, each buyer's need state must be assessed and the selling effort adjusted to it.

need state A psychological state arising when one's desired state of affairs differs from one's actual state of affairs.

netizens Users who spend considerable time on the Internet.

new task buying decision A new purchase decision, typical for infrequently purchased items, that is characterized by extensive information search.

newly industrialized countries Countries whose economies are defined by change, where modern consumer cultures have emerged in a relatively short time.

newspaper sampling Process in which free samples are distributed to consumers through newspapers.

noise Any disturbance that inhibits message transmission to the intended receiver.

nonusers A market segment made up of consumers who do not use a particular product or service.

normative test scores A measure of how well a particular advertisement or promotion scored against average campaigns of its type that were tested previously.

O

objective-and-task approach A method of advertising budgeting that focuses on the relationship between spending and advertising objectives by identifying the specific tasks necessary to achieve different aspects of the advertising objectives.

objective-and-task method A method of establishing a budget for the personal selling effort that is most effective, allowing management to assess the objectives established for the overall selling effort.

off-invoice allowances Program in which marketers allow wholesalers and retailers to deduct a set amount from the invoice they receive for merchandise; a price reduction offered to the trade on a particular marketer's brand.

on-package sampling A type of sampling in which a sample item is attached to another product package.

order taking Accepting orders for merchandise or scheduling services either in written form or over the telephone.

out-of-home media The combination of transit and billboard advertising.

outside order taker The person who typically calls on business buyers or members of the trade channel and performs routine tasks related to orders for inventory replenishment or catalog orders.

overview A document that sets out what is to be covered in a promotion plan and structures the context.

P

packaging The container or wrapping for a product; can affect consumer behavior relating to brand evaluations and the level of use, and provide strategic benefits to marketers as well as values to the trade and consumers.

pages or page views On the Web, the pages (actually the number of html files) sent to a the requesting site.

pay-for-results Payment plan that ties the advertising or promotion agency compensation to a pre-agreed-upon achievement of specified objectives.

percentage-of-sales approach An advertising budgeting approach that calculates the advertising budget based on a percentage of the prior year's sales or the projected year's sales.

perception The manner in which an individual interprets stimuli from his or her environment.

peripheral cues Features of a message other than the actual arguments about a brand's performance.

permanent long-term displays Advertising displays intended for use for more than six months.

permission marketing The process of sending advertising e-mails to users who have signed up for them and given permission for their receipt.

personal selling The presentation of information about a firm's products or services by one person to another person or small group of people.

physiological measures Techniques that use body responses to detect how consumers react to messages.

picturing Communicating with visual images rather than words.

pilot testing Pursuing message evaluation with experimentation in the marketplace.

platforms The ways in which e-commerce transactions are initiated and culminated: direct purchase, catalogs, auctions, e-mails, and barter models.

point-of-purchase (P–O–P) or point-of-purchase advertising Materials used in the retail setting to attract shoppers' attention to a marketer's brand, convey primary brand benefits, or highlight pricing information.

pop-up ad An Internet ad that appears as a Web site page is loading or after a page has loaded.

portal A starting point for Web access and searches; they can be vertical (serving a specialized market or industries); horizontal (providing access and links across industries); or ethnic or community based.

positioning strategy The key themes or concepts an organization features for communicating the distinctiveness of its product or service to the target segment.

positioning The process of designing a product or service so that it can occupy a distinct and valued place in the target consumer's mind, and then communicating this distinctiveness through branding.

posttest message tracking Assessing the performance of advertising during or after the launch of an ad campaign.

potential ad impressions Opportunitiees to be exposed to ads.

premiums Items featuring the logo of a sponsor that are offered free, or at a reduced price, with the purchase of another item.

presumptive close Technique in which a salesperson asks a question like "What address should appear on the invoice?" to make it seem a deal has been agreed upon.

price discrimination The practice of charging different prices to different trade buyers who are buying similar quantities of goods.

price fixing The illegal practice of setting prices in concert with competitors.

price-off deal A type of sales promotion that offers a consumer cents or even dollars off merchandise at the point of purchase through specially marked packages.

primary data Specific information acquired for a particular promotional situation.

primary demand Demand for an entire product category, not just the brand.

prior experience The extent to which a consumer has either direct or indirect experience with purchasing and using products in a product category.

proactive public relations strategy An approach guided by marketing objectives that seeks to publicize a company and its brands, and takes an offensive rather than defensive posture in the public relations process.

product differentiation The process of creating a perceived difference, in the mind of the consumer, between an organization's product or service and the competition's.

production facilitators Group that offers essential technical services both during and after the production process in a promotion.

production services Group of producers (and sometimes directors) who take creative ideas and turn them into ads, direct-mail pieces, or events.

professionals One of the five types of audiences for advertising, defined as doctors, lawyers, accountants, teachers, or any other careerpeople who require special training or certification.

profiling The process of tracking and cataloging the behavior of customers in an e-commerce setting.

promotion The communications process in marketing that is used to create a favorable predisposition toward a brand of product or service, an idea, or even a person.

promotion agencies Agencies that provide specialized services not typically available from advertising agencies.

promotion plan The analysis, strategy, and tasks needed to conceive and implement an effective promotional effort.

promotion research A specialized form of marketing research that focuses on the development and performance of promotional materials.

promotional mix A blend of communications tools used by a firm to carry out the promotion process and to communicate directly with target markets.

psychogalvanometer A machine that measures galvanic skin response (GSR), minute changes in perspiration that indicate arousal to some stimulus—in this context, an advertisement.

psychographics A form of market research that emphasizes the understanding of consumers' activities, interests, and opinions.

public relations (PR) A marketing and management communication function that deals with the public issues encountered by firms across a wide range of constituents.

public relations firm A firm that handles the needs of organizations regarding relationships with the local community, competitors, industry associations, and government organizations.

public relations plan A strategy that identifies the objectives and activities related to the public relations communications issued by a firm.

publicity Unpaid-for media coverage of events related to a firm's products or activities.

puffery The use of absolute superlatives like "Number One" and "Best in the World" in advertisements.

pull strategy Plan in which a marketer uses advertising to stimulate demand among consumers, who then demand it from retailers, who in turn demand it from wholesalers, who then order it from the manufacturer.

pull tactics An approach to advertising in which consumers have control over advertising by seeking information at their own expense; the most common strategy on the World Wide Web.

pulsing A media-scheduling strategy that combines elements from continuous and flighting techniques; advertisements are scheduled continuously in media over a period of time, but with periods of much heavier scheduling.

purchase intent A measure of whether or not a consumer intends to buy a product or service in the near future.

push money A form of trade incentive carried out through a program in which retail salespeople are offered a financial reward for featuring a marketer's brand with shoppers.

push strategy A sales promotion strategy in which marketers devise incentives to encourage purchases by members of the trade to help push a product into the distribution channel.

Q, R

qualifications The combination of skills and training that relate to effective performance.

rational branding An approach that stresses the need for a brand's Web site to provide some unique informational resource to justify consumers visiting it.

rational decision style A decision style characterized by an effort on the part of the buyer to maximize the value of the purchase.

reach The number of people or households in a target audience that will be exposed to a media vehicle or schedule at least once during a given period of time. It is often expressed as a percentage.

reactive public relations strategy An approach dictated by influences outside the control of a company that focuses on problems to be solved rather than opportunities, and requires a company to take defensive measures.

rebate A money-back offer requiring a buyer to mail in a form requesting the money back from the manufacturer.

recall test The most common method of advertising research, which measures the success of an ad or campaign by whether or not consumers remember it.

receivers The consumers or business buyers targeted by a firm in its STP strategy.

reference group Any configuration of other persons that a particular individual uses as a point of reference in making his or her own consumption decisions.

regional advertising Advertising carried out by producers, wholesalers, distributors, and retailers that concentrate their efforts in a particular geographic region.

relationship marketing In the world of supply chain management, the benefits that result from partnerships.

reliability In promotional research, consistency of findings over time.

repeat purchase A second purchase of a new product after trying it for the first time.

repositioning Returning to the process of segmenting, targeting, and positioning a product or service to arrive at a revised positioning strategy.

resonance test A measure of the extent to which a message resonates or rings true with target-audience members.

RFM analysis An analysis of how recently and how frequently a customer is buying from an organization,

and of how much that customer is spending per order and over time.

riding the boards Assessing possible locations for billboard advertising.

rituals Repeated behaviors that affirm, express, and maintain cultural values.

robots Automated programs that do the "legwork" for the consumer by roaming the Internet in search of information fitting certain user-specified criteria.

S

sales force automation (SFA) The process of automating the sales process through the incorporation of computers, cell phones, pagers, the Internet, and other technologies.

sales management Controlling sales at every point in the process, from establishing objectives for the selling effort to the creation of the staff to performance evaluation.

sales promotion The use of incentive techniques that create a perception of greater brand value among consumers or distributors.

salient beliefs A small number of beliefs that are the critical determinants of an attitude.

sampling A sales promotion technique designed to provide a consumer with a trial opportunity.

search engine A software tool used to find Web sites on the Internet by searching for keywords.

secondary data Information obtained from existing sources for use in a promotion.

selective attention The mind's capacity to screen out information that is deemed irrelevant.

selective comprehension Process by which a receiver interprets a message in a way that is consistent with his or her existing attitude and belief structure, resulting in rejecting as biased or untruthful any information that contradicts or challenges this structure.

selective distribution Targeted placement of a product; frequently retailers and manufacturers collaborate on such placements.

selective exposure The ability to allow stimuli into the field of awareness.

selective retention The process of choosing to store only some of the information that is attended to and comprehended.

self-liquidating premium A sales promotion that requires a consumer to pay most of the cost of the item received as a premium.

self-reference criteria (SRC) The unconscious reference to one's own cultural values, experiences, and knowledge as a basis for decisions.

self-regulation The advertising industry's attempt to police itself.

seminar selling An approach designed to reach a group of customers, rather than an individual customer, with information about a firm's products or services.

share of market/share of voice Approach in which a firm monitors the amount spent by significant competitors on promotion and allocates an equal amount or an amount proportional to (or slightly greater than) the firm's market share relative to the competition.

shopping goods Higher-priced items with multiple features such as automobiles, televisions, and clothes.

short-term promotional displays Advertising displays intended for use for six months or less.

single-source tracking measures Ways of providing information from individual households about brand purchases, coupon use, and television advertising exposure by combining grocery store scanner data and devices attached to the households' televisions (called peoplemeters), which monitor viewing behavior.

single-source tracking services Research services that offer information not just on demographics but also on brands, purchase size, prices paid, and media exposure.

situation analysis In an advertising plan, the section in which the advertiser lays out the most important factors that define the situation, and then explains the importance of each factor.

slander Oral defamation; in the context of promotion, this could occur during television or radio broadcast of an event involving a company and its employees.

slice-of-life advertisements Depictions of a common scene from everyday life that suggest the benefits and satisfaction to be gained by using a brand.

slogans Linguistic devices that, due to their simplicity, meter, rhyme, or other factor, link a brand name to something memorable.

slotting fees A type of trade-market sales promotion in which manufacturers make direct cash payments to retailers to ensure shelf space.

social class A person's standing in the hierarchy resulting from the systematic inequalities in the social system.

society A group of people living in a particular area who share a common culture and consider themselves a distinct and unified entity.

source In communication, the marketer of the brand, and in personal selling, the salesperson who represents the marketer.

source credibility The receiver's perception that the source of the message is knowledgeable, believable, trustworthy, and unbiased and has the knowledge to offer relevant information.

spam To post messages to many unrelated newsgroups on Usenet or, unsolicited, to e-mail addresses.

specialty goods High-priced luxury items such as designer clothes and expensive watches that consumers specifically seek out by brand name.

spider An automated program that "crawls" around the Web and collects information.

split-cable transmission A kind of pilot testing that allows testing of two different versions of an ad through direct transmission (via television) to two separate samples of similar households within a single, well-defined market area.

split-list experiment A test of the effectiveness of various aspects of direct-mail advertising pieces.

split-run distribution Similar to split-cable transmission, except that the print medium is used.

ssponsorship Funding an event or a charitable cause, or creating an event in order to highlight a firm's brand to a specific target audience.

standardized (globalized) campaign Campaigns that use the same appeal and creative execution across all (or most) international markets.

sticky site A site on the Internet that can attract visitors repeatedly and keep them for a long time.

STP marketing (Segmenting, Targeting, Positioning) A marketing strategy employed when advertisers focus their efforts on one subgroup of a product's total market.

straight rebuy A situation in which a buyer is purchasing an item on a routine basis and engages in little information search.

straightforward close The best approach to closing a deal in which a salesperson must "sense" when to ask for an order in a straightforward, courteous manner, without tricks, presumptions, or innuendo.

strategy A mechanism by which something is to be done.

subliminal Below the threshold of consciousness.

support media Media used to reinforce a message being delivered via some other media vehicle.

supportive communications Various ways—for instance, directories, specialty advertising items, and brochures—in which a marketer communicates with target audiences outside of mainstream or electronic media.

surfing The act of directed or random browsing of the Internet especially the World Wide Web. Derived from the TV channel surfing idiom.

sweepstakes A sales promotion in which winners are determine purely by chance.

switchers, or variety seekers A market segment made up of consumers who often buy what is on sale or choose brands that offer discount coupons or other price incentives.

system selling An approach that entails selling a set of interrelated components that fulfill all or a majority of a customer's needs in a product or service area.

T

target audience A particular group of consumers singled out for an advertisement or advertising campaign.

target segment The subgroup (of the larger market) chosen as the focal point for the marketing program and advertising campaign.

team selling A type of selling in which a group of people within the organization are assembled as a team to call on a particular customers.

telemarketing A direct-marketing medium that involves using the telephone to deliver a spoken appeal.

testimonial An advertisement in which an advocacy position is taken by a spokesperson.

theater test A measure of consumer likes and dislikes taken in a small theatre, usually set up in or near shopping malls.

third-country national An employee who is a citizen of one country, employed by a corporation from a second country, and working for that corporation in a third country.

thought listing Also called cognitive response analysis, message research that tries to identify specific thoughts that may be generated by an ad.

top-of-the-mind awareness An indicator of consumer ability to recall one brand before another.

trade partners Traditionally, the wholesalers, distributors, and retailers who help carry out the promotion for a brand through personal selling and in-store promotions.

trade reseller All organizations in the marketing channel of distribution that buy products to resell to customers.

trade sales promotions Specialty promotions such as incentive programs, trade shows, sales force contests, and in-store merchandising and point-of-purchase materials aimed at wholesalers, retailers, and vendors.

trade shows Events where several related products from many manufacturers are displayed and demonstrated to members of the trade.

transformational advertising messages Messages that attempt to create a brand feeling, image, or mood that is activated when a consumer uses a brand.

transit advertising Advertising that appears as both interior and exterior displays on mass transit vehicles and at terminal and station platforms.

trial close Technique in which a salesperson poses a question like "Would you like this gift wrapped?" to encourage a potential buyer to close the sale.

trial offers A type of sales promotion in which expensive items are offered on a trial basis to induce consumer trial of a brand.

trial usage An advertising objective to get consumers to use a product new to them on a trial basis.

trustworthiness In promotional research, the honesty of the data gathered.

tying agreements Illegal attempts to bind a buyer to the purchase of additional products as a condition of buying a desired product.

U

unduplicated audience measurement See *reach*.

unique selling proposition (USP) A promise contained in an advertisement in which the advertised brand offers a specific, unique, and relevant benefit to the consumer.

unit-of-sales approach An approach to advertising budgeting that allocates a specified dollar amount of advertising for each unit of a brand sold (or expected to be sold).

Usenet A collection of more than 100,000 discussion groups on the Internet.

user positioning A positioning option that focuses on a specific profile of the target user.

users Also known as unique visitors, the number of different "people" visiting a Web site (a new user is determined from the user's registration with the site) during a specified period of time.

V, W

validity In promotional research, proof that generated information is relevant to the research questions being investigated.

values The defining expressions of culture, demonstrating in words and deeds what is important to a culture.

variety seeking The tendency of consumers to switch their selection among various brands in a given category in a seemingly random pattern.

vertical cooperative advertising An advertising technique whereby a manufacturer and dealer (either a wholesaler or retailer) share the expense of advertising.

vertical market segmentation The process of segmenting the market based on identifying potential customers within a single organizational type or industry.

viral marketing The process of consumers marketing to consumers over the Internet through word of mouth via e-mails and listservs.

virtual mall A gateway to a group of Internet storefronts that provides access to mall sites by simply clicking on a storefront.

visits On the Web, the number of occasions in which a user X interacted with site Y after Z time has elapsed.

voice response analysis A high-tech research procedure that measures inflections in the voice when consumers are discussing an ad; used to determine excitement and other states.

within-vehicle duplication Exposure to the same advertisement in the same media at different times.

World Wide Web (WWW) A universal database of information available to Internet users; its graphical user environment (GUI) makes navigation simple and exciting.

INDEX

NAME/BRAND/COMPANY

INDEX

SUBJECT

Page references in **bold** print indicate ads or photos. Page references in *italics* indicate tables, charts, or graphs. Page references followed by "n" indicate footnotes.

PHOTO CREDITS

319 http://www.focalex.com
320 http://www.toshiba.com
321 http://www.crayola.com (left).
      http://www.mall.com (right).
322 http://www.iwon.com
324 Courtesy of Screaming Media. Art
      Director: Nick Cohen; Copywriter: Mikel
      Reich; Designer: Agatha Sohn;
      Photographer: Joseph Cuttice.
325 Courtesy RealNames Corporation.
327 Thank you to BrassRing.com for
      excellence in advertising (left). Courtesy
      Hyperion (right).
329 MyEvents.com.
333 e-centives, Inc. In-House Agency.

Chapter 10

341 Courtesy Nextcard.com
342 http://www.gap.com (left).
      Platform.net/A. Boatwright (right).
345 Courtesy Oreck (left). Client: Digital
      Island; Agency: Zuckerman Fernandes &
      Partners. Writer: Ben Deily; Art Director:
      Roselle Rapadas (right).
348 Courtesy of JBL, Inc.
349 © Nissan 1995. Reproduced by
      permission. Q45, J30, G20, & Infiniti logo
      are registered trademarks of Nissan (all).
350 Courtesy of Living X Bicycles.
352 Courtesy *Spin* magazine.
358 Courtesy Jasmine.com. Photo by Fabrizio
      Ferri. Grey Landon; Creative Director
      Barbara Nokes.
362 Creative Director/CW: Glenn Kaplan;
      Creative Director/AD: Gary Goldstein;
      Photographer: Fabrizio Gianni
363 Courtesy VISA USA, Inc.
367 Courtesy Nextcard.com
370 Courtesy z.central.com
373 http://www.esky.com
374 http://www.isky.com/index.html

Chapter 11

381 Courtesy of Marriott International, Inc.
382 Courtesy Toys R Us.
384 Reproduced with permission of PepsiCo,
      Inc., 1998, Purchase, New York.
387 Photograph Jeff Greenberg.
389 Ad: "Instant Coffee"; Client: Peet's Coffee
      & Tea; Agency: VITROROBERTSON;
      Creative Directors: John Robertson, John
      Vitro; Art Director: Dave Huerta;

Copywriter: John Robertson; Inset Image:
      Chuck Eaton; Letterpress: Ken
      West; Account Executive: Del Bracht (left).
393 JELL–O and JIGGLERS are registered
      trademarks of Kraft Foods, Inc.; used with
      permission (left). Courtesy of The Gillette
      Company (right).
397 Courtesy General Motors Corporation.
398 Courtesy of Marriott International, Inc.
401 Courtesy of Jelly Belly Candy Company,
      Inc.
402 Photograph by Jeff Greenberg.
405 Courtesy Omega-Swiss made since 1848
      (left). Courtesy of Goldmine Software
      Corporation (right).
408 Heater Advertising, Boston, MA for
      Promotions.com, Inc.

Chapter 12

415 © 1997 James Clinton Davis.
416 © Kevin Fleming/Corbis
421 Courtesy of JBL, Inc.
424 Insignia Systems, Inc.
426 Courtesy of JVC Company of America.
428 Courtesy of The Bettmann Archive.
429 Courtesy of Horst Salons. Carol
      Henderson, Art Director; Luke Sullivan,
      Writer: Fallon McElligot, Minneapolis,
      agency (top). Courtesy of the Museum of
      Flight, Seattle, Washington (bottom).
431 © Joe Higgins/South-Western (top).
      Chris T. Allen, photographer (bottom).
432 © Bob Kramer/Stock Boston.
433 Chris T. Allen, photographer (top). © 1997
      James Clinton Davis (bottom).
435 Bell Atlantic Electronic Commerce
      Services, Inc. Portions © Netscape
      Communications Corporation, 1999.
437 Courtesy Montblanc Boutique
444 Courtesy Noxzema.

Chapter 13

469 Courtesy of Allstate Insurance.
450 © 1999 Microsoft Corporation. All rights
      reserved. Photography by Julian Broad.
451 Courtesy Microsoft Corporation
455 Reprinted with permission of PepsiCo
      Inc., 1996, Purchase, New York.
459 http://www.clothesline.com (left).
      Reproduced with permission of AT&T
      (right).
460 Courtesy of Burson-Marsteller.

465 Courtesy of Coopers & Lybrand lld. (left).
      Courtesy of DuPont (right).
466 Courtesy Hewlitt Packard
467 Courtesy Huntsman Chemical
      Corporation (left). Courtesy of Bayer
      Corporation (right).
468 Courtesy of Chevron Corporation.
469 Courtesy of Allstate Insurance.

Chapter 14

475 Courtesy Docent.
476 http://www.dell.com/us/en/biz/default.
      htm
480 Ad copy created by Dan Metzger, Sr. VP
      Sales & Marketing, Worldtrak Corporation
      Design and layout created by Nygard &
      Associates.
485 Courtesy Cambient.
488 Courtesy infoUSA.
489 © 2000 by Miller Heiman, Inc. All rights
      reserved. Designer: Lawrence Lim;
      Copywriter: Jennifer Vodehnal.
493 http://www.salesforce.com/tour/index/
      html
499 Courtesy of the TerrAlign Group, Metron,
      Inc., Reston, VA 800-437-9603.
502 Courtesy Docent.
505 Courtesy Trilogy

Chapter 15

513 Courtesy of E∗Trade Securities.
514 Courtesy of the Goodyear Tire & Rubber
      Company.
519 © 1998 Pharmacia & Upjohn Consumer
      Healthcare. Agency: Jordan McGrath Case
      & Partners/Euro RSCG.
522 © 1994 B. Kramer/Custom Medical
      Stock Photo.
527 JELL–O is a registered trademark of Kraft
      Foods, Inc.; used with permission.
528 Reprinted with permission of General
      Motors Corporation (left). Courtesy of
      Ford Motor Company (top right).
      Reprinted with permission of General
      Motors Corporation (bottom right).
531 Courtesy NetRatings, Inc.
532 Courtesy Crain Publications.
533 Courtesy Media Metrix.
536 Courtesy of E∗Trade Securities.
537 Courtesy Unilever.
539 ©2000 Deloitte Consulting.